THE MOVIE STARS STORY

EDITED BY
ROBYN KARNEY

OCTOPUS BOOKS

The Editor

ROBYN KARNEY was educated at the University of Cape Town and is a
former film and theatre critic and feature writer. Now resident in London,
she worked as a television script editor and film story consultant. She has
edited the popular Octopus Books series of Hollywood studio histories and
Glamorous Musicals, and is co-compiler and editor of *Movie Mastermind*

The Writers

RONALD BERGEN was born in South Africa and was educated in the
Cape, New York, Paris and London. He lectured in film studies in Paris and
at the University of Lille, and is a regular contributor of reviews and articles
to film magazines. He has published *The A to Z Of Movie Directors*, *Sport In
The Movies*, *Glamorous Musicals* and *Movie Mastermind*.

ROBIN CROSS is a freelance author and broadcaster. His books on the
cinema include *The Big Book Of B Movies or How Low Was My Budget* and
The Big Book Of British Films. He is also the author of *The Bible According to
Hollywood* and *The Hollywood History of World War II*, co-author of *The
Worst Movie Posters Of All Time*, and contributor to *Movie Mastermind*.

JOEL W. FINLER, an American educated at London University, is
primarily a film historian. He has published *All Time Movie Greats*, a book
on the work of actor/director Erich von Stroheim and is currently preparing
a book on Hollywood directors. He contributed to *Anatomy Of The Movies*
and is a considerable picture archivist.

MARK LE FANU was educated at Cambridge University. He is a freelance
writer and critic who has contributed to a number of publications including
'Monogram', 'Films and Filming', 'Sight and Sound', 'Encounter' and
'Positif'. His book on actor Robert De Niro is expected shortly and he is
presently working on a study of the Russian director Andrei Tarkovsky.

DAVID MALCOLM – a *nom de plume* of a well known film writer, novelist
and broadcaster – has worked in the European film industry, is a translator
of film scripts, and regularly contributes articles and criticism to English
and European film journals.

First published 1984 by Octopus Books Limited
59 Grosvenor Street London W1

© 1984 Octopus Books Limited

ISBN 0 7064 2092 6

Printed in West Germany by Mohndruck

CONTENTS

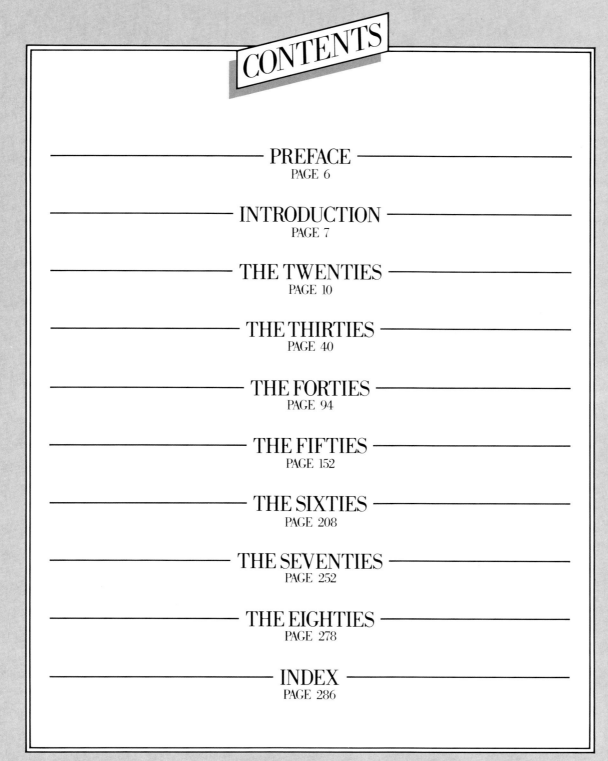

PREFACE

In telling *The Movie Stars Story*, we are attempting to accord the actors and actresses of the screen their rightful place in the history of the cinema. The studio system grew up hand-in-hand with the star system, each being, for a considerable period, indispensable to the other. The films that poured from Hollywood in vast quantities during the Golden Years, both the good and the bad, were often essentially vehicles for the stars; stories were constructed with a priority to display the particular gifts or personalities of particular individuals, and these individuals not only reflected the styles and customs of their time, but often influenced or dictated them. Women, for example, began to wear trousers because the glamorous Marlene Dietrich wore trousers. The studio system is no more. The day of the independent producer and the free-lance star is here to stay, but the place of the screen actor or actress is still of great importance. If the fashions are dictated by Diane Keaton's Annie Hall rather than by Dietrich, nonetheless, the power to influence remains intact.

This book, then, is not merely another directory of stars. We have apportioned our five hundred stars to seven decades in an attempt to give each of them their place in an appropriate social and historical cinematic context. The decisions were not all obvious or easy. While nobody would dispute that Valentino belongs to the 20s, or that John Travolta is significant to the 70s, where is the rightful position of Bette Davis or Katharine Hepburn or Cary Grant – the great durables whose careers have spanned several decades during which they remained at the top of their profession? In such cases, the choice had to be determined by some aspect of a star's life within a decade that seemed, at least, to carry some extra and specific weight. Anomalies do occur, but they are at least intended to be interesting, and consistent with the spirit of the book. Thus, the venerable Sir John Gielgud features in the 1980s, the decade during which after a very long and very distinguished career, he has come, with his Academy award for *Arthur* (1981), to be widely recognised for his contribution to cinema acting.

The major editorial difficulty in assembling *The Movie Stars Story* has been that of selection. There have been many 'stars' in the celluloid firmament who are immediately identifiable as such – names whose capacity to draw the public, to excite interest, to occupy the headlines, has never been in question, and who live on as legends in cinema history. All of these are here. But, having dealt with the obvious choices, the term 'star' ceases always to be a very useful guide, and becomes only a loose definition within which we have broadened the book's horizons. The five hundred, then, include the unchallenged giants of each era. The balance of actors and actresses has been chosen on various grounds: box-office status, or special achievements, or for a uniquely individual – even quirky – talent. We have left the narrow definition behind. *The Movie Stars Story* is, indeed, a story – of success, of failure, of talent, and lack of it; changing styles and customs in an ever-changing world. Every person recorded here is a fragment in the vast kaleidoscope that makes up the history of Hollywood film. The omissions – necessarily subjective – are no reflection on those missing from these pages. There just are not sufficient pages to accommodate all the contenders. We have tried to give a lively and informative account of the life and times of our five hundred, encouraging our writers to retain their individual biases and perspectives to create a book that is a worthy addition to the shelves of the devotees, as well as a valuable introduction for readers new to the world of cinema books.

Robyn Karney

Acknowledgements

The writers who contributed to this book fully deserve my sincere thanks for the cooperative way in which they responded to my often difficult requests. For the energy and enthusiasm that he showed in searching out stills from his collection, special thanks are due to Joel Finler; also in this regard Tom Graves helped considerably, as did the Kobal Collection and Flashbacks. I would also like to express my appreciation to Neil Hornick and Tammy Collins for their assistance, to Clive Hirschhorn for his advice, and to George Baxt who gave unstintingly of his photographic memory. Robin Cross originated the idea of the book and David Burn, my in-house editor, controlled its progress with exceptional skill – to both of them my gratitude is recorded. RK

INTRODUCTION

The movie industry began in the penny arcade kinetoscopes of the 1890s. You dropped a penny in the slot of a squat box-like machine, peered into a stereoscopic viewer and savoured, for a full minute, the delights of Fatima, the belly-dancing sensation of the 1896 Chicago World's Fair or the more restful pleasures of 'Surf At Dover Beach'. On 28 December 1895, in Paris, the Lumière brothers gave the first show of moving pictures projected on to a screen before a paying audience. The film was the prosaically entitled 'A Train Entering the Gare de Ciotat', but as the locomotive puffed towards an amazed audience, it was pulling behind it the infant film industry.

In America the first publicly screened show was held on 23 April 1896 at Koster and Bial's Music Hall in New York. Until 1900, movies were principally screened in vaudeville theatres and were straightforward records of the famous acts of the day. But the turn of the century saw the appearance of the 'nickelodeons' – improvised film theatres which sprang up in small stores, ballrooms and disused halls all over America. By 1908 there were about 9,000 nickelodeons, providing romance and escapism for millions of working class Americans, particularly the immigrants from southern and central Europe whose lack of English discouraged them from theatregoing.

Neither the exhibitors, nor the audience who crowded into their nickelodeons, knew the names of the heroes and heroines who flickered on the screen. But their favourites quickly emerged: 'The Fat Man' or 'The Girl With The Golden Curls' – the first indication of the fusion of physical attributes and personality which became the foundation of the star system in the silent cinema.

The early film production companies, among them the New York-based Edison, Vitagraph and Biograph, and the Chicago-based Selig, were each churning out several one-reelers a week. The breakneck shooting schedules and the swift arrival of films on the screen accelerated the process of identification. The exhibitors, and the men who ran the burgeoning film exchanges which supplied them with their product, were canny entrepreneurs who quickly grasped that familiarity was an asset. But the corporation lawyers and businessmen who financed the film companies were completely out of touch with the nickelodeon audiences, whom they privately

Silent slapstick comedian Ben Turpin was one of the first screen personalities to be publicised by name in a 1909 trade magazine article.

regarded as little more than rabble. They saw their operations as profitable but shoddy enterprises, and their principal concern was for a standardised product. Preserving the actors' anonymity was a simple way of keeping salaries, and costs, down. The actors' own attitudes were more complex. Many of them contemplated work in films only as a last resort, particularly since they were expected to be jacks of all trades: little distinction was made between acting and directing, and many a would-be matinée idol, for example Wallace Reid, had to step behind the camera. At the start of her career, Norma Talmadge doubled as a seamstress in the Vitagraph property department. When young Mary Pickford expressed horror at the prospect of seeking work in 'the flickers', her mother reassured her with the promise that 'It's only to tide us over'.

But in 1909 the barriers began to fall. On 3 April of that year in 'The Moving Picture World', an early trade magazine, Ben Turpin appeared under his own name in an article detailing the life of a 'Moving Picture Comedian'. He assured readers that despite having 'my eyes blackened, both ankles sprained and many bruises .... This is a great life'. The fat comic John Bunny and the ersatz cowboy Broncho Billy Anderson were starring in their own films, Bunny because he was an established stage performer and

Strength and stamina were among the attributes demanded of the early silent stars – even the heroines. Here Helen Holmes prepares to leap aboard a train in The Hazards Of Helen *(1914)*

Florence Lawrence, 'The Biograph Girl', in Pawns Of Destiny *(1914)*

Anderson because he owned his own production company. Movie columns began to appear in the newspapers. In May 1910, Florence Turner, who had been dubbed 'The Vitagraph Girl', first saw her name on a poster advertising a film, a novelty item in which she boxed a round with Gentleman Jim Corbett. Even more popular than Turner was Florence Lawrence, 'The Biograph Girl', whose salary had reached the dizzy heights of $25 a week. In 1910 she fell out with Biograph and into the welcoming arms of Carl Laemmle, head of the Independent Motion Picture Company (IMP), at a salary of $1,000 a week.

Like many of the audience for whom he catered, and in common with many a movie mogul, Laemmle was an immigrant. He had arrived in America from Germany in 1884 and for years had worked in menial jobs. He had turned a nickelodeon into a successful distribution business and then moved into production, taking on the 'Trust', a grouping of the major film companies which had formed The Motion Picture Patents Company with the object of defending their exclusive rights in Edison's, and other patents, in

motion picture equipment. Unlike the stuffed shirt directors of the 'Trust's companies, Laemmle was a showman, in tune with his audience, who instinctively grasped the potential of films. His acquisition of Florence Lawrence established him as the first man to sell the stars rather than the motion pictures.

Then Laemmle pulled off a remarkable publicity stunt. A newspaper article – which he planted – appeared, reporting that Florence Lawrence had been killed in a street car accident in St Louis. It was immediately followed by an advertisement in the trade press – headlined WE NAIL A LIE – claiming that the story was a rumour put about by IMP's competitors. Florence Lawrence was triumphantly produced, and despatched to St Louis to make a personal appearance – the first by a film actor – with King Baggott, a local boy and popular matinee idol. Hundreds of fans turned out to greet the stars, and in the crush enthusiastically tore the buttons off Miss Lawrence's coat. Shortly afterwards a Sunday magazine devoted a lengthy interview to her, complete with photographs and references to her hobbies, fan mail and salary – all of which were to become the staples of the Hollywood fan magazine.

Carl Laemmle, one of the creators of the star system, at the opening day of his newly founded Universal Studios in 1915.

Vitagraph had already started a fan magazine, The 'Motion Picture Story Magazine', established in 1909 by J. Stuart Blackton, and leading 'name' players were sending autographed photos to admirers. 'Motion Picture Story Magazine' started by covering only Vitagraph films, but soon widened its range to include articles about the films and stars of other companies.

On 21 November 1913, 'Variety' observed, 'The stars are scrapping for the spotlight'. The stars, in fact, were moving to the centre of every new film, and their salaries were becoming the most conspicuous element of the budget. At the same time the particular

America's Sweetheart, as Mary Pickford became known, was featured on many a cover of the fan magazines which were proliferating by the mid-teens.

demands of cinema were creating a new breed of screen actor. The merciless, pin-sharp lenses of the day cruelly exposed every line and wrinkle in the faces of the well-upholstered leading ladies of the stage who tried their hand at films. The intimacy of the medium defeated the melodramatic style of distinguished thespians like Sir Herbert Beerbohm Tree, who suffered the indignity of being replaced in many shots by a screen actor, Monte Blue.

When the great Eleanora Duse saw herself in the 1916 *Cenere*, she remarked, 'something quite different is needed'. At Biograph, D.W. Griffith assembled a company of youthful actors with the stamina, and sufficiently well-defined personalities, to handle the exhausting schedule of a two-reeler every week. Among them were Mary Pickford, Blanche Sweet, Lillian and Dorothy Gish and Mae Marsh. Griffith's 'little mothers' and innocent, virginal heroines were among the first great screen archetypes, instantly recognisable to audiences who, like Griffith himself, were steeped in the sentimentality of Victorian theatre and popular fiction. They were mooned over by juvenile leads like 'country boy' Robert Harron, and escorted by older matinée idols such as J. Warren Kerrigan and Maurice Costello – in those days, audiences preferred their leading men to be on the mature side.

The introduction in 1914 of feature-length films, and the erection of huge picture palaces in which to show them, further

enhanced the importance of the stars. The film business was on the point of becoming a mass-production industry, and the rewards held out to leading players had rocketed skywards. In 1913, Adolph Zukor told Mary Pickford's formidable mother, 'If feature pictures succeed, we expect to pay according to the drawing power of the box office'. By 1915, 'Little Mary's drawing – and bargaining – power had raised her salary from an initial $500 to $10,000 a week. In 1919 she went to First National at $350,000 a picture, plus $50,000 for her mother. These immense sums were made possible by the banks' confidence in the studios' collateral, their stars. On the basis of Chaplin's name alone, The Bank of America was willing to loan First National $250,000 towards the cost of *The Kid* (1921). The picture was such a hit that the money came back in six weeks.

If you couldn't buy a star, you could create one. In 1914, William Fox and his supremely inventive press agents transformed an obscure stage actress called Theodosia de Coppet into Theda Bara, the screen's first sex symbol, the original 'vamp', and the foundation stone of Fox's fortunes. Bara's career is one of the early examples of the standardisation of both a star's image and her screen vehicles. When Theda stepped out of character to play a sympathetic role in *The Two Orphans* (1915), the film was a flop. In the following year, 'Motion Picture Story Magazine' published an intriguingly frank article cataloguing the tricks of the trade applied to 'Making a Movie Queen', including faked disappearances and planted fan mail in the movie magazines. Although Hollywood and the dominance of the giant studios was not yet a reality, the star system had been firmly established.

D.W. Griffith, the directorial genius of America's silent cinema and creator of many of the early stars, instructing his young protegée, Lillian Gish, at a rehearsal for Battle Of The Sexes *(1914). Behind them is Robert Harron.*

The correspondence between the stars and the society from which they spring cannot be simply defined. Nevertheless, in some measure, stars undeniably become the repositories of the impulses and daydreams of the great mass of people. The impulses remain constant – the desire for success or fame, the worship of heroes or the secret admiration of certain types of villain – but the form which they take is determined by changing fashion and economic circumstance. Douglas Fairbanks Sr's ebullient go-getters caught the confident mood of America in the World War I years; Tom Mix's daredevil auto chases and Harold Lloyd's cliff-hanging encounters with skyscrapers celebrated the onrush of technology which in the early 20s was transforming the life and landscape of America. Basking in the postwar glow of romantic escapism were Rudolph Valentino and his exotic Latin Lover imitators. The stage was set for the flamboyant golden years of Hollywood in the 20s – the Hollywood of myth and legend.

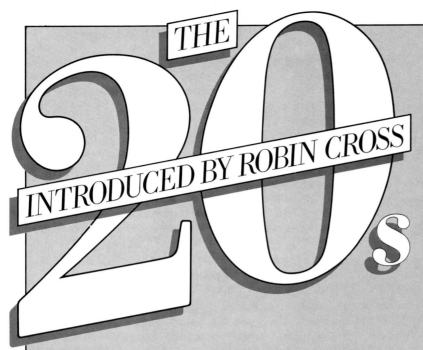

THE 20s

INTRODUCED BY ROBIN CROSS

formed by the merger of the Metro Company, the Goldwyn Company and Mayer Productions. MGM were soon to boast that on their roster there 'were more stars than there are in the heavens'.

Enormous care was now taken to package the stars as glamorous figures whose lives were lived on a different plane to those of ordinary folk. When in 1918 a divorce case revealed the hitherto unknown existence of Francis X. Bushman's corpulent wife Josephine and their five children, his career as a leading man was finished overnight. The public wanted their celluloid idols to be different, and so they were. It was sometimes difficult to discern where, if at all, the fantasy on the screen gave way to real life. When important visitors were shown around the United Artists lot, they were invariably greeted by Mary Pickford smiling away in a Pollyanna outfit. In 1925, the 'Girl With The Golden Curls' was a woman in her early 30s. Gloria Swanson's gold bath tubs, fabulous jewels and exotic wardrobe were merely an extension of the lush decor and costumes of her films with Cecil B. DeMille. The most striking confusion of image and reality was accomplished by Sam Goldwyn who, in 1927, stage-managed the wedding of Vilma Banky and Rod La Rocque as if it were the climax of one the romantic films in which Banky had co-starred with Ronald Colman.

As far back as the winter of 1907, the Selig Company of Chicago sent a troupe of actors and a film crew to Los Angeles to complete *The Count of Monte Cristo*. They used the beach at Santa Monica for location shooting and built interior sets in the back of Sing Loo's Chinese laundry. Such were Hollywood's humble beginnings. In the early 1900s it was a sleepy outcrop of Los Angeles, surrounded by orange groves. The big event of 1905 was the opening of its first store, The Hollywood Cash Grocery, at Sunset and Cahuenga. Fifteen years later it was a factory town, the film capital of the world producing dreams, rather than citrus fruit, for sale. The first studio proper, Horsley's Centaur Film Company, was established in 1911 by an Englishman, David Horsley. In 1915 Carl Laemmle

The ubiquitous Mary Pickford receiving the Best Actress Oscar for her first talkie Coquette *(United Artists, 1929). The Academy Awards were instituted in 1927.*

To stimulate interest in the expanding industry, Carl Laemmle gave the public the opportunity to watch the stars at work on the sets at Universal Studios. Seats in the gallery at the left cost 25 cents and were very popular but this type of promotion had to be dropped when sound came.

opened Universal City, then California's largest studio, in the San Fernando Valley. At this time a stagecoach was still required to complete the last leg of the journey to Thomas Ince's studio in the Santa Ynez Canyon, but Hollywood's age of innocence was rapidly coming to an end.

By 1920 the picture business was America's fifth-ranking industry. For the next 25 years, movies would flourish around two intertwined elements, the studio and the star systems. A crucial moment came in 1924 when Loew's Inc. appointed Louis B. Mayer vice-president and general manager of MGM, which had been

The fantastic wedding cake which dominated the reception was just a papiér mâché prop, as disconcerted guests discovered when they tried to eat it. Asked by a reporter what name she favoured for her first child, Banky replied, 'I don't know, you'll have to ask Mr Goldwyn'. Later, George Cukor satirised the extraordinary junketings in *What Price Hollywood?* (1932).

Stars were often encouraged by their studios to overspend. By putting themselves in debt, they effectively mortgaged the prospect of independence held out by their enormous, and virtually untaxed salaries. Conspicuous consumption was the order of the day. Swanson was heralded as the second woman to earn a million (Pickford was the first) and the first to spend it. In Tom Mix's palatial spread, a fountain in the hall sprayed water alternately coloured blue, pink, green and red. Among the attractions at John Barrymore's rambling home, 'Bella Vista' – virtually a small village – were a trout pond, two swimming pools, a bowling green, a skeet-shooting range, an aviary filled with exotic birds (including Barrymore's pet vulture, Maloney) and quarters for a dozen servants. Hard-drinking guests, of whom there was no shortage, could drown their sorrows in a replica English tavern or a Frontier bar which Barrymore had had shipped from Alaska.

Scandal came bubbling to the surface at the same time as this huge new wealth enabled stars to indulge a lavish private lifestyle instead of living in the movie colony hotels which had characterised the early years of Hollywood. Night life sprang up to cater for celebrities and would-be celebrities. In May 1921, The Cocoanut Grove opened at the Ambassador Hotel, decorated with several palm trees left over from the set of *The Sheik*.

Of this period, Anita Loos wrote: 'To place in the limelight a great number of people who ordinarily would be chambermaids

An early Vitaphone sound studio – actually a silent studio adapted for sound, with the noisy camera housed in a mobile booth and curtains in the rafters to deaden the echoes.

and chauffeurs, and give them unlimited power and wealth, is bound to produce lively results'. They were not slow in coming. In 1923, drug addiction killed athletic leading man Wallace Reid. In the previous years, Mabel Normand and Mary Miles Minter had been caught up in the unsolved murder of director William Desmond Taylor. The biggest scandal of them all was occasioned in 1921 by the manslaughter trial of comedian Roscoe 'Fatty' Arbuckle, then at the height of his fame. Only a few weeks before, Arbuckle had been one of the celebrity guests at a Hollywood dinner organised by Carl Laemmle, to butter up fourteen of the most important censors from the Eastern states. Laemmle was just about to premiere Von Stroheim's *Foolish Wives* in New York and was determined to smooth its path to the screen. In the backlash of the Arbuckle scandal, *Foolish Wives* was held up for a year and then released in a heavily cut version. Even more damaging to Arbuckle was the disclosure, during his trial for the manslaughter of Virginia Rappe, that four years earlier he and a number of top movie executives had been involved in another scandalous party which had been hushed up with some generous bribes. The studio bosses' own hypocrisy was exposed, and this was unforgiveable. Arbuckle was tossed to the wolves.

In the wake of 'Fatty's' fall from grace, Will Hays, President Harding's Postmaster General, was appointed as a kind of moral overseer of Hollywood. Studios began to insert 'morality clauses' into their contracts. When Dorothy Cummings signed to play the Virgin Mary in DeMille's *King of Kings* (1927), her contract stipulated that for seven years she was to live her life in such a way as to 'prevent any degrading or besmirching' of the role she was about to play. When she sued for divorce shortly afterwards, this clause was held to be an infringement of personal liberty.

With the passage of time, the studios' attitude to scandal became more flexible. When Elinor Glyn was asked, in the wake of the Arbuckle affair, what would happen next, she replied 'Whatever

makes most money'. In 1928, Irving Thalberg even suggested to a horrified Lillian Gish that MGM invent a scandal to spice up her starchy screen image.

By then the studios had been provided with a new means of disciplining unruly stars – sound. As Adolphe Menjou remarked, 'For the first time, movie actors were conscious of their vocal chords'. After the success of *The Jazz Singer* (1927), a trade newspaper concluded, 'Thirty three per cent of film actors are out'. Inevitably, things were not quite so simple. Initially, no big new stars were created by the 'talkers' as they were at first called – Al Jolson was already a huge vaudeville star – and, indeed, the coming of sound enabled some fading favourites to make a comeback. Among them was Betty Compson, whose star had fallen, along with her salary, from $3,500 to $500 a week. But she gave a sufficiently impressive performance in *The Barker* (1928) to jump back to $2,500 a week. The big stars hung back, unwilling to commit their voices to the crude new microphones and recording technology.

Just as the film camera imposed its own demands on screen actors in cinema's infancy, so the microphone posed a new interaction between the stars and the technology which brought them to the public. When Douglas Fairbanks Sr recorded a spoken prologue for his last silent feature, *The Iron Mask* (1929), his bravura delivery forced the removal of the microphone to a distance of some 30 feet. The marriage of voice and personality was the key factor in the introduction of sound and the determinant of success or failure. The choice of film for a talkie debut was all-important. Norma Talmadge, the epitome of 20s glamour, made the transition – after a year of preparation – in *New York Nights* (1929), but then failed hopelessly to match her New York twang to the 18th-century costumes of *Du Barry, Woman Of Passion* (1930). John Gilbert, heir to Valentino, fell spectacularly at the first fence. The silent conventions of *His Glorious Night* (1929), Gilbert's first talking feature, were completely at odds with the addition of sound. His intense, passionate style – so electric at his peak – now seemed faintly absurd. The Great Lover had loved and lost. F. Scott Fitzgerald captured the sudden and devasting sense of loss at the passing of an era in 'The Last Tycoon'. A leading lady, swept aside by the arrival of sound, reflects on the twilight of her glory: 'I had a beautiful place in 1928. All spring I was up to my ass in daisies'.

Former US President, Calvin Coolidge (right), visits the giant of the studios, MGM. His host, looking deceptively mild mannered, is mogul Louis B. Mayer.

Roscoe 'Fatty' Arbuckle

Born **Smith Center, Kansas, 24 March 1887**
Died **1933**

Few people remember Roscoe 'Fatty' Arbuckle's films, but his name lives on in the scandal which ruined his career. On Labor Day, 1921, during a wild party in a San Francisco Hotel, the 300lb comedian locked himself in a room with starlet Virginia Rappe. Three days later she died, murmuring 'He hurt me, Roscoe hurt me'. There were allegations of rape, and a theatrically staged arrest on a murder charge engineered by a politically ambitious DA. Three sensational manslaughter trials followed, submerging the fat man in a rising tide of innuendo. In March, 1922, Arbuckle was acquitted by the court, but not by the public, to whom he became a symbol of Hollywood's decadence.

Arbuckle was destroyed at the peak of his fame. He started in films in 1908 as an extra with the Selig Polyscope company. In 1913 he signed with Mack Sennett and, that same year, had a custard pie thrown at him by Mabel Normand in *A Noise From The Deep*. The roles were quickly reversed and Arbuckle soon became the foremost pie-hurler in the business. Between 1913 and 1916 he appeared in at least 106 Keystone films, and within a year of joining Sennett was writing and directing his own material. His placid baby face and enormous bulk belied an inventive mind and nimble body. Louise Brooks recalled that dancing with him was like 'floating in the arms of a giant doughnut'.

Arbuckle's limited humour was leavened with moments of dextrously handled slapstick. He was always the fat working class boy who got the girl at the end; he also adored dressing in drag to play middle-aged, flirtatious matrons with elephantine grace. In 1917, Arbuckle signed with Joseph Schenck at $1000 a week plus 25% of the profits, and complete artistic control of the films made by his Comicque Film Corporation. Among Comicque's 21 two-reelers was *The Butcher Boy* (1917), which introduced Buster Keaton to the screen. The more restrained humour of the later Comicque films reflects Keaton's influence on Arbuckle's roughouse style.

Roscoe was then persuaded by Adolph Zukor of Famous Players Lasky (later Paramount) to move on to feature-length comedies. The former plumber's assistant became a millionaire, adopting a lifestyle to match. Among his many cars was a custom built Pierce Arrow complete with cocktail bar and toilet.

Then came the scandal: the trial revealed Miss Rappe as an alcoholic good-time girl, pregnant, and suffering from venereal disease. Although Arbuckle

went free, prurient minds dwelt on fantasies of the helpless young beauty at the mercy of the slavering fat beast. A Hearst writer offered a sickening valedictory: 'Little Virginia Rappe, the "best dressed girl in the movies", whose up-to-the-minute clothes have been the admiration and envy of thousands, today wears the oldest garment in the world. It is a shroud'.

The trial finished Arbuckle. Paramount withdrew his films from circulation and consigned two others recently completed to the vaults. It cost them $1 million. After the dust had settled, old friends like Keaton and Marion Davies gave Arbuckle the chance to direct under the name of William B. Goodrich. Among his credits were the 1927 Davies feature *The Red Mill* and Eddie Cantor's *Special Delivery* (1927). He embarked on a disastrous vaudeville tour of Europe and was cruelly booed in Paris. In 1931 he signed with Warners to produce a series of two-reel comedies, but there was no comeback – he died in 1933, leaving less than $2000. RC

in the retrospective Days Of Thrills And Laughter *(20th Century-Fox, 1961)*

Arbuckle (right) with the Keystone Cops in In The Clutches Of A Gang *(Mutual, 1913)*

Richard Arlen

Real name **Richard van Mattimore**
Born **Charlottesville, Virginia,
1 September 1889**
Died **1976**

Richard Arlen was the only actor who literally broke into movies. Working in Hollywood as a messenger in the early 20s, he broke a leg crashing his motorcycle into the gates of Paramount studios. When the personable former World War I pilot left hospital, the studio made amends by giving him a contract. He progressed through the ranks to feature roles, but not without setbacks. His part in *Coast Of Folly* (1925) with Gloria Swanson, was left on the cutting room floor. Cast as the romantic lead opposite Bebe Daniels in *Volcano* (1926), he was replaced by Ricardo Cortez three days into shooting.

On loan to Columbia, he completed a sea melodrama, *The Blood Ship*, (1927), and then successfully tested for William Wellman's *Wings* (1927) – one of the last silent epics and the first feature to win an Academy Best Picture Award – being cast as the young pilot who is accidentally shot down by his best friend. Arlen appeared in three more Wellman films: *Beggars Of Life* (1927), *Ladies*

Of The Mob (1928) co-starring with Clara Bow, and *The Man I Love* (1929). In *The Virginian* (1929), he was reunited with Gary Cooper who had played one brief scene in *Wings*. Now Cooper was the star and Arlen his sidekick.

Arlen survived sound, but lack of ambition and limited range confined him to supporting roles in big features, and rugged two-fisted leads in action-packed programmers. In 1935 he went freelance, and in 1939 signed with Universal to co-star with Andy Devine in a series of 13 cut-rate actioners.

In 1941 Arlen moved to the independent Pine-Thomas production unit pumping out fast-paced adventures for Paramount release. He made 13 films for them then, in 1949, a growing deafness forced him to memorise his fellow actors' lines and lip read on the set. An operation restored his hearing and, seemingly ageless, he played heavies in B Westerns and featured roles in big films like *The Mountain* (1956). In the 60s he received a new lease of life from A.C. Lyles, an enterprising producer packaging a series of second feature Westerns crammed with fading stars, among them Rory Calhoun, Lon Chaney Jr and Johnny Mack Brown. Lyles had been an office boy at Paramount when Arlen was a leading man. Now, in the twilight of his career, Arlen made 15 Lyles films on the Paramount lot. RC

Vilma Banky

Real name **Vilma Lonchit**
Born **Naygroog, Budapest, 9 January 1898**

In *Sunset Boulevard* (1950) William Holden, casting a cynical eye over Gloria Swanson's empty, rat-infested swimming pool, muses, 'Vilma Banky and Rod La Rocque must have swum there a thousand midnights ago'. A powerful evocation of a vanished golden age, it conveniently ignored the fact that Banky could not swim a stroke.

She was already a European star when she was spotted by Sam Goldwyn on a 1925 talent hunt. Signed to a five-year contract with Goldwyn, his publicity machine made much of 'The Hungarian Rhapsody's' fractured English. Which was fine just as long as pictures remained silent. Immediately paired with Ronald Colman in George Fitzmaurice's *The Dark Angel* (1925), Vilma's refined blond beauty perfectly complemented his dark good looks. It was an unashamed tearjerker – blinded war hero returns home and rejects his girl – but the Banky-Colman chemistry marked the beginning of one of the great romantic parternships of the 20s.

Banky co-starred with Valentino in *The Eagle* (1925) and his last film, *The Son Of The Sheikh* (1925), before being reunited with Colman in Henry King's *The Winning of Barbara Worth* (1926), a modern Western shot on location in Nevada's Black Rock desert. Then came a Hollywood version of medieval Spain in *The Night Of Love* (1927), with Banky as a Spanish princess kidnapped and wooed by Colman's gypsy outlaw. Rave reviews greeted their next film, *The Magic Flame* (1927), and Goldwyn – never a man to quit while he was ahead – invented an off-screen love affair for his two stars, which was torpedoed when Banky announced her engagement to Rod La Rocque. Her last film with Colman was Fred Niblo's *Two Lovers* (1928), a handsomely mounted historical melodrama with sound and synchronised musical score (no dialogue) added, as in her next film *The Awakening* (1928), directed by Victor Fleming.

By now the mangled English which had once provided so much amusing copy, was becoming a serious embarrassment, and Banky was given an ultimatum by Goldwyn: talk or quit. The result was *This Is Heaven* (1929), which cleverly exploited Vilma's foreign accent by casting her as a Hungarian immigrant flipping hotcakes in the window at Child's restaurant. But her career came to a swift end. She toured with her husband in a play, then went to Germany to make *The Rebel* (1932), her last film, before exchanging the troublesome sound stage for the more agreeable frustrations of the golf course, playing to near-championship standard. RC

in Lady Audley's Secret (Imp, 1912)

Theda Bara

Real name **Theodosia Goodman**
Born **Cincinnati, 1890**
Died **1955**

Theda Bara was the first million-dollar star to be presented as an object of sexual fantasy. The Fox Film company's fortunes were founded on her over-ripe brand of sultriness, and her fame added the word 'vamp' to the language. The ballyhoo began when Fox acquired a 1910 stage hit, *A Fool There Was*. The title came from the first line of Kipling's poem 'The Vampire', inspired by Burne-Jones's painting of a deadly female. Overnight an appropriately lurid image was created for Theodosia de Coppet, the little known 25-year-old stage actress chosen to play the film's vampire woman.

Her name was changed to Theda Bara by contracting her first name and borrowing from her Swiss grandfather's middle name of Barranger. An extravagant life history was invented for her. Theda Bara, according to the publicists, was born in the shadow of The Sphinx, the daughter of an Italian sculptor and a desert princess. Ancient hieroglyphs foretold her coming, and her very name was an anagram for 'Arab Death'. Photographs showed her on all fours drooling over the skeletons of her male victims. Her dark hair, sensual mouth, and huge staring eyes rimmed with black against a layer of dead white make-up, provided an irresistible icon of female wickedness. Years later she wrote, 'To understand those days you must consider that people believed what they saw on the screen. Nobody had destroyed the grand illusion'.

The studio went to some lengths to preserve 'the grand illusion'. Her contract stipulated that she could only appear in public heavily veiled and must never visit a Turkish bath. On a sweltering summer's day she held a press conference swathed in furs. 'Miss Bara', declared the publicist, 'was born in the shadow of The Sphinx . . . it is very hot there, and she is very cold.'

Between 1915 and 1919 Bara made 39 films for Fox, 22 of them directed by J. Gordon Edwards, grandfather of Blake. *A Fool There Was* (1914) is the only one to survive intact. Most of them were florid moral tales with Theda a wronged woman taking frightful revenge on the male sex. In *The Devil's Daughter* (1915) she was 'La Gioconda', deserted by her lover and declaring, 'My heart is ice, my passion consuming fire. Let men beware'. She was a Russian revolutionary in *Rose Of The Blood* (1917), assassinating job lots of aristocrats and leaving red roses on their corpses. Celebrated vamps of the past were given the Bara treatment in *Cleopatra* (1917) and *Salome* (1918). The wickedness in her films was limited to lolling around in overstuffed interiors and some heavy staring and back-arching, but at the time it was enough to fuel a million fantasies of forbidden delights.

By 1919, tired of her image, she demanded the title role of *Kathleen Mavourneen*, as a sweet Irish Colleen. Hibernian societies went on the rampage, stoning theatres and disrupting performances with stink bombs when they learned that a Jewess was playing the symbol of Irish womanhood. Bara's final film for Fox was *The Lure Of Ambition* (1919). She returned to the stage in a melodrama. 'The Blue Flame', extinguished after 48 performances, then attempted a comeback in a poverty row comedy drama, *The Unchastened Woman* (1925), and sent herself up in a Hal Roach short, *Madame Mystery* (1926). It was her last film but, in a curious way, she remained a star. Returning to the stage in 'Bella Donna', she was applauded for five solid minutes on her entrance. RC

John Barrymore

Real name **John Blythe**
Born **Philadelphia, 15 February 1882**
Died **1942**

In 1926, shortly after settling in Hollywood, 'The Great Profile', John Barrymore, wrote to a friend, 'The most wonderful accident that ever happened to me was my coming out to this God-given, vital, youthful, sunny place'. Barrymore's arrival in this West Coast paradise was not strictly by chance. At 44, the youngest member of the famous theatrical Barrymore family was bored with the stage. An already failing memory caused by his drinking, and the ever-present need for money, brought him hurrying to Tinsel Town.

He was the veteran of some 15 films, the first of which had been Famous Players' *An American Citizen* (1913). With the exception of *Dr Jekyll and Mr Hyde* (1920) they were of little consequence, but on the strength of *Beau Brummel* (1924) Warners signed him at a fee of $76,250 per picture. For a while he prospered. *The Sea Beast* (1926) introduced him to the beautiful Dolores Costello whom he married in 1928. *Don Juan* (1926), the first feature to be released with a synchronised musical score, was a big success and, with his beautiful voice, negotiating the coming of sound, an insurmountable hurdle for many silent stars, proved no problem for him.

Warners renegotiated with him for five films at

in Grand Hotel *(MGM, 1932)*

$30,000 per week plus a percentage. The results failed to justify the considerable outlay: *General Crack* (1929), a ponderous costumer; *The Man From Blankley's* (1930), a lukewarm comedy; *Moby Dick* (1930). Barrymore disappeared under a pair of ping-pong eyeballs and a Fagin-like make-up in *Svengali* (1931), repeating the formula in *The Mad Genius* (1931) with his portrayal of a club-footed puppeteer and mesmerist.

Warners let him go and, for a time, he joined his brother Lionel at MGM. Over the next three years, Barrymore gave some of his finest performances, underplaying brilliantly while Garbo went over the top in *Grand Hotel* (1932). His approaching decline, and a young Katharine Hepburn on the threshold of stardom, lent added poignancy to RKO's *A Bill Of Divorcement* (1932). By now, drink was taking its toll; The Great Profile was beginning to sag, and soon he would require large cue cards to be held up on the set. The turning point came with *Dinner At Eight* (1933), in which he played a drunken fourth-rate actor carefully arranging his own suicide and botching his final moment of melodrama with a sad sprawl onto the hotel room carpet. There was a final, brilliant flaring in Howard Hawks's *Twentieth Century* (1934). As Oscar Jaffe, egomaniac producer and ham supreme, Barrymore both celebrated and savaged the notion of 'acting' in a relentless upstaging competition with Carole Lombard. Thereafter, alcohol took over.

Almost two years elapsed until his portly, lecherous Mercutio in MGM's *Romeo and Juliet* (1936), which was followed by an inexorable slide into supporting roles and B features. He could still occasionally – and effortlessly – steal a scene, as he showed in Paramount's *True Confessions* (1937), a Carole Lombard vehicle in which he was cast at her insistence. At Paramount he was Inspector Neilson in three 'Bulldog Drummond' programmers, his unfocussed eyes gazing beyond the prompt cards to the ruins of his career. He pulled himself together for Garson Kanin's *The Great Man Votes* (1939), an alcoholic college professor rehabilitated by the love of his children, and was excellent with Claudette Colbert and Don Ameche in *Midnight* (1939). It was the last flicker of the old talent before a sardonic descent into self-parody in a grisly touring play, 'My Dear Children', which 20th Century-Fox re-fashioned into *The Great Profile* (1939).

His last film was the wretched *Playmates* (1941) where, when the time came to film a scene in which he recites Hamlet's soliloquy, the theatre's once-great Prince of Denmark couldn't remember the lines. Turning from the crew, he mumbled, 'It's been a long time'.

Barrymore died a year later, penniless. RC

with Marian Marsh in Svengali *(Warner Bros., 1931)*

Richard Barthelmess

Born **New York City, 9 May 1895**
Died **1963**

Lillian Gish said of Richard Barthelmess that he had 'the most beautiful face of any man who went before the camera'. In stills his features seem somewhat dour, but at his peak the motion picture camera captured, in his sad spaniel eyes, a range of reticent emotions which verged on spirituality.

Barthelmess came from a theatrical family and was given his chance in films by the Russian actress Nazimova who had been coached in English by Richard's mother. In 1919, he signed a three-year contract with D.W. Griffith and, in the same year, became a big star in *Broken Blossoms*. As the pathetic Limehouse Chinaman hopelessly in love with Lillian Gish's downtrodden skivvy, he displayed an uncanny ability to submerge himself in the physical aspect of a character.

In 1920 he played a country boy in Griffith's *Way Down East*, hopping over the ice floes of a frozen river to rescue 'fallen woman' Lillian Gish in one of

the most famous climaxes in screen history. Then he formed his own company – Inspiration Pictures – to produce *Tol'able David* (1921), in which he shone as the eponymous mountain lad who saves the US mail from a vicious outlaw gang.

Richard went on to repeat the country boy formula in a number of films, notably, *The Little Shepherd Of Kingdom Come* (1928), in which, aged 33, he played a none-too-convincing adolescent. He survived into sound, bringing an appropriately glum quality to Howard Hawks's *The Dawn Patrol* (1930), a grim tale of World War I airmen and, in 1931, he was voted sixth at the box office polls. But his days as a big star were numbered, and he was unable to adapt his technique to the fast-talking films of the early 30s. Only one of his later talkies is remembered – Hawks's *Only Angels Have Wings* (1939), in which he excelled as a pilot whose nerve has cracked, though he gave fine performances in *The Last Flight* (1931), *Heroes For Sale* (1933) and *Massacre* (1934).

Retiring from films in 1942 (his last was *The Spoilers*), Barthelmess joined the Naval Reserve, and enjoyed prosperity until his death. RC

in The Cabin In The Cotton *(First National, 1932)*

Warner Baxter

Born **Columbus, Ohio, 29 March 1891**
Died **1951**

In the 30s Warner Baxter was the mature, well-tailored, responsible type. Playing Janet Gaynor's middle-aged benefactor in *Daddy Long Legs* (1931) or saving Helen Vinson from an oily European adventurer in *As Husbands Go* (1934), he fluttered the hearts of his female fans.

Baxter began his show business career aged 10, mounting a soapbox in his back yard and inviting friends to watch him swallow worms at a penny a time. He was signed by Paramount in 1924 and played Jay Gatsby in *The Great Gatsby* (1926), but remained in the ranks of featured players until *Ramona* (1928). Then an Oscar-winning role fell

into his lap as The Cisco Kid in Fox's *In Old Arizona* (1929) when director-star Raoul Walsh lost an eye on location. By 1930 Baxter was one of Fox's biggest stars. He continued to alternate between mature romantic roles and exotic actioners, but was at his best as a man under pressure—for example, the harassed director bawling at Ruby Keeler in Warner's *42nd Street* (1933), or the hapless *Prisoner of Shark Island* (1936).

Real pressure finally got to Baxter, long celebrated as one of Hollywood's great worriers, and a nervous breakdown in the early 40s was followed by a swift descent into B pictures. In Columbia's 'Crime Doctor' series, he played a reformed mobster turned criminal psychologist. It was a relatively dignified end to his career, requiring him to do little more than stand around while the complicated plots swirled about his weary figure. RC

Wallace Beery

Born **Kansas City, 1 April 1885**
Died **1949**

Wallace Beery was so familiar as a purveyor of comic villainy that even his Pancho Villa seemed like a lovable old rogue in fancy dress. His early career was somewhat bizarre – circus elephant trainer, leading man in musical comedy, then a start in films done up as a hulking Swedish maid in the 'Sweedie' series. In *Sweedie Goes To College* (1915) the young ingenue was Gloria Swanson. They married a year later, briefly and unhappily, and Beery's career seemed becalmed until the serial *Patria* (1917). With cropped hair, and a wicked leer splitting his corrugated features, he played a succession of Beastly Huns, trying to rape Blanche Sweet in *The Unpardonable Sin* (1919). He once remarked that 'my mug has been my fortune'.

Paramount steered Beery back to comedy in *Behind The Front* (1926), the first in a series of knockabout army romps but, despite a subtle performance in *The Beggars Of Life* (1928), they lost interest in him, and when sound arrived he was one of the victims of a wholesale studio purge. Thalberg signed him for MGM, casting him in a prison melodrama, *The Big House* (1930), and – with Marie Dressler – *Min And Bill*, one of 1930's top grossers.

Then Beery won an Oscar for *The Champ* (1931) and found himself among the roster of MGM stars in *Grand Hotel* (1932)—a marvellous performance as an industrialist at the end of his tether—and *Dinner At Eight* (1933) as another tycoon whose problem this time was a flighty Jean Harlow. After *Viva Villa* (1934), however, he slipped into a string of 'mush and muscle' vehicles. Marjorie Main stepped into Dressler's capacious boots in *Barnacle Bill* (1941) and stayed with Beery throughout the 40s in a series of modest programmers, the last of which was *Big Jack* (1949). It was his last film, and it was released posthumously, following his death from a heart attack. RC

Eleanor Boardman

Born **Philadelphia, 19 August 1898**

Graceful, intelligent and patrician, Eleanor Boardman once complained that, 'They always gave me such goody-goody parts, and I do so want to play character'. She appeared in 31 silent films, but had to wait until the end of the 20s to play the drab heroine of King Vidor's classic of social realism, *The Crowd* (1928).

She arrived in Hollywood, aged 24, as the 'Eastman Kodak Girl', making an early impact in *Souls For Sale* (1923), an engaging melodrama in which she played Remember Stodden, a bride who, on her wedding night, runs away from her villainous husband and is rescued by Richard Dix's film unit. She played Amelia Sedley in *Vanity Fair* (1923) – typical of the insipid roles which she resented – then

made her first film with King Vidor, *Three Wise Fools* (1924). After two more films with Vidor, *Wife Of The Centaur* (1924) and *Bardelys The Magnificent* (1926), both with the rising John Gilbert, she married the great director. Garbo and Gilbert had planned to make it a double wedding, but at the last minute Garbo changed her mind, and Gilbert attended as a disconsolate guest.

The Vidors separated in 1930, the year in which Eleanor made her all-talking debut in the Technicolor *Mamba*. She was in John Gilbert's ill-fated *Redemption* (1930) and Charles Brabin's elegant historical drama, *The Great Meadow* (1931), set in the wilderness of 18th-century Kentucky. Her last American film was DeMille's third attempt at *The Squaw Man* (1931), with Warner Baxter, Charles Bickford and the fiery Lupe Velez; and her career ended with *The Three-Cornered Hat* (1932), made in Spain. In 1940 she married director Harry d'Abbadie d'Arrast. RC

in Women Love Once *(Paramount, 1931)*

Clara Bow

Born **Brooklyn, New York, 25 August, 1905**
Died **1965**

Clara Bow was the provocative figure at the heart of The Jazz Age's long, wild party. She was the new, emancipated woman, with that mysterious quality – 'It' – perfectly embodied in her ripe, sexy body, big saucer eyes and mass of red hennaed hair. Young men drank from hip flasks decorated with her pouting face, while Bow herself barrelled down Wilshire Boulevard in her red roadster accompanied by a pair of lap dogs dyed to match her hair.

For all that, Clara was the girl next door, feverishly self-confident and bursting with boop-boop-a-doop. She was also the first screen sex symbol who does not seem ridiculous today. The shopgirls she often portrayed formed the majority of her female audience; her swimsuits and skimpy outfits guaranteed a strong male following, too, but she always remained a girl out for a good time rather than a good-time-girl, reserving a sock on the jaw for the guy who got too fresh.

Her life reads like a scenario for one of her films: a poverty-stricken Brooklyn childhood; first prize in a beauty contest; then a bit part in a film which ended up on the cutting room floor. She landed a bigger role in *Down To The Sea In Ships* (1923) when director Elmer Clifton spotted her picture in a fan magazine. She was taken up by B.P. Schulberg who put her through 14 films in 1925, including *The Plastic Age* in which she was billed as 'The Hottest Jazz Baby In Films'. She accompanied Schulberg to Paramount where she had a hit with *Mantrap* (1926). By now she was a big enough star for the studio to construct a film around her, and the result was Elinor Glyn's *It* (1927), in which she was the lingerie salesgirl who sets her cap at the boss (Antonio Moreno). She was a top Paramount star for the next three years, and made a relatively smooth transition to sound in *The Wild Party* (1929) – though her restless habit of dashing all over the set posed problems for the crude apparatus of the day.

Then scandal struck. In 1930 she disclosed that she had paid off a doctor's wife for 'alienation of affections'. She ran up a $14,000 gambling debt in a Nevada casino without realising what she was doing and, in 1931, she took her former secretary, Daisy de Voe, to court for theft and embezzlement. Daisy counter-attacked by producing evidence of Clara's penchant for booze, drugs and gigolos. Though Clara won the case the public turned its back on its Jazz Baby, she suffered a nervous breakdown, and was dropped by Paramount.

Bow made her last film, *Hoopla* (1933) for Fox, before retiring to Nevada with her husband, B-picture cowboy star Rex Bell. Every year she sent a Christmas card to gossip columnist Louella Parsons on which was written in a spidery hand, 'Do you remember me?'. RC

Louise Brooks

Born **Cherryvale, Kansas, 14 November 1906**

Louise Brooks was a 'lost' star for over twenty years. In the late 20s she was an exquisitely hard-boiled flapper with a unique hairstyle. Women copied her bangs, but in all other respects she was inimitable. Today, she remains a tantalising figure, whose magic eludes analysis. When talkies were taking hold in America, she went to Europe and gave two of the most bewitching performances in silent cinema. On her return, her own wilfulness brought her career into decline, and an understandable but fatal refusal to allow Columbia boss Harry Cohn to exercise his Hollywood version of *droit de seigneur*, booked her a passage to oblivion.

At 15, she started as a dancer in New York with Ruth St Denis. She was in 'George White's Scandals', danced at London's Café de Paris, and became one of Ziegfeld's most popular beauties. Walter Wanger spotted her, and she spent two years at Paramount playing shop girls, jazz babies and *femmes fatales*. Loaned to Fox, she was an overnight

in Beggars Of Life (Paramount, 1928)

success in Howard Hawks's *A Girl In Every Port* (1928), as Mam'selle Godiva, a predatory circus artist casting a spell over men. In William Wellman's *The Beggars Of Life* (1928), dressed as a man and riding the freight trains with Richard Arlen, she added to Mam'selle's cat-like sexuality an ambiguous, androgynous quality which today seems contemporary. The German director G.W. Pabst cast her as Lulu in his silent production in Berlin of *Pandora's Box* (1929). As the nymphomaniac who dies at the hands of Jack The Ripper, she showed great skill in combining amorality and innocence in a performance which Paul Rotha called 'one of the phenomena of the cinema'.

After starring in Pabst's *Diary Of A Lost Girl* (1929), she returned to Paramount, who were uninterested in her European triumphs. Talkies were in, and they wanted Brooks to dub her part in a Philo Vance mystery she had made earlier. She refused, returning to Europe where she starred in her first talkie, *Prix de Beauté* (1930). Back in America her career declined sharply. Broke, she was reduced to playing in a two-reel comedy *Windy Riley Goes To Hollywood* (1931), directed pseudonymously by Fatty Arbuckle. Wellman wanted her for *Public Enemy* (1931), but she capriciously turned it down. 1936 found Louise wearing a blonde wig in a Buck Jones B Western, then Harry Cohn took his revenge. Offering her a place in the chorus of a Grace Moore musical, *When You're In Love* (1937),

Cohn unleashed the full cruelty of his publicity department, releasing stills of Brooks in the chorus line, captioned, 'Louise Brooks, former screen star, who deserted Hollywood seven years ago.... Louise courageously begins again at the bottom'. Her last film was a John Wayne oater, *Overland Stage Raiders* (1938). There followed a series of dead-end jobs, and then retreat into the 'intense isolation' that had been so characteristic of her acting.

In the 50s she was rediscovered. Henri Langlois' exhibition 'Sixty Years Of Cinema' was dominated by a huge portrait of Brooks's matchless profile, and Langlois declared, 'There is no Garbo! There is no Dietrich! There is only Louise Brooks!'. From her New York home, Brooks wrote a string of penetrating articles on film and, in 1982, published a fascinating memoir, 'Lulu In Hollywood'. RC

in Graustark (Essanay, 1915)

Francis X. Bushman

Born **Norfolk, Virginia (or Baltimore, Maryland), 10 January 1883**
Died **1966**

Long before Clark Gable was crowned King Of Hollywood, the athletic, jut-jawed Francis X. Bushman was the monarch of the silver screen. Bushman's first appearances were in the beefcake pictures flashed onto the safety curtain in the intervals of vaudeville shows. In 1911 he was signed by Essanay. In his first ten films he co-starred with Dorothy Phillips, but in 1912 he was teamed with Beverley Bayne in *A Good Catch* and they were quickly established as a popular romantic partnership.

In 1914 'Ladies World' magazine invited readers to nominate the leading man for a film version of their serial 'One Wonderful Night'. Bushman won by half-a-million votes and, the following year, consolidated his popularity with *Graustark*, a Ruritanian romance. He cruised around Hollywood in a 23ft long Marmon limousine with his name embossed on its sides, habitually smoked 8-inch lavender cigarettes, and was always accompanied by five Great Danes. The other 295 he kept on his 280-acre Maryland estate.

Bushman's career was wrecked when he divorced his wife to marry Beverley Bayne. The disclosure of an 18-year marriage and five children was too much for his fans and, despite a last fling as Messala in *Ben-Hur* (1926), he never re-established himself. But he never lost his flair for publicity stunts. In 1931 he offered to auction himself to the highest female bidder prepared to maintain him in his extravagant style. There were no takers. RC

Harry Carey

Real name Henry DeWitt Carey II
Born **The Bronx, New York, 16 January 1878**
Died **1947**

Most cowboy stars of the early silent days were the real thing. Tough, weather-beaten men, they rode off the range and into the movies. When they hit the jackpot, they abandoned the great outdoors for the wide open spaces of the stucco haciendas that studded Beverly Hills.

Harry Carey was a middle-class Easterner obsessed with the West. When he became a star at Universal, he moved away from Los Angeles to 1700 acres of virgin territory near Newhall where he established a thriving ranch. At Universal, Carey's stern determined features cast him in the William S. Hart mould as a strong, silent sagebrush hero. He developed a sinewy, naturalistic style which flourished in an association with John Ford – beginning with *Straight Shooting* (1917) – with

whom he made 26 films, frequently as a character known as Cheyenne Harry, a 'good' badman.

By the mid-20s, however, Carey had been eclipsed by the flamboyant Tom Mix, the relaxed Buck Jones and the deadpan comedian Hoot Gibson. His career had petered out when he made an impressive comeback at MGM as the lead in W.S. Van Dyke's *Trader Horn* (1930). After that, Carey joined many Western old-timers on the serial trail: *Vanishing Legion, The Devil Horses, Last Of The Mohicans*. Then he had a new lease of life as a character actor. He was outstanding in *Kid Galahad* (1937), and Frank Capra used close-ups of his lived-in smiling face to great effect as a sympathetic senator in *Mr Smith Goes To Washington* (1939), a role which earned him an Oscar nomination.

But it was as a cowboy that John Ford remembered Carey. *Three Godfathers* (1948) opens with a clip of Carey on horseback, shot against a glowing sunset and accompanied by the dedication, 'To the memory of Harry Carey, bright star of the early Western sky'. RC

Lon Chaney

Real name Alonso Chaney
Born **Colorado Springs, 1 April 1883**
Died **1930**

'Don't step on it, it may be Lon Chaney', was the advice proffered by director Marshall Neilan to a studio workman whose foot was poised over a spider. The legendary remark paid tribute to its legendary subject, The Man Of A Thousand Faces, but obscured the actor who lay behind the gallery of monsters and grotesques he created with consummate skill and almost masochistic relish.

Chaney was born of deaf mute parents, and his genius for pantomime was acquired in childhood when he mimicked the day's events for his bedridden mother. Against his parents' wishes, he followed his brother John into the theatre, serving a long apprenticeship in touring stock companies and vaudeville, and acquiring his unsurpassed mastery of make-up. He began in films in 1912, a utility actor on the Universal lot, and his first billing was in a comedy, *Poor Jack's Demise* (1913). On the weekly payroll for five years, he played everything from society seducers to Italian fishermen, and in 1915 directed six two-reelers.

He seemed an unlikely candidate for stardom at Universal where he was 'just another player', and went on to Paramount to make *The Miracle Man* (1919), the first film in which he experimented with grotesque make-up. As 'The Frog', a partially paralysed beggar, he combined the talents of make-up artist, actor and contortionist. Already he was employing the painful methods which were later retailed with drooling glee in countless magazine articles. In Goldwyn's *The Penalty* (1920), he was the legless gangster 'Blizzard'. His stumps were created by binding his ankles to his thighs, cutting off the circulation. The strange joy Chaney found in meeting these outlandish challenges was beginning to take its toll. To create the Oriental features of the ruthless Ah Wing in Tod Browning's *Outside The Law* (1921) he used a crude and toxic rubber moulding which permanently damaged his eyesight.

By 1923 he was a big star with a string of successes behind him, including a malevolent Fagin in *Oliver Twist* (1922). A contrite Universal brought him back in a two-picture deal, the first of which was Lambert Hillyer's *The Shock* (1923). While it was in progress, the massive sets were going up for *The Hunchback Of Notre Dame* (1923) in which Chaney was Quasimodo. For this great role, he donned a 30lb breastplate, harnessed to which was a hump modelled from 40lb of rubber. Over the harness – which was so painful that it had to be removed between takes – was stretched a hairy rubber skin. Quasimodo's crooked nose and misaligned eyes were sculpted on with mortician's wax. Irving Thalberg was the production manager on the

film and, when he moved to MGM, immediately signed Chaney to a long-term contract.

He was reunited with Tod Browning in the bizarre crime melodrama, *The Unholy Three* (1925), doubling as Echo the ventriloquist and 'the little lady who sells parrots'. After *The Monster* (1925), he returned to Universal for *The Phantom Of The Opera* (1925) in perhaps his most famous role as the hideously disfigured composer who haunts the sewers beneath the Paris Opera.

MGM now planned to co-star Chaney with Garbo in a Browning screenplay, *Alonso The Armless*, but they soon had second thoughts about this intriguing pairing, and the film was finally made as *The Unknown* (1927) with Joan Crawford taking Garbo's place. Chaney's later MGM career combined rather mechanical variations on his genius for grotesquerie with some impressive straight roles, including *Tell It To The Marines* (1927), one of his personal favourites in which he played a grizzled Marine sergeant.

Chaney resisted sound for as long as he could. In the end, an ironic fate allowed him just one talkie, a remake of *The Unholy Three* (1930), in which he spoke in five different voices and, as a publicity stunt, swore an affidavit to this effect. It was signed on 30 May. On 26 August, Lon Chaney succumbed to throat cancer and, for his remaining days, was forced back on mime. Thus it was that he went to his grave as a great silent star. RC

in The Hunchback of Notre Dame *(Universal, 1923)*

17

Charlie Chaplin

Born **London, 16 April 1889**
Died **1977**

By the time of his death, Charlie Chaplin's seeming unassailability as the greatest of screen comedians, and universal artist, had been considerably undermined by the rediscovery of Buster Keaton. Keaton, however, was unstinting in his praise: 'At his best, and Chaplin remained at his best for a long time, he was the greatest comedian who ever lived'.

Doubtless Chaplin would have agreed. One of the least appealing aspects of his work is his rapt self-absorption, the genius in isolated contemplation of himself. Early in his career he assumed complete control over his films, and this he retained, throughout the heyday of the great studios and to the very end. In his last film, *A Countess From Hong Kong* (1966), he insisted on instructing its stars, Marlon Brando and Sophia Loren, in the minutest details of business in every scene. Significantly, *The Great Dictator* (1940), his first venture into dialogue, was also the first film in which he felt obliged to rely on a well-balanced cast. His natural inclination was to assemble a stock company of loyal mediocrities and ingenues, who spared him both expense and competition. When Keaton threatened to upstage him in *Limelight* (1952), much of his footage ended on the cutting room floor.

In *Limelight*, Chaplin made a sentimental return to the Victorian music hall, and to the seedy South London back streets in which he grew up. Nowadays he is much criticised for the 'Victorian sentimentality' of his work, which is full of blind flower girls and crippled heroines. But the turn-of-the-century stews of London were his spiritual home, providing him with a deep artistic reservoir on which he drew throughout his career. His closeness to this vanished world ensured his closeness to the working class in the early part of his career, whose culture sprang from the same source. The Little Tramp – sly, sometimes violent, not above stealing, mooning over pretty young girls – embodied the fears and daydreams of working-class people. Chaplin's portrayal was real and not patronising; the Little Tramp's pathetic quest for food, warmth and security had been his own.

His childhood was like a nightmare from a Victorian temperance tract. A drunken father, and a mother who spent long periods in lunatic asylums, condemning Charlie to a Dickensian orphanage. His mother's suffering haunted him throughout his life and her mental illness was later displaced into the physical disabilities suffered by the heroines of some of his most personal films – blindness in *City Lights*

(1931), paralysis in *Monsieur Verdoux* (1947) and *Limelight* (1952). His stage career began at the age of seven, in a clog dancing troupe, and he had toured America twice as a star of Fred Karno's vaudeville company when he went to work for Mack Sennett at Keystone in 1914. On Sennett's sprawling Glendale lot, in nearby Westlake Park, in the streets and on the waterfront of Venice, the Little Tramp evolved, making an embryonic appearance in *Kid Auto Races At Venice* (1914). By his twelfth Keystone film, *Caught In The Rain* (1914), Chaplin was directing himself, and he became a star as the dapper conman fleecing Marie Dressler in the six-reel comedy, *Tillie's Punctured Romance* (1914). Billed as 'The World's Greatest Comedian', he moved to Essanay at $1,250 a week. *A Night Out* (1915) marked the debut of Edna Purviance, the first – and most durable – of Chaplin's young 'discoveries'. *The Tramp* (1915) saw the first of the classic fade-outs in which the shabby, indomitable little figure skitters away into the distance.

Mutual then offered him $10,000 a week, plus a $150,000 bonus. In a remarkable burst of creativity, he made 12 films between May 1916 and October 1917, including *The Floorwalker, One AM, The Rink, Easy Street* and *The Immigrant*. The Tramp was now assuming a life of his own, in cartoons, comic strips and Chaplin contests. There were also imitators, including a young Stan Laurel, who had been

Charlie's understudy with Karno. The enormous success of Chaplin's Mutual comedies led to the celebrated 'million-dollar' contract with First National. Chaplin had contracted to make eight comedies in 18 months, but his output was slowing down and in the next 12 months he produced only two films, *A Dog's Life* (1918) and *Shoulder Arms* (1918), an answer to criticism about his lack of involvement in the war effort. There followed *A Day's Pleasure* (1919), and in *Sunnyside*, in the same year, a Pan-like Chaplin pranced through bosky groves accompanied by nubile wood-nymphs, a nod in the direction of Nijinsky who had praised his work as 'balletic'. Then he spent over a year on *The Kid* (1921), in which the bewitching little foundling (Jackie Coogan) raised by The Tramp is Chaplin walking hand-in-hand with his adult self.

He was not free of his commitment to First National until 1922, but in 1919 he joined Fairbanks, Pickford and D.W. Griffith in the formation of United Artists (UA). His first UA film was *A Woman Of Paris* (1923), a drama starring Edna Purviance, in which he played a cameo role. It was a critical success but a commercial failure, and it spurred him on to *The Gold Rush* (1925), in which The Tramp, alone and adrift in the Frozen North, improvises his sad little cabaret with two forks and a couple of bread rolls. *The Circus* (1928) is a scrappy film, and Chaplin's teetering adventures on the high wire owe a debt to Harold Lloyd's 'thrill comedy'. Nevertheless, it won him a special Oscar. At the same ceremony another award was made – to *The Jazz Singer*. Three years later, in *City Lights* (1931), Chaplin triumphantly resisted the talkies, adding only a musical soundtrack. It was the tale of a blind flower girl whose sight is restored by an operation paid for by The Tramp, whom she believes to be a millionaire. In the final shot she is confronted with her pathetic little benefactor, his face lit with a nervous smile which combined both hope and apprehension. James Agee thought it 'the highest moment in cinema'.

Chaplin had long been lionised by the likes of George Bernard Shaw, and now he turned his attention to The Great Problems Of The Day. *Modern Times* (1936) pitched The Tramp into the neon-lit world of automation, although at the end he toddles off into the rural never-never land of his Mutual days, accompanied by Paulette Goddard, his latest gamin (and his third wife). *The Great Dictator* (1940) was prompted by Alexander Korda's observation of the physical similarity between The Tramp and Adolf Hitler. The resemblance was perhaps more than skin deep: both Chaplin and Hitler were auto-didacts of monstrous ego who channelled their own brands of self pity into an idealisation of 'the little man'. Chaplin's films can be seen as his own version of 'Mein Kampf'; ideally he should have played the destitute young Hitler of his pre-1914 Vienna days rather than the posturing Adenoid Hynkel of *The Great Dictator*. After World War II he drifted away from his audience, but made his most fascinating film, *Monsieur Verdoux* (1947). He abandoned The Tramp to play a worldly wife-murderer, second cousin to Adolphe Menjou's cynical Pierre in *A Woman Of Paris*. It is full of Chaplin's underlying misogyny, the result of broken marriages and paternity suits, and the mirror image of The Tramp's sentimental vision of women. By turns wordy and mawkish, it is nonetheless years ahead of its time.

Limelight was his last American film before official hostility to his mild espousal of Communism drove him to settle in Switzerland. *A King In New York* (1957), filmed at Pinewood, was a belated riposte to the treatment he had received at the hands of his adopted country. His last screen role was, appropriately, a silent cameo as a seasick steward in *A Countess From Hong Kong*. Nine years later, in 1975, there was a reconciliation with Hollywood – a triumph of Tinsel Town's limitless capacity for cosmic humbug – and a special Oscar. He was knighted in the same year. RC

with Claire Bloom in Limelight *(United Artists, 1952)*

in The Gold Rush *(United Artists, 1925)* ▷

Ronald Colman

Born **Richmond, England, 9 February 1891**
Died **1958**

Ronald Colman was a stockbroker-belt dream, the courteous professional man whose soft voice and perfect manners hinted at inner depths of strength and mystic introspection. Calm, elegant of dress and demeanour, readily given to wry understatement, he could always be relied upon to 'do the right thing'. He was the kind of Englishman who lived by the unwritten codes of an Empire long since vanished. He was ever an elegant Imperial standard bearer, and there is a melancholy irony in the small cameo he played in his penultimate film, *Around The World In 80 Days* (1956) when, immaculate in solar topee, white ducks and swagger stick, he greets Robert Newton, Cedric Hardwicke and David Niven with the words, 'I'm sorry, Gentlemen, this is the end of the line'. His durability was remarkable. He became a romantic star at the age of 32 and, nearly 20 years later his tact, timing, and incomparable restraint defied time to triumph over the absurdities of plot in *Random Harvest* (1943).

Colman took up acting after being invalided out of World War I. In 1920 he abandoned a mildly successful stage and film career in Britain and sailed to America with £8 in his pocket, three spare collars and two letters of introduction. His first film role was in a Selznick production, *Handcuffs Or Kisses* (1921), well down the cast list. While working on stage with Ruth Chatterton in 'La Tendresse', he was spotted by Lillian Gish, who offered him the male lead in *The White Sister* (1923), directed by Henry King. The moustache he grew for the role was to become part of the architecture of his famous face, and he only abandoned it twice. He made a second film with Gish, *Romola* (1924), then signed with Goldwyn who put him in *Tarnish* (1924) with May McAvoy. Goldwyn loaned him out to star in romantic dramas with Blanche Sweet and light comedies with Constance Talmadge and then teamed him with his new Hungarian star, Vilma Banky, in a wildly successful weepie, *The Dark Angel* (1925). It was to prove a turning point in Colman's career.

A year elapsed before he resumed his partnership with Banky, but the time was well spent: Henry

in A Tale Of Two Cities *(MGM, 1936)*

King's *Stella Dallas* (1925), as the socialite who marries and then rejects vulgar Belle Bennett; Lord Darlington in Lubitsch's *Lady Windermere's Fan* (1925); Norma Talmadge's leading man in Clarence Brown's *Kiki* (1926); and then a definitive performance in the title role of *Beau Geste* (1926). Henry King's *The Winning Of Barbara Worth* (1926) launched Banky and Colman as one of the great romantic partnerships of the 20s. They made three more films together: *The Night Of Love* (1927), a swashbuckler in which Colman played a gypsy

prince; *The Magic Flame* (1927), which cast him in the dual role of circus clown and monocled aristocratic heavy; and *Two Lovers* (1928), a lavish piece of hokum set in 17th-century Europe.

Despite the enormous popularity of these films, Colman was basically miscast as a romantic swashbuckler. Sound changed his screen personality and proved his greatest asset. His cultured, beautifully modulated voice perfectly matched the graciousness that was occasionally at odds with his silent roles. His first talkie, *Bulldog Drummond* (1929), was chosen and rehearsed with great care. In Colman's hands, Sapper's semi-Fascist clubland thug became a debonair and cultivated adventurer, the prototype of the mature, amused romantics which the star copyrighted in the 30s. The long association with Goldwyn ended in 1932, after a press release (reputedly written by Goldwyn himself) which suggested that Colman warmed up for love scenes by getting drunk. Thereafter he never tied himself to a long-term contract, and in 1937 formed his own production company, Renowned Artists. His first film after leaving Goldwyn was, appropriately enough, Fox's *Bulldog Drummond Strikes Back* (1934), which he followed with an older Imperial theme in *Clive Of India* (1935), for which history required him to shave off his moustache. Colman's quiet sense of conviction was at its best when playing a character singled out for a tragic end, and in the same year his performance as Sydney Carton held together a spectacular but lumbering production of *A Tale Of Two Cities* (1935). There was a quality of fragility about his voice which was noticeably moving in his delivery of Carton's speech from the scaffold.

The Fox contract ended with *Under Two Flags* (1936), in which Colman played an insouciant Foreign Legionnaire torn between Rosalind Russell and Claudette Colbert in Frank Lloyd's cracking version of Ouida's romantic novel. His first year as a freelance proved an *annus mirabilis*. In Frank Capra's *Lost Horizon* (1937) he was Robert Conway, the soldier-diplomat who wrestles with inner doubts and finally finds peace in the lost kingdom of Shangri La. Then Selznick chose him for the famous dual role in John Cromwell's classic screen version of *The Prisoner Of Zenda*. It was the dream factory at its smoothest and most beguiling and led to a seven-year contract with Selznick, an arrangement which sadly failed to produce a single film. Colman continued to freelance, at Paramount in *If I Were King* (1938) and *The Light That Failed* (1939), and at RKO in two lacklustre comedies, *Lucky Partners* (1940) and *My Life With Caroline* (1941). In the 40s he devoted a great deal of time to his duties as President of the British War Relief Association of Southern California. He chose his parts with care though not always with wisdom – he turned down both *Intermezzo* and *Rebecca* – but returned to form in *The Talk Of The Town* (1942), and recaptured his classic style in *Random Harvest* (1942), playing an amnesiac who contrives to marry Greer Garson twice. He received an Oscar nomination, but had to wait five years before gaining the Best Actor award for *A Double Life* (1947) as a Shakespearian actor who succumbs to schizophrenia and assumes the character of the role he is playing, in this case Othello, with fatal results for his off-stage Desdemona, Shelley Winters.

There was one more good role in *Champagne For Caesar* (1949), an amusing spoof on television quiz shows. Although his charm remained undimmed, Colman was now rapidly ageing and he settled into semi-retirement, starring with his second wife Benita Hume in a radio and television series, 'The Halls Of Ivy'. His last film was the muddled *The Story Of Mankind* (1957), in which he played The Spirit Of Mankind. A year before he had been asked by a reporter if it was true that he had received a Cadillac limousine as remuneration for a day's work on *Around The World In 80 Days*. 'No,' he replied quietly, 'for a lifetime's work.' RC

in Random Harvest *(MGM, 1942)*

Gary Cooper

Real name **Frank Cooper**
Born **Helena, Montana, 7 May 1901**
Died **1961**

In his early silent days he was languorous and swooningly beautiful. In the 30s, as he matured, he became a virile hero, shy and soft spoken, radiating sincerity and integrity. In his own words, he strove to play 'a fellow who answered the description of a right guy'. Firmly in the mainstream of American archetypes, he was a kind of grown-up Tom Sawyer. Finally, in the 50s, Tom Sawyer grew old; doubt, and the cancer gnawing within him, seamed his face and gave him a moving frailty which found its perfect expression in *High Noon* (1952).

To begin with, Gary Cooper was a 'personality star', but he became the most complete 'natural' actor the cinema has seen. Sam Wood, who directed him in *Casanova Brown* (1944), remarked, 'On the screen he's perfect, yet on the set you'd swear that it's the worst job of acting in the history of motion pictures'. Villainy was outside his range, but his natural deliberation was well suited to comedy, and his versatility is attested by the impressive tally of directors with whom he worked – Hawks, Von Sternberg, Capra, DeMille, Lubitsch, Borzage, King Vidor, Anthony Mann.

He was born of British parents, and was educated in Britain in the years leading up to World War I. Back home in Montana, he worked as a ranch hand and then joined his family in Los Angeles, where he put his equestrian skills to good use as an extra in dozens of Westerns, and Valentino's *The Eagle* (1925) as a Cossack. Then his agent persuaded him to change his name to 'Gary' (after her home town in Indiana) and secured him a bit part in a Ronald Colman-Vilma Banky vehicle, *The Winning Of Barbara Worth* (1926). When the second lead failed to turn up, Cooper took over, died in Colman's arms, and caught the attention of the critics. He was signed by Paramount and given a small part in *It* (1927) with Clara Bow. Well-known for his virility, he had a passionate affair with the man-eating Clara and, at her insistence, was given a bigger role in Paramount's *Children Of Divorce* (1927), where he 'froze' in a romantic persona. *Wings* (1927) gave him another attention-grabbing death scene. His progress was now sure and steady. Three years after working as an extra in a Florence Vidor film, *The Enchanted Hill* (1925), he was her co-star in *Dooms-day* (1928). Paramount then tried, not very successfully, to turn Cooper and Fay Wray into a romantic team (they were paired three more times) in *The Legion Of The Condemned* (1928).

Cooper's first all-talkie was *The Virginian* (1929), back in the saddle in the title role and giving Walter Brennan the immortal warning, 'When you call me that, smile!'. *The Spoilers* (1930) featured his climactic fight with William Boyd, and by the time he made *Morocco* (1930), a Foreign Legion romance with Dietrich, he was an established star. Cooper did not enjoy the experience – or the second-billing – but he was happily reunited with Marlene in Frank Borzage's *Desire* (1936). He moved easily from buckskins in *Fighting Caravans* (1931) to lounge suits and salon comedy with Carole Lombard in *I Take This Woman* (1931), and then played the soldier hero of Hemingway's *A Farewell To Arms* (1932). He survived a sticky patch – which included Coward's *Design For Living* (1933), with Miriam Hopkins, and *Now And Forever* (1934), with Shirley Temple – to re-emerge in a rich period which began with Henry Hathaway's glorious imperial fairy tale *The Lives Of A Bengal Lancer* (1935). Frank Capra's *Mr Deeds Goes To Town* (1936) gave him a part which fitted him like a glove, that of the hick who inherits $20 million and wants to spend it all on the poor in Depression-hit America. A string of hits – *The General Died At Dawn* (1936), *The Plainsman* (1936), *Bluebeard's Eighth Wife* (1938), *Beau Geste* (1939) and *The Westerner* (1940) – saw him approaching his peak. There was only one flop, the

absurd *Adventures Of Marco Polo* (1938), his first film for Goldwyn. In Howard Hawks's *Sergeant York* (1941), he epitomised 'the right guy', a country boy who progresses through rowdy high spirits, religion and pacifism to battlefield heroics on the Western Front. It won Cooper an Oscar, and he was teamed again with Hawks in a memorable comedy, *Ball Of Fire* (1942), co-starring Barbara Stanwyck. *Pride Of*

The Yankees (1942) is probably the central film in the Cooper canon, a thoughtful portrayal of Lou Gehrig, the hesitant, sensitive baseball star who had died of multiple sclerosis in 1941. After *For Whom The Bell Tolls* (1943), in which he played at Hemingway's special request, the quality of his films fell away, although his popularity remained constant. Following DeMille's enjoyably idiotic costume drama *Unconquered* (1947), he was saved by King Vidor's full-blooded melodrama, *The Fountainhead* (1949). During the filming he had a love affair with his co-star, Patricia Neal, which nearly destroyed his marriage. Once again he lost his way, in dire vehicles like Warner's *Bright Leaf* (1950) and *You're In The Navy Now* (1951). He returned to form with *High Noon* (1952), the second of three Westerns he made that year. It was a great performance in an over-rated film. Troubled, decent, racked with anxiety – his Sheriff Will Kane could serve as a metaphor for Cooper's declining years. It won him a second Oscar and ushered in a final flourish with *Blowing Wild* (1953), an interesting oil-rig drama with Barbara Stanwyck, *Vera Cruz* (1954) and *Friendly Persuasion* (1956). Anthony Mann's *Man Of The West* (1958) cast him as a reformed outlaw who is forced to destroy his former colleagues. Cooper's performance was resonant with echoes of his long line of reticent heroes struggling to square their basic decency with the corruption abroad in the world. His last film was *The Naked Edge* (1961). By the time it was released, Cooper was dead. A month earlier at the 1960 Academy Awards ceremony he had been awarded an honorary Oscar for services to the film industry. RC

with Marlene Dietrich in Morocco *(Paramount, 1930)*

Ricardo Cortez

Real name **Jacob Krantz**
Born **Vienna, 19 September 1899**
Died **1977**

Ricardo Cortez was groomed as a Latin Lover, but there wasn't a drop of Spanish blood in his veins. He was born of Hungarian and Austrian parents who later emigrated to New York. Young Jack worked as a Wall Street runner and then trained as an actor before arriving in Hollywood. Tall, dark and handsome, he was taken up by Paramount as the heir to Valentino, but the manufactured star could never equal the great original, and type casting limited his silent career to rather wooden performances in suitably romantic vehicles. Nevertheless, he had the distinction of being the only Hollywood actor to be billed above Garbo, in her first American film, *The Torrent* (1926). He provided another small footnote to film history when, in 1931, he played Sam Spade as a seedy ladies' man in the first screen version of Dashiell Hammett's *The Maltese Falcon*.

His relaxed playing in James Cruze's *Pony Express* (1925) suggested a wider range but, with the coming of sound, Cortez found himself relegated to B pictures where he lent a silky menace to gangsters and bent attorneys. His performances were frequently better than the films in which he appeared, and he can be seen to advantage in such disparate second features as *Mr Moto's Last Warning* (1939) – in which he tried to blow up the French fleet in the Suez Canal – and John Brahm's flashback extravaganza, *The Locket* (1946).

In the late 30s Cortez turned director, delivering a number of stylish programmers including *Inside Story* (1938) and *Heaven With A Barbed Wire Fence* (1939), starring a young Glenn Ford and Richard Conte. He always remained aloof from the movie community, mixing with businessmen and financiers and, when he retired from films, he returned to Wall Street as a banker. RC

Bebe Daniels

Real name **Phyllis Daniels**
Born **Dallas, Texas, 14 January 1901**
Died **1971**

Bebe Daniels made her screen debut aged seven, and at 13 was signed by Pathe as a foil for Harold Lloyd in the 'Lonesome-Luke' two-reelers. Bright and hardworking, she graduated to features with Cecil B. DeMille before becoming one of the most versatile Paramount stars of the 20s, equally adept at light comedy and more sultry roles. In DeMille's *Male And Female* (1919) she played a concubine; in *Everywoman* (1919) she symbolised Vice. She was an accomplished partner for Wallace Reid in *The Dancing Fool* and *Sick Abed* (both 1920), and *The Affairs Of Anatol* (1921). In 1921 she was arrested for speeding. She served 10 days in jail but luxuriated with a Persian rug on the cell floor, and received nearly 800 visitors!

At Paramount Daniels starred in everything from Westerns to costume dramas, the most famous of which was Valentino's *Monsieur Beaucaire* (1924). In 1927 she parodied the Valentino legend in *She's A Sheikh*, playing an Arabian princess who kidnaps handsome Foreign Legionnaire, Richard Arlen.

In 1928 she was abruptly dropped by the studio in the purge which accompanied the coming of sound. She bounced back, singing, in RKO's lavish musical *Rio Rita* (1929). Moving to Warners she appeared in *The Maltese Falcon* (1931), starred opposite Edward G. Robinson in *Silver Dollar* (1932) and John Barrymore in *Counsellor-At-Law* (1933), and was in *42nd Street* (1933). In 1936 Bebe settled in England with husband Ben Lyon, whom she had saved from a life of crime in *Alias French Gertie* (1930). When war broke out they stayed, starring in the 'Hi, Gang!' radio show. After D-Day, she was the first female civilian to go ashore in Normandy, interviewing troops for the 'Stars And Stripes' radio programme.

In 1945 the Lyons returned to Hollywood, where she became a producer. But the tug of London, and a popular radio and TV series there, 'Life With The Lyons', proved too strong. In 1948 they abandoned the fleshpots of Beverly Hills for the homely rigours of austerity Britain. RC

Marion Davies

Real name **Marion Douras**
Born **Brooklyn, New York, 3 January 1897**
Died **1961**

Marion Davies's films are all but forgotten but the memory of Orson Welles's cruel parody of her in *Citizen Kane* (1941) lingers on. Davies was the mistress and protégée of powerful newspaper baron William Randolph Hearst, and *Citizen Kane* a thinly disguised account of his career. Davies provided the model for Kane's second wife, a girl with a Brooklyn accent and a reedy soprano, thrust unwillingly on to the opera stage.

A former showgirl, the real Davies had rather more talent. Her first film was *Runaway Romany* (1917). Hearst established Cosmopolitan Pictures to showcase Davies, instructed his papers that her name was to be mentioned at least once in every issue, and acquired a stream of romantic properties which were entirely unsuited to her limited talents as a light comedienne. No expense was spared with a

Cosmopolitan production – *When Knighthood Was In Flower* (1922) cost Hearst $1,500,000 – but even the hyperbolic efforts of ace gossip columnist Louella Parsons failed to turn Davies into box-office. Perhaps the only person to profit from her was Louise B. Mayer who, in 1925, negotiated an agreement with Hearst to finance her films and pay her salary in exchange for MGM press publicity. At MGM, Davies at last found her way into comedy, notably in King Vidor's *Show People* (1928). In spite of a pronounced stutter, she survived the arrival of sound. Her period at MGM ended in 1934 after a bitter row between Hearst and Mayer over *The Barretts Of Wimpole Street* in which Davies wanted to play Elizabeth. The magnificent bungalow built for Marion at Culver City was dismantled, and re-erected at Warner's after Hearst made Jack Warner an offer he could hardly refuse.

After four films at Warners, the last of which was *Ever Since Eve* (1937), Davies called it a day. Hearst died in 1951, and four months later his loyal mistress married – 'for the first time', as the papers coyly put it. RC

Viola Dana

Real name **Virginia Flugrath**
Born **Brooklyn, New York, 28 June 1897**

Viola Dana was one of a trio of acting sisters, the other two being Shirley Mason and Edna Flugrath. She began a stage career as a dancer and actress while still a child, and was already a stage veteran when she appeared in her first film, Edison's *A Christmas Carol* (1910). Five years later she became a star in *The Stoning* (1915), the tragic tale of a small-town girl whose illegitimate child drives her to suicide.

Her own life was haunted by tragedy. Her husband, director John Collins, died in 1918, and in the space of a few years her mother and both her sisters' husbands died. Then her boyfriend, ace pilot Orme Locklear, was killed in a 'plane crash as she watched him stunting.

She was a star at Metro from 1916 to 1924, 'playing the same part in the same comedy, under different names and slightly different circumstances until my brain reeled'. She left Metro for Paramount where she was rewarded with her most memorable role, the zany stunt girl 'Flips' Montague in James Cruze's *Merton Of The Movies* (1924). Her first talkie was, alas, also her last. She appeared with her sister, Shirley Mason, in Warners' *Show Of Shows* (1929), but by then she was considered a has-been. She retired after a poverty row outing in *Two Sisters* (1929), produced by Rayart, the forerunner of Monogram. RC

Richard Dix

Real name **Ernest Brimmer**
Born **St Paul, Minnesota, 18 July 1894**
Died **1949**

Stalwart and stern-jawed are words that readily spring to mind when considering Richard Dix. Slightly stodgy too – and the engagingly frank Dix would not have demurred. When Sam Goldwyn 'chose' him from 80 candidates to play the lead in *The Christian*, Dix informed the press that he had got the part because everyone else had turned it down. A major star of the 20s, he doggedly clung to his celebrity in the following decade, before being put out to pasture in B features.

His first film was *Not Guilty* (1921), but it was *The Christian* (1923), made in Britain, which established him as a promising young actor. That year Paramount signed him as a replacement for Wallace Reid, and his first film was a typical Reid vehicle, the auto racing drama, *Racing Hearts* (1923).

Dependable and rugged, he was at his best playing reluctant all-American heroes, although he showed a light touch in several romantic comedies directed by Gregory La Cava, including *Womanhandled* (1926) and *Say It Again* (1926). His relations with Paramount were fairly stormy and, in 1929, after three indifferent talkies, he went to RKO, where he had his biggest hit as Yancy Cravat in *Cimarron* (1931), for which he received a 'best actor' Oscar nomination. There were 27 more films at RKO; in *The Lost Squadron* (1932), he was one of a quartet of stunt flyers victimised by director Von Stroheim, and this set the pattern for a succession of formula outings as two-fisted aviators, ace newshounds and US Marshals. His last film for RKO was Val Lewton's B classic, *The Ghost Ship* (1944).

Thereafter his career coasted gently downhill at Columbia, where *The Whistler* (1944) was the first in a series of eight inventive programmers derived from a popular CBS radio programme. Dix starred in all but one, before dying prematurely of a heart attack at the age of 55. RC

Douglas Fairbanks

Real name **Douglas Ulman**
Born **Denver, Colorado, 23 May 1883**
Died **1939**

Douglas Fairbanks was the greatest exponent of the principle that the movies are about movement. Diving off ocean liners, vaulting through the glades of Sherwood Forest, or sliding down the sails of a Spanish galleon, he was in almost perpetual motion, a sword clenched between his teeth, his arm raised aloft, a devil-may-care grin plastered across his sunburnt face. But everyone knew that underneath the exotic costumes there was 'Doug', the all-American optimist and regular guy, a bit of a schoolboy who found in the almost limitless resources of silent cinema's golden age the biggest adventure playground of them all.

When he was signed by the Triangle Corporation Fairbanks was a successful Broadway juvenile lead. His first film was *The Lamb* (1915), loosely based on one of his Broadway hits and something of an ordeal. Feeling his way into the movies, Fairbanks armed himself with an exaggerated Chaplinesque walk, and concealed his sunburnt face under a layer of ghastly white make-up. D.W. Griffith, who supervised filming, was unimpressed and suggested that his talents would be better used in Mack Sennett comedies. Nevertheless, Triangle chose *The Lamb* to be shown at the Knickerbocker Theatre at regular theatre prices, a move designed to reach an audience beyond the nickelodeon market. The camera liked Fairbanks, and the critics singled him out for particular praise.

In a series of satirical comedies, directed by John Emerson and scripted by Anita Loos, Fairbanks created a character who crystallised the impulses and daydreams of American moviegoers. With their muscular moral tone the films resembled gymnastic sermons, their plots pointed skits on current fads and fashion, laced with generous bouts of stunting.

At the end of 1916 Fairbanks started his own production company. In 1917 a peak was named after him in Yosemite National Park. In 1919 he joined Chaplin, D.W. Griffith and Mary Pickford to form United Artists. Marriage to Pickford followed in 1920. *The Mark Of Zorro* (1920), his thirtieth starring feature, launched him as a swashbuckler. It was a risky business as exhibitors were wary of historical drama, but the costumer was a hit. There was a hint of the old 'Doug' in the storyline, but the grey flannel suits and fisticuffs were replaced by black leather and swordplay. The rapiers flickered again in *The Three Musketeers* (1921). Fairbanks so identified with his part that for the rest of his life he retained D'Artagnan's pencil moustache. From 1916, he was the controlling spirit behind his silent films, and *Robin Hood* (1922) revealed his genius as a producer. Bankrolled with his own money at a time

of studio slump, it cost $1 million, much of it spent on the vast set of Nottingham Castle.

In 1929 Fairbanks made his last silent, *The Iron Mask*. He was well-equipped for the talkies, but age was beginning to show. He was a vigorous Petruchio in *The Taming Of The Shrew* (1929), opposite a subdued Pickford, but his sound career failed to catch fire. His final film – *The Private Life Of Don Juan* (1934) – was made in England, and there is a poignant irony in Fairbanks's performance as the aging lover, attempting to resume his fabled career. At the end of the film Don Juan returns to his wife. In real-life, Fairbanks's marriage to Pickford was on the rocks and ended in divorce in 1935. 'Doug' – snobbish, insecure and a puritanical teetotaller – was unable to cope with Mary's drinking, and drifted into a series of affairs. The golden years with America's Sweetheart haunted him for the rest of his life. Marriage to the bland Sylvia, Lady Ashley was no substitute for the adulation of the 20s, when his appearance with Pickford would stop the traffic in any city in the world and bring 300,000 Muscovites out to see them at a time when their films were officially banned in Soviet Russia. RC

with Gino Corrado (left) in The Iron Mask *(United Artists, 1929)*

Greta Garbo

Real name Greta Gustafsson
Born Stockholm, 18 September 1905

Greta Garbo is perhaps the greatest of all female screen legends, the love affair of her extraordinary face with the camera remaining, in the opinion of many, unsurpassed. Clarence Brown, who directed six of her films, called her 'the prototype of all stars', and her life, legend and films are now all but inseparable. It is a testament not only to Garbo's elusive personality, but also to the achievement of the MGM machine in exploiting, enhancing and sustaining her as an unattainable screen goddess. Significantly, when filming the closing scene of *Queen Christina* (1933), Rouben Mamoulian told her to keep her face blank, a beautiful *tabula rasa* on which those watching in the dark could write their own thoughts. William Daniels, the cameraman who lensed 19 of her films, has remarked that her gawky, broad-shouldered, slightly masculine figure did not always show up well in medium shot, and that he preferred to work with her in long shot and close-up. Which is, of course, the perfect metaphor for a star of such enigmatic remoteness, so near and yet so far away.

The roots of Garbo's famed reticence lay in her poverty-stricken upbringing, and in the death in 1928 of the director Mauritz Stiller, her father figure, mentor and lover. All the other men in her life were pale echoes of the Svengali who fashioned her. In the early 20s Stiller dreamt of creating a new kind of woman, 'sophisticated, scornful and superior', but beneath the glittering surface warm and vulnerable. He had already chosen the name 'Garbo' when he spotted his protégée in a gaggle of extras and cast her as the second lead in *The Atonement Of Gosta Berling* (1924). In Berlin he prepared her daily for Pabst's *The Joyless Street* (1925) and, in the same year, accompanied her to Hollywood and MGM, where a sceptical Louis B. Mayer told Garbo, 'American men don't like fat women'. At first MGM had no idea what to do with their two European imports, and Stiller returned to Europe after being taken off Garbo's second film, *The Temptress* (1927).

Irving Thalberg was unimpressed with Garbo's screen tests, and cast her in *The Torrent* (1927), a stunning piece of nonsense in which she played a Spanish prima donna. Most of her silent films were 'vehicles' in the truest sense of the word – subtract Garbo and there is very little left. She was usually cast as a woman of intrigue – the secret agent of *The Mysterious Lady* (1928) or the dangerous seductress in *Flesh And The Devil* (1927), the first of her films with John Gilbert.

Garbo – and MGM's – last silent film was *The Kiss* (1929). Immense care was taken over her introduction to sound. In *Anna Christie* (1930) 40 minutes elapse before she utters the famous line, 'Gif me a visky, ginger ale on the side – and don't be stingy, baby'. The husky, masculine timbre of her voice hinted at the ambiguity of her sexual nature and this was brilliantly exploited by Mamoulian in *Queen Christina* (1933), dressing his star in delicious 17th-century doublet and high boots.

Queen Christina marked a watershed in her career. It ended a run of indifferent films and launched the series of tragic roles on which her reputation as a great actress rests: Tolstoy's *Anna Karenina* (1935), Dumas' *Camille* (1937) opposite Robert Taylor, and *Marie Waleska* (1938), in which she met her match in Charles Boyer. She had now discarded the amused self-sufficiency of the 20s and, in the process, her male audience had largely forsaken her. Women, however, revelled in her suffering.

By 1937 she was in box-office trouble, and the lavish expenditure on her films was justified only by her popularity in Europe. MGM successfully reversed the trend in *Ninotchka* (1939), in which her glum Russian commissar was charmingly unfrozen by Melvyn Douglas. Garbo had laughed (though by no means, as the publicity claimed, for the first time), but the studio blundered with *Two-Faced Woman* (1940), a disastrous attempt to turn her into a comedienne. The War closed the European markets to her and, at the same time, she began her long process of withdrawal, eventually becoming the most famous hermit in New York. The continuing fascination she exerts would seem to defy the widely held belief that absence from the screen is akin to cinematic death. RC

John Gilbert

Real name John Pringle
Born Logan, Utah, 10 July 1895
Died 1936

In 1929 John Gilbert, the heir to Valentino and The Great Lover of the silent screen, made his talking picture debut in *His Glorious Night*. It was anything but. Audiences snickered with embarrassment as Gilbert passionately whispered, 'I love you, I love you, I love you', to a wooden Catherine Dale Owen. The voice of one of the silent screen's most romantic figures was not the voice that audiences had heard in their minds as they watched Gilbert march off to war in *The Big Parade* (1925) or make love to Garbo in *Flesh And The Devil* (1927). The microphone, sadly, reduced the intensity of his love-making to mere posturing.

It was a shattering blow to a star who had lived his life through his films. If he was playing a Cossack prince, Gilbert would fill his Hollywood home with balalaika orchestras and serve his guests with the finest Beluga caviar. He submerged his volatile personality beneath these operatic gestures without any sense of irony. He was the original movie-struck screen star for whom the tinsel on the inside was every bit as real as the tinsel on the surface.

Stardom came after a long, hard apprenticeship which began with work as a $15-a-week extra at Inceville. Later Gilbert wrote scripts for Maurice Tourneur and did some directing, before signing a three-year contract with Fox. In 1924 he moved to the newly formed MGM and was immediately put into an adaptation of Elinor Glyn's *His Hour*. Within a year he was a star and, after Valentino's death in 1926, the screen's most popular romantic leading man. He had a big nose and rather close-set eyes, but his piercing gaze, flashing smile, and hint of vulnerability beneath the glittering exterior, were an irresistible combination. The sexual electricity which crackled in his screen romances with Garbo in *Love* (1927), *Flesh And The Devil* and *A Woman Of Affairs* (1928) led to a brief, celebrated romance which prompted columnist Walter Winchell to coin the phrase 'Garbo-Gilberting' as a convenient shorthand for torrid affairs. When sound arrived, he appeared with Norma Shearer in *The Hollywood Revue Of 1929*, lending a laconic touch to a cod version of the balcony scene from 'Romeo And Juliet', and revealing a pleasant if unexceptionable

Garbo and Gilbert in Love *(MGM, 1927)*

middle-range voice. He signed a new contract with MGM, guaranteeing him $2 million, and made the all-talking *Redemption* (adapted from Tolstoy's 'The Living Corpse') but tension forced his voice into the higher register technicians called 'white'.

When *Redemption* was released in 1930, Gilbert was on the way to becoming a living corpse himself. He had thrown himself into his final role – that of tragic failure – and taken to drinking heavily. The studio did little to help him adapt his bravura style to the more naturalistic requirements of the early 30s. He had earned the undying enmity of Louis B. Mayer after becoming the unwitting dupe in a scheme by Nicholas Schenck to sell off part of MGM to William Fox over Mayer's head. His contract ran out in 1933 with Tod Browning's *Fast Workers*. A few months later he returned to MGM to play opposite Garbo in *Queen Christina* (1933). It was a pairing born of sentiment, but a melancholy feeling clings to the film, and all the confidence and attack which Gilbert had displayed six years earlier had drained away. He was snapped up cheaply by Columbia to make his last film, *The Captain Hates The Sea* (1935), in which he was billed below both Victor McLaglen and Walter Connolly.

John Gilbert died of a heart attack brought on by his excessive drinking. After his death his effects were auctioned. Marlene Dietrich, an old friend, successfully bid for 30 bedsheets, but no one bought The Great Lover's bed. RC

Lillian Gish

Born **Springfield, Ohio, 14 October 1896**

Like Mary Pickford, Lillian Gish made her stage debut at the age of five, joining a touring theatre company with her sister Dorothy and her actress mother. And it was 'Little Mary' who, in 1912, introduced the Gish family to D.W. Griffith Biograph. The same day, the two sisters found themselves in their first film, *An Unseen Enemy*.

Gish was the perfect Griffith heroine, a combination of virginal purity and spiritual strength, and starred in more of his films than any other actress. Her sharp intelligence and technical skill helped to leaven the heavy Victorian sentimentality of the helpless self-sacrificing heroines she played. *The Birth Of A Nation* (1915), *Sold For Marriage* (1916), *Hearts Of The World* (1918), *Broken Blossoms* (1919) and *Way Down East* (1920), are all given a glowing inner life by her fierce concentration and professionalism.

In 1920 Lillian directed Dorothy in *Remodeling Her Husband*, but after *Orphans Of The Storm* (1921), left Griffith after a quarrel over money. She made two films for Inspiration, *The White Sister* (1923) and *Romola* (1924) – both directed by Henry

King and co-starring Ronald Colman – and then signed with MGM for six films at a fee of $800,000. She made *La Bohème* (1926) with John Gilbert, and gave one of the great silent performances in Victor Seastrom's *The Scarlet Letter* (1926). But MGM had decided that Gish's austere image was out of step with the vogue for flappers and jazz babies and, to her horror, Irving Thalberg suggested manufacturing a scandal to pep up her box-office appeal. The studio tried to humiliate her with *Annie Laurie* (1927), but she managed one more masterpiece, Seastrom's *The Wind* (1928), a prairie drama filmed on location in immensely difficult conditions. Edged out by the growing stardom of Garbo, she left MGM for United Artists, for whom she made her first talkie, the Art Cinema production *One Romantic Night* (1930), before returning for a spell in the theatre.

After *His Double Life* (1933) there was a nine-year gap before she slipped back in a supporting role in *The Commandos Strike At Dawn* (1942). Since then she has enlivened a number of films with incisive character performances: *Duel In The Sun* (1946), *The Cobweb* (1955), *The Night Of The Hunter* (1955), *The Comedians* (1967) and *A Wedding* (1978). In 1971 (at the ceremony for the films of 1970) she received a well-deserved special Academy Award. RC

William S. Hart

Born **Newburgh, New York, 6 December 1870**
Died **1946**

In *Tumbleweeds* (1925) William S. Hart breasts a rise, reins in his horse, and gazes sadly at the dust-choked plain below where herds of cattle are making way for the incoming wave of homesteaders. 'Boys,' he says to his companions, 'it's the last of the West.' It was also the last of William S. Hart.

Hart came to films in his mid-40s after a long stage career in Shakespearian roles, and an interpreter of cowboy heroes in 'The Squaw Man' and 'The Virginian'. Although born in New York, he grew up in the Old West, whose life and landscape he later filtered through his own deeply romantic vision of the past. He made his first Western in 1914, playing a badman in a two-reeler made at Thomas Ince's studio, then became a star after *The Bargain* (1914). Given a free hand by Ince to produce Westerns with his own stock company, he revealed himself as a director almost in the Griffith class, and a unique star personality. Hart's screen character was that of the 'good badman', persuaded to turn from his evil ways by the love of a plucky woman. This gave him ample scope to indulge his stock-in trade – lingering close-ups of his craggy, hawk-like face racked with remorse as the moment of redemption draws near. As he gazes on Clara Williams's placid features for the first time in *Hell's Hinges* (1916) – his masterpiece – the caption explains, 'One Who is Evil, Looking for the First Time on that Which is Good'.

He eventually split with the penny-pinching Ince

over the use of his pinto pony Fritz, the first equine star and precursor of Roy Rogers's Trigger. Hart's films were later released by Paramount, and then he formed his own company. Its first film was *The Toll Gate* (1920) in which he was once again an outlaw reformed by a pure woman. By now, however, his supremacy was being challenged by Tom Mix's all-action Westerns. Hart eschewed stunting, and his insistence on courting leading ladies who were young enough to have been his grandchildren stretched credulity to its limits.

When Paramount demanded that Hart submit to studio control, the principled veteran left. His last film, *Tumbleweeds*, was made for United Artists with King Baggott credited as co-director. But the film was pure Hart, austere and realistic, and edited with mathematical precision and rhythmic beauty. He had not lost his touch but, although the film was a success, United Artists deliberately mishandled its distribution after quarrelling with Hart over its length. He took them to court and won, but it was a Pyrrhic victory.

After *Tumbleweeds*, Hart rode slowly off into the sunset. He made a brief guest appearance in *Show People* (1928), and after the success of *Stagecoach* (1939), *Tumbleweeds* was reissued with a new soundtrack and a ten-minute prologue by Hart filmed at his ranch. In one of the most remarkable and moving speeches in film history Hart, a misty film covering his eyes, delivers his reminiscences in his deep and melodious voice. At 70, his commanding presence and steely gaze hint at what he might have achieved in talking pictures had he been a younger man. RC

Sessue Hayakawa

Born **Chiba, Japan, 10 June 1889**
Died **1973**

Humphrey Bogart said of Sessue Hayakawa's performance in *Toyko Joe* (1949), 'He has a wonderful faculty of transmitting a feeling of terror and disaster to any audience, just by the ominous inflections in his voice or by a repressed play of emotions across his otherwise lugubrious countenance'. This sense of restraint also distinguished the Japanese actor's playing in silent films, and his delicate style has been characterised as a mixture of Method and Zen.

His American film career began while he was taking his theatrical troupe, The Japanese Imperial Company, on a tour of the West. He was spotted by Thomas Ince, and scored a big hit in *The Typhoon* (1914), co-starring with his wife Tsuru Aoki, and became a star as the villainous Oriental playboy of Cecil B. DeMille's *The Cheat* (1915). He left Hollywood in 1923 to film in France (where he remade *The Cheat* in 1937) and Japan. He was in France in June 1940, and rather than make films for the Third Reich, he went underground in Antibes. In 1949, Bogart suggested Hayakawa for the role of the scheming baron in *Toyko Joe*, and Louella Parsons launched a search for the actor, who was found exhibiting his paintings in Paris. He then made a number of telling appearances as a character actor, notably as the commandant of the POW camp in *Bridge On The River Kwai* (1957), which gained him an Oscar nomination. RC

in The Gun Fighter *(Triangle, 1923)*

Emil Jannings

Real name **Theodor Janenz**
Born **Rorschach, Switzerland, 23 July 1884**
Died **1950**

Everything about Emil Jannings was massive and slightly ponderous. In the late 20s he hovered over Hollywood, bearing the heavy label 'Great Actor', but his first talkie, *The Betrayal* (1929), revealed a fatal flaw – the German actor's English was virtually

incomprehensible. He was packed off to Europe by Paramount, clutching the Academy Award he had won in 1928 for his performance as the broken Czarist general in *The Last Command*.

Between 1914 and 1926 – when he sailed for America – Jannings made 27 feature films in Germany, seven of them directed by Lubitsch. He played everything from Othello to a comic Haroun al Raschid in Paul Leni's *Waxworks* (1924), but his Teutonic gravitas was particularly suited to a string of heavyweight historical despots who included Peter the Great and Nero. In 1924 Jannings starred in F.W. Murnau's *The Last Laugh*, as an elderly hotel doorman who is demoted to the position of lavatory attendant. The film provided him with the kind of role with which he became identified, that of a respectable man brought down by bad luck or weakness. After the star's return to Germany, he played the stuffy schoolmaster bewitched, then broken and humiliated, by Marlene Dietrich's incomparable nightclub slut in Von Sternberg's *The Blue Angel* (1930).

When Hitler came to power, Jannings fell in with the Nazis and in 1933 was appointed head of Tobis, Germany's second largest film company. Then in 1940 he was put in charge of UFA and starred as the Boer leader Paul Kruger in *Ohm Kruger* (1942), a piece of anti-British propaganda scripted by Josef Goebbels. After the war he underwent de-Nazification, was forbidden to perform in Germany and retired to Austria where he died, a lonely and embittered man. RC

Buster Keaton

Real name **Joseph Keaton**
Born **Piqua, Kansas, 4 October 1895**
Died **1966**

Nothing could be more misleading than the notion of Buster Keaton as 'The Great Stone Face'. He could express passion with the subtlest droop of his eyelids or the slow tossing of his hat into the air. When asked why he never smiled, he replied, 'I had other ways of showing I was happy'. Keaton's comedy is closely in tune with modern films, but they are doggedly unsentimental. His heroes encounter a string of perils, but react to each reversal with an exquisite economy of expression.

He began performing as a toddler in his parents' vaudeville act. Billed as 'The Human Mop', he acquired the deadpan quality and matchless physical elasticity perfected in his great years. In *Cops* (1922) he is pursued by an entire police force. In a single, brilliantly timed movement, he hitches a ride on a passing car, shooting out his right arm to catch its tailboard, and disappears off-screen with his feet flying parallel to the ground. Keaton had made his film debut at Fatty Arbuckle's Comicque studios, in *The Butcher Boy* (1917). In 1919 he formed a

partnership with Joseph Schenck, distributing through MGM. Keaton had complete artistic control, and between 1919 and 1923 was director in all but name of a series of classic two-reelers which included *One Week* (1920) and *The Boat* (1921). In 1923 *The Three Ages* inaugurated a fertile sequence of features; among them *Our Hospitality* (1923), *The Navigator* (1924), *The General* (1927) and *Steamboat Bill Jr* (1927).

Fascinated by machinery, Keaton revelled in mechanical props, but when Schenck persuaded him to join MGM in 1928 he was confronted with a machine he could not control, a huge studio. After *The Cameraman* (1928) and *Spite Marriage* (1929) there was a rapid falling away, hastened by Keaton's drinking and MGM's lack of co-operation. Cast into the wilderness, he made two films in Europe, and kept going with comedy shorts, and bit parts in B features, notably *San Diego I Love You* (1944).

After the War the French rediscovered him, and he appeared in *Sunset Boulevard* (1950) – as one of the bridge-playing Hollywood 'waxworks' – and with Chaplin in *Limelight* (1952).

His genius was finally recognised at the 1965 Venice Film Festival. Behind the cheers there remained a terrible sense of waste. Keaton remarked, 'Sure it's great, but it's all 30 years too late'. RC

in Our Hospitality *(Metro, 1923)*

Al Jolson

Real name **Asa Yoelson**
Born **St Petersburg, Russia, 26 May 1886**
Died **1950**

'I'm going, I'm going,' Al Jolson murmured shortly before he died. It was the old trouper's final performance, and the end of a long career.

He was a hugely popular vaudeville star of nearly 15 years' standing when he made his first film, D.W. Griffith's *Mammy Boy* (1923), an unsuccessful attempt to catch his inimitable barnstorming style. In 1926 he sang in Dr Lee de Forest's experimental short, *April Showers*, released by Warners. The ailing studio decided to gamble on a part-talkie feature, choosing George Jessel's Broadway hit, 'The Jazz Singer'. Jessel backed out, Eddie Cantor turned it down, and it fell to Jolson – the son of a Jewish cantor – to play the son of a Jewish cantor who becomes a vaudeville star. Warners offered Jolson company stock, but he demanded cash – $75,000.

in The Jazz Singer *(Warner Bros., 1927)*

The Jazz Singer (1927) returned $3,500,000 at the box-office. Al sang 'Mammy', told the audience 'You ain't heard nothin' yet', and caused a sensation. *The Singing Fool* (1928), in which he belted out 'Sonny Boy', grossed $5,500,000. Next came *Say It With Songs* (1929) and *Mammy* (1930), with Jolson billed as 'the world's greatest entertainer'.

However, by *Big Boy* (1930) public interest was flagging. Always happiest with a live audience, he retained his popularity in vaudeville and radio but his films described a descending curve: *Hallelujah I'm A Bum* (1933), *Wonder Bar* (1934), *Go Into Your Dance* (1935) – in which he co-starred with his wife, Ruby Keeler – and *The Singing Kid* (1936). There was a brief revival in *Rose Of Washington Square* (1939), and the Stephen Foster biopic *Swanee River* (1940). In 1946, Larry Parks took the title role in Columbia's sentimental version of Al's life, *The Jolson Story*, with Jolson dubbing the songs, a task he repeated in a follow-up, *Jolson Sings Again* (1949). He died in harness the following year, shortly after returning from entertaining US troops in Korea. RC

Laura La Plante

Born **St Louis, Missouri, 1 November 1904**

Laura La Plante must have been the only movie star to travel to Latvia to obtain a divorce. In 1934 she chose Riga, rather than Reno, to end her marriage to William Seiter, who had directed many of her comedy hits in the early 20s.

Blonde, determined, and sporting a shingled, slightly masculine hairstyle, she was often cast as the girl next door. She had a nimble comic touch but is now best remembered as the young heiress nearly driven insane by a grasping cousin in Paul Leni's *The Cat And The Canary* (1927). She was 15 and a Christie Comedy bathing girl when she entered films. Following a stint at Fox, during which she played opposite Tom Mix in *Big Town Round-Up* (1921), she signed with Universal. She quickly climbed the ladder in a series of brisk two-reelers, a couple of action-packed serials, and a spell supporting sagebrush heroes. She made a big impression in *Crooked Alley* (1923), a Boston Blackie adventure, and displayed her comedy flair with Reginald Denny in *Sporting Youth* (1924). She emerged as a star in

Excitement (1924) and the following year was teamed again with Denny in a minor comedy classic, *Skinner's Dress Suit* (1926). *Poker Faces* (1926), with Edward Everett Horton, established her as one of the most talented comediennes of her time, but she was miscast as a Russian ballet dancer in *Midnight Sun* (1926).

Although she described Universal's new sound stages as a chamber of horrors, she had little trouble in adapting to the talkies. After playing Magnolia in the 1929 *Showboat*, she made her all-talkie debut in *Hold Your Man* (1929). In 1930, disenchanted with Universal, she walked off a William Wyler project, and it was with some relief that the near-bankrupt studio terminated her contract. In 1934 she married the head of Warner's operations in Britain and settled there for a while, co-starring with Margaret Lockwood and Douglas Fairbanks Jr in a 1935 quota quickie *Man Of The Moment*. Back in Hollywood she was briefly in the running to take over from Myrna Loy in the 'Thin Man' films, but had to wait until Fred Zinnemann's *Little Mister Jim* (1946) for a comeback. Her last film was *Spring Reunion* (1957), in which she effortlessly scored points off Dana Andrews and Betty Hutton. RC

Rod La Rocque

Real name **Roderick la Rocque de la Rour**
Born **Chicago, 29 November 1896**
Died **1969**

'The wildest jazz, the strongest drama, the real heart appeal and passionate love making'. This is how a contemporary reviewer saw a typical Rod La Rocque movie of the 20s. *Feet Of Clay* (1924) involved a surfboard race, a killer shark, one death, and two suicides whose souls return to their bodies to be given another chance: a combination of *Jaws* and *Between Two Worlds*.

A tall, dashing, matinée idol, La Rocque's career began as a $3-a-day extra at Essanay. At first variously billed as Roderique, Roderick, Rod and even Bob La Rock, he then became a solid Goldwyn leading man. Later, at Paramount, he was cast by Cecil B. DeMille in *The Ten Commandments* (1923). When DeMille left to form Producers Distributing Corporation, La Rocque went with him to star in such films as *Braveheart* (1925) and *Gigolo* (1926). He managed the transition to sound less painfully than some of his contemporaries, and his foxy good looks carried him through to the early 40s in a variety of character roles. His last film was *Meet John Doe* (1941).

La Rocque's 41-year marriage to Vilma Banky was the happiest in Hollywood. They acted together only once, in a 1930 play, 'The Cherries Are Ripe'. RC

Harry Langdon

Born **Council Bluffs, Iowa, 15 June 1884**
Died **1944**

In the 40s a strange, sad little figure haunted Hollywood, eking out a living in B pictures. In the late 20s Harry Langdon had been a big star, a silent comedian ranked with Chaplin and Keaton. By 1933 his fall was so complete that his name was not even included in 'The Picturegoer's Who's Who'. Broken and bankrupt, Langdon, from the depths of his painful obscurity, dreamed of a comeback which unfortunately never happened.

Harry joined Mack Sennett in 1923, already a veteran of more than 20 years in medicine shows, circuses and vaudeville, where he had created an act in which a pathetic, baby-faced man presides over the collapse of his automobile. In a series of one and two-reelers at Sennett, director Harry Edwards and gagmen Arthur Ripley and Frank Capra developed the character on the screen. Langdon's was the comedy of helplessness and indecision. He was just 'a crumb from the sponge-cake of life', as he is charmingly introduced in a Sennett short, *Saturday Afternoon* (1926). He was an innocent abroad, a whey-faced elf with dead-white make-up and rosebud mouth, whose beseeching eyes, fluttering hands and tiny twitching motions of his child-like body betrayed a universe of puzzlement and dither. Often married in his films, he nevertheless remained a child-husband to whom sex was an abstraction.

Langdon left Sennett, forming his own company for a six-picture deal with First National, and taking Edwards, Ripley and Capra with him. Edwards directed *Tramp, Tramp, Tramp* (1926), a big hit in which Langdon set out on a cross-country walking race to win the hand of a young Joan Crawford. Capra took over for *The Strong Man* (1926) and *Long Pants* (1927), after which he was fired by Langdon, who broke up his old team and assumed control over his films. Inevitably he was accused by both Capra and Sennett, of self-destructive egotism and extreme financial incompetence. The charges were exaggerated. The remaining pictures were brought in on time and within budget. The problem was that they were not funny. Langdon may have been able to do more with less than any other comedian, but without his collaborators, he was frozen by his limitations. After *Heart Trouble* (1928), his contract with First National ended, and he began the long, slow slide into obscurity. He was killed off by his own reputation for intransigence, combined with the arrival of sound. His last film role was a bit part in Republic's *Swingin' On A Rainbow*, released in 1945 when Langdon was already dead of a cerebral haemorrhage. RC

Laurel and Hardy

Stan Laurel:
Real name **Arthur Jefferson**
Born **Ulverston, England, 16 June 1890**
Died **1965**

Oliver Hardy:
Born **Harlem, Georgia, 18 January 1892**
Died **1957**

'I am Mr Hardy, and this is my friend, Mr Laurel.' Thus with bowler hat daintily perched on his elbow and an ingratiating beam splitting the fat folds of his face, Oliver Hardy would launch another doomed venture. In Laurel and Hardy's short films – over 60 of them – the task in hand was always disarmingly simple, and the results inevitably and hilariously chaotic. Their bowler hats were the endearing symbols of Stan and Ollie's pretensions to middle-class respectability, but their innocence, forgetfulness and perpetual squabbling marked them out as big babies. The violence they unleashed – like the studious wrecking of James Finlayson's house in *Big Business* (1929) – has all the gleeful concentration of small children.

They came together quite casually. Hardy was a former cinema proprietor who drifted into films as a bit player and heavy, appeared in and co-directed a number of Larry Semon comedies and then joined Hal Roach's Comedy All-Stars. Laurel was a graduate of the English music hall who had come to America with Fred Karno in 1910 and 1913. Laurel worked at Universal and for Broncho Billy Anderson, then joined Roach, making over 50 shorts. He was directing *Get 'Em Young* (1927) when he had to fill in for Hardy who had scalded himself preparing a joint of meat. They were cast in a series of James Finlayson films and were then paired by Roach in *Putting Pants On Philip* (1927), the first official Laurel and Hardy picture. In the next three years they averaged a short a month, many directed by Leo McCarey. Laurel was the creative force in the partnership, and earned twice as much as Hardy,

Laurel (left) and Hardy in Bonnie Scotland *(MGM, 1935)*

although their most cherishable moments invariably revolve around the havoc cascading over Ollie.

They carried their heavily visual style into the talkies without difficulty. The Oscar-winning *Music Box* (1932) showed their ease with the new medium. They moved into features with *Pardon Us* (1931), a short stretched into a feature because of its expensive sets. Initially the demands of feature length outran their comic invention, but they established themselves with *Sons Of The Desert* (1933), *Babes In Toyland* (1934) and *The Bohemian Girl* (1936). After *Blockheads* (1938) they parted company with Roach and became nomads. They went to RKO for *Flying Deuces* (1939), then made two more for Roach at United Artists before moving to Fox and MGM. Now age and the disciplines of the big studios overtook them, and their films were laboured B features. Their final film was a botched French effort, *Atoll K* (1951), in which they looked desperately tired and ill.

When Roach sold their films to television in 1957, it was reported that they did not receive a penny, but Laurel was given some belated recognition in 1960, when he was presented with a special Academy Award 'for his creative pioneering in the field of cinema comedy'. RC

Harold Lloyd

Born **Burchard, Nebraska, 20 April 1893**
Died **1971**

Harold Lloyd's bespectacled hero was the comic version of Douglas Fairbanks' breezy young go-getters, an all-American boy, but one to whom hilarious and hair-raising things happen.

The comedian and his creation caught the boundless optimism of the 20s, and its excitement with the new technology of automobiles and tall buildings. The skyscrapers to which Lloyd clung so alarmingly were thrilling but slightly disquieting, apt metaphors both for the dreams and pitfalls of the Jazz Age. 'Getting the girl' drove Lloyd to become a human fly in *Safety Last* (1923), and left him 12 storeys up, clinging to the sagging arm of a clock, but behind it all beckoned the lure of success and the approval of his peers. In *The Freshman* (1925) his college-boy hero survives the savage humiliations of his classmates to score the winning touch-down in front of a cheering crowd.

Lloyd came into films by way of the legitimate theatre, first working as an extra with Edison and then Universal, where he met Hal Roach. In 1915 Roach used a small legacy to set up a film company with Lloyd playing 'Willie Work', and then a character called 'Lonesome Luke'. In 1917, after over 100 Lonesome Luke one and two-reelers, Lloyd developed a new character, a college-boy type whose ordinariness was mitigated only by his trademark, a pair of horn-rimmed spectacles. In 1918–19 he made 90 one-reelers in his new role, then moved into two-reelers with *Bumping Into Broadway* (1919) and *Captain Kidd's Kids* (1919). In 1920 a prop bomb Lloyd was holding in a publicity shot for *Haunted Spooks*, exploded in his face,

in Doctor Jack *(Hal Roach, 1922)*

removing the thumb and forefinger of his right hand. He returned to finish the film after six months in hospital, and in all his subsequent films wore a prosthetic device, complete with rubber thumb and fingers, concealed by a flesh-coloured leather glove.

Undaunted, he was soon experimenting with spectacular stunt work, moving on to three-reelers with *Now Or Never* (1921) and *Never Weaken* (1921). *A Sailor-Made Man* (1921), a two-reeler which grew into four reels, was his first feature. Lloyd's genius was essentially organisational rather than comic. His normal method was to work backwards from an elaborate gag sequence and devise a plot to accommodate it. *Why Worry* (1924) sprang from the initial idea of a giant with toothache. Lloyd exercised complete control over his films, and the contributions of Roach and, later, gag-men-turned-directors Fred Newmeyer and Sam Taylor were limited to filling in the details. Lloyd also shrewdly retained ownership of the negatives of his films which guaranteed enormous wealth. He was the first major comedian to release a talkie, *Welcome Stranger* (1929), made as a silent and then completely refilmed. It was a big success, principally because audiences were curious to hear him talk. He followed it with *Feet First* (1930), which contains his most nerve-jangling encounter with the topography of a high building. At 37, Lloyd was getting a little old for eager young thrusters. Nevertheless, he played a version of his youthful self in *Movie Crazy* (1932), a satire on Hollywood in which he relived his movie-struck past.

He retired after *Professor Beware* (1938), but in 1947 made an ill-judged come-back in Preston Sturges's *Mad Wednesday* (originally titled *The Sin Of Harold Diddlebock*). In 1952 Harold Lloyd was awarded a special Oscar as 'master comedian and good citizen'. RC

Bessie Love

Real name **Juanita Horton**
Born **Midland, Texas, 10 September 1898**

She has enjoyed one of the longest of screen careers, from *Intolerance* (1916) to *Ragtime* (1981). An exquisite gamin, her long nose giving her a solemn look, Bessie Love never quite made the big time, but her ebullience and wit carried her through an immense variety of roles.

Her father was a Texas cowboy who became a Hollywood chiropractor. Bessie auditioned for Griffith, who gave her a small part in *Intolerance*. Griffith kept her busy in 1916, playing 'little mothers' (*Sister Of Six*) and plucky little orphans (*Cheerful Givers*). The same year she appeared with Fairbanks in *The Good Bad Man* and *Reggie Mixes In*, and William S. Hart in *The Aryan* (1916), before moving on to comedy-dramas at Vitagraph. In the 20s, she graduated to more mature dramatic roles. In *Human Wreckage* (1923) she played a dope-crazed mother who fears the transmission of her addiction to her baby, then had an illegitimate child in Marshall Neilan's *The Eternal Three* (1923) and was a gangster's moll in *Those Who Dance* (1924). She performed the first screen Charleston in *The King On Main Street* (1925), battled with prehistoric monsters in *The Lost World* (1925) and, in the

following year, gave one of her best silent perform-ances in *Dress Parade*, one of Cecil B. DeMille's characteristically lavish productions.

When talkies arrived, Bessie bounced into MGM's *Broadway Melody* (1929), the first backstage musical, singing 'You Were Meant For Me' and winning an Oscar nomination. She continued in musical vein in *The Hollywood Revue Of 1929*, *Chasing Rainbows* and *Good News* (both 1930). After this her career fell away, and in 1935 she settled in England, where she made *I Live Again* (1936) with Noah Beery. During the war she entertained the troops and worked as a continuity girl at Ealing Studios in 1943. Fifteen years later she contributed a telling cameo to the last Ealing film made in Britain, Seth Holt's *Nowhere To Go* (1958). RC

May McAvoy

Born **New York City, 18 September 1901**

Hollywood can be cruel. In 1926 when May McAvoy, a petite, pretty brunette with large Irish-blue eyes, appeared opposite Ramon Novarro in *Ben-Hur*, she was earning $3,500 a week and her name was up in lights. In the 1959 remake, she was a $100-a-week extra in the crowd. She took this reversal philosophically: 'After all, it's 20 years since I retired, and that's 1,000 years in Hollywood'.

She began as she ended – as an extra, in 1916. She made her featured debut as an ingenue in *Hate* (1917), and after the success of *Sentimental Tommy* (1921) signed with Paramount. Specialising in inno-cent heroines, she suffered a career setback when she backed out of Cecil B. DeMille's *Adam's Rib* (1923) after being asked to appear in the scantiest of costumes.

May successfully turned freelance, co-starring with Richard Barthelmess in *The Enchanted Cottage* (1924) and Ronald Colman in *Lady Windermere's Fan* (1925). After Esther in *Ben-Hur* she was Al Jolson's leading lady in *The Jazz Singer* (1927), but did not survive the onslaught of sound. In 1929 she settled into retirement, re-emerging in 1940 to sign with MGM as a bit player. RC

in Sentimental Tommy (Paramount, 1921)

Victor McLaglen

Born **Tunbridge Wells, England,
10 December 1886**
Died **1959**

Victor McLaglen's early life was as action-packed as his later screen career. At 14 he went to South Africa to enlist against the Boers. Fatherly concern kept him out of the War, but he was still under age when he was discharged, having become the regi-mental boxing champion.

He made his screen debut in 1920, playing a prizefighter in a British film, *The Call Of The Road*, and carved out a niche as a picturesque roughneck in a number of films. He crossed the Atlantic in 1925 to star in *The Beloved Brute*. The title perfectly describes his screen persona, the lovable plug-ugly windmilling his way through a series of barroom brawls. The formula was enormously successful in Raoul Walsh's *What Price Glory?* (1926), a World War I adventure in which McLaglen played a boisterous Marine captain. In Von Sternberg's *Dis-honored* (1931) he proved that he could really act, but it was with John Ford that he achieved his greatest success. In *The Lost Patrol* (1934) McLaglen regained his position as a top star, having been dropped by Fox the previous year. In 1935 he won an Oscar for his performance as Gyppo Nolan in Ford's Irish classic, *The Informer*.

As a kilted NCO in Ford's *Wee Willie Winkie* (1937), he was putty in the hands of the diminutive Shirley Temple, but got his own back as the two-fisted Sergeant Quincannon in *Fort Apache* (1948), the first of Ford's great cavalry trilogy. In *She Wore*

A Yellow Ribbon (1949), Ford celebrated McLaglen's lachrymose delight in self-indulgent fisticuffs in an epic saloon brawl. In *The Quiet Man* (1952) Ford burlesqued the process in McLaglen's marathon punch-up with John Wayne.

This finally took the wind out of the old tusker's sails, and McLaglen ended his career in a string of mediocre actioners. RC

Mae Marsh

Real name **Mary Marsh**
Born **Madrid, New Mexico,
9 November 1895**
Died **1968**

Lillian Gish wrote that Mae Marsh had 'a quality of pathos in her acting which has never been equalled'. This was already evident in an early film, *The Sands Of Dee* (1912), and was fully developed when she played the 'Little Dear One' in D.W. Griffith's *Intolerance* (1916).

She was discovered by Griffith when she was 16, and her first leading role was that of a bare-legged prehistoric girl in *Man's Genesis* (1912). She de-veloped a successful partnership with Robert

Harron, who appeared with her in *The Birth Of A Nation* (1915) in which Marsh played Flora, the ill-fated younger sister – one of her most enduring roles, for which she received $35 a week.

After *Intolerance*, Goldwyn signed her to a $2,500-a-week contract. The Goldwyn period was unhappy and marked her last appearance with Harron in *Sunshine Alley* (1917). In 1922 she was one of the first American stars to film in Europe, travelling to England for Herbert Wilcox's *Flames Of Passion* and *Paddy The Next Best Thing*. There followed a memor-able performance in Griffith's *The White Rose* (1923). Her last British film was *The Rat* (1925), produced in Islington by Michael Balcon. In 1932 she made a come back as the mother in Henry King's *Over The Hill* and then settled down to play cameo roles. Her last appearance was in *Arabella* (1967). RC

Adolphe Menjou

Born Pittsburgh, 18 February 1890
Died 1963

In the 20s, Adolphe Menjou was the prince of lounge lizards, playing sleek, exquisitely groomed seducers who were all rolled into one in *The Ace Of Cads* (1926). His smooth man-of-the-world character extended to his personal life, and he was acknowledged as one of the world's best-dressed men. He was obsessive about his appearance, even refusing a role in a British film because the director had the effrontery to ask him to shave off his cryptic little moustache.

He began at Vitagraph in 1914, but it was not until 1921 that he made his first big impression in *The Faith Healer, Courage,* and *The Sheik.* Chaplin's drama, *A Woman Of Paris* (1923), gave him the chance for a suave portrayal of cynicism, and in Griffith's *The Sorrows Of Satan* (1926) he was cast as an elegant Devil.

His approach to acting was, on the surface, equally cynical. Louise Brooks recalled 'He never felt anything. He used to say 'Now I do Lubitsch number one. Now I do Lubitsch number two'.' But the will was there, as he showed in *Morocco* (1930), cocking an amused eye at Marlene Dietrich, and in *The Front Page* (1931), as the tyrannical news editor for which he received an Oscar nomination. By the end of the 30s he had slipped from leads and romantic roles into supporting parts, and in the 40s lent his dapper presence to musicals and screwball comedies: *You Were Never Lovelier* (1942), *Hi Diddle Diddle* (1943), and *Step Lively* (1944).

In the early 50s he was excellent in two thrillers, Anthony Mann's *The Tall Target* (1951) as an assassin out to shoot Abraham Lincoln, and Edward Dmytryk's *The Sniper* (1952). The old cynicism showed through in Stanley Kubrick's *Paths Of Glory* (1957), in which he played a calculating French general in World War I. Ironically, in his last role he dropped the dapper look to play a dishevelled eccentric in *Pollyanna* (1960). RC

Colleen Moore

Real name Kathleen Morrison
Born Port Huron, Michigan, 19 August 1900

'I was the spark that lit up flaming youth', wrote Scott Fitzgerald, 'Colleen Moore was the torch. What little things we are to have caused all that trouble'. Colleen Moore was the first of the up-to-the-minute jazz babies, a thoroughly modern miss who was *The Perfect Flapper* (1924). The exuberant but fundamentally innocent flavour of her most popular films was caught in their titles, *We Moderns* (1925), *Naughty But Nice* (1927) and *Synthetic Sin* (1928). Her Dutch bob hairstyle was imitated by millions of women, cosmetics and clothes bore her name, and there was even a Colleen Moore doll.

Colleen got into films in return for a favour done for D.W. Griffith by her uncle Walter Howey, editor of 'The Chicago Examiner', who was later immortalized by Hecht and MacArthur in 'The Front Page'. In two early 1917 films – *Bad Boy* and *An Old-Fashioned Young Man* – she played the city girl who comes to a small town and vamps an innocent young man. She was Tom Mix's leading lady in several Westerns, had the lead in *Little Orphan Annie* (1919) and developed her comedic talents in a series of Al Christie two- and five-reelers. She became a star as the jazz-mad heroine of *Flaming Youth* (1923), but later alternated flappers with more serious roles, in *So Big* (1925), and *Lilac Time* (1928), co-starring with Gary Cooper.

One of Hollywood's highest paid silent stars, she never really made it into the talkies, although she gave a compelling performance in *The Power And The Glory* (1933), and retired after a mediocre remake of *The Scarlet Letter* (1934). RC

Tom Mix

Born Mix Run, Philadelphia, 6 January 1880
Died 1940

Not content with being the most colourful cowboy of them all, Tom Mix embellished his extravagant screen image with a largely fictional account of his adventurous early life: Rough Rider, US Marshal, freedom fighter in the Boer War, and in the Mexican Civil war of 1910. The legend was so persuasive that many reference books still record these imaginary exploits as fact. In truth, his Army days ended in desertion and his cowboy days were marked by an arrest for horse stealing.

He broke into pictures in 1909 while he was working for the splendidly named Will A. Dickey Circle D Ranch Wild West Show and Indian Congress. The Selig film company used the show and gave Mix the chance to appear as a broncho buster in a semi-documentary film, *Ranch Life In The Great South West.* Between 1911 and 1917 Mix made over 100 one- and two-reelers for Selig, many of which he directed himself. He became a big star when he joined Fox in 1917 and was promoted as a rival to William S. Hart. His Fox films were the complete opposite of Hart's relentlessly plotted melodramas of revenge. Crisply handled by such

capable directors as Lambert Hillyer and Lynn Reynolds, they were slick and streamlined, high on action and low on logic. Packed with spectacular fights and chases (but virtually devoid of shoot-ups), they established the ground rules for all the B

Westerns ground out in the 30s and 40s.

Mix strode through this amiable fantasy of the Wild West sporting an increasingly outrageous wardrobe: huge white sombreros, embroidered shirts, skin-tight white pants studded with diamonds, and pearl-handled Colt .45s transformed him into a veritable Beau Brummel of the range. At the height of his popularity he was earning $20,000 a week and the profits from his films were keeping the Fox studio afloat. At the end of the mile-long drive to his palatial home, a big neon sign winked his famous initials into the night. In 1927 Mix moved to FBO studios, where he quickly bit the dust. With the coming of sound, Western programmers were thought to be a thing of the past and he was dropped. After a spell touring with a circus, he signed with Universal where he made his first talkie, *Destry Rides Again* (1932). His last film was *The Miracle Rider* (1935), a Mascot serial.

Five years later, Mix died in a spectacular auto crash which might have come from one of his best films. His body was pulled from the wreckage unmarked and impeccably dressed, his pockets stuffed with cash and cheques. In the pile-up, a metal suitcase had struck him on the back of the neck, killing him instantly. The last of the legends surrounding Mix's flamboyant life filled the case with a hoard of gold $20 pieces. RC

Mae Murray

Real name **Marie Koening**
Born **Portsmouth, Virginia, 10 May 1885**
Died **1965**

'None of us floozies was that nuts', was Mae Murray's reaction to Billy Wilder's *Sunset Boulevard* (1950). Yet of all the silent stars Murray came closest to Norma Desmond, the epitome and the prisoner of stardom. At a time when outrageousness and eccentricity were considered the essentials of a star's life, she rode in a gold-fitted Rolls Royce attended by liveried footmen, and went through $1,500,000 in eight years.

Murray, with her bee-stung lips and shimmering blonde hair, was a talented dancer, the first Ziegfeld girl to become a star. She befriended Valentino when he was a dancer, and later co-starred with him in *The Delicious Little Devil* (1919). Her speciality was chorus girl, or 'terpsichorean', roles. In *The Gilded Lily* (1921) she was a cabaret dancer saved from a disastrous affair; in *Jazzmania* (1923) she played the queen of a small European country who becomes the dancing queen of an American jazz palace; she had the title role in *The Merry Widow* (1925), during which she dubbed director Erich von Stroheim 'the dirty Hun'.

In 1926 her career was wrecked by a third and ruinous marriage to a fortune-hunting Russian

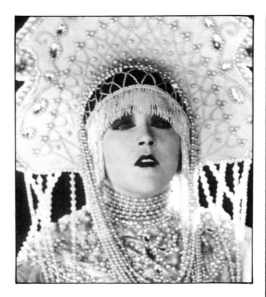

prince, David Mdivani. He encouraged her to walk out on MGM, after which she had great difficulty in obtaining roles. Looking older, and increasingly mannered, she staggered into the talkies, and her last film was RKO's *High Stakes* (1931). Forgotten but not gone, she lingered on, lost in a fantasy world in which she was still a star. RC

in Forbidden Paradise *(Paramount, 1924)*

Pola Negri

Real name **Barbara Apollonia Chalupiec**
Born **Janowa, Poland, 31 December 1894**

Pola Negri was the first big European star to come to Hollywood. Paramount built her up as a modified vamp, while their press agents concocted a phoney feud between her and Gloria Swanson. Negri was cast as the heavy, an image which backfired. To the public she seemed an over-exotic foreign interloper, snootily retreating into books and music and generally taking herself too seriously. The final straw was her melodramatic cross-country dash to Valentino's death bed, and her claim that he died with her name on his lips.

Negri invented a fictitious early life for herself – including a gypsy father exiled to Siberia by the Tsar – actually, she began her career with the Russian Imperial Ballet in St Petersburg. She had made several films in Poland when she became a star in a 1917 Max Reinhardt Berlin stage production. Screen stardom followed, and with it a fruitful collaboration with Ernst Lubitsch. Lubitsch's *Madame Dubarry*

(1919), retitled *Passion*, was a big success in America and led her to Paramount.

Her first vehicle, *Bella Donna* (1923), struck a rich vein of absurdity. She played a scarlet woman, abandoned by her husband and lover, who stalks off to the desert where she is eaten by a panther. She played Catherine the Great in Lubitsch's *Forbidden Paradise* (1924), but her popularity continued to decline. Her last big success was *Hotel Imperial* (1927), then sound killed her Hollywood career.

In England she made *The Woman He Scorned* (1929 – her voice dubbed), and made an unsuccessful Hollywood comeback in *A Woman Commands* (1932). She returned to Germany in the mid-30s, brandishing her Aryan credentials in the face of Goebbels's accusation that she was a Polish Jewess, and made a number of films for UFA. When her name was linked with Hitler's she said, 'Why not? There have been many important men in my life'.

During World War II Negri worked for the Red Cross in France, before making another assault on Hollywood in a screwball comedy, *Hi Diddle Diddle* (1943). In 1964 she was reunited with a big cat – in Walt Disney's *The Moonspinners*. RC

Mabel Normand

Born **Boston, Mass., 16 November 1894**
Died **1930**

Madcap Mabel was the only comedienne of the silent cinema who enjoyed the popularity of a Chaplin or a Lloyd. A disarming little gamin with a dazzling smile, she radiated a captivating and completely natural charm. Her first film was a Vitagraph two-reeler, *Over The Garden Wall* (1910), which starred Maurice Costello. Then her career took off at D.W. Griffith's Biograph studios, and so did the intrepid Normand. In *A Dash Through The Clouds* (1912), she became the first actress to be filmed flying in an aeroplane. At Biograph she worked in split-reel comedies directed by Mack Sennett who was absolutely devoted to his radiant star. When, in 1912, Sennett set up his Keystone Company in California, Normand went with him. By 1914, aged only 20, she was co-directing films with Sennett's big star, Charlie Chaplin, among

in The Extra Girl *(Associated Exhibitors, 1923)*

them *Caught In A Cabaret*, *Mabel's Busy Day* and *Mabel's Married Life*, all released in 1914, but spent most of 1915 partnering Fatty Arbuckle.

But there was a serious actress struggling to get out. The six-reel *Tillie's Punctured Romance* (1914) had whetted her appetite for more ambitious subjects, and Sennett responded with *Mickey*, a feature-length comedy-drama. *Mickey* was dogged by delays, disagreements and financial problems, and it was not until 1918 that it received widespread distribution and became a smash hit. By then Normand had left Mack Sennett and signed up a new contract with Goldwyn.

After 18 crisply produced five- and six-reelers, she was back on the Keystone lot for *Molly O'* (1921). Its release was overtaken by scandal when the director, William Desmond Taylor, was found murdered, and it emerged at the inquest that Normand was the last person to see him alive. Her next film was the appropriately named *Oh, Mabel Behave* (made in 1917 but not released until 1922). But the price of Mabel's penchant for wild living was another scandal, in which her chauffeur shot and wounded an alcoholic oil millionaire with her pistol. Although under enormous pressure, Sennett refused to drop her, doggedly going ahead with the release of *The Extra Girl* (1923). Shortly afterwards, however, she was cited as co-respondent in a divorce case and, reluctantly, he let her go. After that there were a few sad two-reelers with Hal Roach and then marriage in 1926 to Lew Cody, who had been her leading man in *Mickey*. It was a doubly dismal affair – both of them died within a few years, Normand of drug addiction and tuberculosis, and Cody of a heart ailment four years later. RC

Ramon Novarro

Real name **Ramon Samaniegos**
Born **Durango, Mexico, 6 February 1899**
Died **1968**

Built up by MGM as a successor to Rudolph Valentino, Ramon Novarro had too finely developed a sense of irony to take himself seriously as a Great Lover. His last film was the 1960 *Heller In Pink Tights* but, despite the length of his career, he remains indisputably a figure of the 20s.

His family fled to Los Angeles from Mexico during the 1916 revolution. After several jobs, including touring in a ballet called 'Attila The Hun', he became a film extra. Between 1917 and 1921 he made over 20 unsuccessful screen tests before moving from the ranks of the dress extras to featured roles. His big break came when Rex Ingram cast him

as Rupert of Hentzau in Metro's *The Prisoner Of Zenda* (1922). At Ingrams' suggestion he changed his name to Novarro and starred in the director's next four films, including *Scaramouche* (1923).

In 1926 he replaced George Walsh in the title role of *Ben-Hur*, his greatest success, and in 1927 starred opposite Norma Shearer in Lubitsch's *The Student Prince*. In the late 20s he made a number of films with Renee Adorée, the last being *Call Of The Flesh* (1930), his first talkie. Nominally still a big draw – he even starred in a couple of musicals – his career rapidly fell away after *Mata Hari* (1932) with Garbo, and by 1937 he was burlesquing his old image in *The Sheikh Steps Out*.

Novarro's later career was restricted to cameo roles, notably as a smooth villain in Don Siegel's *The Big Steal* (1949). His life ended tragically when he was beaten to death in his apartment by a pair of teenage hustlers. RC

Mary Pickford

Real name **Gladys Smith**
Born **Toronto, Canada, 8 April 1893**
Died **1979**

During *Rebecca Of Sunnybrook Farm* (1917) Mary Pickford reaches for a slice of forbidden blackberry pie. Her mischievous eyes light briefly on a framed sampler admonishing 'Thou Shalt Not Steal', before moving on to another with a more encouraging message – 'God Helps Those Who Help Themselves'. Without more ado, the little heroine tucks in.

The second commandment encapsulates the main themes of Pickford's career. Planned, purposeful, sometimes painful, it made her the most famous

and highly paid woman in the world. The price was the public's refusal to allow golden-haired Little Mary to grow up. She was a young woman of 24 when she essayed the 11-year-old tomboy Rebecca. Six years later in 'Photoplay Magazine' she asked her fans which roles they wanted her to play. Twenty thousand replies flooded in, most of them suggesting the adolescent heroines of children's literature. Child roles represented only seven of her 52 feature films. In *Heart O' The Hills* (1919) she joined the Ku Klux Klan and fell in love with young John Gilbert, but it was as *The Poor Little Rich Girl* (1917), *The Little Princess* (1917), and *Pollyanna* (1920) that her public desired to see her.

As five-year-old Gladys Smith, Pickford made her stage debut in Toronto in 'The Silver Key'. The success of 'Baby Gladys' pulled her widowed mother

Charlotte, brother Jack and sister Lottie into show business, and when the little girl replaced the infant Lillian Gish in a touring show the whole family was hired for $20 a week. In 1907 she opened on Broadway in David Belasco's 'The Warrens Of Virginia', and it was the great impresario who suggested that she change her name to Mary Pickford. When the show closed in 1909, dwindling funds drove the family breadwinner to the then demeaning expedient of extra's work at D.W. Griffith's Biograph film studios in New York. Griffith thought at first that she was 'too little and too fat', but she was soon earning over $100 a week. In *The Little Teacher* (1910), the subtitles identified 'Little Mary' for the first time, and soon exhibitors were deluged with requests for more of her films. The curls and impish grin seen in countless nickelodeons transformed Pickford into the first universally recognisable figure thrown up by the technology of the mass society. When she returned to Broadway in 1913, the theatre was besieged by crowds who had come to see a film star. Adolph Zukor's future Paramount empire grew up around Pickford, and when they parted in 1918, her salary had risen to $10,000 a week guarantee against 50% of the profits.

Her move to First National at $675,000 a year, did nothing to undermine the image of America's Sweetheart. In 1919 she joined D.W. Griffith, Charlie Chaplin and Douglas Fairbanks to form United Artists, and in the following year married Fairbanks. The couple became the uncrowned King

and Queen of Hollywood and their home, 'Pickfair', a West Coast White House. By now Pickford had become a complete actress with a clear idea of her aims. Her performances were acutely observed, and almost Method-like. In *Stella Maris* (1918) she played the pathetic skivvy Unity Blake with one shoulder sagging and the other too high, the result of her observation that such a character would have been deformed by carrying young children on her hip. At United Artists, Pickford moved into straight roles eg a gypsy spitfire in Lubitsch's *Rosita* (1922), but then she returned to the scenes of her own 'lost' childhood in *Little Annie Rooney* (1925), and *Sparrows* (1926).

Her image had not prepared her for the coming of sound. She won an Academy Award for her first talkie, *Coquette* (1929), but was an uncertain Kate opposite Fairbanks' Petruchio in *The Taming Of The Shrew* (1929). His moody behaviour on the set undermined her confidence and hinted at the tension gnawing away at their marriage. *Secrets* (1933), her last film, is haunted by the ghost of 'Little Mary' defying Pickford to become a woman of the world. After her divorce, she married Charles 'Buddy' Rogers. Enormously wealthy, she was content to look after her business interests and dabble in production.

By the early 70s 'Pickfair' was an immaculate sarcophagus in which the Girl With The Golden Curls had become a bed-ridden recluse, seeking solace in astrology, television and the ever-present whisky bottle. RC

with Eugene O'Brien in Rebecca Of Sunnybrook Farm *(Paramount, 1917)*

Charles Ray

Born **Jacksonville, Illinois, 15 March 1891**
Died **1943**

Among the personal tragedies of early Hollywood, one of the most heartbreaking was that of Charles Ray, the archetypal 'Country Boy' star of pictures celebrating the rustic innocence of an American Arcadia. The titles of his most successful films – *The Clodhopper, The Village Sleuth, Egg Crate Wallop* – convey the character he played: a guileless, warm-hearted bumpkin, invariably wearing a battered straw hat and patched dungarees, whose determination and good nature triumphed over the machinations of slickers and sophisticates. With his baby face and hesitant manner, he was a kind of naturalistic Harry Langdon, with the same fatally limited range. The popularity of Ray's farm hands took him in five years from the $35 a week he earned with Thomas Ince in 1913 to a $35,000 per picture contract with Triangle. Success quickly followed at Paramount, for whom Ray made nine films in 1919, but the writing was already on the wall.

Off the set, Ray's lifestyle was anything but bucolic. A snappy dresser, he set a trend for neat English suits and heavy silk shirts with a dark stripe. The most famous feature of his opulent Beverly Hills mansion was a bathroom decorated with black marble and gold leaf and boasting a cut glass tub. Success went to his head. He formed his own company, and after some success with *The Old Swimmin' Hole* (1921) and *The Girl I Loved* (1923), embarked on a historical epic, *The Courtship Of Miles Standish* (1923), adapted from Longfellow's poem. It lost $1 million. Declared bankrupt, he threw one of the most lavish parties Hollywood had seen. When asked how he was going to pay for it, he replied 'Credit'. But credit was not forthcoming. In the age of the Latin Lover, the public lost interest in Charles Ray. Struggling to keep his career alive, he turned to men of the world and tough guy roles. He made some downgrade versions of his old farmyard triumphs, but by now age was thickening his figure and eroding his looks.

After a second bankruptcy in the early 30s, Ray announced, 'I'm not staging a comeback, I'm looking for work'. His reward was a bit part as a doorman in a Cary Grant comedy *Ladies Should Listen* (1934). His last years were spent in misery, eked out with walk-ons and filled with dreams of a triumphant return. Death, following a wisdom tooth operation, was a merciful release. RC

in 1921

Wallace Reid

Born **St Louis, Missouri, 15 April 1891**
Died **1923**

Wallace Reid was the first, but by no means the last, big star to die of drug addiction. It was medical negligence rather than hedonism which led to his death, but the newspapers had a field day, filling their inside pages with imaginative reconstructions of the padded cell in a mental home in which a half-naked Reid supposedly gibbered his life away. The particular irony of his death was that the charming and athletic Reid specialised in breezy, all-American types. No one typified the clean-cut, collar-ad go-getter better than Wally Reid, one of Paramount's most bankable stars of the early 20s.

He was the son of Hal Reid, a writer and theatre producer who moved into films before World War I. Genial and multi-talented, Wally began his film career with Selig, working as a stuntman with another young hopeful Tom Mix. At Vitagraph he moved on to bit parts and frequently set the mood for a scene with his expert violin playing. He worked as a cameraman and tried his hand as a director, employed on *Harvest Flame* (1913) with Marshall Neilan, another doomed butterfly of the silent era who, unlike Reid, lingered on into the 50s, a hopeless alcoholic. Wally's first big role was in *His Only Son* (1912), but when he married his co-star Dorothy Davenport shortly afterwards, the trade press headlined the wedding as 'Film director weds leading lady'.

Reid had more than 100 films to his credit when D.W. Griffith chose him to play a small but important role in *The Birth Of A Nation* (1915). Jesse Lasky attended the premiere and was so impressed with Reid that he quickly signed him to Famous Players. Reid's first release for the company was *The Chorus Lady* (1915), directed by Frank Reicher. In 1917 Reid was *The Squaw Man's Son* in the sequel to DeMille's big 1913 hit, directed by Edward J. Le Saint.

Wally was perfectly at home in prestige productions like *Forever* (1922), a version of *Peter Ibbetson*, and *Carmen* (1915), one of a number of films in which he starred with opera star Geraldine Farrar, but the public preferred to see him behind a steering wheel as the jaunty hero of a series of comedy thrillers filled with breakneck car chases. A typical entry was *The Roaring Road* (1919) which climaxed in a duel between Reid's roadster and a locomotive.

Success trapped Reid on a treadmill of cheaply produced starring vehicles and the hectic pace helped to kill him. It was while filming *The Valley Of The Giants* (1919) in the High Sierras that he was given morphine to relieve the pain of a back injury sustained in a train crash. The treatment continued in hospital and Reid became addicted. For a while he managed to keep up appearances, but by the time he made his last film, *Thirty Days* (1922), he was wasting away and could hardly stand. Fearing the worst, the studio insisted that a doctor accompany him day and night for two weeks, but the hapless medic succumbed to the actor's effortless charm and reported that all was well. Reid died in the arms of his wife, who later supervised and played in *Human Wreckage* (1923), a film based on her husband's experiences as an addict. RC

with Ann Little in Believe Me Xantippe *(Paramount, 1918)*

Gilbert Roland

Real name **Luis Antonio Damaso de Alonso**
Born **Juarez, Mexico, 11 December 1905**

In a 1929 interview, Don Alvarado reflected, 'We Latin Lovers, South of the Border types, have little to do in Hollywood now. Valentino's days are over. I see little or no future for this type of man, including myself'. But one who *did* survive – and became one of Hollywood's most attractive and experienced featured players was Gilbert Roland, whose screen name was a combination of the surnames of two of his early idols, John Gilbert and Ruth Roland.

Roland took the time-honoured path to stardom, working as an extra in Hollywood. His first featured role was in Wesley Ruggles's *Plastic Age* (1926), with whose star Clara Bow he had a well-publicised love affair. Accomplished and darkly handsome, he scored his first big success opposite Norma Talmadge in *Camille* (1927), a role he later played on stage with Jane Cowl. He starred with Talmadge in

three more films, the last of which was *New York Nights* (1929), where he was cast against type as a racketeer. When sound arrived, he appeared in the English and Spanish versions of Hal Roach's *Men Of The North* (1930), and was memorable as Rafaela Ottiano's 'secretary' in Mae West's *She Done Him Wrong* (1933). In the early 30s Roland was kept busy making Spanish-language films at Fox, but his prospects looked poor when Fox merged with 20th Century in 1935, and passed him over for the male lead in *Ramona* (1935) in favour of Don Ameche. But his adaptability, experience and good looks, which improved with age, ensured him 40 years of steady work as a supporting player.

He stayed South of the Border in *Juarez* (1939), and later played the Cisco Kid in a number of above-average Monogram Bs. His relaxed air of authority added weight to a host of unconsidered actioners, and was used to good effect in Budd Boetticher's atmospheric *The Bullfighter And The Lady* (1951), in which he taught Robert Stack the true art of the matador. RC

Norma Shearer

Real name **Edith Shearer**
Born **Montreal, 10 August 1900**
Died **1983**

'How can I compete with Norma when she sleeps with the boss?' Joan Crawford's *cri de coeur* only partly explains Shearer's supremacy in the early 30s as MGM's 'First Lady Of The Screen'. Her marriage to Irving Thalberg was, to say the least, a wise career decision, but Shearer shared her husband's practicality, ambition, and keen awareness of the importance of packaging and publicity. Every Norma Shearer film was an event, and its leading lady a paradigm of poise, elegance and Hollywood class. In her day she was considered a great actress, but she merely posed as one. Behind the marketing there was a hard-working actress, a diligent chameleon who made a little go a very long way in a carefully rationed series of starring vehicles. *His Secretary* (1926), in which she played a Plain Jane who becomes a raving beauty, might have been a blueprint for her own career. Perhaps the most damning comment on her style was delivered by Lillian Hellman, who described her face as 'unclouded by thought'.

Silent films accounted for more than half of Shearer's output. She had a pushy mother whose persistence secured Norma extra work in *The Flapper* and *Way Down East* (both 1920). She was rewarded with a leading role in *The Man Who Paid* (1922). In 1923 she was signed by Louis B. Mayer but had to wait until her success as Consuela, the bareback rider in *He Who Gets Slapped* (1924) before she began to get the star treatment. 'Sophisticated' roles were established as her trademark in films like *A Slave Of Fashion* (1925), *The Waning Sex* (1926) and *The Devil's Bride* (1927), but Mayer remained unimpressed, planning to drop her, when she married Thalberg. He shrewdly put her into a piece of Lubitsch froth, *The Student Prince* (1928), and then stage-managed her introduction to the talkies, casting her against type as a hard-boiled showgirl in *The Trial Of Mary Dugan* (1929). She completed the year on more familiar territory in *The Last Of Mrs Cheyney*, and a brief, embarrassing appearance in *The Hollywood Revue* of 1929.

Shearer was then teamed with MGM's resident clothes horse, Robert Montgomery, in a series of glossy entertainments playing cynical women of the world who suffered fetchingly in mink. They paid a handsome dividend when, in 1930, *The Divorcée* brought her an Oscar. An adaptation of Noel Coward's *Private Lives* (1931) starred Shearer as Amanda and Montgomery as Elyot. Coward diplomatically called the results 'charming'. Next on the list of classics was Eugene O'Neill's *Strange Interlude* (1932), with Clark Gable, then a serviceable remake of the old Colman-Banky tearjerker *Smilin' Through* (1932), with Fredric March. She suffered nobly as

with Clark Gable in Strange Interlude *(MGM, 1932)*

Elizabeth in *The Barretts Of Wimpole Street* (1934), and then ventured a somewhat over-aged Juliet in George Cukor's dull version of Shakespeare's play. After Thalberg's death in 1936, Shearer's position at MGM became as shaky as that of Marie Antoinette, whom she played in a lavish biopic of 1938. Rumour had it that the studio had tried to sabotage the project and force her to sell her MGM stock, but she soldiered on, starring with Gable in *Idiot's Delight* (1939) – more idiotic than delightful – and giving a good performance in Cukor's *The Women* (1939), the best film of her career. The role of Scarlett O'Hara almost came her way, but she dithered and then turned it down, a boon for cinema if not for Shearer. Several years later she compounded the error by rejecting *Mrs Miniver*, although by then she had retired from the screen, her last film being a final outing with Cukor, *Her Cardboard Lover* (1942). RC

Gloria Swanson

Real name **Gloria Swenson**
Born **Chicago, 27 March 1897**
Died **1983**

The year was 1925, high summer of the silents, and according to Gloria Swanson, 'I was … the most popular female personality in the world, with the possible exception of my friend Mary Pickford'. This splendidly back-handed insult to 'Little Mary' is characteristic of the Swanson style – at its best on the screen when she played girls who fought for everything they had, could look after themselves, and would take no nonsense from anyone. Her resilience is perfectly captured in a possibly apocryphal incident. After allowing a live lion to stand over her in *Male And Female* (1919), a hysterical Gloria came to Cecil B. DeMille to announce that she was in no condition to work the following day. DeMille pulled out a jewellery box and suggested that she select a trinket to calm her nerves. Swanson recalled, 'I picked out a gold-mesh evening bag with an emerald clasp and immediately felt much better'.

Time, and the distorting lens of *Sunset Boulevard*, have cast Swanson in the role of *Boulevard*'s Norma

in Bluebeard's Eighth Wife (Paramount, 1923)

with Nancy Olson (left), William Holden (2nd left) and Erich von Stroheim in Sunset Boulevard (Paramount, 1950)

Desmond, a mad silent movie queen, haunting a decaying mansion in which thousands of images of herself gather the remorseless dust of ages. Billy Wilder's dissection of Hollywood's past was crammed with references to Swanson: Norma, talons clawing the air, caught in the flickering light cast by *Queen Kelly*, whose director Erich von Stroheim was cast in *Sunset Boulevard* as her butler and former husband and director; Norma's visit to Swanson's old stamping ground, Paramount, where the real Cecil B. DeMille is directing *Samson And Delilah* and calls her 'young fellow', just as he had addressed Gloria in the dream time when they were making *Male And Female*; a repeat of the marvellous Chaplin imitation from *Manhandled* (1924).

Norma Desmond only dreamed of an impossible comeback. Gloria accomplished at least three. She began as an extra at Essanay, then was teamed with Bobby Vernon in a series of romantic comedies. She played in several 'Sweedie' comedies with Wallace Beery, whom she married (the first of six husbands), and accompanied in 1916 to the Sennett studios in California. Sennett decided to make her another Mabel Normand, but Gloria didn't want to be

another anybody, and the final straw came when she had to submit to being cuddled by a paunchy, bathing-suited Mack Swain in *The Pullman Bride* (1916). She left Sennett for Triangle where she was mollified with dramatic roles in eight films, all of which were released in 1918.

In 1919, divorced from Beery, she signed with Cecil B. DeMille, who was releasing through Paramount. At the time DeMille was making lavishly mounted moral tales of marital infidelity, decked out with a nicely calculated degree of titillation. There were six films with DeMille, in all of which Swanson appeared as an extravagantly gowned sophisticate – a shopgirl's vision of idle luxury – but usually more sinned against than sinning. Their last film together was *The Affairs Of Anatol* (1921), with the ill-fated Wallace Reid.

By now Swanson was an international star. *The Great Moment*, directed by Sam Wood who handled her next nine films at Paramount, was the first in which her name appeared above the title. In 1922 she was with Valentino in *Beyond The Rocks*, and the following year negotiated a new contract with Paramount which gave her a say in the choice of roles. She insisted on *Zaza* (1923), directed by Allan Dwan, playing a gamine-like Parisienne soubrette, and racing through an outlandish parade of costumes. Careful to keep her fans guessing, she played a gum-chewing shopgirl in Dwan's *Manhandled* (1924), and then made a Ruritanian romance, *Her Love Story* (1924), wearing a bridal outfit which was said to have cost $100,000. At the end of 1924 she made *Madame Sans-Gene* (1925) in Paris. She returned in triumph with a new husband, the Marquis de la Falaise de la Coudraye. At the New York première of *Madame Sans-Gene*, a gigantic Stars and Stripes and Tricolour flew over the Rivoli Theatre, while the entire facade was filled with Swanson's name in lights. Making a royal progress across America, she wired ahead to Paramount, 'Am arriving Monday with Marquis. Arrange ovation'. It was proof, if proof was needed, of her early vow that, 'When I am a star, I will be every inch and every moment the star. Everybody from the studio gateman to the highest executive will know it'.

In 1926 Paramount offered to renew Swanson's contract at a fabulous $18,000 a week, but the star wanted to produce her own pictures and, funded by her then lover, Joseph Kennedy, she went to United Artists at $20,000 a week. She indulged her passion for extravagance in her first independent production, *The Loves Of Sunya* (1927), but then met her match in Erich von Stroheim, who directed the ill-fated *Queen Kelly* (1927). Von Stroheim spent $600,000 on this baroque paean to sado-masochism before Swanson pulled the plug. Undaunted, she made *Sadie Thompson* (1928) – a version of Jeanne Eagels's *succès de scandale* 'Rain', retitled to outflank the Hays office – and nearly won an Oscar. It was a big commercial success, as was *The Trespasser* (1929), her first talkie, in which she sang 'Love Your Magic Spell Is Everywhere'. Allan Dwan's *What A Widow* (1930) followed, but only four years and four films later she was shuffled off into a reluctant retirement. There had been quarrels with Goldwyn at United Artists and bad advice from a band of sycophantic admirers, but the principal reason was her association, in the Depression years, with a fast-receding era of reckless extravagance. After *Music In The Air* (1934) there was a seven-year gap before *Father Takes A Wife* (1941), a doomed attempt to recall the Swanson of the 20s.

Despite her absence from the screen, Swanson remained a star by force of her remarkable personality. After *Madame Sans-Gene*, she had wondered, 'What's left? How can I top it?'. The answer came 25 years later with *Sunset Boulevard* (1950), earning her an Oscar nomination but proving an impossible act to follow. There was a dismal Warners programmer *Three For Bedroom C* (1952), then a bizarre Italian toga epic, *Nero's Weekend* (1956). After this there was nothing left but to play herself, which she did with aplomb in *Airport 1975* (1974). RC

in Airport 1975 (Universal, 1974)

Blanche Sweet

Born **Chicago, 18 June 1895**

In Mervyn Le Roy's *Showgirl In Hollywood* (1930) Blanche Sweet, playing a silent star on the skids, sang 'There's A Tear For Every Smile In Holly-wood'. The poignancy of it was underlined by the fact that to all intents and purposes it was her penultimate film. A small part in RKO's *The Silver Horde* (1930) marked the end of a movie career which began in 1909.

She was 14 years old when she made her debut in Edison's *A Man With Three Wives* (1909) and had been in the theatre for 12 of them. The experience paid off: skinny little Blanche was one of the wives. When she started at Griffith's Biograph studios she was a pale adolescent of almost Dresden-like beauty. She soon filled out and carved a niche for herself in resilient roles, notably in *The Lonedale Operator*

in 1922

(1911) as a plucky telegraph girl holding off a payroll gang. In *Judith Of Bethulia* (1913) she was the heroine, drugging an evil warlord and cutting off his head.

In 1917, after making 92 films in eight years, she retired, making an ill-timed return in *The Unpardonable Sin* (1919), a war film which was overtaken by the Armistice. Her great success of the 20s was in *Anna Christie* (1923). This was followed by *Tess Of The D'Urbervilles* (1923), directed by her husband Marshall Neilan. In 1929 she was again the victim of bad timing when she made Herbert Wilcox's *The Woman In White* in London. A silent, it was left stranded by the growing popularity of talkies. With Garbo about to make a triumphant sound debut in *Anna Christie* (1930), Sweet was making the transition in a one-reel Vitaphone comedy short. After retiring from films, she enjoyed a good run in the Broadway production of 'The Petrified Forest', and had a bit part in *The Five Pennies* (1959). RC

Norma Talmadge

Born **Niagara Falls, New York, 26 May 1897**
Died **1957**

Once upon a time there were three sisters: Norma, Natalie and Constance. They were all extremely beautiful and their frail but determined mother watched carefully over their Hollywood careers. Constance was an adept comedienne, the perfect flapper; Natalie married Buster Keaton, co-starred with him in *Our Hospitality* (1923) and went on to make his life a misery. Norma married Keaton's boss and became the biggest star of the three, the queen of the great indoors, suffering magnificently – amid scenes of splendour – for her celluloid sins.

Norma began at Vitagraph in *The Household Pest* (1910), playing a young girl kissing a photographer under the camera cloth. In three years she made about 100 films, mostly playing light comedy, but was not billed until *Under The Daisies* (1913). After a popular series of melodramas with Antonio Moreno, and a brief flirtation with National Pictures, she made seven films in eight months for Griffith's Fine Arts company. In 1916 she married Joe Schenck,

who persuaded her to go independent under the banner of the Norma Talmadge Film Company. Its first film, *Panthea* (1917) directed by Allan Dwan, demonstrated the archetypal Talmadge role – a brave heroine who finds her way to redemption via a series of stunning costume changes. A popular series of films co-starring Eugene O'Brien, the first of which was *Poppy* (1917), established her as a star second only to Mary Pickford.

Her golden period began with *Yes Or No?* (1920) and she reached the peak of popularity in 1922 with *Smilin' Through* and *The Eternal Flame*, an elaborate costumer. Then came *Secrets* (1924), *Graustark* (1925), *The Lady* (1925) and, perhaps her most famous film, *Kiki* in 1926. Her last silent was *The Woman Disputed* (1928), principally memorable for its battle scenes and a surprise walk-on by Charlie Chaplin. Constance then offered Norma some sensible advice: 'Get out now and be thankful for the trust funds that Mama set up'. Nevertheless, there were two talkies, *New York Nights* (1929) and *Du Barry, Woman Of Passion* (1930).

Talmadge was finally destroyed by the reality of the microphone. Her last years were spent confined to a wheelchair, suffering from arthritis. RC

Conway Tearle

Real name **Frederick Levy**
Born **New York City, 17 May 1878**
Died **1938**

If a producer wanted a really low-down heel, there was always Conway Tearle's foreign nobleman, generally afflicted with a disagreeably rare disease, trailing abandoned mistresses in his wake as he moved in on rich, innocent young heiresses – though he did progress to sophisticated but dependable 'hero' roles.

Although a New Yorker, Tearle came from a family of English actors (he was Godfrey Tearle's half-brother) and went back to England to study with his father, the distinguished Shakespearian Oswald Tearle. His first opportunity came when his father fell ill during a performance of 'Hamlet' and young Conway stepped into the breach. He was an instant success and graduated to the London stage, where he played juvenile leads under the tutelage of the famous Shakespearian actor-manager Sir Herbert Beerbohm Tree.

He arrived in Hollywood in 1914 and became an accomplished leading man to some of the great ladies of the silent screen: Mary Pickford in *Stella Maris* (1918); Constance Talmadge in *A Virtuous Vamp* (1919); Pola Negri in *Bella Donna* (1923); Alice Terry in *The Great Divide* (1925). His versatility earned him the title of 'The Man Of Many Moods', and his stage training enabled him to make a smooth transition to the talkies, which included *Vanity Fair* (1932), *Should Ladies Behave?* (1933) and *Klondike Annie* (1936). RC

together in The Great Divide *(MGM, 1924)*

Alice Terry

Real name **Alice Taafe**
Born **Vincennes, Indiana, 24 July 1899**

Alice Terry once told an interviewer, 'I never had the slightest ambition to go into the movies. I didn't lie awake nights dreaming of a call from some great director, and I never had the slightest desire to see how my name would appear in electric lights'.

But the cool, auburn-haired beauty with large thoughtful eyes did get the call – from director Rex Ingram. In 1921 he cast her opposite Rudolph Valentino in *The Four Horsemen Of The Apocalypse* and *The Conquering Power*. She married Ingram that year and subsequently limited her appearances to his films. She started in movies in 1916, at Triangle, and her ability to weep at will was quickly put to good box-office use. Later, Ingram cast her as virtuous heroines in *The Prisoner Of Zenda* (1922) and *Scaramouche* (1923), but she longed to try her hand at wicked ladies. She finally got her chance in *Mare Nostrum* (1926), playing an Austrian temptress and secret agent.

Mare Nostrum was made in the Mediterranean where Ingram and Terry had settled in 1925. At Ingram's studio in Nice, they made *The Magician* (1926), a 'lost' film adapted from a Somerset Maugham novel. In 1927 Rex and Alice went to North Africa to film *The Garden Of Allah*, the old warhorse in which a sophisticated woman discovers that her husband is a Trappist monk on the run. The husband and wife team failed to survive the sound takeover, but in Morocco they co-directed one talkie, *Baroud* (1933). RC

Rudolph Valentino

Real name **Rodolfo Guglielmi**
Born **Castellaneta, Italy, 6 May 1895**
Died **1926**

Rudolph Valentino, like James Dean, is one of the Great Dead whose premature exit from this life was, in retrospect, the shrewdest of career decisions. Death froze him for ever in the attitude of The Great Lover. It came at a time when he faced scandal and ruin, but the hysterical response of his fans to the tragedy of his passing, ensured his continuing legend. Most people have never seen even a frame of *The Sheik*, but they *have* seen grainy newsreel footage of the heaving crowds who threatened to overwhelm his lying-in-state and who wept at his funeral.

The way for Valentino was paved by Douglas Fairbanks, whose swashbucklers – the first of which was *Robin Hood* (1922) – fed post-war America's voracious appetite for escapism. 'Doug' was always careful to retain his husky Americanism beneath the feathered hats and doublets, but Valentino supplied a powerful dose of sleek and graceful Latin eroticism. He did not create the Latin Lover tradition singlehanded – it had already been established in the movies by a succession of smooth society seducers whose brilliantined hair and flashing smiles were the trademarks of their villainy. Valentino's achievement was to make romantic villainy attractive to women without threatening them. He was a seducer who

in The Sheik *(Paramount, 1921)*

could be treated like a gentleman. In *The Sheik* (1921) he turns out to be an Earl, and the prospect of rape which hangs over the film is, at the story's end, about to be transformed into the conventional ending in the marriage bed.

Nearly 60 years after his death, the legendary magnetism is hard to define. The flared nostrils and fixed stare seem at times to be absurd and interminable. Even in the 20s, male cinemagoers found the camp opulence of his films a little tiresome, nicknaming him 'The Pink Powder Puff', and it is this androgynous quality which remains most striking about him today. In public he was forced to cultivate a facade of arrogant machismo, but he was in reality weakwilled and malleable, an easy prey for the two dominating women who fashioned his career: June Mathis, the influential casting director at MGM; and his second wife, Natacha Rambova, a quintessentially idiotic 20s figure (she was in fact Winifred Shaughnessy from Salt Lake City) who was Nazimova's costume designer and exercised a baleful influence over a number of Valentino's films.

He was born of peasant stock, the son of a veterinary surgeon. He arrived in America, steerage class, in 1913, and after working as a gardener in Central Park, became a dancer in a New York nightclub. For a while he replaced Clifton Webb as

the partner of exhibition dancer Bonnie Glass. In this shadowy world, he dispensed sexual favours on both sides of the fence, was involved in petty crime and blackmail, and played a prominent role in a society divorce scandal in which a famous Latin American beauty shot her wealthy husband. After this, he sensibly made his way to San Francisco with a touring theatrical troupe, and then travelled on to Los Angeles. Mae Murray, an old friend, found him work in *Alimony* (1918), and Universal gave him leads in *A Society Sensation* (1918), *All Night* (1918) and Mae Murray's *A Delicious Little Devil* (1919), before he was relegated to gangsters and oily heavies. In *Eyes Of Youth* (1919) he sailed close to the course he had charted in New York, playing a professional co-respondent employed to romance Clara Kimball Young. Shortly afterwards, his first marriage, to actress Jean Acker, collapsed on their wedding night.

Valentino's performance in *Eyes Of Youth* had

caught the attention of June Mathis, who suggested him for the second lead in Rex Ingram's *The Four Horsemen Of The Apocalypse* (1921). In this World War I adventure, Valentino played a wastrel who becomes a war hero, and by the end of filming his part had been built up into the starring role. When the sensational box-office returns started coming in (they finally reached $4,500,000), all the prints were recalled and Valentino's name brought to the head of the cast list. He made three more films at MGM, the last of which was Nazimova's modern dress *Camille* (1921), extravagantly designed by Rambova, whom Valentino married in 1923. Then MGM let him slip through their fingers and, accompanied by June Mathis, he went to Paramount, who rewarded him with *The Sheik*. Valentino was the prince of the desert, Ahmed Ben Hassan, and Agnes Ayres the object of his erotic emoting. Women in the audience fainted in the aisles, and 'Sheik mania' swept America, influencing interior design and inspiring the hit song 'The Sheik Of Araby'.

After *Moran Of The Lady Letty* (1922), he made *Beyond The Rocks* (1922) with Swanson, a romantic extravaganza concocted by Elinor Glyn and filled with stunning period costumes, but the bull-fighting saga *Blood And Sand* (1922), directed by Fred Niblo, was his next big success. Then he fell victim to Rambova's artistic pretensions in *The Young Rajah* (1922), rigged out in a turban, gold jock strap and a sackful of pearls the size of tennis balls. Encouraged by his wife, he demanded artistic control over his films and, while Paramount wrangled, embarked on a nationwide tour giving tango exhibitions. He returned to Paramount, gaining complete artistic control with an independent supervisor appointed. Under Rambova's tutelage, his character became increasingly effeminate, and after *Cobra* (1925), he moved to United Artists for two films with Vilma Banky, *The Eagle* (1925) and *The Son Of The Sheik* (1925). Their success restored some of his by-now flagging popularity, but a perforated ulcer resulting in inoperable peritonitis cut short his life at the age of 31. In tune with his chaotic life he died $200,000 in debt. Two attempts to rekindle the flame have been made, in *Valentino* (1951), with Anthony Dexter in the title role, and a 1977 biopic starring Rudolf Nureyev. Too remote from us in time and fashion, Valentino stubbornly defies revival, although the legend lives on. RC

in The Four Horsemen Of The Apocalypse *(Metro, 1921)*

Conrad Veidt

Born **Potsdam, Germany, 22 January 1893**
Died **1943**

The films of Conrad Veidt can be summarised in the title of that indispensable book on German cinema, 'From Caligari To Hitler'. Weimar Germany, decadent and neurotic, was the perfect environment for the young Veidt. His gaunt frame, wild eyes and feverish, ravaged features were a Romantic corrective to the over-upholstered performances of Emil Jannings. He was a tortured hero straight from the pages of Edgar Allan Poe, driven to destruction by the demonic power of secret knowledge. Not surprisingly, he was a magnificent Reinhardt 'Faust'.

In his early films he played a succession of sinister Gothic roles, including Death in Richard Oswald's *Unheimliche Geschichten* (1918), and culminating in his haunted performance as the somnambulistic Cesare in Robert Wiene's *The Cabinet Of Dr Caligari* (1920), He was Ivan the Terrible in Paul Leni's *Waxworks* (1924) and the crippled concert pianist who gets a distressing hand transplant in the first version of *The Hands Of Orlac* (1924). The Faustian role in *The Student Of Prague* (1926) established his international reputation, leading to

an offer from Universal. In his first Hollywood film he was cast as the superbly decadent Louis XI opposite John Barrymore in *The Beloved Rogue*, released by United Artists in 1927.

When sound arrived his thick accent cut short his Hollywood career, and he returned to Germany where he became *persona non grata* with the Nazis. *Die Andere Seite* (1932) – a version of 'Journey's End' in which he played Stanhope – was condemned as pacifist. In 1932 he signed with Gaumont British and went to England, where his 30s films included *Rome Express* (1932), *The Wandering Jew* (1932), *I Was A Spy* (1933), *The Passing Of The Third Floor Back* (1935) and *Dark Journey* (1937). A visit to Germany in 1934 to make *William Tell* nearly ended in internment when he announced plans for his next film, *Jew Süss* (1934). At the beginning of World War II he was well cast by Michael Powell in *The Spy In Black* (1939) and *Contraband* (1940), before travelling to Hollywood to complete *The Thief Of Bagdad* (1940) in which he played the Grand Vizier. He gave a performance of mesmeric evil as Joan Crawford's sinister mentor in *A Woman's Face* (1941) and, among a number of Nazi roles, was notable as the reptilian Gestapo man in *Casablanca* (1942), a year before his death of a heart attack. RC

Erich von Stroheim

Real name **Erich Oswald Stroheim**
Born **Vienna, Austria, 22 September, 1885**
Died **1957**

He was popularly known as 'The Man You Love To Hate' from his portrayal of brutal German army officers on the screen during World War I. A famous 20s photograph shows him in an impeccable, white, officer's uniform, his head shaven, a monocle in one eye and a cigarette holder in his hand. But Erich von Stroheim's true character was far removed from his on-screen image. Born into a middle-class Jewish family in Vienna, he emigrated to the US in 1906 after a brief stint in the army. Sensitive, intelligent, and immensely gifted, he quickly established himself in Hollywood during the mid-1910s as a bit player, assistant director, military advisor and art director.

In 1918 he managed to interest producer Carl Laemmle, head of Universal, in a script he had written, and he went on to make a remarkable debut as director of *Blind Husbands* (1918) in which he also starred. During the following years he developed into one of the leading Hollywood directors and helped boost the prestige of Universal Studios.

directing Greed *(Metro-Goldwyn, 1923)*

Foolish Wives (1922) turned out to be the high point of his early directorial career, and featured his most fully realised performance in the role of a villainous Continental rogue and bogus officer. He did not appear in his naturalistic masterpiece, *Greed* (1924), which was only released by MGM in a severely truncated form. However, the hit version of *The Merry Widow* for MGM in 1925 restored Von Stroheim to favour and he was given the opportunity to star in and direct *The Wedding March* (1928) for Paramount, playing a more sympathetic character, an aristocrat. Again, as had happened with *Foolish Wives* and *Greed*, the picture was taken away from him and never released in the two-part form he had planned. The studios would not countenance his massive overspending and autocratic manner and thus, his career as a director-star reached a premature end.

Two further opportunities did arise to direct – *Queen Kelly* (1928) produced by and starring Gloria

Swanson, and *Walking Down Broadway* (1932) for Fox – but they, too, ran into difficulties. Meanwhile, he had resumed his career as an actor, making a chillingly effective sound debut as *The Great Gabbo* (1929). In *The Lost Squadron* (1932), he played a megalomaniacal film director, a role loosely based on the popular image of him behind camera, and he appeared opposite Garbo in *As You Desire Me* (1932). But he was unhappy in a Hollywood dominated by the big studios.

An offer to film in France in 1936 led him to take up residence in that country, where he spent most of the remainder of his life, and where he married the French actress Denise Vernac who appeared in a number of films with him. Most notable among his later performances were the upper class prison camp commandant in Jean Renoir's *La Grande Illusion* (1937), Rommel in *Five Graves To Cairo* (1943), and the ex-film director turned butler to his former star (Gloria Swanson) in *Sunset Boulevard* (1950). JF

THE 30s

INTRODUCED BY JOEL W. FINLER

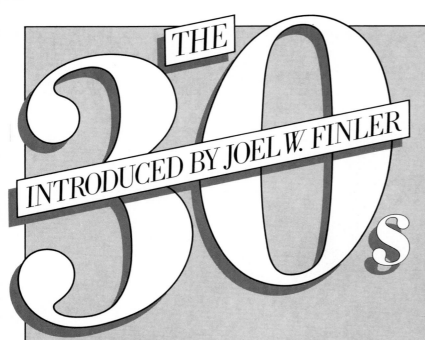

'Have the talkies killed screen romance?' asked a popular fan magazine of the time. It was true that the nature of screen acting and romance was drastically altered by the changeover to sound. Valentino had died in 1926; other romantic stars attempted to carry on into the 1930s with varying success. Ramon Novarro, for example, recognised the need for a change of image and made the transition from Latin lover to musical comedy star and then to character actor with a gradual decline in status; John Gilbert was unable – or unwilling – to make a similar adjustment. Clara Bow was so closely identified with a particular 20s flapper image that it was difficult for her to fit into the new moods and fashions of the 30s, and, in the case of Fairbanks and Pickford, the coming of sound merely speeded retirement that was imminent due to age.

Among the leading film companies, United Artists suffered most from the arrival of the talkies. Of the four original founders of the company – Pickford, Fairbanks, D.W. Griffith and Charles Chaplin, Chaplin alone survived, but on a 'semi-retired' basis, producing each new film at five or six-yearly gaps. Vilma Banky, Norma Talmadge, Gloria Swanson – all went into decline. This state of affairs at UA reflected a trend towards a greater concentration of power in a smaller number of large studios – studios which not only led the field in film production, but

Flanked by MGM's Irving Thalberg (left) and President of the Academy, director Frank Capra (centre right), Bette Davis wins her first Best Actress Oscar for Dangerous (1935). On the right, the Best Actor Oscar winner, Victor McLaglen (for The Informer).

dominated distribution and exhibition as well. Thus, MGM, formed in 1924, now challenged Paramount as the top studio, while Warner Bros. pioneered the introduction of sound and grew rapidly. The last of the majors, RKO, was formed specifically to exploit the newly booming demand for sound pictures, and the coming of the talkies led to a massive new investment in sound equipment and cinemas.

But the 30s were dominated by the Depression and its aftermath. The relative prosperity and optimism of the 20s had been fuelled by consumer buying on credit and stock market speculation. The banks had so extended themselves that when the Wall Street crash came in October, 1929, the effects were cumulative and the entire banking system was in danger of collapse. The mood of the country changed. Millions of people suddenly found themselves unemployed or on short time. Far-reaching changes in the economic and political climate led eventually to the Democrat's sweeping victory in 1932 and the New Deal.

Not surprisingly, these changes were reflected in the kind of movies that were made. During the late 20s, the cinema had developed into a major new industry which brought the beginning of a golden age of filmgoing. Audiences averaged 100 million people per week during 1929–30 and, initially, the industry was cushioned from the effects of the Depression by the popularity of

Adrian was Hollywood's most influential and glamorous dress designer of the decade, gowning Garbo, Shearer, Crawford and Harlow, to name but a few.

the new talkies. Aside from two bad years in 1931 and 1932, attendances during the 30s averaged a healthy 8 million per week. The studios exercised their power by creating a new group of superstars. Some of them had risen from the ranks of the silent bit-players, many more were newly signed up from the theatre. The major studios proved remarkably adept at promoting their new discoveries, who developed their skills by appearing in star vehicles, specially designed for them, year after year. The stars created at this period were to prove extraordinarily durable, with careers that spanned thirty years or more – Dietrich, Davis, Stanwyck, Cagney, Cooper, Gable, to name but a few.

The new breed of stars were more in tune with the harsh realities of life than their silent romantic counterparts. Movies still provided escapism, but escapism of a different sort. Moviegoers now identified with the rise to power of a 'Little Caesar' or a 'Public Enemy' who had grown up on the tenement streets. The convention of the criminal as hero was born. Warner Bros. in particular presented topical subjects which reflected the headlines: prohibition, organised crime, the cruelties of the chain gang, the excesses of the gutter press all proved grist to the Warners mill. Even a number of the studio's lavish musicals were set against a Depression background, with the golddigging showgirls portrayed as wisecracking victims of the times.

Public adulation of the stars was now firmly established. Here Basil Rathbone is besieged by a throng of young autograph hunters in 1936.

Thus, the romantic silent heroes were replaced by tough, down-to-earth types like Cagney, Edward G. Robinson and Paul Muni at Warner Bros., Gable and Wallace Beery at MGM. There were also, of course, the sophisticated and polished leading men, often of a theatre background, who could handle dialogue with ease – stars such as Ronald Colman, William Powell, Fredric March. Naturally, the men had their female counterparts. The era of the new 'modern' 30s woman had dawned and with it the fast talkers and spunky wisecrackers like Joan Blondell, Ginger Rogers, Glenda Farrell; the versatile sophisticates and queens of melodrama – Bette Davis, Barbara Stanwyck, Joan Crawford; the blonde bombshell sex symbols as personified by Jean Harlow and Mae West. The decade was characterised by a sophisticated and glamorous feminine image. The age of the designer had arrived in Hollywood, led by Adrian at MGM, Travis Banton at Paramount, Orry-Kelly at Warner Bros., who ensured that the leading ladies they dressed would be recognised throughout the world as the best-dressed, most stylish of women.

Throughout the decade the studio system and the star system flourished together. Studio power was related to star power and, first and foremost among the star-studded majors was MGM. Their roster of leading players dominated the Oscar nominations during the early years of sound – Norma Shearer, Marie Dressler, Lionel Barrymore and Wallace Beery all won awards, Garbo was nominated twice. There were Best Picture awards, too, and the strength of the studio was very clearly demonstrated during 1931–34 when the industry was most badly hit by the Depression. MGM alone never fell into the red. In contrast to MGM, Paramount turned to the theatre and signed up a large number of new sound stars at one fell swoop. Fredric March, Claudette Colbert, Sylvia Sidney, Kay Francis and the Marx Brothers all came from the Broadway stage, while Jeanette MacDonald and Maurice Chevalier proved a hit musical pairing. The arrival of Dietrich from Germany, Chevalier from France, plus directors Ernst Lubitsch and Josef von Sternberg, as well as art director Hans Dreier, combined to give the studio its uniquely European touch. There was nothing European, however, about Mae West. She arrived in Hollywood in 1932 and took it by storm. She was undeterred by the moguls' insistence that her preference for 'Gay Nineties' costumes and settings would never appeal to the primarily youthful filmgoers, and her first two starring pictures were smash hits which saved Paramount from going bust.

Mae's wittily suggestive dialogue shocked the censors, just as sexy Jean Harlow was making her mark at MGM, and while Busby Berkeley was putting large numbers of scantily clad chorus girls through their paces at Warner Bros. The result, unfortunately, was a stricter enforcement of the industry's self-censorship code beginning in 1934. But by this date, at least the studios were on their way to recovering from the effects of the Depression. The recovery was – during the mid and late 30s – given lift-off by the popularity of a new group of musical star pairings. Having been done to death during the early sound years, musicals were virtually dropped by most of the studios (with the notable exception of Warner Bros.), but suddenly came back into fashion. The stylish cycle from RKO, boasting the biggest star coupling in screen musical history – Fred Astaire and Ginger Rogers – led the way. Operetta-style musicals from MGM starred Jeanette MacDonald and Nelson Eddy, while Shirley Temple helped to revive the ailing Fox and Deanna Durbin gave a vitally needed boost to the declining fortunes of Universal. At the same time, more generous budgets became the order of the day for selected prestige productions at MGM such as *Romeo And Juliet*, *Mutiny On The Bounty* and *The Great Ziegfeld*, to mention but a few. Even Warner Bros., with its reputation for tight budgeting, began upgrading its product with a series of action-costumers, most often starring the studio's talkies' successor to Fairbanks, Errol Flynn, with Olivia de Havilland or Bette Davis among the women, and making use of the new Technicolor.

Darryl Zanuck demonstrated the efficacy of the star system when he took over the reins at Fox – renamed 20th Century-Fox. In the interests of rebuilding the studio's fortunes, he developed a new group of distinctive star personalities, including Tyrone Power, Alice Faye, Don Ameche and ice-skater Sonja Henie. By the late 30s, Fox had regained its former position as one of the leading Hollywood studios. At RKO Ginger Rogers branched out into comedy and dramatic roles and replaced Katharine Hepburn as that studio's leading female star. RKO's feminine bias during the 30s reflected the strength of its contract list on the distaff side. Smaller, less fortunate rivals like Columbia depended on loanouts from the majors for their prestige productions. This practice often enabled stars to break away from the typecasting that their own studios insisted upon as a means of creating and maintaining a particular image. Indeed, it was while reluctantly on loanout to Columbia for *It Happened One Night*, that Colbert and Gable won Oscars in 1934 for their comedy performances.

By the late 30s a number of leading stars were going independent, or otherwise rebelling against the restrictive nature of their exclusive studio contracts. Top directors like Frank Capra, Howard Hawks, Leo McCarey and George Stevens began to function as 'producer-directors' and, in addition, the giant com-

The lavish Hollywood parties thrown by William Randolph Hearst's mistress, the actress Marion Davies, in the early 30s no doubt helped to lighten the dismal days of the Depression. Photographed at one of them are (left to right) Gloria Swanson, Marion herself, Constance Bennett and Jean Harlow.

panies were under threat from the government for their monopolistic and restrictive practices. Finally, the already independent producers, such as Samuel Goldwyn, Walter Wanger, David O. Selznick and Walt Disney, were becoming very successful. The nominations for the Best Picture Oscar in 1939 were dominated for the first time by independent productions; and, for the first time in the Academy's history, the winner was an independent production: David Selznick's *Gone With The Wind*.

Don Ameche

Real name **Dominic Amici**
Born **Kenosha, Wisconsin, 31 May 1908**

'We have a young lad on the lot who has a marvellous radio voice, and he can act better than John Barrymore ever thought of doing. He's as handsome as Robert Montgomery and as pious as a monk. He has the male lead in *Ramona*, and when the director got stuck at the Mass part in the marriage ceremony because the altar boys couldn't recite Latin he offered to stand off camera and recite the prayers.'

This paragon of virtue was Don Ameche, a former radio star who signed with Fox in 1936. His screen debut, playing Jean Hersholt's two sons in *The Sins of Man* (1936) was serious enough, but the studio preferred to throw away his breezy, good-natured talent in featherweight Sonja Henie, Alice Faye and Loretta Young vehicles. He was also condemned to lose the girl to Tyrone Power. It was Loretta Young in *Love Is News* (1937), for whom Ameche grew the elegant pencil moustache which became his trademark. In *The Story of Alexander Graham Bell* (1939), he invented the telephone. In the 40s, his butterscotch baritone carried him through a number of plush, undemanding musicals, including *Down Argentine Way* (1940), *That Night In Rio* (1941) and *Moon Over Miami* (1941). His sense of fun insulated him from the clowning of the Ritz Brothers in *The Three Musketeers* (1939), in which he was a swashbuckling D'Artagnan. When given the chance, he was adept at sophisticated

with Claudette Colbert in Sleep My Love *(United Artists, 1948)*

comedy – Lubitsch deployed his talent perfectly in *Heaven Can Wait* (1943). It was Ameche's last big film at Fox.

He left the studio after *Wing And A Prayer* (1944), to freelance – none too successfully. Douglas Sirk handled his last two films of the 40s: *Sleep My Love* (1948), an efficient variation on the *Gaslight* theme; and *Slightly French* (1949), a snappy musical co-starring Dorothy Lamour. In the 50s, he had two Broadway hits, 'Silk Stockings' (1955) and 'Goldilocks' (1958), the latter a burlesque of the silent days which recalled *Hollywood Cavalcade* (1939), in which Ameche had played a washed-up old time director. He made a return to the screen in 1966 in a Bert I. Gordon quickie, *Picture Mommy Dead*, but since then has given relaxed performances in *Suppose They Gave A War And Nobody Came* (1970) and the very successful *Trading Places* (1983). RC

George Arliss

Real name **George Andrews**
Born **London, 10 April 1868**
Died **1946**

The early 30s were distinguished by some unlikely box office attractions: Jackie Cooper crying his eyes out to order; Wallace Beery and Marie Dressler, grizzled plug-uglies surrounded at MGM by the sleek romancing of Shearer, Gable and Crawford. But the strangest of all was George Arliss, veteran British thespian, the monocled curator of a portrait gallery of Great Figures From History. He was hailed as 'The First Gentleman Of The Screen', but as film historians Griffith and Mayer wryly observed, 'According to Arliss, Disraeli, Voltaire, Richelieu and even Alexander Hamilton all looked exactly alike, except for details of costume, and all were crafty but benevolent gentlemen who spent most of their time uniting unhappy lovers.'

He arrived in America in 1901 and became a star

in the 1908 production of Molnar's 'The Devil'. In the 20s he was persuaded to put some of his famous performances on celluloid. Among them was *Disraeli* (1922). With the arrival of sound and the stampede to sign up stage actors, he repeated the role for Warners and won the 1929 Best Actor Award.

Today Arliss seems a richly camp figure, but he had three good years at Warners, at $10,000 a week. But an unrelieved diet of ham, however succulent, eventually palls, and he was released from his contract after *Voltaire* (1933).

There were three films for Darryl F. Zanuck – *The House of Rothschild* (1934), *The Last Gentleman* (1934) and *Cardinal Richelieu* (1935) – and then Arliss returned home to Gaumont British, for whom he had already played an epicene Wellington in *The Iron Duke* (1935). By now he was considered an anachronism, and his high falutin' ways did not endear him to the studio chief, Michael Balcon. His career rapidly petered out, and his last film was *Dr Syn* (1937). RC

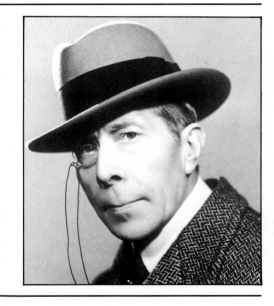

Jean Arthur

Real name **Gladys Greene**
Born **New York City, 17 October 1905**

Jean Arthur's career is a shining example of the importance of timing. She served a long, grinding apprenticeship before the mid-30s fashion for tongue-in-cheek drollery revealed her talents as a comedienne, and made her one of Columbia's biggest stars.

She made her debut in John Ford's *Cameo Kirby* (1923) and spent the rest of the 20s marooned in second string horse operas and comedy shorts. At Paramount in the early 30s she vied with Mary Brian for the ingenue roles turned down by Nancy Carroll. After *The Lawyer's Secret* (1931), she left Hollywood for Broadway. Columbia proved her saviour, giving her a good role in a Jack Holt melodrama, *Whirlpool* (1934), and signing her to a long-term contract. Then John Ford's drama *The Whole Town's Talking* (1935) cast her in the role she was to patent – the fresh-faced, energetic, white-collar girl of the Depression years, warm-hearted, loyal and nobody's

fool. Determined and adaptable, the Arthur heroine took everything in her stride, even when, in *Easy Living* (1937), a mink coat descended on her from the heavens and turned her life upside down. Her husky voice had a beguiling quaver, and under the buoyant good spirits there was an astringency which owed much to her jaundiced view of Hollywood. Her glowing common sense permeates Frank Capra's late-30s classics *Mr Deeds Goes To Town* (1936), *You Can't Take It With You* (1938) and *Mr Smith Goes To Washington* (1939); and her fierce independence made her a memorable Calamity Jane in DeMille's *The Plainsman* (1936), and tempered Howard Hawks's sentimental notions of male cameraderie in *Only Angels Have Wings* (1939).

Until the arrival of Rita Hayworth, Arthur was the queen of the Columbia lot. She won an Oscar nomination for her performance in George Stevens's *The More The Merrier* (1943), but she had grown weary of her long-running feud with Columbia's boss, Harry Cohn, and quit the studio after *The Impatient Years* (1944). She made only two more films, Billy Wilder's *A Foreign Affair* (1948) and George Stevens's *Shane* (1953). RC

Fred Astaire

Real name Frederick Austerlitz
Born Omaha, Nebraska, 10 May 1899

'I just put my feet in the air and move them around,' explained Fred Astaire, the greatest dancer in the history of the cinema, who remains unsurpassed in virtuosity, invention and elegance. The top hat, white tie and tails with black cane that he sported, gave him an image that 'simply reeked of class.' He even walked with a jaunty, dance-like strut. His light, carefree, expressive singing voice inspired top songwriters such as George Gershwin, Cole Porter, Irving Berlin and Jerome Kern.

Astaire began his dancing career at the age of seven in a vaudeville act with his sister Adele. They became Broadway's supreme dancing team, and the toast of the international set. Fred taught the Prince of Wales to tap, and it was rumoured that he was sneaked into Buckingham Palace to do so. When Adele married into the English aristocracy in 1932, Fred entered films. A studio talent scout commented notoriously on his first screen test, 'Can't act. Can't sing. Slightly bald. Can dance a little', but David O. Selznick at MGM took a chance and gave him a guest spot in *Dancing Lady* (1933) in two production numbers with Joan Crawford. He was teamed up with Ginger Rogers for the first time in *Flying Down To Rio* (1933). Although Dolores Del Rio and Gene Raymond were the nominal leads, Fred and Ginger made the greatest impression, dancing 'The Carioca'. There followed another eight black-and-white RKO musicals between 1933 and 1939, set in fashionable resorts, luxurious hotels and ornate nightclubs with black, glass floors over which the couple glided to enduring stardom and huge box-office receipts.

Fred was a perfectionist, and the gruelling rehearsals often put a strain on his relationship with Ginger, never very amicable at the best of times. However, on screen they were transformed into lovers, their superb dance duets being symbolic representations of love-making. Katharine Hepburn commented, 'He gives her class and she gives him sex.' This is best demonstrated in 'Night And Day' from *The Gay Divorcee* (1934), 'Cheek To Cheek' from *Top Hat* (1935), and the wistful 'Never Gonna Dance' from *Swing Time* (1936). Astaire's solos were also highlights as in the title number from *Top Hat* in which he taps spectacularly, donned in his famous attire. In 'Slap That Bass' from *Shall We Dance* (1937), he dances in the spotless engine room of an ocean liner, his taps synchronised with the pounding pistons. His devastating dexterity is shown in *Carefree* (1938), where he manages to hit eight golfballs in a row straight down the fairway, dancing and singing at the same time. *The Story Of Vernon And Irene Castle* (1939), the final film in the remarkable sequence, was the least successful, and Fred and Ginger decided to go their separate ways.

The following five years were unsatisfactory for Fred. His films were inferior to the RKO musicals, and, except for Eleanor Powell and Rita Hayworth, he had to make do with uninspiring dancing partners such as Paulette Goddard, Virginia Dale and Joan Leslie. The first of Astaire's many new partners had been MGM's top dancing star, Eleanor Powell, and the highlight of *Broadway Melody Of 1940* was their 'Begin The Beguine' duet. *You'll Never Get Rich* (1941) and *You Were Never Lovelier* (1942) were relatively successful collaborations with Columbia's Rita Hayworth. From the peak of the 30s musicals, through the valley of the early 40s, Fred Astaire then managed to leap with exceptional ease into the more integrated form of the new Technicolored MGM musicals. The whimsical *Yolanda And The Thief* (1945) contained an audacious sixteen-minute surreal ballet, and in the all-star revue *Ziegfeld Follies* (1946), Fred partnered Lucille Bremer in two 'dance stories' that brought a tragic dimension to his dancing. After *Blue Skies* (1946), with Bing Crosby, Fred declared he was retiring from the screen.

After two years of inactivity, he was called back to MGM for *Easter Parade* (1948) when Gene Kelly broke an ankle. Fred and Judy Garland turned out to be an interesting combination, and in the clownish duet, 'A Couple Of Swells', he played against his polished persona by impersonating a tramp with a battered top hat and missing front teeth. Garland and Astaire were to be linked again in *The Barkleys Of Broadway* (1949), but because of Judy's erratic behaviour, she was removed from the picture. Producer Arthur Freed contacted Ginger Rogers for

a reunion with Astaire after ten years, and they played a bickering husband-wife dance team, slightly parodying their own personalities.

Astaire continued to experiment with slow-motion, multiple images and trick photography to extend the range of his dancing. In *Royal Wedding* (1951), he completely disregarded the law of gravity, dancing on the walls and ceilings of his hotel room, and in *The Belle Of New York* (1952), he floated to the top of Washington Square arch and then danced on passing clouds, after a kiss from Vera-Ellen. He gave his finest performance as an ageing song-and-dance man in *The Band Wagon* (1953), one of his best films. In fact, he was miserable during shooting. His wife, Phyllis, mother of his two children Fred and Ava, was dying of cancer. He also found Cyd Charisse the heaviest of dancing partners, and came to dread the lifts. Nonetheless, it was one of his best pairings and they were teamed again in *Silk Stockings* (1957). Fred was now nearly sixty and decided to enter the less spectacular realms of character acting, his only return to the musical being *Finian's Rainbow* (1968) in which he sang and danced a little.

While always enlivening any film with his presence, none of his 'straight' roles particularly added to his reputation. He played a motor-racing scientist in *On The Beach* (1959), Debbie Reynolds' debonair father in *The Pleasure Of His Company* (1961), an amusing detective in *The Notorious Landlady* (1962), and was one of the many stars trapped in *The Towering Inferno* (1974). Fred recently married again after almost three decades of widowhood. Besides making rare appearances on TV, he keeps occupied with his race-horses. His last film appearance was as narrator with Gene Kelly in MGM's auto-tribute *That's Entertainment Part 2* (1976), in which some of his past glories were recalled. RB

in Daddy Long Legs (20th Century-Fox, 1955)

in Smart Woman *(RKO, 1931)*

Mary Astor

Real name **Lucille Langhanke**
Born **Quincy, Illinois, 3 May 1906**

Mary Astor was at her best playing devious seductresses and demure bitches. One has only to think of her in *Red Dust* (1932), angling for Clark Gable while her weak-willed husband (Gene Raymond) is cracking up in the jungle; or in *The Maltese Falcon* (1941) as the pathological liar Brigid O'Shaughnessy, almost but not quite retaining our sympathy as the lift doors close over her face and she is carried away from a regretful Sam Spade.

Later, she played an interminable series of matronly roles at MGM, the 'Metro Mothers', as she scathingly called them, although they were invariably illuminated by her warm skills. Ironically, both aspects of her career were given an added nuance by her troubled private life which, in the mid-30s, kept the scandal sheets working overtime. In 1936, during a custody fight over her daughter with her second husband, newspapers began publishing what they claimed to be pages from her diaries, retailing the torrid details of her affair with playwright George S. Kaufman. In her 1959 autobiography Astor claimed that they were imaginative forgeries, but she never denied one disclosure, that she loathed Hollywood. Of those years she later wrote, 'I was sick, spoiled and selfish, prowling like some animal seeking monetary satisfaction. Sexually I was out of control'.

Legend, and occasionally life, provides a mixed-up Hollywood goddess with a ruthlessly ambitious mother. Astor had a father who singlemindedly thrust his teenage daughter into films. She was tested and rejected by Griffith, signed by Famous Players, dropped after six months and three bit parts, and then taken up by the studio again in 1923. The ravishingly beautiful 17-year-old caught John Barrymore's roving eye and she starred with him in *Beau Brummell* (1924). Off the set she was less demure, and conducted an affair with Barrymore which had cooled by the time they were teamed again in 1926 in *Don Juan* (by now he was infatuated with Dolores Costello, his co-star in *The Sea Beast* (1926), and his behaviour during filming was icily correct).

Astor was charming as Fairbanks's leading lady in *Don Q, Son of Zorro* (1925) and in the same year was chosen as a Wampas Baby Star. Among the bevy of young hopefuls selected that year by the Western Association of Motion Picture Advertisers were Joan Crawford, Janet Gaynor and Dolores Del Rio. Publicised as the 'cameo girl', Mary made *The Rose Of The Golden West* (1927) with Gilbert Roland and was now on the rung just below the big time. In 1928 her salary at Fox was $3,750 a week. But when sound came, the ladder was twitched away. She was

dropped by Fox, who considered her unsuitable for talkies, and spent several months out of work before appearing on stage with Edward Everett Horton in 'Among The Married'. She was soon back on the screen, working as a freelance after turning down an offer from RKO, cannily observing, 'Once your name goes above the title of a picture, it must never come down or your prestige is gone'. Instead, she remained unclassifiable, and unfailingly stylish, playing parts big and small in films which ranged from MGM's *Red Dust* (1932), with Gable and Harlow, to Universal's *Straight From The Heart* (1935), with Baby Jane Quigley, a cut-rate answer to Shirley Temple.

The diaries scandal boosted rather than damaged her career, and she was superb in *Dodsworth* (1936), providing Walter Huston with a refuge from Ruth Chatterton. She was a prize bitch in MGM's *Woman Against Woman* (1938), giving Herbert Marshall a hard time, and then turned her acid-tongued attentions to Claudette Colbert in *Midnight* (1939). She completed a memorable trio of harpies in Warners' *The Great Lie* (1941), a Bette Davis vehicle in which she stole the film from under the star's nose after her part had been built up at Davis's insistence. Astor's deceptive talent was not lost on Davis. Twenty-three years later, while filming *Hush, Hush Sweet Charlotte* (1964) – Astor's last film – Bette told director Robert Aldrich, 'Turn her loose, you might learn something'. *The Maltese Falcon* was the peak of her career, in which she created the definitive two-faced *femme fatale*. She showed a delightful flair for comedy in Paramount's *The Palm Beach Story* (1942), as Rudy Vallee's husband-hungry sister, and then went to MGM. Here she played mother to all the studio's resident ingenues: Susan Peters (*Young Ideas*), Kathryn Grayson (*Thousands Cheer*), Judy Garland (*Meet Me In St Louis*), Elizabeth Taylor (*Cynthia*), and Esther Williams (*Fiesta*). The distressing absence of malice was finally remedied in the 1947 *Desert Fury*, in which she was Lizabeth Scott's mother, a vicious saloon bar queen. However, the last straw came with *Little Women* (1949). A brood consisting of June Allyson, Elizabeth Taylor, Janet Leigh and Margaret O'Brien was too much and she

left MGM in the following year.

A drinking problem and a long period in analysis limited Astor's film roles in the 50s, although she was good as Robert Wagner's neurotic mother in Gerd Oswald's weird little psycho-drama *A Kiss Before Dying* (1956). In *Return To Peyton Place* (1961) she displayed all her old scene-stealing skills. She retired in 1964 to write novels. RC

with George Arliss in A Successful Calamity *(Warner, 1932)*

with Philip Dorn and Gloria Grahame (right) in Blonde Fever *(MGM, 1944)*

Gene Autry

Born **Tioga, Texas, 29 September 1907**

Gene Autry was not the first singing cowboy, but in the late 1930s he pioneered a new brand of Western in which a sagebrush hero's tonsils were more important than his skill with a shooting iron.

The 'Yodelling Cowboy' made his screen debut in a 1934 Ken Maynard oater, *Old Santa Fé*, a second feature for Nat Levine's Mascot company. In 1935 Levine gave Autry the starring role in *Phantom Empire*, a bizarre 12-part serial which combined science fiction with a tale set in the modern West.

When Mascot merged with Republic, Autry became an overnight star in *Tumbling Tumbleweeds* (1935), the first of 58 features he made for the studio. They all conformed strictly to his 'Cowboy Code': Gene would never slug anyone smaller than himself or take unfair advantage, he would keep his word, would not smoke or drink, and would never

kiss the leading lady (a commandment he occasionally broke). He always played himself, bland and poker-faced, usually leaving the acting to comic sidekick Smiley Burnette and his horse Champion. In the final reel he would reluctantly put down his guitar for a brief dust-up with the heavies – all this limiting the action somewhat. In the 66-minute *Gaucho Serenade* (1940), it takes 44 minutes for anyone to get on a horse, 50 minutes for a punch to be thrown and nearly an hour for a gunshot to interrupt the range warbling.

After Autry returned from war service, he had to cede top place at Republic to Roy Rogers. He made five more Republic features and then formed his own Flying A company, releasing through Columbia. In the early 50s the B-Western was thundering down the dusty trail to extinction and Autry's final Flying A film was, appropriately, *Last Of The Pony Riders* (1953). He turned to television and, immensely rich, retired from the screen in 1960 after a cameo role in *Alias Jesse James* (1959). RC

Lew Ayres

Born **Minneapolis, 28 December 1908**

Even when playing the white-haired inter-stellar patriarch of *Battle Star Galactica* (1979), Lew Ayres retained the open-faced, boyish good looks which had catapulted him to stardom 49 years earlier in *All Quiet On The Western Front* (1930). His calmness belied a blighted career, much of which was spent in B pictures.

Having first studied medicine at the University of Arizona, he was spotted singing in Ray West's orchestra by Pathé executive Paul Bern, who signed him for a small part in *The Sophomore* (1929). When Bern went to MGM, he hired Ayres for a featured role in Garbo's *The Kiss* (1929). His performance won him the part of the German boy soldier sickened by war in *All Quiet On The Western Front* (1930). He was effectively cast as Constance Bennett's seducer in *Common Clay* (1930), but by the mid-30s he had slipped down to second features at 20th Century-Fox. At Republic he directed *Hearts*

in Don't Bet On Love (Universal, 1933)

In Bondage (1936) and then drifted through a dismaying series of programmers at Columbia and Paramount. Republic's *King Of The Newsboys* (1938) was the nadir, from which he was rescued by a good part in *Holiday* (1938), as Katharine Hepburn's wastrel brother. MGM signed him, and his second film there was a B, *Young Dr Kildare* (1938), with Ayres as the crusading medic. Ayres became the patron saint of hypochondriacs everywhere and made eight more Kildare films, the last of which was *Dr Kildare's Victory* (1941).

In World War II he registered as a conscientious objector, a move which resulted in a public boycott of his films. Experience as a non-combatant deepened his acting range in *Dark Mirror* (1946), *The Unfaithful* (1947) and *Johnny Belinda* (1948), as the doctor caring for deaf-mute Jane Wyman. After *Donovan's Brain* (1953), Ayres retired to make a religious documentary, *Altars Of The East* (1955). In Preminger's *Advise And Consent* (1962), he played the US Vice President suddenly elevated to the highest office, and in *Damien – Omen II* (1978) he came to a sticky end under an ice lake. RC

Tallulah Bankhead

Born **Huntsville, Alabama, 31 January 1903**
Died 1968

Tallulah Bankhead spent a lifetime playing herself, from the tawny-haired darling of 20s London society to the raddled but indomitable old crone of her later years. Her gravel-throated cry of 'Daaahling' passed into the language, and her genius for scurrilous repartee was part of showbusiness folklore. In part self-mockingly, Tallulah strove mightily to preserve a reputation 'as pure as the driven slush', but the effort overshadowed her considerable gifts as an actress. Tennessee Williams wrote 'A Streetcar Named Desire' with Bankhead in mind as Blanche Dubois. Sadly, when she came to play the part in the 50s, she was too old.

The daughter of a wealthy Alabama businessman and politician, she made her stage debut at the age of 16 in 'Squab Farm'. In 1922 she went to London for 'The Dancers', and instantly became the toast of the town, followed everywhere by a small army of besotted fans known as 'the gallery girls'. Towards the end of her long stay in Britain she made two films, *His House In Order* (1928) and *A Woman's Law* (1928), and in 1931 signed with Paramount. The studio had no idea what to do with her and crassly tried to turn her into a second Dietrich in George Cukor's *Tarnished Lady* (1931). This was followed by a succession of turkeys, including a 1931 remake of the old Sessue Hayakawa vehicle *The Cheat*, and *The Devil And The Deep* (1932), Charles Laughton's first Hollywood film. After *Faithless* (MGM, 1932), with Robert Montgomery, Tallulah returned to Broadway.

She showed just how good an actress she was in Lillian Hellman's 'The Little Foxes' and Thornton Wilder's 'The Skin Of Our Teeth'. Then, in 1944, she gave a richly comic performance in Alfred Hitchcock's *Lifeboat*, a film notable for confining itself to the smallest acting space of any movie ever made, the craft of the title. Despite the difficult circumstances, Tallulah contrived to look a million dollars and, naturally, called everyone 'Daaahling'.

Bette Davis' *monstre sacrée*, Margo Channing, in *All About Eve* (1950) bore more than a passing resemblance to Bankhead. When it was released Tallulah told radio listeners on 'The Big Show', 'When I get hold of her, I'll tear every hair out of her moustache'. Ironically, her last film appearance was in a cut-rate Hammer shocker *Fanatic* (1965), which attempted to cash in on Davis' Gothic horror success in *Whatever Happened To Baby Jane?* (1962). RC

in Tarnished Lady (Paramount, 1931)

Lionel Barrymore

Real name **Lionel Blythe**
Born **Philadelphia, 28 April 1878**
Died **1954**

Lionel Barrymore was the first of the famous acting clan to make films, and one of the first stars of the legitimate theatre to carve out a movie career. He joined Biograph in 1909, and in the years before World War I played in many of D.W. Griffith's early films, including *The Musketeers Of Pig Alley* (1912) and *Judith Of Bethulia* (1913). He also made script contributions and directed several features.

In 1926 he signed with MGM, with whom he stayed to the end of his career. By the end of the 20s Barrymore had exchanged leading man status for that of forceful character player, notably as the benighted Atkinson in Raoul Walsh's *Sadie Thompson* (1928). With the arrival of sound he returned to directing, with *Madame X* (1929) and *His Glorious Night* (1929). After handling *The Rogue Song* (1929), *The Unholy Night* (1929) and *Ten Cents A Dance* (1931), he won an Oscar for his performance as Norma Shearer's drunken father in *A Free Soul*

(1931). Then he embarked on a long line of bravura, and frequently hammed up, eccentrics: the harassed little pen pusher who makes off with Joan Crawford at the end of *Grand Hotel* (1932); Rasputin in *Rasputin And The Empress* (1933); the Devil's Island escapee who shrinks his human captives to miniature size in *The Devil Doll* (1936); and the head of the over-winsomely loopy household in *You Can't Take It With You* (1938).

The latter-day Barrymore specialised in more rough-hewn patriarchs, usually with hearts of gold. He was Judge Hardy in *A Family Affair* (1937), which initiated the 'Andy Hardy' films, but the role for which he is best remembered is that of Dr Gillespie, whom he played 15 times in MGM's long-running Dr Kildare series. The irascible Gillespie perfectly suited Barrymore's crusty screen persona and, in the late 30s, accommodated his arthritis which confined him to a wheelchair. Despite his increasing infirmity, Barrymore slogged on through the 40s, looking ever more frail and waxy-faced as he drove Lillian Gish to drink in Selznick's *Duel In The Sun* (1946) and went *Down To The Sea In Ships* (1949) in Henry Hathaway's whaling saga. His last film was *Main Street To Broadway* (1953). RC

Freddie Bartholomew

Real name **Frederick Llewellyn**
Born **London, 28 March 1924**

That Hollywood is truly the land of dreams is proved by the career of Freddie Bartholomew, who was Greta Garbo's son in *Anna Karenina* (1935) and, in *Lloyds Of London* (1936), grew up to be Tyrone Power. In the mid-30s, California was a happy hunting ground for a regiment of expatriate British actors of all ages. Chief of the juniors was Freddie, a little lordling with dimples to rival Shirley Temple, cut glass vowels and perfect manners.

His origins were quite humble. He was born in London to lower middle-class parents and brought up in Wiltshire by his grandparents. His Aunt Cissie remorselessly pushed him into a career as a child actor and secured him small parts in two films made on location in the West Country, *Fascination* (1930) and *Lily Christine* (1932).

In 1934 she took her 10-year-old nephew to America, ostensibly to visit relatives, and signed him with MGM for *David Copperfield* (1935) at $175 a week. After *Anna Karenina* his weekly salary was raised to $1000.

In David O. Selznick's *Little Lord Fauntleroy* (1936), Bartholomew was teamed for the first time with street-wise Mickey Rooney, a perfect foil to Freddie's prissy gentility. They were reunited in MGM's *Captains Courageous* (1937) in which Bartholomew gave his best performance as the spoilt

brat who falls off an ocean liner into Lionel Barrymore's fishing schooner. The boys were together again in *Lord Jeff* (1938), but by then Freddie's career was in decline, and the $1 million he had earned since 1934 was being dissipated by 27 ruinously expensive lawsuits fought by his aunt and his parents over the spoils of his brief stardom.

By 1942, *A Yank At Eton* starred Rooney. Bartholomew had slipped to fourth billing. After a couple of Bs, he became a US citizen and joined the USAAF. After the war he made two films for RKO, *Sepia Cinderella* (1947) and *St Benny The Dip* (1951), and then went into television. Today he is a top Madison Avenue advertising executive. RC

with Lionel Barrymore (left) in Captains Courageous *(MGM, 1937)*

Constance Bennett

Born **New York City, 22 October 1904**
Died **1965**

Constance Bennett had three careers: Paramount's *Code Of The West* (1925) made her a popular leading lady of the silents; in the early 30s she was the queen of the 'confession' film, second only to Garbo at the box office and – briefly – the highest paid woman in Hollywood. Today, she is chiefly remembered in her final incarnation as the elegant, unruffled exponent of high 30s comedy.

Her silent career ended abruptly after *The Pinch Hitter* (1926), when she eloped with steamship and railroad heir Philip Bland. After three years in the international set, she was coaxed back to Pathé in 1929 by one of its executives, the Marquis de Falaise de la Coudraye, whom she married in 1932 after his divorce from Gloria Swanson. *This Thing Called Love* (1929) was her introduction to the talkies, followed by the appropriately titled *Rich People* (1930). Then she starred in the old Cleves Kinkead

tearjerker *Common Clay* (1930), as a parlour maid seduced and abandoned by wicked rich boy Lew Ayres. The success of this casting against type led to a string of martyrdoms including *Bought* (1931), made on loan to Warners at $30,000 a week. Bennett was far too brittle and articulate to play suffering stenographers and victimised artists' models, but this seeming contradiction only increased the popularity of her films. Her husky voice and deadpan, wisecracking skill were equally well suited to a string of classic comedies, which climaxed with Hal Roach's *Topper* (1937) with Cary Grant, and *Merrily We Live* (1938), a variation on *My Man Godfrey* (1936) with Brian Aherne.

Thereafter her popularity declined, although she continued to work throughout the 40s. In 1946 she produced and starred in *Paris Underground*, whose co-star, Gracie Fields, provided one of cinema's oddest pairings. Her last film of the decade, Republic's *Angel On The Amazon* (1949) was an unashamed B. She died of a cerebral haemorrhage shortly after completing her last film, *Madame X* (1965). RC

Joan Blondell

Born **New York City, 30 August 1909**
Died **1979**

Joan Blondell's career can be summarised thus: from hash-slinger in *Steel Highway* (1931) to soda jerk in *Grease* (1978). She described herself perfectly as 'the happy go lucky chorus girl, saucy secretary, flip reporter, dumb blonde waitress, I'll-stick-by-you broad.' Pert and big-eyed, she was the snappiest example of that 30s phenomenon, the gold-digger, wisecracking her way through a man's world with her eyes often fixed firmly on the money rather than the men.

In 1929 Blondell was appearing in a Broadway play, 'Penny Arcade', with James Cagney. Warners turned it into *Sinners' Holiday* (1930) and gave them both starring roles. Blondell was a superb foil for Cagney. Far too knowing to be taken in by his restless banter, she soaked up his explosive energy in *Public Enemy* (1931), *Blonde Crazy* (1931) and

with Jayne Mansfield (left) in Will Success Spoil Rock Hunter? (20th Century-Fox, 1957)

Footlight Parade (1933). Warner Bros. was a male-dominated studio, and while Cagney quickly became a star, Blondell remained a supporting player, although her 53 films from 1930–9 are a fair indication of her indispensability. In the early 30s she played second leads in musicals, singing of her 'Forgotten Man' in *Gold Diggers of 1933*, then moving to fast-paced comedy, regularly partnering Pat O'Brien and Dick Powell.

In 1937 she had a big success opposite Leslie Howard in *Stand In*, playing the lady of the title and helping Howard's stuffy banker to save 'Colossal Pictures' from bankruptcy. Two years later she finally rebelled against the happy-go-lucky chorus girl image, and left Warners to freelance. But in the 40s Veronica Lake set the style for blondes, bloodless rather than gutsy, and Blondell's work became increasingly intermittent. In the next 10 years there were only 13 films. Blondell was superb in the war melodrama *Cry Havoc* (1943) as a burlesque queen

turned nurse in the Philippines. However, after playing Aunt Cissy in Elia Kazan's *A Tree Grows In Brooklyn* (1945), she spiralled down to programmers, supports in big features like *Adventure* (1945), and character roles, notably as a cynical carnival queen in *Nightmare Alley* (1947).

In the 50s there was theatre work, including a musical version of *A Tree Grows In Brooklyn*, and some engaging appearances as slightly blowsy, sozzled-looking middle-aged dames. She was a fading vaudeville star in *The Blue Veil* (1951) and Eleanor Parker's drunken aunt in *Lizzie* (1957). She provided Jayne Mansfield with a cynical companion in *Will Success Spoil Rock Hunter?* (1957), hitting the bottle to forget a disastrous affair with a milkman. Fortunately, she meets ulcerated advertising executive Henry Jones, and they set off together on a milk-quaffing future. In her last film she moved up a social notch or two, playing a society lady in *The Champ* (1979). RC

William Boyd

Born **Cambridge, Ohio, 5 June 1898**
Died **1972**

William Boyd's long, switchback career took him from Cecil B. DeMille silent epics to an Indian Summer of TV stardom as Hopalong Cassidy of the Bar 20 Ranch. Few of the viewers who enjoyed his small-screen adventures of the early 50s remembered that he had been one of DeMille's favourite leading men, the star of *The Volga Boatman* (1926) and Simon of Cyrene in *King Of Kings* (1927).

At first untroubled by the coming of sound, he maintained his star status on the Paramount lot and took the lead in D.W. Griffith's part-talkie, *Lady Of The Pavements* (1929). But in the early 30s his slipping popularity was dealt a seemingly mortal blow when the scandalous off-screen antics of another actor with the same name – William 'Stage' Boyd – were frequently attributed to him. He was rescued from poverty row by independent producer Harry Sherman, who offered him the part of the heavy in the first of a series of Westerns based on Clarence E. Mulford's Hopalong Cassidy stories. James Gleason was earmarked to play Mulford's wizened whisky-sodden old timer, but when he pulled out the part was offered to Boyd. In his hands Hopalong became an elegant gentleman of the range, clad from head to foot in dark blue, which offset his silver hair, and sporting distinctive double holsters and white cowhead bandana grip.

in 1932

The first in the series was *Hop-A-Long Cassidy* (1935) (the hyphens were subsequently dropped), and over the next 13 years there were 66 Cassidy adventures, 28 of them directed by one of the unsung heroes of the Bs, Lesley Selander. James Ellison, and later Russell Hayden, played Hopalong's youthful sidekick; up to 1939 comic relief was supplied by the peppery, bearded George 'Gabby' Hayes, and in the 40s by Andy Clyde. The Cassidy series reached a peak in the early 40s, although some of the plots were hardly conventional Western fare: in *Secrets Of The Wasteland* (1941) Hoppy and the boys from the Bar 20 discover a lost Chinese city, a kind of cut-rate prairie version of Shangri-La.

The Hopalong Cassidy films were originally released by Paramount. In 1942 distribution was taken over by United Artists. Four years later Boyd bought the rights to the series and formed his own production company, but by then the best years were over, and the stresses and strains of plummeting budgets were plain to see. Late entries like *The Dead Don't Dream* (1948) were little more than feeble thrillers given a vaguely Western flavour and shot almost entirely indoors. The series ended with *Borrowed Trouble* (1948).

It looked as if Boyd was washed up a second time, but television came galloping to the rescue. The revival of the old Sherman features by NBC and a new series of 52 30-minute adventures restored Boyd's fortunes. His last screen appearance was a cameo as himself in DeMille's *The Greatest Show On Earth* (1952). RC

in 1935

Charles Boyer

Born **Figeac, France, 28 August 1897**
Died **1978**

The French have never felt at home in Hollywood. Charles Boyer is the exception that proves the rule, but his stardom was not won without initial setbacks which might have discouraged a less determined and professional actor. At his peak in the late 30s, he was a suave exotic amid an army of all-American leading men, his bedroom eyes and intriguing accent evoking memories of the Latin Lovers of the silent screen.

Boyer studied at the Sorbonne and the Paris Conservatoire, and by his mid-20s was established as a star of the French theatre and cinema. In 1928 he signed with UFA to make French versions of German films made in Berlin. Shortly afterwards he was enticed to Hollywood by MGM to play in French versions of *The Trial Of Mary Dugan* (1929) and *The Big House* (1930). The introduction of subtitles, and his heavy accent, made him difficult to cast and, after being loaned to Paramount for *The Magnificent Lie* (1930), he went back to UFA. He returned to Paramount in 1932 for *The Man From Yesterday* and then played Jean Harlow's chauffeur in *Red-Headed Woman* (1932). Unhappy with the result, he again returned to Europe.

In 1934, Fox saw his English version of *Thunder In The East* and were sufficiently impressed to invite Boyer back to Hollywood for 'a series of romantic yarns of the Valentino type'. The result was a terrible flop, *Caravan* (1935), with Loretta Young. The disconsolate Boyer bought out his contract and was snapped up by Walter Wanger, who gave him a featured role in *Private Worlds* (1935), with Claudette Colbert. Wanger signed Boyer to a personal contract and began to build up his reputation for sultry, slightly roguish romancing in *Break Of Hearts* (1935), *Shanghai* (1935), again with Young, and *The Garden Of Allah* (1936). Boyer showed that he was equally at home with humour in Frank Borzage's *History Is Made At Night* (1937), with the delightful Jean Arthur, and there was more comedy in *Tovarich* (1937), which was sandwiched between Boyer's two biggest films of the 30s: *Conquest* (GB: *Marie Walewska*), with Garbo, in which he gave the most enduringly popular impersonation of Napoleon; and *Algiers* (1938), Hedy Lamarr's sensational introduction to Hollywood. Then Wanger dropped him, under pressure from exhibitors who were unwilling to book foreign stars, but he remained popular – *Love Affair* (1939) and *When Tomorrow Comes* (1939), both with Irene Dunne as his leading lady, were immensely successful.

Boyer was in France when war broke out. He was quickly dispatched to the US by the French government, which saw his value as a propaganda asset (he became an American citizen in 1942). The pattern of his wartime films was set by *All This And Heaven Too* (1940), in which he was a French count yearning after secretary Bette Davis. A smooth stream of women's pictures was finally interrupted by a svelte performance in *Gaslight* (1944) as Ingrid Bergman's villainous husband. In the following year he was effective as Graham Greene's *Confidential Agent* (1945), but his appeal as a romantic leading man was now receding as rapidly as his hairline. After *Arch Of Triumph* (1948) he left Hollywood for Broadway, returning in 1951 – minus toupee and as a character actor – in *The Thirteenth Letter*.

Thereafter he worked steadily in Europe and Hollywood, although he was seldom given the chance to display his versatility. A notable exception was Max Ophuls's *Madame de . . .* (1953). His sheer professionalism redeemed a number of mediocre films, including *The Buccaneer* (1957), *Love Is A Ball* (1962) and *How To Steal A Million* (1965), but even Boyer sank without trace in the ghastly remake of *Lost Horizon* (1973). He contributed an incisive cameo to Alain Resnais' *Stavisky* (1974) and two years later appeared in his last film, *A Matter Of Time* (1976). RC

with Greta Garbo in Conquest *(MGM, 1937)*

George Brent

Real name **George Nolan**
Born **Shannonsbridge, Ireland, 15 March 1904**
Died **1979**

The 30s was the era of high-powered leading ladies. George Brent once remarked that all a leading man needed was a good haircut, as the back of his head was the only part of him that an audience was ever likely to see. Brent's hairstyling remained immaculate, and the nape of his neck can be savoured in a succession of 'women's pictures' in which he provided an urbane, if somewhat bland, prop for Kay Francis, Barbara Stanwyck, Myrna Loy, Ann Sheridan and, notably, Bette Davis, with whom he appeared in 11 pictures, including *Jezebel* (1938) and *Dark Victory* (1939). Davis's passion for him in *The Great Lie* (1941) may now seem a little strained, but Brent unfailingly absorbed the high-voltage emotion with all the panache and animation of a well-mannered sponge. He was never good enough to capture a film himself. When he was placed centre-stage, as in *Honeymoon For Three* (1941), in which he played Don Juan, the results were predictably limp.

Brent spent his youth in New York, then returned to Ireland where later he claimed to have been a dispatch rider for the IRA leader Michael Collins in The Troubles. During this period he also gained some experience at Dublin's Abbey Theatre before touring the US in 'Abie's Irish Rose'. He was one of the few actors to emerge from the undergrowth of the serials into the big-time, surviving an early encounter with Rin Tin Tin in Mascot's *The Lightning Warrior* (1931) to give a good performance in Warner Bros'. *The Rich Are Always With Us* (1932). Immediately after the film he married its star, Ruth Chatterton, a mere 24 hours after her divorce, which raised a few eyebrows at the time. The marriage only lasted a couple of years, and Brent later married another Warners star, Ann Sheridan (he managed six wives in all!). In the late 40s his smooth good looks became haggard and jowly, and the good parts began to dry up. He strolled through a number of B features, and then – like many another failing star – it was back to Britain. In *The Last Page* (1952), even a spirited vamping by a busty young Diana Dors failed to dispel Brent's air of weary gloom, and he returned to America to make *Mexican Manhunt* (1953), a serviceable little programmer and his last film. RC

Johnny Mack Brown

Born **Dothan, Alabama, 1 September 1904**
Died **1974**

Johnny Mack Brown began his career in tuxedos as a silent leading man, but in the 30s he exchanged evening dress for buckskins and became one of the biggest stars of the B Western. A football star of the 20s, Brown was the only Hollywood leading man to be elected to The Football Hall Of Fame. His gridiron triumphs led to a contract with MGM and a film debut in *Slide Kelly Slide* (1926). He squired Greta Garbo, Norma Shearer and Marion Davies, and in 1928 was flapper Joan Crawford's playboy halfback boyfriend in *Our Dancing Daughters*.

His Western career began in spectacular fashion, playing the title role in King Vidor's wide-screen *Billy The Kid* (1930), and using a six-shooter reputedly owned by the legendary badman. But in the early 30s his MGM career foundered as he was elbowed out of the way by a rising Clark Gable. By 1933 he was making Westerns on poverty row, starring in the Mascot serial *Fighting With Kit*

Carson (1933). Then he moved over to A.V. Hackel's Supreme Pictures, for whom he churned out 16 sagebrush second features between 1935 and 1937. After three serials with Universal, beginning with *Wild West Days* (1937), he embarked on a long series of programmers for the studio, the first six of which co-starred Bob Baker. Some of the early Universal entries are particularly interesting: *Boss of Bullion City* (1941) co-starred Maria Montez; and several were directed by Joseph H. Lewis, revealing a fluency uncharacteristic of the Bs, with *Arizona Cyclone* (1941) outstanding.

After *The Lone Star Trail* (1943), Brown moved to Monogram where he made a total of 66 oaters, in many of the earlier entries playing 'Nevada Jack McKenzie', with Raymond Hatton from Monogram's 'Rough Riders' series. He plugged on gamely, gaining a little avoirdupois every year, until *The Marshal's Daughter* (1953). He worked in television and, falling on hard times, took a job as the *maitre d'hotel* in a Los Angeles restaurant. In the 60s he made a brief comeback in A.C. Lyles Westerns, and his last film role was as a cowardly sheriff in *Apache Uprising* (1966). RC

in 1932

Jack Buchanan

Born **Glasgow, Scotland, 2 April 1891**
Died **1957**

Genial, modest, always the complete professional, Jack Buchanan was the model of the dapper Mayfair man-about-town of the 20s and 30s. He had no peer on the English stage, enjoyed a good run in Hollywood in the early 30s, and 20 years later, as his career was drawing to a close, made a triumphant return in *The Band Wagon* (1953).

Buchanan made his stage debut in Glasgow in 1912, and by the mid-20s was Britain's top musical comedy star. In 1924 he triumphed on Broadway with Gertrude Lawrence in 'Charlot's Revue of 1924', but it was not until 1927 that he had his first British film success with a melodrama, *Confetti*. *Toni* (1928) was a silent version of his musical comedy hit of 1924 and then he travelled to Hollywood to make *Paris*, a musical co-starring Irene Bordoni. He guested in Warners' 1929 *Show Of Shows*, then took over a role originally intended for Chevalier in

Paramount's *Monte Carlo* (1930), co-starring Jeanette MacDonald. Back in Britain he played the Austrian army officer who falls for flower girl Anna Neagle in Herbert Wilcox's *Goodnight Vienna* (1932). Most of his films of the 30s were amiable, frothy concoctions with the emphasis on farce. At his peak in the mid-30s, the film and the stage version of *This'll Make You Whistle* (1937) were running at the same time in London's West End. *Bulldog Sees It Through* (1940) was a jaunty spy thriller, but this kind of frolic was soon overtaken by a greater realism, and Buchanan was off the screen until his marvellous performance in *The Band Wagon*, as a flamboyant impresario who joins forces with Fred Astaire, Cyd Charisse, Oscar Levant and Nanette Fabray to produce the ultimate musical.

He returned to Britain to make two more films, but by now he was a very sick man. His last film appearance was in the title role of Preston Sturges's tragic misfired comeback, *Les Carnets De Major Thomson* (1955) filmed in France. By the time it was exported, in a mutilated version, Sturges and Buchanan were both dead. RC

Billie Burke

Real name **Mary William Ethelbert Appleton Burke**
Born **Washington D.C., 7 August 1885**
Died **1970**

Billie Burke was cinema's favourite featherbrained aunt, with an inimitable silvery, fluting voice. But long before her film career began she was one of Broadway's greatest beauties, whose escorts included J.M. Barrie, Caruso and Somerset Maugham.

Her father was the internationally famous clown Billy Burke, and much of her childhood and youth were spent in London where, in 1903, she made her first legitimate stage appearance. In 1907 she was brought to America by Charles Frohman to star in 'My Wife', and quickly became the toast of Broadway, marrying the great impresario Florenz Ziegfeld in April, 1914. In 1915 she was signed by Thomas Ince at $10,000 a week to make *Peggy*, a Scottish romance, at his California studios. After *Gloria's Romance* (1916), a serial filmed on location in Florida, Burke signed with Paramount Artcraft, for whom she made 14 films in the next four years, all of them shot in New York.

In the 20s she settled into semi-retirement, but the Wall Street Crash – which wiped out Ziegfeld's fortune – brought her back to her profession. She appeared in some Pathé Rodeo shorts in 1930 and was cast as John Barrymore's feckless wife in RKO's *A Bill of Divorcement* (1932). She was the hapless hostess in MGM's *Dinner At Eight* (1932), followed

in She Couldn't Take It *(Columbia, 1935)*

by Joan Crawford's daffy aunt in *Forsaking All Others* (1934) and the pixillated Mrs Topper in three *Topper* films from 1937–1941. Miss Burke took in Brian Aherne's bogus tramp in *Merrily We Live* (1938) and won an Oscar nomination. She was charming as Oliver Hardy's wife in *Zenobia* (1939), and in the same year played Glinda the Good Fairy in *The Wizard Of Oz*, her favourite role. Monty

Woolley drove Burke and her family to distraction in *The Man Who Came To Dinner* (1941), but she soldiered on into the 50s, as disarmingly vapid as ever, in *Father Of The Bride* (1950) and *Father's Little Dividend* (1951). Her career ended with a flourish in John Ford's *Sergeant Rutledge* (1960). As a witness for the prosecution, she gave her familiar fluttering old lady a memorably rancid edge. RC

James Cagney

Born **New York City, 1 July 1899**

James Cagney is the most irresistibly charming of all film stars. Typecast by Warner Bros. as the little tough guy who manhandles women and makes them like it, his stylised swagger and bravado overrode his gangster films' ostensibly 'realistic' content. His bounce, and terrier-like dynamism, owed much to his beginnings as a dancer, as if Cagney's impish spirit was picking up secret harmonies which other less intuitively sensitive actors could not hear. Like a dancer, his performances were always superbly choreographed: playfully slapping The Dead End Kids around a tenement baseball court in *Angels With Dirty Faces* (1938); barnstorming through *Yankee Doodle Dandy* (1942) as if, in David Thomson's memorable phrase, he was 'a toy running wild'; as Cody Jarrett in *White Heat* (1949), reeling around his cell, delirious with one of his 'headaches'.

He was born on New York's Lower East Side and, after a succession of humble jobs, got his start in vaudeville. In the late 20s he moved from cabaret to the legitimate theatre and, in 1929, while co-starring with Joan Blondell in 'Penny Arcade', Warners acquired the rights to the show, brought the stars to Hollywood, and turned it into *Sinners' Holiday* (1930). The studio signed Cagney at $400 a week and put him into a Lew Ayres gangster melo, *Doorway To Hell* (1930). Director William Wellman was impressed with his performance in *Other Men's Women* (1931) and he was rewarded with the second lead in *Public Enemy* (1931), as bootlegger Edward Woods's buddy and partner in crime. After three days they exchanged roles. Cagney went on to dominate the film, pulping a grapefruit in Mae Clarke's face and finally crashing dead in his mother's hallway. Cagney made violence and a life of crime magically seductive, and *Public Enemy* made him Warners' number 2 gangster, second only to Edward G. Robinson.

The studio rushed him into a string of cheaply made melodramas, all of them animated by Cagney's raw energy as hoodlum, ex-con, or tough, cynical hero battling the rackets: *Blonde Crazy* (1931), *Taxi* (1932), *The Crowd Roars* (1932) and *Winner Takes All* (1932). But he was dissatisfied with these parts, referring to them as 'dese, dem and dose' roles, and he took on Warners in a running battle for better films and a higher salary. They settled at $1,750 a week and he came back in *Hard To Handle* (1933),

as a hustler who organises a dance marathon for a publicity stunt. In *Footlight Parade* (1933) he was a hustling theatre producer, closing the film with a stunning Busby Berkeley routine, 'Shanghai Lil'. *Lady Killer* (1933) gave him another chance to rough-house Mae Clarke, dragging her across the floor by her hair.

Cagney was just too much for most of Warners' leading ladies – only Joan Blondell and, later, Ann Sheridan, had the humour and resilence to stay the course. As a result, in *Here Comes The Navy* (1934), Warners teamed Cagney with the reassuringly solid Pat O'Brien. Among the films they made together were two classics: Howard Hawks's *Ceiling Zero* (1936), in which they played rival airline pilots; and Michael Curtiz's *Angels With Dirty Faces*. In the pulsating *G-Men* (1935), he was on the right side of the law, joining the FBI when his pal is rubbed out by the mob. He was an excellent Bottom in Max Reinhardt's *A Midsummer Night's Dream* (1935), but he was working up to another row with the studio. After completing *Ceiling Zero*, he took himself off to Grand National for two minor films, *Great Guy* (1936) and *Something To Sing About* (1937). But Cagney and Warners needed each other – by now he had crept into the box office top ten – and he returned to the studio for *Angels With Dirty Faces*. *Boy Meets Girl* (1938) was a pacy, screwball spoof of

in Public Enemy (Warner Bros., 1931)

Hollywood directed by Lloyd Bacon, who also handled *The Oklahoma Kid* (1939), an unlikely but enjoyable excursion, co-starring Humphrey Bogart. The year ended with *The Roaring Twenties*. His contract ran out in 1940, and although anxious to form his own production company, the star was persuaded to sign for another two years. His partnership with O'Brien ended with *The Fighting 69th* and *Torrid Zone* (1940). Raoul Walsh's *The Strawberry Blonde* (1941) is a minor classic, with Cagney outstanding as the small-town dentist infatuated with gold-digger Rita Hayworth.

By the time he made *Captain Of The Clouds* (1942), Cagney was the second highest paid US citizen (Louis B. Mayer was No 1), but he was attracting criticism from right-wingers for what they saw as his 'Communist' leanings. His reply was *Yankee Doodle Dandy*, the biopic of the strutting ultra-patriot, livewire song and dance man George M. Cohan, a non-stop performance which won him an Oscar.

With his brother William he then went independent, releasing through United Artists. *Johnny Come Lately* (1944) was an attempt to mellow his image, playing a hobo helping Grace George to run a small newspaper. *Blood On The Sun* (1946) was more traditional Cagney fare – a melodrama set in pre-war Tokyo with journalist Cagney stumbling on Japanese plans for world domination.

After *The Time Of Your Life* (1948), Warners asked him back for *White Heat* to play the mother-fixated psychopath Cody Jarrett. 'Top of the world, Ma' he yells just before he perishes in a gigantic petrol tank explosion – an ending which, once seen, is never forgotten.

It was the final flourish before the slow falling away in an uneven series of films. *Kiss Tomorrow Goodbye* (1950) was a turgid evocation of his gangster days, and in *Come Fill The Cup* (1951) he gave a restrained performance as a journalist trying to lick alcoholism. *A Lion Is In The Streets* (1953) provided him with a challenging role as a demago-

in Ragtime (Paramount, 1981)

gue in the Huey Long mould; he was the neurotic captain in *Mister Roberts* (1955), and had a walk-on as George M. Cohan in Bob Hope's *The Seven Little Foys* (1955). After *These Wilder Years* (1956), with Barbara Stanwyck, he played Lon Chaney Sr in *Man Of A Thousand Faces* (1957), then directed *Short Cut To Hell* (1957), an undistinguished remake of *This Gun For Hire*. He was excellent as a surgeon caught up with the IRA in *Shake Hands With The Devil* (1959), and then played Admiral Halsey in a biopic, *The Gallant Hours* (1960), directed by his old friend Robert Montgomery. He bowed out with a characteristically demonic burst of energy in Billy Wilder's *One Two Three* (1961), as a manic Coca-Cola salesman. In 1981 he came out of retirement to appear in *Ragtime*. RC

in Yankee Doodle Dandy (Warner Bros., 1942)

in Show Business *(RKO, 1944)*

Eddie Cantor

Real name Edward Iskowitz
Born New York City, 31 January 1892
Died 1964

Nicknamed 'The Apostle Of Pep', Eddie Cantor made 14 films between 1926 and 1948. But the saucer-eyed vaudeville star never wholly succeeded in transferring his frantic style to the screen.

Born over a Russian tea house in a New York ghetto, his was the classic rags-to-riches story. He caught the show business bug after winning first prize in an East Side amateur night, and in 1907 made his professional debut at the Clinton Music Hall as one half of a song and dance team. Later he worked as a singing waiter, with a piano player named Jimmy Durante. In vaudeville he established his reputation singing his friend Irving Berlin's songs, and then became a Ziegfeld star in such hits

as 'Whoopee' (1928) which he made into a movie version in 1930.

He made his screen debut in *Kid Boots* (1926), with Clara Bow. Several films, and several hundred thousand dollars later, disaster struck – the Wall Street Crash. Cantor lost everything. Undeterred, he sat down and wrote a best-seller about the experience, 'Caught Short'. His films were usually in the 'underdog outwits the bullies' mode, full of chases and madcap stunts. There was a bullfight in *The Kid From Spain* (1932), a chariot race in *Roman Scandals* (1933), and an 80-mile-an-hour chase on a scenic railway in *Strike Me Pink* (1935).

Cantor was also one of America's biggest radio stars, hosting his own show for two decades. He was forced into early retirement after a heart attack in 1952. In the same year Keefe Brasselle starred in a biopic, *The Eddie Cantor Story*. In 1956, he was honoured with a special Academy Award 'for distinguished services to the film industry'. RC

Madeleine Carroll

Real name Marie-Madeleine O'Carroll
Born West Bromwich, England,
26 February 1906

Madeleine Carroll was one of Britain's most glamorous exports to Hollywood. A cool and exquisitely beautiful blonde, her acting ability was limited, but perfectly suited to the romantic make-believe of films like *The Prisoner Of Zenda* (1937). Her studied lack of animation also provided Hitchcock with an 'ice maiden' prototype in two of his best films of the

30s, *The Secret Agent* (1936) and *The Thirty-Nine Steps* (1936).

A graduate of Birmingham University, she began by modelling hats, then made her debut on the West End stage in 'The Lash' (1927). The *Guns Of Loos* (1928) was her first film and, by the time of *The W Plan* (1930), she was Britain's biggest female star. After *I Was A Spy* (1933), she went to Fox to appear in John Ford's *The World Moves On* (1934), a lumbering family saga co-starring Franchot Tone then, back in Britain, her career went into the doldrums. It was revived by *The Thirty-Nine Steps* and *The Secret Agent*. Alexander Korda sold her contract to Walter Wanger and 20th Century-Fox, and Miss Carroll returned to Hollywood for *The Case Against Mrs Ames* (1936). She was well-served by the films of her peak Hollywood years: *The General Died At Dawn* (1936); *Lloyds Of London* (1937) in which George Sanders and Tyrone Power fought over her; *The Prisoner Of Zenda*, a perfect vehicle for her porcelain good looks; *Honeymoon In Bali* (1939), the second of three enjoyable films with Fred MacMurray; and *My Son, My Son* (1940), in which she gave her best acting performance. She married rugged actor Sterling Hayden, and in 1941 they made a handsome couple in *Bahama Passage*, which contains the immortal moment when, to Carroll's suggestion that they make love, Hayden replies, 'No, let's fish'.

After co-starring with Bob Hope in *My Favourite Blonde* (1942), she returned to Britain to concentrate on war work. Her film career never picked up after 1945. She made a British weepie, *White Cradle Inn* (1946), and returned to Hollywood for *Don't Trust Your Husband* (1948), a limp marital romp with Fred MacMurray. Her last film was Otto Preminger's *The Fan* (1949). RC

Ruth Chatterton

Born New York City, 24 December 1893
Died 1961

In the early 30s George Arliss was the First Gentleman of the Screen and Ruth Chatterton the First Lady. Her films were generally superior weepies in which she was a mature woman, enduring tragedy with unruffled serenity and often with some humour.

She had a long Broadway career behind her when, in 1925, she accompanied her actor husband, Ralph Forbes, to Hollywood. Her film debut came in 1928 when Emil Jannings requested her for Paramount's *Sins Of The Fathers*. With the arrival of sound, her stage training stood her in good stead, and Paramount put her into *The Doctor's Secret* (1929) and *The Dummy* (1929). On loan to MGM, she starred in *Madame X*, according to 'Picturegoer', 'The most poignant thing the Talkies have given us to date'.

She returned to Paramount a big star, and *Charming Sinners* (1929), *The Laughing Lady* (1929) and *Sarah And Son* (1930) saw her approaching her peak. MGM borrowed her for *Lady Of Scandal* (1930), then back at Paramount in *Anybody's Woman* (1930), she was a chorus girl who reforms alcoholic lawyer Clive Brook. In *The Right To Love* (1930) she skilfully accomplished the classic dual-role formula reserved for Great Ladies of the Cinema, ageing to play both mother and daughter.

in The Laughing Lady *(Paramount, 1930)*

By now a new star was rising on the Paramount horizon, Marlene Dietrich, and Chatterton signed with Warners, working out her contract with three commercial disasters, *The Magnificent Lie* (1931), *Once A Lady* (1931) and *Tomorrow And Tomorrow* (1932). She never recovered her star status, and rapidly became a support for her second husband, George Brent, whom she married after they co-starred in *The Rich Are Always With Us* (1932). They appeared together in three more films, then *Journal Of A Crime* (1934) with Adolphe Menjou marked the end of her Warners contract, and also the end of her marriage.

It was two years before Chatterton worked again: in Columbia's *Lady Of Secrets* (1936) and Fox's *Girls' Dormitory* (1936). She was excellent as Walter Huston's egocentric wife in Goldwyn's *Dodsworth* (1936), then went to Britain for her last two films, *The Rat* (1938) and *Royal Divorce* (1938). She returned to the theatre and began writing in the 50s, when four of her novels were published. RC

Maurice Chevalier

Born **Paris, 12 September 1888**
Died **1972**

Maurice Chevalier was over 40 when he made his Hollywood debut in *Innocents In Paris* (1929). He immediately became one of Paramount's most popular stars. With his straw hat perched at a roguish angle, his jutting lower lip, and a French accent as broad as the Champs Elysées, he personified the sexually confident, Parisian boulevardier, a role he exploited right into his old age.

He had been a star of the French music hall, often appearing at the Folies Bergère with chanteuse Mistinguette, with whom it was said he had a love affair. His gallic charm was the perfect complement to the Anglo-Saxon reserve of Jeanette MacDonald in four lavish boudoir operettas, *The Love Parade* (1929), *Love Me Tonight* (1932), *One Hour With You* (1932) and MGM's *The Merry Widow* (1934). MacDonald was cast by director Ernst Lubitsch in the title role of the latter, against the wishes of Chevalier who didn't really get on with his co-star. He wanted Grace Moore for the part. MGM promised to team him up with Miss Moore in his following film, but Chevalier refused when he found out he was to get second billing. *The Merry Widow* emerged as one of the screen's most polished musicals, and Chevalier was at his bawdy best singing of going to Maxim's 'where all the girls are dreams.' His famous straw boater was used as a motif in a production number of *Folies Bergère* (1935), his last film before returning to Europe.

Chevalier had wanted to return two years previously, but found the large American salaries difficult to resist. His wife, Yvonne, who had joined him in Hollywood in 1931, had never been happy in the film colony. Rumours of love affairs between Maurice and other women, including his co-star Claudette Colbert in *The Smiling Lieutenant* (1931), finally led to divorce. He made two films in France and two in England, one being René Clair's comedy *Break The News* (1937), co-starring Jack Buchanan, just before the war. During the Occupation, he confined himself to entertaining on the Paris stage. There were uncomfortable suggestions of collaboration but, at the Liberation, he managed to clear his name. Immediately after the war, Chevalier gave one of his best straight performances in René Clair's *Le*

Silence Est D'Or (1947). He made a few more films in France, before being recalled to Hollywood for a second American career at the age of 69.

In over a dozen schmaltzy romantic comedies, Chevalier spread his French, avuncular personality rather thickly, whether as Audrey Hepburn's private-eye father in *Love In The Afternoon* (1957), an ingratiating priest in *Jessica* (1962), or Frank Sinatra's mentor in *Can Can* (1960). However, he was outstanding as Louis Jourdan's elderly *roué* uncle in *Gigi* (1958) (he had been a personal friend of Colette, the author of the novella on which the musical was based). Stanley Kauffmann in the 'New Republic' wrote, 'Every time Chevalier approaches, one mutters, 'No, it's too silly, I'm not going to be charmed by a man who deliberately sets out to charm me', and every time Chevalier prevails.' His captivating smile and enduring charm dispel any unpleasantness from the subject as he sings 'I'm Glad I'm Not Young Anymore' and 'Thank Heaven For Little Girls.' In addition to the film's nine Oscars, Chevalier was given a special Academy Award 'for his contribution to the world of entertainment for more than half a century'. RB

with Louis Jourdan (left) and Leslie Caron in Gigi (MGM, 1958).

in Maid Of Salem (Paramount, 1937)

Claudette Colbert

Real name **Claudette Chauchoin**
Born **Paris, 13 September 1905**

In the 30s she was often cast in sultry roles: the cruel Poppaea, bathing in asses milk in DeMille's enjoyably ludicrous *The Sign Of The Cross* (1932); slinking mischievously through an art deco Egypt in the title role of his *Cleopatra* (1934). But Claudette Colbert – fresh-cheeked and big-eyed, with a warm purring laugh which effortlessly conveyed brittle sophistication – was at her best in comedy. On set, she could be difficult, adamantly refusing any right-profile shots, but on screen she was enchanting.

Her parents came to America when she was six, and she made her stage debut in 'The Wild Westcotts' (1923). By the late 20s, she was a leading Broadway actress with one silent film to her credit, First National's *For The Love Of Mike* (1927), directed by Frank Capra. The coming of sound, and her stage background, secured her a contract with Paramount, for whom her first film was *The Hole In The Wall* (1929). Her first big film was a melodrama, *Manslaughter* (1930), co-starring Fredric March, and she widened her range in Lubitsch's *The Smiling Lieutenant* (1931) – tangling with Miriam Hopkins over Maurice Chevalier – and *The Man From Yesterday* (1932), in which Clive Brook and Charles Boyer tangled over her. Comedy was clearly her forte, as she showed in Elliott Nugent's charming Depression comedy *Three-Cornered Moon* (1933).

Then she was loaned to Columbia to play the runaway heiress in Capra's Oscar-studded comedy *It Happened One Night* (1934), carrying away the Best Actress award.

Colbert stayed at the top for the next ten years, and in 1938 was listed as the highest paid Hollywood star, at a salary of $426,944. She chose her parts with great care, initially alternating sentimental dramas like *Imitation Of Life* (1934) with brisk comedies like *The Gilded Lily* (1935). She was Cigarette, the saucy mascot of the Foreign Legion, in *Under Two Flags* (1936), but thereafter comedy won out: *I Met Him In Paris* (1937), *Tovarich* (1937), *Bluebeard's Eighth Wife* (1938), the delightful *Midnight* (1939) and MGM's *It's A Wonderful World* (1939). She reached her peak in Preston Sturges's comic masterpiece *The Palm Beach Story* (1942), but was an unlikely choice as the Average American Wife in *Since You Went Away* (1944).

Her association with Paramount ended after *Practically Yours* (1944). The postwar pursuit of 'realism' was at odds with her flair for romantic comedy, and her playing became increasingly mannered in minor films like *Guest Wife* (1945) and *Without Reservations* (1946). Her last big hit was *The Egg And I* (1947), a comedy which introduced Ma and Pa Kettle to the screen. After *Let's Make It Legal* (1951), she went to Britain to make *The Planter's Wife* (1952), and then to France for two films. After a B-film, RKO's *Texas Lady* (1955), Colbert returned to Broadway and, six years later, turned up as Troy Donahue's mother in *Parrish* (1961). RC

Jackie Coogan

Born **Los Angeles, 24 October 1914**
Died **1984**

The five-year-old Jackie Coogan was spotted by Charlie Chaplin parodying his father's tap-dancing act in an Annette Kellerman revue. As Chaplin watched, the idea for his first six-reeler sprang – almost fully formed – into his mind. After trying out Coogan in the two-reel *A Day's Pleasure* (1919), he cast him as the bewitching little ragamuffin, raised and then lost by the Tramp in *The Kid* (1921).

By the time Coogan made *Daddy* (1923) he was one of Hollywood's top earners. In the same year he moved from First National to MGM in a four picture, $1 million deal. His first offering was *Long Live The King* (1923), in which he played 'a lovable little prince', Otto of Lavonia. Age began to take its toll, and in 1927 his famous tousled bob was sheared off in front of the cameras; the event was celebrated in *Johnny Get Your Hair Cut* (1927).

In Hollywood terms, senility had overtaken him by the time he was 13. Jackie showed that he was a capable actor in *Tom Sawyer* (1930) and *Huckleberry Finn* (1931), but by the mid-30s he had slipped into an obscurity from which he was yanked by that *sine qua non* of all child stars' careers, an unseemly squabble over money. He had made $4 million at his peak, but when he asked his mother for the money, she told him that under Californian law it was all hers. After a series of bitterly fought court cases, he came away with a mere $126,000. A by-product of this little tragedy was The Child Actors Bill, popularly known as 'the Coogan Act', which attempted to outlaw such exploitation.

After World War II, Coogan turned up in bit parts in B films, notably the Albert Zugsmith–Mamie Van Doren exploiters, *High School Confidential* (1958) and *Sex Kittens Go To College* (1960). In the 60s, balding and paunchy, he played Uncle Fester in TV's 'Addams Family.' RC

in The Kid *(First National/Warner Bros., 1920)*

in Sooky *(Paramount, 1931)*

Jackie Cooper

Real name **John Cooper Jr**
Born **Los Angeles, 15 September 1921**

In his autobiography, 'The Moon's A Balloon', David Niven recounted with great humour his inability to summon up the tiniest tear at Merle Oberon's death bed in *Wuthering Heights* (1939). He should have taken lessons from child star Jackie Cooper, who could cry at will. As one critic wrote in 1934, 'Jackie Cooper's tear ducts having been more or less in abeyance for the past few months, have been opened up to provide an autumn freshet in *Peck's Bad Boy*'.

He got his start in Bobby Clark and Lloyd Hamilton comedy shorts and, in 1927–8, was 'the little tough guy' in Hal Roach's 'Our Gang' series. He was a veteran of 10 when he won an Oscar nomination for his performance in *Skippy* (1931), based on Percy Crosby's cartoon strip. Cooper lost out, but the film's director (and his uncle) Norman Taurog, picked up the Best Director Award. At MGM, Cooper formed a memorable partnership with Wallace Beery in *The Champ* (1931), and three years later was Jim Hawkins to Beery's Long John Silver in *Treasure Island* (1934). *The Bowery* (1933) and *O'Shaughnessy's Boy* (1935) were weak copies of *The Champ*. In adolescence, Cooper played Clifford Goldsmith's gormless small town hero Henry Aldrich in two films, *What A Life* (1939) and *Life With Henry* (1941).

After war service Cooper tried a comeback in B features like *Kilroy Was Here* (1947), co-starring with another former child star, Jackie Coogan. He later played on Broadway and in summer stock, but he was more successful in television, starring in 'The People's Choice' and 'Hennessy'. He became a director and executive producer on the M*A*S*H series, for which he won an Emmy award. He made a return to the big screen in *Superman* (1978), as Perry White, editor of the 'Daily Planet'. RC

Larry 'Buster' Crabbe

Real name **Clarence Lindon Crabbe**
Born **Oakland, California, 17 February 1907**
Died **1983**

Like Johnny Weissmuller, Buster Crabbe swam his way into films. The 400-metre gold medallist in the 1932 Olympics, he drifted into movies as a stunt-man and extra while studying law. MGM's Tarzan was the rage in 1932, and Buster was soon cast as a thinly disguised version of Edgar Rice Burroughs's ape man in Paramount's *King Of The Jungle* (1933). Speech training lowered his high-pitched voice to a growl, and in the same year he was thrown into his first serial, Sol Lesser's *Tarzan The Fearless*. Crabbe proved athletic and decorative, but his dialogue was confined to meaningless grunts, which put paid to his chances of major stardom. Paramount signed him for a series of Zane Grey B Westerns and his stalwart qualities persuaded Universal to bleach his hair and cast him as space hero Flash Gordon in the 1936 serial, based on Alex Raymond's immortal

in Flash Gordon *(Universal, 1936)*

comic strip. Crabbe soared through space in his spluttering rocket, his mission being to foil the schemes of power-crazed Ming the Merciless. In episode twelve, Ming came to a sticky end in 'The Tunnel Of Terror', but *Flash Gordon* had been so successful that he was resurrected for two sequels, *Flash Gordon's Trip To Mars* (1938) and *Flash Gordon Conquers The Universe* (1940). Buster did further serial duty as comic strip heroes Red Barry (1938) and Buck Rogers (1939), the latter a handsomely mounted attempt to repeat the Flash Gordon formula.

Throughout the 40s, he plugged away in poverty row actioners and Westerns, such as PRC's *Frontier Outlaws* (1944). After World War II, he toured the world in his Aqua Show and then set sail as Captain Silver in a location-shot Columbia serial, *The Sea Hound* (1947). His ninth and last serial was *King Of The Kongo* (1952). After a long-running TV show, *Captain Gallant Of The Legion* (in which he co-starred with his son Cuffy), he went into comfortable semi-retirement, buckling on his holster for the occasional B Western. RC

Joan Crawford

Real name **Lucille Le Sueur**
Born **San Antonio, Texas, 23 March 1904**
Died **1977**

'Movie star!' The words were invented for Joan Crawford, as she progressed from Jazz Baby to Shopgirl's Dream to the Bitch Goddess whose savage slash of a mouth and devouring eyes loomed out of the women's magazines. Her hairstyles and make-up changed with chameleon-like rapidity, but underneath she remained a combination of strength and vulnerability, a shade vulgar, a little obvious. She was at her best in trash, absorbing the clichés like blotting paper.

Her monolithic qualities were heightened by the Joan Crawford No 1 Plot: determined girl from the wrong side of the tracks claws her way to the top and sacrifices love and happiness in her fight to stay there. Doomed in romance and the victim of predatory men, her film heroines were the paradigms of her own unhappy life and manic success drive. Three failed marriages, to Douglas Fairbanks Jr, Franchot Tone and Philip Terry; several miscarriages, and then the bizarre rearing of four adopted children recounted in grisly detail by Christina Crawford in 'Mommie Dearest'. The complete fusion of art and life came in Michael Curtiz's *Mildred Pierce* (1945), in which Crawford's relentlessly over-achieving heroine suffers for the sins of her spoilt brat of a daughter.

She started as a dancer, and was spotted in the chorus line of a Broadway musical by MGM's Harry Rapf. Placed under contract, she made her screen debut doubling for Norma Shearer in *Lady Of The Night* (1925). As Lucille Le Sueur she appeared in a Jackie Coogan vehicle, *Old Clothes* (1925), and then MGM launched a publicity campaign to find her a new name. Transformed into Joan Crawford, she embarked on a more drastic metamorphosis, dieting ferociously to give her face that angularity which became the foundation of her enduring stardom.

Crawford became a star in *Our Dancing Daughters* (1928), playing the definitive flapper. There were more flapper roles, but by the time of *Our Blushing Brides* (1930) she was demanding meaty parts. *Paid* (1930) established the Crawford archetype, a shop girl falsely jailed and hell bent on revenge. In *Possessed* (1931) she was a small-town girl on the make, ensnaring politician Clark Gable, and in *Grand Hotel* (1932) she was a hard-boiled typist-cum-whore. Then, in an attempt to overhaul her rivals, she overreached herself, as Sadie Thompson, in Lewis Milestone's *Rain* (1932). *Dancing Lady* (1933), with Gable, quickly restored her popularity, but the formula-bound repetitiveness of her films began to undermine her status. *The Last Of Mrs Cheyney* (1937) showed that she was at home in more sophisticated roles, but a year later she was

declared 'box office poison' in the notorious full-page advertisement placed by exhibitors in 'The Hollywood Reporter'. With characteristic tenacity she embarked on *The Shining Hour* (1938), weathering stiff competition from Margaret Sullavan, survived *Ice Follies Of 1939* and stole the show in George Cukor's *The Women* (1939). She gave one of her best performances in Frank Borzage's *Strange Cargo* (1940) and, in Cukor's *A Woman's Face* (1941), underlined her capacity for suffering.

But the quality of her films at MGM rapidly declined, and in 1943 she went to Warners. Following a brief appearance in *Hollywood Canteen* (1944), she triumphed in *Mildred Pierce* (1945), winning the Best Actress Oscar. Now typed as a driven queen bitch on the verge of middle age, she smothered John Garfield in *Humoresque* (1946) and succumbed to schizophrenia over Van Heflin in *Possessed* (1947). In *Flamingo Road* (1949) and *The Damned Don't Cry* (1950) she stalked stonily through her old woman-on-the-make routine, and was put through the mill in *This Woman Is Dangerous* (1952). Younger men now became figures of menace: her husband Jack Palance in *Sudden Fear* (1952) and her lover Jeff Chandler in *Female On The Beach* (1955). In the 50s she seemed determined to play both the male and the female leads, but Nicholas Ray used her basilisk humourlessness with great skill in *Johnny Guitar* (1954).

Robert Aldrich handled the two most effective films of her later career, *Autumn Leaves* (1956) and the Grand Guignol *Whatever Happened To Baby Jane?* (1962). The latter's success led to a rash of ill-judged appearances in cheap shockers, the last one of which was *Trog* (1970). RC

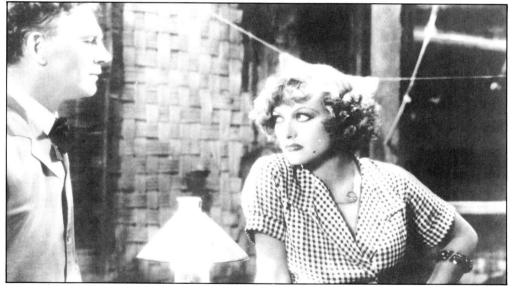

with Walter Huston in Rain *(United Artists, 1932)*

Bing Crosby

Real name **Harry Lillis Crosby**
Born **Tacoma, Washington, 2 May 1904**
Died **1977**

Bing Crosby's film career floated 'straight down the middle' with the lazy, effortless parabola of one of his golf drives. It was a triumph of the art that conceals blandness, as deceptive as the unwavering quiff of the toupée which hid his receding hairline.

Amiable, unassuming and relaxed, he moved smoothly from singing with Paul Whiteman to Mack Sennett shorts, and then his feature debut in *King Of Jazz* (1930). Signed by Paramount in 1931, he crooned his way through the 30s in a string of musicals, of which the best were *We're Not Dressing* (1934), *Anything Goes* (1936) and *Doctor Rhythm* (1938). In 1940 he was teamed with Bob Hope and Dorothy Lamour in *The Road To Singapore*, the first of the seven freewheeling 'Road' films in which Crosby ran good-natured rings around the

blustering Hope. *Holiday Inn* (1942), with Astaire, cemented his position as one of America's most popular entertainers, and two years later he climbed to No 1 at the box office, playing the singing priest Father O'Malley in Leo McCarey's *Going My Way* (1944). There was an equally successful sequel, *The Bells Of St Mary's* (1945), in which he encouraged a serene Ingrid Bergman to 'dial O for O'Malley if you're ever in trouble'.

In the late 40s and early 50s the abrasive MGM Technicolor musicals made Bing's collegiate style seem a little pallid, an old raccoon coat on a rack of sharkskin suits. *White Christmas* (1954), awash with sentimentality, restored his fortunes at the box office, and encouraged him to take on the role of the failed singing star in *The Country Girl* (1954), a beautifully judged performance opposite Grace Kelly. After *High Society* (1956), he coasted through a handful of mediocre ventures. His screen career ended with a forgettable remake of *Stagecoach* (1966). Enormously wealthy, his life was appropriately concluded after a good round of golf. RC

in 1934

Bette Davis

Real name Ruth Elizabeth Davis
Born Lowell, Massachusetts, 5 April 1908

Bette Davis once told an interviewer that the reason she worked so hard was that there were so few *real* actresses in films. Her temperament, her fierce belief in her own ability, and her distinctive looks marked her out from her great contemporaries. She did not possess the enigmatic glamour of Garbo; the hint of the bully in her ruled out the 'waif' image established for Janet Gaynor; and she was far too talented to substitute costume changes for acting in the manner of Norma Shearer. Bette Davis has never allowed us to forget this – just as she has assiduously promoted herself as a pawky New Englander and great screen *actress* rather than movie star. She has made much of her constant battle with Warner Bros. for good parts, but in her pulsing eyes and angular manner-isms there was always a streak of vulgarity and melodrama which fed on the absurdities of some of her best films, *Jezebel* (1938), *The Letter* (1940) and *All About Eve* (1950), in which her Margo Channing is quintessential Davis. She despises 'cheap senti-ment', but her survival depends upon it.

She studied acting at the John Murray Anderson School and had the distinction of being fired from her first job by George Cukor. She went on to a big success in 'Broken Dishes', failed a Goldwyn screen test, and was then signed by Universal who put her in *Bad Sister* (1931). She was the mousy little good sister in the film, and this condemned her to a string of 'Jenny Wren' roles at the studio in *Seed* (1931), *Waterloo Bridge* (1931) and *The Menace* (1931), for which she dyed her hair blonde. After *Hell's House* (1931), a programmer for Capital, she went to Warners as George Arliss's leading lady in *The Man Who Played God* (1932). It was a crucial break, but she remained in supporting roles in *The Rich Are Always With Us* (1932) and *So Big* (1932). She returned to leading lady status in *The Dark Horse* (1932) and *Cabin In The Cotton* (1932), in which she played the first of her 'bitch on wheels' roles, an absurdly exaggerated small-town Southern tramp, flouncing all over country boy Richard Barthelmess, and talking about 'washin' ma hayuh'. She worked her way determinedly upward through *Three On A Match* (1932) and *20,000 Years In Sing Sing* (1933) to *Ex-Lady* (1933), her first starring vehicle and, according to Davis, 'a piece of junk'. Then it was back to programmers, with *Fog Over Frisco* (1934) a snappy thriller.

Reluctantly, Warners lent her to RKO for John Cromwell's *Of Human Bondage* (1934). Davis had

in The Anniversary (20th Century-Fox, 1968)

begged for the role, and her performance as the ruthless waitress who enslaves Leslie Howard won universal praise. In *Bordertown* (1935) she was a prize bitch bumping off husband Eugene Pallette for love of Paul Muni and cracking up in court in spectacular fashion. In *Dangerous* (1935) she was an alcoholic star on the skids, rehabilitated by Franchot Tone, and it won her the Best Actress Oscar which had eluded her the previous year. She followed that with *The Petrified Forest* (1936), and then two turkeys – *Golden Arrow* (1936), a comedy with George Brent, and *Satan met A Lady* (1936). This brought her simmering feud with Warners to the boil. She refused *God's Country* and *The Woman* and went to England to film outside her contract. Warners slapped an injunction on her and she returned, a well-publicised but unrepentant martyr, for *Marked Woman* (1937), *Kid Galahad* (1937), *That Certain Woman* (1937) and *It's Love I'm After* (1937), a charming comedy in which she played a temperamental and over-bearing stage star.

Then with childlike glee, Davis plunged her hands into the brantub of smoothly crafted melodra-ma and came up clutching *Jezebel*, the first of her great vehicles whose lurid absurdities are overcome by her passionate conviction. Her performance as the tempestuous Southern belle won her a second Oscar and launched a series of films in which she played tortured, unhappy women: she was deserted by Errol Flynn in *The Sisters* (1939); lost her illegitimate child to Miriam Hopkins in *The Old Maid* (1939); climbed the stairs to die in blindness in *Dark Victory* (1939); and went mad in *Juarez* (1939).

in All About Eve (20th Century-Fox, 1950)

with Leslie Howard in Of Human Bondage *(RKO, 1934)*

The series came to a climax with her performance as The Virgin Queen in *The Private Lives Of Elizabeth And Essex* (1939).

The star stayed in costume for *All This And Heaven Too* (1940), playing a 19th-century gover-ness who falls for her employer, Charles Boyer. Somerset Maugham's colonial piece, *The Letter* (1940), opened in splendid style with Davis empty-ing her revolver into her lover. In *The Great Lie* (1941), she brought up Mary Astor's child as her own. Then she returned to steamy goings-on in Southern mansions, bringing expertise to the appal-ling Regina – passionate, thwarted and tyrannical – in the screen version of Lillian Hellman's *The Little Foxes* (1941). She showed a sure comic touch in *The Man Who Came To Dinner* (1942) and then, in *Now Voyager* (1942), was transformed from dowdy, disturbed spinster into the chic recipient of Paul Henreid's lighted cigarettes. These were the golden years – she even sang in *Thank Your Lucky Stars* (1943) – then gave an admirably restrained perform-ance in *Watch On The Rhine* (1943), allowed Miriam Hopkins the bitchery in *Old Acquaintance* (1943) and sailed through the grand soap opera of *Mr Skeffington* (1944), supported by Claude Rains.

The Corn Is Green (1945), overwhelmed by its serious intentions, marked a watershed in her career. After *A Stolen Life* (1946), there were three stinkers in a row – *Deception* (1946), *June Bride* (1948) and *Winter Meeting* (1948). Her Warners contract ended with King Vidor's *Beyond The Forest* (1949).

All About Eve was a stunning answer to those critics who thought she was finished, but the comeback faltered, undermined by her poor choice of films and her increasingly mannered acting. After *The Star* (1952), Richard Winnington observed that the price of Davis's long fight to preserve her integrity was an over-weening egotism – 'only bad films are good enough for her'. And bad films were what she got: The *Virgin Queen* (1955), *Storm Center* (1956), and *The Catered Affair* (1956); an unhappy British venture with Alec Guinness, *The Scapegoat* (1959); and Capra's *Pocketful Of Miracles* (1961).

Then came a bizarre renaissance in Robert Aldrich's *What Ever Happened To To Baby Jane?* (1962), which cunningly exploited the sado-maso-chistic elements in the careers of Davis and her co-star Joan Crawford. *Hush, Hush, Sweet Charlotte* (1964) was in the same mould, with Davis as a cracked old Southern belle, Jezebel gone gaga. Hammer wheeled her out in *The Nanny* (1965) and *The Anniversary* (1967), a grotesque attempt at comic horror with an eye-patched Davis playing a monstrous matriarch. She yearned for meaty parts, but had to content herself with dismal films like *Bunny O'Hare* (1970), dressing up as a hippy to rob a bank. In a cameo in *Death On The Nile* (1978) she was, happily, allowed to dispense a flash of her old vitriol. RC

in The Little Foxes (RKO, 1941) ▷

Olivia de Havilland
Born **Tokyo, 1 July 1916**

Dainty, pretty and immensely hard-working, Olivia de Havilland, the elder sister of Joan Fontaine, was born of British parents, who separated when she was six. She was brought up by her mother in California and, while still a student, was chosen by Max Reinhardt to play Hermia in his Hollywood Bowl production of 'A Midsummer Night's Dream' and in the subsequent Warner Bros. film. The studio signed her to a seven-year contract, and her first release for them was *Alibi Ike* (1935).

Warners worked her hard, principally as the demure foil for Errol Flynn's dash in a series of classic swashbucklers and actioners including *Captain Blood* (1935), *The Charge Of The Light Brigade* (1936), *The Adventures Of Robin Hood* (1938) – as the most captivating of Maid Marions – *The Private Lives Of Elizabeth and Essex* (1939), *Dodge City* (1939), and *They Died With Their Boots On* (1941). There was also a delightful excursion into comedy in *Four's A Crowd* (1938). Flynn fell in love with de Havilland but, sensibly, she resisted him, later

in Gone With The Wind *(MGM, 1939)*

observing, 'I'm not going to regret it – it could have ruined my life'.

Away from the fairytale romancing with Flynn, she occasionally showed her inexperience. She was out of her depth opposite Fredric March in *Anthony Adverse* (1936), but a year later gave an entrancing performance as a dizzy society girl in a featherweight comedy, *It's Love I'm After* (1937). By the time she was cast as Melanie in David O. Selznick's *Gone With The Wind* (1939) she had grown sufficiently as an actress to make a fully rounded character out of that butter-wouldn't-melt-in-her-mouth paragon. She opened out, as James Cagney's gentle wife in *The Strawberry Blonde* (1941) and as a shy spinster wooed and married by cynical gigolo Charles Boyer in *Hold Back The Dawn* (1941). It won her an Oscar nomination but, ironically, she lost out to Joan Fontaine (*Suspicion*). *Princess O'Rourke* (1943) marked the end of de Havilland's Warner contract, but the studio begged to differ, claiming an extra six months because of suspensions. But the star proved tougher than she looked, taking on and defeating Warners in a long court battle which determined that, in future, seven years would be the upper limit for any film contract and, furthermore, this would be inclusive of any suspensions.

She went to Paramount for *The Well-Groomed Bride* (1946) and *To Each His Own* (1946), the latter an immaculately judged performance revealing a warmth untapped in her Warners days and winning her the Best Actress Oscar. Now she began to spread her wings, first in Robert Siodmak's *The Dark Mirror* (1946), playing two sisters, one good, the other not so good. *The Snake Pit* (1948) was a searing drama set in a mental institution. Then she netted a second Oscar for her performance as the gauche spinster in *The Heiress* (1949). In the 50s she seemed to lose interest in filming, acting on Broadway and, in 1955, settled in France with her husband Pierre Galante, editor of 'Paris-Match'. She co-starred with Alan Ladd in *The Proud Rebel* (1958) and was invincibly ladylike in Anthony Asquith's *Libel* (1959). She returned to Hollywood to make an efficient chiller, *Lady In A Cage* (1964), and stayed to replace Joan Crawford in *Hush, Hush, Sweet Charlotte* (1964) when the latter fell ill. In the disastrous *Pope Joan* (1972), she was Liv Ulmann's Mother Superior. Then came two 'disaster' movies proper, *Airport '77* (1977) and *The Swarm* (1978), in which she joined a hapless bunch of stars menaced by bees. RC

with Joseph Cotten in Hush . . . Hush, Sweet Charlotte *(20th Century-Fox, 1964)*

Dolores Del Rio
Real name **Lolita Negrette (married Del Rio)**
Born **Durango, Mexico, 3 August 1905**
Died **1983**

One of the great images of the 30s is that of Dolores Del Rio photographed in the house designed by her husband Cedric Gibbons, premier art director at MGM. In the streamlined, ultra-modern living room, her lush dark beauty gives her the quality of a hothouse flower blooming in a Hollywood vision of the Bauhaus. She was one of the world's most beautiful women, but her exotic looks typecast her as Latin *femmes fatales* or madonna-like peasant girls. David O. Selznick summed it up when he told director King Vidor, 'I want Del Rio and McCrea in a South Seas romance. Just give me three wonderful love scenes like you had in *The Big Parade* and *Bardelys The Magnificent*. I don't care what story you use, so long as we call it Bird Of Paradise and Del Rio jumps into a flaming volcano'.

A second cousin to Ramon Novarro, she married at 16 into a wealthy and aristocratic Mexican family, and went to live in Mexico City. There she was spotted by film director Edwin Carewe, who persuaded her to come to Hollywood, put her under personal contract and gave her a small part in *Joanna* (1925). A year later she played Charmaine (the temptress of the hit song) in Raoul Walsh's *What Price Glory?* (1926), her extraordinary beauty glowing amid the heavy male horseplay of co-stars

Edmund Lowe and Victor McLaglen. She showed she could act in Carewe's *Resurrection* (1927) and became a big star in his *Ramona* (1928). There was a less successful attempt to repeat the formula in *Evangeline* (1929), her last film with Carewe and a tentative introduction to the talkies.

In 1930 Del Rio signed with United Artists and made her first all-talking picture, *The Bad One* (1930). She portrayed a denizen of a Marseilles brothel for whom sailor Edmund Lowe understandably jumps ship. Shortly after the film she married Gibbons and then suffered a nervous breakdown, possibly a delayed reaction to her break-up with Carewe and the death of her first husband in a European sanatorium. Happily, she recovered, and signed with RKO, but now she seemed to be posing rather than acting, and she was dropped after *Flying Down To Rio* (1933). When she came to England in 1936 to make *Accused* with Douglas Fairbanks Jr, C.A. Lejeune wrote, 'Miss Del Rio, who has to act but doesn't, goes through the motions of rage and despair and tenderness with mathematical accuracy'.

After the mangling of her role in *Journey Into Fear* (1943) – and the end of her affair with its producer, Orson Welles – she returned to Mexico where she became Latin America's top screen star. She appeared in John Ford's *The Fugitive* (1947), filmed in Mexico, but did not return to Hollywood until the 1960 *Flaming Star* in which she played Elvis Presley's Indian mother. A role more worthy of her was that of the 'Spanish Woman' in John Ford's Red Indian drama, *Cheyenne Autumn* (1964). RC

in Journey Into Fear *(RKO, 1943)*

Marlene Dietrich

Real name **Maria Magdalene von Losch**
Born **Berlin 27 December 1901**

Marlene Dietrich's career divides into three very unequal parts: her early film and theatre work in the 20s; the five years with Josef von Sternberg, during which he directed her in seven masterpieces; and the years from 1935 to the present day in which her talent and intelligence were often misunderstood and misused. The legend remained, but with the passing of the years she sometimes seemed to be more like a brilliant female impersonator acting out a Dietrich role rather than the real woman of *The Blue Angel* (1930).

Dietrich used to claim that *The Blue Angel* was her first film, but her screen debut was in the 1923 *Der Kleine Napoleon*. She was 28, and a mother, when Von Sternberg spotted her in a Berlin play, 'Two Neckties', and cast her as Lola Lola, the promiscuous dance hall singer who enslaves and destroys schoolmaster Emil Jannings. Her performance was a masterpiece of indolent, sluttish sensuality; wearing men's evening dress, Dietrich tantalized a lesbian countess and, when she half-spoke, half-sang 'Falling In Love Again', James Agate wrote that 'Reason tottered on her throne'.

Paramount announced that they had signed Dietrich for one film, Von Sternberg's *Morocco* (1930), a Foreign Legion adventure in which she gave up Adolphe Menjou for Gary Cooper, following him into the desert in her evening dress. The film was a huge hit, and America was swept by a craze for the mannish suits and slacks which Dietrich wore with such insolent panache. Paramount retained her at $125,000 a picture, and Von Sternberg embarked on a remarkable series of films in which Dietrich became the enigmatic centrepiece of his obsession with light and pictorial composition. The overhead lighting in *Dishonoured* (1931) threw the incomparable bone structure of her face into glorious relief, and also disguised her lumpy nose (it was later altered by surgery). Cameraman Lee Garmes won an Academy Award for his work on *Shanghai Express* (1932), a bewitching exercise in muted eroticism in which she played a supremely worldly prostitute. In *Blonde Venus* (1932) she emerged from a gorilla suit, donned a fuzzy white wig and serenaded Cary Grant with 'Hot Voodoo'. In *The Scarlet Empress* (1934), she was the nymphomaniac Empress, Catherine of Russia. Their last collaboration was *The Devil Is A Woman* (1935), set in so outlandish a fantasy of Spain that the Spanish government of the day forced Paramount to withdraw the film, but not before it had already failed at the box office.

Dietrich has tried to play down the years with Von Sternberg, but the cabaret act which she mounted in the mid-50s was little more than a distillation of that legendary period. No director served her so well. Lubitsch turned her into a light comedienne in *Desire* (1936) and *Angel* (1937), but when Paramount made the discovery that she had slumped to No 126 at the box office, they bought out her contract. She was off the screen for two years until she played Frenchie, the saloon bar queen in *Destry Rides Again* (1939). At Universal in the 40s she was reduced to the exotic decoration fought over by the likes of John Wayne and Randolph Scott in *The Spoilers* (1942). At MGM she was painted gold for a campy dance sequence in *Kismet* (1944), and had to wait until Billy Wilder's *A Foreign Affair* (1948), set in postwar Berlin, for a good part. There was a hint of the old magic when she was cast as the ageing but still eminently desirable bandit queen in Fritz Lang's baroque Western *Rancho Notorious* (1952), financed by Howard Hughes, and, in 1958, she had a marvellous cameo in Orson Welles's *Touch Of Evil*, playing a fortune teller and purveyor of hot chili to the director/star's bloated hulk of a detective. She bowed out after *Judgement At Nuremberg* (1961), but in the 70s made an ill-advised return in *Just A Gigolo* (1978), which starred a new androgyne, David Bowie. RC

Robert Donat

Born **Manchester, England, 18 March 1905**
Died **1958**

In a hoarse, slurred voice Robert Donat delivered the last line of *The Inn Of The Sixth Happiness* (1958) to a tearful Ingrid Bergman: 'We shall never see each other again, I think. Farewell'. The words were prophetic. Donat was rushed to hospital and died three weeks later from the chronic asthma which had plagued him since the early 30s. That voice is remembered today: expressive and melodious, with a suggestion of fragility and romantic diffidence – ironically, as a child he had to take elocution lessons to get rid of his broad Lancashire accent and, even more surprisingly, a painful stammer.

In 1932, when his British stage career was taking off, he turned down a Hollywood offer from Irving Thalberg. It was characteristic of the indecision which blighted his career and lay at the root of his illness. He made only 19 films, and turned down 10 times that number including *Robin Hood, Romeo and Juliet, Magnificient Obsession* and *A Double Life*.

He became an international star after playing

Culpeper in Korda's *The Private Life Of Henry The VIII* (1933). This led to his only Hollywood film, as Edmund Dantes in the Edward Small production of *The Count Of Monte Cristo* (1934). Thereafter all his films were made in Britain. His worsening asthma made his work increasingly intermittent, but there were some notable performances: a relaxed, quizzical Richard Hannay in Hitchcock's *The Thirty-Nine Steps* (1935); the dual role in René Clair's *The Ghost Goes West* (1936); the idealistic young doctor in *The Citadel* (1938), the first of a four-film deal with MGM; and the gentle pedagogue of MGM's (and James Hilton's) *Goodbye Mr Chips* (1939), for which he won a Best Actor Oscar.

The Adventures Of Tartu (1943), and the 1945 *Perfect Strangers* completed his MGM contract. Three years later he gave a brilliant performance as counsel for the defence in *The Winslow Boy* (1948). After *The Magic Box* (1951), a muted Festival Of Britain tribute to film pioneer William Friese-Green, he was gradually overwhelmed by illness. This lent added poignancy to his penultimate film, Ealing's *Lease Of Life* (1954), in which he played a dull country parson who decides to speak his mind when told that he only has six months to live. RC

Melvyn Douglas

Real name **Melvyn Hesselberg**
Born **Macon, Georgia, 5 April 1901**
Died **1981**

The most nimble and elegant of 30s farceurs, Melvyn Douglas had a spectacular start in movies, co-starring with Gloria Swanson in Sam Goldwyn's *Tonight Or Never* (1931). Then in quick succession he squired Ann Harding in *Prestige* (1931), Claudette Colbert in *The Wiser Sex* (1932) and Lupe Velez in *The Broken Wing* (1932). However, after *As You Desire Me* (1932), with Garbo, Goldwyn concluded that Douglas was a carbon copy of William Powell and relegated him to poverty row productions like Majestic's *The Vampire Bat* (1933).

He was rescued by a meaty role opposite Claudette Colbert in Columbia's *She Married Her Boss* (1935), which led to a seven-year contract. Loaned out to co-star with Joan Crawford in MGM's *The Gorgeous Hussy* (1936), he so impressed the studio that they bought a share of his contract. It was flattering but frustrating. Columbia had neither the resources nor the inclination to showcase Douglas in a top production, and MGM consigned him to playing second fiddle to William Powell. To relieve the highly paid stagnation, Douglas kept himself busy, and made seven films in 1936. Nevertheless, his assured playing made him much more than a run-of-the-mill leading man. His enigmatic grin, arched eyebrow and delicately shaded vocal inflection were sufficient to romance a bored Marlene Dietrich in *Angel* (1937), repel the post-pubescent advances of Deanna Durbin in *That Certain Age* (1939), and unfreeze Garbo in *Ninotchka* (1939).

After distinguished war service, Douglas's days as a romantic leading man were over. After a long spell on Broadway, and on tour in the US and Australia, he returned to give a memorable performance in *Billy Budd* (1962), was Paul Newman's grizzled cattle baron father in *Hud* (1963), for which he won an Oscar, and thereafter settled down to play a string of crotchety patriarchs in *I Never Sang For My Father* (1970), *The Candidate* (1972), *The Seduction Of Joe Tynan* (1979) and *Ghost Story* (1981). RC

in Nagana (Universal, 1933)

Marie Dressler

Real name **Leila Koerber**
Born **Coburg, Canada, 9 November 1869**
Died **1935**

Throughout her career Marie Dressler was the butt of jokes aimed at her bulky figure and battered face. In *Tillie's Punctured Romance* (1914), Mabel Normand compared her to a Ringling Brothers elephant. Beneath the homely exterior, however, there was a sharp and worldly woman. She began in opera and straight theatre, where Nature cast her as Mrs Malaprop when she was still in her 20s. She became a vaudeville star and in 1910 had a big hit with 'Tillie's Nightmare'. Four years later Mack Sennett turned it into the six-reel comedy *Tillie's Punctured Romance*, in which Charlie Chaplin's dapper conman danced attendance on Dressler's rich farm girl. Her first film career never took off, and her stalwart role in the chorus girls' strike of 1917 placed her on the blacklist of the major theatrical impresarios.

Dressler was forced to find work in France in one-reel comedies, and was contemplating suicide when Allan Dwan gave her a small part in Fox's *The Joy Girl* (1927). In Hollywood, she was helped by the influential screenwriter Frances Marion, who persuaded Irving Thalberg to co-star her with Polly Moran in *The Callahans And The Murphys* (1927). An Irish boycott killed the film, but Dressler gradually regained her popularity as a featured player in *Breakfast At Sunrise* (1927), *Bringing Up Father* (1928) and *The Patsy* (1928).

Sound was the making of Marie Dressler, rounding out her weatherbeaten, sceptical personality. Once again Marion was a decisive influence, securing her the part of Marthy, the waterfront crone in MGM's *Anna Christie* (1930). She returned to dockland in the same year as the rough and ready landlady of a sleazy flophouse in *Min And Bill*. Wallace Beery co-starred, and the film was a massive hit, propelling Dressler into the ranks of the top box-office draws. In 1933 she headed the 'Motion Picture Herald' poll and, that year, made *Dinner At Eight* and *Tugboat Annie*. By then the cancer from which she had been suffering since the mid-20s was making her haggard and drawn. Her last film was *The Late Christopher Bean* (1933). RC

Irene Dunne

Born **Louisville, Kentucky,
20 December 1898**

Douglas Fairbanks Jr, who worked with her on RKO's *Joy Of Living* (1938), said of Irene Dunne, 'She's a dream, an absolute dream, one of the most professional women I've ever known'. Equally adept at light comedy and three-handkerchief weepies, she was as resourceful and witty as the indomitable British governess she portrayed with such charm in *Anna And The King Of Siam* (1946).

She studied singing at the Chicago College Of Music and moved smoothly into Broadway musicals. Her Magnolia in the road show version of 'Show Boat' led to a contract with RKO and *Leathernecking* (1930). Richard Dix insisted on her for the role of Sabra Cravat in *Cimarron* (1931), which won her an Oscar nomination. She played Ricardo Cortez's crippled sweetheart in *Symphony Of Six Million* (1932) and established her credentials for noble, ladylike suffering. She was John Boles's self-sacrificing mistress in *Back Street* (1932); and in *Magnificent Obsession* (1935) was accidentally blinded by playboy Robert Taylor.

Stingaree (1934), an Australian outback drama, gave her a chance to sing, and she then made a number of musicals, including *Roberta* (1935), and *Show Boat* (1936) recreating her old part of Magnolia. Her talents as a comedienne were revealed in Leo McCarey's sparkling comedy of divorce, *The Awful Truth* (1937). McCarey also directed *Love*

with Charles Boyer in Love Affair *(RKO, 1939)*

Affair (1939), a shipboard romance 'women's picture' co-starring Charles Boyer which launched Miss Dunne on a string of sentimental films, including *When Tomorrow Comes* (1939), reunited with Boyer, and *The White Cliffs Of Dover* (1943). She was charming with Cary Grant in *My Favourite Wife* (1940) and *Penny Serenade* (1941).

Dunne had two big postwar successes, *I Remember Mama* (1947) and *Life With Father* (1948), then disappeared under several layers of make-up to play Queen Victoria in *The Mudlark* (1950), filmed in Britain. Despite her rubber mask, she gave a good performance, but the film was a box office disaster and effectively ended her career. She made only two more (modestly budgeted) films – *Never A Dull Moment* (1952) and *It Grows On Trees* (1952) – before turning her considerable energy and intelligence to work at the United Nations. RC

Deanna Durbin

Real name **Edna Mae Durbin**
Born **Winnipeg, Canada, 4 December, 1921**

'Just as a Hollywood pin-up represents sex to dissatisfied erotics, so I represented the ideal daughter millions of fathers and mothers wished they had,' recalled Universal Picture's wholesome singing star Deanna Durbin. Deanna's own father was a blacksmith with the Canadian Pacific Railway, who took the family to California when she was a baby. At an early age, the little girl demonstrated a remarkable singing talent, so her parents scraped up enough money to give her a classical training. At the age of 15 she attended an audition at the Disney Studios for the voice of Snow White, but was told she didn't sing like a child.

Then an agent recommended her to MGM who put her in a musical short called *Every Sunday* (1936) with another young hopeful, Judy Garland. The story goes that Louis B. Mayer phoned an executive after a screening and said 'Drop the fat one.' Durbin was dismissed and Garland given a contract. In fact, Mayer had meant Judy to be dropped, but Deanna created a sensation by singing on the Eddie Cantor radio show, and was signed up by Hungarian-born producer Joe Pasternak at Uni-

in It Started With Eve *(Universal, 1941)*

with Adolphe Menjou and Mischa Auer (right) in One Hundred Men And A Girl *(Universal, 1937)*

versal for *Three Smart Girls* (1936), his first American production.

The picture struck gold at the box-office, literally saving the ailing studio from bankruptcy. The young star became their most bankable asset through the rest of the decade, and she was dubbed 'The Watteau Shepherdess of Universal'. Pasternak proceeded to guide her through nine more economical, light-hearted musicals in which she soothed Depression-weary adults with her bell-like voice and Pollyanna personality. She reconciled her divorced parents in *Three Smart Girls*, married off her sisters in *Three Smart Girls Grow Up* (1938), and charmed Leopold Stokowski into conducting her father's orchestra of unemployed musicians in *One Hundred Men And A Girl* (1937).

Deanna was everybody's ideal teenager, whose modestly cut dresses were imitated by young girls throughout the country. Her popularity abroad is poignantly demonstrated by the fact that her photo, cut from a movie magazine, was found above Anne Frank's bed in her attic in Amsterdam where the young diarist was hiding from the Nazis. In 1938, she was given a special Oscar, as was Mickey Rooney, for 'bringing to the screen the spirit and personification of youth'. Deanna slipped into the

pubescent age in the appropriately titled *That Certain Age* (1938), in which she had a crush on sophisticated journalist Melvyn Douglas, but had to settle for unsophisticated Jackie Cooper.

By 1939, the teenager was slowly but very surely blossoming into young womanhood, and her screen image gently began to match her growth. She received her first screen kiss, amidst much newspaper-headlined ballyhoo, from Robert Stack in *First Love* (1939). The question mark in *Nice Girl?* (1941) was irrelevant because nice Deanna ended up with boy-next-door Robert Stack rather than older man Franchot Tone, but she finally got Tone in *His Butler's Sister* (1943), after reaching her majority. Durbin's mentor Joe Pasternak left for MGM after *It Started With Eve* (1941), a romantic comedy with Charles Laughton as a crusty millionaire naturally charmed by the young star, and her career began to falter. 'I couldn't go on forever being Little Miss Fixit who burst into song,' she explained, but her attempts to gain sophistication lost her her public. She also refused to trim down her figure. Indeed, Walter Plunkett who designed the period dresses for her only colour film, *Can't Help Singing* (1944) recalls saying to her, 'Dear, aren't you getting a bit heavy?'. Deanna replied, 'It doesn't matter, dear, you can

always let my dresses out at the sides'.

Her efforts in straight roles met with little success. Jean Renoir left *The Amazing Mrs Holliday* (1943) because he found her unresponsive to his direction; Robert Siodmak's *Christmas Holiday* (1944), in which she played a nightclub singer helping her killer husband Gene Kelly, is a curiosity. As a witness to a murder in *Lady On A Train* (1945), she was directed by Charles David, whom she later married. In one of her last films, *Because Of Him* (1946), she played a stage-struck waitress who convinces ham actor Charles Laughton that she's good enough to be his leading lady in a dramatic role. Cinema audiences were not so convinced. Deanna Durbin decided to retire from the screen in 1948, because 'I was the highest paid star with the poorest material'. After two broken marriages, she wed David in 1950 in France where she has lived happily ever since. RB

in Something In The Wind *(Universal, 1947)*

in 1936

Frances Farmer

Born **Seattle, Washington,
19 September 1913**
Died **1970**

Howard Hawks, who directed part of *Come And Get It* (1936), recalled that Frances Farmer had 'more talent that anyone I ever worked with'. A big, commanding blonde with a firm jaw and a marvellously husky voice, she was, for a brief moment, Paramount's hottest leading lady but, by the 40s, the lovely Miss Farmer had already pressed the self-destruct button and descended into a 10-year nightmare in the lower depths of America's most horrifying mental institutions.

While at high school in Seattle, she won a national essay competition with an entry entitled 'God Dies'. Newspaper headlines declared 'Seattle Girl Denies God, Wins Prize'. It was an early introduction to controversy, which flared again in the spring of 1935 when Seattle's 'The Voice Of Action' – a Communist newspaper – sponsored her on a trip to the Soviet Union. On her return from Russia, Farmer tried unsuccessfully to join New York's radical Group Theatre. She was given a screen test by Paramount, and signed at $100 a week. For the serious-minded, idealistic young actress, Hollywood was something less than second best, and from the moment of her arrival in California she made no secret of her contempt for the Dream Factory. After a couple of Bs, she was Bing Crosby's love interest in *Rhythm On The Range* (1936), and was then loaned to Goldwyn for *Come And Get It*, an Edna Ferber lumberjacking saga in which she played the dual role of a raunchy saloon bar queen and her daughter. Then, to her disgust, she was little more than an elegant set decoration in RKO's *The Toast Of New York*, and on her home lot, *Exclusive*, and *Ebb Tide* (all 1937).

While the studio pleaded with her to adopt the sable and limousine style appropriate to a star, Farmer refused to give interviews, drove around Hollywood in an old jalopy, and raised money for the Loyalists in the Spanish Civil War. In 1937 she left California to play in a stock production of 'The Petrified Forest.' Her fame now opened the doors of the Group Theatre and, later that year, in New York, she played Lorna Moon opposite John Garfield in Clifford Odets's 'Golden Boy'. On her return to Paramount, she did punishment duty in a B-feature, *Ride A Crooked Mile* (1938), before travelling back to New York and a doomed affair with Odets. At this point she lost her way, fatally undermined by the realisation that the Group Theatre radicals could be as cynically manipulative

as the Hollywood vulgarians. Her movie career never recovered, and after Warners' *Flowing Gold* (1940) with Garfield, she slid back into the Bs, including *World Premiere* (1941) with a sozzled John Barrymore, and replaced Maureen O'Hara as Tyrone Power's co-star in a Fox costumer, *Son Of Fury* (1942), her last appearance on celluloid for 16 years.

Farmer's mental balance had already been unhinged by a deadly combination of amphetamine (to control her weight) and alcohol (to control her

with Fay Holden (left) in Exclusive (Paramount, 1937)

nerves). On 19 October 1942, while en route to a party thrown by Deanna Durbin, she was arrested on a minor traffic violation and charged with drunken driving. On 13 January 1943, she was dragged from her hotel bed, and in a Los Angeles night court charged with failing to report to her parole officer. Kicking and screaming, she was carried away and put in a straitjacket. Certified as 'mentally incompetent', the next seven years saw an appalling cycle of release and recommittal by her mother, during which she was subjected to insulin therapy, electro-convulsive treatment, hydrotherapy (a fancy word for immersion for hours on end in

freezing water) and, in all probability, an unauthorised frontal lobotomy. At the Western State Mental Hospital, Washington, she was confined, naked and shaven-headed, in a ward for the incurably insane. She was released in 1950, found work in a laundry and later married an engineer (her first marriage had been to actor Leif Erickson). The marriage did not last and she settled down to a life of alcoholic seclusion in Eureka, California.

In 1957 she was spotted by a small-time agent, Lee Mikesell, who married her and coaxed her into a comeback of sorts, including an embarrassing appearance on 'This Is Your Life'. She played in stock and made a film – a Z-grade 'teen agony' quickie, *The Party Crashers* (1958). Divorced again, she hosted an afternoon television show in Indianapolis devoted to B movies. In 1968–9 she was actress in residence at Purdue University. Her constant companion, Jean Ratcliffe, penned most of her autobiography, 'Will There Really Be A Morning?', which provided the title of a 1982 biopic starring Susan Blakely. The rival production, *Frances* (1982), starred Jessica Lange. RC

Glenda Farrell

Born **Enid, Oklahoma, 30 June 1904**
Died **1971**

'Hi, slug', was Glenda Farrell's affectionate greeting to Frank McHugh in Warner Bros.' *Mystery Of The Wax Museum* (1933). It was a typical Farrell role – hardboiled, wisecracking reporter, with golden hair and a heart to match. At Warners in the 30s she was always billed below the studio's top-line leading ladies, such as Kay Francis, Bette Davis and Barbara Stanwyck, but in films like *Travelling Saleslady* (1935) and *Miss Pacific Fleet* (1936) she formed a live-wire partnership with fellow gold-digger Joan Blondell, a liaison which earned them the tag of the 'gimme girls'.

In 1929 she was signed by Warners after scoring a big hit on Broadway in 'Life Begins' (she repeated the role on film in 1932). She made her screen debut playing a bit part in *Lucky Boy* (1929), and then was a gangster's moll in *Little Caesar* (1930). Her brisk style made her an excellent support for Paul Muni in *I Am A Fugitive From A Chain Gang* (1932) and *Hi, Nellie!* (1934), once again as a sharp-witted newshound. She carried the characterisation over into *Smart Blonde* (1937), the first of a snappy little B series in which she played Torchy Blane, a fast-talking girl reporter whose constant and energetic quest for scoops was always getting in the way of her policeman boyfriend, Barton MacLane.

Her studio contract ran out in 1939, and in the 50s, weary of being typecast, she made a deft transition to playing matronly character roles on television, on Broadway, and in a number of films, including *The Girl In The Red Velvet Swing* (1955), *The Middle Of The Night* (1959) *Kissin' Cousins* (1964) and *Tiger By The Tail* (1970). RC

Alice Faye

Real name Alice Jeanne Leppert
Born New York City, 5 May, 1912

The blonde who dominated Fox musicals from the mid-30s to the early 40s was singing star Alice Faye. She had a little turned up nose, pouting mouth, and sang in a deep mellow voice. She could belt out the title song from *Alexander's Ragtime Band* (1938), or seduce with a tender ballad like 'You Say The Sweetest Things, Baby' from *Tin Pan Alley* (1940). She could act too, usually playing gutsy ladies who fell for the wrong guy, either Tyrone Power or John Payne. Alice also featured in a few non-musical roles such as a female flyer in *Tail Spin* (1939), and, most effectively, as murder suspect Dana Andrews's wife in Otto Preminger's *Fallen Angel* (1945). Generally, however, she appeared in opulent period sagas such as *Rose Of Washington Square* (1939), based on the life of Fanny Brice; the 'disaster musical' *In Old Chicago* (1938); and *Hello, Frisco, Hello* (1943), in which she sang the Oscar-winning song, 'You'll Never Know'.

The daughter of a policeman, Alice Faye began singing professionally at the age of fourteen. Rudy Vallee picked her out of the chorus line of 'George White's Scandals', and signed her to tour with his band as a singer. Her screen debut was as his leading lady in Fox's *George White's Scandals* (1934), but she was soon the centre of a scandal, named by Vallee's wife in his divorce trial. In 1936 she married singer Tony Martin with whom she co-starred in *Sally, Irene And Mary* (1938). Faye clashed frequently with Fox studio boss Darryl F. Zanuck over policy, although he took her side in a dispute with top

costume designer Travis Banton on *That Night In Rio* (1941). When Alice demanded flashier decoration on her costumes like Marlene Dietrich's, Banton informed her that Dietrich had the style to carry it off, but such dresses would make Faye look like 'a carnival hootch.' She immediately phoned Zanuck who reprimanded the designer for his rudeness. Banton never worked for her or Fox again.

Faye divorced Tony Martin in 1940, married bandleader Phil Harris in 1941, and they now have four grandchildren. She retired from the screen in 1944, making a comeback 18 years later in *State Fair* (1962), in which she sang one song. She returned to the stage in 1973 in a revival of 'Good News' with her one-time screen partner John Payne. RB

W.C. Fields

Real name William Dukenfield
Born Philadelphia, 10 February 1879
Died 1946

A turn of the century poster for his juggling act describes W.C. Fields as 'Different From The Rest'. He was not merely different, but unique – a comic genius and American tank town Lear whose bloodshot eye was turned with malevolent accuracy on the absurdities and pettiness of life. Drink-sodden, florid of speech and nose, a relentless misogynist and inveterate child hater, women and children loomed large in the Fields demonology. The chiselling, work-shy shopkeepers he habitually played were inevitably saddled with wives and daughters whose mouths were alternately filled with food and venom.

in Tillie And Gus *(Paramount, 1933)*

The private Fields was inseparable from his curmudgeonly creations. He ran away from his poor and unhappy home when he was 11, and his teenage years, spent hustling in the seedier streets of Philadelphia, fixed for ever his suspicious view of the world. Whatever it was, Fields was against it. In his later years, his paranoia led him to stash away his savings in over 700 bank accounts all over the world. By the time he was 21, he was an international juggling star. In 1914 he joined the 'Ziegfeld Follies' and made his first film, *Pool Sharks*, in 1915. Then there was a nine-year gap before he returned to the screen in a Marion Davies film, *Janice Meredith* (1924). D.W. Griffith's *Sally Of The Sawdust* (1925) was an adaptation of Fields's stage success 'Poppy' in which he created the archetypal Fieldsian character: Eustace McGargle, the conman and ventriloquist, whose speciality was selling 'talking dogs' to gullible hicks. He signed with Paramount, and in *It's The Old Army Game* (1926) played the inept small-town druggist who recurred in various incarnations in several of his subsequent films.

He was dropped by Paramount when the talkies arrived. Ironically, since Fields's rasping voice put the finishing touch to his comic personality. He had to wait until 1932 before he found regular work again, with Mack Sennett in four classic shorts: *The Pharmacist*, *The Dentist*, *The Fatal Glass Of Beer* and *The Barber Shop*. They were distributed by Paramount, with whom the comedian signed a long-term contract following his success in their *International House* (1933).

Paramount never succeeded in accommodating Fields's genius, and initially he remained a star turn in other people's films with little control over his material. *If I Had A Million* (1932) paired him in an episode with Alison Skipworth, nonchalantly destroying the cars of road hogs. *Tillie And Gus* (1933) was an attempt to turn them into a Beery–Dressler-style partnership, and also introduced Baby LeRoy. Fields was reunited with his small antagonist in *The Old Fashioned Way* and *It's A Gift* (1934). On loan to MGM, he played a masterly Micawber in *David Copperfield* (1935), but by now his drinking was taking its toll. He was consuming more than two quarts of alcohol a day, and his travel wardrobe

with Freddie Bartholomew in David Copperfield *(MGM, 1935)*

consisted of three trunks – one for clothes and two for liquor. After *Poppy* (1936), he was off the screen for two years. Paramount released him from his contract after *The Big Broadcast Of 1938*, and he went to Universal at $150,000 a film, $25,000 of which was for scriptwriting. This consisted of random jottings on the backs of envelopes and on toilet paper. His screen credits were under the names Mahatma Kane Jeeves and Otis Criblecoblis. Universal let Fields do as he liked, provided it didn't cost too much. The results were *You Can't Cheat An Honest Man* (1939); *My Little Chickadee* (1939), with Mae West; *The Bank Dick* (1940, his masterpiece), and *Never Give A Sucker An Even Break* (1941). The last was his calculatedly incoherent farewell to the insanities of Hollywood. Polyneuritis prevented more features, although he played a few cameos. His last appearance was in *Sensations Of 1945*. With exquisite timing, he died on Christmas Day. RC

Errol Flynn

Born **Hobart, Tasmania, 20 June 1909**
Died **1959**

As a young man Errol Flynn tried a variety of jobs and bummed around the world before he was first attracted to acting. After a brief period on stage in England, at Northampton Rep and in the West End, he was signed to a film contract by Warner Bros. He arrived in Hollywood in 1935 at the age of 25 with a reputation as a maverick and hell-raiser which he was never able to live down and which was reinforced by his first, tempestuous marriage to the French actress Lili Damita.

When Robert Donat declined to appear in a planned production of *Captain Blood* (1935), based on the novel by Rafael Sabatini, Jack Warner decided to take a chance on the new and relatively untried young actor. Tall, athletic, and strikingly handsome, Flynn appeared made for the role of the English doctor forced to turn rebel and pirate leader. He was happily teamed with another rising young Warner Bros. star, Olivia de Havilland, and when the picture turned out to be a big success, he became a star virtually overnight. Clearly Flynn was set for a career as a dashing hero of adventure movies and brought to his roles a lively sense of humour and a flair which soon marked him as the top swashbuckling star of the sound cinema, carrying on the tradition of the legendary silent star, Douglas Fairbanks Sr.

Flynn had arrived at Warners just as the studio was recovering from the Depression and was planning to expand its output of expensive prestige productions. As the studio's top costume star he appeared in such pictures as *The Charge Of The Light Brigade* (1936), *The Private Lives Of Elizabeth And Essex* (1939), and *The Sea Hawk* (1940), most often directed by Michael Curtiz and with Olivia de Havilland as his co-star. Most memorable of all was *The Adventures Of Robin Hood* (1938), in which Flynn's lively and exhilarating performance was ably supported by a fine cast drawn from the studio's top contract players and with Olivia de Havilland as Maid Marian. This, the costliest Warner Bros. picture and the most expensive Technicolor movie made up to that date, turned out to be the high point of his career and the only one of his pictures ever nominated for a Best Picture Oscar. (Flynn himself was never nominated for an Oscar.)

Never happy in his role as Hollywood 'superstar', he always hoped to break out of the typecast mould which the star system had forced on him. His stage experience in England had led him to believe that he could play a much wider variety of roles, and in 1936 he had even naively hoped he might be cast opposite Norma Shearer in the MGM version of *Romeo and Juliet*. (The role of Romeo eventually went to Leslie Howard.) As he wrote in his autobiography – with a rare bit of insight: 'I was full of ambition at the time. I wanted to create something important ... As the months, the years rollicked on, and as I went from one picture to another, the stereotyped roles I played stamped out of me my ambition to do finer things or to expect to be able to do them in Hollywood ... I do not know to what extent this stereotyping of me – this handing me a sword and a horse – led to my rebellions, high jinks and horsplay over the globe, but I think it had plenty to do with it.'

Flynn failed to make much of an impact in his few contemporary pictures, or in serious roles like the unfortunate newspaperman married to Bette Davis in *The Sisters* (1938). And when Miss Davis pulled out all the stops in her suitably larger-than-life performance as Queen Elizabeth the following year, she all but acted Flynn's Essex off the screen. As early as 1938 Flynn had made his mark in the first of his war roles, as Capt Courtney, one of the hard-drinking and fatalistic World War I air aces of the Royal Flying Corps in *The Dawn Patrol* – an excellent remake of Howard Hawks' 1930 original. In addition, he managed to develop into a Western

with Olivia de Havilland in Dodge City (Warner Bros., 1939)

star, beginning with the lavish Technicolor *Dodge City* (1939) with de Havilland co-starring. Other Westerns followed, most notably *They Died With Their Boots On* (1942), his first with Raoul Walsh who took over as his favourite director during the early 40s, and became a close personal friend as well. As recalled by Walsh, 'I saw a lot of Errol Flynn and every time we went out somewhere, I was sure to get into trouble. As soon as we set foot in some bar, people started picking on him. With Flynn one always went on an adventure and you never knew what would happen next.'

Perhaps their best film together was a long (2½ hour), tough and surprisingly naturalistic war picture, *Operation Burma* (1945), which holds up remarkably well today. Flynn led an all-male cast as the captain of an American ranger platoon preparing the way for the main Burmese offensive. It provided him with one of his rare opportunities to sustain a serious contemporary part with the emphasis on character rather than action. As the only star in the cast, and without the usual romantic interludes to fall back on, he gave an excellent performance, and

in later years regarded the picture as one of the few he was proud of having done.

During the early 40s Flynn divorced Lili Damita and contracted his second unsatisfactory marriage to Norah Eddington. He shared a bachelor apartment with his friend, David Niven, who had co-starred with him in *The Dawn Patrol*, and by the the time the two met again after the war, in the words of Niven, 'although he still looked in good physical shape and gave the outward impression of being the same ... there was something infinitely sad about him, something missing.' But Errol managed to light up the screen once more, swashbuckling his way through *The Adventures Of Don Juan* (1949), and had a small but effective role in MGM's production of *Kim* (1950) based on the book by Rudyard Kipling. However, his star was clearly on the wane.

Shortly after his second divorce came through, he married the young actress Patrice Wymore, who stuck by him and provided much needed support during the difficult times ahead. After 18 years with Warner Bros. he broke with the studio and had hopes of embarking on a new career as an independent producer-star during the early Fifties. Unfortunately, he lost all his money on his first major venture, an Italian-based production of the William Tell story which was never completed. In ill health and no longer in demand as a star, he made something of a comeback during the late 50s, playing the kind of drunk roles which came easily to him at this stage in his career. He was hired by producer Darryl F. Zanuck to appear as Mike Campbell in *The Sun Also Rises* (1957), based on the Hemingway novel, then followed this with *Too Much Too Soon* (1958). Adapted from Diana Barrymore's autobiography, Flynn here played the role of her father, John Barrymore, who had been a close personal friend and drinking partner of his during the late 30s. Another Zanuck production, *The Roots Of Heaven* (1958), adapted from Romain Gary's book and directed by John Huston, virtually brought his career to an end, although he was involved in one last minor picture entitled *Cuban Rebel Girls* (1959), a kind of semi-documentary tribute to Fidel Castro which Flynn wrote, narrated and co-produced.

At the age of 50, Errol Flynn had burned himself out – his body already looked like that of an elderly man – but he did manage to complete his autobiography, *My Wicked, Wicked Ways*, shortly before his death in 1959. JF

in The Adventures Of Don Juan (Warner Bros., 1949)

in Montana (Warner Bros., 1950) ▷

in I Dream Too Much *(RKO, 1935)*

Henry Fonda

**Born Brand Island, Nebraska, 16 May 1905
Died 1982**

Tall, dark and soft-spoken, Henry Fonda projected a quiet power and sincerity on the screen which was perfectly suited to his many roles as the likeable American hero and man of the people. In the course of his long career he came to represent a very special embodiment of the American spirit, a kind of American Everyman figure.

Fonda got his first acting experience in the Omaha Community Playhouse, but soon headed east to play in summer stock and join the University Players company which included among its members Joshua Logan, James Stewart and Margaret Sullavan, who became Fonda's first wife. He gained much-needed experience on the New York stage during the early 30s and, following his success as the lead in 'The Farmer Takes A Wife', (1934) was given a film contract by the independent producer Walter Wanger. Not surprisingly, he landed his first part in the film version of this play in 1935 and had his first big hit with *The Trail Of The Lonesome Pine* the following year. This latter was the first outdoors Technicolor picture, and when he was invited to appear in England in the first British Technicolor picture, *The Wings Of The Morning* (1937), followed by the first colour western, 20th Century-Fox's *Jesse James*, filmed in 1938, he could rightly claim to be the cinema's very first Technicolor star. However, his best picture during these early years was *You Only Live Once* (1938) directed by Fritz Lang, a socially conscious thriller set against the Depression background. Fonda was excellent in the role of a young man – basically a good guy, but with the cards stacked against him – who is forced by circumstances to turn criminal on the run together with his devoted wife, played by Sylvia Sidney.

In 1936 a rich New York divorcée, Frances Seymour Brokaw, became the second of Fonda's five wives. Their daughter Jane was born in December 1937, followed by a son, Peter, born early in 1940 at a time when his father was firmly establishing himself as one of the top American film stars. In fact, 1939 had marked a major turning point in Fonda's career and the beginning of his close collaboration with director John Ford, starting off with three films in a row. In the case of *Young Mr Lincoln* (1939), Fonda was initially reluctant to play the great Lincoln on the screen until Ford convinced him that he was not playing the President of US but rather a young 'jackleg' lawyer from Springfield. It turned out to be one of Fonda's best films. He and Ford followed this with another historical picture, *Drums Along The Mohawk* (1939), set during the American War of Independence and Ford's first venture into colour. Fonda's sensitive and intelligent performance as the pioneering homesteader who is forced to take up arms against the Indians and the British helps to lift the picture above the level of the usual westerns of the period. He was ably supported by Claudette Colbert as his wife. Finally, the Ford-Fonda pairing reached its peak with *The Grapes Of Wrath* (1940), Oscar-nominated as Best Picture and the most honoured of all Fonda's early films. Ford won an Oscar as did Jane Darwell for her appealing supporting role portrayal of Ma Joad, while Fonda received his first nomination, but lost out to his friend James Stewart (who won for his performance in *The Philadelphia Story*). As Tom Joad, Fonda gave his definitive portrayal of the grassroots American, buffeted by fortune but willing to stand up for his rights. The role provided a 20th century American counterpart to his 18th and 19th century portraits of Lincoln and Frank James.

Having succeeded in preserving his independence early in his career, Fonda had had no choice but to sign a contract with 20th Century-Fox in order to get the coveted role of Tom Joad. As a result, his career unfortunately wound down during the 40s, as a result of being forced into a number of pictures he would not have chosen to make. At least he was able to reduce the length of his contract by three years of war service. After the war he rejoined Ford to play another legendary American figure, sheriff Wyatt Earp, in *My Darling Clementine* (1946). In fact, the

in Firecreek *(Warner Bros., 1968)*

western had been undergoing a major revival both before and after the war, and Fonda was one of the key figures in developing a more serious and adult treatment of western characters and themes. Aside from his work with Ford, he was at his convincing best in the title role of Fritz Lang's sadly underrated *The Return Of Frank James* (1940); and in *The Oxbow Incident* (1943) Fonda's moving performance contributed immeasurably to the picture's impact as one of the first of a new breed of adult westerns.

After one last Ford western, *Fort Apache* (1948), Fonda's career took a new direction. He returned East to create the title role of 'Mr Roberts' on the Broadway stage and, seven years later, starred in the successful film version, followed by the role of Pierre in a lavish, Italian-based production of Tolstoy's *War And Peace* (1956). He then went back to New York for a pair of memorable contemporary roles – as the nightclub musician wrongly accused of being a criminal in Hitchcock's *The Wrong Man* (1957), and as 'juror no 8' in *Twelve Angry Men* (1957). He continued active throughout the 60s, but his ill health forced him to wind down during the 70s, although he was well cared for by his fifth wife, Shirlee. He was awarded a special honorary Oscar in 1981 and had one last triumph that same year, playing opposite Katharine Hepburn and joined by his daughter Jane in *On Golden Pond*. His Oscar for this role was accepted on his behalf by his daughter, for he was too ill to attend the ceremony. Sadly, he died a few months later. JF

with James Cagney (left) in Mr. Roberts *(Warner Bros., 1955)*

Preston Foster

Born **Ocean City, New Jersey,**
24 October 1902
Died **1970**

Preston Foster, tall and rugged looking, was a reliable action star, yet proved himself capable of giving sensitive performances in dramatic roles as well. After trying a number of different jobs in his youth, Foster first became interested in acting during the late 20s, and enjoyed some moderate success on Broadway. He appeared in a number of pictures at Warner Bros. during the early 30s, but got his big break at RKO in 1935. A sympathetic role as Dan Gallagher in John Ford's much acclaimed production of *The Informer* was followed by the lead role of Marcus the blacksmith in the studio's

in 1939

lavish production of *The Last Days Of Pompeii*, and he also shared the romantic lead with Barbara Stanwyck in *Annie Oakley* – all this in 1935. He was reteamed with the prolific Miss Stanwyck the following year in a relatively disappointing film adaptation of Sean O'Casey's *The Plough and the Stars* directed by John Ford.

But it was all downhill from this point on, although his name can be spotted in the cast list of such 40s productions as *Northwest Mounted Police* (1940) and *The Harvey Girls* (1946). JF

Jean Gabin

Real name **Jean-Alexis Moncorgé**
Born **Meriel, France, 17 May 1904**
Died **1976**

His physical presence on the screen could be compared with that of Spencer Tracy or the mature Humphrey Bogart, yet Jean Gabin's claim to stardom during the thirties rests on a relatively small number of films. Clearly, he was a natural film actor and one of the few 'superstars' produced by the French cinema; by the time of his death his career had spanned almost half a century and he had become virtually a French institution.

Initially reluctant to follow in the footsteps of his parents who were music hall entertainers, he finally took the plunge as a young man, but abandoned the stage during the early thirties as soon as he realised that his true *forte* was the cinema. He was fortunate in working with three of the leading French directors. In *Pépé Le Moko* (1937), directed by Duvivier, he played the archetypal figure of the French gangster on the run, romantic and realistic, tough yet sensitive, but fatalistic and doomed to die a violent death. He also died memorably in his two pictures with Marcel Carné, and it was rumoured that he demanded an effective death scene as part of his contract. But he managed to survive two of his three films with the great Jean Renoir, who discovered new depths in the Gabin persona and did not need to fall back on the clichés of the period. As Renoir noted, 'Gabin was at his most expressive when he did not have to raise his voice. Magnificent actor that he was, he got his greatest effects with the smallest means'. In *La Grande Illusion* (1937) Gabin even wore Renoir's old World War I pilot's tunic, and his exceptional performance was undoubtedly the major factor that turned *La Bête Humaine* (1938) into a believable and moving picture.

The outbreak of war halted his film career, although he made two pictures in the US, *Moontide* (1942) and *The Impostor* (1944). By the time he re-emerged as a major star, it was the mid-fifties, and one was seeing a new Gabin on the screen, now transformed into a gruff, stocky and more respectable figure. He carried on for 20 more years, acting in pictures up to the end of his life. JF

Kay Francis

Real name **Katherine Edwina Gibbs**
Born **Oklahoma City, Oklahoma,**
13 January 1903
Died **1968**

A stylish actress who specialised in sophisticated dramatic roles during the 30s, Kay Francis is one of those many film stars of the second rank who are all but forgotten today. She gained her first acting experience on the stage during the 20s, going by the name of Katherine Francis. With the coming of sound she was screen-tested and signed by Paramount in 1929, and soon developed into one of their leading stars. Of the number of pictures on which she was teamed with William Powell, including *Jewel Robbery* and *One Way Passage*, which they made for Warners in 1932, *One Way Passage* (1932) is probably best remembered. She played a fatally ill baroness and he a gentleman burglar. Their tragically doomed love affair served as the centrepiece of the picture which was highly thought of at the time, even winning an Oscar for best original screenplay, but it has not stood the test of time.

As a contract star, Kay Francis appeared in many minor programmers and rarely landed a role in anything memorable. In Lubitsch's *Trouble in Paradise* (1932) she was the rich 'other woman', ripe for fleecing, while Miriam Hopkins revelled in the more promising part of the female thief and co-conspirator with conman Herbert Marshall. Miss Francis was one of the most highly paid stars in the 30s, and since Paramount was particularly well supplied with leading actresses, they were happy to let her go to Warner Bros. during a period of financial crisis. If Jack Warner was pleased to acquire her services, he was less pleased with her huge salary which far exceeded that of Bette Davis during the late 30s. Also, she had become too closely identified with a type of romantic dramatic movie which had become passé. Her career clearly ran out of steam by the end of the decade. In the mid-forties, she co-produced and starred in three low-budget B's and toured in stock companies before retiring from her profession. Her last screen appearance was in *Wife Wanted* (1946). Miss Francis died of cancer, leaving the bulk of her $1 million fortune to charity. JF

in 1930

Clark Gable

Born Cadiz, Ohio, 1 February 1901
Died 1960

The beginning of the 30s saw the arrival of a new type of screen hero, sporting a distinctly tougher and more earthy image. Warner Bros. had Cagney and Robinson, but MGM had Clark Gable!

He had been a slow developer at first, but was given some timely assistance early in his career by his first two wives, both of whom were a number of years his senior. On the screen he had to depend on his undoubted charisma to make up for those qualities he lacked as an actor. 'I can't act worth a damn,' he once observed in a typically self-deprecating mood. But it wasn't really true. Without a *Little Caesar* (1930) or a *Public Enemy* (1931) to shoot him to instant stardom, Gable gained his first film experience during the early 30s playing a variety of roles in a large number of relatively undistinguished movies, often handled by second-rate directors. He specialised in down-to-earth characters, especially gamblers and gangsters, but also essayed the occasional lawyer, reporter, and even a minister (in *Polly Of The Circus*, 1932). But he was at his best in roles which provided him with suitably snappy dialogue and required him to be hardboiled but likeable. Like Cagney, he often mistreated his on-screen girlfriends, but ended up paying a high price. In *A Free Soul* (1931), for example, he slapped Norma Shearer, around but was himself bumped off by the male lead (Leslie Howard).

Three pictures teamed with Joan Crawford, a pair with Shearer and one with Garbo all added to his self-confidence as he gradually developed into MGM's top male star. He obviously benefitted from the opportunity of playing opposite many of Hollywood's leading ladies. Paired with Jean Harlow shortly after her arrival at the studio, the success of *Red Dust* (1932) gave a big boost to both their careers. Her particular brand of earthy humour and sexiness nicely complemented his. *Dancing Lady* (1933) was the best of the early Crawford–Gable pictures (and even introduced Fred Astaire to the screen), followed by *It Happened One Night* (1934) co-starring with Claudette Colbert. Ironically, he made this picture under protest, loaned out to the tiny Columbia studio (for the first time) as a punishment. And he was not even their first choice for the tough, cocky, but good-natured newspaper reporter who tames and wins an heiress on the run. Clearly, the role was made to order for him and gave him a chance to work with Frank Capra who was just developing into one of Hollywood's leading directors. The picture turned out to be a surprise hit and the year's top Oscar winner, providing a big boost to Columbia. Gable was awarded his only Oscar, along with Colbert, and director Capra.

Although MGM finally gave him a long overdue hike in salary, during the years which followed he continued to be cast in far too many second-rate movies. 1935, however, was a good year for him with *Call Of The Wild* (on loan to 20th Century), *China Seas*, his third picture with Harlow, and *Mutiny On The Bounty*, based on the novel by Nordhoff and Hall. A convincing performance as Fletcher Christian earned Gable his second Oscar nomination and offered proof, if proof were needed, of his ability to shine in a role which was not ideally suitable for him. *Mutiny On The Bounty* won the Oscar for Best Picture of the year, though Gable missed out on his.

In *San Francisco* (1936) Gable's stylish performance proved he could hold his own on the screen, even in the company of the formidable Spencer Tracy whose acting abilities he admired. Although quite different in style and temperament, they got on well together and were re-teamed in *Test Pilot* (1938), directed by Gable's old friend, Victor Fleming. But it was as if Gable, during these years, was marking time, waiting for that picture which was to cap his career in 1939 – *Gone With The Wind*. He was the unanimous choice for the much-coveted role of Rhett Butler, the Southern adventurer and man of fortune who finally weds and beds Scarlett O'Hara, but leaves her in the end. Gable here proved himself a fully mature and convincing actor, earning a well-deserved third Oscar nomination. The picture virtually swept the board at the Oscar ceremony, gaining

with Vivien Leigh in Gone With The Wind *(MGM, 1939)*

awards to Vivien Leigh and director Victor Fleming, and for Best Picture, but Gable was left out. Yet 1939 had been a good year and, with his marriage to actress Carole Lombard, as well, he had lived up to his unofficial title as the 'King of Hollywood'. For him, however, 'The King stuff' was 'pure bull'. 'I'm just a slob from Ohio who happened to be in the right place at the right time.'

After *Gone With The Wind*, his return to undistinguished MGM programmers was clearly a letdown, although the studio did provide him with two new attractive young co-stars, Lana Turner and Hedy Lamarr. Shattered by the death of Carole Lombard in a plane crash in 1942, he promptly joined the US Air Force for the duration of the war. Back at MGM in 1945 his new co-stars were Greer Garson – 'Gable's Back and Garson's Got Him' went the advertising slogan for *Adventure* (1945) – and Deborah Kerr, who joined him in a somewhat more interesting picture, *The Hucksters* (1947). But MGM was already a studio in decline. The old formulas and contract directors could no longer be depended on to succeed with the new and more sophisticated film audiences. A potentially outstanding adult western, *Across The Wide Missouri* (1951), was, for some unexplained reason, severely cut by the studio. In 1953 MGM came up with the unlikely-sounding idea of remaking the old 1932 movie, *Red Dust*, in Technicolor, with Gable reprising his own role 20 years on. Ava Gardner, and the relatively inexperienced Grace Kelly – this was only her second major

with Montgomery Clift (left) and Marilyn Monroe in The Misfits *(United Artists, 1961)*

part – were cast in those roles originally played by Mary Astor and Jean Harlow. In the capable hands of veteran director John Ford the film turned out to be Gable's last big MGM success and proved that his old magic was still there. The following year he left MGM after 23 years with the studio.

With his mature style and appearance, Gable easily fitted into the western revival of the fifties. He had a hit with *The Tall Men* (1955), the first of three pictures with director Raoul Walsh. And his one last memorable picture turned out to be a 'modern' western directed by John Huston – *The Misfits* (1960). This picture occupies a very special and sad place in the history of the cinema. Arthur Miller had written the script for his wife, Marilyn Monroe, as their marriage was breaking up. It turned out to be her last completed film and the last for Gable as well. As the aging but still rebellious cowboy who ropes and captures wild stallions for a living, Gable's role was physically extremely demanding. The picture was a big success, but a few weeks after filming was completed, Gable died of a heart attack. Two years later Marilyn Monroe tragically, was dead, too, of an overdose of pills. JF

Faithfully yours
Clark Gable

Janet Gaynor

Real name **Laura Gainor**
Born **Philadelphia, Pennsylvania,
6 October 1906**

Petite and sweet, Janet Gaynor has the distinction of being the first winner of a Best Actress Oscar. She won it for her combined work in *Sunrise* (1927), *Seventh Heaven* (1927) and *Street Angel* (1928). The latter two were sentimental romances directed by Frank Borzage, in which she played misguided women who are reformed through love. The object of her affections in both (and nine other) films was the ineffectual Charles Farrell, and together they became known as 'America's favourite love-birds.' She was poignant as the wife whose husband tries to kill her for another woman in F.W. Murnau's poetic masterpiece, *Sunrise*.

After graduating from high school, Gaynor went to Hollywood in the early 20s, where she worked for four years as an extra before appearing in Hal Roach comedy shorts and two-reel westerns. Her first feature was *The Johnstown Flood* (1926) for Fox, and she soon became one of the studio's biggest stars in the late 20s and early 30s, mostly playing a series of waifs such as the orphan girl in *Daddy Long Legs* (1931). In two of her musicals, *Sunny Side Up* (1929) and *Delicious* (1931), in which she sang and danced a bit, Janet was a poor girl, falling for millionaire Farrell. She broke away from Fox in 1936, giving one of her finest performances for David O. Selznick, in *A Star Is Born* (1937) as a rising Hollywood star with an alcoholic husband. Gaynor's own first marriage to an attorney had broken up. In 1939, when she married Adrian, MGM's top costume designer, she retired from the screen. She returned to films once, to play Pat Boone's mother in *Bernadine* (1957). RB

Paulette Goddard

Real name **Marion Levy**
Born **Great Neck, New York, 3 June 1911**

Without a doubt, Miss Paulette Goddard has had an interesting and unusual life. A strikingly attractive and vivacious brunette, she was a teenage showgirl and a Ziegfeld Girl, and first married at the age of 14. She arrived in Hollywood after her divorce in 1931 and met Charlie Chaplin the following year. They were secretly married in 1936 but had split up before the release of their second film together, *The Great Dictator* (1940).

Chaplin has written of his first discovery of her acting talent and his attraction to her 'gamine' quality which first inspired the idea of *Modern Times* (1936). The film was a big hit and she was tipped as the leading candidate for the role of Scarlett O'Hara in *Gone With The Wind* before Selznick's discovery of Vivien Leigh. She got *The Cat And The Canary* (1939) at Paramount instead, opposite Bob Hope, and was given the Southern belle lead in DeMille's Technicolor epic, *Reap The Wild Wind* (1942). For a few years, Miss Goddard was one of Paramount's top stars, but by the late 40s her film career was virtually over. In 1942 she had married actor Burgess Meredith, with whom she gave one of her best performances in *Diary Of A Chambermaid* (1946), but they were divorced in 1950. In 1958 the famous German novelist, Erich Maria Remarque, became her fourth husband. JF

in Unconquered (Paramount, 1947)

in Prestige (RKO, 1932)

Ann Harding

Real name **Dorothy Gatley**
Born **Fort San Houston, Texas, 7 August 1901**
Died **1981**

Ann Harding was a strikingly patrician beauty, with a beguilingly deep voice. She once told an interviewer, 'Perhaps I am that unfortunate creature known as a highbrow', and it was this rather smug determination to bring a touch of class to the martyred characters she specialised in which cut short her career as a star.

A talented stage actress, she came to Hollywood as the talkies were taking hold, and became one of the cosmopolitan ladies showcased by Pathé. She made her debut in *Paris Bound* (1929) opposite Fredric March. *Condemned* (1929) established her as a star and Pathé paid Ina Claire $55,000 to make way for Harding in *Holiday* (1930). In *East Lynne* (1931) she suffered divorce, rejection by society and blindness with stately resignation, but was soon quarrelling with RKO, with whom Pathé had merged, and was so upset by *Prestige* (1932) that she tried to buy the print from the studio.

By 1933, her decline was commencing. She had been at her best exchanging calculated insults with Myrna Loy in *The Animal Kingdom* (1932) and *When Ladies Meet* (1933), but she quickly sank under the weight of sob-strewn formula films like *The Right To Romance* (1933) and *The Life Of Vergie Winters* (1934). Relentlessly nudged out by Katharine Hepburn, she became an over-priced asset and between 1936 and 1942 made only one film, the British *Love From A Stranger* (1937). Her comeback was an efficient B thriller, *Eyes In The Night* (1942). She then settled back into matronly featured roles in modest ventures and, in 1956, was reunited with Fredric March in *The Man In The Grey Flannel Suit*, but her film career came to an inglorious end that year with two programmers, *Strange Interlude* and *I've Lived Before*. RC

Cedric Hardwicke

Born **Lye, England, 19 February 1883**
Died **1964**

A fine actor who was trained for the stage at RADA and held a low opinion of the cinema, Cedric Hardwicke first established his reputation on the stage in England during the 20s at Birmingham Rep, and then in the West End. Later he divided his time between plays and (mainly British) films. Knighted in 1934, he made his Broadway debut in 1937 and established himself in Hollywood as a leading character actor from 1939 on. Sir Cedric was not a natural film actor, but made up for it with sheer professional skill. In roles like the middle-aged French priest in *Cross Of Lorraine* (1944) or the father in Hitchcock's *Rope* (1949), he appeared intelligent and sympathetic, but he could project a tough, acerbic, even wicked quality which made him

a natural villain. In *The Moon Is Down* (1943), for example, he played the leading role of an authoritarian nazi officer who commands the German troops occupying a Norwegian town.

After the war he divided his time between England and the US and was much in demand for large-scale costume pictures. He played Tiberius in *Salome* (1953), Edward IV in *Richard III* (1955), King Priam in *Helen Of Troy* (1955) and Pharaoh in *The Ten Commandments* (1956) and rounded out his Hollywood career as the sleazy gangster doctor in *Baby Face Nelson* (1957) – to the surprise of director Don Siegel who had not realised that this 'great Shakespearian actor' had always wanted to play a gangster on the screen. JF

Jean Harlow

Real name **Harlean Carpentier**
Born **Kansas City, Missouri, 3 March 1911**
Died **1937**

Her dress catches in a taxi door in *Double Whoopee* (1929) and is whipped off to reveal her delicious rear view and a terrific pair of legs. For many movie-goers this brief sequence in an early Laurel and Hardy short introduced them to a young starlet who shot to stardom in three years, but was to die tragically and unnecessarily only five years later.

Jean Harlow's remarkable appearance – peroxide blonde hair, shapely figure and unnaturally white skin which appeared to glow under the gaze of the camera – would have guaranteed her a career in pictures as an extra or bit player. But, although she had no formal training as an actress, she had a lively sense of humour and a refreshingly detached atti-tude toward her screen image and striking sex appeal, and developed into a fine comedienne. In her early pictures she was type-cast as a tough, brassy, blonde. In Howard Hughes's *Hell's Angels* (1930) she delivers the memorable line, 'Excuse me while I slip into something more comfortable', and we are treated to a glimpse of her creamy white shoulders and bare back as she disappears into the bedroom. She played a gangster's moll in *The Secret Six* (1930) and, again, in *The Public Enemy* (1931) opposite

with Clark Gable in Saratoga *(MGM, 1937)*

Cagney where, although her part was only a small one, she got to share the film's well-known poster with him. Up-and-coming Columbia had the idea of exploiting her already famous image in a Frank Capra picture called simply *Platinum Blonde* (1931). But she was miscast as a spoilt rich girl, while Robert Williams and Loretta Young had the best lines and stole the show.

In 1932 MGM purchased her contract from Howard Hughes and this marked a major turning point in her career. Irving Thalberg brought in Anita Loos, who had written *Gentlemen Prefer Blondes*, to provide a suitably witty and entertaining script for Jean. Given the opportunity to demonstrate her natural gift for comedy, she sparkled in the role of the *Red-Headed Woman* (1932), a gold-digging good-time girl who climbs the social ladder, in spite of Jack Conway's heavy-handed direction. Was it mere coincidence that her first big hit came out just as Mae West was completing her first picture at Paramount? The impact of this pair of unconven-tional and wisecracking blondes from the two top studios, both embodying a daringly lighthearted attitude to sex, undoubtedly played a major role in the formation of the Catholic Legion of Decency in 1934, and a stricter enforcement of the motion picture Production Code.

In *Red Dust* (1932) Jean had a better director (Victor Fleming), as well as Clark Gable, and took a famous bath in a wooden rain barrel. The role of a cheap but likeable floozie fitted her like a glove. She

was reteamed with Gable in *Hold Your Man* the following year, then Fleming cast her in his satirical comedy about 30s Hollywood, *Bombshell* (1933). She played a sexy but exploited movie star, not too far removed from her true self, and followed this with a

small but effective role as the endearingly vulgar young wife of crooked businessman Wallace Beery in an all-star version of *Dinner At Eight* (1933). This last rounded out a remarkable two years at MGM.

Off screen, however, it was one of the most difficult periods of her young life. Her second husband, MGM producer Paul Bern, committed suicide in 1932. Her follow-up marriage to cin-ematographer Harold Rosson was over virtually before it began, while she still had trouble coping with her difficult mother and stepfather who had caused her much grief during her youth.

If the pictures which followed were less than inspired, reflecting, perhaps, her inability to extend her range, she still gave an excellent performance in the 1936 screwball comedy *Libelled Lady*. The stellar cast included Spencer Tracy, Myrna Loy and William Powell. She and Powell had an off-screen affair going at the time, and her friend Anita Loos has suggested that her premature death in 1937 was not only due to the behaviour of her Christian Scientist mother, who prevented her getting im-mediate medical treatment, but to her depression at the breakup of her relationship with Powell. Her last picture, *Saratoga* (1937), was completed by the studio after her death by making use of a stand-in. It was a smash hit. JF

Sonja Henie

Born **Oslo, Norway, 8 April 1912**
Died **1969**

A pert and friendly ice skating champion, Sonja Henie's natural charm and athletic ability made up for those qualities she lacked as an actress. She arrived in Hollywood in 1936 just as Darryl Zanuck was developing a new group of stars to boost the fortunes of his new studio, 20th Century-Fox. He took a chance on a first Henie picture, *One In A Million* (1936), signing her to a contract once he realised that her pictures could be filmed quickly and cheaply and would be profitable at the box office. Most of her films were concentrated between 1937 and 1939, and contributed to the studio's revival. Generally in the light romantic vein, the slim plot lines were designed so as to not get in the way of the ice skating displays which were the main highlight. Her various male co-stars included Tyrone Power, Ray Milland and Don Ameche and, in her most memorable picture, *Sun Valley Serenade* (1941), she played a war refugee with John Payne as

in It's A Pleasure (RKO, 1945)

her foster parent and shared top billing with Glenn Miller and his Orchestra. Her success obviously paved the way for Esther Williams who was just breaking into movies as Sonja's career was winding down. She died of leukemia, aged 57. JF

Katharine Hepburn

Born **Hartford, Connecticut, 9 November 1907**

From her first appearance on the screen co-starring opposite John Barrymore in *A Bill Of Divorcement* (1932), it was clear that a new star had arrived in Hollywood. Katharine Hepburn burst onto the screen like a breath of fresh air. Tall and slim, with high cheekbones, clean-cut features and aristocratic bearing, she was not conventionally attractive, but more than made up for it through her talent as an actress, and her personal, distinctive style. She could appear positively radiant on the screen, as in *The Little Minister* (1934), when she played the role of a lovely gypsy girl, a wild, untamed creature of the forest. First seen from a distance she looks like a stunning apparition from another world, and one can easily understand why the young minister hero, who is captivated by her charisma, immediately falls in love with her.

But this picture was not at all typical. Early on in her career at RKO it became clear that she was developing in two different directions. On one hand there were the pictures based on popular plays or novels like *A Bill Of Divorcement, Morning Glory* (1933), *Little Women* (1933), and *Alice Adams* (1935), which were all box office hits. She won her first Oscar for her vibrant performance in *Morning Glory* as Eva Lovelace, a young actress who comes to New York determined to succeed in the theatre, and was a natural for the role of Louisa May Alcott's Jo. As director George Cukor noted, 'Kate had come from a large New England family like the one in the story, and had so identified with the novel's spirit of familial feeling that she had cast a magic spell over the entire production'. The picture emerged as RKO's biggest hit of the decade. In 1935 she received her second of twelve Oscar nominations for her Alice Adams.

On the other hand, her feminist qualities and individuality led her to star in such roles as the aviatrix in *Christopher Strong* (1933) and the girl disguised as a boy in *Sylvia Scarlett* (1935). She was *Mary of Scotland* in 1936, and joined the Victorian suffragette movement in *A Woman Rebels* later that same year. But these pictures all flopped badly at the box office and provoked a hostile reaction from

many critics at the time. The failure of the studio's prestige production of *Quality Street* (1937) and the delightful Howard Hawks comedy, *Bringing Up Baby* (1938), in which she starred opposite Cary Grant, finally brought her association with RKO to an abrupt end. She was labelled 'box office poison' by a survey of film theatre owners, and it took her many years to live this down.

In typical Hepburn fashion she returned to the theatre, scored a big hit on Broadway in *The Philadelphia Story* in a role specially written for her, then returned to Hollywood in triumph. She starred in the film version of the play in 1940, making a fresh start at a new studio (MGM) and earning another Oscar nomination. In *Bringing Up Baby* she had represented the Dionysiac spirit, irrational, self-propelled, drawing the dull, bookish Cary Grant into her world of scrambled identity, and liberating his libido. But in *The Philadelphia Story* their roles were neatly reversed. *She* is the respectable one trying to keep everything under control and has to be liberated by the unconventional tactics of her ex-husband (Grant). The following year, 1941, MGM teamed her with Spencer Tracy for the first time in

Woman Of The Year. She was Oscar-nominated again, and was clearly well on her way to revitalising her film career.

Although Hepburn and Tracy were very different types, they developed a legendarily successful partnership both on and off the screen. In contrast to Tracy's purely instinctive approach to his roles, she was more methodical and analytical. She loved to rehearse and do many takes of a scene, while Tracy would be at his best on the very first take. Although the studio did not appear to take much interest in Miss Hepburn's career during these years – none of her non-Tracy pictures were at all memorable – the partnership managed six MGM films together during the 40s when they were both at their peak. The best of the series were the last two. *State Of The Union* (1948) was a political comedy based on a play by Howard Lindsay and Russel Crouse, directed by Frank Capra. Tracy had the lead role of a potential Presidential candidate, but Hepburn, making her entrance relatively late in the picture as his estranged wife, clearly stole the acting honours. As co-star Angela Lansbury recalled, 'What was exciting about Tracy and Hepburn was their presence ... Their personalities as well as their talents were orchestrated so marvellously. I began to think of them as one person, really; I suppose most people did'.

Then, in *Adam's Rib* (1949), she and Tracy played married lawyers who find themselves on opposing sides in a husband–wife case of attempted murder. The witty script specially written for them by their friends, the husband-and-wife team of Garson Kanin and Ruth Gordon, provided Kate with her best feminist role. She is totally convincing as the shrewd lawyer who makes ingenious use of the equality of the sexes as the basis for her defence, claiming that the law and society apply different standards of behaviour for women and for men. The accomplished playing of the couple turned the picture into an entertaining and often hilarious comedy without detracting from the serious underlying themes.

For her third memorable film in a row, *The African Queen* (1951), the star travelled abroad to join director John Huston and co-star Humphrey Bogart on location in Africa. For all three of them this was their first venture into Technicolor. Kate played a middle-aged missionary thrown into close quarters with the vulgar master of a small, beaten-up boat as they travel along a Congolese river, evading and outwitting the Germans during World War I. Mixing comedy and adventure, it was a two-character film, in which she gave a fine demonstration of her ability to develop within a role. The sensitive interaction between her and Bogart (in an unfamiliar guise) undoubtedly benefitted from her many films with Tracy. (She earned yet another Oscar nomination, while Bogart's performance won him his only Oscar.)

At this stage in her career, Miss Hepburn's liberated, modern ladies of a type most often found in the Tracy movies, tended to be replaced by the more repressed, spinsterish heroines of *The African Queen, Summer Madness* (US: *Summertime,* 1955) and *The Rainmaker* (1956). A smallish part in the film version of Tennessee Williams's *Suddenly Last Summer* (1959) was followed by a more meaty and satisfying role in an adaptation of Eugene O'Neill's *Long Day's Journey Into Night* (1962). Her qualities as an actress were now so highly regarded in Hollywood that she was Oscar-nominated for all five of these roles.

After a brief retirement from the screen, she joined Tracy for the one last picture that was written specially for them, *Guess Who's Coming To Dinner?* (1967). Her sympathetic performance earned her second Oscar and she immediately won her third the following year for her Eleanor of Aquitaine in *The Lion In Winter.* Although she continued acting in the occasional film and television movie throughout the Seventies, her one last triumph on the screen came in 1981 when she and her co-star, Henry Fonda, both won Oscars for their performances in *On Golden Pond.* JF

with Adolphe Menjou in State Of The Union *(MGM, 1948)*

with Spencer Tracy (left) and Gig Young in Desk Set *(20th Century-Fox, 1957)* ▷

Miriam Hopkins

Born **Bainbridge, Georgia, 18 October 1902**
Died **1972**

A gushy blonde who cultivated an overly gracious and 'refined' manner on the screen which perfectly suited her roles as a schemer or social climber – Miriam Hopkins first got her big break at Paramount during the early 30s. Signed up from the Broadway theatre – she had started out as a showgirl 10 years earlier – Miss Hopkins had the good fortune to work with leading directors like Lubitsch and Mamoulian. She played the floozie in Mamoulian's superbly realised *Dr Jekyll And Mr Hyde* (1931), opposite Fredric March, and was Herbert Marshall's scheming and crooked accomplice in the very Lubitschian *Trouble In Paradise* (1932). By late 1934 Paramount had let her go, but she got the opportunity to work with Mamoulian once again when he took over the first feature in the new three-strip Technicolor –

in Becky Sharp *(RKO, 1935)*

Becky Sharp (1935). Although Thackeray's scheming heroine was made to order for her, it also showed up her limitations as an actress and her inability to carry a film on her own. Signed up by Goldwyn, she had her most sympathetic role, and gave her best performance, in *These Three* (1936) directed by Wyler, as a school teacher involved in an unhappy triangle relationship and the victim of small-town intolerance. She played a scheming architect in *Woman Chases Man* (1937), opposite Joel McCrea, in a weak attempt to broaden her range to screwball comedy. But she was not a natural comedienne. By the late 30s she had failed to develop as an actress, and her performances were becoming increasingly mannered. She was most often cast in unsympathetic roles, like Bette Davis's unscrupulous rival in *The Old Maid* (1939) and again in *Old Acquaintance* (1943). By this time Miss Hopkins had also become increasingly difficult to handle on the set and her career as a star was over; she made only seven more pictures, her last being *The Chase* (1966). JF

Leslie Howard

Real name **Leslie Stainer**
Born **London, 24 April 1893**
Died **1943**

During the course of his distinguished career on both sides of the Atlantic, Leslie Howard came to embody the image of the ideal Englishman on the screen, tall, slim, fair-haired, sensitive and intelligent. Yet he was, in fact, the son of Hungarian Jewish immigrants who had settled in England not long before he was born.

Howard was already in his mid-twenties when he first became interested in acting, but within a few years he had made his name on the stage both in London and New York. For his first film role, an adaptation of *Outward Bound* in which he had already starred on Broadway, he was allegedly offered an amazing $5,000 a week by Warner Bros. in 1930. Soon MGM were bidding for his services. He appeared opposite Norma Shearer in a pair of pictures, then received his first Oscar nomination for his assured performance in an extremely successful Hollywood version of yet another British play which he had previously done on the stage – *Berkeley Square* (1933). He returned periodically to work in Britain, but only had his first big British hit as *The Scarlet Pimpernel* in 1935.

At the peak of his career Howard was much in demand, but was very choosy about the roles he accepted and only averaged about two films per year. He made a good try at Romeo opposite Norma Shearer in 1936, then triumphed two years later with his Professor Higgins in *Pygmalion* which he also co-directed. (The picture ended up with five

in Gone With The Wind *(MGM, 1939)*

Oscar nominations including one for his performance and Best Picture.) Although he returned to the US to play in *Intermezzo* and *Gone With The Wind* in 1939, the outbreak of war stimulated him to devote all his energies to supporting the British war effort via radio broadcasts, articles and films. He directed and starred in the anti-Nazi *Pimpernel Smith* (1941), a tribute to the men who flew the Spitfires in the

RAF – *The First Of The Few* (1942) – and directed *The Gentle Sex* (1943), which was dedicated to the women's ATS.

He died tragically in 1943 when his unarmed plane was shot down by a squadron of German fighters. C.A. Lejeune wrote, 'Howard was more than a popular actor ... He had become something of a symbol to the British people'. JF

with Irene Dunne in Ann Vickers *(RKO, 1933)*

Walter Huston

Real name **Walter Houghston**
Born **Toronto, Canada, 6 April 1884**
Died **1950**

A tall, rugged type who was trained as an engineer, Walter Huston projected a feeling of strength allied with shrewdness and intelligence. He tended to be cast as a figure of authority in many of his pictures, especially as he was in his mid-forties by the time sound had arrived. He was much in demand during the early 30s, having previously established himself as a leading figure on the American stage, and played an assortment of fathers, judges and businessmen, and even the occasional villain. He first made his mark on the screen with an impressive performance as *Abraham Lincoln* (1930) which revealed him to be an outstanding natural film actor who made subtle and effective use of his face, voice and body and had not been 'spoiled' by his earlier years on the stage.

Huston played the lead in a number of topical,

socially conscious pictures like Frank Capra's *American Madness* (1932) and *Gabriel Over The White House* (1933). Then he scored his biggest success of the decade on the stage and in the follow-up film version of *Dodsworth* (1936). Adapted from the novel by Sinclair Lewis about a retired American businessman who discovers a new life in Europe, the picture was produced with great care by Sam Goldwyn and directed by William Wyler. It earned half-a-dozen Oscar nominations, including one for Best Picture and for Huston's performance, but unfortunately it brought him no new offers of note, and he returned to the stage. His next outstanding film role, as a crusty, irascible yet likeable incarnation of the Devil in *All That Money Can Buy* in 1941 earned his second Oscar nomination. And that same year he made a brief appearance in the first feature directed by his son John (*The Maltese Falcon*).

In 1948 both Hustons won their first Oscars, John for directing and Walter for his definitive performance as a grizzled but wise old prospector, in *The Treasure Of The Sierra Madre*, one of his last appearances. JF

Boris Karloff

Real name **William Pratt**
Born **Dulwich, London, 23 November 1887**
Died **1969**

A gentle, cultured, cricket-loving Englishman, Boris Karloff was the unlikeliest of stars. Most of the films he made were cheap horror movies and, in the A features in which he appeared, he was invariably a supporting player.

Karloff's enduring fame rests on a series of immaculate performances in the early 30s, mostly for Universal – *Frankenstein* (1931), *The Mummy* (1932) and *The Old Dark House* (1932) – but no

in Frankenstein *(Universal, 1931)*

matter how meretricious some of his later vehicles, he always remained wryly conscious of his own legend, and brought a touch of self-deprecating humour on to the set. He was not a great actor, but lent something of his gravity and deliberation to the monsters, mad scientists and necromancers he created. He displayed his professionalism in his relatively few straight parts, notably as a mobster in *Scarface* (1932) and as the religious maniac in RKO's *The Lost Patrol* (1934). He also revealed a deftly humorous streak in *The Secret Life Of Walter Mitty* (1947).

The son of a well-to-do diplomat he emigrated to Canada in 1909, joined a touring theatre company and took the name Boris Karloff. After 10 years of

barnstorming on the kerosene circuit, he found himself in Los Angeles, unemployed, and took work as an extra. In the 20s, his gaunt features and rawboned figure secured him unspectacular but steady work as villainous Orientals, native chiefs, Western desperados and the occasional fur trapper. Sometimes he worked as a labourer to make ends meet, consoling himself with back numbers of Wisden, the cricket lover's Bible. It is an indication of his obscurity that when Howard Hawks cast him as the trusted convict who turns killer in *The Criminal Code* (1931), 'Picturegoer' assumed he was making his screen debut. Thereafter the parts improved, particularly in two Warner films, *Five Star Final* (1931) and *The Mad Genius* (1931), but he was still just a hard-working heavy. Karloff was playing a murderer in *Graft* (1931) when he was spotted in the Universal commissary by director James Whale who was casting *Frankenstein*. Whale had found his monster: 'Boris Karloff's face fascinated me ... his physique was weaker than I could wish, but that queer penetrating personality of his, I felt, was more important than his shape, which could be easily altered'. The process was completed by make-up man Jack Pierce who built up the Monster's head – square and flat like a box – with layers of rubber and cotton. The livid scar across the forehead showed where the brain of a dead man had been inserted. The two metal electrodes on Karloff's neck were fixed so tightly that he retained tiny scars there for years afterwards. The Monster's legs were stiffened with steel struts, and on Karloff's feet were boots normally worn by asphalt spreaders. The combined weight of the outfit was nearly 50lbs, and it took three and a half hours to put on and an hour and a half to remove after shooting. Beneath the make-up, which Universal sensibly copyrighted, Karloff presented a feeling and vulnerable Monster, groping pathetically for the sun as a trapdoor in Frankenstein's laboratory slides back. One only has to compare his performance with those of later interpreters – Lugosi, Glenn Strange, Lon Chaney Jr, Christopher Lee – to realise its depth and subtlety. It made him a star overnight.

He cemented his position as the king of horror in Whale's *The Old Dark House* (1932), then had a

speaking role as the hissing Oriental criminal mastermind in *The Mask Of Fu Manchu* (1932) before playing the 3,700-year-old Ardeth Bey, the bandaged menace of Karl Freund's *The Mummy* (1932). In the mid-30s, the steam was running out of the horror cycle, and after Whale's marvellous black comedy, *The Bride Of Frankenstein* (1935), with Elsa Lanchester as Karloff's assembly-kit bride, he moved gently into starring roles in B features. He was the heavy in an excellent entry in Fox's Charlie Chan series, *Charlie Chan At The Opera* (1936), then went to Monogram to play a rival Oriental sleuth, the scholarly Mr Wong, in a series of brisk programmers. He bade farewell to Frankenstein's Monster in *Son Of Frankenstein* (1939) and at Columbia embarked on a series of 'mad doctor' roles with Nick Grinde's *The Man They Could Not Hang* (1939). An outstanding entry was *The Devil Commands* (1941), directed by Edward Dmytryk. Karloff was well used in Val Lewton's distinguished B horror unit at RKO, in *The Body Snatcher, Isle Of The Dead* (1945) – a mesmeric performance as a disillusioned Greek general succumbing to plague – and *Bedlam* (1946). He saw out the 40s with a mixed bag: *Lured* (1947), a stylish melodrama directed by Douglas Sirk and starring Lucille Ball; *Unconquered* (1947), in which he played an Indian chief; *Dick Tracy Meets Gruesome* (1947), as, needless to say, Gruesome; *Tap Roots* (1948), in another Indian role; and *Abbott And Costello Meet The Killer* (1949). He marked time in the 50s, alternating television work with some undistinguished programmers and, in 1958, returned to England for two superior chillers, *The Haunted Strangler* (1958), and *Corridors Of Blood* (1958), released in 1963.

In the 60s Roger Corman and AIP gave him a new lease of life in *The Raven* (1963), *The Terror* (1963) and *Comedy Of Terrors* (1964). Because he owed the parsimonious Corman a couple of days work he made Peter Bogdanovich's *Targets* (1968). As Byron Orlock, an elderly horror star, he was a thinly disguised version of himself, 'his skin a blend of California tan, jaundice and the old parchment of Gothic castles'. Karloff went on to make four more films in Spain, all of them unreleased, but *Targets* remains his testament. RC

with Katherine Emery in Isle Of The Dead *(RKO, 1945)*

Ruby Keeler

Born **Halifax, Canada, 25 August, 1909**

In 1970, thirty years after she had retired from the screen, Ruby Keeler returned to Broadway in a revival of 'No, No, Nanette'. She was still remembered for her role as the demure chorus girl who takes over from the injured star in *42nd Street* (1933), and to whom director Warner Baxter says, 'You're going out a youngster, but you've got to come back a star.' She did just that, becoming the female lead in a further eight spectacular Warner Bros. 'backstage' musicals in the 30s, usually as Dick Powell's sweetheart. Keeler's face is the motif of the 'I Only Have Eyes For You' number in *Dames* (1934), and she danced with James Cagney in 'Shanghai Lil' from *Footlight Parade* (1933), two of several Busby Berkeley routines she featured in. However, her singing voice was squeaky and her round-shouldered tap dancing was only just adequate.

Ruby came from a poor family who somehow managed to pay for her dancing lessons. At fourteen she got into the chorus line of a Broadway show, and for the next three years danced in nightclubs and on stage. While appearing in Los Angeles, she met Al Jolson, who followed her back to New York and married her in 1928. They appeared in only one film together, *Go Into Your Dance* (1935). In 1937, she left Warners with her husband after he had quarrelled with them, and her career petered out. She divorced Jolson in 1940 and after *Sweetheart Of The Campus* (1941), a Columbia cheapie, married a real estate broker and left show business. RB

Elissa Landi

Real name **Elizabeth Marie Christine Kuehnelt**
Born **Venice, Italy, 6 December 1904**
Died **1948**

Elissa Landi is the best known of that group of stunningly attractive European starlets, like Anna Sten and Gwili Andre, who were tempted by Hollywood during the early 30s in the wake of Garbo and Dietrich. All but forgotten now, their days of stardom were numbered due either to unsuitable pictures, absurd publicity or lack of talent – sometimes a combination of all three.

At least Miss Landi had every opportunity to develop as an actress. Although born in Venice, she was educated in England and had her first success there on the stage in the 20s and in a few films, most notably in *Underground* (1929), directed by Anthony Asquith. An appearance on Broadway led to a

in The Sign Of The Cross (Paramount, 1932)

contract with the Fox studio which was desperately searching for new star talent. She was rushed into a number of weak efforts during 1931–32, of which only *Yellow Ticket* (1931), in which she starred as a Russian peasant girl and was supported by Laurence Olivier and Lionel Barrymore, was at all memorable. She sparkled briefly as the heroine of two costume epics – DeMille's *The Sign Of The Cross* (1932) and *The Count Of Monte Cristo* (1934), but by 1935 her brief movie career was virtually over. JF

Priscilla Lane

Real name **Priscilla Mullican**
Born **Indianola, Iowa, 12 June 1917**

An attractive and likeable starlet, Priscilla Lane was signed to a contract by Warner Bros. in 1937 and appeared in a number of the studio's most interesting pictures between 1938 and 1941. Lacking any formal training – (she had first made her name as a vocalist with her two sisters) – she did all that was

in Brother Rat And A Baby (Warner Bros., 1940)

required of her, namely, she looked attractive and provided sympathetic support to the studio's top male stars.

She played an assortment of daughters, girlfriends and fiancées, but rarely made it to the altar. Teamed with Wayne Morris in three 1938 releases, she also helped John Garfield shoot to stardom in *Four Daughters* that year, and played Cagney's nightclub singer girlfriend in *The Roaring Twenties* (1939). As Cary Grant's fiancée in *Arsenic And Old Lace* (filming in 1941 but not released until 1944) she had little to do but look attractive and frightened. Ditto Hitchcock's *Saboteur* (1942), in which she was forced to join the fugitive hero on the run (Robert Cummings). She was not really right for the part, and Hitchcock claimed that he was forced to use her. It proved to be her last film of any interest. JF

Elsa Lanchester

Real name **Elizabeth Sullivan**
Born **Lewisham, England, 28 October 1902**

A delightful and accomplished character actress whose film career was inevitably overshadowed by that of her famous husband Charles Laughton, Elsa Lanchester's movie appearances have spanned a remarkable 50-year period from 1927 up to *Murder By Decree* in 1976.

She first lit up the screen in Korda's *The Private Life Of Henry VIII* (1933) which had been planned as a vehicle for Charles Laughton and herself – they had married four years earlier. She played the fourth wife, Anne of Cleves. The roles of the other wives were expanded, leaving Elsa's role small but effective, and she provided the comic high point of the picture. Speaking with an extraordinary Dutch accent, she first greets the king with 'Oh Heinrich', and waits for him patiently in bed while munching on an apple. 'The things I've done for England', he exclaims as he arrives at the door. But their

in Bride Of Frankenstein (Universal, 1935)

encounter turns into a hilarious and witty sequence as they end up playing cards in bed, and she keeps winning. As if to make up for this unflattering caricature of a role, she was offered a more sympathetic part in *Rembrandt* (1936) and was superb, although the picture flopped. In the meantime she had made a striking appearance as a mate designed for the monster in *Bride Of Frankenstein* (1935), in which she was also seen in the prologue as gothic novelist Mary Shelley, author of the original book.

In Hollywood during the 40s she specialised in middle-aged, eccentric ladies. In *The Big Clock* (1947), starring Laughton, she gave a superb cameo as an unconventional painter, reprising this role in *Come To The Stable* (1949) – 'Miss Amelia Potts, Religious Paintings' – to win her first supporting actress Oscar nomination. The second came in 1957 when she played Laughton's strict, no-nonsense nurse in *Witness For The Prosecution*. After Laughton's death in 1962 Miss Lanchester appeared in supporting roles in a number of Disney pictures including *Mary Poppins* (1964), and has also found time to write a book on their life together, 'Charles Laughton and I'. JF

Charles Laughton

Born **Scarborough, England, 1 July 1899**
Died **1962**

Charles Laughton possessed truly remarkable qualities as an actor and was equally good in a wide range of roles during the course of his thirty plus years as a movie star. His sensitive and convincing performances won over film audiences in spite of the nastiness of some of the characters he portrayed on the screen – like Captain Bligh or Quasimodo – and made one forget his bulky shape and unattractive appearance. Yet he was extremely insecure and self-conscious, and could be un-cooperative at times. Acting did not come easily to him, and many film directors found him difficult to work with, although the end result generally made it all worth while. As Alexander Korda sarcastically expressed it, 'With him acting was an act of childbirth. What he needed was not so much a director as a midwife'. Hitchcock put it even more succinctly: 'You can't direct a Laughton picture. The best you can hope for is to referee.'

Trained at RADA, Laughton made his name on the West End stage during the late 20s and had parts in a number of British films. Then his successes on Broadway, along with his wife Elsa Lanchester (they married in 1929) led to offers from Hollywood, and he was immediately cast as the lead in an unusual group of pictures including *The Old Dark House* (1932) and *Island Of Lost Souls* (1932). That year he also gave an entertaining, over-the-top performance as Nero in DeMille's *The Sign Of The Cross* (1932). Throughout the decade he continued to divide his time between Hollywood and England, where he returned in 1933 to play the title role in Korda's *The Private Life Of Henry VIII* (1933). Although cheaply made and looking it, Laughton's commanding presence could redeem the weakest of pictures. He won an Oscar for his performance, and the unexpected success at the box office gave a big boost to the fortunes of Korda's London Films company, as well as to Laughton himself.

Clearly reaching an early peak in his career, Laughton then excelled in five very different roles in a row from 1934 to 1936, beginning with Elizabeth Barrett's strict Victorian father in *The Barretts Of Wimpole Street* (1934) for MGM. He gave a delightful comedy performance as an English butler transposed to the American far West in *Ruggles Of Red Gap* (1935), followed by the doggedly persevering Inspector Javert in *Les Miserables* (1935). His portrayal of the ruthless Captain Bligh in *Mutiny On*

in Rembrandt *(United Artists, 1936)*

The Bounty (1935) is justly famous and earned him a second Oscar nomination, while the picture itself was a big hit and won the Best Picture Oscar. He returned to England to play the title role of *Rembrandt* (1936) for Korda, and was again outstanding in a film which was not widely seen nor did it receive the appreciation it deserved.

His uncompromising performance as Quasimodo, *The Hunchback Of Notre Dame*, in 1939, evokes both pity and terror, while he was suitably villainous in a memorable thriller, *The Big Clock* (1948). Back in England again, he starred in David Lean's excellent production of *Hobson's Choice* (1954), before his only film as director, *The Night Of The Hunter* (1955). An accomplished and imaginative work, over the years it has gained a reputation as a cult classic. Finally, in 1957, Laughton received his third Oscar nomination for his polished portrayal of the crafty middle-aged lawyer in the film version of Agatha Christie's *Witness For The Prosecution*. Not one to rest on his laurels, he next gave a choice portrayal of a Roman patrician in *Spartacus* (1960). His last appearance was as the wily Southern senator in *Advise And Consent* (1962). JF

in The Sign Of The Cross *(Paramount, 1932)*

Carole Lombard

Real name **Jane Alice Peters**
Born **Fort Wayne, Indiana, 6 October 1908**
Died **1942**

First spotted playing baseball on the street by director Allan Dwan, Carole Lombard was given her first film part at the age of 12. Thus began the movie career of the actress who was to develop into the leading Hollywood comedienne of the 30s, and who, although stunningly attractive, never entirely lost her tomboyish qualities.

Under contract to Paramount, Carole played in a large number of weak pictures by second-rate directors, but one of the few exceptions was *No Man Of Her Own* (1932). This was the only time she starred with Clark Gable whom she later married. In 1934 she was cast opposite John Barrymore in *Twentieth Century*, directed by Howard Hawks. Perhaps a bit self-conscious about her lack of formal training, she prepared thoroughly for her role. A little too thoroughly for, early on in the filming, Hawks and Barrymore were taken aback, and they both worked hard to convince her to stop 'acting' and be more natural, which she did. From that point on she was superb as a temperamental actress, a role tailor made for her. The give and take between her

and Barrymore made the sparks fly, and Hawks concluded that 'she's probably going to be a big star . . . if we can just keep her from acting'.

One of the earliest screwball comedies, the picture marked a turning point in Lombard's career, demonstrating for the first time her outstanding natural abilities as a film comedienne, extremely modern in style and in the expressive use of her voice and body. Unfortunately, her talents were often wasted. She had to wait two years for *My Man Godfrey* (1936) in which she played a spoilt rich girl in a crazy household who is sorted out by an unlikely new butler played by the debonair William Powell. (In real life, Powell had been Carole's first husband.) For her performance she received her only Oscar nomination. The following year she had another memorable role as the small-town girl thought to be dying of radium poisoning in *Nothing Sacred*. A hilarious black comedy, it reunited her with writer Ben Hecht, who had scripted *Twentieth Century*, and was her only picture filmed in Technicolor.

For the last picture before her untimely death in a plane crash, she got one of Hollywood's leading directors, Ernst Lubitsch, at the peak of his form. She played a Polish actress helping to outwit the German occupying forces in *To Be Or Not To Be* (1942), and this superb anti-Nazi satire stands as a fitting final tribute to her gifts. JF

with Raymond Massey (left) in Arsenic And Old Lace *(Warner Bros., 1944)*

Peter Lorre

Real name **Laszlo Löwenstein**
Born **Rosenberg, Hungary, 26 June 1904**
Died **1964**

Peter Lorre's genius was for the incongruous and the grotesque, his eyes alternately beseeching, or bulging with unrestrained terror. Small, squat and a prisoner of his early fame, he was typecast by Hollywood, but remained a riveting screen presence, hovering compellingly on the edge of big films like *Strange Cargo* (1940) or starving in intriguing, off-beat B features like Robert Florey's *The Face Behind The Mask* (1941).

Fritz Lang's *M* (1931), based on the career of the Dusseldorf mass killer Peter Kurten, was Lorre's first film. His performance as the corpulent, hunted psychopath was a masterpiece of mime and suggestion – he had only 12 lines of dialogue. In 1934 the Nazis forced him to leave Germany. In Paris he appeared in G.W. Pabst's *De Haut En Bas* (1934), then moved to London to play memorably sinister parts in two Hitchcock films, *The Man Who Knew Too Much* (1934) and *The Secret Agent* (1936). Sandwiched between these was his Hollywood debut, as Dr Gogol in MGM's *Mad Love* (1935). At Columbia he was Raskolnikov in Von Sternberg's *Crime And Punishment* (1935), and in 1936 was signed by 20th Century-Fox. Almost immediately he was cast as the nimble, self-effacing Japanese sleuth Mr Moto in *Think Fast, Mr Moto* (1937), the first of a series of eight programmers.

In 1941 he played the gardenia-scented Joel Cairo in Warners' *The Maltese Falcon*, the first of several films in which he formed an unholy alliance with Sydney Greenstreet. In the war years he capitalised on his genius for neuroticism, playing an assortment of refugees, spies and sadistic Nazis, notably in *Casablanca* (1942), *Background To Danger* (1943) and *The Cross Of Lorraine* (1943). His immediate post-war films were hit and miss affairs, enlivened by a marvellous study in hallucination in Florey's *The Beast With Five Fingers* (1946).

In 1951 he returned to Germany to produce, direct and star in *Der Verlorene*, a haunting exorcism of the recent Nazi past but a commercial failure. Swollen by a glandular complaint, Lorre coasted through character roles in a string of undistinguished films, relieved only by *Beat The Devil* (1954) and *Silk Stockings* (1957). The latter revealed his talent for comedy, well used to parody himself in three Roger Corman films including *The Raven* (1963). His last film was *The Patsy* (1964). RC

Anita Louise

Real name **Anita Louise Fremault**
Born **New York City, 9 January 1915**
Died **1970**

She was beautiful as a little girl, blonde and blue-eyed, and first appeared on the screen as a child actress during the 20s, but Anita Louise, like many other child stars of the cinema, was never able to make the transition to mature, adult roles. After a brief stage career, she was signed by RKO to appear in a number of forgettable roles in second-rate pictures. Her best at RKO was her last, playing Constance Bennett's sister in *Our Betters* (1933) directed by George Cukor. Stunningly attractive she kept busy throughout the decade providing a bit of clean, wholesome glamour or romantic interest in secondary roles as a succession of daughters, sisters or girlfriends. (She rarely made it to the altar.)

Taken up by director William Dieterle (and Warner Bros.) in 1934, Miss Louise went on to make four pictures for him during 1934–36. She played a young Marie Antoinette in *Madame Du-Barry* (1934) and Paul Muni's daughter in *The Story Of Louis Pasteur* (1936), but had her biggest

in Everything Is Rosie *(RKO, 1931)*

opportunity as Titania in the studio's prestigious production of *A Midsummer Night's Dream* (1935). She was ethereally beautiful, but otherwise failed to make an impression. Warners kept her on for a number of years and found her particularly suited to costume roles, but by 1940 she was reduced to appearing in B-pictures and, at the age of 25, her film career was virtually over. JF

Myrna Loy

Real name **Myrna Williams**
Born **Raidersburg nr Helena, Montana, 2 August 1905**

'Not only was I supposed to have a pet python, but I had my father's male victims turned over to me for torture, stripped; I then whipped them myself, uttering sadistic gleeful cries.' Thus Myrna Loy recalled the last of her Oriental roles as Fah Lo See, daughter of the notorious Fu Manchu which marked the end of her early period in Hollywood. During the years 1926 through 1932 when she appeared in *The Mask Of Fu Manchu*, Miss Loy averaged nine films per year. She played a remarkable and varied assortment of gypsies, slave girls, spies, and, due to her expressive, almond-shaped eyes, got more than her fair share of Orientals. A slim, attractive brunette, she had originally trained as a dancer, but

the chorus line at Grauman's Chinese (sic) Theatre had propelled her into the movies.

Reference to Miss Loy's early career became a standard Hollywood bad joke after she became a major star. In fact, in 1932 she was first signed by MGM, and by the following year there was a marked improvement in her roles. In *Topaze* (1933), opposite John Barrymore, she demonstrated her comedic talent, but the turning point came when she was teamed with William Powell and Clark Gable in *Manhattan Melodrama* (1934) directed by W.S. Van Dyke. Sensing something special between Powell and Loy, he immediately reteamed them in *The Thin Man* (1934), and thus began an acting partnership which flourished for over 10 years. Aside from the Thin Man sequels, they appeared together in *The Great Ziegfeld* (1936), *Libelled Lady* (1936), a delightful screwball comedy, and many others. But Miss Loy is undoubtedly best remembered today as the female half of the Thin Man detective couple, Nick and Norah Charles. Although she is outclassed by Powell in the acting department, it is the interaction between them which counts. She rarely initiates anything – her playfulness is responsive, as is her drinking, and she is pushed out of the way whenever danger threatens. Their affectionate banter, mutual tolerance, and unsentimental concern is both touching and funny. Are there any other films of the period in which a *married* couple get on so well together, swapping badinage and trying to outdrink each other? Reviewed today their relationship appears as fresh, truthful and unusual as it must have seemed when the pictures were first shown although, inevitably, some of the later entries in the cycle deteriorated badly.

After a gap of a few years, Loy combined her wifely qualities, cast opposite Fredric March, with motherly ones in *The Best Years Of Our Lives* (1946) which won the Best Picture Oscar. She had one last big hit as the mother of twelve coping valiantly in *Cheaper By The Dozen* (1950), before slipping into smaller roles and cameos, including an appearance in *Airport '75* (1974). JF

Bela Lugosi

Real name **Béla Blasko**
Born **Lugos, Hungary, 20 october 1882**
Died **1956**

'I am Dracula, I bid you welcome,' announces Bela Lugosi, as with sinister deliberation, he advances on Dwight Frye down the cobweb-clogged, bat-infested staircase of his ancestral home. And so he remained for the rest of his life. In Lugosi's later, desperate years, the role which in the early 30s brought him easy fame and fortune became part lifeline, part millstone around his neck as he tottered through an increasingly grisly series of low budget encounters with characters such as the East Side Kids in *Spooks Run Wild* (1941) and Mother Riley in *Mother Riley Meets The Vampire* (1952). Once the studios found him difficult to cast, he was condemned to humiliating repetitions of his early triumph.

A Max Reinhardt leading man, he had a brief film career, as Arisztid Olt, in Hungary before coming to the US in 1921 with a theatrical touring company. In New York he learnt his part in 'The Red Poppy' phonetically, 'like the music of a song', which partly explains the curious, drawn-out cadences of his voice. His first American film was *The Silent Command* (1923), and in 1927 he played Dracula on Broadway. A turning point came when he appeared as the courtly, sinister Inspector Delzante in Tod Browning's first talkie, *The Thirteenth Chair* (1929).

in The Black Cat *(Universal, 1934)*

Browning was to direct the screen version of *Dracula* (Universal, 1931) with Lon Chaney, but Chaney died and Lugosi stepped in. His performance is one of the classics of cinema – absurd, but made utterly compelling by Lugosi's weird conviction and inimitably deliberate phrasing. With the deathly pallor of his face heightened by evening dress, opera cloak and jet-black skullcap of brilliantined hair, he was a hypnotic vision from beyond the grave. Lugosi was

tested at Universal for the Monster in *Frankenstein*. The make-up made him look like a cross between The Golem and something from *Babes In Toyland*, and he turned down the part in favour of the hypnotist in *Murders In The Rue Morgue* (1932).

Perhaps the greatest irony of Lugosi's career was that almost as soon as he was established as the first big horror star of the talkies, he began to feel the clammy hand of poverty row on his shoulder. After two major films he was reduced to the Halperin's low-budget *White Zombie* (1932), and then loped off to Columbia for an unashamed B, *Night Of Terror* (1933). Throughout the 30s, however, Lugosi still managed to secure parts in interesting films such as *The Raven* (1935) and *The Invisible Ray* (1936), but the films, alas, grew inexorably cheaper and the parts smaller and, by the early 40s, he was down among the dead men in PRC cheapies. After a charming comic performance as one of Garbo's compatriots in *Ninotchka* (1939), Lugosi moved to Sam Katzman's Banner Pictures – Monogram's B unit, if such a thing were possible. He could no longer afford to be choosy, and gratefully accepted Frankenstein's Monster in Universal's *Frankenstein Meets The Wolf Man* (1943).

But grimmer ordeals lay ahead for he was now in the grip of drug addiction. Lugosi finally lost his moorings and drifted into the subliminal outer limits of fringe film-making eg *Bela Lugosi Meets A Brooklyn Gorilla* (1952) and a sad, posthumous appearance in *Plan 9 From Outer Space* (1959). RC

Jeanette MacDonald

Born **Philadelphia, 18 June, 1901**
Died **1965**

'Today, anything that has a suggestion of sentiment is quickly dismissed as corn,' Jeanette MacDonald explained in an interview in 1964. 'Frankly, what's wrong with it? ... Sentiment, after all, is basic. Without it there is no love, no life, no family.' And there would certainly not have been the eight lavish sentimental operettas that she made with Nelson Eddy at MGM, including *Naughty Marietta* (1935), *Rose Marie* (1936), *Maytime* (1937) and *Sweethearts* (1938). Although she was animated and he was wooden, her trilly soprano blended well with his stolid baritone in duets such as 'Ah, Sweet Mystery Of Life!' and 'The Indian Love Call'. Known as 'America's Sweethearts' or, not too complimentarily, 'The Singing Capon and the Iron Butterfly', they formed one of the most popular musical partnerships in motion picture history.

Jeanette was a Broadway chorus girl in her teens, soon reaching stardom in stage musicals and operettas. Ernst Lubitsch, at Paramount, chose her to star in his first talkie, *The Love Parade* (1929), opposite Maurice Chevalier, the first of four sumptuous saucy screen operettas she was to make with the Frenchman. Tall, titian-haired MacDonald had a self-mocking air, whether as a princess pining for love in

with Nelson Eddy in Rose Marie *(MGM, 1936)*

her chateau in Rouben Mamoulian's *Love Me Tonight* (1932), or when discarding her widowhood in the title role of Lubitsch's MGM production of *The Merry Widow* (1934). As Chevalier aptly puts it in the latter movie, 'Your right eye says yes, and your left eye says no.' Other co-stars were Jack Buchanan in *Monte Carlo* (1930), and Allan Jones in *The Firefly* (1937), a romantic musical set in Napoleonic Spain where Jeanette was a somewhat unlikely spy posing as a cafe dancer. When Clark Gable was asked to co-star with her in *San Francisco* (1936), he at first refused because he had heard about her 'high-toned' attitude from his friend Nelson Eddy, and snubbed her whenever they were not filming. The film, however, allowed her to sing a few operatic arias,

literally bringing the house down. MacDonald, who played the coquettish ingenue, on and off screen, way into her thirties, would hog all the best camera angles from her male partners. John Barrymore reacted to her scene-stealing on the set of *Maytime*, by shouting, 'If you wave that loathsome chiffon rag you call a kerchief once more while I'm speaking, I shall ram it down your gurgling throat!'

MacDonald married actor Gene Raymond in 1937. During the war her popularity waned, and MGM terminated her contract. Nevertheless, she returned to the studio to play Jane Powell's mother in *Three Daring Daughters* (1948) and, in her last movie, *The Sun Comes Up* (1949), she co-starred with Lassie. RB

Fredric March

**Real name Ernest Frederick McIntyre Bickel
Born Racine, Wisconsin, 31 August 1897
Died 1975**

'To me characterisation is the whole fun of acting,' Fredric March once wrote. '*Every* part is a character part.' This statement nicely sums up his attitude to acting, and in the course of his forty plus years in films he appeared in a wide variety of roles, comedy and drama, contemporary and period, and even starred in a few action pictures and swashbucklers.

in Strangers In Love *(Paramount, 1932)*

Tall, handsome and intelligent-looking, with an exceptionally fine voice, he could impose his authority on a role, even as a young man when he was gaining his first stage experience touring throughout the US and appearing in summer stock. After his marriage to the actress, Florence Eldridge, they formed their own touring repertory company and played together regularly on the stage and, later on, in a few films. In 1928 with the coming of sound, March was one of the first stage actors to be signed by the film companies. He had a contract with Paramount for five years and appeared in almost thirty pictures during that time. Although most of them were far from memorable, his John Barrymore impersonation in *The Royal Family Of Broadway* (1930) earned him his first Oscar nomination and, two years later he gave a remarkable performance in

the dual role of *Dr Jekyll And Mr Hyde*. March succeeded in portraying both Jekyll and Hyde as fully developed characters, making effective use of his bodily movements and gestures as well as his voice. In an extraordinary chase sequence near the end of the film, Hyde swings adroitly down the bannisters like the ape-man he is, providing us with perhaps the best of the many film interpretations of this role.

March won his first Oscar for this performance and suddenly found himself much in demand. This allowed him to become more selective in his choice of roles, and he worked with a number of Paramount's leading directors – DeMille, Lubitsch, and Mitchell Leisen. In *The Barretts Of Wimpole Street* (1934) at MGM, Laughton stole the acting honours, but he and March were more evenly matched, and at their stellar best, in the excellent 1935 production of *Les Miserables*. Throughout his career March had to fight to keep from being type-cast and attempted, for example, to cut down on the large number of costume roles requested of him. He was excellent in

the World War I picture, *The Road To Glory* (1936), and he brought real substance to the slightly clichéd character of the alcoholic and fading film star, Norman Maine, in *A Star Is Born* (1937) which earned him his third Oscar nomination. He demonstrated his comic flair in two delightful screwball comedies, *Nothing Sacred* (1937) with Carole Lombard and *I Married A Witch* (1942), the lady in question being Veronica Lake. From 1942 on, he cut back further on his film commitments to an average of only one picture per year. Two of his most solid and moving performances in the mature, fatherly roles which were now being offered to him earned him two further Oscar nominations – for *The Best Years Of Our Lives* (1946) and *Death Of A Salesman* (1951). (He landed his second Oscar for the former, but lost out to Bogart in 1951.) March continued in pictures throughout the 50s and 60s and contributed one last memorable performance in the American Film Theatre version of O'Neill's *The Iceman Cometh* (1973). JF

with Linden Travers (left) and Kathleen Ryan during the shooting of Christopher Columbus *(Rank/Universal, 1949)*

Herbert Marshall

**Born London, England, 23 May 1890
Died 1966**

Herbert Marshall was the least likely of 30s movie stars. A dependable but distinctly diffident Englishman, he had lost a leg in World War I, but managed to disguise this quite effectively. The possessor of a soft but richly melodious and distinctive voice, he first developed into a leading star on the stage on both sides of the Atlantic during the 20s. In 1928 he married the actress, Edna Best, and they became an extremely popular stage couple.

Between theatre appearances, he had his initial Hollywood success in a supporting role in *The Letter* (1929) adapted from Maugham and starring Jeanne Eagels. Back in England he was excellent in an early Hitchcock talkie, *Murder* (1930), but his career really took off in a big way in 1932 at Paramount. That year he played opposite Claudette Colbert in *Secrets Of A Secretary*, followed by Von Sternberg's *Blonde Venus* in which he was Marlene Dietrich's long-suffering husband, and Lubitsch's *Trouble In Paradise* as a gentleman thief torn between Miriam Hopkins and Kay Francis. These pictures set the pattern for his subsequent career. Clearly his sober,

sensitive image served to highlight the glamorous qualities of Hollywood's most stunning female stars.

After one last trip back to England, he settled firmly in Hollywood. However, Paramount was disappointed with his failure to develop into a top romantic star, and he moved on to MGM and three more leading ladies – Norma Shearer, Constance Bennett and Greta Garbo – all in one year (1934). But Marshall was clearly in danger of falling into a rut as he continued to play a repetitive selection of ill-used husbands, kindly understanding fathers and elderly, well-behaved lovers, and his under-stated style easily tended to appear dull and mannered on the screen. His private life was less conventional. He had a taste for drink, and an intense affair with no less than Gloria Swanson threatened his marriage.

Marshall's career underwent a brief revival during the early 40s when he played Bette Davis's betrayed husband in two of her best pictures, *The Letter* (1940, a remake of the 1929 version) and *The Little Foxes* (1941), both directed by William Wyler. He was Laraine Day's sympathetic father in *Foreign Correspondent* (1940) but, in a nicely Hitchcockian twist, turned out to be the villain. His last outstanding role was that of Somerset Maugham, the author, as narrator in *The Moon And Sixpence* (1942), a part he repeated in *The Razor's Edge* (1946). JF

Marx Brothers

Real name **Leonard (Chico)**
Born **26 March 1886. Died 1961**

Real name **Arthur (Harpo)**
Born **21 November 1888. Died 1964**

Real name **Julius Henry (Groucho)**
Born **2 October 1890. Died 1977**

Real name **Herbert (Zeppo)**
Born **25 Feb 1901. Died 1979**

(all were born in New York City)

left to right: Zeppo, Groucho, Chico and Harpo in Cocoanuts *(Paramount, 1929)*

Groucho wore a large, false moustache, glasses and a frock coat and walked with a strange loping gait. He was called Rufus T. Firefly, Hugo Z. Hackenbush or Otis B. Driftwood, but they were all variations on the same character, famous for his one-liners. Caught in a compromising position by an irate husband in *Monkey Business* (1931) – 'Sir, this is an outrage, breaking into a man's home ... I'm not in the habit of making threats but there'll be a letter about this in 'The Times' tomorrow morning.' Taking Harpo's pulse in *A Day At The Races* (1937), he exclaims, 'Either this man is dead or my watch has stopped.'

Harpo wore a curly reddish-blonde wig and a top hat and carried an old taxi horn to honk at appropriate moments, when he was not playing the harp or chasing nubile young starlets. Chico affected an Italian accent, wore a Tyrolean style hat and appeared marginally more sane, but the real 'straight man' in the early pictures was Zeppo, the fourth and least interesting brother.

Their characters had been refined and developed through trial and error in front of live audiences over a period of many years. Thus, by the time they first reached the screen in 1929 with *The Cocoanuts*, a film version of one of their big stage successes, they were already highly seasoned vaudevillians. On the stage they were totally uninhibited and irrepressible, since there was no one around to control them, but in filming there was always a director to call a halt after each take. Yet they demonstrated that they could convey a similar sense of spontaneity, and even improvise a little in bringing their particular zany and surreal world to life on the screen, while sticking to a written script and keeping within the area marked out for the camera.

By shooting their first two pictures at Paramount's Astoria studios on Long Island, they were able to continue performing on the stage during the evenings while filming during the day. But in 1930 they made the move to Hollywood where they completed their last three movies for Paramount. Most notable of the group was the anarchic satire, *Duck Soup* (1933), on which they had an apportunity to work with a major director (Leo McCarey) for the first time. When their contract lapsed, producer Irving Thalberg was quick to step in. The MGM pictures which followed were more polished and slightly less wacky, yet both *A Night At The Opera* (1935) and *A Day At The Races* (1937) are regarded as classic Marx Bros comedies. After the death of Thalberg, however, it was clear that they had passed their peak, although they continued to make pictures together, at irregular intervals, for another thirteen years, after which Groucho made a few solo appearances. JF

Burgess Meredith

Born **Cleveland, Ohio, 16 November 1908**

A talented and versatile character actor, Burgess Meredith first made his name on the stage during the 30s, coming to Hollywood in 1936 to recreate his successful role of Mio, the young man who wants to clear his father's name in *Winterset*. He landed the leading role of George in the successful film version of John Steinbeck's *Of Mice And Men* (1939) which was nominated for a Best Picture Oscar, and led to his playing a number of eccentric or comic roles in such pictures as Lubitsch's *That Certain Feeling* (1941), and *Tom, Dick And Harry* (1941), in which he was the lively, working-class non-conformist Harry who won the girl (Ginger Rogers). Effective as the war correspondent-observer-commentator Ernie Pyle in *The Story Of GI Joe* (1945), he went on to produce and co-star in *The Diary Of A Chambermaid* (1946) with his third wife, Paulette Goddard. In 1949 Meredith co-starred opposite Charles Laughton and directed *The Man On The Eiffel Tower*, adapted from Simenon and filmed in the new Ansco colour process on location in Paris—a combination he used to appealing visual effect.

Blacklisted during the 50s, his career was later revived by producer-director Otto Preminger and he found himself much in demand for elderly eccentric character parts. He was nominated for a supporting actor Oscar two years running for his performances as Karen Black's ex-vaudevillian father in *The Day Of The Locust* (1975) and as Mickey, the tough, old manager in *Rocky* (1976). JF

Robert Montgomery

Real name **Henry Montgomery Jr**
Born **Beacon, New York, 21 May 1904**
Died 1981

In the 30s Robert Montgomery was MGM's resident all-American playboy, steering the studio's Great Ladies through a series of glossy light comedies and drawing room dramas. No one was more sleekly groomed (when playing an air-express pilot in *Night Flight*, 1932, he wore evening dress under his flying clothes) or had a more persuasive way with smooth seducers and cowardly scions of the Park Avenue set. In *The Divorcée* (1930) he helped himself to Norma Shearer as casually and effortlessly as if she were a proffered cocktail.

Signed by MGM in 1928, he worked continuously for the studio until 1941. He was often cast in 'English' roles, notably in *Privates Lives* (1931) and *Busman's Honeymoon* (1940) as Dorothy L. Sayers's aristocratic sleuth, Lord Peter Wimsey. By 1937 Montgomery was chafing at his ladies' man image. After *The Last Of Mrs Cheyney* (1937), his sixth film with Joan Crawford, he badgered MGM into giving him the part of the homicidal maniac Danny in *Night Must Fall* (1937). The studio willed the film to fail, but it was a considerable critical and commercial success. Nevertheless, Montgomery had to look elsewhere for interesting roles, which he found in RKO's *Mr and Mrs Smith* (1941), and Columbia's *Here Comes Mr Jordan* (1941).

He joined the US Navy in 1941, returning to make John Ford's *They Were Expendable* (1945). He quarrelled with MGM over *Desire Me*, a 30s throwback with Greer Garson, and walked out soon after shooting started to direct himself as Philip Marlowe in *The Lady In The Lake* (1946).

Montgomery got out while the going was good after directing and starring in *Eye Witness* (1949). He prospered in television and became President Eisenhower's small-screen coach. In 1960 he directed *The Gallant Hours*, a biopic of Admiral Halsey, played by his old friend James Cagney. RC

Paul Muni

Real name Muni Weisenfreund
Born Lemberg, Austria, 22 September 1895
Died 1967

At his peak on the screen during the 30s, Paul Muni was one of the most highly respected film actors in the world, and was equally at home in contemporary pictures and in costume roles. In fact, his films neatly divide into two groups – the socially conscious dramatic pictures and thrillers like *Scarface* (1932) and *Black Fury* (1935) can be contrasted with the later group of costume films in which he played

such characters as Louis Pasteur, a Chinese peasant (in *The Good Earth*, 1936), Emile Zola, and the Mexican leader, Benito Juarez. Although he won an Oscar nomination for *I Am A Fugitive From A Chain Gang* in 1932, it was the later group which drew most praise at the time, including an Oscar for his performance as Pasteur in 1936, and both an Oscar nomination and the New York Film Critics Best Actor award for Zola the following year. Yet today it is the earlier group which is more highly regarded, *Scarface* most of all.

Muni's performance as the gangster, Tony Camonte, loosely based on Al Capone, exudes an incredible energy and vitality as he ruthlessly carves his way to the top only to die in a hail of bullets. He is like an overgrown child who delights in every acquisition, whether fancy clothes, a new girlfriend, or more sinister symbols of his status like a bullet-proof car or a new Tommy gun, which he treats like a toy. The picture made his name, and that of George Raft who played one of his gangster henchmen. But for Muni *Scarface*, filmed in 1931, marked a comeback to movies after a two-year gap.

He had originally appeared on the stage with his actor parents as a child, before emigrating to the US and establishing himself as a star of the Yiddish Art Theatre and on Broadway before being invited to Hollywood in 1929. He received an Oscar nomination for his first film, *The Valiant* (1929), but made only one more before returning to the stage until Hollywood beckoned again.

After *Scarface* Muni landed the superb role of the innocent man who is turned into a criminal on the run in *I Am A Fugitive*. Offered a contract on extremely favourable terms by Warner Bros., he selected his parts carefully, averaging only one or two pictures per year. By 1936 when the studio began to expand its production of prestige costumers and biopics, Muni had developed a special fondness for hiding behind disguises. To Bette Davis, who co-starred with him in *Juarez* (1938), this was a great mistake. 'The film audience wants to become familiar with certain physical attributes that are ever present in each performance,' she wrote in

her autobiography. 'There is no question that his technique as an actor was superb . . . (but) Mr Muni seemed intent on submerging himself so completely that he disappeared.' The failure of *Juarez* at the box office, followed by another flop, convinced Warner Bros. that Muni's star was on the wane and his contract was allowed to lapse. He had always been a difficult man to handle, and even his most successful pictures had been expensive to make. As producer Hal Wallis remarked, 'Every time Paul Muni parts his beard and looks down a telescope, this company loses two million dollars.'

He returned to the stage and had a hit with 'Key Largo', travelled to London to do 'Death Of A Salesman' in 1949, and had another hit in 1955 with 'Inherit The Wind'. He appeared in only a handful of pictures during the 40s, including the Oscar-nominated *Stage Door Canteen* (1943). His last, and notable, performance on film was as a sympathetic, slum doctor in *The Last Angry Man* (1959), for which he received his final Oscar nomination. JF

Muni (left) in I Am A Fugitive From A Chain Gang *(Warner Bros., 1932)*

Jack Oakie

Real name Lewis Delaney Offield
Born Sedalia, Missouri, 12 November 1903
Died 1978

A jolly, lively, slightly plump figure, Jack Oakie flourished on the screen during the late 30s and early 40s as a staple character actor, most often cast as the genial, but slightly dim-witted friend of the hero. He got his early stage experience in vaudeville and was signed by Paramount in 1928 when the talkies arrived. He had a leading role in the 1932 parody of the Olympics, *Million Dollar Legs* opposite W.C. Fields, provided friendly support to rivals Fredric March and Cary Grant in *The Eagle And The Hawk* (1933), and was once again Grant's genial but incompetent side-kick in *The Toast Of New York* (1937), RKO's biopic about the notorious Wall Street financier, Jim Fisk.

During the following years Oakie really came into his own. His hilarious take-off on Mussolini in the role of Benzini Napoloni in Chaplin's *The Great Dictator* (1940) earned him an Oscar nomination. Signed up by 20th Century-Fox, he played Shirley Temple's step-father in *Young People* (1940). Paired with Charlotte Greenwood as a small-time vaudeville couple, he claimed that the dance numbers were the most energetic of his film career and caused him to lose a stone in weight. In *Tin Pan Alley* which followed in 1940, Oakie gave one of his best performances as the songwriting partner of John Payne, the pair of them pursuing singer Kate Blane to London during World War I. Throughout the 40s, Oakie turned up in supporting roles but, after 1950 he worked only occasionally in films and on television. He had a cameo role in Mike Todd's *Around The World In Eighty Days* (1956), and made his last screen appearance in 1962 in the Doris Day comedy, *Lover Come Back*. JF

in The Toast Of New York *(RKO, 1937)*

Merle Oberon

Real name **Estelle Merle O'Brien Thompson**
Born **Bombay, India, 19 February 1911**
Died **1979**

A petite, exotic-looking and strikingly beautiful brunette, Merle Oberon arrived in England at the age of 17. She succeeded in establishing a totally fabricated version of her origins, claiming that she had been born in Tasmania and that her Eurasian mother who accompanied her was her maid. She worked as a café hostess, calling herself Queenie O'Brien, before becoming a film extra and bit player.

She was given her big chance by producer Alexander Korda, with a small but effective part as Anne Boleyn in *The Private Life Of Henry VIII* (1933) and as Lady Blakeney in *The Scarlet Pimpernel* (1934). She became much in demand in Holly-wood, and it was soon clear that she was the single most successful star ever discovered and developed by Korda, whom she married in 1939, two years after her near-fatal car crash had caused Korda to abandon his ambitious, half-completed *I Claudius*. Commuting between London and Hollywood, Merle alternated weak vehicles designed for her by Korda, like the Technicolored *Over The Moon* (1937) and *The Divorce Of Lady X* (1939), with more prestigious American productions. She gave a fine performance in *These Three* (1936) and had her best role ever as the beautiful Cathy in *Wuthering Heights* (1939). Although she had real style, her talent as an actress was limited. In spite of some good roles in the 40s (she divorced Korda in 1945) her career was in decline and was virtually over by 1948, but for a handful of appearances, including in a film called *Interval* (1973) which she produced and co-edited, before confining herself to a fourth husband. JF

Warner Oland

Real name **Werner Ohlund**
Born **Umea, Sweden, 3 October 1880**
Died **1938**

'Not always wise to accept simple solution. Mind like parachute. Only function when open'. Such allegedly Chinese aphorisms delivered at a suitably measured pace by a tall, bulky, Oriental gentleman in a white hat and tropical suit, sporting a pencil-thin moustache, conjures up the vision of that inscrutable Chinese detective of the screen, Charlie Chan, otherwise known as Warner Oland.

Although other actors played Chan, it was Oland who made the role his own from 1931 up until his death in 1938. A Swede who came to the US aged 10, be began his career in the theatre, designing sets, translating Strindberg and acting. He entered silent films in 1912, appeared in numerous serials, played many character heavies and soon became type-cast as an Oriental. He did land other parts occasionally, like that of Jolson's rabbi father in *The Jazz Singer* (1927). But it was Josef von Sternberg who gave him his best role, as Chang, the villainous, half-caste warlord in *Shanghai Express* (1932). JF

ZaSu Pitts

Born **Parsons, Kansas, 3 January 1898**
Died **1963**

A small, dark figure sits wrapped in her shawl, a finger placed pensively on her lips as she thinks up a new way to outwit her honest but simple-minded husband. This classic image of ZaSu Pitts as Trina, the heroine of Erich von Stroheim's silent master-piece, *Greed* (1924), draws attention to one of the outstanding, subtle characterisations of the silent cinema. By the end of the picture Trina appears prematurely aged, totally transformed in appearance from the young, single girl of the opening. Clearly, ZaSu was a fine actress.

She went on to play a leading role in Stroheim's *The Wedding March* (1927) and the hero's mother in *All Quiet On The Western Front* (1930), but even by this early date her dramatic parts had been forgotten and she had begun to be typecast as a comedienne. Thus, ZaSu was replaced by a far inferior actress in the final version of the film and went on to appear mainly in comedies thereafter. As a small, pert, slightly dotty spinster type of indeterminate age she appeared in a series of Hal Roach comedy shorts with Thelma Todd during 1931–33. Many more pictures followed, ranging from the W.C. Fields comedy, *Mrs Wiggs Of The Cabbage Patch* (1934) though to the Doris Day–James Garner spoof, *The Thrill Of It All*, and Stanley Kramer's *It's A Mad, Mad, Mad, Mad, World* (both in 1963). By the time of her death in 1963 she had been in pictures for almost half a century, having started out with Mary Pickford in 1917. JF

in Their Big Moment *(RKO, 1934)*

Dick Powell

Born **Mountain View, Arkansas,**
14 November 1904
Died **1963**

Dick Powell was known in the 30s as a boyish, energetic, wavy-haired tenor in a stream of Warner Bros. musicals; in the 40s as a tough guy in *films noirs*; and in the 50s as the host of 'The Dick Powell Show', a pioneering series of TV Drama. He also directed a number of films including the ludicrous *The Conqueror* (1955), with John Wayne as Genghis Khan, and two competent war films with Robert Mitchum, *The Enemy Below* (1957) and *The Hunters* (1958). Most memorably, Powell was the wide-eyed, juvenile lead partnering naive Ruby Keeler in the Busby Berkeley musicals, *42nd Street* (1933), *Gold Diggers Of 1933*, and *Dames* (1934). He usually introduced a song in his dangerously high voice, before Berkeley went into his flights of choreo-graphic fantasy. It is Powell's leering face that bursts through a picture of girls reclining in the title number of *Dames*, and is seen at the end of a tunnel of female legs in *42nd Street*. His second wife, Joan Blondell, also appeared with him in several Warner Brothers musicals.

After seven years with Warners, he began to get more variable and demanding roles, as in René Clair's clairvoyant comedy, *It Happened Tomorrow* (1944). His image soon changed from soft tenor to hardboiled private eye in *Murder My Sweet* (1944), and he continued with craggy roles in low-budget dramas such as *Johny O'Clock* (1947), and, at MGM, co-starred with his third wife June Allyson in *Right Cross* (1950) and *The Reformer And The Redhead* (1950), and played the best-selling novelist in *The Bad And The Beautiful* (1952). He ended his screen career in *Susan Slept Here* (1954), a strained sex comedy with fifty-year-old Powell as young Debbie Reynolds' father figure/lover. RB

Eleanor Powell

Born Springfield, Massachusetts, 21 November, 1912
Died 1982

Billed as 'The World's Greatest Tap Dancer' and 'The Queen of Ra-Ta-Taps', Eleanor Powell beat a tattoo through ten MGM musicals between 1935 and 1943. Leggy, toothy, ever-smiling Eleanor began dancing at the age of 11 and reached Broadway at 17, where she became a hit in Ziegfeld shows and 'George White's Scandals'.

She came to Hollywood for the role of the switchboard operator in *Broadway Melody Of 1936*, but so impressed Louis B. Mayer that he offered her the romantic lead. 'Oh, Mr. Mayer, you can't do that,' she told him. 'I don't know anything about the camera. You have a girl in this picture who dances, sings, is sexy and everything – she's magnificent. You'd just be wasting your time.' Mayer insisted, got the studio's cosmeticians to beautify her homely

in 1936

features, and she became a star overnight. Powell went on to make two more *Broadway Melodies* (1938 and 1940), and the appropriately titled *Born To Dance* (1936), all backstage stories the finales of which mainly involved Eleanor in silver top hat and spangled tuxedo on a battleship with sequined cannons and hundreds of singing and dancing sailors. (Her singing voice was always dubbed). 'When I danced at Metro,' she recollected. 'Everybody used to come over and watch, including other stars. It was like playing to a live audience. You'd hear applause, and people would yell out, 'Go Ellie. Show 'em.' It egged you on like a racehorse.'

After *Lady Be Good* (1941), Powell continued at MGM to lesser effect in two Red Skelton comedies, *Ship Ahoy* (1942) and *I Dood It* (1943), the latter being one of Vincente Minnelli's first assignments. She retired from the screen shortly after marrying Glenn Ford in 1943, only reappearing in a guest spot in *The Duchess Of Idaho* (1950). They divorced in 1959 and Eleanor, who never remarried, spent her time doing charitable work. RB

William Powell

Born Pittsburgh, Pennsylvania, 29 July 1892
Died 1984

The typical, well-remembered image of William Powell as the debonair, middle-aged gentleman, with his neatly trimmed moustache and immaculate dress, first became familiar to film audiences during the 30s. But it was not always so. He had been in pictures for a decade or so before his sophisticated image began to catch on. In the silents he had been playing villains since 1922, when he was first cast as Moriarty in the John Barrymore version of *Sherlock Holmes*. But Powell made the most of things, stealing many of the pictures he appeared in, for the villain was often the most interesting part.

At Paramount for seven years (1924–31), Powell appeared in two last memorable silents directed by Josef von Sternberg in 1928 – *The Last Command* and *The Dragnet* – then had a major success with his second talkie, *The Canary Murder Case* (1929) in which he played the gentleman detective Philo Vance for the first time. (He later appeared in three sequels.) Drawing on his early stage experience, Powell, was one of the few silent stars whose career was boosted by the coming of sound. He had a fine

voice and was clearly maturing into an exceptional film actor, but he was unhappy with the kind of roles which Paramount was giving him, although they did put him in two pictures with Carole Lombard who became his second wife in 1931. Powell's short stint at Warner Bros. (1931–34) was not much better. Then, in 1934, he made his first for MGM, *Manhattan Melodrama* with Myrna Loy and Clark Gable. He and Miss Loy worked well together and were immediately paired in the highly successful *The Thin Man* and again in *Evelyn Prentice* (both 1934), followed by *Reckless* in (1935) in which Powell appeared with his new fiancée, Jean Harlow, for the first time. (He had divorced Lombard in 1933; Harlow died without them having married).

For Powell 1936 was his peak year. He was reteamed with Loy and Harlow (and Tracy) in the delightful screwball comedy, *Libelled Lady*, followed by the successful *After The Thin Man*. *The Great Ziegfeld* with Powell in the title role won the Best Picture Oscar, while he was nominated for the second time for his performance in *My Man Godfrey*. The first had been for *The Thin Man*, and his third came in 1947 for his delightful performance in *Life With Father*. His screen appearances now became fewer but continued into the mid-50s, ending with the role of Doc in *Mr. Roberts* (1955). JF

Tyrone Power

Born Cincinatti, Ohio, 5 May 1913
Died 1958

Tyrone Power grew up in show business and was the third actor in his family to bear that name. His great-grandfather had been a distinguished Irish actor in the early 19th century, while his father, who was born in London and emigrated to the US, was a famous matinee idol who appeared in many silent pictures prior to his death in 1931. Tall, dark, and strikingly handsome, Power was a likeable star of limited talent who made most of his pictures for one studio, 20th Century-Fox. He was discovered by producer Darryl Zanuck and the studio's leading contract director, Henry King, who directed him in eleven pictures beginning with *Lloyds Of London* in 1936 which first shot the young actor to stardom. During the following years he was cast in many of the studio's prestige productions – costume drama, musicals and the occasional western during the late 30s, progressing to action pictures and swashbucklers during the 40s.

Power's genial but relatively bland personality served to blend well with his co-stars. During his earliest period as a star, he was cast in romantic roles in forgettable pictures designed to boost new female stars like Loretta Young, Sonja Henie and Alice Faye. His three films with the contrastingly blonde Faye were the best, and included the studio's tribute

to Irving Berlin, *Alexander's Ragtime Band* (1938). When the studio ventured into Technicolor, he was the star of the first hit, *Jesse James* (filmed in 1938) and went on to appear in a pair of extremely stylish costumers, *Blood And Sand* (1941) with Rita Hay-

worth and *The Black Swan* (1942) with Maureen O'Hara. (Each won the Oscar for colour cinematography in consecutive years.) He gave adequate performances in both, but was at his best as a swashbuckler in the dual leading role in *The Mark Of Zorro* (1940) – demonstrating the affected airs of a fop in public but secretly operating as a masked avenger by night.

After war service, Power attempted to broaden his range with dramatic pictures (*The Razor's Edge*, 1946, *Nightmare Alley*, 1947)) and comedies (*The Luck Of The Irish* and *That Wonderful Urge*, both 1948) mixed in with the costumers, but without much success. His career was clearly running out of steam, and many of the studio's best roles with Power's favourite director, Henry King, were going to Gregory Peck. He was originally meant to do *The Robe* (1953), the first CinemaScope film, but ended up with the undistinguished *The King Of The Khyber Rifles* (1953) instead. During this period he occasionally returned to the stage, and he had one last memorable role in *Witness For The Prosecution* (1958), but could not really compete in the acting stakes with his more illustrious co-stars Laughton, Lanchester and Dietrich.

Power may not have been a great actor, but in private life he was, according to David Niven, 'everybody's favourite person ... that great rarity – a man who was just as nice as he seemed to be.' He died prematurely of a heart-attack while location filming in Spain. JF

George Raft

Born **New York City, 26 September 1895**
Died **1980**

Raised in the notorious Hell's Kitchen district, George Raft was a small-time boxer and ballroom dancer with supposed underworld connections, before breaking into films in 1929. Although his range as an actor was extremely limited, he managed to establish himself as a star by projecting a strikingly mean and insolent image which he hardly varied from film to film. As one of Paul Muni's gangster associates in *Scarface* (1932), he first made his mark on the screen with the coin-flipping gesture which became his trademark, a gesture which – according to director Howard Hawks – was meant to symbolise a new kind of cool defiance and hostility. His portrait of a tough but nattily dressed nightclub boss in *Night After Night* (1933) helped further to establish his screen persona, although the picture is better remembered today for Mae West's cinema debut. He spent his early years at Paramount, but appeared to fit in better at Warner Bros. where he played Cagney's prison sidekick in *Each Dawn I Die* (1939) and was teamed with Bogart as a trucker in *They Drive By Night* (1940). He sent up his own image in *Some Like It Hot* (1959), meanwhile having become heavily involved in owning gambling casinos, and was the subject of a feeble biopic, *The George Raft Story* (1961). JF

in Song Of Surrender (Paramount, 1949)

Claude Rains

Born **London, England, 10 November 1889**
Died **1967**

It is surprising that the cinema took so long to discover him. On the stage since his youth, by the 20s Claude Rains had developed into a leading actor, widely acclaimed on both sides of the Atlantic. As a young man director Vincent Sherman recalled observing Rains at work, a slow but meticulous craftsman. 'His voice was outstanding: deep, rich, and resonant with a mellow dignity', and his performance expressed his 'special brand of humour and irony, sly looks and gestures'. In fact, these were qualities which only became evident to film audiences a decade later. For, with the coming of sound, when film studios were signing up all the available stage talent, he was ignored. Of course, he was very short and not at all handsome, and was reaching middle age, yet he was such a fine and intelligent actor with so strong a 'presence' that this neglect is difficult to understand.

It was a back-handed compliment to Rains's ability that, given his big chance by British director James Whale as *The Invisible Man* (1933), he was so successful through the use of his voice alone. He continued to alternate between stage and film, but the quality of his pictures improved after he signed with Warner Bros. in 1936. The studio was just embarking on a series of prestigious costumers and found Rains ideally suited for them, although he was most often cast as a 'heavy'. He appeared in *Anthony Adverse* (1936), *The Prince And The Pauper* (1937) and *The Adventures Of Robin Hood* (1938), in which he and Basil Rathbone made a superbly villainous English pair. The following year he received the first of his four Supporting Actor Oscar nominations for his performance as a corrupt senator in Frank Capra's *Mr Smith Goes To Washington*.

Rains continued active in pictures throughout the 40s, averaging two to three per year and maintaining an extremely high standard in a wide variety of roles. He earned a well-deserved second Oscar nomination for his suave but opportunistic chief of police in *Casablanca* (1943), and was nominated again the following year for *Mr Skeffington* opposite Bette Davis. After starring with Vivien Leigh in a disastrously expensive British production of *Caesar And Cleopatra* (1945), he was again Oscar-nominated for his portrayal of one of the most memorable of Hitchcock villains in *Notorious* (1946). 'He was extremely human,' François Truffaut noted, 'It's rather touching – the small man in love with a taller woman.' To which Hitchcock replied, 'Yes, Claude Rains and Ingrid Bergman made a nice couple, but in the close shots the difference between them was so marked that if I wanted them both in frame, I had to stand Rains on a box.' He made several screen appearances in the 50s and 60s, including one as Herod in *The Greatest Story Ever Told* (1965), and even managed to intersperse his busy career with no fewer than five marriages. JF

Luise Rainer

Born **Vienna, Austria, 12 January 1910**

An established star on the Viennese stage with a few minor movies to her credit, Luise Rainer was brought to Hollywood in 1935 by MGM and shot to stardom the following year, winning successive Oscars during 1936–37. But by 1938 her brief film career was virtually finished, bringing to an end one of the most baffling of Hollywood success stories.

An attractive, petite brunette with soulful and expressive eyes, her film performances gave little indication of any great talent as an actress. She was most effective in romantic dramatic roles in films such as *Escapade* (1935), or *The Great Ziegfeld* (1936) in which she co-starred with William Powell. Her Oscar for the latter is all the more surprising in that her performance as Anna Held was so small a role as to hardly qualify for more than 'supporting actress' consideration. Another role as a long-suffering wife, although far removed from the glamorous world of Florenz Ziegfeld – that of a Chinese peasant in *The Good Earth* (1937), earned her second Oscar. A handful of later pictures during 1937–38 were anti-climactic, and she sank into obscurity as swiftly as she had reached stardom. JF

Basil Rathbone

Born **Johannesburg, South Africa,
13 June 1892**
Died **1967**

Tall, slim, angular and athletic, Basil Rathbone was one of the most durable of screen villains. His career spanned almost half a century from *Innocent* (1921), a British silent, to *Hillbillys In A Haunted House* (1967). An early stage career in Britain led to Broadway and on to Hollywood in the 20s. He divided his time between films and theatre for many years until the introduction of sound when he could make use of his fine voice in such pictures as *The Last Of Mrs Cheyney* (1929), one of MGM's first talkies, co-starred with Norma Shearer.

His film career nonetheless moved slowly – until 1935. That year marked a major turning point, with Rathbone establishing himself as the screen's leading villain. He played the nasty Mr Murdstone in *David Copperfield*, was Garbo's snobbish, cold and hypocritical husband in *Anna Karenina*, then Pontius Pilate in *The Last Days Of Pompeii*, and finally a rival

French pirate captain who fought a memorable duel to the death with Errol Flynn in *Captain Blood*. Nominated for an Oscar for the relatively small role of Tybalt in *Romeo And Juliet* in 1936, the year that a new Oscar category had been created for 'supporting actor', it is reasonable to assume that this honour was not just for this performance alone, but a recognition of his previous screen achievements.

Rathbone's portrayal of the hunchback king in *If I Were King* in 1938 earned him a second Oscar nomination, but again he lost out (to Walter Brennan). That same year he had two of the most memorable roles of his career at Warner Bros. as the villainous Sir Guy in *The Adventures Of Robin Hood*, and as the uncompromising but guilt-ridden major in *The Dawn Patrol*. It was a chance remark at a Hollywood party that apparently gave Darryl Zanuck the idea of signing Rathbone to star as Sherlock Holmes. He closely fitted author Arthur Conan Doyle's description as tall and lean with penetrating eyes and a hawk like nose. The cycle of 14 pictures which followed established Rathbone for all time as the definitive Holmes, with Nigel Bruce as Dr Watson. JF

in Bathing Beauty (MGM, 1944)

in Little Caesar (First National, 1930)

Edward G. Robinson

Real name **Emmanuel Goldenberg**
Born **Bucharest, Rumania,
12 December 1893**
Died **1973**

Probably the best Hollywood actor and most important star never to be so much as *nominated* for an Oscar, Edward G. Robinson was small and ugly, but he had great style and screen presence, and was one of the most dedicated and hard-working of actors. An extremely intelligent and cultured man, he spoke many languages and built up one of the finest private art collections in the world. But in spite of being a big star, he had little interest in the cinema and was overly dismissive of his own great contribution to it.

Having emigrated to the US as a child, he developed an interest in the theatre which was interrupted by war service. During the 20's, however, he emerged as an outstanding actor and regarded the theatre as his true *métier*. After his first big hit, playing a gangster in 'The Racket', he was inundated with film offers. He agreed to do a few

in My Daughter Joy (British Lion/Columbia, 1950)

pictures, mainly for the money, but after one of his plays flopped badly, he signed a contract with Warner Bros. and did not appear on the stage again for over twenty years.

Originally cast in a relatively small role in *Little Caesar* (1930), he apparently had to convince producer Hal Wallis that the lead role of Caesar Enrico Bandello was made for him. As an early talkie the picture may seem crude by modern standards, yet it had action, punchy dialogue and the remarkable menace and vitality of Edward G. Robinson. A big box office success, it turned him into a star overnight and set the tone for the many gangster movies which followed. Unfortunately, it also meant that he had to fight against being typecast as a heavy throughout the rest of his career. But he did succeed in playing a wide range of roles, and his outstanding performances succeeded in lifting many otherwise second-rate pictures.

Robinson was excellent as the tough newspaper editor in *Five Star Final* (1931) and was instrumental in earning the picture an Oscar nomination as Best Picture. In *The Whole Town's Talking* (1935) he gave a virtuoso performance in the dual role of a tough gangster and a timid, look-alike bank clerk. He struggled to get Warner Bros. to do one of his pet projects, *Confessions Of A Nazi Spy* (1939), an excellent and topical film made in semi-documentary style which was ahead of its time. Yet Robinson himself was apparently disappointed at the result. Of all his plays and films, he was proudest of *Dr Ehrlich's Magic Bullet* (1940), a picture with a strong social theme in which he proved he could match Paul Muni in his ability to submerge himself in a historical role. Although he hesitated before accepting third billing (below Barbara Stanwyck and Fred MacMurray) in *Double Indemnity* (1944), he clearly stole the picture with one of his most memorable screen portraits, as the shrewd but sympathetic insurance claims investigator.

Unfairly victimised by the post-war 'Red scare' in the US, Robinson found it difficult to get work for a time. As he wrote in his autobiography, 'I was doomed, both by age and former political leanings, to a slow graveyard. The top directors and producers wouldn't have me ... What I needed was recognition again by a top figure in the industry.' That figure turned up in the unlikely shape of Cecil B. DeMille, who cast Robinson in the major role of Nathan in *The Ten Commandments* (1956). Thus, he was able to round out his long and distinguished career in style, with leading character roles in such pictures as *A Hole In The Head* (1959), *Two Weeks In Another Town* (1962), *The Cincinnati Kid* (1965) and finally *Soylent Green* (1973), released just 50 years after his first picture in 1923. Robinson was awarded a special honorary Oscar in 1973, but died shortly before it was due to be presented. JF

Ginger Rogers

Real name **Virginia McMath**
Born **Independence, Missouri, 16 July, 1911**

'He gives her class and she gives him sex', remarked Katharine Hepburn on Ginger Rogers' glorious partnership with Fred Astaire. They two-stepped into the dance-hall of fame in nine RKO musicals beginning with *Flying Down To Rio* (1933) and ending with *The Story Of Vernon And Irene Castle* (1939). The cheeky, pert blonde proved the perfect foil to debonair Astaire in these tuneful, lighthearted comedies of errors, the best being *The Gay Divorcee* (1934), *Top Hat* (1935) and *Swing Time* (1936).

From early childhood Ginger was groomed for stardom by her divorced mother. At the age of 15 she began singing and dancing on the vaudeville circuit, later with her first husband Jack Pepper, billed as Ginger and Pepper. She started in pictures playing wise-cracking blondes for various studios in such films as Warners' *Gold Diggers Of 1933*. Ginger got the role in *Flying Down To Rio* only because Dorothy Jordan decided to get married rather than dance with the relatively unknown Fred Astaire. Despite her success in musicals, she was anxious to prove herself a serious actress. She showed her range playing working girls from the wrong side of the tracks, and moving into higher circles in two Gregory La Cava social comedies, *Fifth Avenue Girl* (1939) and *Primrose Path* (1940), and won a Best Actress Oscar in the title role of *Kitty Foyle* (1940). However, her forté was comedy as she demonstrated in George Stevens's *Vivacious Lady* (1938), where she pretended to be a student in professor James Stewart's class; and impersonated a 12-year-old in Billy Wilder's *The Major And The Minor* (1942). In *Lady In The Dark* (1944), Rogers played a fashion editor with her hair up, who had Freudian dreams

in Sitting Pretty *(Paramount, 1933)*

with her hair down.

Her films after the war were rather mediocre, excepting Howard Hawks's *Monkey Business* (1952). Ginger has since appeared on stage in Broadway musicals, 'Hello Dolly' and 'Mame'. In the early 70s, she became fashion consultant to the J.C. Penny retail chain store. Her second husband was actor Lew Ayres, her fourth was Frenchman Jacques Bergerac, 16 years her junior, and her fifth was actor-producer William Marshall. RB

Mickey Rooney

Real name **Joe Yule Jr**
Born **New York, 23 September 1920**

In 1938, the extraordinary, multi-talented 18-year-old Mickey Rooney was America's Number One box-office star, earning more than $300,000 annually. In the same year, he was awarded a special Oscar (as was Deanna Durbin) for his 'spirit and personification of youth.' In 1962, Rooney declared himself bankrupt, revealing that he has nothing left of the $12 million he had earned over the years. After being an MGM luminary for a decade, he was forced to appear in dozens of B movies to pay off his debts and alimony payments (he has been married eight times; Ava Gardner was his first wife, Martha Vickers his third.) But the pint-sized performer came bouncing back, making his Broadway debut in the highly successful 'Sugar Babies' in 1979.

Mickey's parents were in vaudeville, and he first appeared on stage at the age of 15 months, soon becoming part of the family act. He made his film debut as a midget in a short, later changing his name to Mickey McGuire, the character he played in a series of two-reel comedies. He became Mickey Rooney in 1932 when, aged 12, he started to appear in features. In 1934, he signed with MGM for whom he played a variety of brash kids, including Clark Gable as a boy in *Manhattan Melodrama* (1934). Loaned out to Warner Bros., he made his first real impact as a delightful Puck in Max Reinhardt's *A Midsummer Night's Dream* (1935), although he broke a leg during shooting and had to be wheeled around on a bicycle by concealed stagehands. Back at Metro, Mickey played tough, working-class boys opposed to prissy, patrician Freddie Bartholomew in *Little Lord Fauntleroy* (1936), *The Devil Is A Sissy* (1936) and *Captains Courageous* (1937).

In a modest comedy called *A Family Affair* (1937), Rooney played Andy Hardy, a small town judge's son continually getting into scrapes. It was the first of fifteen vastly popular Hardy Family films

– idealised, over-sentimental views of American family life. He was also effective as the bad boy reformed by priest Spencer Tracy in *Boy's Town* (1938), and in other examples of warm-hearted Americana such as *The Adventures Of Huckleberry Finn* (1939), *Young Tom Edison* (1940) and *The Human Comedy* (1943). As a youngster, Rooney's exuberance and talents were amply displayed in several lively musicals co-starring Judy Garland such as *Babes In Arms* (1939), *Strike Up The Band* (1940), and *Girl Crazy* (1943), in which he sang, danced, played a number of instruments, did imitations and handled comic and emotional scenes with equal aplomb. In 1944, he joined the army, but when he returned three years later, he had outgrown his juvenile roles and his popularity waned. He left MGM in 1948 and as a free-lance proved himself an able character actor in *Baby Face Nelson* (1957) and *Requiem For A Heavyweight* (1962). RB

in Girl Crazy *(MGM, 1943)*

in 1937)

Sylvia Sidney

Real name **Sophia Kosow**
Born **Bronx, New York, 8 August 1910**

Although Sylvia Sidney's film career was concentrated in the 30s decade, she was fortunate in working with many of the leading directors of the period – Lang, Hitchcock, Vidor, Sternberg, Wyler and Mamoulian among others.

She had left Broadway for Hollywood in 1930, was placed under contract by Paramount, and rushed into *City Streets* (1931) when Clara Bow fell ill. She was fortunate to have the sympathetic Rouben Mamoulian as director: 'He taught me, took care of me, and . . . gave me good training adjusting to a camera', she recalled. Petite and attractive, Miss Sidney had the most strikingly expressive blue-green eyes, but there was a slight sadness about her which led her to be cast most often in unhappy roles as the long-suffering, sad-eyed heroine of such pictures as *An American Tragedy* (1931), *Fury* (1936), and *Dead End* (1937). She was particularly memorable as Henry Fonda's faithful wife who joins him on the run in *You Only Live Once* (1937). Sylvia returned to the theatre in the 40s, but has made occasional film appearances since then and was nominated for a supporting actress Oscar for her touching performance as Joanne Woodward's mother in *Summer Wishes, Winter Dreams* (1973). JF

Barbara Stanwyck

Real name Ruby Stevens
Born Brooklyn, New York, 16 July 1907

One of the most professional and hard working of Hollywood actresses, Barbara Stanwyck has had a long and distinguished career playing a wide variety of roles in pictures of widely varying quality. Yet she herself always gave of her best and was highly regarded by the directors and others she worked with, who invariably have the nicest things to say about her. Cecil B. DeMille's remark that 'I have never worked with an actress who was more cooperative, less temperamental and a better work-man' (sic) draws attention to her tough, resilient, and self-reliant qualities. And director Joseph H. Lewis notes that, 'Miss Stanwyck has always been a down-to-earth, gutsy type of gal. It dates back to her childhood, from what I understand. She admired the pioneers who travelled west (which may explain why she made so many westerns).' As one of the most convincing of the female western stars, she never looked out of place in male garb and doing a man's work, yet she could be extremely feminine and funny, too. Slim and attractive, with shapely legs, she sported the body of an ex-dancer (which she was). Yet her beauty was slightly unconventional, and matched by her distinctive 'cracked-ice' voice. From early in her career she projected a real style and individuality, blending charm with toughness, intelligence with vulnerability.

Stanwyck had a difficult childhood. Orphaned at the age of five, she was brought up by an elder sister who also introduced her to show business. She became quite successful on the stage as a dancer and made the transition to straight acting roles during the late 20s, first on the stage and then in films. Fiercely independent, even at that early stage in her career, she refused to sign an exclusive contract, but mainly worked alternately between Columbia and Warner Bros.

She was excellent in the title role in *Night Nurse* (1931), opposite a young Clark Gable and directed by William Wellman, who handled a number of her early Warners pictures. But best known of her early roles is that of the young heroine in *The Bitter Tea Of General Yen* filmed in 1932. She played an

American woman who has just arrived in China and who develops an extraordinary love-hate relationship with a ruthless Chinese warlord, played by Nils Asther, who holds her captive, and by whom she is both attracted and repelled. A very atmospheric picture, making liberal use of soft focus photography, it appears a bit dated today, but Miss Stanwyck's performance already projects that mixture of independence and vulnerability which became her trademark in later years. And she was sexy.

The last and best of a group of her pictures directed by Frank Capra at Columbia, *General Yen* reflected the kind of Oriental theme which was very much in vogue at the time. (*Shanghai Express* with Dietrich, *The Mask Of Fu Manchu* with Myrna Loy and *The Hatchet Man* are some other examples of the same period). Similarly, her gold-digger role in *Baby Face* (1933) coincided with Jean Harlow's *Red Headed Woman* and Mae West's *I'm No Angel*, not to mention the *Goldiggers Of 1933*. In fact, Stanwyck's early career reads like a history of 30's Hollywood genre cycles, including, for example, a series of early

gangster-prison-thriller pictures: *The Locked Door* (1930), *Illicit* (1931) and *Ladies They Talk About* (1933). She had her first western role as *Annie Oakley* at RKO in 1935, and contributed to the brief pre-war reappearance of the A-Western, cast in *Union Pacific* (1939) with Joel McCrea. Here she demonstrated her ability to handle difficult, and sometimes dangerous, action sequences, much to the delight of old C.B. DeMille and true to her image as a tough and resilient actress who would develop into an authentic western star during the 50s revival of that genre.

She proved her range in handling dramatic roles with a moving and sympathetic portrait of the long-suffering wife and mother in Goldwyn's remake of *Stella Dallas* (1937). This performance earned her an Oscar nomination for the first time, and it was clear that she was reaching her peak as an actress. Much in demand, she alternated between good dramatic roles in pictures like *Golden Boy* (1939), *Remember The Night* (1940), and *Meet John Doe* (1941) which reunited her with director Frank Capra, and . . . screwball comedies! This was a genre in which Stanwyck the star excelled, and which was highly popular at the time. *Breakfast For Two* (1937) with Herbert Marshall was followed by *The Mad Miss Manton* (1938) opposite Henry Fonda; and she was reteamed with Fonda in *The Lady Eve* (1941), she as a worldly-wise con woman, he as a bumbling, absent-minded but rich scientist who falls in and out of love with her. In the follow-up picture, *Ball Of Fire* (also 1941) Gary Cooper was the professorial type who falls for her gum-chewing gangster's moll, Sugarpuss O'Shea, who is hiding out from the cops and her gangster boyfriend. The culmination of her personal comedy cycle, this performance duly earned her a scond Oscar nomination.

In *Ball Of Fire*, she wore a sexy, slit dress. She displayed her legs more fully and gave another excellent performance as the *Lady Of Burlesque* (1943), again directed by Wellman, then turned on the sex appeal to ensnare Fred MacMurray in *Double Indemnity* (1944). Although the conception of her part as a deadly blonde *femme fatale* was a bit shallow, her performance was exceptional and earned her a third Oscar nomination. In addition, it marked a new stage in her career. She became one of the leading stars of 40's *film noir*, as reflected in the leading roles which she now played. *The Strange Love Of Martha Ivers* with Van Heflin and Kirk Douglas (making his film debut) was followed by *The Two Mrs Carrolls* with Bogart (both 1946). *Sorry, Wrong Number* (1948) was the best of that group of pictures in which she played a vulnerable woman menaced, here by Burt Lancaster, and it won her a fourth Oscar nomination. Then *The File On Thelma Jordan* in 1949 brought the cycle full circle in a re-working of the *Double Indemnity* set-up, but with Wendell Corey in the Fred MacMurray role as the man she exploits.

A major western revival during the 50s gave a boost to many of the middle-aged male stars like Stewart, Gable and, of course, Wayne. But Stanwyck was one of the few actresses who proved herself capable of matching the men at their own game. During the last active period of her film career she established herself as a hard-boiled, no-nonsense Western 'heavy' in such pictures as *Cattle Queen Of Montana* (1954) with Ronald Reagan, and *The Violent Men* (1955) opposite Edward G. Robinson. And she rounded off the cycle with *Forty Guns* (1957), in a role made for her, as the tough boss of the county with 40 hired gunmen by her side. Reaching the age of 50, she had lost none of her adventurous, spunky qualities. Director Sam Fuller tells how his stuntmen were a bit wary of doing one of the most dangerous stunts in the picture. But Stanwyck did it herself – falling off her horse and being dragged along the ground with her foot caught in the stirrup.

She had her biggest success during the 60s in her own TV Western series, 'The Big Valley', and in 1981 she was awarded a special – and very well-earned – honorary Oscar. JF

with Gary Cooper in Meet John Doe *(Warner Bros., 1941)*

with Ray Milland (seated right) in California *(Paramount, 1947)* ▷

Anna Sten

Real name Annel (Anjuschka) Stenskaja Sudakevich
Born Kiev, Russia, 3 December 1908

Best remembered today as the Russian-born actress whom producer Sam Goldwyn was unable to turn into a star, Anna Sten was strikingly attractive, with a well-developed figure to match. She had a brief career on the stage and spent some time with Stanislavsky's famous Moscow Art Theatre before appearing in a number of silent films. Miss Sten first came to the attention of the international public as an appealing Grushenka in a German version of 'The Brothers Karamazov' retitled *Der Mörder Dimitri Karamasoff* (1931).

Signed by Goldwyn the following year and

in A Woman Alone (Rank, 1936)

brought to Hollywood, she was cast in the role of Zola's *Nana*. Unfortunately, the weak script hardly bore any relation to the original novel and Miss Sten had trouble with her English. The original director was replaced by the more sympathetic Dorothy Arzner (in 1933) but the script problems were never solved. In the role of the fallen woman, Anna Sten appeared on the screen as a pale imitation of Marlene Dietrich with even an attempt at a deep, Dietrich-like singing voice. In spite of an elaborate publicity campaign, the picture was a flop, and Miss Sten's two followup vehicles, *We Live Again* (1934) with Fredric March and *The Wedding Night* (1935) cast opposite Gary Cooper, fared no better. Goldwyn released her from her contract and she made a few more pictures, including one or two for British producers, but her film career was effectively over before it had begun. JF

Margaret Sullavan

Real name Margaret Brooke
Born Norfolk, Virginia, 16 May 1911
Died 1960

Dedicated to the theatre throughout her life, Margaret Sullavan was a reluctant film star. During the years 1933–41 she made only a dozen or so pictures, dividing her time between Universal and MGM, and returning to her first love, the theatre, whenever possible.

Small and frail-looking with a distinctively husky voice, she was attractive in a simple, unaffected and down-to-earth manner which led her to be cast most often as the nice, girl-next-door type. She specialised in portraying suffering heroines on the screen, in adaptations of the romantic fiction of the period like *Little Man What Now?* (1934) and *Next Time We Love* (1936) with James Stewart. Her peak years came at MGM, beginning with *Three Comrades* in 1938 in which she played the tragically ill heroine suffering nobly in post-war Germany. Through the

quality of her playing she was able to give greater depth and meaning to such potentially saccharine roles – here earning her only Oscar nomination, along with the New York Film Critics Award.

This was but one of four pictures she made with director Frank Borzage, widely regarded as the Hollywood master at bringing this type of tragic romantic story alive on the screen. Miss Sullavan was re-teamed with James Stewart in three more pictures – *The Shopworn Angel* (1938), and *The Shop Around The Corner* (1940) both delightful bittersweet comedies, and *The Mortal Storm* (1940), directed by Borzage, in which she returned to her more tragic roles. A big success on Broadway in 1943 with 'The Voice Of The Turtle' confirmed her undiminished love of the theatre, and she spent most of her last years on the stage, only returning for one last film in 1950, ironically titled *No Sad Songs For Me*. She died of an overdose of barbiturates, following on a fraught personal life, aged 49. JF

Robert Taylor

Real name Spangler Arlington Brugh
Born Filley, Nebraska, 5 August 1911
Died 1969

Robert Taylor spent almost his entire film career at MGM and this immediately tells a lot about him. He was a modest and accommodating man, a star who fulfilled his studio assignments with a minimum of fuss. He retained fond memories of his early years at MGM, recalling in 1964: 'I wish today's young actors had a studio and boss like I had. It groomed us carefully, kept us busy in picture after picture, thus giving us exposure, and made us stars.' And with regard to Louis B. Mayer: 'He was kind, fatherly, understanding and protective. He gave me picture assignments up to the level that my abilities could sustain at the time, and was always there when I had problems.'

Inevitably, the progress of Taylor's career was closely wedded to the fortunes of the studio. As a handsome, romantic leading man he appeared opposite Harlow, Garbo, Shearer, Crawford, Margaret Sullavan and Hedy Lamarr. Variety was the keynote – he rarely had the same co-star twice and never became part of a romantic pairing like Gable–Harlow or Powell–Loy. He was first spotted performing in amateur theatricals at college and was signed by MGM in 1934. He shot to stardom during 1935–36 in a series of major pictures which included *Broadway Melody Of 1936* with Eleanor

Powell and *Magnificent Obsession* opposite Irene Dunne (both 1935) followed by co-starring roles with Janet Gaynor, Loretta Young and Joan Crawford and finally played Armand in *Camille* (1936). A classic example of miscasting opposite Garbo, with Lionel Barrymore as his father, he here demonstrated an ability to submerge himself in a role even if his limitations as an actor meant that he did not have anything positive to contribute.

It was around this time that Taylor made two pictures with Barbara Stanwyck whom he married in 1939. (They divorced 12 years later.) He was *A Yank At Oxford* in 1938, married Margaret Sullavan in *Three Comrades* later that year, then joined Vivien Leigh on *Waterloo Bridge* in 1940. But the weakness of many of his early 40s vehicles already reflected the beginning of the decline at MGM. (During these years the studio lost Garbo, Shearer and Crawford and began to concentrate more on musicals.) This became even more apparent when Taylor returned to the studio after war service.

Although he never developed as an actor, as he matured he became noticeably less bland and was offered more complex and interesting roles. He was at his best in an unusual part as a hard-done-by American Indian in *Devil's Doorway* (1950), the first of his many 50's Westerns. He followed this with the lead roles in MGM's two big costume hits of the period, *Quo Vadis?* (1951) and *Ivanhoe* (1952). But from this point on, his star, like that of the studio, was noticeably on the wane, although he continued acting in pictures virtually up to his death. JF

Shirley Temple

Born **Santa Monica, California, 23 April 1928**

Franklin D. Roosevelt stated in 1935, 'During this Depression, when the spirit of the people is lower than at any other time, it is a splendid thing that for just fifteen cents an American can go to a movie and look at the smiling face of a baby and forget his troubles.' (She smiled most of the time, anyway!)

The President was, of course, referring to the world's biggest and smallest star from 1934 to 1938, Shirley Temple. She was a bright-eyed, curly-topped dimpled cherub, whose chirpy singing and toddler's tap-dancing were perfect antidotes to the Depression. Her message was 'Be Optimistic' which she sang in *Little Miss Broadway* (1938). Her biggest hits were 'On The Good Ship Lollypop' from *Bright Eyes* (1934) and 'Animal Crackers In My Soup' from *Curly Top* (1935), sung while skipping between tables at an orphanage lunch. In *Stowaway* (1936), she displayed her considerable talents by impersonating Eddie Cantor, Al Jolson, and Ginger Rogers (dancing with a Fred Astaire doll).

Shirley made her first screen appearance before she was four in a series of one-reelers called 'Baby Burlesks', imitating Marlene Dietrich and other stars. With her ambitious mother behind her, she was signed by Fox, making an impression singing 'Baby Take A Bow' in *Stand Up And Cheer* (1934). She soon became a national institution and, after her first year in movies, she received a special Oscar 'in grateful recognition of her outstanding contribution to screen entertainment during the year 1934.' 'I stopped believing in Santa Claus when I was six' she remembers, with a mixture of amusement and regret. 'Mother took me to see him in a department store and he asked me for my autograph.'

John Ford directed her in *Wee Willie Winkie* (1936), changing the sex of Kipling's little hero to suit Shirley. However, as she approached her second decade, Fox, and the public, began to lose interest in her, though she continued to make films until 1949

in Little Miss Marker *(Paramount, 1934)*

for various studios. She was the bobby-soxer with a crush on Cary Grant in *The Bachelor And The Bobby Soxer* (1947) and worked for Ford again in *Fort Apache* (1948) co-starring her husband, John Agar. Shirley divorced him in 1949 and married businessman Charles Black in 1950. Known officially as Shirley Temple Black, she went into politics, becoming the US representative to the UN in 1968, and ambassador to Ghana from 1974 to 1976. RB

Franchot Tone

Real name **Stanislas Pascal Franchot Tone**
Born **Niagara Falls, New York, 27 February 1905**
Died **1968**

Most often cast as the successful and cultivated gentleman, a rich playboy or an upper class cad, Franchot Tone's roles reflected his own background. He was born into a well-to-do family, and educated at Cornell University where he first developed an interest in the theatre. Signed by MGM in 1933, he appeared in an average of five to six films per year, most often typecast in supporting roles. He had one memorable year, however, in 1935, when he gave an excellent performance as a devil-may-care officer friend of Gary Cooper in *The Lives Of A Bengal Lancer*, supported Bette Davis in her first Oscar-winning role in *Dangerous*, and was nominated for an Oscar himself for his playing of midshipman Roger Byam in *Mutiny On The Bounty* (which won the Best Picture Oscar). He also married Joan Crawford, but divorced her in 1939, the year he left MGM. Among his later films of note were *Five Graves to Cairo* (1943) in which he played a British officer disguised as a waiter and *Phantom Lady* (1944) as a psychopathic murderer. He worked mainly in the theatre during the 50s, but returned to Hollywood in 1962 to play the weak and aging US President in Preminger's *Advise And Consent*. JF

Spencer Tracy

Born **Milwaukee, Wisconsin, 5 April 1900**
Died **1967**

The most solid and durable of film stars, Spencer Tracy appears to have been incapable of giving a bad performance, although one may suspect that his seeming expertise was a bit too easy. He was rarely called upon to stretch himself as an actor and, in his mature years, became increasingly difficult to work with and did too few movies of note. Yet he was undoubtedly one of the great natural film actors. Surprisingly, he was screen tested by a number of the studios during the late 20s and considered unsuitable, possibly due to his rugged, chunky appearance. It was not until he had a big hit on the stage as Killer Meers in 'The Last Mile' coinciding with a new interest in gangster pictures, that he was signed by Fox in 1930.

Such was the pace of events that, even before he reached California, MGM had released a prison movie, *The Big House* (in June 1930), which required a rethink of Tracy's first picture, a similar prison yarn called *Up The River* (1930). According to the film's director, John Ford, the script was 'junk' anyway, but Ford set about turning it into a comedy with the help of his two talented new stars, Bogart and Tracy, who were both appearing in their first feature: 'There was no awkwardness at all. Spence was as natural as if he didn't know a camera was there, or as if there had *always* been a camera when he acted before.'

Although Tracy made a few interesting pictures at Fox during the following years, such as *The Power And The Glory* (1933) scripted by Preston Sturges, his best roles were generally on loan-out to other studios – *20,000 Years In Sing Sing* filmed by Warner Bros. in 1932, *A Man's Castle* (1933) for Columbia. Fox had been badly hit by the Depression, and did not really recover until Zanuck took over the reins in 1935. But by that time Tracy had signed a new contract with MGM where he soon emerged as a star of the top rank. In 1936 he starred with Sylvia Sidney as an innocent man accused of murder in Fritz Lang's *Fury*, supported Powell, Harlow and Loy in *Libelled Lady*, demonstrating his talent for comedy, and won his first Oscar nomination as the down-to-earth priest in *San Francisco*. Choosing his roles carefully, he only appeared in two or three pictures per year, but won

consecutive Oscars for *Captains Courageous* (1937) in which he played a Portuguese fisherman, and *Boys Town* (1938), as Father Flanagan, the first of his biopic roles. He followed with Stanley (to Hardwicke's Livingstone) in 1939 and played *Edison, The Man* in 1940.

Late in 1941 Tracy's career (and life) was changed by his teaming with Katharine Hepburn in *Woman Of The Year*. Their close personal relationship lasted till the end of his life; the best of their many pictures together during the 40s was *Adam's Rib* in 1949. Tracy received his fourth Oscar nomination for his likeable, gruff performance as *The Father Of The Bride* (who was Elizabeth Taylor) in 1950. He was equally convincing as the tough, one-armed avenger figure in *Bad Day At Black Rock* (1955). Chalk up Oscar nomination number five, while number six followed soon after for his *The Old Man And The Sea* (1958). Difficult to work with and in ill health, most producers considered him unusable, but Stanley Kramer disagreed and cast him in four of his last five pictures. These included further Oscar-nominated performances for *Inherit The Wind* (1960), *Judgment At Nuremberg* (1961) and, posthumously, *Guess Who's Coming To Dinner*. He died a few weeks after filming was completed. JF

Johnny Weissmuller

Born Windber, Philadelphia, 2 June 1904
Died 1984

Olympic historians cherish Johnny Weissmuller as the winner of five gold medals, in 1924 and 1928, and the holder of 67 world records. Everyone else remembers him as Tarzan, churning through the lakes of a make-believe rain forest to grapple with giant crocodiles or swinging through the tree-tops to protect his jungle subjects from white hunters, ivory poachers and Nazi agents. Nobody was ever so completely identified with a role. Esther Williams was a star when she put on a bathing suit, Weissmuller had his carefully arranged loincloth. He may have been crammed into a business suit for *Tarzan's New York Adventure* (1942), but the 'Big Apple' was just a 'stone jungle', and he was soon happily diving off the Brooklyn Bridge. His one attempt to break the mould, in *Swamp Fire* (1946), is forgotten.

Weissmuller got the part of Edgar Rice Burrough's jungle hero without a screen test. His graceful physique was considered sufficient, since the dialogue was limited to grunts and monosyllables – to the dismay of Rice Burroughs, whose novels portrayed the ape man as the cultivated Lord

in Tarzan Triumphs *(RKO, 1943)*

Greystoke. For all his years with Maureen O'Sullivan's loquacious Jane (and later the lively Brenda Joyce) Weissmuller's Tarzan never became one of the screen's great raconteurs. The first three Tarzan films – *Tarzan The Ape Man* (1932), *Tarzan And His Mate* (1934) and *Tarzan Escapes* (1936), were solid productions, but after the death of Irving Thalberg in 1936 the budgets on the Tarzan features were cut back. In *Tarzan Finds A Son* (1939), Weissmuller and O'Sullivan acquired a child companion, 'Boy' (Johnny Sheffield). In 1942, after six films, O'Sullivan left the series and in the same year Weissmuller moved from MGM to RKO.

The first RKO feature, *Tarzan Triumphs* (1942), struck a topical note, pitting Johnny against a gang of Nazi agents. He declared 'Now Tarzan make war', an unusually verbose utterance, but he might just as well have said 'Now Tarzan make Bs'. At RKO production values took a spectacular nosedive and Weissmuller finally bowed out after *Tarzan And The Mermaids* (1948). He exchanged his loincloth for a safari suit in Sam Katzman's Jungle Jim series – 'Tarzan with clothes on', as one wag put it. Between 1948 and 1956 he appeared in 20 'Jungle Jim' adventures, rock-bottom second features whose imaginative use of all kinds of stock footage gave the series a uniquely surreal charm. RC

Mae West

Born Brooklyn, New York, 17 August 1892
Died 1980

Perhaps the most remarkable thing about Mae West was her sublime ability to turn all the conventional notions about sex on their heads while at the same time prowling around, with that marvellous swaying matelot's roll, like one of the 'grandes horizontales' of the 1890s. The Edwardian era was her spiritual home, and her epigrammatic dexterity the equal of Oscar Wilde's. Her body had the fullness and ripe, flowing lines of Art Nouveau, rounded out still further with feather boas and enormous hats frothing with feathers. She was comfortable. She never needed to paw her men – she just sat back and drank them in, especially if the object of her attention was the stunning young Cary Grant of *She Done Him Wrong* and *I'm No Angel*. There is very little obvious sex in her films. It was something to be savoured rather than described, smouldering away in West's monumental languor and drawling innuendo, both of which encouraged the mind's eye to conjure up visions of steamy encounters either just concluded or about to begin. The last laugh, however, was always on the audience. A revealing moment comes at the beginning of *I'm No Angel*. As West glides into the wings of a circus sideshow, having wowed the open-mouthed hicks with 'They Call Me Sister Honky Tonk', she murmers, 'Suckers'.

She started on the stage at the age of six in Hal Clarendon's stock company. By 1914 she was a vaudeville star billed as 'The Original Brinkley Girl'. She invented the 'shimmy' dance, and in the 1920s began to write, produce and direct her own plays. The first of them, 'Sex' (1926), earned her a 10-day jail sentence on an obscenity charge. She was already celebrating the ambiguities and absurdities of the aforementioned subject – most of the characters in 'The Pleasure Man' were female impersonators, a delicious irony when one considers that West's playful caricature of female glamour forms the bedrock of all drag acts. Her first film was Paramount's *Night After Night* (1932). She was fourth billed, but earned $5,000 a week for 10 weeks work and wrote her own lines. Later, the film's star, George Raft, recalled, 'Mae West stole everything but the cameras'.

Paramount increased her salary to $8,500 a week and turned her loose on *She Done Him Wrong* (1933), a screen version of her play 'Diamond Lil', set in her favourite stamping ground, the gay 90s. In *I'm No Angel* (1933) she was outrageous as a lady lion tamer – 'a girl who lost her reputation but never

in She Done Him Wrong *(Paramount, 1933)*

missed it'. No star ever had the buildups Mae awarded herself, and the formula worked. *I'm No Angel* grossed $3 million and saved Paramount from bankruptcy. But the prudes were beginning to close in: *Belle Of The Nineties* (1934) was subjected to the stricter enforcement of the Hays Office production code. Nevertheless, 'Photoplay' described it as 'a triumph of Mae over matter', and Paramount came up with a new contract for two films at $300,000, including $100,000 for the story (in 1935 she was the highest paid woman in America). *Goin' To Town* (1935), with Mae as a rustler's widow trying to crash society, managed to drive a coach and horses through the Hays Code, but in her later films her ample comedy was encased in a straitjacket. In *Every Day's A Holiday* (1938) the double entendres were banished altogether, and the results were predictably dull. After her stormy collaboration with W.C.

Fields in *My Little Chickadee* (1939), she made only one more film, *The Heat's On* (1943), a low-budget nightclub musical. She had to content herself with the thought of all those downed airmen bobbing about in the drink wearing their inflatable 'Mae West' life-savers.

After the war, she toured in 'Diamond Lil' and worked up a marvellous cabaret act in which she surrounded herself with muscle men. She was Billy Wilder's first choice for Norma Desmond in *Sunset Boulevard* (1950) – Miss West was not flattered – but she had to wait another 20 years before her comeback in *Myra Breckinridge* (1970), adapted from Gore Vidal's sex-change satire. It was a dismal film, but Mae stayed gloriously afloat while the rest of the cast sank without trace. Alas, the kindest thing one can say about her last film, *Sextette* (1978), is that it was a mistake. RC

Fay Wray

Born **Alberta, Canada, 15 September 1907**

Long before she became the scream queen of the 30s and the apple of King Kong's monstrous eye, Fay Wray was a raven-haired ingenue in silent Westerns at Universal, providing the love interest for a host of cowboys. She was chosen as a Wampas Baby Star in 1926, and the following year she moved from oaters into the big time in Erich von Stroheim's *The Wedding March* (1927).

Paramount paired her in several films with Gary Cooper, and in the early 30s she co-starred with action hero Jack Holt in *Dirigible* (1931), *The Woman I Stole* (1933), *Master Of Men* (1933) and *Black Moon* (1934). Inevitably, these have been overshadowed by the series of classic horror films on which her fame rests today. In Tod Browning's *Doctor X* (1932) she narrowly escaped death at the hands of Preston Foster's 'Moon Monster'. In Michael Curtiz's *The Mystery Of The Wax Museum* (1933) Lionel Atwill was intent on turning her into one of his exhibits. Worse was to follow in *The Vampire Bat* (1933), in which he almost succeeded

in giving her a disagreeable transfusion of his blood substitute.

In RKO's *The Most Dangerous Game* (1932) she fled through jungle sets with Joel McCrea, pursued by a mad Russian aristocrat. The same sets were then lined up for a more ambitious project. Producer Merian C. Cooper told Wray that she was going to have 'the tallest, darkest leading man in Hollywood'. Anticipating Clark Gable, she got King Kong. There may have been better and more beautiful actresses than Kong's miniature leading lady, but as Ann Darrow, Wray provided an unforgettable combination of sex appeal and vulnerability as she wriggled helplessly in his outsize fist, and she certainly possessed the necessary lung-power for the role.

After *King Kong* (1933) there was a slow decline. In 1939 she divorced her husband, screenwriter John Monk Saunders, who had become a drug-sodden alcoholic. In 1942 she married producer Robert Riskin and retired, but made a comeback in the 50s after nursing him through a long, fatal illness. She appeared in TV's 'Pride Of The Family' series, and as a harassed member of the older generation in a number of 'teen agony' exploitation Bs, including *Rock Pretty Baby* (1956). RC

Diana Wynyard

Real name **Dorothy Cox**
Born **London, 16 January 1906**
Died **1964**

Stately and gracious, Diana Wynyard brought an understated warmth to the films she made in Hollywood in the early 30s.

She made her London stage debut in 1925, with a walk-on part in 'The Grand Duchess'. Seven years later she enjoyed a long, triumphant run on Broadway in 'The Devil Passes', with Basil Rathbone. MGM signed her to play the Princess Youssoupoff in *Rasputin And The Empress* (1932) and, surrounded by the colourful antics of the Barrymores, she gave a performance of great natural charm. She went to Fox for Frank Lloyd's meticulous recreation of Noel Coward's *Cavalcade*, one of the surprise hits of 1933, in which Coward found her 'entrancing', and for which she was Oscar-nominated. At MGM she made *Men Must Fight* (1933), with Lewis Stone,

in An Ideal Husband (*British Lion, 1947*)

and *Reunion In Vienna* (1933) with a teetering John Barrymore. Then she was loaned to RKO for *Where Sinners Meet* and *Let's Try Again* (both 1934), two rather wordy films with Clive Brook. By now she was typecast in 'British' subjects, and her next film was Universal's *One More River* (1934).

Disenchanted with Hollywood, Miss Wynyard returned to Britain, remaining off screen until the 1939 *On The Night Of The Fire*, with Ralph Richardson. In the same year she was Mrs Disraeli in *The Prime Minister*, then gave a luminous performance as Anton Walbrook's persecuted wife in *Gaslight* (1939), the original screen version of Patrick Hamilton's chiller, directed by Thorold Dickinson. *Freedom Radio* (1941) was a phoney Resistance drama, and *The Prime Minister* (1941) a lumbering piece of wartime moral uplift. *Kipps*, also 1941, was directed by Carol Reed, whom she married in 1943 (they were divorced in 1947). She continued to grace the English stage until her premature death through illness, making very few films, her last being Fox's *Island In The Sun* (1957). RC

Loretta Young

Real name **Gretchen Michaela Young**
Born **Salt Lake City, Utah, 6 January 1913**

She was known as 'Hollywood's beautiful hack', a tag earned by her durable, well-defined and rather empty glamour. In the early 30s her lovely profile was often blurred by floods of tears in films in which she portrayed young working girls who marry older men. But she also had a serviceable comic touch and, beneath the apple cheeks and big, swimming eyes there was a tough professional – her husband Grant Withers called her 'the steel butterfly'.

Loretta Young was one of four sisters, all of whom were put to work as extras by their mother. Her first acting role came by chance, when she stood in for her sister Polly Ann in a Colleen Moore vehicle, *Naughty But Nice* (1927). She was adored by Lon Chaney in *Laugh Clown Laugh* (1928), and then signed with Warners for whom her first starring role was in the all-talking *The Squall* (1929). In *The Careless Age* (1929), she formed an effective partnership with Douglas Fairbanks Jr which continued in *The Fast life* (1929), *The Forward Pass* (1930), *Loose Ankles* (1930), *I Like Your Nerve* (1931) and *The Life Of Jimmy Dolan* (1933). In *Road To Paradise* (1930) she was married to an elderly Conway Tearle, a pattern repeated in *The Right Of Way* (1931), with Conrad Nagel, *Too Young To Marry* (1931), with Grant Withers, and *The Hatchet Man* (1923), with Edward G. Robinson.

Some of the best films of her career came in this

early period, including *Platinum Blonde* (1931), in which she was Jean Harlow's rival; *Taxi* (1932), a snappy outing with Cagney; *Zoo In Budapest* (1933), and *Man's Castle* (1933).

In 1934, Miss Young moved to Zanuck's new 20th Century, where she had a big success in *The House Of Rothschild* (1934) and looked beautiful in *Clive Of India* (1935). Then, at Paramount, she made *The Crusades* (1935), once again marrying an older man, this time Henry Wilcoxon.

After *Ramona* (1936), she moved into comedy with *Ladies In Love* (1936) and *Love Is News* (1937), both with Tyrone Power, but grew restless with the studio (now 20th Century-Fox), quarrelled over parts and pay, and left after *Wife, Husband And Friend* (1939).

She was out of work for a year until Columbia's *The Doctor Takes A Wife* (1940). The once expensive star took a salary cut, then second place to Alan Ladd at Paramount in a wartime actioner, *China* (1943), and a gooey romance *And Now Tommorrow* (1944), in which she was a deaf socialite. She co-starred with Gary Cooper in *Along Came Jones* (1945) and played fugitive Nazi Orson Welles' wife in *The Stranger* (1946). She was becalmed when, to everyone's surprise, she won the Best Actress Award for her performance as a Swedish farm girl in *The Farmer's Daughter* (1947). It failed to arrest the decline, and MGM's *Key To The City* (1950) was her last big film. Her career petered out in the early 50s with a string of Bs, the last being *It Happens Every Thursday* (1953), after which she slid happily into a long-running TV show. RC

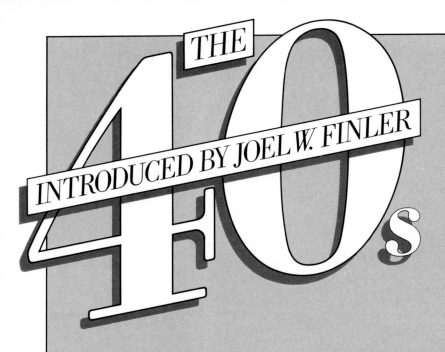

THE 40s

INTRODUCED BY JOEL W. FINLER

Havilland won a landmark court case against Warner Bros. in 1945, which meant that the severely restrictive and punitive provisions of the contract system were now outlawed by the courts.

First off the mark in producing war pictures had been, not surprisingly, Warner Bros. With its outstanding line-up of action directors and tough male stars, and a special interest in bringing topical subjects to the screen, the studio could easily switch from thrillers and gangster movies to war pictures and war-related spy thrillers. *Confessions Of A Nazi Spy* starring Edward G. Robinson appeared early in 1939, while as early as 1938 the studio had begun fighting the Germans again in a series of World War I films beginning with *The Dawn Patrol* starring Errol Flynn and David Niven.

The top hits and Oscar winners tended to be patriotic, 'war-related' pictures rather than actual combat films. Cooper and Bergman fought the Fascists in Spain in *For Whom The Bell Tolls* (1943) and Selznick's *Since You Went Away* (1944), starring Claudette Colbert and Jennifer Jones, depicted the trials and tribulations of a family on the home front. But the biggest hit of the 40s was Goldwyn's *The Best Years Of Our Lives* (1946) about the experiences of a group of servicemen returning to civilian life after the war. A starry cast was led by Fredric March, Myrna Loy, Dana Andrews and Teresa Wright, and included real-life soldier Harold Russell who, thanks to World War II, had hooks for hands. The picture clearly demonstrated Goldwyn's ability to gauge the tastes of contemporary audiences. These pictures introduced a new, younger generation of film stars, alongside those established stars from the 30s who were still at their peak.

MGM, the studio which had dominated the 30s, had its biggest

The outbreak of war in Europe toward the end of 1939 had a major effect on the United States, and finally brought the economic problems of the 30s to an end. The war years saw a return to full employment for the first time since the beginning of the Depression and, correspondingly, a boom in film attendance. In a decade full of contradictions, Hollywood had its most profitable and successful years during the early and mid-40s, but attendances fell back toward the 70 million mark by the end of the decade. In addition, the studios were troubled by union problems and strikes during the postwar years, followed by the 'Red scare' investigations which led to the notorious blacklist. At the same time the government's 'consent decree' of 1948 forced the large studios to sell off their film theatres and give up their previous 'monopolistic practices' such as the system of block booking which forced exhibitors to take movies they didn't want.

After the war people turned to new interests and activities. A boom in car buying meant mobility, and a greater choice for those no longer looking to their neighbourhood cinema for entertainment, but, at the same time, this resulted in the growth of drive-in cinemas. A similar boom in home building, and in the sale of radios, gramophones and many other home appliances, reflected an expansion of activity in and around the home, even before the arrival of television. The nature of filmgoing changed from a regular, habitual activity to a more selective one, in which a visit to the cinema became something of an occasion. Wartime restrictions had caused a fall in the number of films being produced, of course, while the important overseas market had shrunk considerably, and many of the leading stars joined the armed services or spent time touring, entertaining troops and selling war bonds. However, the quality of the pictures improved. Newly developed lenses, faster film stock and improved methods of sound recording and mixing were put to good use by talented directors and technicians, following the example of new arrival Orson Welles and his cameraman Gregg Toland. The 40s represented the high point of studio film-making, although there was a trend toward shooting more on location during the postwar years. Although the studios themselves were still in a relatively strong position, their power was being eroded as the decade developed. More stars and directors were opting for independent status. The studios were forced to loosen their grip, allowing a greater artistic freedom to the large number of directors turned producer-director, such as Wyler, Hitchcock, Curtiz, Ford and King Vidor, and a new prestigious group of writer-directors, including Welles, Wilder, Huston, Mankiewicz, Rossen and Preston Sturges, who had proved their worth. Between them, these men accounted for the vast majority of the Oscar winners and top box office hits of the decade. Olivia de

Marlene Dietrich, appropriately garbed, was one of dozens of stars who did their bit for the war effort. Here, she is with troops at the Olympic Stadium in Berlin, during a visit to the resident garrisons in 1945.

hit and only Oscar winner of the decade with *Mrs Miniver* (1942) starring Louis B. Mayer's new discovery, Greer Garson. A superior propaganda picture which showed how a British middle-class family coped with the Blitz and the effects of the war, it contributed immensely to the tide of pro-British sentiment sweeping the US during the dark days of 1942. But MGM was already beginning to slip from its top spot and experienced a major turnover in stars around this time. Garbo, Shearer and Crawford were gone, along with James Stewart, the Marx Brothers, Robert Montgomery and Robert Young, and even Gable was lost – to the armed services for three and a half years. New stars of note included Lana Turner, Hedy Lamarr, Van Johnson, Elizabeth Taylor and Robert Walker, but most important of all was the studio's expanded schedule of musical productions developed by executive producers Arthur

Rehearsing on set at RKO studios in 1943, the inimitable Fred Astaire. The film was The Sky's The Limit, *his partner, not Ginger this time, but Joan Leslie.*

Freed and Joe Pasternak. This was the area in which the studio emerged as the undisputed leader during the mid-40s, with an impressive new line-up of talent that included Gene Kelly, Esther Williams, June Allyson and Kathryn Grayson. Frank Sinatra and Lucille Ball arrived from RKO, while Fred Astaire was coaxed out of semi-retirement, and Judy Garland emerged as one of the superstars of the decade.

The glossy Technicolor musical had first been promoted in a big way by 20th Century-Fox during the early 40s with a mainly new group of stars led by Betty Grable, Carmen Miranda and Alice Faye. MGM took up the challenge but, Vincente Minnelli apart, the studio clearly suffered from a lack of outstanding directors, and failed to maintain the quality of its black-and-white pictures.

Although filming in colour grew only slowly, all the studios got in on the act – mainly with musicals and other escapist fare which appealed to wartime audiences. The small Columbia used Technicolor to promote its new star discoveries, led by Rita Hayworth and Cornel Wilde. Over at Universal, Maria Montez was cast in a series of exotic colour fantasies, followed later in the 40s by the sultry Yvonne de Carlo. Even Sam Goldwyn had his own Technicolor star, the redheaded Danny Kaye, one of a large number of redheads who suddenly began to brighten up the movie screens. (Others included Maureen O'Hara, and the new British star, Deborah Kerr, in addition to Rita Hayworth, Lucille Ball, and Rhonda Fleming). Yet two of the top studios were surprisingly slow to take advantage of the possibilities offered by colour. At Paramount Bing Crosby was the top box-office star of the decade, but appeared in relatively few colour pictures. Most of his hits were in black-and-white, including a number of the popular 'Road' series with Bob Hope and Dorothy Lamour. Similarly, Warner Bros. interest in colour only developed toward the late 40s to spotlight the talents of a fresh blonde musical star – Doris Day.

If the colour musicals of the 40s represented the icing on the cake, the bread and butter was still the solidly crafted black-and-white film-making which was extending in new directions. The vast majority of the leading directors preferred it, as did many of the top stars like Bette Davis, Humphrey Bogart, John Garfield, Katharine Hepburn, and others who were rarely or never seen on the screen in colour prior to the 50s. A few stars like Joan Crawford and Claudette Colbert were even convinced that they didn't look well in colour, and managed to avoid it until relatively late in their careers.

It was the black-and-white pictures which reflected most accurately the mood of the time. There was little of the optimism and complacency after the war of the sort which had fuelled the isolationism and excesses of the post-World War I years. The explosion of the atomic bomb had ushered in a new era, and the Cold War kept international tensions high. Returning veterans in vast numbers faced problems, the status of the Negro was improving, and more women were employed in full time jobs. The New Look introduced by Dior marked a return to traditional feminine glamour. The 'Red scare' paranoia of the post-war years, inflamed further by the media, led to spurious loyalty tests and witch hunts. The most notorious was that of HUAC (House Un-American Activities Committee) which was assured of spectacular headlines when it set out to investigate the supposed Communist infiltration of Hollywood. Unfortunately, this came at the very time (1947) when the studios were introducing serious political and social themes into their pictures. In 1947 *Gentleman's Agreement*, dealing with the problem of anti-semitism, won the Best Picture Oscar.

But most important of all was the emergence of *film noir* during the mid-40s, a style of crime thriller which served to introduce many important new stars like Burt Lancaster, Robert Mitchum, Robert Ryan, Alan Ladd, Veronica Lake, Richard Widmark, while giving a new boost to the careers of established stars like Stanwyck, Bogart, Dick Powell, Joan Crawford, Joan Bennett, Edward G. Robinson, Claire Trevor and Ida Lupino. Within the low-keyed (and relatively low-budget) thriller or gangster framework, many of the leading script-writers and directors of the time found that they could express their concern with the current state of American society. Most favoured themes dealt with the corruption of police, politicians, and businessmen. The hero was often a returned war veteran disturbed by what he found – like Van Heflin in *The Strange Love Of Martha Ivers* (1946), or Bogart in *Dead Reckoning* (1947). Similarly, the theme of anti-semitism was tackled in the 'noir' thriller *Crossfire* (1947). Many of the *film noir* writers, directors and stars were among those singled out for attack by HUAC. The 'Hollywood Ten', all of whom served short prison sentences for their refusal to co-operate with the witch hunt, happened to include the producer (Adrian Scott) and director (Edward Dmytryk) of *Crossfire*, while writer Albert Maltz had the scripts of *This Gun For Hire* (1942) and *The Naked City* (1948) to his credit. Other leading contributors to *film noir* who were later blacklisted for their left-wing associations included John Garfield and Edward G. Robinson, and directors Joseph Losey and Abraham Polonsky. One of the sorriest episodes in the history of Hollywood, the blacklist came at a time when the film industry could ill afford to lose so many of its leading creative talents. Thus, the 40s decade ended on a distinctly downbeat note.

Photographed at Washington Airport, Humphrey Bogart (left), Evelyn Keyes and Danny Kaye, members of a large protest delegation of stars, confer before seeing the House Unamerican Activities Committee.

with Marie Windsor in Abbott And Costello Meet The Mummy *(Universal, 1955)*

Abbott and Costello

Real name **William A. Abbott**
Born **Ashbury Park, N.J., 2 October 1895**
Died **1974**

Real name **Louis Francis Cristillo**
Born **Paterson, N.J., 6 March 1906**
Died **1959**

Early in his career, chubby little Lou Costello was a stuntman who once doubled for Dolores Del Rio. This unlikely combination now seems funnier than anything in the films Costello made in the 40s with his partner, straight man Bud Abbott. Of all the top screen comics, theirs is the humour that has least improved with age; it remains firmly fixed in the cross-talk patter routines of their burlesque days, the most famous of which was the 'Who's On First' sketch, which concerns a first baseman with the name of Who.

Abbott and Costello came up the hard way in the 30s. Years in burlesque were rewarded with a spot on Kate Smith's radio show, and their sudden popularity led to a 1939 Broadway revue, 'The Streets Of Paris'. In 1940, Universal signed them for supporting roles in their first film, *One Night In The Tropics*, an adaptation of the Earl Derr Biggers story 'Love Insurance' starring Allan Jones, Robert Cummings and Nancy Kelly. Universal had some bizarre saviours over the years – Bela Lugosi, Deanna Durbin, Ma and Pa Kettle, Francis the Talking Mule. In the 40s the studio thanked God for Abbott and Costello. After *One Night In The Tropics*, they were signed to a long-term contract and put into uniform for *Buck Privates* (1941), which featured two of their favourite routines, 'The Dice Game' and 'Army Drill', and the Andrews Sisters, who sang

ing players and musical interludes: the Andrews Sisters returned for *In The Navy* (1941) and were joined by Dick Powell, who didn't mind slumming it as long as he retained his star billing; *Ride 'Em, Cowboy* (1942) co-starred Johnny Mack Brown and Dick Foran and had Ella Fitzgerald and the Merry Macs singing 'A Tisket A Tasket'; *Pardon My Sarong* (1942) was enlivened by the Ink Spots, Lionel Atwill and Virginia Bruce.

Production values were higher on MGM's *Rio Rita* (1942), an updated version of the old Broadway musical, with Nazis taking over the ranch where Bud and Lou were working. It was the first of three films at Culver City, the other two being *Lost In A Harem* (1944) and *Abbott And Costello In Hollywood* (1945). In 1942, Bud and Lou were No 1 at the box-office, but their enormous success was rapidly outrunning their comic invention which, in truth, now consisted of little more than stringing together their familiar old burlesque turns. Moreover, while fat, frightened Lou could handle slapstick with ease, weasel-faced Abbott was a straight man pure and simple, with no talent for physical comedy.

Abbott (left) and Costello in The Time Of Their Lives *(Universal, 1946)*

'The Boogie Woogie Bugle Boy Of Company B'. Intended as a flat rental B picture, *Buck Privates* hit a note of topicality – it opened with a shot of President Roosevelt signing the draft law in a Universal news clip – and was a smash hit. By the end of 1941, theatre owners voted Bud and Lou No 3 at the box-office, after Mickey Rooney and Clark Gable. All their early films were beefed up with good support-

In the late 40s, Universal tried to revive the duo's flagging popularity by teaming them with the monsters from the studio's classic horror films. The first in an uneven and increasingly low-budget series was *Abbott And Costello Meet Frankenstein* (1948), with Lon Chaney, Bela Lugosi and Glenn Strange as the Monster. Vincent Price turned up at the end as the voice of the Invisible Man. The film's success prompted Universal to team the boys with Boris Karloff in *Abbott And Costello Meet The Killer, Boris Karloff* (1949), a comedy-thriller through which Karloff paced with wary dignity as a fake medium. Later, the Invisible Man, Dr Jekyll and Mr Hyde and the Mummy were press-ganged into co-starring with Bud and Lou, along with Captain Kidd (played by Charles Laughton, repeating his 1946 role as the dreaded privateer) and the Keystone Kops. Only the Creature from the Black Lagoon had the good taste to avoid the buffoonery.

Their first colour film was *Jack And The Beanstalk* (1952), directed by an old B feature hand, Jean Yarbrough. By the mid-50s, however, they had slipped down to poverty row status. Their last film together was *Dance With Me, Henry* (1956), which they produced themselves and released through United Artists. The threadbare plot, which revolved around an old amusement park, was about as run down as their screen partnership. After their split, Costello made one last, sad solo effort, *The Thirty-Foot Bride Of Candy Rock* (1959). RC

in Pardon My Sarong *(Universal, 1942)*

June Allyson

Real name **Ella Geisman**
Born **New York City, 7 October 1917**

In the 40s, many an MGM movie was enlivened by the peppy presence of June Allyson. In the 50s, she regularly played the little, lip-quivering waiting wife. She waited for hubby James Stewart in three films – to recover from a leg amputation in *The Stratton Story* (1949), to return from the war in *The Glenn Miller Story* (1954), and from a flying mission in *Strategic Air Command* (1955). She looked up at the sky again in *The McConnell Story* (1955) as husband Alan Ladd tested jets, and exuded sweet wifely support to Van Heflin in *A Woman's World* (1954) and William Holden in *Executive Suite* (1954), both trying for job promotion. Jose Ferrer had the audacity to cast this embodiment of marital patience as a nagging wife in *The Shrike* (1955).

Petite and husky-voiced, Allyson trained as a dancer and was a Broadway chorus girl in her teens, also appearing in several two-reel shorts. MGM offered her a contract for *Best Foot Forward* (1943), after she had been in the Broadway version. June was soon being given girl-next-door roles in *Two Girls And A Sailor* (1944) and *Music For Millions* (1944), and played Kathryn Grayson's protective sister in the turn-of-the-century *Two Sisters From Boston* (1946). Her best musical role was in the bouncy, campus caper *Good News* (1947), a remake of the 1930 Bessie Love vehicle, and she gave a good account of herself as the tom-boyish Jo in *Little Women* (1949), a part played previously by Katharine Hepburn. Allyson also suffered by comparison with Claudette Colbert in the musical remake of *It Happened One Night*, entitled *You Can't Run Away From It* (1956), directed by her husband Dick Powell. June gave up films in 1959, did some TV work, then retired after Powell's death in 1963. RB

Dana Andrews

Born **Collins, Mississippi, 1 January 1909**

Dana Andrews was already thirtyish when he broke into films, but he quickly established himself as a star during the mid-40s, dividing his time between Goldwyn and 20th Century-Fox. Quiet, deliberate and calm, he always appeared slightly less than secure, in spite of his good looks, and was often cast as a basically good guy who turns out a loser. Thus, in his first notable role in *The Oxbow Incident* (1943) he was the innocent victim of a lynch mob. He had the best role of his career as the dedicated detective in *Laura* (1944), directed by Otto Preminger who also used him as the sleazy hero of *Fallen Angel* (1945) and a compromised cop in *Where The Sidewalk Ends* (1950).

Andrews's career peaked in 1946 with one of the best of World War II films, *A Walk In The Sun*, followed by the Oscar-winning *The Best Years Of Our Lives*. He had nothing new to offer during the 50s, appearing in Fritz Lang's last two American productions, both 40s-style thrillers. From then on he was cast mainly in routine roles, setting the pattern which he has maintained ever since, as a reliable supporting actor in occasional pictures throughout the 60s and 70s. JF

in 1947

Eve Arden

Real name **Eunice Quedens**
Born **Mill Valley, California, 30 April 1912**

After some stage experience and bit parts in a few films, Eve Arden's screen persona was established in her first major picture, *Stage Door* (1937), as a sophisticated, wordly, wise-cracking character actress. 'It would be a terrific innovation if you could get your mind to stretch a little further than the next wisecrack' Katharine Hepburn remarks at one point. To which Eve replies, 'You know, I tried that once, but it didn't snap back into place.'

Most often playing the friend, confidante, sister or secretary to the hero or heroine, she became a fixture in dozens of Hollywood movies during the 40s and 50s, from the acrobatic Peerless Pauline tricking Groucho in *At The Circus* (1939) to James Stewart's faithful and efficient secretary in *Anatomy Of A Murder* (1959). She usually got the best lines, occasionally stole the picture, and was invariably peeved at the attitude of the other characters towards her. As she complained to Joan Crawford, 'I'm awfully tired of men talking to me man to man.' The picture was *Mildred Pierce* (1945) and she received an Oscar nomination for her performance. During the 50s she became well known as the star of 'Our Miss Brooks' on radio, TV and in a 1956 film. Unfortunately, her screen appearances since 1960 have been few and far between. Most recently she brought a bit of much needed class to *Grease* (1976) as the high school principal. JF

Richard Attenborough

Born **Cambridge, England, 29 August 1923**

Small in stature, with boyish looks and a slightly scared, insecure quality, Richard Attenborough was almost inevitably type cast in his early pictures. His screen debut was as a frightened young stoker in *In Which We Serve* (1942); he played a youthful gangster in *Brighton Rock* (1947), and, at 26, gave an excellent and convincing performance as a bullied schoolboy half his real age in *The Guinea Pig* (1949). Having appeared in far too many second-rate pictures during the 50s, he formed his own production company in 1959 with writer-director Bryan Forbes. Their first together was *The Angry Silence* (1960), but *Seance On A Wet Afternoon* (1964) was a far better film, although Attenborough's own performances were excellent in both.

in The Gift Horse *(British Lion, 1952)*

It was already clear that Attenborough aspired to directing himself. He made a successful debut in that capacity with *Oh What A Lovely War!* (1969) and devoted more of his time and energies to directing during the 70s, although he still acted occasionally. Preferring large scale productions based on true characters and events, he directed *Young Winston* (1972), *A Bridge Too Far* (1977) and then had a phenomenal success with *Gandhi* (1982), which won a number of Oscars including Best Picture and director. JF

Lauren Bacall

Real name **Betty Joan Perske**
Born **New York City, 16 September 1924**

'You know you don't have to act with me, Steve. You don't have to say anything, and you don't have to do anything. Not a thing. Oh, maybe just whistle. You know how to whistle, don't you Steve? You just put your lips together and blow.'

These words were spoken by a tall, slim, tawny blonde with almond-shaped eyes in one of the most astonishing of Hollywood film debuts in *To Have And Have Not* (1944). Lauren Bacall (who prefers to be addressed as Betty) was only 19-years-old at the time and had done virtually no acting before. She had worked mainly as a model in New York City and her photograph had been spotted by the wife of producer-director Howard Hawks. Just a glance at that famous 1943 'Harper's Bazaar' cover immediately convinces one of the veracity of the story, for she already had that special, modern 40s look about her, appearing wise beyond her years and with a slightly insolent quality which Hawks was to bring so effectively to life on the screen. But it was hard work. As Hawks recalled, 'Bacall had about four months of the toughest kind of training before we put her in *To Have And Have Not*... She really worked. You had to give her credit.' Mostly the training involved lots of reading aloud, out of doors, off by herself, developing the low register of her voice until it became natural. On the set she was not only aided by Hawks but by her co-star Humphrey Bogart. As the filming progressed, the relationship between them became closer and this, too, made the filming easier. By the time the picture was completed, it was clear that Hawks had succeeded in creating a new screen image, making effective use of her sexy, sultry, speaking voice – a kind of 40s answer to Dietrich and Mae West – and she even got a few songs to sing. (It *was* her own voice, although Hawks had experimented with dubbing.) Her relationship with Bogart had become more serious at the time that his tempestuous marriage to Mayo Methot was reaching the end. Thus, not only did Betty Bacall shoot to instant stardom when the picture was released, widely acclaimed for her performance, but she was also involved in one of the great, true, Hollywood love stories, a kind of follow-up to the Chaplin marriage the year before. (Although she was not quite as young as Oona O'Neill, and Bogart was ten years younger than Chaplin, there was still a 24-year gap between them.)

Hawks immediately rushed them into another picture together, *The Big Sleep*, which began filming in October 1944 and was completed before they married in 1945. If anything the chemistry worked

with Humphrey Bogart in Dark Passage *(Warner Bros., 1947)*

even better here. Certainly it is a far better film, Bacall is more assured in her playing, and again she and Bogie make a terrific team. She matches him well and her scenes with him are sharp, ironical and suggestive, with a sophisticated edge and the feel of a real relationship developing both within and apart from the Chandler world of hoodlums, blackmail and violence.

After such an incredible start to her film career, the pictures which followed had to be something of a letdown. In fact, she immediately got dreadful notices for her first without Bogart, *Confidential Agent* (1945), which brought her down to earth. Although she hoped to continue her career after her marriage, she turned down most of the weak scripts offered to her and was continually in dispute with Warner Bros, the studio which had bought her contract from Howard Hawks. Two more good, but

not exceptional, thrillers with Bogie confirmed their position as Hollywood's leading *film noir* couple. But in the 50s they each went their separate ways – on the screen, that is. She got a chance to demonstrate her qualities as a stylish and attractive actress on her own in a group of glossy colour pictures filmed during the middle years of the decade – *How To Marry A Millionaire* (1953), teamed with Marilyn Monroe and Betty Grable, and more serious roles in *The Cobweb* (1955), *Written On The Wind* (1956) and *Designing Woman* (1957) with Gregory Peck. Unfortunately, she had few memorable parts offered to her during later years, after Bogie's death in 1957. She achieved her greatest success on the stage, in 'Cactus Flower' in 1966, and in 'Applause', the musical stage version of the 1950 film, *All About Eve*, in 1970. From 1961 to 1969 she was married to actor Jason Robards Jr. JF

Lucille Ball

Born **Jamestown, New York, 6 August 1911**

More than most movie stars, Lucille Ball's fame rests on her immensely successful TV shows, rather than on her roles on the big screen. Lucille was an RKO contract player in comedy supporting parts in low budget movies, when she met Cuban bandleader Desi Arnaz on a set in 1940, marrying him the following year. In 1951, they began the 'I Love Lucy' series and six years later their TV company, Desilu Productions, bought up the studio where they had met. After their divorce in 1960, Arnaz sold his interest to her and she eventually sold out to Gulf and Western (owners of Paramount Studios, whose lot was situated next to RKO's) for over $10 million, a business deal curiously at odds with her screen persona as the dizzy redhead.

Lucille's mining engineer father and concert pianist mother had sent her to New York when she was 15 to study drama with John Murray Anderson. Between stage engagements, she worked as a secretary, waitress and model. The latter job helped her become a Goldwyn Girl in *Roman Scandals* (1933),

followed by two years of bit parts before working her way up to featured roles at RKO. Her best chance came in Dorothy Arzner's *Dance, Girl, Dance* (1940) as a burlesque queen, stealing the picture from the leads with her rendition of 'Oh, Mother, What Do I Do Now?' From 1943, her bright red hair became a feature in Technicolored MGM musicals such as *Best Foot Forward* (1943) *Ziegfeld Follies* (1946), seen whipping girls in cat suits in the opening number, and *Du Barry Was A Lady* (1943), but she wasn't given much scope for her clowning in any of them. As a freelance, she got more interesting and challenging roles in two *films noirs*, *The Dark Corner* (1946) and *Lured* (1947), and proved herself to be a perfect comic partner to Bob Hope in *Sorrowful Jones* (1949), *Fancy Pants* (1951), *The Facts Of Life* (1960) and *Critic's Choice* (1963).

Lucy's film appearances have been rare since 1960. Any ravages of time were covered by fuzzy soft-focus photography in the musical *Mame* (1974), but failed to disguise, even for those who love Lucy, that she was miscast. In 1961, she married nightclub comedian Gary Morton. Desi Jr and Lucie Arnaz, her children from her first marriage, are both in show business. RB

Anne Baxter

Born **Michigan City, Indiana, 7 May 1923**

Anne Baxter is best remembered today as the overly ingratiating and 'humble' schemer of *All About Eve* for which she won an Oscar nomination in 1950. This honour represented the culmination of a remarkable decade in which she had worked with many of the top Hollywood directors. She played the young heroine in Jean Renoir's superb and under-rated *Swamp Water* (1941), and appeared in Welles's *The Magnificent Ambersons* (1942) as well as *Five Graves To Cairo* (1943) for Billy Wilder. She also won a supporting actress Oscar for her performance as Sophie in Edmund Goulding's version of Maugham's *The Razor's Edge* (1946).

Attractive, charming and talented, Miss Baxter

never developed a strong personality on the screen, and inevitably her parts became more routine during the 50s. She appeared in less distinguished efforts of Hitchcock (*I Confess*), and Fritz Lang (*The Blue Gardenia*), both released in 1953, but landed the major role of Nefertiti in DeMille's *The Ten Commandments* (1956) which should have given a much-needed boost to her career, but it didn't. Although she continued acting in films, during later years she began to appear more frequently on television. Apparently doomed to remain in the shadow of the major stars, she took over from Lauren Bacall on stage in 'Applause', adapted from her own early film success, *All About Eve*, and replaced the real Bette Davis – *All About Eve's* Margo Channing – in the TV series, *Hotel*. Most recently (1983) she served as the narrator of a film about her grandfather, the famous architect Frank Lloyd Wright. JF

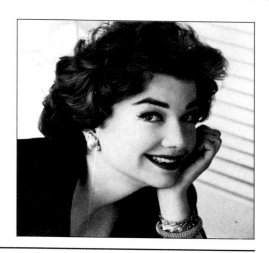

William Bendix

Born **New York City, 4 January 1906**
Died **1964**

Having flirted with show business for a number of years while holding down a variety of other jobs, William Bendix was over 30 by the time he experienced his first success in the theatre. A big hit as the cop in the Theatre Guild's production of Saroyan's 'The Time of Your Life' in 1939 led to offers from Hollywood. He arrived in California two years later, aged 35, and immediately established himself as a leading 'heavy' in a typical mixture of war pictures, thrillers and comedies. Signed by Paramount, he won an Oscar for his performance as a tough marine in his third picture, *Wake Island* (1942) and followed this with *The Glass Key* (1942). Here he played a thug opposite Alan Ladd, and a similar relationship was developed between them in *The Blue Dahlia* a couple of years later. They made a number of other films together including *Two Years Before The Mast* (1946), *Calcutta* (1947) and *The Deep Six* (1958).

Heavy-set, and square-jawed with a thick Brooklyn accent, Bendix was most often cast as the dumb but likeable sidekick of the hero. But he also starred in some minor pictures like *The Hairy Ape* (1944) and *The Babe Ruth Story* (1948), and in a popular radio and then TV show (with a film version in 1949), *The Life Of Riley*. During his later years he mixed the occasional film and stage appearance with more regular work on TV. JF

in Calcutta *(Paramount, 1947)*

Joan Bennett

Born **Palisades, New Jersey, 27 February 1910**

Life imitates art or, perhaps, art imitated life in the real life adventures and career of Joan Bennett. She ran away from home to get married at 16, was a mother at 17, and divorced at 18, later becoming Hollywood's youngest grandmother. In 1952 she was involved in a bizarre scandal when her husband, Walter Wanger, was jailed for shooting her agent.

She was born into a show business family, daughter of matinee idol Richard Bennett, who also acted in films, and younger sister of movie star Constance Bennett. An attractive petite blonde, Joan broke into films in 1928 but fell under the shadow of her more famous sister during the 30s and appeared in relatively few films of note. She played demure sister Amy to Katharine Hepburn's Jo at RKO in *Little Women* (1933) and appeared opposite Bing Crosby in *Mississippi* (1935). Married to scriptwriter Gene Markey for a time, her career began to pick up during the late 30s under contract to producer

Walter Wanger who was to become her third husband. She scored her greatest success during the 40s and early 50s as a brunette and working with a better class of director – Renoir, Ophuls, Minnelli and, especially, Fritz Lang. For him she appeared in a number of sluttish roles – the streetwalker in *Manhunt* (1941), the object of Edward G. Robinson's attentions in *The Woman In The Window* (1944) and *Scarlet Street* (1946). In this latter she is most convincingly cruel and nasty to Edward G. while masochistically loving the roughing up which her tough-guy boyfriend Dan Duryea, regularly dishes out to her.

Miss Bennett became more respectable and middle class in her later films – in *The Reckless Moment* (1949) she is excellent as a mother threatened by James Mason's sleazy blackmailer, and very respectable indeed married to Spencer Tracy with Elizabeth Taylor their daughter in *The Father Of The Bride* (1950), and its sequel *Father's Little Dividend* (1951). During later years she mixed film work with TV and the stage, and made a recent appearance in an Italian horror flic, *Suspiria* (1976) directed by Dario Argento. JF

in The Texans *(Paramount, 1938)*

Ingrid Bergman

Born Stockholm, Sweden, 29 August 1915
Died 1982

In 1938 producer David Selznick bought the remake rights to a romantic Swedish picture called *Intermezzo* (1936) with the idea of casting Ronald Colman or William Powell, or even teaming Charles Boyer and Loretta Young in the lead roles. He also signed up the picture's Swedish star, Ingrid Bergman, who arrived in the US in May 1939. Selznick did not like her name, which sounded German, and wanted to change it. He thought her too tall, and, although there was nothing he could do about her height, he planned a few changes in her appearance of the kind which were deemed necessary in 30s Hollywood – eyebrows plucked, teeth capped, etc. But she refused. Since it was clear that she was serious in her objections and was ready to return to Sweden, where she had already established herself as a leading star of stage and screen, Selznick changed his tack. He proceeded to promote her as a new kind of natural, unspoilt and unglamourised type of star. He then cast her in the remake of her own earlier movie, *Intermezzo: A Love Story* (1939) which closely followed the original and, not surprisingly, served as a suitable vehicle for launching his new star. Sensitively handled by director Gregory Ratoff with support from co-star Leslie Howard, her spontaneous charm and intelligence came across in this short, 70-minute feature designed to introduce her to the American public.

Unfortunately, after *Gone With The Wind*, *Intermezzo* and *Rebecca*, all made in 1939, Selznick gave up producing pictures for a few years and Miss Bergman's Hollywood career got off to a rather slow start. She was loaned out to other studios for a couple of minor pictures and enjoyed the opportunity to make her Broadway debut with Burgess Meredith in 'Liliom'. A step up was provided by the cockney barmaid part opposite Spencer Tracy in MGM's prestigious remake of *Dr Jekyll And Mr Hyde* in 1941. Originally cast as the nice, upper-class girl, Bergman wished to demonstrate her range as an actress and had successfully negotiated a swap in roles with Lana Turner.

Following another stage appearance, in the title role of O'Neill's 'Anna Christie', she was cast in *Casablanca* at Warner Bros. in 1942. This, finally, was her big break, although it may not have seemed like it at the time. The production was plagued by

many problems, including an unsatisfactory script which was being rewritten as the film was being shot. She and Humphrey Bogart turned out surprisingly effective as a romantic couple, and the picture gave a propitious boost to both their careers, although they never played together again. Miss Bergman succeeded in giving real substance to the slightly clichéd role of a woman torn between love and duty. Her beauty, warmth and intelligence shone forth from the screen and captivated a large popular audience for the first time – it turned out to be the first of her many 40s hits and winner of the Best Picture Oscar.

Within a matter of days after completing the filming of *Casablanca*, Ingrid was out on location in the Californian Sierra Nevada Mountains with a new, close-cropped haircut, playing Maria in Paramount's film version of *For Whom The Bell Tolls* (1943), a last minute replacement for Vera Zorina. It was her first big budget production and the only one of her early pictures to be filmed in colour. (The serious dramatic pictures and thrillers in which she was most often cast were invariably shot in black-and-white during this period.) Her lovely complexion, using a minimum of make-up, photographed well in colour and the film revealed her fresh,

natural beauty on the screen more clearly than ever before. As critic James Agee wrote at the time, 'Miss Bergman not only bears a startling resemblance to an imaginable human being; she really knows how to act, in a blend of poetic grace with quiet realism which almost never appears in American pictures.' Visually impressive and well acted, the picture gained Oscar nominations for Best Picture and for all four leading members of the cast including Gary Cooper, Ingrid Bergman – her first – and Katina Paxinou, the Greek actress and the only winner. It was also a big hit, as was the less memorable follow-up, *Saratoga Trunk*, in which she was again cast opposite Cooper. (Filmed in 1943 it was not released until 1946.)

Back at MGM in 1944 Bergman was given the starring role in a stylish remake of the stage thriller *Gaslight*, based on the play by Patrick Hamilton. Again she gave a fine performance as the attractive young wife in Victorian London gradually being driven insane by her husband (Charles Boyer). It won her her first Oscar. She benefitted from the fact that she was under contract to Selznick rather than to one of the big studios and thus was not forced to do pictures she did not like. But he was doing so few films of his own that, during the early years, she was unhappy to be working so little. Once she became well known, however, she was able to select her roles carefully and only averaged one or two pictures per year. Selznick attempted to find quality vehicles for her, and even got Hemingway to endorse her as his choice for Maria in *For Whom The Bell Tolls*. In fact, she turned out to be an extremely profitable property for Selznick, who received substantial fees for loaning her out to other studios, while her salary was not as high as other top stars. But she cared less about money than the quality of her parts.

Finally, in 1944, Selznick put together his first production for her since *Intermezzo*, pairing her with his new young male star, Gregory Peck, and his top director, Alfred Hitchcock. *Spellbound* reflected a growing interest in psychiatry at the time. She was convincing as a psychiatrist, Peck less so, but the picture was a hit, and Selznick immediately loaned her to RKO to play a down-to-earth nun in *The Bells Of St Mary's* (1945) opposite Bing Crosby's priest. Planned as a sequel to *Going My Way* (1944) it turned out an even bigger success and the top hit of her career, earning her a third Oscar nomination. (During this period she appeared in more top hit movies than any other female star.) Miss Bergman's seven-year contract with Selznick ended on a high note with a superb Hitchcock picture, *Notorious*, (1946), in which she was cast opposite Cary Grant and Claude Rains. Now on her own, she was not very successful in her choice of roles. After three flops in a row, including the extremely expensive *Joan Of Arc* (1948) which gained her a 4th Oscar nomination, she left for Italy to work with film director Roberto Rossellini. She bore his child illegitimately, heaping scandal upon her head in puritan America, and became an outcast from Hollywood for several years, although they did marry subsequently. They made a number of pictures together, of which *Voyage To Italy* (1953) with George Sanders, an intense marital drama, was the best received. After her relationship with Rossellini broke up, she returned to favour and, in 1956, played the title role in *Anastasia* which earned her a second Oscar. She married Swedish producer Lars Schmidt in 1958 and, during the following years she continued to be active in Europe, mixing the occasional film with regular theatre appearances and a few TV specials. She rounded off her career in the 70s by winning a supporting actress Oscar for her performance as an elderly spinster in *Murder On The Orient Express* (1974). She returned to Sweden in 1977 to work with the outstanding Swedish director, Ingmar Bergman, and actress Liv Ullmann in *Autumn Sonata*, her first Swedish film for almost 40 years. Finally, she took the title role in a two-part American TV production on the life of the Israeli prime minister, Golda Meir, which was completed shortly before her death, after a long illness. JF

with Humphrey Bogart in Casablanca *(Warner Bros., 1942)*

in Joan Of Arc *(RKO, 1948)* ▷

Ann Blyth

Born **Mt Kisco, New York, 16 August 1928**

Diminutive, dark-haired Ann Blyth with her slightly oriental eyes and pleasant lyric soprano voice, had a rather patchy film career, appearing mostly in insipid roles. However, she made an impression for the first time as Joan Crawford's spoilt-brat daughter in *Mildred Pierce* (1945) for which she was nominated for a Best Supporting Actress Oscar.

Ann made her professional debut at the age of five, singing on the radio. Although she studied voice and later sang with the San Carlo Opera Company, Hollywood gave her little chance to sing operatically except in three MGM CinemaScope operettas, *Rose Marie* (1954), *The Student Prince* (1954), and *Kismet* (1955). She had been borrowed from Universal for *The Great Caruso* (1951), because Kathryn Grayson refused to work with temperamental Mario Lanza again. Ironically, the most

successful song in the film, was 'The Loveliest Night Of The Year' which was sung by Blyth, playing the part of Caruso's wife, while waltzing with her husband at an Italian restaurant.

Previously, she had been given the occasional ditty in minor Universal musicals co-starring Donald O'Connor, and smiled sweetly at Bing Crosby in *Top O' The Morning* (1949). Meatier roles came in Lillian Hellman's *Another Part Of The Forest* (1948) – (At 13, Ann had appeared on Broadway in Hellman's 'Watch On The Rhine'), and as the condemned murderess in Douglas Sirk's melodrama, *Thunder On The Hill* (1951). Otherwise, she provided feminine decoration for lusty male adventures such as *The World In His Arms* (1952) and *All The Brothers Were Valiant* (1953). After making *The Buster Keaton Story* (1957), she was badly miscast as the great torch singer of the twenties in *The Helen Morgan Story* (1957) – her voice was dubbed by Gogi Grant – she retired from the screen to devote herself to light operas and stage musicals. RB

in Tokyo Joe (Columbia, 1949)

Humphrey Bogart

Born **New York City, 25 December 1899**
Died 1957

Bogart today is regarded as an almost mythic figure of the cinema, the archetypal anti-hero, tough and cynical on the surface, but uncorrupted and incorruptible, and capable of sensitivity, tenderness, and even love. But it wasn't always so. It was a long, slow process by which Humphrey Bogart, the young stage and film actor, was transformed into Bogey, the mature movie star of the 40s. Of course, some of his pre-Bogey gangster films of the 30s are reasonably familiar, like *The Petrified Forest* (1936) and *Dead End* (1937). But who has seen such early clinkers as *A Devil With Women* (1930), *Bad Sister* or *A Holy Terror* (both 1931). The titles say it all.

Having experienced some measure of success on Broadway during the late 20s, Bogart was brought out to Hollywood, a conventional, good looking and reasonably competent actor. But he failed to click in a number of mainly second-rate pictures such as those mentioned above, and returned to the theatre to find that good parts there were also few and far between. Finally he got his big break in 1935 when he landed the part of the gangster, Duke Mantee, in *The Petrified Forest* and was cast in the film version, too, due to the efforts of its star, Leslie Howard. Although Bogart now had a contract with Warner Bros., he was apparently doomed to play supporting heavy roles, forever in the shadow of the studio's top gangster stars – Edward G. Robinson, James Cagney and George Raft.

The turning point for Bogart came during the early 40s when, through both perseverance and good luck, he began to get larger parts, better scripts

and good directors. Raoul Walsh cast him with George Raft and Ida Lupino in *They Drive By Night* in 1940, followed by *High Sierra* later that year. Here he had the lead, portraying the last days of a gangster on the run and the doomed relationship with a girl he meets (Ida Lupino again). And in *The Maltese Falcon* (1941) he put his own personal stamp on the character of Dashiell Hammett's detective, Sam Spade. Clearly Bogey had arrived, although he had only gotten his big break because George Raft had turned down both roles. Nominated for Oscars for Best Picture, screenplay and supporting actor (Sydney Greenstreet), *The Maltese Falcon* made the names of all those associated with it, including John Huston, here directing his first picture and the first of many he was to make with Bogart over the years. Co-star Mary Astor, working with him for the first time, was impressed with his acting ability, and his involvement in the role of Spade: 'It is true his personality dominated the character he was playing – but the character gained by it. His technical skill was quite brilliant. His precision timing was no accident. He kept other actors on their toes...'

Bogart's role as Rick, the expatriate American in *Casablanca* (1943) marked another landmark in his career and earned his first Oscar nomination. There was a shift in focus to emphasize the romantic side of Bogart's screen persona which was softened somewhat, especially in his love scenes with Ingrid Bergman. Bogart fell in love in real life, too, when, in

1944, director Howard Hawks teamed him with a new young girl named Lauren Bacall whom he had discovered working as a model in New York. The partnership paid off: they made two excellent pictures in a row, *To Have And Have Not* (1944) and *The Big Sleep* (1946), which confirmed Bogie's position as Warner Bros. top star, and in 1945 he and Betty (as she was known) were married. (He had previously been married to Helen Menken, Mary Philips and Mayo Methot, all actresses.)

Reunited with director John Huston and his actor father Walter, Bogey pulled out all the stops in playing an obsessive gold hunter in *The Treasure Of The Sierra Madre* (1948). He and Huston then went on to make three more together: *Key Largo* (1948) in which Bogey's heroics were ably supported by a cast which included Bacall, Edward G. Robinson and Lionel Barrymore; an entertaining spoof thriller, *Beat The Devil* (1954), and *The African Queen* (1951) their first in Technicolor. Cast as a likeable rogue in this latter, he was given a rare opportunity to demonstrate his range as an actor, more than holding his own opposite the formidable Katharine Hepburn. Bogey won his only Oscar for this performance, but gained a further nomination for his Captain Queeg in *The Caine Mutiny* (1954). Although his health was deteriorating, he continued to acquit himself well in six more films, including *Sabrina* (1954), *The Desperate Hours* (1955) and his last, a boxing movie, *The Harder They Fall* (1956) in which he played a hack sports writer. JF

in The Treasure Of The Sierra Madre (Warner Bros., 1948)

John Carradine

Born **New York City, 5 February 1906**

A leading Hollywood character star for over 50 years and the father of three film actor sons – David, Keith and Robert – John Carradine has played a wide variety of roles in upwards of 200 pictures. He is probably best known for his appearances in countless horror movies ranging from *The Bride Of Frankenstein* (1935) through *Billy The Kid Vs Dracula* (1966) – he played Dracula, up to the recent *House Of Long Shadows* (1983). During the 40s he was one of a group of familiar contract players who lent a touch of class to the extensive Universal horror output of the period.

But on a more serious level, Carradine had been a leading member of John Ford's movie stock company during 1936–40. As a gentleman gambler along for the ride in *Stagecoach* (1939) his manners were impeccable. He made a formidable villain in *Drums Along The Mohawk* (1940), an evil renegade leader identified by the black patch he wears over one eye. But most memorable of all is the tall, wiry figure of Casey, the lapsed preacher turned union organizer in *The Grapes of Wrath* (1940), who joins the Joad family on their trek west because, 'There's somethin' happenin' out there an' I'd like to try to learn what it is.' JF

in Frontier Marshall *(20th Century-Fox, 1939)*

Jack Carson

Born **Carmen, Manitoba, Canada, 27 October 1910**
Died **1963**

Before he established himself in vaudeville and then in the movies, Jack Carson worked as a salesman, a construction worker and an emcee. That says it all. For his film image was that of the brash and bulky guy with the smiling face whom you never could quite trust. A fast talking wise guy, in other words, who was often cast as the hero's sidekick or rival.

Under contract to RKO during the late 30s, he arrived at Warner Bros. in 1941 and immediately stole James Cagney's girl (Rita Hayworth) in *The Strawberry Blonde*, but ended up the loser, as usual. He had a good role in *Mildred Pierce* (1945) with Joan Crawford, but was most often cast in the studio's comedies and musicals paired with Jane Wyman, Dennis Morgan, Ann Sheridan or Doris Day. He was notable as the cynical press agent slinging off James Mason in *A Star Is Born* (1954), and his other good 50s role was that of Paul Newman's older brother in *Cat On A Hot Tin Roof* (1958). Married to the formidable Madeleine Sherwood with a collection of bratty kids, he keeps trying to be reasonable, but cannot control his wife. Although cast as the 'heavy', one feels that he deserves our sympathy more than contempt. During the late 50s Carson alternated between TV and films, averaging only one picture per year up to his early death. JF

Lon Chaney Jr

Real name **Creighton Chaney**
Born **Oklahoma City, 10 February 1906**
Died **1973**

A chip off the old hump, Lon Chaney Jr never escaped the long, grotesque shadow thrown by his father. Billed as Creighton Chaney, he entered films as a stock player at RKO, after the great man's death. He starred in the studio's only serial, *The Last Frontier* (1932), but was dropped in 1935. After two years on 'poverty row', he was signed by Fox, who renamed him Lon Chaney Jr and put him to work as a hulking heavy in B features like *Charlie Chan In City Of Darkness* (1939) and *Mr Moto's Gamble* (1939). In the same year he got his big break, repeating his stage performance as the retarded, itinerant farmworker Lennie in *Of Mice And Men*, then played Akhoba, the one-eyed leader of the Rock People, in Hal Roach's *One Million BC*, stealing the film from his prettier co-stars, Carole Landis and Victor Mature, and landing a five-year contract with Universal.

First came *Man Made Monster* (1941), followed by a Dick Foran serial, *Riders Of Death Valley* (1941). Then the moment arrived for a startling metamorphosis. Chaney dropped the Jr and disappeared under make-up wizard Jack Pierce's layers of rubber moulding and yak hair to emerge as the loping lycanthrope of *The Wolf Man* (1941). In the

Elisha Cook Jr

Born **San Francisco, California, 26 December 1906**

Although he was a little guy, he generally packed a rod and tried to act tough, as in *The Maltese Falcon* (1941) in which he made his first impact on the screen as a hired gun, perpetually surprised by Humphrey Bogart. He was good at reacting, with his clear blue eyes which were expressive even in black-and-white. – a talent which brought him work with most of the Hollywood majors.

As the archetypal victim or fall guy of 40s *film noir*, Elisha Cook Jr was often called upon to express surprise, hurt or pain before he got bumped off, as in *Phantom Lady* (1944) or in *The Big Sleep* later that same year. He had a good supporting role as a tough homesteader in *Shane* (1953) where, although his animated blue eyes reflected his determination to stand up to the cattle men, he was cruelly mowed down by Jack Palance. And Stanley Kubrick gave him a memorable part in *The Killing* (1956), as the double-crossed husband of Marie Windsor. Already over 30 by the time *The Maltese Falcon* was released, Cook went on to make appearances in a further 80 movies and was still going strong over 30 years later in a send-up of the picture, *The Black Bird* (1974), as well as in *St Ives* (1976), *The Champ* (1979), and *Hammett* (1982). JF

in The Maltese Falcon *(Warner Bros., 1941)*

next two years he played the complete range of Universal monsters: a robotic Frankenstein monster in *The Ghost Of Frankenstein* (1941); the anagrammatically named vampire Count Alucard in *Son Of Dracula* (1943); and Kharis, the 3000-year-old bandaged one in *The Mummy's Tomb* (1942), *The Mummy's Ghost* (1944) and *The Mummy's Curse* (1944). The Wolf Man remained his favourite and in later years he referred to him as 'my baby'. As the hapless Lawrence Talbot, he succumbed to the spell of the wolfbane in four more films. In *The House Of Dracula* (1945) he was cured by Onslow Stevens, but three years later suffered an understandable relapse on encountering Abbott and Costello in *Abbott And Costello Meet Frankenstein* (1948). By then the steam had run out of Universal's horror cycle. Chaney was dropped and quickly found himself down among the B people. In the 50s he contributed telling cameos to *High Noon* (1952) – as the drunken sheriff – and *Not As A Stranger* (1955), playing Robert Mitchum's washed-up father. The rest of the time was spent in horror cheapies alongside veteran actors and directors who had seen better days, the pathetic echo of Lennie clinging to many of his later cut-rate monsters. One of A.C. Lyles's stock company of old-timers recruited for a series of 60s western programmers, Chaney was still talking about making a horror comeback when, like his father, he died of throat cancer. RC

Joseph Cotten

Born **Petersburg, Virginia, 15 May 1905**

An occasional theatre critic before he became an actor, Joseph Cotten achieved his greatest success on the stage during the late 30s, playing the lead opposite Katharine Hepburn in 'The Philadelphia Story' and as a member of Orson Welles's Mercury Theatre company. When Welles brought the company to Hollywood and RKO to take part(s) in his first feature, *Citizen Kane* (1941), Cotten naturally came with them. Welles cast him in the important role of Jedediah Leland, Kane's friend and 'conscience', and the newspaper's theatre critic (a little joke recalling Cotten's early years). Cotten was excellent, and was even better as the *nouveau riche* inventor and suitor who is ill-treated by the aristocratic Amberson family in Welles's masterly but mangled (by RKO) *The Magnificent Ambersons* (1942).

When RKO terminated its relationship with Mercury, Cotten signed with producer David Selznick. Alfred Hitchcock, the leading Selznick director, immediately (and perversely) cast him as the sophisticated and friendly Uncle Charlie who comes to visit his small town relatives in *Shadow Of A Doubt* (1943), but who turns out to not be quite what he seems – revealed, in fact, as one of Hitchcock's most memorable villains. Selznick, however, had different ideas and cast the tall, dis-

in Duel In The Sun *(Selznick, 1946)*

tinguished looking actor as a romantic leading man opposite Jennifer Jones in a number of pictures. Cotten's career declined after one last, memorable appearance opposite Orson Welles in *The Third Man* (1949), although he continued to appear in films for many years up to the late 70s. JF

Yvonne De Carlo

Real name **Peggy Yvonne Middleton**
Born **Vancouver, B.C., Canada,
1 September 1922**

A dark-haired and attractive star, Yvonne De Carlo arrived at Universal during the mid-40s after a number of bit roles at other studios. She was just in time to take over from Maria Montez as Universal's leading female Technicolor star, cast in similar exotic roles like *Salome – Where She Danced* (1945), *Song Of Scheherezade* (1946) and *Slave Girl* (1947). She had been a dancer since childhood, and appeared in nightclubs and theatres before her screen debut in 1942. A better actress than Montez, Miss De Carlo branched out successfully into westerns and adventure roles.

However, her best part during this period was in a black-and-white picture, *Criss Cross* (1948), in which she met a violent death, caught between nasty Dan Duryea as her current husband, and Burt Lancaster, her ex. During the 50s she filmed on both sides of the Atlantic. A lively foil to Alec Guinness in *The Captain's Paradise* (1953), she then landed the major role of Sephora in DeMille's *The Ten Commandments* (1956). Miss De Carlo continued to appear in occasional films and TV movies throughout the 60s and 70s, including *McLintock* (1963) and *Won Ton Ton, The Dog Who Saved Hollywood* (1975) but is best known recently for her starring role on TV in 'The Munsters'. JF

Dan Dailey

Born **New York City, 14 December 1914**
Died **1978**

When Dan Dailey belted out the title song from *There's No Business Like Show Business* (1954), he really sounded as though he meant it. The six foot five inch hoofer had been in show business since he was a child, appearing first in minstrel shows, later in vaudeville and with Minsky's burlesque troupe. He so impressed in the lead of 'Stars In Your Eyes' on Broadway, that MGM offered him a contract. After playing small parts in five movies (he was the ex-boxer in *Ziegfeld Girl*, 1941), Dailey left the studio to join the army.

He returned a lieutenant, and joined Fox who gave him his first starring role in the Betty Grable vehicle, *Mother Wore Tights* (1947). Dailey became the studio's leading male dancer, lending his gawky appeal to a series of backstage sagas such as *When My Baby Smiles At Me* (1948) – for which he was nominated as Best Actor as a burlesque comedian who hits the bottle – *My Blue Heaven* (1950) and *Call Me Mister* (1951), all co-starring Grable. Away from the corny, colourful musicals, Dan Dailey brought gusto and pathos to the role of baseball star Dizzy Dean in *The Pride Of St Louis* (1952) and in three John Ford movies in which he was cast in military uniform: *When Willie Comes Marching Home* (1950), as a hick hero, *What Price Glory?*

in It's Always Fair Weather *(MGM, 1955)*

(1952) and *Wings Of Eagles* (1957), as the wartime buddy of James Cagney and John Wayne respectively. With the decline of the screen musical in the late 50s, Dailey turned to the stage, cabaret and TV. His last film was *The Private Files Of J. Edgar Hoover* (1977), in which he was touching as Hoover's lifelong companion. It was a far cry from the grinning song-and-dance man of yesteryear. RB

in Hotel Sahara *(United Artists, 1951)*

in Blackbeard The Pirate *(RKO, 1952)*

Linda Darnell

Real name **Monetta Eloyse Darnell**
Born **Dallas, Texas, 16 October 1921**
Died **1965**

The 40s was Linda Darnell's decade. Only a teenager when the decade began, she had arrived in Hollywood the year before and signed a contract with 20th Century-Fox. Linda had her first leading role in a major production opposite Tyrone Power in *The Mark Of Zorro* (1940), but by the end of 1950 she had reached the end of her contract and her career as a star was virtually over. A strikingly attractive brunette, although her acting talent was limited, she made a sympathetic heroine in a variety of 40s pictures working with a number of the leading Fox directors. She played Tyrone Power's childhood sweetheart and young wife in *Blood And Sand*

(1941), sensitively directed by Rouben Mamoulian, and had her best western role as the girl torn between various men in John Ford's *My Darling Clementine* (1946). After three with Otto Preminger, including the lead in Technicolored box-office hit, *Forever Amber* (1947), she got her best opportunities as Rex Harrison's wife in a lively Preston Sturges comedy, *Unfaithfully Yours* (1948); and in *A Letter To Three Wives* (1949), written and directed by Joseph Mankiewicz, as the tough lower-class girl who has hooked a rich husband. She made a few more films during the early 50s and did some later TV work. Then in 1965, Miss Darnell met a truly appalling end. While on a visit to her former secretary in Chicago, she was watching a television showing of *Star Dust*, a movie which she had made twenty-five years earlier. The house caught fire, and Linda Darnell was burned to death. JF

Brian Donlevy

Born **Portadown, Ireland, 9 February 1899**
Died **1972**

A soldier and adventurer in his youth, Brian Donlevy was well prepared for the kind of roles he was to play in innumerable films. Square-jawed, heavy-set and most often sporting a pencil moustache, he developed – after some experience on the stage – into one of Hollywood's most dependable tough guy stars during the 30s. In *In Old Chicago* (1938) Donlevy played a tough political boss who is Tyrone Power's unscrupulous rival, and two years later writer-director Preston Sturges developed the same kind of character into *The Great McGinty* (1940), an enjoyable political satire. Donlevy brought to the part an appropriate blend of charming rascality with a no-nonsense toughness which he

carried over from his more heavy roles – such as his tough-as-nails sergeant in *Beau Geste*, which had earned him his only Oscar nomination – as Best Supporting Actor – in 1939.

Donlevy was much in demand for villainous roles throughout the 40s and appeared in a mixture of thrillers, war pictures and westerns. However, in 1943, MGM had enough confidence in his box office appeal to star him in King Vidor's $3 million Technicolor production, *An American Romance*. He was excellent as Steve Dargos, a penniless immigrant who rises to the top of the American steel industry, a kind of upbeat and more socially acceptable MGM variation on the ruthless McGinty. But the picture flopped, and Donlevy went back to playing heavies. Still a stylish actor during the 50s when the B-pictures started to out-number the 'A's, his later efforts, including *The Curse Of The Fly* (1965), and three A.C. Lyles westerns, are best forgotten. JF

Paul Douglas

Born **Philadelphia, Pennsylvania,
4 November 1907**
Died **1959**

A most unlikely looking film star, Paul Douglas had an unusual film career to match. Tall, craggy and heavy set, he played professional football in his youth, then graduated to sports broadcaster and bits of acting on radio, making use of his fine voice. He had done relatively little stage work before he experienced a phenomenal success creating the role of Harry Brock, the boorish scrap metal dealer, in *Born Yesterday* on Broadway opposite Judy Holliday. But he turned down the film part which went to Broderick Crawford instead.

Already in his 40s, he signed a contract with 20th Century-Fox and was immediately cast as Linda Darnell's rich beau, then husband, in *A Letter To*

in 1949

Three Wives (1948). The kind of tough talking but warm-hearted character which he played here can be seen as a typical Paul Douglas role. In *Everybody Does It* (1949), a delightful comedy, he was married to Celeste Holm and discovered he had a literally smashing singing voice. During the following years he divided his time between cops, crooks and sporting roles, but was excellent as Barbara Stanwyck's solid, dependable, but naive husband in Fritz Lang's *Clash By Night* (1952). This part gave him one of his best opportunities to demonstrate his sensitivity and intelligence as an actor. In 1954 he came to Britain to play the lead in Alexander Mackendrick's entertaining Ealing comedy, *The Maggie*. As a blustering, grumpy American businessman, he served as a suitable target for the disruptive tactics of the Scottish locals determined to do things their own way. Back in the US he had one last good comedy role, reunited with Judy Holliday and again playing a business tycoon, in *The Solid Gold Cadillac* (1956). Unfortunately, his talent was wasted in the mainly routine roles he was subsequently offered, although he continued active in films up to his death in 1959. JF

Dan Duryea

Born **White Plains, New York,
23 January 1907**
Died **1968**

Dan Duryea is best remembered today as a distinctly nasty type, one of those slimy creatures spawned by 40s *film noir*, a flashy dresser with slicked back blonde hair and a high, whining voice. He acted

with Joan Bennett in Scarlet Street *(Universal, 1945)*

cynical and tough, especially when there were ladies about, but was strictly a small time operator who often came to a bad end.

Duryea had first worked in advertising before he became interested in acting and was well into his 30s by the time of his first big Broadway stage success, creating the role of the unlikeable son, Leo, in Lillian Hellman's *The Little Foxes* in 1939. He made his film debut in the movie version two years later. His first gangster role (albeit in a comedy) in *Ball Of Fire*

(1941) immediately followed, and he was one of the nasties terrorizing Ray Milland in Fritz Lang's *Ministry Of Fear* (1944). In two further Lang pictures he graduated to lead heavy opposite Joan Bennett in *The Woman In The Window* (1944) and *Scarlet Street* (1945). Here Duryea developed a taste for exploiting not so lady-like ladies and gave Mary Beth Hughes some of the same rough treatment in *The Great Flamarion* (1945), ditto Yvonne De Carlo in Siodmak's violent melodrama *Criss Cross* (1949).

By the late 40s he was mixing his hoodlum roles with western baddies, as in *Winchester '73* (1950) and *Ride Clear Of Diablo* (1954), and even landed the title role of a reformed baddie in *Al Jennings Of Oklahoma* (1951). As he grew older there was a softening of his character and he played more sympathetic parts in such pictures as *Battle Hymn* (1957) and *The Flight Of The Phoenix* (1965) while working regularly in television appearing in, among other series, 'Peyton Place'. JF

Joan Fontaine

Real name **Joan de Beauvoir de Havilland**
Born **Tokyo, Japan, 22 October, 1917**

Joan Fontaine got her big break in 1939 when producer David Selznick cast her in the lead role in his prestige production of *Rebecca*. She was still relatively unknown, and young enough to make a special impact on the screen as the clumsy and naive young heroine of Daphne du Maurier's popular novel. As director Alfred Hitchcock noted, 'In the early stages of filming Joan was a little self-conscious, but I could see her potential for restrained acting and I felt she would play the character in a quiet, shy manner.'

In fact, Joan had already been acting in films, for over three years. As George Cukor recalled, '...she had been at RKO playing not too interesting leading women, and she was not terribly good.' The younger sister of Olivia de Havilland, she had begun her acting career on the stage on the West Coast before being signed up for films. In her only picture of note at RKO, she had been merely adequate playing an upper class British heiress opposite Fred Astaire in *Damsel In Distress* (1937), but after she left RKO George Cukor offered her a supporting role in *The Women* (1939). He felt that she emerged as a convincing screen actress for the very first time, singling out for special praise one sequence in particular – the telephone conversation in which she discovers that she is still in love with her husband. 'She did this scene with the most tremendous force and feeling. It was a thrilling moment when she realised that she was an actress... She had been acting for four years and not very successfully. Suddenly there was this breakthrough.'

Later that year Cukor advised Selznick to cast her in *Rebecca* in preference to the many other actresses being considered for the part, among them Vivien Leigh, Anne Baxter and Margaret Sullavan. Miss

Fontaine's sensitive and moving performance as the timid second wife of Max de Winter (Laurence Olivier) earned her an Oscar nomination, while the picture itself won the Best Picture Oscar in 1940. Not surprisingly, she produced a more assured performance in a similar role as an insecure wife (to Cary Grant) in the follow-up picture, *Suspicion* (1941), again directed by Hitchcock, and was rewarded with an Oscar.

At her peak of popularity, she still looked young enough to play teenage heroines in such pictures as *The Constant Nymph* (1943), earning yet another Oscar nomination, and *Jane Eyre* (1944). Both were based on romantic English novels and again Miss Fontaine was sensitively handled by British direc-

with Charles Boyer in The Constant Nymph *(Warner, 1943)*

tors, Edmund Goulding and Robert Stevenson. In danger of being typecast – Charlotte Brontë's heroine, Jane Eyre, was very much in the *Rebecca* mould – she managed a change of direction in her next movie, *Frenchman's Creek* (1944) as a rather different type of Du Maurier heroine. Portraying a more liberated and independent woman, she looked more attractive than ever in 17th century costume. The film was a lavish $4 million swashbuckler in Technicolor, and Miss Fontaine's first appearance in colour suited her. She even acquitted herself well in a few of the action sequences. (In real life she is an accomplished sportswoman.)

Having divorced her first husband, actor Brian Aherne, in 1945, the star was involved for a time with producer John Houseman, then married another producer, William Dozier, who produced a number of her later pictures beginning with *From This Day Forward* (1946). She was pleasantly appealing as Mark Stevens's wife in this socially conscious little picture about a young couple coping with the Depression during the late 30s. But she was little more than an attractive foil for Bing Crosby in Billy Wilder's sugary *Emperor Waltz* (1948) which was, however, quite successful at the box office. Soon after this, she made her most memorable and interesting picture of the late 40s, *Letter From An Unknown Woman* (1948), starring opposite Louis Jourdan. According to John Houseman it was made within a kind of 'family atmosphere' as Joan, her executive producer husband and writer Howard Koch were all old friends. The opening sections recalled her earlier successes playing 'an adolescent girl in thrall to an older man,' as Houseman described it. But the collaborative efforts of the team, with a major contribution from director Max Ophuls, deepened and developed the central theme. Koch credits Miss Fontaine with having made important suggestions regarding the portrayal of her character who is seen at three different stages in her life. According to him, 'Joan Fontaine was one of the few actresses capable of making the intensely romantic Lisa a credible character, and I still regard the performance she eventually gave as one of the most brilliant I've ever seen on film...'

Unfortunately, Miss Fontaine never again found a role which could match this, nor worked with another director who was quite as gifted as Ophuls. She was attractive and appealing as Lady Rowena in *Ivanoe* (1952), and as a foil for Bob Hope in *Casanova's Big Night* (1954). She rounded out her film career during the late 50s and early 60s in a series of pictures made for 20th Century-Fox, including *Island In The Sun* (1957), *A Certain Smile* (1958), and *Tender Is The Night* (1962), after which she returned to periodic work in the theatre. JF

with Louis Jourdan in Letter From An Unknown Woman *(Universal, 1948)*

Glenn Ford

Born **Quebec, Canada, 1 May 1916**

Glenn Ford began his film career with over a dozen mainly B pictures and westerns between 1939–43 and failed to make much of an impact. In his youth he had tried a variety of jobs before becoming interested in the theatre, and was acting on the West Coast when he was signed to a contract by Columbia Pictures. When he returned to films after war service, Ford was immediately cast in a pair of A pictures, opposite Rita Hayworth in *Gilda* (1946) and Bette Davis in *A Stolen Life* (1946), and was revealed as an attractive, personable and intelligent leading man. During the following years he proved to be a versatile actor and appeared in a variety of roles, but his career failed to really take off until the mid-50s.

With Fritz Lang's excellent thriller, *The Big Heat* (1953), Ford brought a quiet authority and sincerity to the role of the obsessive ex-cop determined to avenge the death of his wife and expose the crooked gang boss. As a firm but sympathetic school teacher in *The Blackboard Jungle* (1955), he refused to be intimidated by a class of delinquent kids, and in *The Teahouse Of The August Moon* (1956) he displayed a great (and previously untapped) gift for comedy. After starring in two fine westerns directed by Delmer Daves, *3:10 To Yuma* (1957) and *Cowboy* (1958), Ford gave another superb performance in the delightful comedy western *The Sheepman* (1958) with Shirley MacLaine.

Cast in a number of major pictures which flopped during the early 60s, including the MGM remakes

in Gilda (Columbia, 1946)

of *Cimarron* (1961) and *The Four Horsemen Of The Apocalypse* (1962), Ford's career went into decline and he appeared in a number of routine westerns. During the 70s he was most often seen on television, starring in *Cade's County* and a number of TV movies, before landing a nice cameo role as Superman's adopted father in *Superman* (1978). JF

John Garfield

Real name **Julius Garfinkle**
Born **New York City, 4 March 1913**
Died **1952**

John Garfield was the last 30s addition to Warner Bros.' already formidable roster of tough male superstars. Dark-haired, solidly built, and with a determined and aggressive look about him, he was most often cast as a rebellious, cynical young man – an image which reflected his own tough New York background. In fact his screen persona was essentially naturalistic and 'modern' – he had more in common with (and was a forerunner of) Brando and Dean than with Cagney or Bogart. Director Elia Kazan, for example, referred to Garfield as 'the first of the natural, off-the-street rebels.'

After studying at drama school, Garfield spent some time bumming around the country before he joined the Group Theatre and made his name on the Broadway stage, most notably in Clifford Odets's *Golden Boy* in 1937. He arrived at Warner Bros. the following year, where his refreshingly caustic and down-to-earth qualities helped to redeem an otherwise sentimental confection called *Four Daughters*. This, his first film role, won him a supporting actor Oscar nomination, but the studio failed to find him the kind of good parts he deserved. He was, of course, typecast as the loner or social outcast in such vehicles as *They Made Me A Criminal* and *Dust Be My Destiny* (both in 1939) – the titles say it all – then played a cocky but doomed gangster in *Castle On The Hudson*, (1940) a remake of the 1933 Tracy picture *20,000 Years In Sing Sing*.

In 1941 Garfield proved he could hold his own with Edward G. Robinson in *The Sea Wolf*, and had a change of pace in 1942 on loan to MGM to play Spencer Tracy's sidekick in *Tortilla Flat*. With America's entry into the war, he immediately found himself cast in a series of war movies beginning with *Air Force*, late in 1942, followed by *Destination Tokyo* (1943). He was typically cast as the tough city wise-guy member of the crew who can handle himself in action, and in *Pride Of The Marines* (1945) starred in the true life story of blinded war hero Al Schmid. Garfield was clearly at his peak. Cast as the loner, drifter and murderer in MGM's *The Postman Always Rings Twice* (1946) Garfield portrayed him as more sensitive, intelligent and weaker (and more sympathetic) than the character in James M. Cain's original novel, whereas Lana Turner came across as harder, colder and tougher. But in spite of this shift in balance, they both gave excellent performances and their love scenes struck a few sparks off the screen.

The two pictures which followed saw Garfield cast in familiar, Golden Boy-type roles as a poor, young, but talented and ambitious violinist/boxer rising to the top while attempting to maintain his integrity – the kind of parts he played so well. The first, *Humoresque* (1946), opposite Joan Crawford completed his Warner Bros. contract, while *Body And Soul* (1947) earned him his second Oscar nomination. His other 1947 picture, *Gentleman's Agreement*, in which he played a supporting role to Gregory Peck won the Best Picture Oscar. *Force Of Evil* (1948) completed an excellent run of pictures for him, but there was a sameness about his performances which suggests that he was never really stretched as an actor. Here he was on the wrong side of the law once again, involved in running a crooked numbers racket. During the following years the parts he was offered were less good. *The Breaking Point* (1950) was a stylish remake of Hemingway's *To Have And Have Not* (1944), while *He Ran All The Way* (1951) turned out, alas, to be his final picture. Garfield's difficulties during his last years, which led up to his premature death from a heart attack were undoubtedly aggravated by the activities of the House Un-American Activities Committee. He was one of the saddest and most tragic victims of the HUAC witch hunt. JF

in Gentleman's Agreement (20th Century-Fox, 1947)

Judy Garland

Real name Frances Gumm
Born **Grand Rapids, Michigan, 10 June 1922**
Died **1969**

From her hospital bed while recovering from drug abuse, Judy Garland and friends listened to a radio broadcast of the Academy Awards ceremony in which Judy had been nominated as Best Actress for her remarkable comeback picture *A Star Is Born* (1954). The champagne was on ice, and her fans waited optimistically, waiting to hear that her great performance and long career had finally – and deservedly – been rewarded that night with an Oscar. However, the coveted statuette went to Grace Kelly for *The Country Girl*. It was just another blow in a life that had given so much pleasure to others but had itself been denied happiness. Garland was to make only three further films during the last fourteen years of her life. A lean period for a trouper who had worked non-stop on stage and in movies since she first trod the boards at the age of three, joining her vaudevillian parents. Born in a trunk, Judy died in the bathroom of her London apartment, aged only a mere 47, of 'an incautious self over-dosage of sleeping pills.'

Billed as 'the little girl with the great big voice', Judy joined her two older sisters in the 'Gumm Sisters Kiddie Act', later changed to the Garland Sisters. When the act broke up, Judy went solo, pushed by her zealous mother – a woman once described by her daughter as 'the real-life Wicked Witch of the West.' At thirteen, she gained an MGM contract and was put into a two-reel short called *Every Sunday* (1936) with another film debutante, Deanna Durbin. Durbin was dropped

in 1946

and Judy kept on. At the start of her long career at MGM, she virtually stole the show in *Broadway Melody Of 1938* when the 'new hot little singing sensation' sang 'Dear Mr. Gable, You Made Me Love You' to a photograph of the star.

Louis B. Mayer wanted Shirley Temple for the role of Dorothy in *The Wizard Of Oz* (1939), but when Fox wouldn't release her, he reluctantly gave 16-year-old Judy Garland the chance to play the little farm girl from Kansas who, after her fantastic adventures, discovers that 'home is best.' Judy brought such warmth and freshness to the role that for it, as well as *Babes In Arms* the same year, she won a special Oscar for 'her outstanding performance as a screen juvenile during the past year'. Mayer continued to derogate Judy, calling her his 'monkey', which didn't do much for her already shaky self-confidence. In a series of 'juvenile' musicals with Mickey Rooney, such as the Busby Berkeley-directed *Babes In Arms, Strike Up The Band* (1940) and *Babes On Broadway* (1941), she often played the

ugly duckling whom Mickey considers a pal, before realising at the fadeout that he really loves her. Rooney later commented paradoxically, 'We had fun all the time together. It was terrible the way we never stopped working.' Berkeley was a hard taskmaster who made Judy feel 'as if he had a big black bullwhip and he was lashing me with it. Sometimes I used to think I couldn't live through the day'.

Judy's hectic schedule aggravated an already nervous disposition. In addition, she had always had a weight problem and the studio put her on a strict diet. Before long she was living on pills. Sleeping pills, pep pills and appetite suppressants. At nineteen, she married the first of her five husbands, bandleader David Rose. They separated after two years, and Judy started seeing a psychiatrist regularly. During the shooting of *Meet Me In St. Louis* (1944), Judy first dated co-star Tom Drake, but the relationship with her director, Vincente Minnelli, grew, despite her emotional outbursts and the way she kept the rest of the company waiting. Before long they were living together, marrying as soon as

in A Star Is Born (Warner Bros., 1954)

her divorce came through in 1945. Judy blossomed into a beauty under Minnelli's loving eye in the four films he made with her. She is at her most radiant in *Meet Me In St. Louis*, whether singing tender ballads like 'The Boy Next Door' or the vigorous 'Trolley Song', characteristically throwing her hair back from her forehead. She is beguiling as a working girl in *The Clock* (1945), a touching realist romance, *Ziegfeld Follies* (1946) and witty in *The Pirate* (1947).

But, although there was joy from their daughter Liza, the Minnelli marriage was soon tottering. While making *The Pirate*, Judy's paranoia and drug dependency became more serious. Hedda Hopper found her one day in a state of hysteria in her trailer, accusing everyone of being against her. She was so overwrought that she had to be carried to her car and driven home, still wearing her costume and make-up. Soon after this incident, she was placed in care in a private sanatorium. Nevertheless, the vibrant young star returned to give of her best with Fred Astaire in *Easter Parade* (1948). Cast opposite Astaire again in *Barkleys Of Broadway* (1949), however, Judy suffered from constant migraine. She recalled, 'I went for days without sleep but I kept on. Then I started to be late for rehearsals and began missing days. Finally I was fired. They didn't give me the courtesy of a call or a meeting or a discussion. They sent me a telegram.' She was replaced by Ginger Rogers. Again, later, she had to be replaced – this time by Betty Hutton on *Annie Get Your Gun* (1950), while she was in hospital for her drug-addiction problems.

After undergoing the frightful experience of amphetamine and barbiturate withdrawal in a Boston hospital, Judy reported for work on *Summer*

Stock (1950). She felt humiliated by the studio's insistence on having a psychiatrist on the set at all times, as well as by fighting a losing battle against her weight. As a result, she was consistently late on the set, or would arrive and say to director Charles Walters, 'Look, buddy, if you expect any acting out of me today, forget it!' But three months later, she came back fifteen pounds lighter and did the 'Get Happy' number in a couple of takes. However, MGM had reached the end of their tether, and her contract was not renewed.

In a state of depression and bitterness, Garland made the first of many suicide attempts, by trying to swallow broken glass. She was helped back to some semblance of stability by the efforts of her third husband, Sid Luft, who became her manager and arranged her triumphant appearances at the London Palladium and New York's Palace Theater. Then came her greatest achievement: George Cukor's *A Star Is Born* in which she extended her emotional and musical range as Vicki Lester, the star with a self-destructive, alcoholic husband, Norman Maine (James Mason). Both characters demonstrated two sides of Judy, and drew from her the most memorable screen demonstration of her great musical and dramatic gifts. However, she and Luft divorced, and a custody battle over their two children ensued.

In 1963, Judy made her final film, *I Could Go On Singing*, almost a parody of her public and private life. Her co-star Dirk Bogarde remembered rather a cruel story. 'When she started working at Shepperton, the whole crew loved her. They were full of awe. "Miss Garland's coming on to the set tomorrow" etc. But, by the end of a few days, they were calling her "It".' Liza commented, 'Mama was showy and she knew it. She once said to a persistent fan, "I've got rainbows up my ass". Liza also recalled that her

in I Could Go On Singing (United Artists, 1963)

mother's husbands all had one thing in common, a sense of humour.

Garland's fourth marriage – to a young actor, Mark Herron – lasted less than a year, and early in 1968 she married a discotheque manager, Mickey Deans. In the same year, she began the most disastrous engagement of her career. At a London cabaret, she was late for performances, cracked up in mid-song, forgot her lines, and made an embarrassing spectacle of herself. Audiences were hostile. Despite this, she had been planning another show in London when she took her life.

Apart from the anguished moments in *A Star Is Born*, and a couple of 'straight' roles, the dumpy hausfrau in *Judgement At Nuremberg* (1961) and the teacher of retarded children in *A Child Is Waiting* (1963), in both of which she excelled, Judy Garland's screen image was of a sunny, spirited, songbird in over twenty-five joyful MGM musicals from 1937 to 1950. That is how her millions of fans prefer to remember her. RB

with Mickey Rooney in Strike Up The Band (MGM, 1940) ▷

Betty Grable

Real name **Elizabeth Ruth Grable**
Born **St Louis, Missouri, 18 December 1916**
Died **1973**

Amongst the more pleasant World War II memorabilia is a picture of the GI's favourite pin-up girl, Betty Grable, in a white bathing suit looking seductively over her shoulder and displaying her 'million dollar legs', the actual amount Lloyds of London insured them for. By her own admission, she could act 'just enough to get by', a phrase that could equally apply to her singing and dancing, but Fox wrapped her up expertly in brightly coloured packages, and made her just the thing to send to the troops at the front.

Betty, who trained at the Hollywood Professional school, was a chorine in Hollywood musicals at the age of 13. She is the shapely Goldwyn Girl who leads the others in the opening number from *Whoopee!* (1930). She continued in bit parts for Sam Goldwyn under the name of Frances Dean, reverting to Betty Grable at RKO as an ingenue in several musicals. In 1937, she married former child star Jackie Coogan. They toured briefly together in vaudeville, but divorced in 1940. When Alice Faye was rushed to hospital with appendicitis, Grable was summoned by Fox from Broadway for the lead in *Down Argentine Way* (1940). This butter blonde with the peaches and cream complexion and beautiful long legs made a vivid impression. She then starred in eighteen undemanding musical frolics during the following decade, including *Moon Over Miami* (1941), *Sweet Rose O'Grady* (1943) and predictably, *Pin Up Girl* (1944). When Betty committed the cardinal sin of failing to show her legs in *The Shocking Miss Pilgrim* (1947), the protests from thousands of fans forced Fox to call her next film, *Mother Wore Tights* (1947).

In the early 50s, with the rise of the new Fox blonde Marilyn Monroe, Grable's popularity declined. In 1965, her 22-year-old marriage to trumpeter Harry James ended. She appeared in a few stage musicals, including 'Hello Dolly', before dying of lung cancer at the age of fifty-six. RB

in Mother Wore Tights (20th Century-Fox, 1947)

Greer Garson

Born **County Down, Ireland, September 29 1908**

Greer Garson was the personal discovery of MGM studio boss Louis B. Mayer who spotted her on the London stage while on a trip to Europe in 1938. The tall, attractive, Irish-born redhead had established herself in the theatre after serving an apprenticeship in rep and on tour during the early and mid-30s.

Her film career got off to a slow (but memorable) start when she was cast in the relatively small part of Robert Donat's wife in *Goodbye Mr Chips* (1939), an MGM British production. She was lively and pleasant and did not have much to do, yet won an Oscar nomination for her performance. Given her first opportunity to demonstrate her talent as an actress (in a costume role), she more than held her own opposite Laurence Olivier in MGM's typically lavish production of *Pride And Prejudice* (1940). A sentimental but stylish Technicolor picture, *Blossoms In The Dust* (1941) followed. Her light complexion and Titian hair photographed well in colour and here she was teamed for the first of many pictures with Walter Pidgeon. Only her fourth movie role, it gathered her a second Oscar nomination, and she actually won the award the following year for her most celebrated performance in the title role of *Mrs Miniver* (1942), which typecast her from then on. She presented an idealised version of a typical upper-middle class British mother and housewife, rather too unbelievably perfect, beautiful, and heroic in coping with the war, and far too young for the role. (She married actor Richard Ney, who played her son in the picture, the year after it was released.)

In *Random Harvest* (1942), another big hit, she was again cast as the wife of a gentlemanly British actor, Ronald Colman. Averaging only one picture per year, she accomplished the unique feat of winning Oscar nominations for three successive performances: She played *Madame Curie* (1943) and *Mrs Parkington* (1944), married to Walter Pidgeon in both, and in *The Valley Of Decision* (1945) was romantically involved with Gregory Peck. Her record of six Oscar nominations within seven years has never been matched and attests to the level of her popularity and prestige at the time – with the powerful support of Louis B. Mayer and MGM behind her, of course. *Adventure* (1946) with Gable was her last hit, and her career began to suffer from being too closely identified with a particular type of sentimentalised character. She failed in various attempts to broaden her appeal, but her memorable Calpurnia in *Julius Caesar* (1953) gave a hint of her capabilities as a classical actress. She retired from films after 1954 but has made occasional comebacks, most notably as Eleanor Roosevelt in *Sunrise At Campobello* (1960) which earned her another Oscar nomination. Among other TV appearances, she played Aunt March in 'Little Women' (1978). JF

in Song Of The Thin Man (MGM, 1947)

Gloria Grahame

Real name **Gloria Grahame Hallward**
Born **Los Angeles, Calif., 28 November 1925**
Died **1982**

An attractive, green-eyed blonde with unusual lips which gave her an insolent, sulky appearance, and with a lisping delivery to match, Gloria Grahame was most often cast as a fallen woman or gangster's moll, but she was a talented actress who often transcended those clichéd parts in which she was cast. After some stage experience, and encouraged by her English actress mother, she was signed by MGM in 1944 and had her first major success, Oscar-nominated for her performance as a bar singer in *Crossfire* (1947). She married Nicholas Ray (her second husband) in 1948, the same year he directed her in *A Woman's Secret*, but their next together was a big improvement: in an inspired piece of casting she was teamed with Bogart *In A Lonely Place* (1950), then landed a leading role in DeMille's *The Greatest Show On Earth* (1952), and won a supporting Oscar for her dissatisfied wife in *The Bad And The Beautiful* later that same year. These were her best years, and she worked with a number of interesting directors, including two films each with Minnelli and Fritz Lang. Miss Grahame played the gangster's moll attracted to Glenn Ford in Lang's *The Big Heat* (1953) and had a delightful change of pace, playing Ado Annie in *Oklahoma!* (1955). During the late 50s she appeared in a few minor movies and, subsequently, mixed the occasional film with stage and TV work. A couple of years before her death she had small roles in *Head Over Heels* and *Melvin And Howard* (both 1980). JF

Farley Granger

Born **San Jose, California, 1 July 1925**

'In Hollywood I was either the neurotic killer or the poor little rich boy or the pathetic poverty-stricken boy, all in a one-dimensional kind of way... I realised that romantic leads were such a bore and that I really wanted to do character things.' Thus, later in life, Farley Granger looked back on his brief period of stardom. He had been typecast because of his youthful good looks and lack of any real acting experience. He had been discovered while in his last year of high school, signed to a film contract by producer Sam Goldwyn and cast in a major Hollywood production, *The North Star* (1943) while he was still a teenager. Although under contract to an independent producer, Granger suffered from some of the same problems as other contract stars. During the postwar years, for example, his Goldwyn pictures, such as *Enchantment* (1948) and *Roseanna McCoy* (1949), were invariably less interesting than his loan-outs – like his first picture after war service, *They Live By Night* filmed at RKO in 1947.

Although still relatively unknown, Granger was selected for the latter by director Nicholas Ray for his ability to project a certain youthful innocence and vulnerability, while appearing tough enough to

make his position, as a young gangster on the run, appear credible and convincing. His fine performance immediately led to a part in the Hitchcock production of *Rope* (1948), in which he played the more sensitive and sympathetic of the two young killers, and appeared to have no trouble coping with the ten minute long takes in spite of his lack of stage experience. He played a thief on the run in *Side Street* (1949) at MGM and finally got his best Hollywood role as the vulnerable, tennis-playing hero of Hitchcock's *Strangers On A Train* (1951), although Robert Walker's convincingly sinister villain stole the picture.

Unhappy with the Hollywood roles which followed, Granger bought himself out of his Goldwyn contract before leaving for Italy to appear in Visconti's *Senso* (1954). In this stunningly beautiful Technicolor production, Granger tried hard but was out of his depth in attempting to sustain a lengthy and unfamiliar part as a 19th-century Austrian soldier, and co-star Alida Valli stole the acting honours. Back in the US he had one more major role, in *The Girl In The Red Velvet Swing* (1955). During the following years he devoted himself more to the theatre and TV, only returning to pictures during the late 60s and early 70s, starring in a number of Continental productions mixed with a few American TV movies. JF

in Edge Of Doom *(RKO, 1950)*

Stewart Granger

Real name **James Stewart**
Born **London, England, 6 May 1913**

Tall, dark and debonair, Stewart Granger specialised in playing dashing romantic leading men, but never took his acting too seriously. He was a medical student at Epsom College when his friend Michael Wilding introduced him to the pleasures of working as a film extra – good pay and attractive girls for a minimum amount of effort. After attending drama school, he gained his first acting experience on the stage during the late 30s. Invalided out of the Black Watch Regiment, he resumed his film career during the war and made his name as the young hero of Gainsborough Pictures' *The Man In Grey* (1943) in which James Mason scored as the dastardly villain. The picture also made the names of Margaret Lockwood and Phyllis Calvert who alternated as the romantic heroines of the successful Granger-Gainsborough vehicles which followed in 1944 – *Fanny*

in The Wild North *(MGM, 1952)*

By Gaslight, *Love Story* and *The Madonna Of The Seven Moons*. He then graduated to a British Technicolor star, appearing in three lavish, but not very successful, colour costumers, playing Apollodorus in *Caesar And Cleopatra* (1945), Thorn in *Blanche Fury* (1947) and the adventurer Konigsmark in Ealing studio's first venture in colour *Saraband For Dead Lovers* (1948). In 1949 he joined Jean Simmons in *Adam And Evelyn*, and they were married the following year in the US after he had completed his first picture under his new contract

with MGM – a colourful and successful remake of *King Solomon's Mines*, on location in Africa and co-starring Deborah Kerr.

A number of costume pictures of variable quality followed. Granger was seen at his swashbuckling best in the title role in MGM's lively and entertaining remake of *Scaramouche* (1952); and another good one was the CinemaScope production of *Moonfleet* (1955), a tale of smuggling and adventure set in 1770's Dorset. A highly unlikely subject for director Fritz Lang, it turned out surprisingly well, with a

major contribution from Granger in the lead. Less good was *Young Bess* (1953) in which he was reunited on the screen with Jean Simmons, while the remake of *The Prisoner Of Zenda* (1952) and *Beau Brummell* (1954) are best forgotten. Granger's MGM contract expired in 1957, and he was less in demand during the years that followed. He continued to average one picture per year throughout the 60s, did some TV work during 1969-71 – including a stab at Sherlock Holmes – and, most recently, played a cameo role in *The Wild Geese* (1978). JF

in Scaramouche *(MGM, 1952)*

Cary Grant

Real name Archibald Alexander Leach
Born Bristol, England, 18 January 1904

It took Cary Grant a number of years to discover his screen persona, and having discovered it and established himself as one of the top Hollywood stars of the late 30s, the story of his later career reflected how long he was able to sustain it. He got better as he matured, and for 30 years his screen image hardly varied from that of the immensely handsome, likeable and elegant star with a nice sense of irony and superb timing which made him ideal in comedy roles and fast-paced comedy-thrillers.

As a young leading man Cary was good-looking but dull, and hardly benefitted from his appearance in Mae West's first two smash-hit movies in 1933, *I'm No Angel* and *She Done Him Wrong*. Apparently Paramount, the studio which had him under contract during the mid-30s did not know what to do with him. Even during his later, mature years, he was not the kind of actor who could create a memorable characterisation out of an otherwise weak role, but had to be cast in the right parts, and he did his best work for a few directors, most notably George Cukor, Howard Hawks and Alfred Hitchcock. Grant had already appeared in twenty movies by the time he made *Sylvia Scarlett*, a quirky and unusual picture, and the first of three with Katharine Hepburn and director George Cukor. He obviously felt comfortable in the role of the Cockney con-man which drew on his previously untapped vitality as an actor. It was as if he had been let loose on the screen for the first time, and he produced an immensely engaging performance which hinted at better things to come. But his emergence as a star of the first rank was still a few years off.

Coming from a broken home, Cary had originally run away at the age of 14 to join a travelling troupe of young knockabout comedians who played in vaudeville houses all over England. He worked hard to perfect his acrobatic and pantomime skills and was selected for a US tour in 1920. Staying on in New York, he graduated into operetta during the late 20s, then headed west to California late in 1931 and ended up signing a five-year contract with Paramount shortly before his 28th birthday. He was immediately averaging six pictures per year, and gained much useful experience opposite a number of top female stars including Marlene Dietrich, Mae West and Sylvia Sidney. But by the time his contract expired, the actor was determined to maintain his independence and arranged a joint deal with Columbia and RKO, both studios that were weak on leading men.

in Hot Saturday (Paramount, 1932)

By 1937 the screwball comedy had become established in Hollywood. This popular new type of movie provided a natural opportunity for him with his special blend of spontaneous vitality and charm, and gift for rapid fire repartee. He and Constance Bennett made a pair of lively and sophisticated ghosts in *Topper* followed immediately by *The Awful Truth*, his second for Columbia and his first major success as a comedy star. (The film received six Oscar nominations including Best Picture.) As his co-star Irene Dunne recalled, 'Cary and I were almost complete strangers when we met on the set... I was instantly impressed with his energy and enthusiasm. As I watched Cary working each day, I marvelled at the excellence of his timing – the naturalness, the ease, the charm... People usually react with skepticism when I say that Cary's intelligence and seriousness of approach were his strongest points as an actor. Behind that carefree and sophisticated man on the screen, there's a painstaking worker and keen mind at work.'

Two delightful comedies with Katharine Hepburn followed – Howard Hawks's *Bringing Up Baby*, and *Holiday* directed by George Cukor (both 1938). Director Hawks who had initiated the screwball comedy cycle with *Twentieth Century* in 1934 recognised Grant's unique talent and the possibilities opened up by teaming him with a strong actress like Katharine Hepburn. As Hawks saw it, 'You take a professor, and you use the girl's part to knock his dignity down. Katie and Cary were a great combination. It's pretty hard to think of anybody but Cary

Grant in that type of stuff.' In fact, the pattern worked so well that Hawks was tempted to use it again, making the underlying sex role reversal theme even more explicit. In *His Girl Friday* (1940) the character of the ace reporter is changed from a man (in the original version known as 'The Front Page') to a woman, played by Rosalind Russell, while in *I Was A Male War Bride* (1949), as the title implies, Cary plays Ann Sheridan's alien spouse, classified by the army bureaucracy as a 'male war bride' with all the comic complications that entails. In each case a strong female star was required to play as naturally as possible with the comedy supplied by Cary's superbly timed 'reacting', as well as by the situation. Hawks again: 'I think it's fun to have a woman dominant and let the man be funniest.'

In 1939 Cary appeared in a pair of highly unusual, but memorable, adventure pictures in which his slightly detached, ironic quality proved a great asset. Archibald Cutter in RKO's tongue-in-cheek version of *Gunga Din* was followed by a more poignant role as the boss of a broken down airline in Central America in *Only Angels Have Wings*. Clearly Cary Grant was hitting his stride during these years, and virtually every picture is of interest. In 1940 he joined Katharine Hepburn (and Cukor) again in *The Philadelphia Story*, cast in a smallish but effective starring role as her charming but cynical ex-husband. And in 1941 he finally won recognition that was long overdue – his first Oscar nomination. Admittedly, it was for one of his less memorable roles, as the dutiful father and husband (to Irene Dunne) in a sentimental tale, *Penny Serenade*. Also in 1941, however, he began a fruitful collaboration with director Alfred Hitchcock who took perverse advantage of his attractive star image to cast him as a likeable playboy type whom Joan Fontaine both loves and fears and marries in *Suspicion*. (Apparently Hitchcock even toyed with the idea of making him a murderer). In 1944 Cary portrayed a genuinely different, downbeat character, a Cockney hustler and drifter named Ernie Mott in *None But The Lonely Heart*, written and directed by Clifford Odets. But although there were some moving moments in the picture, the star was not capable of getting inside the character in the manner of a Garfield or a Brando, which was what was required, although he did gain a second Oscar nomination. Reunited with Hitchcock on *Notorious* (1946), Cary was teamed with Ingrid Bergman and the result was a knockout. They made a most attractive couple on the screen, and their tormented and passionate love relationship, complicated by wartime suspense and danger, was extremely moving. The picture was a great success, but during the following years Cary returned to the kind of likeable but unremarkable comedy roles which he managed so easily. The best of the bunch were a pair with Howard Hawks, *I Was A Male War Bride* and *Monkey Business* (1952), a kind of pre-LSD comedy in which he was teamed with Ginger Rogers and Marilyn Monroe. In 1949 he married actress Betsy Drake, his co-star the previous year in, you guessed it, *Every Girl Should Be Married*. She became the third of his five wives, one per decade. The others included Virginia Cherrill (mid-30s), heiress Barbara Hutton (mid-40s), actress Dyan Cannon (60s), and most recently Barbara Harris (not the actress of the same name). Although his career wound down during the 50s, there were two more pictures with Hitchcock, the pleasantly diverting *To Catch A Thief* (1955) with Grace Kelly, and a last masterpiece, *North By Northwest* (1959), opposite Eva-Marie Saint, in which he proved that he could still light up the screen. Even imitation Hitchcock provided some fun, with Audrey Hepburn, in Stanley Donen's sparkling *Charade* (1963). A clear indication of the lasting power of Cary Grant's romantic screen image was the fact that he could be paired so easily with Grace Kelly and Audrey Hepburn, both of whom were 25 years his junior. But the star retired from the screen after *Walk Don't Run* (1966) and has served as a part-time cosmetics executive during recent years. He was awarded a well-merited special Oscar in 1969. JF

with Joan O'Brien in Operation Petticoat *(Universal, 1959)*

in To Catch A Thief *(Paramount, 1955)* ▷

Kathryn Grayson

Real name **Zelma Kathryn Hedrick**
Born **Winston-Salem, North Carolina,
9 February, 1922.**

When coloratura soprano Kathryn Grayson sang five songs, including an aria from 'La Traviata', in MGM's all-star patriotic parade, *Thousands Cheer* (1943), she began her ten-year reign as the prima donna of Hollywood. (Jeanette MacDonald and Deanna Durbin were now over the hill.) With her china-doll features, little turned-up nose and patrician manner, Grayson raised the tone of over a dozen MGM musicals. (Seven produced by Joe Pasternak, Durbin's mentor.) Although opera managers did not beat a path to her door, her clear, slightly shrill, small voice carried well on film in the popular classics and operatic scenes. She got to sing at the Met with real-life opera star Lauritz Melchior in *Two Sisters From Boston* (1946), and duets with Mario Lanza in *That Midnight Kiss* (1949) and *The Toast Of New Orleans* (1950).

Kathryn Grayson's classically trained voice did not lead her to the opera house but to the radio and The Eddie Cantor Show, on which she was discovered by an MGM talent scout at the age of 18. In her first film, she played the title role in *Andy Hardy's Private Secretary* (1941), and the following

in Lovely To Look At *(MGM, 1952)*

year starred in *Seven Sweethearts* and *Rio Rita* with Abbott and Costello. But her career, like her voice, hit the heights after *Thousands Cheer*. Kathryn teamed up with Frank Sinatra in three movies,

Anchors Aweigh (1945) in which she spent over two hours trying to get a singing audition with Jose Iturbi; *It Happened In Brooklyn* (1947), as a music teacher, and the dismal *The Kissing Bandit* (1948), enlivened only by her rendition of 'Love Is Where You Find It'.

After Grayson refused to work with Lanza again, because of his boorish behaviour, she found her best partner in virile baritone Howard Keel in *Show Boat* (1951). She had already played Magnolia in the 'Show Boat' sequences of *Till The Clouds Roll By* (1946), and was perfect casting in the colourful remake of Jerome Kern's classic. Unwisely, she left MGM after *Lovely To Look At* (1952), also with Keel, for a four-picture contract with Warners. This was terminated after two mediocre vehicles, *The Desert Song* (1953) and *So This Is Love* (1953), making a fine attempt in the latter to play Grace Moore, opera and film star of the 30s. Kathryn returned to her old studio to triumph in *Kiss Me Kate* (1953), proving that there was more fun in her than she had been credited with. She let her hair down in the acerbic 'I Hate Men', and matches Howard Keel in 'So In Love' and 'Wunderbar'.

But the kissing for Kate Grayson had to stop and, after one further film *The Vagabond King* (1956), she appeared only in nightclubs and on stage. She had been married to actor John Shelton and singer Johnny Johnston. RB

Sydney Greenstreet

Born **Sandwich, England,
27 December 1879**
Died **1954**

'A dead man on the floor. A doomed man in front of me. A Strauss waltz on the radio. What could be more entertaining?' Thus does Sydney Greenstreet's massive Colonel Robinson find himself with the edge on George Raft in *Background To Danger* (1943), combining cultured irony, bogus *bonhomie* and single-minded, steely villainy.

With the exception of Ealing's Katie Johnson, no actor became a film star so late in life. After a distinguished stage career, and at the age of 61, Greenstreet was chosen by John Huston to play Caspar Gutman in *The Maltese Falcon* (1941). He was so nervous before his first scene that he asked Mary Astor to hold his hand and tell him that, 'I won't make an ass of meself'. His menacing bulk, rumbling chuckle, florid Edwardian manner and amused irony were very close to Hammett's original and his pairing with Peter Lorre was one of Hollywood's happiest strokes of casting: a ponderous clubman Lear danced attendance by a gardenia-scented Fool.

Over the next eight years he made up for lost time with 24 pictures for Warners. In *They Died With Their Boots On* (1941) he played the gourmandising general who launched Errol Flynn's General Custer on his inglorious career; his cultured spy, Dr Lorenz, in *Across The Pacific* (1942) was a small masterpiece of self-absorbed ruthlessness; he was the acceptable face of corruption in *Casablanca* (1942). He was memorably teamed with Lorre in *The Mask Of Dimitrios* (1944), *Three Strangers* (1946) and, their last film together, *The Verdict* (1946), an efficient thriller set in Victorian London and Don Siegel's first feature film as director. He personified big-business egomania in MGM's *The Hucksters* (1947).

Warners tried Greenstreet in comedy, but films like *Pillow To Post* (1945) and *That Way With Women* (1947) were unworthy of his talent. However, the romantic and the aesthete lurking within his huge frame made him a perfect Count Fosco in *The Woman In White* (1948). By the time he appeared as the evil Sheriff Titus Semple in *Flamingo Road* (1949), Greenstreet was a very sick man. It was his last appearance on film except for a cameo in *It's A Great Feeling* (1949) and a character part in *Malaya*, an MGM actioner released in 1950. Doubtless the search for the Falcon still goes on – 'I leave you the *rara avis* on the table as a little memento'. RC

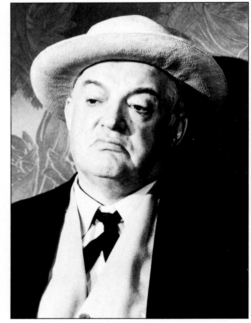

in The Hucksters *(MGM, 1947)*

Rex Harrison

Born **Huyton, England, 5 March 1908**

A tall, stylish stage actor who has had an uneven career in films, Rex Harrison first discovered the theatre while at school. He worked his way up from rep to touring companies to West End success in 1936. Signed to a film contract by Alexander Korda, he appeared in the long running Terence Rattigan play, 'French Without Tears', in the evenings while filming during the day. He starred as a young journalist opposite Vivien Leigh in *Storm In A Teacup* (1937) and had major roles in *Night Train To Munich* (1939) and *Major Barbara* (1941) before serving in the RAF. Immediately after the war he was cast in a part made for him, as the sceptical writer haunted by his ex-wife in a delightful Technicolor version of Noel Coward's *Blithe Spirit* (1945), and went on to play the lead in *The Rake's Progress* (1945) joined by the first of his six wives, Lilli Palmer, in their first film together. He had clearly matured as a film star and accepted an offer from Hollywood where he and Palmer did a number

of pictures, but at different studios. Although obviously miscast as the king in *Anna And The King Of Siam* (1946), his first American film, he gave a surprisingly good performance, but was better as the ghostly British sea captain romantically attached to Gene Tierney in *The Ghost And Mrs Muir* (1947).

Glad to get back to the stage during the 50s, he met and fell in love with Kay Kendall while filming *The Constant Husband* (1955), and she joined him in New York where he had the biggest success of his stage (and later film) career in the role of professor Higgins in 'My Fair Lady'. In spite of the problems involved, he managed to develop a unique style of half-speaking, half-singing on pitch which he used to great effect in the show, which he played for three years on stage. In 1964 he won an Oscar for the movie version. Cast as Caesar in the troubled epic production of *Cleopatra* (1963), he provided some much needed stylish acting which earned him an Oscar nomination. Aside from a lavish musical production of *Dr Dolittle* (1967), his later pictures were not at all memorable, including, most recently, a remake of *The Prince And The Pauper* (1977) and *Ashanti* (1979). JF

in Unfaithfully Yours *(20th Century-Fox, 1948)*

Rita Hayworth

Real name **Margarita Carmen Cansino**
Born **Brooklyn, New York, 17 October 1918.**

'It's true, I made a lot of mistakes,' says Rita Hayworth in her dying breath, to Orson Welles, after a shoot-out in a hall of mirrors at the end of *The Lady From Shanghai* (1948), a line which the actress might endorse today. The life of Rita Hayworth, a star who epitomised 40s Hollywood glamour, reads like the script of a far-fetched soap opera, more melodramatic, more romantic than any film she appeared in. Hers is the tale of someone in the hall of fame, but actually caught in a hall of mirrors where everything is illusory.

The daughter of Spanish dancers, dark-haired Rita began dancing in her parents' act at the age of twelve. In her teens, under the name of Rita Cansino, she danced with her father in nightclubs at Californian resorts and in Tijuana, Mexico, before being spotted by Fox production boss, Winfield Sheehan. In 1935, she made her screen debut in *Under The Pampas Moon*, followed by other bit parts, usually appearing as an exotic dancer.

In 1937, she married Edward Judson, a businessman twenty-two years her senior, who gave up car selling to concentrate on his wife's career, and succeeded in gaining her a seven-year contract with Columbia. The studio set to work on her subsequently famously glorious hair: they raised the hairline on her forehead by electrolysis, and turned her into a redhead, after which she also emerged anglicised as Rita Hayworth. She continued to appear in a number of B films until Howard Hawks cast her in *Only Angels Have Wings* (1939). Her beauty glowed in the South American jungle where she made eyes at Cary Grant while her husband, Richard Barthelmess, was off on a flying mission. This brought her a number of parts as the vampy second female lead. Columbia loaned her out to Warner Bros. where she was a gold digger in *The Strawberry Blonde* (1941), and 'the other woman' in *Affectionately Yours* (1941), and at Fox, looking ravishing in Technicolor, she had little difficulty in luring bullfighter Tyrone Power away from faithful Linda Darnell in *Blood And Sand* (1941).

In a change of pace back at Columbia, Rita returned to dancing – as Fred Astaire's superb partner in *You'll Never Get Rich* (1941) and *You Were Never Lovelier* (1942). She, indeed, was never lovelier than in the Fox musical, *My Gal Sal* (1942),

in Affair In Trinidad (Columbia, 1952)

during which she fell in love with her co-star, Victor Mature. This was part of the disturbing cycle of falling in and out of love with various men which was to characterise her private life. Rita obtained a divorce from Judson in order to marry Mature, but decided, instead, to marry director-actor Orson Welles in 1943. She was now becoming Hollywood's leading 'Sex Goddess', and millions of pin-ups of her were sent to American servicemen overseas.

It was Columbia director Charles Vidor who brought out Hayworth's healthy eroticism best, in *Cover Girl* (1944), in which she danced with Gene Kelly, but most of all in *Gilda* (1946). Married to nasty scar-faced casino owner, George Macready, she sang (with Anita Ellis's voice) 'Put The Blame On Mame', after a few drinks, peeling off her long black gloves in a symbolic striptease as Glenn Ford, and millions of hot-blooded men all over the world, lusted for her. Rita was later to say, 'Every man I knew had fallen in love with Gilda and wakened with me.' In Vidor's listless Bizet-less *The Loves Of Carmen* (1948), she was a sexy Spanish gypsy to Glenn Ford's Don José.

The tempestuous marriage to Orson Welles had broken down when he directed her in *The Lady*

From Shanghai (1948), a misogynistic *film noir*, in which Rita as an icy, predatory woman entraps Welles in a web of intrigue. The same year, she met and fell in love with Aly Khan, the handsome, multi-millionaire playboy son of the Aga Khan, and spiritual leader of millions of Moslems. Though the Prince was not legally divorced, they travelled around Europe together and, heady with her new-found wealth and romance, Hayworth informed Columbia that she was retiring from films for a while, thus giving up an annual salary of a quarter of a million dollars. She and Aly were married in France in May, 1949. Two years later, Rita returned to Columbia, divorced and contrite, begging Harry Cohn, the tough studio head, to restore her contract.

At the age of thirty-four, she continued to bring a voluptuousness to inferior vehicles such as the fallen woman in *Affair In Trinidad* (1952), again with Glenn Ford, and *Miss Sadie Thompson* (1954), enticing priest José Ferrer to sin. As *Salome* (1953), she stripped only to the fourth veil, dancing to save the head of John the Baptist, in this version. Meanwhile, an acrimonious relationship with Harry Cohn continued. She was dissatisfied with the films he was giving her, and he was unhappy about her waning popularity and her fourth marriage to

in The Loves Of Carmen (Columbia, 1948)

vocalist Dick Haymes in 1953. The Argentinian-born Haymes got into financial difficulties due to alimony payments to three former wives, and had problems with immigration officials, because he had avoided the draft in World War II by giving up his American citizenship. They were divorced in 1955.

After a three-year absence, Rita returned to the screen, but her bloom was fading. In 1941, when Columbia had hoped to film *Pal Joey*, she was offered the role of the nice chorus girl. When they filmed it in 1957, Hayworth played Frank Sinatra's world-weary 'sugar-mommy.' She was quite affecting as Burt Lancaster's ex-mistress begging for another chance in *Separate Tables* (1958), and the shady lady surrounded by men in *They Came To Cordura* (1959). Between pictures, she found time to marry producer James Hill for the statutory two years. In the sixties the films, and her appearances in them, became more and more insignificant, among them Claudia Cardinale's mother in *Circus World* (1966), and an embittered woman in *The Money Trap* (1966), who turns to alcohol for solace.

Sadly, in 1976, it was revealed that Rita Hayworth had become an alcoholic and that her business affairs had been taken over by the authorities. Pictures of a dishevelled, distraught woman appeared on the front pages around the world. Gradually, she was rehabilitated with the help of friends and especially her daughter Princess Yasmin Khan, whose looks evoke memories of her mother, now tragically senile, in the flower of youth. RB

with Glenn Ford in The Money Trap *(MGM, 1966)*

Van Heflin

Born **Walters, Oklahoma, 13 December 1910**
Died **1971**

A solid, dependable actor who never made it as a big star, Van Heflin is best remembered as the hard working rancher married to Jean Arthur in the classic Hollywood Western *Shane* (1953) or as the mentally disturbed bomber in *Airport* (1970), his last picture. Heflin's stage experience during the 30s led him to Hollywood where he appeared in a number of movies. But his career did not take off until he was signed by MGM at the age of thirty. He immediately won a supporting actor Oscar for his second MGM film, playing Robert Taylor's drunken, Shakespeare-quoting sidekick in *Johnny Eager* (1942). Heflin appeared in a large number and variety of pictures during the 40s, ranging from thrillers (*The Strange Love Of Martha Ivers*, 1946) to costumers (Athos in *The Three Musketeers*, 1948) and even musicals. His roles during later years were less interesting, although he developed into a western star with memorable performances in *Shane*, *3:10 To Yuma* (1957) and *Gunman's Walk* (1958) despite a sameness of theme and character. His few films during the 60s included some unfortunate choices – George Stevens's epic flop, *The Greatest Story Ever Told* (1965) and a disastrous remake of the western classic, *Stagecoach* (1966). JF

in Under Ten Flags (Paramount, 1960)

Paul Henreid

Born **Trieste, 10 January 1908**

'And will you be happy, Charlotte?'
'Oh Jerry, don't let's ask for the moon. We have the stars.' Max Steiner music wells up; fade to black; end title. This classic exchange after Paul Henreid does his cigarette trick – putting two cigarettes in his mouth and lighting them before passing one to Bette Davis – at the end of *Now Voyager* (1942), represents Henreid's most celebrated moment on the screen. He had arrived in the US in 1940 from England where he had appeared on the stage and in a few films. Immediately recognised as the archetype of the tall, handsome and sophisticated European leading man, RKO cast him with Michele Morgan in a film about the French resistance, *Joan Of Paris* (1941). *Now Voyager* followed and then *Casablanca* (1943) cast as a dedicated European resistance leader, married to Ingrid Bergman. Tired of playing noble but dull characters, he tried a change of tack in 1945, swashbuckling his way through *The Spanish Main*, RKO's first Technicolor production. Blonde-haired Henreid gave a suitably virile and athletic

in Major Barbara (United Artists, 1941)

Wendy Hiller

Born **Bramshall, Cheshire, England, 15 August 1912**

Wendy Hiller first made her name on the stage during the mid-30s, and in films playing forthright and determined young ladies like Shaw's Eliza Doolittle and Major Barbara. She won an Oscar nomination for Eliza, perfectly cast opposite Leslie Howard's Professor Higgins in *Pygmalion* (1938), in which she made a touching and convincing transition from Cockney flower seller to self-assured and stylish young lady. In Powell and Pressburger's *I Know Where I'm Going* (1945) Miss Hiller demonstrated her ability to give a subtle and moving performance in a film original not based on a literary source. Continuing to divide her time between stage and films during the 50s, she won a supporting actress Oscar for her performance in another play adaptation, Rattigan's *Separate Tables* (1958), and was excellent in the unhappy role of Paul Morel's mother in *Sons And Lovers* (1960). *A Man For All Seasons* won half a dozen Oscars in 1966 and she was nominated yet again for her smallish role as Thomas More's wife. She was created a Dame in 1975 and more recently appeared in *Voyage Of The Damned* (1976), a weak remake of *The Cat And The Canary* (1979), and *The Elephant Man* (1980). JF

in 1942

performance, taming haughty Maureen O'Hara and foiling the villainous Walter Slezak, and the picture was a surprise hit. But his career went downhill after this and he turned to directing B-pictures during the mid-50s. JF

Celeste Holm

Born **New York City, 29 April 1919**

Celeste Holm's screen image combined the wise-cracking, witty qualities of Eve Arden with the softer, friendlier touch and musical talent of Betty Garrett whom she closely resembled in appearance. Most often cast in supporting roles as the spinster friend, sister or confidante of the star, she only settled in Hollywood for a relatively short period during the late 40s when she was under contract to 20th Century-Fox. For most of her professional life she was a stage star, but did some work on radio, TV and on the night-club circuit. Miss Holm was signed up in 1946 after Broadway successes as Ado Annie in 'Oklahoma!' and as the star of 'Bloomer Girl'. She

in Champagne For Caesar (United Artists, 1950)

made an auspicious debut dressed in bright red two-thirds of the way through *Three Little Girls In Blue* (1946) and stole the show with a lively Ado Annie-type number, 'Je suis toujours la dame' (Always a Lady). The following year she won a well-deserved supporting Oscar for her sympathetic fashion editor in *Gentleman's Agreement*. Her short stay at Fox concluded with further Oscar nominations for her performances in *Come To The Stables* (1949) and *All About Eve* (1950) as Bette Davis's close friend. She returned to the New York stage, but was back in Hollywood to play Sinatra's sympathetic friend in a couple of MGM musicals, *The Tender Trap* (1955) and *High Society* (1956). During later years Miss Holm appeared in a handful of comedy roles, and a number of TV movies during the 70s, and was most recently seen as Aunt Polly in *Tom Sawyer* (1973) and in a small part in Larry Cohen's *The Private Files Of J. Edgar Hoover* (1978). JF

Tim Holt

Born **Beverly Hills, 5 February 1918**
Died **1973**

Born into a famous movie western family just as his father, Jack Holt, was developing into one of the top western stars of the silents, Tim Holt appeared in a number of his father's pictures as a child, then became a B-western star himself at RKO during the 40s at about the same time that his sister, Jennifer Holt, was starring as a B-western heroine. By the time he retired in 1952 he had appeared in about fifty, mainly minor, westerns, although he did have small roles in John Ford's *Stagecoach* (1939) and *My Darling Clementine* (1946).

However, Holt is best remembered today for his fine performances in two dramatic roles: He played the lead in Orson Welles's *The Magnificent Ambersons* (1942), where Welles took advantage of his boyish, curly-haired good looks to turn him into the spoilt, bratty young hero who gets his 'come-uppance' in the end. And five years later he gave a sympathetic performance as Curtin, the youngest of the three gold prospectors, in John Huston's *The Treasure Of The Sierra Madre* (1947). Holt returned to the screen for one last memorable role, starring in *The Monster That Challenged The World* (1957), before retiring from the screen. JF

in Storm Over Wyoming *(RKO, 1950)*

with Dorothy Lamour in Road To Morocco *(Paramount, 1942)*

Bob Hope

Born **Eltham England, 29 May 1903**

Bob Hope's years as a film star merely represent an interlude in his long career as a stand-up comedian on radio, stage and TV. Although born in England, Hope grew up in Cleveland, Ohio in the US. After trying his hand at various jobs, he went on the stage, first in vaudeville, then in comedy roles, and finally had his biggest success on the radio. Coming to films from radio he never really developed as a movie actor, but relied heavily on dialogue, verbal jokes, and gags prepared by his large staff of contract writers. Writer-director Melville Shavelson recalled that there were as many as thirteen writers first hired by Hope to supply him with material for his radio programme, 'The Pepsodent Show' in 1938. 'Until this point there was no distinct 'Bob Hope character.' It was our group that created him. He didn't realise it at the time, but we based the character, to a large extent on Bob himself. And the character hasn't changed in forty years.'

The typical Hope character is a timid weakling and coward who, through mistaken identity, suddenly finds himself in an extremely awkward and dangerous situation. He is frequently in the position of trying to cope with a heroine who is smarter and stronger than himself, in an amusing variation on the sex reversal theme. Through good luck, rather than intelligence or bravery on his part, he generally emerges victorious in the end and wins the girl. In *My Favourite Brunette* (1947) with Dorothy Lamour he is a baby photographer next door to, and mistaken for, a private eye. He acquires a reputation as a gunslinger in *The Paleface* (1948), but is really a travelling dentist, and the real sharpshooting is done by the formidable Jane Russell. *My Favourite Spy* (1951) has him playing opposite Hedy Lamarr as a comedian who is the exact look-alike of a notorious spy. And in *Casanova's Big Night* (1954) he is a timid tailor's assistant induced into attempting to masquerade as Casanova, with Joan Fontaine as the tough and resourceful heroine.

In his first picture, *The Big Broadcast Of 1938*, Hope sang the Oscar-winning song, 'Thanks for the Memory' which has been associated with him over the years. Quickly established as a star at Para-

Trevor Howard

Born **Cliftonville, England,
29 September 1916**

One of the most intelligent and reliable of that group of British actors who emerged after the war, Trevor Howard first made his name in films as the sensitive, decent doctor who has an affair with housewife Celia Johnson in *Brief Encounter* (1946). He played a similar role in *Passionate Friends* (1948) for the same director, David Lean, but his romantic image was soon left behind. With his determined look, rasping voice and slightly abrasive personality, he was most often cast during the following years in thrillers or war pictures playing tough, authoritarian types. He was the cynical but dedicated intelligence officer

in 1951

pursuing Orson Welles in *The Third Man* (1949), an impressive Capt Bligh in the remake of *Mutiny On The Bounty* (1962), the tough British general, Lord Cardigan, in *The Charge Of The Light Brigade* (1968), and most recently played Cartwright in *The Sea Wolves* (1980). The kind of solid, dependable performer who is often forgotten when the awards are passed out, he did receive the British Film Academy award in 1958 for his seagoing captain in *The Key* and was nominated for an Oscar for his bitter, irascible Morel Sr in *Sons And Lovers* (1960), a fine version of D.H. Lawrence's novel. JF

mount, where he stayed for almost twenty years, he brought his stable of radio writers with him '…to take scripts (which somebody else had written) and punch jokes into them', according to Shavelson. Bob then introduced them in such a way that he appeared to be ad-libbing in front of the camera. He had his first hit with Paulette Goddard in *The Cat And The Canary* in 1939 and that same year served for the first of many times as the emcee of the Oscar ceremony. The following year he received the first of four honorary Oscars for his services to the Academy and the motion picture industry. And *Road To Singapore*, also in 1940, with Bing Crosby and Dorothy Lamour, began the highly successful and entertaining series of *Road* movies, which ran for six titles over twelve years and included *Road To Morocco* (1942) and *Road To Bali* (1952). A dedicated golfer and an immensely wealthy man, Hope reduced his film appearances during the 60s and virtually retired after the failure of *Cancel My Reservation* (1972), but played a cameo role in *The Muppet Movie* (1979) and continued active with personal appearances, most recently visiting Beirut to entertain the US Marines stationed there over Christmas 1983. JF

Betty Hutton

Real name **Betty June Thornburg**
Born **Battle Creek, Michigan,
26 February 1921**

Among the frenetic, ear-splitting female vocalists of the 40s, the most popular was 'The Blonde Bombshell' Betty Hutton. She worked almost exclusively for Paramount, for whom she knocked herself out in explosive numbers in musicals such as *The Fleet's In* (1942), *Happy Go Lucky* (1943) and *The Stork Club*

(1945). She also remained very much herself as Texas Guinan, nightclub hostess of the 20s, in *Incendiary Blonde* (1945), Pearl White, silent screen serial queen, in *The Perils Of Pauline* (1947), and Blossom Seely, vaudeville star, in *Somebody Loves Me* (1952), all rags-to-riches Technicolored biopics.

Hutton's life could be the subject of a similar Hollywood biopic, but with more pathos than most. As a child, after the death of her father, she was forced to sing in the streets to support her family. At 15 she was singing with big bands, including the Vincent Lopez Orchestra. After her success on Broadway in 'Two For The Show' in 1940, Paramount offered her a contract. But MGM gave her her greatest chance in *Annie Get Your Gun* (1950) when Judy Garland was suspended.

She returned to Paramount for *Let's Dance* (1950) with Fred Astaire, and was the trapeze artist in Cecil B. DeMille's *The Greatest Show On Earth* (1952). Shortly after, she left Paramount after the studio refused her demand that her second husband Charles O'Curran, a choreographer, direct all her movies. She would make one more film, and appear occasionally on stage or in nightclubs, but because of an old shoulder injury and emotional problems, Betty became unreliable. In 1967, she walked out of a B western and filed for bankruptcy. Married and divorced five times, she retreated to a Rhode Island Catholic rectory, where she lived and worked as a cook and housekeeper, only leaving it once in five years to undergo psychiatric treatment in a mental hospital. She recovered, and was hired as a hostess at a Connecticut sports centre in 1978. RB

in 1949

Celia Johnson

Born **Richmond, England, 18 December 1908**
Died **1982**

After training at RADA, Celia Johnson went on the stage and established herself as a leading and accomplished actress in the West End during the 30s. Her film career got off to an auspicious start with three Noel Coward roles during the 40s. A small but effective part as the wife of naval captain Noel Coward in *In Which We Serve* (1942) was followed by a more substantial role as Robert Newton's wife in *This Happy Breed* (1944). In her most famous part, attracted to doctor Trevor Howard in *Brief Encounter* (1945), she again appeared as the archetype of the dutiful, dependable, middle-class British wife who generally keeps her feelings to herself. Her sensitive performance suggested the emotions which lie beneath the surface and won her an Oscar nomination and the New York Film Critics best actress award. Miss Johnson returned to the stage and did not make another film for four years. Working mainly in the theatre, she occasionally appeared in plays on TV and films, but by the time of her death had acted in less than a dozen pictures, including as Alec Guinness's homey wife who lets her hair down in *The Captain's Paradise* (1953) and, in marked contrast, the severe headmistress in conflict with Vanessa Redgrave in *The Prime Of Miss Jean Brodie* (1969). JF

John Ireland

Born **Vancouver, Canada, 30 January 1914**

An experienced stage actor by the time he landed his first film role, John Ireland made a notable debut as Windy, the thoughtful member of the platoon headed by Dana Andrews in *A Walk In The Sun* (1945). He won a supporting actor Oscar nomination for his performance as Jack Burden, the important reporter character in *All The King's Men* which won the Best Picture Oscar in 1949. Tall and thin, he could be mean looking, too, and spent much of his later career playing heavies in a variety of gangster pictures and westerns. He was on the wrong side of the law in two different versions of the Earp vs Clanton shoot-out, playing Billy Clanton in *My Darling Clementine* (1946) and Johnny Ringo in *Gunfight At The OK Corral* (1957), and was gangster Lee J. Cobb's gunsel in *Party Girl* (1958). Ireland was one of Kirk Douglas's original band of gladiator slave rebels in *Spartacus* (1960) but looked a bit old (he was 45) and thin for the part. Other epics followed, most notably *55 Days At Peking* (1963) and *The Fall Of The Roman Empire* (1964) but most of his later pictures are of little interest. He continued to be active in films and TV movies throughout the 70s, playing an ageing police detective in *Farewell My Lovely* (1974) and again in *Incubus* (1981). JF

in The Good Die Young (United Artists, 1954)

Gloria Jean

Real name **Gloria Jean Schoonover**
Born **Buffalo, New York, 14 April 1926**

Three years after Deanna Durbin made her successful screen debut, Universal introduced into its ranks another child soprano in the cheery, well-scrubbed shape of Gloria Jean in *The Underpup* (1939). Although she had a certain young following, Gloria never achieved the popularity or fame of her predecessor, appearing mostly in quickie musicals and programme fillers.

Gloria Jean had been singing in vaudeville and on radio since she was three. She followed in Durbin's dainty footsteps in Little Miss Fixit roles, occasion-

ally breaking into song. Little Miss Jean's partners were generally Donald O'Connor and Peggy Ryan, the other two leading teenage talents on the Universal lot, demonstrating their musical precocity in vacuous vehicles entitled *Get Hep To Love* (1942), *Mr Big* (1943) and *When Johnny Comes Marching Home* (1943). More senior co-stars were Bing Crosby in *If I Had My Way* (1940), and W.C. Fields in *Never Give A Sucker An Even Break* (1942).

Gloria's limited talents did not survive the transition to ingenue roles, and Universal dropped her. After several low-budget movies for United Artists and Colombia, she retired and became a receptionist and switchboard operator for a California cosmetics firm. She left her desk to appear in Jerry Lewis's *The Ladies' Man* (1961). RB

in A Little Bit Of Heaven (Universal, 1940)

Van Johnson

Real name **Charles Van Johnson**
Born **Newport, Rhode Island,
25 August, 1916**

in 1949

Throughout the 40s, a blue-eyed, sandy-haired, freckle-faced actor of innocent charm was so idolised by screaming bobby-soxers that he was called 'The Voiceless Sinatra'. Van Johnson only sang and danced a little, and acted with not much depth yet, in 1945, he was the second biggest box-office star in Hollywood after Bing Crosby. He appeared so often in uniform that perhaps wartime America pinned its hopes on the boy-next-door-gone-to-war type that Johnson represented.

'Mrs Johnson's boy, Van', first joined up cinematically in *Pilot No. 5* (1943), but got his big chance in *A Guy Named Joe* (1943), as the fledgling pilot watched over by the ghost of former flyer Spencer Tracy. A few months into shooting, Van had a serious car accident, and had to have a metal plate put in his forehead. While the company waited for him to recover, Louis B. Mayer, head of MGM, announced his intention to replace him, but Tracy threatened to walk off the film unless Mayer waited for Van. The picture boosted his popularity and MGM gave him star billing in *Thirty Seconds Over*

Tokyo (1944), again as a heroic pilot. He flew under Brigadier Clark Gable in *Command Decision* (1948), held out against the Nazis in William Wellman's *Battleground* (1949), and flew off on bombing missions in North Korea in *Men Of The Fighting Lady* (1953). Actually, the former chorus boy never saw any real fighting. (Because of his accident he was given a military deferment.) Johnson was first noticed in 1940 in 'Pal Joey' on Broadway, which starred Gene Kelly. After one minor film at Warners, *Murder In The Big House* (1942), he joined MGM where he remained for 12 years. Away from the war, Van proved the ideal, uncomplicated beau for June Allyson in *Two Girls And A Sailor* (1944) and *The Bride Goes Wild* (1948); for Esther Williams in four films including *Easy To Wed* (1946) and *Easy To Love* (1953), and for Judy Garland in *In The Good Old Summertime* (1949).

After leaving MGM in 1954, Van tried to put his famous freckled face to less boyish use. He played one of the instigators of *The Caine Mutiny* (1954), a blind playwright trying to solve a murder in *Twenty-Three Paces To Baker Street* (1956), and appeared in two mystical, sentimental wartime love stories, *The End Of The Affair* (1955) and *Miracle In The Rain* (1956). His film career petered out in the 60s, but he continued to appear regularly on stage (largely the dinner-theatre circuit) and TV. RB

with Humphrey Bogart in Beat The Devil *(United Artists, 1953)*

Jennifer Jones

Real name **Phyllis Isley**
Born **Tulsa, Oklahoma, 2 March 1919**

Jennifer Jones was discovered by producer David Selznick and placed under contract in 1940. He kept her in New York '…while she received extensive training, and would not let her come to Hollywood until she was ready.... I refused to launch her until exactly the right role came along.' That turned out to be the starring part of the young French peasant girl who sees a vision of the Virgin Mary in *The Song Of Bernadette* (1943) which won her an Oscar. She was then cast opposite her husband Robert Walker as the girl in love with a young soldier in *Since You Went Away* (1944). Her role grew with each rewrite of the script by writer-producer Selznick, and he was still playing the same game almost 20 years later on their last film together, *Tender Is The Night* (1962). According to director Henry King, 'David lost all judgement. He thought that the more there was of Jennifer the better the film would be.'

Undeniably beautiful, Jennifer won a supporting

actress Oscar nomination for her performance in *Since You Went Away*, and by the time the picture was released, she had broken up with her husband and embarked on a new relationship with her mentor, Selznick. Having started out as the youngest and least experienced of the Selznick stars and his one true discovery, she became his second wife in 1949, and much of his activity as a producer was devoted to providing her with suitable roles. After a romantic part in *Love Letters* (1945) opposite Joseph Cotten which earned her another Oscar nomination, she was cast in Selznick's *Duel In The Sun* (1946) as a wild and sexy half-breed girl, in marked contrast to her previous roles, and earned a fourth Oscar nomination. She was similarly wild and untamed in Michael Powell's *Gone To Earth* (1950) and King Vidor's *Ruby Gentry* (1952), having portrayed *Madame Bovary* in 1949, and won a last Oscar nomination in 1955 for her performance as a Eurasian girl in love with William Holden in *Love Is A Many Splendoured Thing*. She virtually retired from the screen after her husband's death in 1965, but had one small role of note during the 70s in *The Towering Inferno* (1974). JF

Danny Kaye

Real name **David Daniel Kaminski**
Born **Brooklyn, New York, 18 January 1913**

A highly successful singer, dancer and comedian in vaudeville and nightclubs, Danny Kaye graduated to the Broadway stage where he had a big hit with 'Lady in the Dark' in 1941. Sam Goldwyn signed him to a film contract, had his hair dyed reddish-blonde and cast him in a series of Technicolor musicals beginning with *Up In Arms* (1944), and including *The Secret Life Of Walter Mitty* (1947) and *A Song Is Born* (1948). Kaye was guided in his career by his wife, Sylvia Fine, who wrote many of his songs and comedy routines. His broad comedy style and characteristically fast delivery of 'patter songs' was popular during the 40s, but has not worn well, although his virtuosity was sometimes astounding and always original. He was provided with perhaps

his best role by the writer-director team of Norman Panama and Melvin Frank as a slightly dotty American ventriloquist in the comedy spy thriller *Knock On Wood* (1953) opposite Mai Zetterling. And he had his biggest box-office hit with Bing Crosby in the first VistaVision production, *White Christmas* in 1954, the year he also received a special Oscar. A tireless worker for UNICEF, he virtually retired from the screen in the early 60s, but was last seen in *The Madwoman Of Chaillot* (1969) and in a few television specials. JF

Gene Kelly

Real name **Eugene Curran Kelly**
Born **Pittsburgh, Pennsylvania,
23 August 1912.**

When Gene Kelly sang 'Gotta Dance, Gotta Dance' in the Broadway ballet from *Singin' In The Rain* (1952), he was uttering his credo. He had danced in his childhood, become a dance instructor (after taking an Economics degree at the University of Pittsburgh), danced on Broadway, and danced in nineteen Hollywood musicals between 1942 and 1957, establishing himself, with Fred Astaire, as the greatest male dancer in motion picture history. In 1951, he received a Special Academy Award 'in appreciation of his versatility as an actor, singer, director and dancer and especially for his brilliant achievements in the art of choreography on film.'

As an actor in 'straight roles', Kelly had had a modicum of success. As if to compensate for his brash and cheery personality, he brought an over-earnestness to the war dramas, *Pilot No. 5* (1943) and *The Cross Of Lorraine* (1943) and the mafia thriller, *The Black Hand* (1950). He was uneasy as Deanna Durbin's ne'er-do-well husband in *Christmas Holiday* (1944) and as Natalie Wood's Jewish beau in *Marjorie Morningstar* (1958), but was happier as the cynical newspaperman in *Inherit The Wind* (1960),

and Liv Ullmann's witty ex-husband in *Forty Carats* (1973) for which he was nominated for a Best Supporting Actor Oscar. Naturally, he was in his element as the swashbuckling D'Artagnan in the choreographed but non-musical version of Dumas's, *The Three Musketeers* (1948).

As a singer, Kelly's light, husky tenor voice put over the beautiful 'Long Ago And Far Away', sung to Rita Hayworth in *Cover Girl* (1944), 'Love is here To Stay' to Leslie Caron in *An American In Paris* (1951), and, of course, the song with which he will always be associated, the title number from *Singin' In The Rain*, later used on the sound-track of Stanley Kubrick's *A Clockwork Orange* (1971) as an ironic counterpoint to the violence.

Of the seven movies he directed solo, only two are musicals. *Invitation To The Dance* (1956), a partially successful attempt to make an all-dancing film, contained three ballets, the last featuring a dance with Kelly and cartoon figures. There are glimpses of the old-time MGM musical magic in *Hello, Dolly!* (1969), but it suffers from overkill and the miscasting of Barbra Streisand in the title role. His non-musicals have two left feet, such as *The Tunnel Of Love* (1958) with Doris Day, the mawkish *Gigot* (1963), and the plodding comedy western, *The Cheyenne Social Club* (1970). However, it is as co-director, with Stanley Donen, of *On The Town*

(1949), *Singin' In The Rain* and *It's Always Fair Weather* (1955) that Gene Kelly can be considered as one of the most creative forces in the musicals of the fifties. (He also co-starred in all three).

Kelly had already choreographed 'Billy Rose's Diamond Horseshoe', and the successful Broadway musical 'Best Foot Forward', and had starred in Rodgers and Hart's 'Pal Joey', before he was invited to Hollywood at the age of 30 by David O. Selznick. Arthur Freed at MGM wanted him for the role of the egotistical dancer in *For Me And My Gal* (1942) with Judy Garland, so 50% of Kelly's contract was bought from Selznick. 'I was a good stage performer, but the movies threw me,' recalled Gene. 'Judy never mentioned this to me, but very quietly helped me. I'll never forget how much I learned about movies during that first picture'. After the film's success, the rest of his contract was bought up and Kelly became a major MGM star, a position he enjoyed for the following 15 years.

Gene and his nineteen-year-old actress wife, Betsy Blair, became part of Hollywood society and

in Singin' In The Rain *(MGM, 1952)*

kept 'open house' on Saturday nights where some of the greatest talents in Hollywood gathered. Meanwhile, Kelly was beginning to widen the scope of his dancing and choreography, with such inventive numbers as the dance with his own reflection in *Cover Girl*, and with Jerry Mouse in *Anchors Aweigh* (1945) in a role which earned him a nomination for the Best Actor Oscar. In *Anchors Aweigh*, teamed with Frank Sinatra, he donned the sailor suit that seemed to become as inseparable from his image as Astaire's was from top hat and tails.

Kelly brought a cocky character and virile athletic dancing to the screen, a combination of acrobatics, tap and ballet. In *The Pirate* (1948), opposite Judy Garland again, he gave a delightful tongue-in-cheek performance as a ham actor mistaken for a blood-thirsty buccaneer; he danced jauntily with street urchins in *An American In Paris* (1951), and on rollerskates in *It's Always Fair Weather*, singing 'I Like Myself' as if he meant it. But, undoubtedly the

most celebrated image of Kelly is with arms outstretched, hanging from a lamp-post, folded umbrella in one hand, and looking up into the pouring rain in the title song from *Singin' In The Rain*.

The peak of Kelly's choreographic genius is reached in the lengthy ballet from *An American In Paris*, but there is an underlying pretentiousness in this, and in the 'Day In New York' ballet from *On The Town*, and others that recall Danny Kaye's lyric in *White Christmas* (1954) that 'chaps who once did taps are now doing choreography'.

Gene Kelly's last film for MGM, *Les Girls* (1957), coincided with the divorce from his wife after seventeen years marriage. Betsy felt that Gene had treated her too much like a daughter, and needed a more mature relationship. Jeannie Coyne, Kelly's second wife, had been married to Stanley Donen, his old friend and colleague. Gene had known her since she was a child at the school where he had taught dancing, then on Broadway, and as a chorus girl in many an MGM musical. They had two children (he had a daughter by Betsy Blair) before Jeannie died

tragically of leukemia in 1973.

Since a skiing accident in the early sixties damaged his knee, Gene has done little dancing, but has often appeared in films as a reminder of the great days of the musical. Always much admired in France (he once choreographed a ballet at the Paris Opera), he was paid homage by French director Jacques Demy who cast him in *The Young Girls Of Rochefort* (1967), a musical about three sailors on leave. In recent years, he has worked on TV, and directed the linking material for *That's Entertainment Part 2* (1976) like a TV special, what critic Pauline Kael called 'The Gene Kelly Memorial Service conducted by Gene Kelly.' Still youthful in appearance and helped by a toupee, he cropped up in two youth movies, *Viva Knievel!* (1977) as a drunken bike mechanic, and *Xanadu* (1980) with Olivia Newton-John where, still smiling broadly, his appearance recalled the days when he was 'laughing at clouds, way up in the sky.' RB

Deborah Kerr

**Born Helensburgh, Scotland,
30 September 1921**

'She was so young and yet she had even then the quality of complete malleability; playing three parts . . . she had the ability to *feel* herself into the changes of role without relying on makeup.' Thus the distinguished British director Michael Powell described the strength of Deborah Kerr as an actress which first led him to star her in his remarkable Technicolor production, *The Life And Death Of Colonel Blimp* (1943) – not to mention the fact that, with her reddish-blonde hair and light complexion, her natural beauty was enhanced by colour.

Miss Kerr had originally studied to be a dancer, but switched to the theatre during the late 30s and made her film debut in Shaw's *Major Barbara* in 1940. She was excellent in a relatively small role as a Salvation Army girl, and appeared in a number of other pictures before *Blimp* launched her to stardom. As a follow-up to *Blimp*, Powell starred her as the Mother Superior of an isolated convent in the Himalayas. Her sensitive performance in this picture, *Black Narcissus* (1947), as well as in *I See A Dark Stranger* (1946), her last two British pictures before leaving for Hollywood, earned her the New York Film Critics' Award for 1947. Two years later she gained her first Oscar nomination for her

performance as Spencer Tracy's wife in *Edward My Son* (1949), her third picture for MGM. As a measure of her status at that studio, she was starred as the Christian, Lygia, opposite Robert Taylor in the epic *Quo Vadis?* (1952). Although she succeeded in projecting the kind of spiritual qualities required by the part, she was rather overwhelmed by the spectacle. She finished off her MGM contract with a

small, but effective, role as Portia in Joseph Mankiewicz's adaptation of *Julius Caesar* (1953).

A real change of direction followed as Miss Kerr welcomed the opportunity to be cast against type as the sexy blonde wife who has an affair with Burt Lancaster in *From Here To Eternity* (1953). Her fresh yet totally convincing approach to the role brought a second Oscar nomination, while the picture itself won the top Oscar. Having matured into one of the leading Hollywood stars, Miss Kerr selected her roles with care and averaged only two pictures per year. Yet she was Oscar-nominated three years running for three very different roles – as the English governess in *The King And I* (1956), her first musical, as a nun stranded on a Pacific island with Marine Robert Mitchum in *Heaven Knows Mr Allison* (1957) and as the plain and timid spinster who falls for David Niven's outcast bogus army officer in *Separate Tables* (1958). During the filming of *The Journey* in 1958 she met scriptwriter Peter Viertel who became her second husband in 1960, the same year that she received her sixth and last Oscar nomination for *The Sundowners*. During the 60s her roles became less interesting and she retired from the screen after making a valiant stab at the thankless part of Kirk Douglas's unsympathetic wife in *The Arrangement* (1969). A few leading stage appearances followed during the 70s, and she continues to do theatre and TV work, her beauty remarkably unimpaired by time. JF

Alan Ladd

**Born Hot Springs, Arkansas,
3 September 1913
Died 1964**

Deborah Kerr who co-starred with Alan Ladd in one picture summed up his appeal thus: 'He was awfully good in putting across what he had, in his looks and in his manner; he had something very attractive – a definite film personality which he had worked hard to perfect.' Ladd was one of the first and biggest of the stars created by 40s *film noir*, and one of the first of a new breed of movie 'anti-hero' types of which Bogart was the most famous. In an inspired bit of casting, prompted by the prodding of Ladd's agent, Paramount gave him his first leading role as the psychopathic killer, teamed with Veronica Lake, in

with Jill Bennett in Hell Below Zero *(Columbia, 1954)*

This Gun For Hire (1942). He became a star overnight, just ten years after his first appearance as a film extra in *Once In A Lifetime* (1932).

Ladd had grown up in difficult circumstances and genuine poverty after the early death of his father. As a young man he knocked around in many different jobs, including work on the fringes of the film industry both in front of the camera, as an extra or bit player, and behind the scenes as a grip (one of the lowliest members of the film crew who rig the

scaffolding and lights on the studio catwalks high above the set). Although he was only five-and-a-half feet tall and his acting experience had been limited, he had the graceful, purposeful movements of an athlete (which he was), a quiet spoken but firm voice, developed during his stints of radio acting, and green-eyed, blonde-haired good looks very different from the other male stars of the period. From the very first he had a style which was uniquely his own. Although Paramount initially had their doubts about him, the enthusiastic public response quickly convinced the studio of his appeal. To capitalise on his initial success, the studio immediately rushed him into another thriller with Veronica Lake, *The Glass Key*, in 1942, and that same year he married his agent, Sue Carol, who had

played such an important part in launching him. During the late 40s he extended his range into dramatic roles like *The Great Gatsby* (1949), and acquitted himself well in a number of westerns which led up to his most famous role in *Shane* (1953). Here his characteristic style of underplaying was put to good use as he portrayed a mysterious blonde gunslinger who comes to the aid of a group of homesteaders in their war with the local cattle baron. But in spite of the picture's great success, the Ladd films which followed were markedly inferior to those which had preceded it. He had one last memorable role as Nevada Smith in *The Carpetbaggers* (1964) shortly before his death. His son, Alan Ladd Jr, became a leading film industry executive during the late 70s. JF

Veronica Lake

Real name **Constance Ockelman**
Born **Brooklyn, New York,
14 November 1919**
Died **1973**

A beautiful petite blonde who, during the 40s introduced to the world a new 'peek-a-boo' hair style matched by a sexy deep voice, Veronica Lake had trained for a short while at drama school, then did film 'walk-ons' before she was 'discovered'. Placed under contract by Paramount Pictures, she shot to stardom in a handful of films during 1941–42. A leading role as a nightclub singer in *I Wanted Wings* was followed by Preston Sturges's depression satire *Sullivan's Travels* (both 1941) in which she played the girl who accompanies film director Joel McCrea. She was then teamed with Alan Ladd in a pair of thrillers which turned them both into major stars, *This Gun For Hire* and *The Glass Key* (both 1942). In both pictures Miss Lake managed to invest her role with her own unique brand of sex appeal and presented the perfect sultry counterpart to Ladd's coolly underplayed tough guys. Thanks to the efforts of Preston Sturges, she was given the opportunity to demonstrate her natural comedy talent, cast as the seductive witch in Rene Clair's delightful *I Married*

in 1946

A Witch (1942). Unfortunately, her career went into swift decline, though she co-starred again with Ladd in *The Blue Dahlia* (1946), and was virtually finished by 1950, although she appeared from time to time on the stage and in a couple of later B-movies. JF

Hedy Lamarr

Real name **Hedwig Kiesler**
Born **Vienna, 9 November 1913**

In the early 40s Hedy Lamarr was thought the most beautiful woman in films and was a byword for glamour. But it was a glamour which lacked the spark of personality, ultimately as stiff and unyielding as the board which held her star-spangled costume in place in *Ziegfeld Girl* (1941).

in 1938

Discovered by Max Reinhardt, she gained international notoriety by appearing fleetingly naked in a Czech film, *Extase* (1932). Her reputation preceded her to London, from where she pursued a reluctant

Louis B. Mayer to America on board the 'Normandie'. Before the liner had docked in New York, she had secured a seven-year contract and a new name. Uncertain of what to do with her, Mayer loaned Lamarr to Walter Wanger for *Algiers* (1938), a sensational first picture in which her beauty lured Charles Boyer from the safety of the Casbah. With instant stardom came Hollywood's top leading men: Robert Taylor in *Lady Of The Tropics* (1939), Spencer Tracy in *I Take This Woman* (1940), Clark Gable in *Boom Town* (1940) and *Comrade X* (1940), a variation on *Ninotchka*; and she turned in probably her best performance opposite Robert Young in *H.M. Pulham Esq* (1941).

Miss Lamarr then slipped into lightweight exotic roles in *Tortilla Flat* (1942) and *White Cargo* (1942), playing the dusky nymphomaniac Tondelayo, slinking all over Walter Pidgeon. Temperamental, and choosy about her parts, she turned down *Casablanca*, *Gaslight* and *Saratoga Trunk* (a blessing for audiences, who got Bergman instead), and wound up her MGM contract with a feeble comedy, *Her Highness And The Bellboy* (1945). She formed her own production company to play sultry *femmes fatales* in Edgar Ulmer's *The Strange Woman* (1946) and *Dishonored Lady* (1947), but was virtually a back number when DeMille chose her as Victor Mature's devious mate in *Samson And Delilah* (1949). It failed to arrest her decline, although Joseph H. Lewis's *A Lady Without Passport* (1950), remains a minor B classic. She was miscast in Bob Hope's *My Favorite Spy* (1951); was an absurd Joan of Arc in *The Story Of Mankind* (1957); and finally virtually played herself as an ageing movie star in *The Female Animal* (1957). In recent years a shoplifting charge (of which she was cleared) and an optimistic $21 million law suit against the ghost writers of her titillating autobiography have kept her fitfully in the headlines. RC

Carole Landis

Real name **Frances Lillian Mary Ridste**
Born **Fairchild, Wisconsin, 1 January 1919**
Died **1948**

'Carole Landis was what might now be called a liberated woman, and she was frowned upon because of it,' according to Rex Harrison. 'She was quite ambitious and wanted to make films, but for reasons which I never got to the bottom of, she couldn't get into any studio.' In fact, by the time that Rex first met Carole, her brief Hollywood career was over. She had started out as a singer-dancer in nightclubs, then worked as an extra before landing the lead as a prehistoric cave girl opposite Victor Mature in Hal Roach's *One Million BC* (1940). She had a good comedy role in *Topper Returns* and joined Betty Grable at 20th Century-Fox in the Technicolored musical *Moon Over Miami* (both 1941). But the best role under her Fox contract was in the tense

in Topper Returns *(MGM, 1941)*

thriller with Victor Mature, *I Wake Up Screaming* (1941). Her later parts were mainly routine, although she did star in *Four Jills In A Jeep* (1944), loosely based on her own story of touring to entertain the troops. Miss Landis's attempts at freelancing were unsuccessful, and after two last British pictures she returned to Hollywood where she committed suicide. Her body was discovered by Harrison, her close friend at the time, and his Hollywood career was cut short by the ensuing scandal. JF

in Tropic Holiday *(Paramount, 1938)*

Dorothy Lamour

Real name **Mary Leta Dorothy Kaumeyer**
Born **New Orleans, 10 December 1914**

Although a sarong has clung to Dorothy Lamour's image as tightly as it clung to her curvaceous figure, she had both a larger range and a larger wardrobe than she is credited with. She was clad in furs in *Spawn Of The North* (1938), an adventure tale set in Russia; she wore slinky gowns as a nightclub singer called 'The Countess' in *The Fleet's In* (1942) and spangled tights in the circus dramas, *Chad Hanna* (1940) and *The Greatest Show On Earth* (1952).

Lamour played Tyrone Power's girlfriend in the low-key gangster movie, *Johnny Apollo* (1940), was a saloon singer in Rouben Mamoulian's musical western, *High, Wide and Handsome* (1937) and *Lulu Belle* (1948), and did the Can-Can in *Slightly French* (1949). But she will be remembered as the pretty bone of contention between Bob Hope and Bing Crosby in six 'Road to...' films, and the girl that GI's dreamed of meeting on a tropical island.

Before becoming Miss South Seas of the 1940s, Miss Lamour was Miss New Orleans of 1931, a band vocalist and radio performer. (She was married to bandleader Herbie Kaye from 1935 to 1939.) The sultry, good-humoured brunette began her long

career at Paramount in a sarong for *The Jungle Princess* (1936), a garment she continued to wear with great success in other tropical island epics such as John Ford's *The Hurricane* (1937), *Aloma Of The South Seas* (1941) and *Rainbow Island* (1944), playing a child-like savage.

Dorothy often sent herself up on the Roads to *Singapore* (1940), *Zanzibar* (1941), *Morocco* (1942), *Utopia* (1946), *Rio* (1947) and *Bali* (1952). She was ungallantly replaced by Joan Collins in *Road To Hong Kong* (1962), but made a brief appearance as herself. She retired in 1953, making occasional films such as John Ford's *Donovan's Reef* (1963) – a homage to her tropical island image. RB

Vivien Leigh

Real name **Vivian Mary Hartley**
Born **Darjeeling, India, 5 November 1913**
Died **1967**

Vivien Leigh was both the luckiest and unluckiest of stars. A petite and stunningly beautiful brunette with striking blue-green eyes, she suffered from recurring bouts of tuberculosis which finally killed her at an early age. She set out to win her man, Laurence Olivier, and succeeded, becoming a famous star at the same time. For a while they were the most attractive and celebrated show business couple in the world. But signs of Vivien's serious mental illness began to appear during the 40s at the height of their fame. A manic depressive, she would suddenly be transformed from a kind, sweet and

in Waterloo Bridge *(MGM, 1940)*

thoughtful wife into a wild, cruel and uncontrollable woman. Olivier increasingly found himself unable to cope, in spite of his love for her, and they were divorced in 1960. An extremely courageous woman, she fought her illness by working, mainly on the stage, as she had few film offers during the later years, and continued acting up to the last years of her life.

According to Vivien herself, she enjoyed dressing up so much as a young child that by the age of seven she was already set on becoming an actress – as she told her slightly older classmate, Maureen O'Sullivan, at the time. Her first role was Mustard Seed in a school production of 'A Midsummer Night's Dream', but she did not get her first break as a grown-up actress until some fifteen years later. During 1934–35 she appeared in her first films, landed a number of good stage roles – enjoying a big hit in a comedy, 'The Mask of Virtue' – and was signed to a film contract by Alexander Korda. Having briefly met Laurence Olivier who was already established as one of the leading young British actors of his generation, she was strongly attracted to him. Their relationship developed rapidly during 1937 when they made two films together, *Fire Over England* and *21 Days* (quickly rushed into production as a follow-up picture), and on the stage she played Ophelia to his Hamlet. She played a dissatisfied and flirtatious wife who has an affair with Robert Taylor in the MGM British production of *A Yank At Oxford* (1938), which co-starred her old school chum, Maureen O'Sullivan. At the opening of *St Martin's Lane* (1938), the last of Vivien's early British films, with Charles Laughton, she was meant to be a cockney busker. But she looked too beautiful and refined and did not manage the accent at all well, only coming into her own and demonstrating her qualities as a film actress in the second half where she is transformed by Laughton into a stage star.

By now Leigh and Olivier were living together and looking forward to marrying once their respective divorces came through. She flew out to join him

in Hollywood in December 1938 just as *Gone With The Wind* was about to go into production with no final decision yet taken on the actress to play Scarlett O'Hara. Producer David Selznick first met Vivien on the set where the burning of Atlanta was being filmed, allegedly introduced by his agent brother, Myron Selznick, who simply said, 'I want you to meet Scarlett O'Hara.' Although she looked perfect for the part, Selznick was only finally convinced by the tests. '... made under George Cukor's brilliant direction (which) showed that she could act the part right down to the ground.' In spite of her limited film experience, her personal dislike of Scarlett who is an irritating and unlikeable heroine, and the fact that the shooting script was being rewritten while filming was in progress, Vivien managed to give an exceptional performance during the long months that the film was in production. 'I'd never have been able to get through without the book and George Cukor,' she recalled. 'I'd keep the book by me, and look up each scene as we filmed it to remind myself where I was supposed to be and how I should be feeling... On Sundays I'd steal over to George Cukor's and discuss with him the bits we'd be working on the next week. It was probably terribly irregular, but I couldn't have finished without him.' (The original director on the picture, Cukor had been replaced by Victor Fleming after only ten days.) In addition Vivien played a small creative role, along with the others working on the film, in selecting from the various dialogue rewrites. She personally insisted on the inclusion of that important and revealing line toward the end when she is drunk and thinks of her mother: 'She brought me up to be kind and thoughtful and ladylike, just like her, and I've been such a disappointment.'

Miss Leigh won a well deserved Oscar for her performance in *Gone With The Wind* which won nine Oscars in all, including Best Picture, and went on to become the biggest hit in movie history. She became a super-star over night, but immediately returned to more modest starring roles in black-and-white pictures like *Waterloo Bridge* (1940), in which she gave a moving performance as Robert Taylor's tragic World War I amour, a former streetgirl who is forced by his family to relinquish marriage to him. Then she and Olivier married and appeared together in 'Romeo and Juliet' – her Broadway debut. *That*

Hamilton Woman for Korda in 1941, in which she played the title role opposite Olivier's Lord Nelson, was a romantic pro-British propaganda piece which reunited them on the screen for the first time in four years but also turned out to be their last screen partnership.

Returning to England where Olivier did a number of films and triumphed as both director and star of *Henry V* (1945), she was hampered by her Selznick contract and illness and did not get to do another picture until Gabriel Pascal's lavish Technicolor version of Shaw's *Caesar And Cleopatra* (1945). She was really too old to play the kittenish young heroine convincingly, but managed better with the more mature Cleopatra; yet her efforts, and those of co-star Claude Rains, were largely negated by an extremely static and misconceived production. Her serious mental illness became more evident about this time. *Anna Karenina* (1948) saw her once again trying to cope with a part which did not suit her. After touring on stage with Olivier and appearances with him in London and New York, she was offered the superb role of Blanche in the film version of Tennessee Williams's *A Streetcar Named Desire* (1951), which she had played on the London stage, directed by her husband. Director Elia Kazan's approach was rather different, and there were some problems, initially, according to Kazan. 'Then ... she and I got together, got an understanding, and she became enthusiastic about what I was saying to her. And we became very close ... I was really awfully glad that she got an Oscar. I think she deserved it.' For Vivien it had been a timely return to Hollywood in a role which had obvious affinities with Scarlett. It brought her opposite the remarkable young Brando in a juxtaposition of two contrasting acting styles, but unfortunately turned out to be her last truly memorable movie appearance. The on-screen ageing process continued as she played progressively older (but nonetheless remarkably beautiful) women – middle-aged ladies, in *The Deep Blue Sea* (1956), *The Roman Spring Of Mrs Stone* (1961) (another Tennessee Williams role) and, finally, an elderly divorcee in *Ship Of Fools* (1965). She had been more active on the stage during these last years and was generally more successful in lighter-weight parts than the heavy dramatic and classical roles that she had attempted with Olivier. JF

with Charles Laughton in St Martin's Lane *(Paramount, 1938)*

relaxing on the set of Gone With The Wind *(MGM, 1939)* ▷

Margaret Lockwood

Real name **Margaret Day**
Born **Karachi, Pakistan, 15 September 1916**

Best remembered today as a popular star of romantic escapist fare during the war and immediate postwar years, Margaret Lockwood was one of the leading lights at Gainsborough Pictures along with Stewart Granger, James Mason and Patricia Roc. An attractive brunette, she specialised in playing a new type of treacherous and sexy heroine – a disloyal, jealous vixen in *The Man In Grey* (1943), the title role, a female highwayman, in *The Wicked Lady* (1945) at the peak of her popularity, and a wild gypsy girl accused of murder in the Technicolored *Jassy* (1947). She began appearing in movies from the age of eighteen and had her first successes with director Carol Reed who cast her in seven pictures, including *Bank Holiday* (1938) and *The Stars Look Down* (1939), playing the first of her nasty heroines. But her best picture of this period was Hitchcock's spy thriller, *The Lady Vanishes* (1938) in which she gave a fine performance as the resourceful heroine teamed with Michael Redgrave. By the late 40s her career was in decline and a series of pictures with producer-director Herbert Wilcox failed to revive it. More recently she has appeared on the stage and TV and played Cinderella's wicked stepmother in *The Slipper And The Rose* (1976). JF

Ida Lupino

Born **London, England, 4 February 1918**

Ida Lupino began an active career in the movies as a teenager, first in Britain in 1933 and then in the US from 1934 on. She appeared in a few films of note like *Peter Ibbetson* (1935) and *The Gay Desperado* (1936), but was mainly cast in weak programmers during the late 30s. Finally, during 1939–42, she was given an opportunity to prove her very real talent in some better parts, beginning with the Cockney girl lead with Ronald Colman in *The Light That Failed* (1939), and then at Warner Bros. where she held her own opposite such studio tough guys as Bogart, Garfield and Robinson. She specialised in portraying experienced, frequently ill-treated, but sympathetic, ladies, like the girl who befriends Bogart's gangster-on-the run in *High Sierra* (1940) or the escaped convict girl in *The Sea Wolf* (1941). She even won the New York Film Critics' award for her performance as the tough older sister of Joan Leslie who pushes her into a show business career in *The Hard Way* (1942). An extremely intelligent actress who was knowledgeable about what was going on on the other side of the camera, when her roles failed to improve during the late 40s, a solution was at hand: she developed a new career as a producer, writer and director of low budget pictures which often dealt with feminist themes, the first being *Not Wanted*

with Irene Dunne in The Silver Cord *(RKO, 1933)*

Joel McCrea

Born **Los Angeles, Calif., 5 November 1905**

There is a conversation which is alleged to have taken place between writer-director Preston Sturges and actor Joel McCrea. Sturges pointed out that a great pianist does not repeat one note over and over again but makes use of all the notes and all the expressive possibilities of the instrument. To which McCrea replied, 'Well, the way I look at it, Preston, Rubenstein and those guys are looking for the one note – and I've already found it.'

McCrea may have been a one-note actor, but he

(1949), which she produced, scripted and co-directed (uncredited). Perhaps her best film as director was *The Bigamist* (1953), in which she also co-starred with Edmond O'Brien and Joan Fontaine. During later years she appeared on TV, has done a few TV movies, and was last seen on the big screen in Sam Peckinpah's *Junior Bonner* (1972) and *The Food Of The Gods* (1976). JF

certainly had a long and varied movie career and worked with many of the leading Hollywood directors including Wyler and DeMille, and made three pictures with Sturges. Educated at USC, he got his first taste of the movies working as an extra and was offered a number of leading roles with the coming of sound in 1929. Tall, handsome and easy-going in the Gary Cooper mould, he moved easily from romantic parts to adventure pictures and comedy at RKO where he had a contract during the early 30s. But his best known early pictures were actioners like *The Lost Squadron* with Erich von Stroheim, as a robust flier, and *The Most Dangerous Game* (both 1932) as an adventurer hunted by Leslie Banks in a serious life and death game. He appeared with Frances Dee in *The Silver Cord* in 1933, and they were married later that year. A new contract with Sam Goldwyn reflected his standing in Hollywood and meant better quality roles. He gave a fine performance in the triangular *These Three* (1936) about small town prejudice, and in *Dead End* (1937) both directed by Wyler. In DeMille's *Union Pacific* (1939) he starred with Barbara Stanwyck whom he regarded as 'the best actress I ever worked with'. (They made six films together.) A modest man who was aware of his own limitations, he noted, 'I turned down as many roles that I thought were beyond my abilities as I did ones I thought weren't good enough.' At Paramount Preston Sturges used him in two of his more serious pictures, *Sullivan's Travels* (1941) as the film director travelling around the US in search of serious subjects, and *The Great Moment* (filmed in 1942), a loosely fictionalized treatment of the discovery of anaesthetics, as well as in *The Palm Beach Story* (1942), McCrea's most delightful screwball comedy in which he is married to Claudette Colbert. He starred in William Wellman's Technicolor western *Buffalo Bill* (1944) and in a remake of *The Virginian* (1946), which put him firmly on course for the final stage of his career, specialising in western roles. Sam Peckinpah's *Ride The High Country* in 1962 teamed him, appropriately, with Randolph Scott as a creaky pair of ageing cowpokes. Virtual retirement followed, although he recently reappeared in *Mustang Country* (1976). JF

Roddy McDowall

Born **London, England, 17 September 1928**

A child actor who arrived in Hollywood in 1940, Roddy McDowall was immediately cast in a number of highly successful pictures like *How Green Was My Valley* (1941) and *My Friend Flicka* (1943). Although working mainly for 20th Century-Fox, he had his most lasting success at MGM as the young boy who loses and then regains his pet collie in *Lassie Come Home* (1943) with the young Liz Taylor. As Roddy noted, 'For what seems like decades I was regarded by the public as Lassie's brother or something.' During the 50s he developed a stage career, only returning to the movies ten years later

with Frances Farmer in Exclusive *(Paramount, 1937)*

in Lord Love A Duck *(United Artists, 1966)*

with leading roles in *Cleopatra* (1963) as Octavian and in *Planet Of The Apes* (1968), heavily made up as a young and sympathetic archaeologist-chimp named Cornelius. As Roddy notes, 'I suppose I officially ceased being Lassie's Brother when *Planet* came out and became such a big hit. I loved my part in that, the make-up was fantastic, and it was a matter of interpreting character and personality . . .' Three *Apes* sequels followed, and Roddy has continued active in films up to quite recently, appearing in *Funny Lady* (1975), *Circle Of Iron* (1979) and *Charlie Chan And The Curse Of The Dragon Queen* (1980), along with a number of TV movies. He is also a skilled stills photographer. JF

Dorothy McGuire

Born **Omaha, Nebraska, 14 June 1918**

Dorothy McGuire's screen image remained the same throughout the twenty odd years that she was starring in pictures, from 1943 through 1964. She started out as a nice, wholesome and attractive type, and quickly found her niche playing a succession of sympathetic wives, sweethearts and mothers. On the stage from an early age, she had her first big success on Broadway in *Claudia* in 1941 as the naive but good-hearted young wife. The film version in 1943 provided her with an ideal starring vehicle opposite Robert Young. They made a likeable screen couple and appeared together again in another sentimental weepie, *The Enchanted Cottage* (1945), and in a sequel to *Claudia* entitled *Claudia And David* (1946). In between she was terrorised in *The Spiral Staircase* (1946) and was miscast (she was too sympathetic) as the puritanical mother in *A Tree Grows In Brooklyn* (1945), but director Kazan used her again in *Gentleman's Agreement* (1947) as Gregory Peck's nice WASP fiancée whose supposedly 'liberal' attitude towards Jews is called into question. She gained her only Oscar nomination for this performance, but during the 50s her roles became less interesting, mainly sympathetic wives and mothers, and she virtually retired from the screen after playing Mary in *The Greatest Story Ever Told* (1965). JF

Fred MacMurray

Born **Kankakee, Illinois, 30 August 1908**

Sugar Kane (Marilyn Monroe): 'You see, I have this thing about saxophone players. I don't know what it is, but they just curdle me . . .' In fact, the many jokes about sax players in *Some Like It Hot* (1959) can probably be traced back to Fred MacMurray. When director Billy Wilder was having trouble casting the role of the murderer in *Double Indemnity* in 1943, he finally turned to Fred who was currently under contract to Paramount. According to Wilder, Fred's first reaction was, 'For Christ's sake, you're making the mistake of your life. I'm a saxophone player. I can't do it.' He turned out to be excellent in the role, combining the qualities of a tall, good looking, but brash get-ahead type with a slightly sleazy, devious quality which was also part of Fred's screen image. His insurance salesman-turned-murderer who falls for Barbara Stanwyck, is double-crossed by her, and comes to a bad end, marks the high point of his very full and long film career.

As a touring sax player and vocalist during the 30s, MacMurray finally ended up on the Broadway stage playing in 'Roberta' and was signed to a contract by Paramount in 1934. He got his first break in a screwball comedy with Carole Lombard in 1935, *Hands Across The Table*, one of nine movies he made for director Mitchell Leisen, but he appeared mainly in a large number of routine pictures, alternating between comedies and actioners. His performance as a kind of gigolo-secretary to Rosalind Russell in a weak role reversal comedy, *Take A Letter Darling* (1942), and as a lecherous bandleader in *And The Angels Sing* in 1943 were the kind of roles which led up to *Double Indemnity*. But in spite of its success, he was back doing programmers during the following years.

He appeared in a few pictures of note during the 50s. He played the smart-guy lieutenant who first sows the seeds of mistrust in *The Caine Mutiny* (1954) with Bogart, and director Douglas Sirk made good use of him as the unhappy family man and harassed hubby who is attracted to old flame Barbara Stanwyck in *There's Always Tomorrow* (1956). He was excellent in a small role, again cast by Billy Wilder, as the cynical boss and family man who likes a bit (Shirley MacLaine) on the side in the Oscar-winning *The Apartment* (1960). Around this time his waning film career took on a new lease of life as he began starring in a series of highly successful Disney-produced family comedy movies like *The Shaggy Dog* (1959) and *The Absent-Minded Professor* (1961), as well as the long-running and popular television series, 'My Three Sons'. He was also seen in the film *The Swarm* (1978). JF

James Mason

Born Huddersfield, England, 15 May 1909
Died 1984

A reliable and sympathetic actor in films for almost fifty years, with a uniquely expressive voice, it is difficult today to think of James Mason as a debonair and romantic villain in such British movies as *The Man In Grey* (1943) and *The Wicked Lady* (1945), and smashing his stick down on Ann Todd's piano-playing fingers in *The Seventh Veil* (1945). But this was where he first made his name, although his best British picture, by far, was *Odd Man Out* (1947), in which he starred as an IRA gunman on the run.

Arriving in the US, Mason's Hollywood career got off to a slow start with two pictures for director Max Ophuls and not much else of interest until a starring role in the superb spy thriller *Five Fingers* (1952), directed by Joseph Mankiewicz. He gave an excellent, underplayed performance as the brilliant valet spy Diello 'Cicero', loosely based on a true incident of World War II. Although he was not a strong enough classical actor to give a fully satisfying

interpretation of Brutus in *Julius Caesar* (1953), he quickly redeemed himself the following year with one of his most memorable and sympathetic performances in *A Star Is Born*, which earned him his first Oscar nomination. He had a second big hit in a row when he played Captain Nemo in the Disney studio's successful version of Verne's *20,000 Leagues Under the Sea* (1954). *Bigger Than Life* (1956) saw him involved as producer, writer (uncredited) and starring as the small-town schoolteacher unbalanced by drug treatments – an interesting and underrated picture. He then rounded out the most successful decade of his career with another fine Verne adaptation (*Journey To The Centre Of The Earth*) and played one of the most memorable of Hitchcock villains, menacing Eva Marie Saint and Cary Grant in *North By Northwest* (both 1959). With his return to Europe in the 60s, Mason's pictures – with the exception of *Lolita* (1962) from Nabakov's novel – became somewhat less interesting, although he won a supporting actor Oscar nomination for his performance as the wealthy man with an eye on Lynn Redgrave in *Georgy Girl* (1966), and continued active in films throughout the 70s. JF

in 1952

Victor Mature

Born Louisville, Kentucky, 29 January 1915

Brooding underneath a fez in *The Shanghai Gesture* (1941), disappearing behind an outsize, blood-stained handkerchief in *My Darling Clementine* (1946) or threatening to burst out of his fetching array of thongs in *Samson And Delilah* (1949), Victor Mature remains one of cinema's most engaging primitives.

He made his debut in a Hal Roach comedy-thriller, *The Housekeeper's Daughter* (1939), but was soon fitted out in a designer loincloth, and put his glistening musculature to work defending Carole Landis from a small army of monstrous, back-projected lizards in *One Million BC* (1940). He was shunted into musicals, first with Anna Neagle in *No No, Nanette* (1940) and then with Betty Grable. In between he provided Von Sternberg with a suitably baroque substitute for Dietrich in *The Shanghai Gesture*, and was framed by Laird Cregar's obese, psychopathic cop in *I Wake Up Screaming* (1941). After war service in the Coast Guard he had a good run: as a consumptive Doc Holliday in Ford's *My Darling Clementine*; fleeing from Richard Widmark's giggling killer in *Kiss Of Death* (1947), and was

memorably anguished in *Cry Of The City* (1948).

Nature created Mature for the role of Samson in DeMille's tuppence-coloured epic, mangling stuffed lions and toppling a pasteboard temple. He played it quite straight, a style he continued throughout the 50s in a string of cloak and sandal sagas: *Veils Of Bagdad* (1953), *The Robe* (1953), *Demetrius And The Gladiators* (1954) and *The Egyptian* (1954). By the mid-50s Hollywood had virtually finished with him, although he was effectively cast in Richard Fleischer's heist thriller *Violent Saturday* (1955), and Anthony Mann's offbeat western *The Last Frontier* (1956). He went to England to make a few films for Warwick, but age was furrowing his ripe features with worry lines, a condition doubtless hastened by the absurdity of films like *Zarak* (1956) and *The Bandit of Zhobe* (1959).

After two films directed by exhausted Hollywood veterans, Frank Borzage's *China Doll* (1958) and Edgar Ulmer's *Hannibal* (1959), Mature subsided into semi-retirement. He re-emerged to reveal a long-concealed and stylish sense of humour in *After The Fox* (1966), virtually playing himself as a fading matinée idol, providing the Monkees with an outsize menace in *Head* (1968), and enjoying himself hugely as a comic gangster in *Every Little Crook And Nanny* (1972) with Lynn Redgrave. RC

Ray Milland

Real name Reginald Truscott-Jones
Born Neath, Wales, 3 January 1905

As a tall, handsome and sophisticated leading man at Paramount for twenty years, Ray Milland was given the opportunity to play opposite many of the most attractive and talented female stars in Hollywood ranging from Claudette Colbert in *The Gilded Lily* (1934), Dorothy Lamour in *The Jungle Princess* (1936) and Frances Farmer in *Ebb Tide* (1937), to Paulette Goddard in *Kitty* (1945) and Marlene Dietrich in *Golden Earrings* (1947). He averaged three to four pictures a year throughout most of the 30s and 40s but his talent as an actor was rarely appreciated. At least he was offered a wide variety of roles and proved he could handle action pictures, drama and comedy with equal facility.

Thus, during the early 40s, when his parts started to improve, he starred in the DeMille Technicolor epic *Reap The Wild Wind* around the same time that he was cast with Ginger Rogers in a delightful, intimate comedy, *The Major And The Minor* (both 1942). Milland starred in a memorable group of thrillers as well, beginning with Fritz Lang's *Ministry Of Fear* (1944) and including *The Big Clock* (1948) and *Alias Nick Beal* (1949), which exploited the darker side of his film personality, as did *The*

in I Wanted Wings (Paramount, 1941)

Lost Weekend (1945). In this last, his sensitive interpretation of an alcoholic writer, an uncharacteristically strong dramatic role, he received the only Oscar nomination of his career and won, as did the picture and director Billy Wilder. Given the opportunity to direct and star in a number of pictures later in his

career, he proved he was no slouch behind the camera either, particularly with *The Safecracker* (1958) and *Panic In Year Zero* (1962). He continued acting in movies throughout the 70s with roles in *Love Story* (1970), *The Last Tycoon* (1976), and *Oliver's Story* (1978) among others. JF

Ann Miller

Real name **Lucille Ann Collier**
Born **Chireno, Texas, 12 April 1919**

It took Ann Miller twelve years and twenty-five films to emerge as the screen's most exciting tap dancer in *Easter Parade* (1948). At the age of 30, the vivacious, rosy-cheeked, raven-haired Amazon, stopped the show with 'Shakin' The Blues Away'. To think that Irving Berlin was initially opposed to casting her in the picture!

A professional dancer from an early age, she entered the movies in her late teens as one of RKO's *New Faces Of 1937*. The following year, Ann Miller played the ballet-dancing daughter of a kooky family in Frank Capra's screwball comedy, *You Can't Take It With You* (1938), and was with the Marx Brothers in *Room Service* (1938). During the war, Miller shook her legs in let's-put-on-a-show-for-the-troops mini-musicals with titles like *Priorities On Parade* (1942),

Reveille With Beverly (1943), and *Hey Rookie* (1944), for various studios. Her big break came at MGM in Arthur Freed's Technicolored productions, although she never actually starred in a major film. She was usually cast as a wise-cracking, cheerful second-lead, most typically in her two best films, *On The Town* (1949) and *Kiss Me Kate* (1953). In the former, she played an anthropologist who throws herself at Jules Munshin whose face she compares to a prehistoric man, before going into a dynamic dance around the museum ending with the collapse of a dinosaur skeleton. In *Kiss Me Kate*, Ann had four splendid numbers beginning with 'Too Darn Hot' in which she is at her sexy, gyrating, spinning-top best, kicking her famous legs at the camera in this made-in-3D movie.

She made her exit from films in 1956, but continued to entertain in nightclubs and on stage, taking over the lead in 'Mame' on Broadway. In 1979, at the age of 60, Ann Miller danced and sang in 'Sugar Babies' with undimmed perfection. RB

John Mills

Born **North Elmham, England,
22 February 1908**

John Mills occupies a special place in the affections of British cinemagoers as a modest and likeable star who never abandoned England for Hollywood, and as a model of the show business husband and father figure – married (since 1941) to writer Mary Hayley Bell and father of actresses Juliet and Hayley Mills. Small and youthful looking and not particularly handsome, he projected a quiet determination which was ideal for playing the typical British enlisted man during the war years when he first made his name in such pictures as *In Which We Serve* (1942), *We Dive At Dawn* (1943), *Waterloo Road* (1944), and *The Way To The Stars* (1945). Although he was already in his late thirties, he still appeared young enough to play the 'juvenile lead' in the first half of *This Happy Breed* (1944) – he ages during the course of the picture and makes a convincing transition from Cockney rating to officer, with a change in accent to match – and he played a twentyish Pip in *Great Expectations* (1946), and gave a performance which demonstrated his ability to handle a costume role.

In fact, Mills's film career can be divided into two parts – the war pictures, and the others. Having experienced his first success during the war, he was never entirely able to shake loose from his close

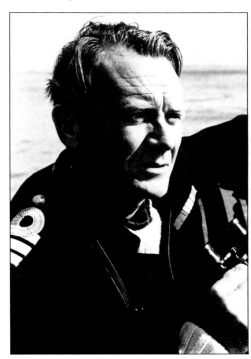

in Above Us The Waves *(Rank/Republic, 1955)*

Carmen Miranda

Real name **Maria da Carmo Miranda da Cunha**
Born **Marco de Canavezes, Portugal, 9 February 1909**
Died **1955**

In the annals of Hollywood, there are few more eccentric phenomena than the flamboyant, exotic, explosive 'Brazilian Bombshell', Carmen Miranda. Her extravagant gestures, costumes and headgear piled with tropical fruit, brightened up the war years and set the nation impersonating her. Mickey Rooney in *Babes On Broadway* (1941) with make-up, bare midriff and fruity hat, takes her off accurately, after having been coached good-naturedly by Senorita Miranda herself. Out of her large mouth issued fractured English and hit songs such as 'Chica, Chica, Boom Chic', 'I Yi Yi Yi Yi' and 'Mama Yo Quiero'. From 1940–1944, this caricature of South American womanhood, was one of the highest paid women in America at $2 million a year, provided by Twentieth-Century Fox.

As a child, Miranda left Portugal with her parents for Rio, where her father ran a fruit business. After being educated at a convent, she began singing on radio and making records, before appearing in four Brazilian musical films. It was because of her success in 'Streets Of Paris' on Broadway, and in cabaret at the Waldorf, that Fox signed Miranda up. Although she played no part in the plot of *Down Argentine Way* (1940), and her three songs were filmed in New York while the rest was made in Hollywood, she created a sensation. She was immediately cast as the second female lead in Alice Faye/Betty Grable musicals such as *That Night In Rio* (1941), *Weekend In Havana* (1942) and *Springtime In The Rockies* (1942), usually playing a nightclub entertainer. In *The Gang's All Here* (1943), Busby Berkeley placed Carmen at the centre of a fantastical, Freudian number called 'The Lady With The Tutti-Frutti Hat', in which she entered, singing the self-descriptive song, while 60 girls did suggestive things with

60 giant bananas. She was top-billed for the first time in *Greenwich Village* (1944) and *Something For The Boys* (1944), but the public began to tire of the sameness of her portrayals.

In her latter years, she co-starred with Groucho Marx in a cheapie called *Copacabana* (1947), a low point in both their careers, and appeared in two Jane Powell musicals for MGM, teaching Wallace Beery to rhumba in *A Date With Judy* (1948) and singing a characteristic song, 'Cha Bomm Pa Pa' in *Nancy Goes To Rio* (1950). The combination of Jerry Lewis and Carmen Miranda was a bit too much in her final film *Scared Stiff* (1953). She died suddenly of a heart attack, aged 46, after doing a number on the Jimmy Durante TV show, and was buried in Brazil. RB

association with the military. War pictures continued to be popular throughout the 50s and 60s and he was cast in films such as *The Colditz Story* (1954), *Dunkirk* (1958) and *Tunes Of Glory* (1960), most often playing officer types, and later promoted to field-Marshal Haig in *Oh What A Lovely War* (1969), and Kitchener in *Young Winston* (1972). Yet his non-military roles of note included a typically cool and capable *Scott Of The Antarctic* (1948), a very likeable Willy Mossop who rebels against his dictatorial boss (Charles Laughton) in *Hobson's Choice* (1954), and a strange and atypical character role as the village idiot in David Lean's *Ryan's Daughter* (1970), which won him a best supporting actor Oscar. JF

Robert Mitchum

Born Bridgeport, Connecticut, 6 August 1917

With his typically self-deprecating sense of humour Robert Mitchum has described his early starring years thus: 'I came into being during the era of the ugly leading man started by Humphrey Bogart just after the war, and I always made the same film. They'd just keep moving new leading ladies in front of me. I'd close my eyes and when I opened them again there was a new leading lady. I woke up once and there was Marilyn Monroe.'

The typical image of Mitchum as a sleepy looking, heavy-lidded, casual type of actor who doesn't take acting very seriously is deceptive. 'It sure beats working' – is his oft-quoted remark. Yet over the years he has revealed himself to be extremely professional, talented and hard working, always early on the set and word-perfect with his lines. (According to director Howard Hawks, half way through their only film together, *El Dorado*, 1967, he accused Mitchum of being 'the biggest fraud I've ever met. You pretend you don't care a damn thing about a scene, and you're the hardest working so-and-so I've ever known.')

With his laid back, relaxed, modern style of

in The Night Of The Hunter *(United Artists, 1955)*

when he was offered a starring role in *The Story of GI Joe*. Although he is typically disparaging about his performance – 'I was lucky. No one could have missed in such a role.' – it earned him his first and only Oscar nomination (as supporting actor). Yet the genre in which he, and his studio excelled, was *film noir*. He played the first of his 'noir' villains in *When Strangers Marry* (1944), anticipating his later psychopathic baddies in *The Night Of The Hunter* (1955) and *Cape Fear* (1962). But once he became a star he was most often cast as a reluctant but capable anti-heroic hero, involved with unpredictable and frequently treacherous women like Jane Greer in *The Big Steal* (1949), Jane Russell in *His Kind of Woman* (1951) and Jean Simmons, who actually kills him and herself at the end of *Angel Face*, Otto Preminger's superb thriller which brought the RKO 'noir' cycle to a dramatic conclusion in 1953. And even Mitchum's westerns, *Blood On The Moon* (1948) and, especially, the highly stylised and psychological *Pursued* (1947), opposite Teresa Wright and directed by Raoul Walsh, stand as excellent examples of late 40s 'noir westerns'.

In a highly publicised incident in 1948, Mitchum was busted and served a short sentence for smoking marijuana in what was later revealed to be a put-up job, but which contributed at the time to the popular image of him as a rebel and hell-raiser, ignoring the

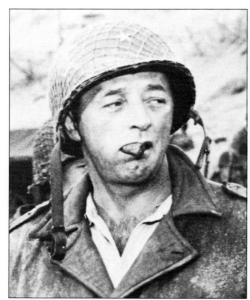

in The Longest Day *(20th Century-Fox, 1962)*

acting Mitchum provided an interesting link between the older generation of actors – the Humphrey Bogart of 40s *film noir* and the John Wayne of westerns – with the newer rebellious types of the 50s like Marlon Brando and Paul Newman. Yet having remained active in the same genres over such a long period means that he has also provided a unique personal link between the 40s and recent years. Thus, he was a key figure in the 70s revival of *film noir*. Such pictures as *The Friends Of Eddie Coyle* (1973), and remakes of *Farewell, My Lovely* (1974) and *The Big Sleep* (1978) recall his own early roles in *Crossfire* and *Out Of The Past* (both 1947) among others. Similarly, his recent war roles in *Anzio* (1968), *Midway* (1976) and the TV spectacular, *The Winds of War* (1983), connect with his 40s World War II movies like *30 Seconds Over Tokyo* (1944) and *The Story Of GI Joe* (1945). These suggest the range and diversity of his career, and it is really not his fault that he has not been in a larger number of good pictures, for his own performance is the best thing to be found in far too many of the movies he has appeared in. However, he has never really been a strong enough actor to carry a film on his own, as John Wayne could. 'He doesn't have anywhere near the force that Wayne has,' director Hawks was once moved to comment.

As one might expect, Mitchum experienced a tough childhood, and, while still a teenager, spent a

with Deborah Kerr in The Sundowners *(Warner Bros., 1960)*

number of years bumming around the country and living rough. A wide variety of jobs followed, including a short stint as a professional boxer, before he broke into films as an extra and bit part player during the early 40s. He appeared in sixteen different pictures released in 1943, although at least two of them – *Corvette K-225* and *Gung Ho!* – make use of some of the same shots of him. The parts gradually got larger, and in 1944 he was signed by RKO: 'They were looking for a journeyman actor,' he recalled. 'They felt I could do a number of things, so by hiring me they'd be getting a lot for the same money. I was a sort of utility man there for ten years ... RKO opened the door for me – and I became their workhorse.' His first big break came in 1945

fact that he was a happily married family man. It did not seem to hurt his career, however. Immediately upon being released he completed *The Big Steal* (1949), which had carried on filming with his stand-in while he was in prison. He continued active in a wide variety of pictures during the years that followed and up to the present date. Among his most memorable performances were the blood-chillingly sinister preacher in *The Night Of The Hunter*, a Marine marooned on a desert island with a nun in the comedy-war-adventure, *Heaven Knows, Mr Allison* (1957), an Australian sheep-shearer, opposite Deborah Kerr in *The Sundowners* (1960), and a hilarious, drunken sheriff, paired with John Wayne in *El Dorado* and demonstrating his sadly underused talent for comedy. JF

Maria Montez

Real name **Maria Africa Vidal de Santo Silas**
Born **Barahona, Dominican Republic,
6 June 1920**
Died **1951**

Maria Montez became a star in Hollywood at a time when Technicolor musicals were all the rage. A strikingly attractive Latin American brunette, she couldn't sing or dance and could only act a little. So Universal invented a new Technicolor genre for her with the emphasis on romantic, costumed exotica. Set in far off, storybook lands, there were generally plenty of dancing girls and spectacular special effects, the villains were cruel, and the hero was tall, dark and handsome. Attired in a variety of exotic costumes ranging from a simple sarong – in competition with Dorothy Lamour at Paramount – to more elaborate garb, like the fantastic snake priestess outfit in *Cobra Woman* (1944), Maria's popularity was at a peak for a short period during the mid-40s.

She had done a bit of acting and modelling before breaking into movies in 1941. Her first Technicolor starring role was as Scheherezade in *Arabian Nights* (1942), followed by *White Savage* and *Ali Baba And The Forty Thieves* (both in 1943) in which she played Princess Amara, the childhood sweetheart of Ali Baba (Jon Hall, who was her regular co-star). Perhaps the best of the lot was *Cobra Woman*, which required her to appear in a dual role as twin sisters, one good and the other an evil priestess. As recalled by director Robert Siodmak, '*Cobra Woman* was silly but fun. You know, Maria Montez couldn't act from here to there, but she was a great personality and believed completely in her roles.' She was married to

in Cobra Woman *(Universal, 1944)*

French actor Jean-Pierre Aumont, and was the mother of an actress daughter, Tina Aumont. Before her sad, premature death, she made her last pictures in Europe such as *The Thief Of Venice* (1950) and *The Pirate's Revenge* (1951), which came her way after she was no longer in demand in Hollywood. JF

Michèle Morgan

Real name **Simone Roussel**
Born **Neuilly-sur-Seine, France,
29 February 1920**

Michèle Morgan never again in her long career appeared in a role which so perfectly suited her as that of the beautiful, mysterious young girl, old beyond her years, who has a brief, tragic affair with Jean Gabin in *Quai Des Brumes* (1938). She was only eighteen at the time, but had already been acting in pictures for three years and had played her first major role opposite Raimu the previous year as the Russian heroine of *Gribouille*. A refined and intelligent-looking beauty with classical features, she was offered a Hollywood contract by RKO, on the basis of *Quai Des Brumes*' success. But she did not leave France until the beginning of the occupation in 1940, then found that 'RKO didn't know what to do with me. I spent the first year perfecting my English, then I made two films, both of them stinkers.' She tested for *Casablanca*, was extremely disappointed at losing out to Ingrid Bergman, then landed the follow-up picture opposite Bogart, *Passage To Marseilles* (1943). Filmed on the Warner Bros. back lot with artificial-looking sets, 'it was a wartime melodrama full of propaganda,' she recalled, 'although Hollywood at that time couldn't have been more remote from the war. I didn't enjoy doing the film. At the time I was single, bored, and unhappy with Hollywood... It seemed very unreal to me then.'

Back in France after the war, she immediately re-established herself as one of that country's leading screen actresses with her performance as the blind girl in the film version of Gide's *La Symphonie Pastorale* (1946) which earned her the best actress award at Cannes. She lent a touch of Continental sophistication to a small role as Ralph Richardson's mistress in *The Fallen Idol* (1948) before resuming her career in France. The parts that followed were rarely worthy of her, apart from a delightfully mature romantic role opposite Gérard Philipe in *Les Grandes Manoeuvres* (1955), and she virtually retired from the screen after *Benjamin* in 1968. JF

in Joan Of Paris *(20th Century-Fox, 1942)*

Anna Neagle

Real name **Marjorie Robertson**
Born **London, 20 October 1904**

It was inevitable that Anna Neagle, the First Lady of the British cinema between 1937 and 1951, should have been created a Dame of the British Empire in 1969. The attractive, aristocratic blonde Neagle, rhymes with regal, made her international reputation as Queen Victoria in *Victoria The Great* (1937) and *60 Glorious Years* (1938), both sentimental, patriotic epics.

In fact, Dame Anna had been a professional dancer since the age of 14, and a chorus girl in Charles Cochran's revues. After appearing in bit parts in two films, she was discovered by producer-director Herbert Wilcox who co-starred her with Jack Buchanan in his film *Goodnight Vienna* (1932). From then on Wilcox took charge of her career, directing all but two of her films. Although a mediocre director, he found a popular formula in which to display his Galatea's rather limited abilities. In 1939, they went to Hollywood to film three luke-warm musical remakes for RKO, *Irene* (1940), *No, No, Nanette* (1940) and *Sunny* (1941), before returning gratefully to England. They were married in 1943. Apart from a few 'naughty' roles such as *Nell*

Gwyn (1934) and *Peg Of Old Drury* (1935), in which she showed a bit of bosom, Anna Neagle played indomitable, historical heroines like *Nurse Edith Cavell* (1939), the pilot Amy Johnson in *They Flew Alone* (1942), French Resistance worker *Odette* (1950), and Florence Nightingale in *The Lady With The Lamp* (1951).

In contrast to the stiff upper-lip dramas, Wilcox paired his wife with insipid Michael Wilding in sugary, snobbish musical comedies and romances with fashionable London areas in the titles such as *Spring In Park Lane* (1948) and *Maytime In Mayfair* (1949), and with a declining Errol Flynn in *Lilacs In The Spring* (1954) and *King's Rhapsody* (1955). In the late 50s Neagle attempted to get 'with it' in painful youth-oriented films such as *My Teenage Daughter* (1956) and *The Lady Is A Square* (1958), and produced (but did not appear in) three pictures featuring the 'teenage' singer Frankie Vaughan, then 30 years old.

Since retiring from films in 1958, Anna Neagle has continued her career on stage in Britain, recently appearing in the revival of 'My Fair Lady' in her old regal form. She was widowed in 1977. RB

David Niven

Born **Kirriemuir, Scotland, 1 March 1910**
Died **1983**

A sophisticated and intelligent actor, tall and slim, generally sporting a moustache and well dressed, David Niven was often called upon to portray the archetypal Englishman on the screen. He had an eventful life which he described in two witty best-selling books of memoirs, 'The Moon's A Balloon' and 'Bring On The Empty Horses'. Educated at a number of prep schools, he finally ended up at Sandhurst, which led to a stint in the Highland Light Infantry before he left England for Canada and the US in his early twenties. After floating around the fringes of high society for a number of years, trying his hand at various jobs and clearly attracted to a glamorous life style which he could not afford, he ended up, not surprisingly, in Hollywood, trying to break into the movies.

Niven started out as a lowly extra – 'Anglo-Saxon type, No. 2008' – and was promptly put into his first film as a Mexican, complete with sombrero, sandals, baggy white suit and false moustache, and sprayed

in 1951

with a brown substance to give his pale skin the required dark hue. As a complete unknown with no previous acting experience, but with a few useful social contacts, he had the good fortune to be signed to a contract by producer Sam Goldwyn in 1935. But he had to prove himself as a film actor, and, during the following years, he slowly and painfully worked his way up from bit parts in pictures like *Barbary Coast* (1935) and *Dodsworth* (1936), to supporting roles before finally achieving star status.

In his book Niven has described his first ever long dialogue scene in *A Feather In Her Hat* (1935). He was so terrified during the first take that everything went wrong, but at the end everyone applauded and the director congratulated him and asked him to do another 'just for safety'. Much more relaxed on the second take, Niven only learned afterwards that the director, Alfred Santell, had briefed everyone on the set while he was in his dressing-room: 'The boy who's playing Leo – this is his first big scene in a picture and we've all got to help him loosen up. After the first take, no matter how bad he is, I want you all to applaud, then I'll put some film in the camera.' The following year (1936) Niven landed his first good roles, in *Thank You Jeeves*, and as a young officer who dies heroically in *The Charge Of The Light Brigade*. This latter part he got by acting insolent to the dictatorial director Michael Curtiz at

the tryout. He became close friends with the star, Errol Flynn, and they ended up sharing an apartment. A few years later, they appeared together in *The Dawn Patrol* (1938), which marked another step up for Niven who obviously benefitted from the fact that British literary and dramatic subjects were a staple part of the Hollywood output during these years. And in his private life, he fitted easily into the large British expatriate colony in Hollywood led by such stalwart and distinguished figures as Ronald Colman, Basil Rathbone and C. Aubrey Smith.

Niven moved easily from dramatic roles like Edgar in *Wuthering Heights* – surviving the torture of director William Wyler's insistence on take after take – to an actioner, *The Real Glory*, and had his first chance to shine in a comedy role opposite Ginger Rogers in *Bachelor Mother*, all in 1939. But the title role of the gentleman thief in *Raffles* (1940) turned out to be his last pre-war Hollywood picture as he returned to England and rejoined the army as a second lieutenant. While serving with distinction he was given leave to appear in three British films of note – *The First Of The Few* (1942) telling the story of the Spitfire, *The Way Ahead* (1944), a superior piece of pro-army propaganda, and Michael Powell's allegorical *A Matter Of Life And Death* (1946) in which he played a brain-damaged RAF pilot, suspended between Heaven and earth.

Returning to the US after the war, he was an established star, yet found it difficult to land good parts, and appeared in a number of undistinguished pictures both in the US and back in England. His break with producer Sam Goldwyn in 1950 left him free to take any offers, but they were few and far between. Niven tried a first-ever role in the theatre opposite Gloria Swanson which turned out disastrously, but did somewhat better in a live TV production of 'The Petrified Forest'. He gave a likeable performance in *The Moon Is Blue* (1953), but his film career did not pick up until he starred as Phileas Fogg in Mike Todd's extremely successful production of *Around The World In 80 Days* which won the Best Picture Oscar in 1956. Two years later Niven himself won an Oscar for his performance as the bogus 'major' in *Separate Tables* (1958) based on the play by Terence Rattigan. A number of comedy roles followed, the best of which was in *Ask Any Girl* (1959) opposite Shirley MacLaine, but he proved that he could still acquit himself well in a demanding action picture like *The Guns Of Navarone* (1961). Later pictures of note included *55 Days At Peking*

in The Guns Of Navarone *(Columbia, 1961)*

(1963) and *The Pink Panther* (1964) with Peter Sellers, in which he played an aristocratic thief. He continued active in pictures throughout the 60s and 70s with a similar mixture of comedies and adventure films up to the end – his last two screen appearances were in *The Sea Wolves* (1980), and the unfortunately titled *Better Late Than Never* which was made in 1981 but not released until some time after his death. JF

with Ginger Rogers in Bachelor Mother *(RKO, 1939)*

Pat O'Brien

Born **Milwaukee, Wisconsin,**
11 November 1899
Died **1983**

Although Pat O'Brien appeared in a large number of pictures during the peak years of his career from 1931 through 1951, he is best remembered for a few key roles. His first big success came in 1931 when he gave a characteristically quiet, assured performance as ace reporter Hildy Johnson, playing 'straight man' to Adolphe Menjou's shrewd and unpredictable newspaper editor in the first of three film versions of Hecht and MacArthur's play, *The Front Page*. O'Brien brought a similar quiet authority to the role of the social reformer priest in *Angels With Dirty*

in Man Alive *(RKO, 1945)*

Faces (1937), pitted against his childhood friend-turned-gangster played by James Cagney.

Originally a song-and-dance man turned dramatic actor, O'Brien fitted well into the Warner Bros. contract roster during the 30s. Best known as a solid, dependable, but unexciting actor, he was paired with the more dynamic Cagney in a number of pictures like *Ceiling Zero* (1936). His likeable performance as Dean Stockwell's grandfather in director Joseph Losey's first feature, *The Boy With Green Hair* (1948) was but one of a number of such appearances in mildly enjoyable pictures during the 40s. But by the 50s his career was clearly winding down. He had smallish roles in *The Last Hurrah* (1958), with his old friend Spencer Tracy and in *Some Like It Hot* (1959), and was seen most recently in *The End* (1978), as well as being reunited for one last time with Cagney in *Ragtime* (1981). JF

with Gale Storm in Curtain Call At Cactus Creek *(Universal, 1950)*

Donald O'Connor

Born **Chicago, Illinois, 30 August 1925**

'Donald O'Connor was always making us laugh', recalled Gene Kelly about *Singin' In The Rain* (1952), 'so I said, Let's do a number called 'Make 'Em Laugh'. It was all improvisation. The dummy he uses in the dance, for example, was lying on a rehearsal stage next door to us. We walked in there one day and Donald started to fool around with it. For half an hour we just roared with laughter. Finally we said, Well, let's put that in the number. All of it came right out of Donald. It was unbelievable. We had to throw out twenty minutes of it.' *Singin' In The Rain* was the high spot in the small, sprightly, explosively talented song-and-dance comedian's 30-year movie career. Oscar Levant had originally been chosen for the role of Cosmo Brown, but the film's directors, Gene Kelly and Stanley Donen insisted on O'Connor. Apart from the sensational 'Make 'Em Laugh' number, Donald danced two dynamic duets with Kelly, 'Fit As A Fiddle' and 'Moses Supposes'.

The son of vaudevillians had come a long way since he joined the family act as a child. The 11-year-old Donald made his screen debut with two of his brothers in a specialty routine in *Melody For Two* (1937). The following year, he signed a contract with Paramount and played Bing Crosby's jockey kid

brother in *Sing You Sinners* (1938), Huckleberry Finn in *Tom Sawyer–Detective* (1938), Fred Mac-Murray as a child in William Wellman's *Men With Wings* (1938) and Gary Cooper as a child in *Beau Geste* (1939). After a couple of years back in vaudeville, he returned to the screen in 1942 in a series of Universal B musicals, becoming popular and well-known as the breezy juvenile lead, mainly opposite the equally lively and youthful Peggy Ryan. Then O'Connor found a new partner in Francis, the talking mule. This puerile but highly successful series began with *Francis* (1950) and continued with *Francis Goes To The Races* (1951), ... *Goes To West Point* (1952), ... *Covers The Big Town* (1953) ... *Joins The Wacs* (1954) ... *In The Navy* (1955) ... O'Connor didn't go on, explaining, 'When you've made six pictures and the mule gets more fan mail than you do ...'

He made two huge Fox musicals, *Call Me Madam* (1953) with Ethel Merman, and *There's No Business Like Show Business* (1954) in which he is driven to drink – in CinemaScope – by Marilyn Monroe. After being given the impossible task of portraying Keaton in *The Buster Keaton Story* (1957), he only appeared in three more films, giving him more time to concentrate on composing music. The Brussels Symphony Orchestra has recorded some of his work, and in 1956 he conducted the Los Angeles Philharmonic in a performance of his first symphony, 'Reflections D'Un Comique'. RB

Maureen O'Hara

Real name **Maureen FitzSimons**
Born **Millwall, Ireland, 17 August 1920**

A lively and strikingly attractive Irish colleen who hailed from a little town near Dublin, Maureen O'Hara was one of a number of redheaded stars who flourished during the Technicolor era of the 40s and early 50s. In fact, much of her early career was divided between colourful escapist entertainments like *The Black Swan* (1942), *Sinbad The Sailor* (1947), *Bagdad* (1949), *Flame Of Araby* (1951) and *Lady Godiva* (1955), and the more serious black-and-white efforts like the Oscar-winning *How Green Was My Valley* (1941) directed by John Ford, Jean Renoir's pro-French Resistance propaganda film *This Land Is Mine* (1943), *The Foxes Of Harrow* (1947) and Ford's *Rio Grande* (1950).

Miss O'Hara had a brief career on the stage with Dublin's famed Abbey Players before she came to London. A featured role opposite Charles Laughton

in *Jamaica Inn* (1939), directed by Hitchcock, led to an offer by Laughton of the gypsy girl lead in his next picture, a major Hollywood production of *The Hunchback Of Notre Dame* (1939) at RKO. Although she played a Welsh girl in her first Ford picture (*How Green Was My Valley*), she later developed into his favourite Irish heroine. In *The Quiet Man* (1952) she gave a delightful performance as the independent-minded Irish lass torn between traditional and modern attitudes to marriage who eventually succumbs to the charms of John Wayne. She was West Point 'Irish' in Ford's *The Long Gray Line* (1955), married to Tyrone Power, and in *Wings Of Eagles*, the last of her five with Ford, she was again married to Wayne. A spirited and robust actress who could stand up to the men, she emerged as an accomplished western star during the 50s, and although she appeared in several non-westerns throughout the 60s this genre sustained her up to the time of her retirement from the screen, her last two having been *Big Jake* (1971) with Wayne and a TV movie remake of *The Red Pony* (1973) with Henry Fonda. JF

Laurence Olivier

Born Dorking, England, 22 May 1907

From his first stage appearance as Brutus in 'Julius Caesar' in 1916 up to his most recent performance on TV in 'A Talent for Murder' opposite Angela Lansbury, Lord Olivier's career has spanned almost 70 years. His first love has always been the theatre. A leading stage actor from the mid-30s, he later turned to directing and producing, was appointed the first director of the British National Theatre in 1973, and was knighted, and subsequently given a peerage, for his services to British theatre. But he has had a long and distinguished career in the cinema as well, developing from a young romantic star into a director-star best known for his Shakespeare adaptations and finally as an extremely successful mature star and character actor.

Olivier became interested in the theatre as a boy and made a first notable appearance as Katharine in a schoolboy production of 'The Taming Of The Shrew'. After a brief stint at drama school, he played a variety of roles at Birmingham Rep and then on the West End stage. He appeared in his first movies during the early 30s and travelled to New York with Noel Coward, Gertrude Lawrence, and his young

in Hamlet *(Rank/Universal, 1948)*

actress wife, Jill Esmond, where they presented Coward's 'Private Lives' on Broadway. Both he and Jill were invited out to Hollywood and given screen tests, like so many of the young stage actors of the period. As an exceptionally handsome, stylish, and charismatic young English actor with a moustache in the Ronald Colman mould, Olivier was cast in a few pictures – *The Yellow Ticket* (1931) with Elissa Landi and *Westward Passage* (1932) opposite Ann Harding – without much success and returned to England. His mixed feelings about the cinema were not improved by the fact that Jill Esmond was more successful in Hollywood than he had been, and a further trip west ended badly when he was replaced by John Gilbert in *Queen Christina* (1933), thus robbing him of the chance to star opposite Garbo.

Olivier continued to develop his skills as an actor, mainly on the stage, in a variety of roles. Finally the big break came with a much acclaimed production of 'Romeo and Juliet' in 1935 in which he alternated with Gielgud in the roles of Romeo and Mercutio. He played Orlando in a weak 1936 film version of *As You Like It* and the following year appeared with Vivien Leigh in the Korda production, *Fire Over England*, and on the stage as Hamlet to her Ophelia. They fell in love and began living together while he continued to establish himself as a leading Shakespearian actor before departing, somewhat reluctantly, for Hollywood once again. Cast as Heathcliffe in a prestige Goldwyn production of *Wuthering Heights* (1939), the picture represented an important turning

point for him. Under director William Wyler he produced his best film performance to date as the tragic romantic hero of Emily Brontë's novel and earned his first Oscar nomination. The picture opened his eyes to the possibilities of the cinema more clearly than before, as he recalled. 'I was snobbish about films until *Wuthering Heights*... Then gradually I came to see that film was a different medium and that, if one treated it as such, one could work in it... It was Wyler who gave me the simple thought – "if you do it right, you can do anything". And if he hadn't said that, I would never have done *Henry V* five years later.'

Vivien visited him in Hollywood and ended up

with Vivien Leigh in Fire Over England *(Warner Bros., 1937)*

with the role of Scarlett O'Hara. Thus, both of them were simultaneously launched on highly successful, though separate, movie careers. Working with Alfred Hitchcock on his first American film, Daphne du Maurier's *Rebecca* with Joan Fontaine, Olivier proved that he had matured into an excellent film actor, and his underplayed performance as the troubled, aristocratic Max de Winter earned him a second Oscar nomination, while *Rebecca* won the Best Picture Oscar for 1940. Although his next picture, *Pride And Prejudice*, took him to MGM where Vivien was filming *Waterloo Bridge* (both 1940), they did not manage to make a film together until Korda's *That Hamilton Woman* (1941) with Vivien in the title role and Olivier as Lord Nelson. Designed as a pro-British propaganda piece, filmed quickly and cheaply, it succeeded admirably in its modest aims, aided by Olivier's fine performance.

Back in England he had fun impersonating a French-Canadian trapper with a convincing French accent playing an unforgettable little cameo role in Michael Powell's *The 49th Parallel* (1942). Not surprisingly, the government decided that he could make a greater contribution to the war effort through his film work than in the services and he was released. When the idea of adapting Shakespeare's *Henry V* (1945) to the screen was first suggested as a suitably patriotic war subject, Olivier approached a number of established directors to work with him. When they declined, he decided, with typical enthusiasm, to forge ahead on his own. In spite of the problems caused by wartime filming, he managed to assemble an experienced group of technicians and an excellent cast. One of a small group of early British Technicolor productions, the picture was not entirely successful in blending stage artifice with screen naturalism, but proved to be a very worthwhile attempt to adapt Shakespeare to the screen, nevertheless. Olivier himself gave a lively,

assured and striking performance which earned him his third Oscar nomination. There was an Oscar nomination for Best Picture, too, and Olivier was awarded a special Oscar for his achievement.

Throughout his career Olivier was characterised by his willingness to take risks, and after his latest stage successes at the Old Vic he regarded a film version of *Hamlet* (1948) as the obvious choice. Although his 'modern' conception of the role and production looks more traditional today, the result, at the time, was just as compelling and successful in its way as *Henry V* had been. Demonstrating a greater assurance as a director and a firmer grasp of the film medium, the result was a better integrated production. His mature and cool performance earned him his only acting Oscar, while *Hamlet* turned out to be the first British production ever to win a Best Picture Oscar.

Concentrating more on his theatre work during the following years, he nevertheless returned to the US and gave another fine performance in a downbeat, elderly character role in *Carrie* (1952). Then back to filming Shakespeare – his famous stage characterisation of *Richard III* (1955) brought to the screen, and another Oscar nomination, although a disappointing production overall (which he directed). The following year he attempted to direct Marilyn Monroe while starring opposite her in *The Prince And The Showgirl*, the kind of stagebound production which does not adapt well to the screen, and it didn't. A surprising change of direction in 1957, and a move away from the 'establishment' theatre saw him starring in a new play by John Osborne, *The Entertainer*, giving an extraordinary impersonation of a broken-down, ageing music-hall star. The film version in 1960 brought a sixth Oscar nomination, and he married his co-star, Joan Plowright, the following year after divorcing Vivien Leigh. He continued to make occasional film appearances, whenever his theatre commitments would allow, in the 60s and 70s, in a wide variety of character roles. He won further Oscar nominations for *Othello* (1965) – the film version of his stage production; for *Sleuth* (1972); and for *The Boys From Brazil* (1978). His most sinister and frightening performance on the screen – as the 'dentist' who terrorizes Dustin Hoffman in *The Marathon Man* (1976) – brought a supporting actor nomination, and he was awarded his second 'special' Oscar in 1978. During recent years, fighting severe illness with notable courage, he has turned his attention to television, but has been seen on the big screen in the remake of *The Jazz Singer* (1980) and *Clash Of The Titans* (1981). JF

in Battle Of Britain *(United Artists, 1969)*

with Claire Bloom in Richard III *(London Films, 1955)* ▷

Lilli Palmer

Real name Lillie Marie Peiser
Born Posen, Germany, 24 May 1914

A sophisticated, yet gentle and intelligent, international star, Lilli Palmer's career as an actress got off to an unfortunate start, for her very first stage success during 1932–33 coincided exactly with Hitler's rise to power. Since she was Jewish she was forced to leave Germany and went to Paris, then England where she found work in the theatre and films. Lilli married Rex Harrison in 1943 and they appeared together in *The Rake's Progress* (1945) before leaving for Hollywood. She gave an excellent performance as Gina, a tough and resourceful member of the Italian resistance who falls in love with OSS agent Gary Cooper, in Fritz Lang's *Cloak And Dagger* (1946). But her teaming with John Garfield in *Body And Soul* (1947) worked somewhat less well, and she did only two other American films before leaving Hollywood. During the 50s she and Harrison appeared on stage together and made *The Fourposter* (1952), an enjoyable comedy, before the break-up of their marriage. Travelling widely during the following years, she starred in a variety of Continental and American films including Jacques Becker's *Montparnasse 19* (1957) with Gérard Philipe, *But Not For Me* (1959) as Clark Gable's wise-cracking ex-wife, and in 1958 married film actor Carlos Thompson. Semi-retired from acting, during the 70s she published her entertaining memoirs, 'Change Lobsters And Dance,' appeared in a German film version of Goethe's *Lotte In Weimar* (1975) and was also in the screen version of Ira Levin's *The Boys From Brazil* (1978). JF

in The Rake's Progress (Rank/Universal, 1945)

Gregory Peck

Born La Jolla, California, 5 April 1916

A famous memo from producer David Selznick in 1941 reads: 'I am sorry to say that I don't see what we could do with Gregory Peck... We would have great difficulty in either using him ourselves or in getting other studios to use him... He photographs like Abe Lincoln, but if he has a great personality, I don't think it comes through...' It was only four years later that Peck became one of Selznick's leading stars and was very much in demand to play leading roles at all the major studios.

Tall, handsome and an established stage actor,

Peck was first signed by producer-scriptwriter Casey Robinson in 1943 for *Days Of Glory* at RKO. Although the picture itself was not very good – a kind of small budget follow-up to Paramount's *For Whom The Bell Tolls* (1943), with Peck in the Cooper role of partisan/guerilla fighter – he learned quickly and appreciated the assistance he got from director Jacques Tourneur. Already in his next film, *The Keys Of The Kingdom* (1944), one can see on the screen for the first time that characteristically dedicated, earnest quality and basic decency which has become Peck's hallmark over the years, and which here earned him his first Oscar nomination. He then played opposite Greer Garson in *Valley Of Decision* for MGM, but was miscast as a mentally

disturbed bogus psychiatrist in Hitchcock's *Spellbound* (both 1945), his first for Selznick; Ingrid Bergman and Michael Chekhov stole the acting honours. Another for Selznick followed – *Duel In The Sun* (1946) – Peck's first western and his first portrayal of a nasty character on the screen. As he recalls, 'Selznick liked the idea of taking me from *The Keys Of The Kingdom* where I had played this saintly maverick priest, and making me a rapist, a forger, a killer, a liar, a thoroughly rotten no-good but with a certain likeability. He enjoyed that kind of switch in my character.'

Duel In The Sun turned out to be Peck's fourth big hit in a row, filmed before, but released shortly after, *The Yearling* (1946) in which he played a young pioneering homesteader. A nice twist had him married to a slightly older wife played by Jane Wyman – both of them receiving Oscar nominations for their performances. A starring role as a dedicated reporter investigating anti-semitism in the Oscar-winning *Gentleman's Agreement* in 1947 brought him his third Oscar nomination in as many years. Again Selznick forced him on Hitchcock, and again he was miscast – as an English barrister defending Alida Valli in *The Paradine Case* (1948).

He appeared in a couple of good westerns, *Yellow Sky* (1949), and *The Gunfighter* (1950) in which he gave his best ever western performance, but the failure of the picture at the box-office was blamed on the fact that he wore a moustache. He had received his fourth Oscar nomination the previous year working for the same director, Henry King, as a harried World War II bomber squadron commander in *Twelve O'Clock High*. In all they did six pictures together including *David And Bathsheba* (1951) and *The Snows Of Kilimanjaro* (1952).

After an excellent run of pictures, with hardly a dud among them, it was inevitable that Peck's career would slacken off during the 50s. He continued to appear in a variety of roles ranging from adventure – a good try at Ahab in *Moby Dick* (1956) and a big hit with *The Guns of Navarone* (1961) – to comedy, most notably *Roman Holiday* (1953) with Audrey Hepburn. He finally won his only Oscar in 1962 in a serious dramatic role as a liberal lawyer in a small southern town who defends a black prisoner in *To Kill A Mockingbird*. In 1967 he received the Jean Hersholt Humanitarian Award from the Academy of Motion Picture Arts and Sciences and served a three-year term as Academy president (1967–70). He tried his hand at producing with *The Trial Of The Catonsville Nine* (1972) and *The Dove* (1974). His most recent performances of note were in *The Omen* (1976), *The Boys From Brazil* (1978) and *The Sea Wolves* (1980). JF

with Ava Gardner in The Snows Of Kilimanjaro (20th Century-Fox, 1952)

Walter Pidgeon

Born **East St John, New Brunswick, Canada,
23 September 1897**

A tall, distinguished looking actor who first made his name on the stage as a baritone, then as a straight actor, Walter Pidgeon broke into silent pictures during the late 20s, briefly became a film musical star, then concentrated on straight acting. By the time of his retirement after two last pictures in the 70s, *Two Minute Warning* (1976) and the ill-judged Mae West vehicle, *Sextette* (1978), his career had spanned over fifty years.

The centrepiece and highlight of Pidgeon's career came during the 40s when he was paired with Greer Garson in a number of pictures at MGM beginning with *Blossoms In The Dust* in 1941, the same year that he played a sympathetic Welsh priest in the Oscar-winning *How Green Was My Valley*. Greer Garson and the picture, *Mrs Miniver*, won the 1942 Oscars, while Pidgeon's sensitive performance as Mr Miniver earned him a nomination. Clearly at his peak in popularity during these years, he and Garson were both nominated again for their dedicated

scientist couple in *Madame Curie* (1943). His best role of the late 40s was as the general in *Command Decision* (1948), and other pictures of note (in over 100 that he made) included *The Bad And The Beautiful* (1952), *Forbidden Planet* (1956) and *Advise And Consent* (1962). JF

Ronald Reagan

Born **Tampico, Illinois, 6 February 1911**

'No, no, *Jimmy Stewart* for governor – Reagan for his best friend,' Jack Warner is alleged to have remarked on hearing that Ronald Reagan was running for governor of California. Now that the former B-picture star has made it to the White House, the bad

actor jokes have proliferated, but he was really a modest, likeable young man in his early days as a contract star at Warner Bros.

Reagan served an active apprenticeship, appearing in 27 pictures during 1938–41 and worked his way up to a starring role in *King's Row* (1941) in which, confronted with his amputated leg, he delivered that immortal line, 'Where is the rest of me?' A competent professional of limited range, his pictures were probably no better and no worse than he deserved. His 1940 marriage to actress Jane Wyman was not helped by a long wartime separation and his growing political activities, and they were divorced in 1948. He served with distinction as the president of the Screen Actors' Guild during the late 40s and 50s and remarried in 1952 another actress co-star, Nancy Davis, now the First Lady. (They played together in *Hellcats Of The Navy*, 1957). More in demand for TV than movies, he had one last film role as the nasty double-crossing heavy in Don Siegel's remake of Hemingway's *The Killers* (1964) just two years before he was elected governor of California. A staunch conservative, he lost the Republican nomination to Gerald Ford in 1976, but made a surprising comeback in 1980 and went on to defeat the incumbent President, Jimmy Carter. JF

Thelma Ritter

Born **Brooklyn, New York, 14 February 1905**
Died **1969**

The most surprising thing about Thelma Ritter is the fact that it took her so long to discover the movies . . . or for the movies to discover her. She did her first acting on the stage during the 20s, and on radio, but was in her mid-forties when director George Seaton asked her to play a small role in *Miracle On 34th Street* (1947). The picture was successful and so was she: best remembered for one scene in which she bawls out a department store Santa. Miss Ritter was immediately signed by 20th Century-Fox, one of the studios which had been in the forefront of the new trend to film on location and give its pictures a more naturalistic feel. *34th St*, of course, was New York City, and a large number of Ritter's films were set there. As an authentically Brooklyn-born New Yorker, gifted with marvellous qualities as a character actress, she brought a genuine New York feel (and accent) to *The Model And The Marriage Broker* (1951), in which her office was on top of the Flatiron Building, *Pickup On South Street* (1953) and *Rear Window* (1954), with its Greenwich Village courtyard setting. She was fortunate in her choice of directors who included Sam Fuller, Hitchcock and Huston. Mankiewicz for ex-

in All About Eve *(20th Century-Fox, 1950)*

ample, put her cynical, worldly-wise qualities to good use in *A Letter To Three Wives* (1949) and *All About Eve* (1950), which earned her the first of her six supporting Oscar nominations, a record, although she never won. She was nominated four years in a row – for *The Mating Season* (1951), *With A Song In My Heart* (1952) and *Pickup On South Street*. Later nominations were for her performances as Doris Day's maid in *Pillow Talk* (1959) and Burt Lancaster's mother in *Birdman Of Alcatraz* (1962), near the end of her career, which also included a role in *The Misfits* (1961). Her last appearance was in *The Incident* (1967). JF

Flora Robson

Born **South Shields, England, 28 March 1902**
Died **1984**

Four years as a welfare officer in a breakfast cereals factory is an unlikely preparation for the role of Queen Elizabeth I, but such an interlude interrupted Dame Flora Robson's promising start in the English theatre. She returned to the stage in 1929 and three years later her film career took off in Anthony Asquith's *Dance, Pretty Lady* (1932). In *Catherine The Great* (1934) Alexander Korda cast her as the Dowager Czarina, the first of her imperious *grande dame* roles and, still only 35, she played Elizabeth I in Korda's *Fire Over England* (1937).

in Holiday Camp *(Rank/Universal, 1948)*

She was at her quietly moving best as Leslie Banks's dying wife in *Farewell Again* (1937), a performance filled with the authority and stillness which characterise her best work. Hollywood beckoned, and Goldwyn cast her as the housekeeper in *Wuthering Heights* (1939), while Warners gave her sinister roles: Paul Muni's domineering wife in *We Are Not Alone* (1939); Ingrid Bergman's half-caste servant in *Saratoga Trunk* (1942). Struggling unsuccessfully to free herself from typecasting, and only a year older than George Raft, she was his mother in *Invisible Stripes* (1939), and played the Virgin Queen in *The Sea Hawk* (1941). In Britain the 1939 *Poison Pen* gave her the first of many 'tortured spinster' roles. Too often, in a long series of films for Rank, she was forced into a narrow range: a sad spinster in *Holiday Camp* (1948), an embittered MP in *Frieda* (1947), a starchy magistrate in *Good Time Girl* (1947). She had sympathetic roles in *Great Day* (1945) and *Black Narcissus* (1947), and then gave a blazing performance as the ageing, vindictive courtesan, Countess von Platen, in Ealing's *Saraband For Dead Lovers* (1948).

In the 50s she concentrated on the theatre. She was the nurse in *Romeo And Juliet* (1954), but the rest of her films were Rank potboilers. Nonetheless, her superb achievements were rewarded with a DBE in 1960. In 1962 she returned to an earlier mode, playing the capricious Chinese Empress in *55 Days At Peking* and a missionary in John Ford's *Seven Women* (1965). Her quality has seen her through a number of preposterous horror features, including *The Beast In The Cellar* (1971), and she was a housekeeper again in *Dominique* (1979). She celebrated her fiftieth film in *Clash Of The Titans* (1981), playing a memorable witch. RC

Roy Rogers

Real name **Leonard Slye**
Born **Cincinnati, Ohio, 5 November 1912**

A Beverly Hills hostess once observed that Roy Rogers had 'the purtiest backside in Hollywood'. At the peak of his popularity the slim, boyish cowboy star looked as if he had been poured into his skin-tight pants, and wore shirts embroidered with flowering roses. But despite the extravagance of the Republic wardrobe department, Rogers remained the epitome of clean-cut wholesomeness, right down to his fancy boots.

He made his debut, as a member of the Sons of the Pioneers singing group, in Liberty Films' *The Old Homestead* (1935). After Paramount's *Rhythm On The Range* (1937), he went solo with Republic under the name of Dick Weston. His first film as Roy Rogers was *Under Western Stars* (1938), directed by Joseph Kane who went on to handle no less than 41 Rogers features in a row.

By 1945 he was No 1 on the Republic lot and 'King of the Cowboys'. From the early 40s, his films became outdoor musical dramas rather than westerns – frequently with a modern setting – though packed with fights and chases, they closed with a ten-minute musical revue. From *Red River Valley* (1941) Rogers was joined by the Sons of the Pioneers, who gave way at the end of the decade to the Riders of the Purple Sage. Burnette was eventually succeeded by whiskery old-timer George 'Gabby' Hayes and then Andy Devine. From *The Cowboy And The Senorita* (1944) romantic interest

was provided by Dale Evans, who played in 20 straight Rogers films before marrying him in 1947. His entourage was completed by his horse Trigger, and Bullet the faithful dog, both of whom can be admired as stuffed exhibits at the Roy Rogers Museum near his ranch at Chatsworth, California. Occasionally Rogers stepped out of character to play a featured role in a non-western, like the musical *Lake Placid Serenade* (1944), although he was woefully miscast in Bob Hope's 1952 comedy *Son Of Paleface*. He had a cameo role in *Alias Jesse James* (1959) and was in *Mackintosh And T.J.* (1975). RC

Rosalind Russell

Born **Waterbury, Connecticut, 4 June 1908**
Died **1976**

A tall, slim, intelligent brunette from New England, Rosalind Russell was already in her mid-twenties when she first arrived in Hollywood with a fair amount of stage experience behind her. She immediately made an impression as the sophisticated, Katharine Hepburn-type of strong-willed woman

although that studio was already well stocked with top female stars. Thus, in her early MGM pictures she was most often called upon to play the 'other woman' – to Maureen O'Sullivan, for example, in *West Point Of The Air*, and to Jean Harlow in *China Seas* (both 1935). Her best role at MGM (and the last under her six year contract) was in *The Women* (1939) when director George Cukor encouraged her to go slightly over the top in her portrayal of an out-and-out bitch. Reaching the peak years of her career in the 40s, she was extremely lucky with her first

in What A Woman *(Columbia, 1943)*

and, during the course of her career, she came to represent Hollywood's idea of a hardboiled career woman. According to Miss Russell's own estimate, she played variations on this same type in 23 different pictures: 'My wardrobe had a set pattern – a tan suit, a grey suit, a beige suit, and then a negligee for the seventh reel, near the end, when I would admit to my best friend on the telephone that what I really wanted to become a dear little housewife.'

Although initially invited to test for Universal, she ended up accepting a better offer from MGM,

picture as a freelance, cast opposite Cary Grant as an ace reporter in *His Girl Friday* (1940). A screwball comedy, it provided her with the very best of her Hollywood career woman roles, and under Howard Hawks's direction, the witty dialogue was delivered at an incredibly rapid pace. But she had to wait two more years for her first Oscar nomination for another enjoyable comedy role in *My Sister Eileen* (1942). Although the pictures which followed were uneven, to say the least, she was duly rewarded for her efforts in two expensive prestige productions in a

Margaret Rutherford

Born **London, England, 11 May 1892**
Died **1972**

One of the great character comediennes of the cinema, Margaret Rutherford could be counted on to enliven any picture she appeared in. With her expressive jowly face and distinctive style of acting, she was most often cast as an eccentric English 'type'. Brought up by two maiden aunts who loved the theatre, she began acting at an early age, but didn't experience her first professional success until the mid-30s when she also began appearing in pictures. During the early 40s she was given better roles in films like *The Demi-Paradise* (1943), leading up to her remarkable and unforgettable performance as the unpredictable medium Madame Arcati in the film version of Noel Coward's *Blithe Spirit* (1945), a role which she had created on the stage. This set her on course to become a staple figure in post-war British film comedy ranging from *Passport To Pimlico* (1949) and *The Happiest Days Of Your Life* (1950) up to *I'm All Right Jack* (1959) and *The Mouse On The Moon* (1963). Along the way she made a delightful appearance as Miss Prism in

in Murder Most Foul *(MGM, 1964)*

The Importance Of Being Earnest and played Agatha Christie's scatty lady detective, Miss Marple, in a number of movies, often joined in the cast by her actor-husband, Stringer Davis. She won a supporting actress Oscar for her performance in *The VIP's* (1963), and was a memorable Mistress Quickly in Orson Welles's *Chimes At Midnight* (1966). JF

more serious vein at RKO – *Sister Kenny* (1946) and Eugene O'Neill's weighty *Mourning Becomes Electra* (1947) – with two further Oscar nominations. (Both flopped badly at the box office, however.)

The lack of suitable film roles led her to return to the stage during the early 50s. Aside from a smallish 'character role' in *Picnic* (1955), she did nothing of note for a few years until given the opportunity to make a triumphant return to Hollywood in the title role of *Auntie Mame* (1958), earning her last Oscar nomination in a big box office hit. But the offers which followed were no better. She got one last opportunity to pull out all the stops – brilliantly – as the most outrageous stage mother ever in *Gypsy* (1962). But the pictures which followed were mainly stinkers and she brought her career to a close with *Mrs Pollifax – Spy* (1971) and a TV movie, *The Crooked Hearts* (1972), co-starring with Douglas Fairbanks Jr. That same year (1972), the Academy presented her with the Jean Hersholt Humanitarian Award for her charity activities. JF

George Sanders

Born **St Petersburg, Russia (British parents),
3 July 1906**
Died **1972**

'I was beastly but I was never coarse. I was a high class sort of cad.' For over 30 years George Sanders padded down a path of silky villainy and purring caddishness, dispensing sneers and disdainful dialogue with the studied weariness of a man who has seen everything and is surprised by nothing. His air of effortless superiority was unique, but the languor was part of an elaborate front which concealed an impressive stamina – between 1940 and 1942 he appeared in 22 films. These survival mechanisms enabled him to steal scenes in good films and survive

in The Saint Strikes Back *(RKO, 1939)*

the stinkers with his reputation intact. In Hitchcock's *Rebecca* (1940), playing the foppish blackmailer Jack Favell, his insinuating drawl seemed to linger in a room long after he had left it. His Charles II in *Forever Amber* (1947) gazed sceptically at Linda Darnell's creamy bosom, happily insulated from the sorry antics around him.

After a chequered early career selling cigarettes in South America, Sanders drifted into radio drama with the BBC and then into films. 20th Century-Fox brought him to Hollywood for *Lloyds Of London* (1936), in which he played Lord Everett Stacy, the first in a long line of velvety villains whose patrician hauteur was a guarantee of evil intentions. He was kept busy playing supporting parts at Fox, and at RKO was those suave amateur sleuths, The Saint and The Falcon. He shrugged off the Saint after four programmers, beginning with *The Saint Strikes Back* (1939), and escaped from the Falcon after four entries, conveniently expiring in *The Falcon's Brother* (1942), which allowed his real-life brother, Tom Conway, to take over the part.

During the war years he alternated gentlemanly British undercover agents with bullet-headed Prussian officers or sinister Gestapo types, stepping out of character to play romantic parts in *Rage In Heaven* (1941) and MGM's *Her Cardboard Lover* (1942). His first star part was as Charles Strickland, the Gauguin figure in Somerset Maugham's *The Moon And Sixpence* (1942). He was perfectly cast as the cynical Lord Henry Wootton in Albert Lewin's stylish *The Picture Of Dorian Gray* (1945), delivering Wilde's epigrams as if they had been written with him in mind, and was equally effective in another Wilde adaptation, Otto Preminger's *The Fan* (1949).

Ann Sheridan

Born **Denton, Texas, 21 February 1915**
Died **1967**

'She outlived some of the worst pictures you've ever known . . . People liked her. They made her a star in spite of the bad pictures. When we made *Male War Bride* she wasn't so young. She'd been through the mill by that time. But if you're going to make a good picture with Cary Grant, you'd better have somebody who's pretty damn good along with him.' Thus director Howard Hawks recalled his work with Ann Sheridan in her best picture, the delightful screwball comedy *I Was A Male War Bride* (1949) which briefly revived her flagging career during the late 40s, for it was a smash hit. A strikingly attractive brunette, she had originally arrived in Hollywood in 1933 as a beauty contest winner. Used as a bit player at Paramount, she appeared in over twenty pictures during 1934–35 until tested by Howard Hawks. He recommended her to Jack Warner and she was given an opportunity to develop into a leading star at Warner Bros. during the following years. Miss Sheridan proved herself in brassy, hard-boiled roles opposite Cagney, Bogart and Co in such pictures as *Torrid Zone* and *They Drive By Night* (both 1940). Her last picture of note was the enjoyable comedy Western *Take Me To Town* (1953). During later years she appeared mainly on TV before her premature death from cancer. JF

After an excursion into Biblical lechery in *Samson And Delilah* (1949), he returned to modern dress as Addison de Witt, the waspish theatre critic whose voice-over provides a barbed commentary to the backstage back-stabbings in Joseph L. Manckiewicz's *All About Eve* (1950). It won him a well-deserved Oscar as Best Supporting Actor, but the success seemed to dismay Sanders into a long, agonisingly protracted decline.

His last big starring role was in *Call Me Madam* (1953) in which he switched on a pleasing baritone to serenade Ethel Merman. Then, clearly bored and operating on auto-pilot, he drifted through a series of chainmail and toga epics, the last of which was *Solomon And Sheba* (1959). By the 60s nobody was writing his kind of parts any more and he resigned himself to sleepwalking through some of the dimmer reaches of cinema. The voyage ended with a stint in drag as a homosexual spy in John Huston's *The Kremlin Letter* (1971) and as Beryl Reid's butler in *Psychomania* (1973), his last film. When it was released, he was already dead from a drugs overdose in a Spanish hotel. His suicide note blamed it all on boredom. Addison de Witt would no doubt have arched a supercilious eyebrow at the news, but in truth it was rather sad. RC

Gale Sondergaard

Born **Lichtfield, Minnesota, 15 February 1899**

A formidable presence on the screen, Gale Sondergaard was initially reluctant to act in films but became one of Hollywood's leading character actresses. University educated, she became successful on the stage during the 20s and was associated with the Theatre Guild where she met director Herbert Biberman. They were married in 1930, and when he was invited to Hollywood, she joined him and soon found herself cast in the role of the deceitful and ruthless Faith Paleologus in *Anthony Adverse* (1936). This, the first of her memorably sinister screen

performances, earned her the first ever Oscar for supporting actress (a newly created awards category). She went on to star in such pictures as *The Life Of Emile Zola* (1937) – a sympathetic role, for a change, as the wife of Dreyfuss, was the scary housekeeper in the delightful remake of *The Cat And The Canary* (1939), and had one extraordinary confrontation scene with Bette Davis in *The Letter* (1940). Oscar-nominated for her performance as Lady Thiang, the prince's mother, in *Anna And The King Of Siam* (1946), she was blacklisted with her husband during the late 40s. She gave a one-woman show off-Broadway in 1965, and reappeared on screen in *Slaves* (1969), directed by her husband, and *The Return Of A Man Called Horse* (1976). JF

in 1952

Ann Sothern

Real name **Harriette Lake**
Born **Valley City, North Dakota,
22 January 1909**

Ann Sothern was a B-picture queen with an A-feature talent. One of the great hard-boiled blondes of the 40s, she began her movie career in 1927 with a bit part in *Broadway Nights*, made in New York. Two years later she joined her mother, a singer, in Hollywood where she had small parts in *Hearts In Exile* (1929) and *Show Of Shows* (1929).

After a short spell at MGM and a stint on Broadway, she signed with Columbia, for whom her first film was a backstage musical, *Let's Fall In Love* (1934). The next four years saw her shuttling back and forth between programmers and A-features. Among the latter were Eddie Cantor's *Kid Millions* (1934) and 20th Century-Fox's *Folies Bergère* (1935), in which she stepped out with Maurice Chevalier. Dropped by Columbia in 1936, she moved to RKO where she was soon marooned in a limp series of features co-starring Gene Raymond, with whom she had first appeared in *Hooray For Love* (1935). She had better luck on loan to MGM in *Dangerous Number* (1937) and at Fox with *Fifty Roads To Town* (1937) and *Danger, Love At Work* (1937). She wriggled out of her RKO contract and stole the show as a tart with a heart in Walter Wanger's *Trade Winds* (1938), and MGM snapped her up for a film originally intended for Harlow, *Maisie* (1939). Sothern played the lady of the title, a brassy, scatter-brained *chanteuse* living on her wits. It established

the formula for the subsequent nine films in the 'Maisie' series, sprightly B-features with Sothern constantly getting into – and out of – scrapes.

Sothern was a wisecracking moll in *Brother Orchid* (1940), co-starred with Eleanor Powell in *Lady Be Good* (1941) and took on the Ethel Merman role in *Panama Hattie* (1942). She was superb in a dramatic role in *Cry Havoc* (1943), and said goodbye to Maisie in *Undercover Maisie* (1947). She was skilfully used by Joseph Mankiewicz in his artful slice of Americana, *A Letter To Three Wives* (1948), but in the 50s the parts dried up and she quit Hollywood for TV after playing Anne Baxter's room mate in Fritz Lang's *The Blue Gardenia* (1953). She returned in 1964, as a sententious, political committee woman in *The Best Man*. Somewhat more plump than in her heyday, she was beastly to Olivia de Havilland in *Lady In A Cage* (1964) and striking as a blowsy part-time hooker in *Sylvia* (1965). In the same mould, she ran a brothel, in *Chubasco* (1968), but her subsequent work has been limited to made-for-TV films, exploitation features and feeble horror outings such as The *Killing Mind* (1973), *Golden Needles* (1974) and *Crazy Mama* (1975). RC

James Stewart

Born **Indiana, Pennsylvania, 20 May 1908**

One of the cinema's outstanding natural actors, James Stewart generally appears so relaxed and easy-going on the screen that his very real talent is taken for granted. But he is one of the most conscientious and hard working of actors. Tall, thin and gangly in his early pictures with a slow, individual drawl, his is the kind of down to earth and likeable film personality with whom film audiences find it easy to identify. Yet he appeared in more than his share of outstanding pictures and had close working relationships with three directors, in particular, Frank Capra, Anthony Mann and Alfred Hitchcock. Stewart is typically modest about his acting accomplishments during the course of a career which stretches almost fifty years from his first bit parts in 1935, up to his most recent film for cable TV, *Right Of Way* (1983), co-starring with Bette Davis for the first time. And he has even been happily married to the same wife for over thirty years.

Stewart gained his first stage experience while a student at Princeton University, but it was not until he graduated, at the age of 24, that he became seriously interested in the theatre. He joined the University Players, a summer stock company, at Falmouth, Massachusetts led by Joshua Logan, Henry Fonda and Margaret Sullavan. Experience on Broadway and on tour led to a screen test and a contract with MGM a few years later in 1935. He was immediately cast in small parts in such glossy studio products as *Rose Marie* and *Wife Vs Secretary*, was an unlikely heavy in *After The Thin Man*, but got an unusual opportunity to sing to dancer Eleanor Powell, giving an acceptable rendition of a superb Cole Porter ballad, 'Easy to Love', in *Born To Dance* – all in 1936.

At its peak during the late 30s MGM was so well supplied with top stars that it failed to appreciate Stewart's talent. He first made his mark during 1938–39 mainly on loan-out to other studios. He starred with Ginger Rogers in an enjoyable light comedy, *Vivacious Lady* (1938) at RKO, and landed the role of the quiet-spoken but effective sheriff who impresses Marlene Dietrich in *Destry Rides Again* (1939) for Universal. But the high point was his collaboration with director Frank Capra on two social comedy hits at Columbia, paired with the delightful Jean Arthur. His part in *You Can't Take It With You* (1938) was not a large one, but he was excellent as the son from a conventional family – in a 'Romeo and Juliet'-type situation – who falls for the girl brought up in a family of eccentrics. The title part in *Mr Smith Goes To Washington* (1939) was something else again, undoubtedly his best of the 30s, playing one of Capra's familiar folk-hero types, the embodiment of small town honesty and integrity who takes on the US Senate. Stewart's assured performance immediately put him in the front rank of Hollywood stars, earning him his first Oscar nomination and the New York Critics' award.

At MGM Stewart appeared in a hilarious screw-ball comedy with Claudette Colbert, *It's A Wonderful World* (1939), not to be confused with the Capra film with a similar title, and a pair with his old friend Margaret Sullavan: *The Shop Around The Corner* was a delightful and delicate comedy directed by the master of the genre, Ernst Lubitsch, while *The Mortal Storm* (also 1940) was one of the more serious and intelligent efforts to dramatise the rise of the Nazi menace developing in pre-war Germany as seen by one family. Then in *The Philadelphia Story* (1940) Stewart's easy-going style nicely balanced the high-key acting of Katharine Hepburn and the cool performance of Cary Grant. In this entertaining triangle comedy, Cary got the girl; Jimmy got his only Oscar.

After a five year break serving with distinction in the US Air Force, Jimmy returned to Hollywood and Frank Capra to play the small town hero in *It's A Wonderful Life* (1946). Although his performance won another Oscar nomination, Capra's type of

folksy social comedy had become dated. Stewart proved during the following years, however, that he was capable of moving with the times and was able to strike out in new directions. His screen image had matured considerably, and his crusading crime reporter in *Call Northside 777* (1948) fitted in well with a new style of more naturalistic, location filming. Although he was miscast in *Rope* (1948) as the teacher whose ideas have had a corrupting influence on two of his students, it was his first opportunity to work with Hitchcock. Stewart continued to appear in a wide variety of pictures – sports (*The Stratton Story*, 1949), action (*Malaya*, 1949), drama (*No Highway In The Sky*, 1951, and DeMille's Oscar-winning *The Greatest Show On Earth*, 1952) and comedy – he won his fourth Oscar nomination for *Harvey* (1950) in a role which he had first created in a rare stage appearance.

That same year (1950) he launched himself on a new career as a western star in a pair of outstanding examples of the genre. In *Broken Arrow* his sincere and moving performance as a military scout who falls in love with an Indian girl gave added depth to one of the first and best of a new group of serious

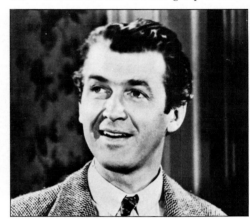

in Harvey (Universal, 1950)

westerns which treated the Indians with respect. And Stewart exercised his power as an independent, free-lance star in choosing Anthony Mann to direct *Winchester 73*, thus beginning an extremely successful actor-director partnership which included eight pictures over a period of six years. But this was not simply the case of a comedy and dramatic star turning his hand to westerns. Although already in his forties, Stewart was in fine physical shape and equal to any demands which a tough director like Mann was likely to make. In the best of their westerns, like *Bend Of The River* (1952) and *The Far Country* (1955), this new rugged physicality is blended with the kind of sensitive and intelligent performances which one has come to expect from Stewart. The best of their non-westerns was a highly successful musical bio-pic, *The Glenn Miller Story* (1954), and that same year Jimmy appeared in the first of his three outstanding pictures with Alfred Hitchcock. In the classic suspense thriller *Rear Window* he gave a virtuoso performance – from the confines of a wheelchair – an incapacitated photographer who suspects that a murder has been committed across the courtyard from his apartment. Stewart's performances in Hitchcock's remake of *The Man Who Knew Too Much* and in the highly original thriller *Vertigo* (1958) qualified him as the director's favourite American star, matched only by the equally attractive Cary Grant.

Stewart rounded out the remarkable 50s decade with the kind of performance as a likeable, folksy, but still sharp, small-town lawyer, which he could do so well, in *Anatomy Of A Murder* (1959), earning one last Oscar nomination. By the time of his appearance in three John Ford westerns during the 60s, both men were beginning to show their age. Stewart wound down his career during the late 60s in a number of westerns, and played a small role in John Wayne's moving last picture, *The Shootist* (1976). JF

with Richard Attenborough (right) in The Flight Of The Phoenix (20th Century-Fox, 1965) ▷

Akim Tamiroff

Born **Baku, Russia, 29 October 1899**
Died **1972**

Short, dark and a bit sleazy looking, Akim Tamiroff turned his slightly sinister appearance and heavy accent to good advantage, developing into a leading Hollywood character actor during the mid-30s, a position he maintained for almost twenty years. He was educated at Moscow University, then attended the Moscow Art Theatre School of Acting. An extensive tour with the Art Theatre in 1923 brought him to New York where he decided to remain. Tamiroff joined Nikita Balieff's Chauve-Souris repertory company and remained active on the stage, appearing in a number of Theatre Guild productions, too, before he left for Hollywood. He landed small parts as Pedro in *Queen Christina* (1933) and the Emir of Gopal in *Lives Of A Bengal Lancer* (1935), but soon worked his way up to larger parts in such pictures as *Anthony Adverse*, and *The General Died At Dawn* (both 1936), earning an Oscar nomination for his performance in a supporting role as the wily Chinese General Tang of the title. As this assortment of roles suggests, he was equally at home playing a wide variety of nationalities, in the best Hollywood tradition, and moved easily between contemporary and costume roles. Signed to a

contract by Paramount, he worked with most of the studio's leading directors, including making two pictures each with Henry Hathaway, Frank Borzage and Preston Sturges, and three pictures with Robert Florey, and Cecil B. DeMille – beginning with *The Buccaneer* (1938) in which he gave what DeMille described as 'one of the screen's most finished and endearing performances as Dominique You, the boastful, soft-hearted 'cannoneer of Napoleon' and Lafitte's first lieutenant.'

Near the end of his Paramount stint, Tamiroff won a second Oscar nomination for his playing of Pablo, the devious partisan leader in *For Whom The Bell Tolls* (1943). He cut back on his film roles during the late 40s, but one of his last in Hollywood saw him cast opposite Orson Welles in *Black Magic* (1949), before he returned to Europe. Welles the film director was to make good use of him during later years, casting him in rather sleazy roles in such pictures as *Confidential Report* (aka *Mr Arkadin*) (1954), *Touch of Evil* (1958), in which he played the crooked boss Joe Grandi, *The Trial* (1962) as the victimised Block, and most intriguing of all, but unfortunately never completed, a production of *Don Quixote* (filmed in 1955) in the role of Sancho Panza. He continued acting in films throughout the 60s – he was in *The Great Bank Robbery* (1969) – and had one last memorable role as the tired, elderly private eye in Jean Luc Godard's *Alphaville* (1965). JF

in 100 Rifles *(20th Century-Fox, 1969)*

in Night And The City *(20th Century-Fox, 1950)*

Gene Tierney

Born **Brooklyn, New York,
20 November 1920**

A stunningly good-looking girl from a well-to-do New York family, Gene Tierney began acting on the stage as soon as she left school and had her first big break early in 1940 playing a small role in 'The Male Animal' on Broadway. Signed to a generous contract by 20th Century-Fox, she was immediately cast as an enterprising young woman reporter in Fritz Lang's superb Technicolor Western *The Return Of Frank James* (1940) starring Henry Fonda. Her exotic, feline, appearance – high cheek bones, reddish-brown hair and striking green eyes – photographed well in colour, and she became one of the studio's leading Technicolor stars. During the following years she had the title role in the romanticised Technicolor Western *Belle Starr* (1941), and appeared with Don Ameche in Ernst Lubitsch's first Technicolor comedy, *Heaven Can Wait* (1943). The culmination of her early Technicolor career came in 1945 when she won her only Oscar nomination for her playing of the mentally disturbed heroine, a paranoid wife driven to murder and suicide by her obsessive jealousy, in the sumptuously photo-

graphed *Leave Her To Heaven*. The picture was also her biggest hit at the box-office.

With regard to the darker, black-and-white side of her career, she was miscast as the wild Georgia country girl in *Tobacco Road* (1941), but director Josef von Sternberg made much better use of her slightly Oriental-looking beauty, casting her as the dissolute heroine, Poppy, in *The Shanghai Gesture* (1941). And she further established her credentials as the classic 40s *film noir* heroine in the title role of *Laura* (1944), as the mysterious career girl whose life-size painting gazes down on, and fascinates, the young detective (Dana Andrews) investigating her murder. Then she suddenly walks through the door halfway through the picture. The picture made the name of producer-director Otto Preminger who cast her in two further thrillers of note – as the beautiful, disturbed wife who comes under the influence of the evil Dr Korvo (José Ferrer) in *Whirlpool* (1949), and as the young widow who finds herself romantically involved with cop Dana Andrews again in *Where The Sidewalk Ends* (1950).

Married during the 40s to top fashion designer Oleg Cassini, who provided the costumes for a number of her films, she was divorced in 1952 at a time when her career was clearly going into decline. She appeared opposite Gable in *Never Let Me Go* (1953) and was still in demand for some big CinemaScope pictures like *The Egyptian* (1954). But she retired from the screen after suffering a nervous breakdown. During later years she appeared occasionally on TV and played a few small film roles, most notably reunited with Otto Preminger for *Advise And Consent* (1962). JF

with Anton Dolin in Never Let Me Go *(MGM, 1953)*

Ann Todd

Born **Hartford, England, 24 January 1909**

An attractive, sophisticated blonde who specialised in playing cool, upper-class British wives, particularly during the post-war years, Ann Todd divided her time between the cinema and her first love, the theatre, throughout much of her career. But during the late 50s, after the break-up of her marriage to director David Lean, she turned her hand to writing, producing, and directing a number of documentaries which continued to appear during the 60s, like *Thunder Of The Gods* (1967) about a visit to the classical site of Delphi in Greece.

Miss Todd studied at the Central School of Speech and Drama in London and, while still in her teens, made her professional debut, at short notice, at the Arts Theatre Club. She soon made her name on the London stage and began appearing in pictures from 1931. Signed by producer Alexander Korda, she missed out on the lead in *Wedding*

in 1952

Rehearsal in 1932 due to an unfortunate auto accident, but played in later Korda productions like *Things To Come* (1936), *Action For Slander* (1937) and *South Riding* (1938). But the big turning point in her film career came with *The Seventh Veil* (1945), in which she gave a memorable performance as the young concert pianist trying to break free of the dominating influence of her brooding, violent, guardian played by James Mason. She was invited to the US to play Gregory Peck's attractive and charming wife in *The Paradine Case* (1948) for Alfred Hitchcock. And in 1949 she married leading British film director, David Lean, and they made three pictures together. He cast her as an unstable, disturbed but elegant heroine in both *The Passionate Friends* (1949) and *Madeleine* (1950), but she returned to a more familiar role as the long suffering upper class wife in *The Sound Barrier* (1952), married to a test pilot. She had one last role of interest as Leo McKern's frigidly refined wife in the heavy-handed *Time Without Pity* (1957) before she turned to making her own films. JF

Claire Trevor

Real name **Claire Wemlinger**
Born **New York City, 8 March 1909**

A sophisticated and intelligent-looking blonde, Claire Trevor always appeared old beyond her years. She started off in pictures in her early twenties portraying career women, especially newspaper reporters, which was Hollywood's idea of the kind of role suitable for a street-wise New York girl. She later 'graduated' to playing a succession of gangster's molls and saloon girls of indeterminate age for over twenty years, providing a real lift to any picture she appeared in – and some of them badly needed it.

Although at first glance Miss Trevor's career appears to lack any shape, a clear underlying pattern can be discerned. After studying at Columbia University and the American Academy of Dramatic Art in New York, she appeared on stage for a few years before being signed by Warner Bros. for some Vitaphone shorts. But she only moved to Hollywood when Fox signed her to a long term (five year) contract in 1933. She soon began starring in programmers, appearing opposite James Dunn in *Jimmy And Sally* and co-starring with Spencer Tracy in *The Mad Game* (both 1933), playing the first of more than half-a-dozen newsgal roles. Although most of these early Fox pictures are of little interest, she did manage to develop a good working relationship with the sympathetic and highly competent director, Allan Dwan. They made six films together during 1935–37 before she left Fox in the hope of landing better roles. She won her first Oscar nomination in a supporting role as Humphrey Bogart's tough ex-girlfriend in the Sam Goldwyn production of *Dead End* (1937). Then, in 1938, she began the western, saloon girl phase of her career with the Technicolored *Valley Of The Giants*, immediately followed by *Stagecoach* in perhaps the best known role of her career. As the likeable but ill-treated Dallas who has been forced out of town by the blue-nosed ladies, she invested her part with a very real and deep feeling in a picture which, in spite of its reputation, deals very much in character stereotypes. She and John Wayne lit up the screen together; her worldly-wise lady makes him appear very young indeed, although he was, in fact, two years her senior. She was reteamed with him playing a tomboyish heroine in *Allegheny Uprising* (1939), and in *Dark Command* (1940) as a snobbish banker's daughter who looks down her nose at Wayne's illiterate cowboy; but he refuses to be put off and ends up saving her, and the town, from Cantrill (Walter Pidgeon) and his raiders.

She had a small role in *Honky Tonk* (1942) with Gable and Lana Turner, and starred in Columbia's first in Technicolor, *The Desperadoes* (1943), as gunfighter Glenn Ford's resourceful ex-girlfriend. But with the emergence of 40s *film noir*, Miss Trevor

suddenly found herself in demand for a very different type of picture and emerged as one of the leading 'noir' stars in a series of pictures made at RKO during 1944–47, beginning with *Murder My Sweet* (1944). The natural culmination of the group of roles was her assured performance as gangster Edward G. Robinson's badly treated, alcoholic mistress in *Key Largo* which earned her a supporting actress Oscar in 1948. (She and Robinson had performed together on radio during the 30s and

were reunited as a husband and wife well past their prime in *Two Weeks In Another Town*, 1962).

Claire continued active in pictures throughout the early and mid-50s and won a last Oscar nomination for her performance as one of the passengers in a disaster-prone airliner, piloted by Wayne, in *The High And The Mighty* (1954). During later years she was seen occasionally on TV, and had one last good film role during the 60s as Richard Beymer's mother in *The Stripper* (1963). JF

with Edward G. Robinson in Two Weeks In Another Town *(MGM, 1962)*

Lana Turner

Born **Wallace, Idaho, 8 February 1921**

Lana Turner was only sixteen years old when she was discovered sitting on a stool at the soda fountain of a Hollywood drugstore, or so one of the most famous of Hollywood stories would have it. A shapely, attractive blonde with no previous acting experience of any sort, her subsequent development serves as a prime example of the Hollywood star-making machinery working overtime. Initially put into bit parts at Warner Bros., she ended up being groomed for stardom at the biggest studio of all, MGM, which was just reaching its peak during the late 30s. First introduced as a juvenile, she was soon upgraded to more mature and sexy roles and found herself promoted as a pin-up and 'the sweater girl' during the war. Although her limitations as an actress were always apparent, she developed a strong screen presence which came across effectively in certain types of roles. Much married and divorced, and the subject of rumours of affairs with a large number of Hollywood leading men, her private life

in Portrait In Black *(Universal, 1960)*

was often in the news, yet it didn't appear to affect her career. Even the biggest scandal of all, when her teenage daughter attacked and murdered her gangster lover, Johnny Stompanato, with a knife in 1958, appeared to benefit her career more than it hurt it. These dramatic events were not far removed from the kind of melodramatic and highly successful pictures she was making at the time – a case, perhaps, of life imitating art. A born survivor, she was still making a few movies in the 70s in a career which, by that time, had spanned a period of forty years, against all the odds and when equally attractive and, it must be said, far more talented girls had fallen by the wayside.

First taken up by producer-director Mervyn LeRoy who cast her in a bit part in *They Won't Forget* (1937), he took her with him when he moved to MGM. There Miss Turner was immediately given a small role in *Love Finds Andy Hardy* (1938), along with Judy Garland and with Mickey Rooney in the title role. Similar parts followed in a number of pictures, including *Dancing Co-Ed* (1939) in which she appeared with bandleader Artie Shaw. He became her first husband the following year, but the marriage only lasted a matter of months. *Ziegfeld Girl* (1941) was designed as a suitable vehicle to promote her, along with a number of the studio's other up-and-coming young stars like Judy Garland and Hedy Lamarr, also playing chorus girls, with James Stewart in tow, and re-using some of the most spectacular footage from *The Great Ziegfeld* (1936). By now it was clear that Lana had achieved star status. She was then teamed with the studio's top male stars. Miscast as the upper-class British girl

engaged to Spencer Tracy in *Dr Jekyll And Mr Hyde* (1941), she fared better in a pair of films with Gable, then made her first venture into *film noir* as the young girl attracted to gangster Robert Taylor in *Johnny Eager* (1942), for which she was reunited with director Mervyn LeRoy. Her performance as the scheming Cora opposite John Garfield in *The Postman Always Rings Twice* (1946) was one of her best, although she came across as a somewhat tougher and cooler sexy type than the heroine of the novel. This picture was one of five straight hits for Lana – the others included *Green Dolphin Street* (1947), *Cass Timberlane* (1947) and *The Three Musketeers* (1948).

MGM attempted to maintain its glamorous image of the 50s with Elizabeth Taylor, Ava Gardner, Cyd Charisse and, of course, Lana, still under contract. She was cast in a lavish but hollow Technicolor remake of *The Merry Widow* in 1952, but was given a better opportunity to prove her acting abilities in *The Bad And The Beautiful* that same year. Director Vincente Minnelli had originally wanted to cast her in his *Madame Bovary* (1949), but was told by a representative of the Breen production code office that her reputation as a sex symbol would make it more difficult for the film to get a code seal. According to producer John Houseman, 'Vincente and I had run several of her old films: we were struck by the fact that she was capable of brilliant individual scenes (as in *Ziegfeld Girl*) but seemed to lack the temperament or the training to sustain a full-length performance. This made our episodic film just right for her.' The quality of her acting in *The Bad And The Beautiful* reflects the abilities of Minnelli who 'called on many ruses and subterfuges to extract a performance from her.' The director recalled, 'as she got more into the picture her nervousness disappeared, and she effectively made the character's transition from tramp to glamour queen.'

Lana's long stay at MGM came to an end after 17 years in 1955 with a pair of weak costumers – she played a sexy high priestess in *The Prodigal* and the title role in *Diane* (de Poitiers), a medieval romance. Her career got a big boost when she was offered a leading role as a mother at odds with her teenage daughter in the film version of the bestselling *Peyton Place* (1958). Miss Turner received her only Oscar nomination for her performance, and the picture's

with Clark Gable in Honky Tonk *(MGM, 1942)*

success was assured by the scandal concerning her own daughter which broke that same year and put her in the headlines. She immediately had another big hit, her last, playing an ambitious actress mother who neglects her daughter in *Imitation Of Life* (1959). The picture was one of Lana's best, sensitively directed by Douglas Sirk. Producer Ross Hunter cast her in two further glossy productions – *Portrait In Black* (1960) and *Madame X* (1966) – but they did not turn out nearly so well. In 1969 she married for the seventh time, but again it didn't last; her fourth during the 50s had been actor Lex Barker, one of Hollywood's Tarzans. She made a few last appearances during the 70s on the stage, on TV and in a couple of 'cheapie' film productions. JF

with John Garfield in The Postman Always Rings Twice *(MGM, 1946)*

Lupe Velez

Real name **Maria Velez de Villalobos**
Born **San Luis Potosi, Mexico, 18 July 1908**
Died **1944**

Lupe Velez was the quintessential Mexican leading lady. On the screen, her hyperactive rhumba cavortings, fractured English, flared nostrils and outrageous mugging made Carmen Miranda look like Little Orphan Annie. Off the screen, her life was devoted to stimulating, if imprudent, diversion: a steamy romance with Gary Cooper, her co-star in *Wolf Song* (1929); and a marriage to Johnny Weissmuller which quickly turned into a non-stop public brawl.

She got her start in Hal Roach comedy shorts before being chosen by Douglas Fairbanks to play 'The Mountain Girl' in *The Gaucho* (1928). The role established a screen character which she played, with minor variations, for the rest of her time in Hollywood – an ebullient termagant whose explosive energy left its mark on a succession of bruised and battered leading men. Peasant girls and South Seas half-castes were her stock-in-trade, and when sound arrived, audiences were delighted with her machine gun bursts of heavily accented English. Abandoning any pretensions to serious acting, she became a novelty personality, shrieking her way through films like *The Half-Naked Truth* (1932), in which she played 'Princess Exotica', a publicity-grabbing actress who keeps a pet lion in her apartment.

Her marriage to Weissmuller ended in 1939, when her career was on the skids. It was rescued by RKO's *The Girl From Mexico* (1939), a low-budget

in The Girl From Mexico *(RKO, 1939)*

comedy built around her personality. As red hot tamale, Carmelita, a Mexican married to a harassed advertising executive, she jabbered her way through eight more 'Mexican Spitfire' films, all co-starring Leon Errol. Riotous Bs with just about every expense spared, they established Lupe as one of RKO's gallery of B-picture queens.

The final entry was *Mexican Spitfire's Blessed Event* (1943), in which Carmelita acquired an ocelot and became pregnant. When Velez herself became pregnant there was no happy fade-out. Terrified by the scandal which would follow the birth of an illegitimate child, she committed suicide with an overdose of sleeping pills. RC

Anton Walbrook

Born **Vienna, Austria, 19 November 1900**
Died **1967**

Anton Walbrook was fortunate in his film career, for although he did not make many pictures, he had the opportunity to work with a few major directors at their peak, most notably Michael Powell and Max Ophuls. A tall, dark and sophisticated actor, he projected a special sense of authority, even arrogance, on film which he had acquired from his early stage experience, and which was particularly effective in costume roles. Born into a family with a long tradition as circus performers, he preferred the theatre and first made his name as an actor in Vienna and Germany during the 20s. Although he appeared in one or two silents, he only began acting regularly in films during the 30s with leading roles in *Viktor Und Viktoria* (1933) (recently remade by Blake Edwards and Julie Andrews), *Masquerade* (1934) and *Michael Strogoff*, in both the German and American versions (1936 and 1937). Back in Britain he played Prince Albert, a distinctly reluctant suitor

for the hand of Queen Victoria, extremely awkward, shy and ill at ease at his first meeting with the young queen – a nicely underplayed and far more convincing performance than that of Anna Neagle in the title role, in *Victoria The Great* (1937). He established himself as a British film star with a charismatic performance as the cold-blooded, criminal Edwardian husband deliberately driving his wife mad in *Gaslight* (1940), opposite Diana Wynyard, and directed by Thorold Dickinson, and in the highly successful *Dangerous Moonlight* (1941). A rewarding collaboration with director Michael Powell began with a small role in *The 49th Parallel* (1941), and he co-starred as Roger Livesey's German rival and friend in the remarkable *The Life And Death Of Colonel Blimp* (1943). But the high point of his career was as the Diaghilev-like ballet impresario in *The Red Shoes* (1948), which was a great critical and box-office success. His later pictures of note included an atmospheric British production of *The Queen Of Spades* (1949) and, back on the Continent, two with Max Ophuls, *La Ronde* (1950), and the lavish *Lola Montez* (1955) in which he played the King of Bavaria. JF

Robert Walker

Born **Salt Lake City, Utah, 13 October 1918**
Died **1951**

'Listen. It's so simple. Two fellows meet accidentally, like you and me. No connection between them at all, never saw each other before. Each one has somebody that he'd like to get rid of. So, they swap murders.' With these words the shrewd, psychopathic Bruno first outlines his ingenious scheme to an incredulous Farley Granger in Hitchcock's *Strangers On A Train* (1951). Here, Robert Walker gave the most remarkable performance of his brief film career. As a sensitive and handsome young actor, he had struggled to break into the movies along with his young actress wife, Jennifer Jones, in 1939 with little success. All he could land were a few bit parts, and it wasn't until four years later that he was signed to a contract by MGM. He had his first success in a leading role in an appealing service comedy, *See Here Private Hargrove* (1944), following closely on

the heels of his wife's big breakthrough with *The Song Of Bernadette* (1943). Producer David Selznick, who would subsequently marry Jennifer, brought them together in *Since You Went Away* (1944), but their marriage had already broken up. Walker was unhappy and finding it difficult to cope at the same time that he had won recognition as a star. MGM cast him mainly in romantic roles in lightweight and frequently bland comedies and musicals during the following years. The best of the bunch was *The Clock* (1945) in which he gave a nicely judged performance, opposite Judy Garland, as a young soldier who falls in love while on leave. But it took Alfred Hitchcock to recognise the troubled and manic qualities which lay beneath the surface, turning Walker into one of the most memorable of Hitchcock villains. Unfortunately, Walker (who had been drinking heavily since 1949, and suffered several nervous breakdowns) only had the opportunity to make use of his new, darker screen persona in one further picture, *My Son John* (1952) before his early death from a heart attack. JF

John Wayne

Real name Marion Michael Morrison
Born Winterset, Iowa, 26 May 1907
Died 1979

As the embodiment of the archetypal western hero John Wayne was tall, handsome, rugged and independent, soft-spoken and slow to anger, but a tough man in a fight. This idealised and romanticised view of the western hero was first established in the popular B-westerns of the 30s when Wayne was gaining his first film experience. In fact, Wayne's characterisations in his better, later pictures like *The Searchers* (1956) and *Rio Bravo* (1959) had a complexity and sensitivity far removed from the cliché of the typical hero of the far west. His long career as a western star, beginning with *The Big Trail* (1930) and closing with *The Shootist* (1976) meant that he appeared in a wide variety of pictures which closely paralleled the ups and downs of the genre as a whole for almost half a century.

Fresh out of USC where he had gone on a football scholarship, Wayne had only appeared in a few bit parts when his friend, John Ford, recommended him to director Raoul Walsh as a good possibility for the lead role in the epic 70mm western, *The Big Trail* (1930). It was one of a small group of prestigious early talkie westerns which included *In Old Arizona*

in Stagecoach *(United Artists, 1939)*

(1929), King Vidor's *Billy The Kid* (1930) and the Oscar-winning *Cimarron* (1931), but this western revival turned out to be a short-lived phenomenon. Only the B western and western serial continued to flourish during the 30s and Wayne was quickly 'demoted' to the B's. Here he served a long, hard apprenticeship 'the leading man had to be there all the time – we never worked less than eighteen hours a day' – in a much despised genre. Things only began to pick up during the late 30s when he was rescued from B westerns at Republic by John Ford, directing his first western for ten years, who offered him the lead in *Stagecoach* in 1938 as the Ringo Kid. Along with his assured handling of the action sequences, Wayne demonstrated his qualities as a sensitive actor in his love scenes with Claire Trevor, and played throughout with characteristically easygoing charm.

Again the experience of Wayne coincided with a general upgrading of the western. Concurrent with the filming of *Stagecoach*, 20th Century-Fox's *Jesse James* was in production as was *Dodge City* at Warner Bros. and C.B. DeMille's *Union Pacific*. King Vidor's *Northwest Passage* (for MGM) and Universal's *Destry Rides Again* were filmed in 1939, while Wayne was rushed into two followup movies with Claire Trevor – *Allegheny Uprising* (at RKO) and *Dark Command*, reunited for the latter with director Raoul Walsh back at Wayne's own studio,

Republic. Wayne's star was clearly ascending. Ford gave another useful boost by casting him in a non-western character role as Ole Oleson, the young Swedish seaman, in *The Long Voyage Home* (1940). An enjoyable ensemble piece without a star role, Wayne fitted in well and was given good support by an experienced group of troupers including Thomas Mitchell and Barry Fitzgerald. Other non-western roles followed including a lead in the DeMille epic *Reap The Wild Wind* (1942). In fact, America's entry into the war had quickly killed off the western revival. Most of the leading action stars were drafted into military service or found themselves cast in the many war movies which began to pour out of the studios. Thus, Wayne too, starred in

in The Longest Day *(20th Century-Fox, 1962)*

such pictures as *The Fighting Seabees* (1944) and John Ford's *They Were Expendable* (1945) about the PT boats fighting in the Phillipines. Here Wayne gave another fine performance, co-starred with Robert Montgomery, but major recognition of his new standing as a top star didn't come until three to four years later.

Even at this relatively advanced date in his career Wayne did not feel confident in his position as a leading star. He had to be pushed into confronting studio boss Herbert Yates and insisting that he be given the role of the tough but sympathetic Sergeant Stryker in *Sands Of Iwo Jima* (1949), according to director Allan Dwan. 'But it worked. And after that picture he was the kingpin . . .' Wayne's performance earned him his first Oscar nomination, while the picture itself was the biggest box-office hit in the history of Republic Pictures.

In the meantime Wayne had also returned to westerns, playing a major part in the most successful revival and development of the western ever, which began during the post-war years and continued throughout the 50s. Although Wayne had graduated to producer-star status with the unremarkable *The Angel And The Badman* (1947), it was the smash hit *Red River* (1948) which first boosted him toward super-star status. Producer-director Howard Hawks, working with him for the first time, had confidence in Wayne's acting abilities, and cast him in the lead role of the ageing trail boss opposite the young Montgomery Clift in his first film. Not only was the central conflict of the picture built on the contrast between two very different characters, but there were two contrasting styles of acting to match – Wayne's more outgoing style vs the internalised approach of Clift. Wayne clearly held his own on the screen under Hawks's sympathetic guidance, and 'he became a goddamn good actor,' in the words of Hawks. 'Well Jack Ford said, 'I never knew that big son of a bitch could act', . . . then Ford put him in two or three good pictures . . . He's so much better an actor than people give him credit for.'

In fact, there were four Ford westerns – *Three Godfathers* (1948) and the so-called cavalry trilogy. As Captain Kirby Yorke in *Fort Apache* (1948) he proved that he could hold his own opposite Henry Fonda's martinet of a colonel, while in the Technicolored *She Wore A Yellow Ribbon* (1949) he gave another excellent performance as an ageing cavalry officer. Both were big hits and, along with *Red River* and *Iwo Jima*, boosted him into the ranks of the top box-office stars. The third cavalry western was *Rio Grande* (1950) in which Wayne played a somewhat older Kirby Yorke and was teamed with Maureen O'Hara for the first time. The second followed two years later – the delightful comedy romance, *The Quiet Man* (1952), again directed by Ford, set in colourful Ireland with Wayne in fine form wooing and winning the wilful Miss O'Hara.

Active during the early 50s in a right wing organisation with the extraordinary title, the Motion Picture Alliance for the Preservation of American Ideals, Wayne produced and starred in one blatantly Red-scare picture, *Big Jim McLain* (1952). Its failure caused him to return to the more familiar action roles. He produced and starred in two more big hits – a 3-D western, *Hondo* (1953) and an early forerunner of the disaster movie, *The High And The Mighty* (1954) in which he played the pilot of an airliner in trouble.

in The Shootist *(Paramount, 1976)*

The maturing of the western during the 50s was reflected in Wayne's two best: *The Searchers* (1956), playing a western loner for Ford, and *Rio Bravo* (1959), as a resourceful sheriff with an odd collection of deputies, a picture which succeeded admirably in mixing a deadly serious situation with some offbeat comedy. A later follow-up with Hawks – *El Dorado* (1967) – was even funnier. Clearly Wayne was no slouch at playing comedy either. He ventured into directing himself with the long and tedious *The Alamo* (1960): 'to remind people not only in America but everywhere that there were once men and women who had the guts to stand up for the things they believed.' And similar politically dubious sentiments lay behind his production of *The Green Berets* (1968), supporting the US involvement in Vietnam. *The Alamo* was typical of the overblown type of western of 1958–62, also represented by *The Big Country* (1958) and *How The West Was Won* (1962) in which Wayne played a cameo role. A decline was perhaps inevitable after the peak 50s years, in spite of the efforts of Wayne. He continued remarkably active in spite of his advanced age, and finally won an Oscar for his lively, larger than life performance as Rooster Cogburn in *True Grit* (1969). He finally began to wind down during the 70s and gave one last moving performance in *The Shootist* (1976) as the ageing gunman dying of cancer as, indeed was the monolithic star himself. JF

with Kim Darby and Glen Campbell in True Grit *(Paramount, 1969)* ▷

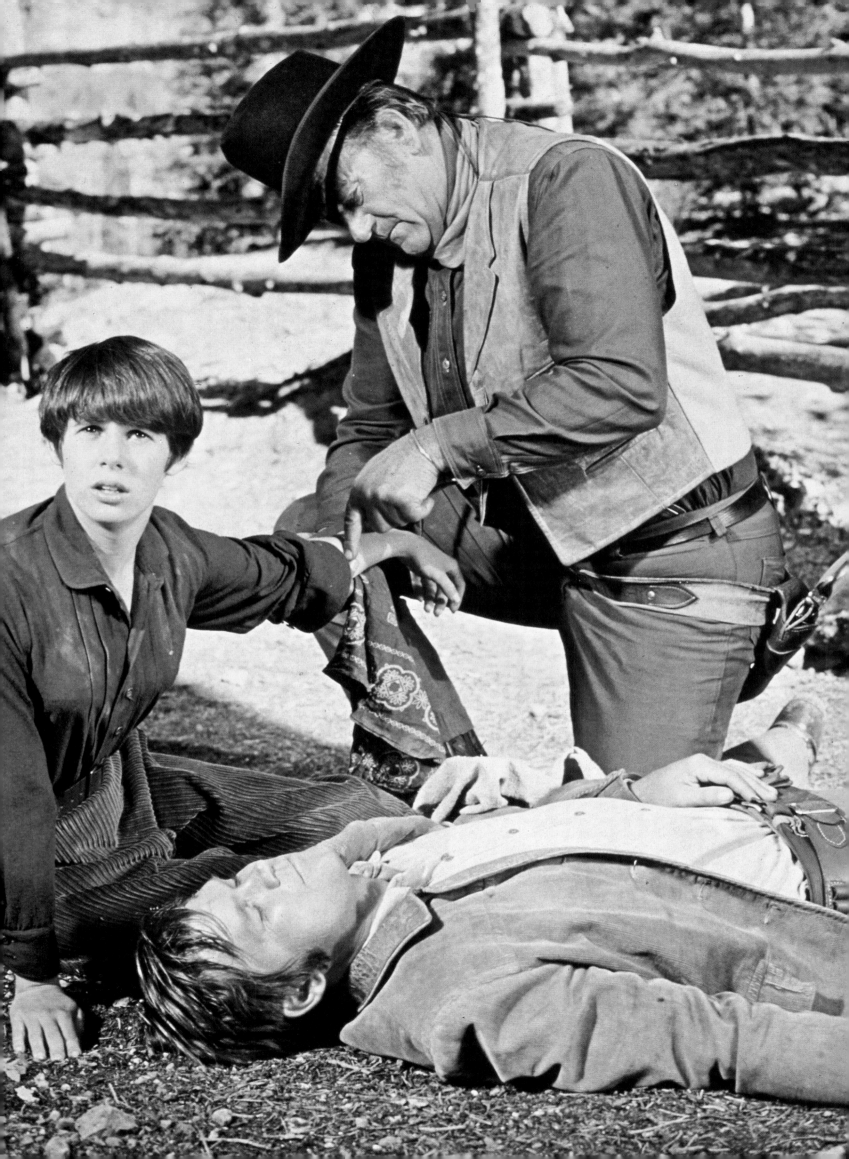

Orson Welles

Born **Kenosha, Wisconsin, 6 May 1915**

One of the giants of the American cinema, as both actor and director, Orson Welles burst upon the film world in 1941 as the star and director (and co-scriptwriter) of the remarkable *Citizen Kane* which set the pattern for his subsequent career. Recognising his own attraction to outsize and extraordinary characters, Welles the director often provided Welles the star with his best film roles. As he explained in a 1958 interview, 'I've played lots of bad characters, you know, some from choice, some not. But they aren't 'little' people, because I'm a natural for 'big characters'. I have to be larger than life. It's a fault in my nature.'

Hailed as a multi-talented boy wonder at an early age, Welles was sixteen when he first went on the stage in Dublin. A charming, handsome, talented and charismatic figure, he first made his name on Broadway and on the radio both as actor and director during the mid-30s. In 1937 he joined with John Houseman to form the Mercury Theatre, and soon extended their activities into radio where they are still remembered for a famous 1938 version of 'The War of the Worlds' which caused some Americans to head for the hills, convinced that the Martians had landed. As Houseman recalled, 'Orson projected a personality on the air that soon made him one of the radio stars of his day and of which he took full advantage before an audience of several millions each week.'

Inevitably Welles was invited to Hollywood, and was given an extremely favourable contract by RKO in 1939. After working on a number of possible projects, he seized on the idea of *Kane* suggested by writer Herman Mankiewicz, and it was set up as the first Mercury Production, drawing on many of the same talents who had worked with Welles in the theatre and on radio. *Kane* emerged as a cinematic tour de force and clearly placed Welles prominently in the vanguard of that new group of writer-directors who were just emerging during the early 40s, including Preston Sturges, John Huston, and Billy Wilder. Welles had transformed Mankiewicz's original script, aided by a talented group of collaborators, while drawing on his own remarkable visual sense and experience with sound on the radio. But the centrepiece of the film was his own fine performance as Kane, playing him at various stages in his life ranging from active young man to reclusive old age. The powerful William Randolph Hearst ordered a

in A Man For All Seasons (*Columbia, 1966*)

virtual embargo on publicity (recognising himself as the story's inspiration) in his newspapers, but, for his efforts, Welles received Oscar nominations (his only ones) as actor and director, and won his only Oscar for his contribution to the script. (*Kane* was also nominated as Best Picture but lost out to *How Green Was My Valley* (1941).)

A change of management at RKO meant that Welles's second production was taken away from him before he had completed it. Yet *The Magnificent Ambersons* was an equally original and accomplished work which he had scripted and directed but did not act in. He immediately demonstrated his talent as a strong character actor with an impressive performance as Rochester in *Jane Eyre* (1944). A third Mercury production, *Journey Into Fear*, (1943) was an atmospheric thriller which he produced, co-scripted and directed in part. He transformed his appearance with a hooked nose and bushy eyebrows playing a supporting role as the sinister Turkish colonel of police. Although one of his lesser 40s efforts, the picture reflected his fascination with playing powerful and evil men and was his first of many ventures into *film noir*. Thus, in *The Stranger* (1946) he played the ex-Nazi villain, Franz Kindler,

and continued his attraction to 'noir' themes and characters on into the 50s. He played the mysterious and powerful *Mr Arkadin* (1955), heavily made up for much of the film, and was virtually unrecognisable as the gargantuan and sleazy police chief Quinlan in *Touch Of Evil* (1958), his best 50s film and sole post-40s opportunity to direct in the US. Welles has explained that he likes to hide himself in a role through the use of make-up, especially when he is directing himself: 'I have to see the rushes, therefore the more I am made up the less I recognise myself, and the more capable I am of making an objective judgement.'

Of special interest are the two parts in which he appeared virtually without make-up. In the excellent thriller, *The Lady From Shanghai* which he made with Rita Hayworth in 1947 after their three-year marriage had ended, he came closest to playing an attractive leading man as the Irish adventurer Michael O'Hara. In *The Third Man* (1949), however, he played one of his best ever villains, the notorious Harry Lime. Although the film was directed by Carol Reed, Welles was given a lot of scope to create his own characterisation and write his own dialogue. According to Welles, 'it was more than just a part for me. Harry Lime is without a doubt a part of my creative work.'

The literary side of Welles as star and director included three cheaply produced Shakespeare adaptations – *Macbeth* (1948), *Othello* (1951) and best of all, *Chimes At Midnight* (1966) in which he played Sir John Falstaff with great gusto. Welles appeared in a supporting role in his heavily stylised version of Kafka's *The Trial* (1962) as the advocate Hastler, and dubbed many of the other male voices in the film himself. In *The Immortal Story* (1966) adapted from Karen Blixen, he returned to playing a very Kane-like character, the rich elderly merchant Clay, while in the entertaining and witty feature-length documentary, *F For Fake* (1975) Welles made a revealing appearance as himself, speculating on the nature of art and fakery.

Over the years Welles has given many memorable performances in pictures for other directors. In addition to Rochester and Harry Lime, he played Cesare Borgia in *Prince Of Foxes* (1949) and gave an impressive cameo performance as the stentorian Father Mapple in *Moby Dick* (1956). He played a sincere and compelling lawyer, modelled on Clarence Darrow, in *Compulsion* (1959) and effectively stole the picture, was a convincing Cardinal Wolsey in the Oscar-winning *A Man For All Seasons* (1966) and an American general in *Catch-22* in 1970, the same year that he was awarded a special Oscar. He continued acting in films during the 70s and in occasional TV commercials. JF

with Rita Hayworth in The Lady From Shanghai (*Columbia, 1948*)

Cornel Wilde

Born **New York City, 13 October 1915**

A handsome and athletic young actor who was an expert fencer, Cornel Wilde had gained some acting experience on the stage, including the role of Tybalt in Olivier's 1940 production of 'Romeo and Juliet', before arriving in Hollywood. He spent four years trying to establish himself as a star, but was cast mainly in programmers before he got his big chance in 1944. The small studio, Columbia, was attempting to upgrade its image with some major productions, including a planned biopic of Chopin entitled *A Song To Remember*, and Wilde landed the lead role. Filmed in Technicolor at a cost of $1.5 million, the picture ended up being a big hit, started a new trend of composer biopics, and made the name of Wilde who received his only Oscar nomination for his performance.

Wilde had proved his talent for playing costume parts, and, as a new 'Technicolor star', he was much

in demand for a few years. He appeared as Aladdin in *A Thousand And One Nights* (1945) and as the son of Robin Hood, putting his fencing and athletic skills to good use, in *Bandit Of Sherwood Forest* (1946); 20th Century-Fox cast him in a couple of lavish costume productions with Linda Darnell, directed by Otto Preminger – the musical *Centennial Summer* (1946) and a film adaptation of the best-seller, *Forever Amber* (1947) – all filmed in colour. But the

in The Naked Prey *(Paramount, 1966)*

best of the group was a contemporary drama, *Leave Her To Heaven* (1945), in which he played a weak writer who falls in love with, and marries, the beautiful but disturbed Gene Tierney.

During the following years he appeared in a variety of poor movies. However, he did have a good part in DeMille's big circus film, *The Greatest Show On Earth* (1952) as a French trapeze artist, although he was afraid of heights. ('I had a terrible time at first

– agonising nightmares for weeks.'). It all came right in the end – he gave a good performance and cured his fear of heights, but the picture's big success failed to revitalise his career. His most interesting films during this period were small, black-and-white thrillers like *Road House* (1948), *Shockproof* (1949) and *The Big Combo* (1955). With this type of film – *Storm Fear* (1955) – he launched his new career as a producer-director-star, playing opposite his actress wife, Jean Wallace, who starred in most of the films he directed like *Maracaibo* (1958), *Lancelot And Guinevere* (aka *Sword of Lancelot*; 1963), and *No Blade Of Grass* (1970). Wilde's undoubted power and originality as a director-star reveals him as a true 'primitive' of the cinema, at his best in the African adventure *The Naked Prey* (1966), and the uncompromisingly naturalistic war movie with a pacifist message, *Beach Red* (1967). JF

Esther Williams

Born **Los Angeles, 8 August 1923**

'Wet she was a star', 'Only on dry land is she truly out of her depth', 'She is a duck in the water, but a fish out of it.' These rather unfair remarks refer, of course, to Esther Williams, 'Hollywood's Mermaid', who swam her way through over a dozen bright MGM musicals in the 40s and early 50s.

Esther was a champion swimmer at 15 and modelled swim suits at a department store, while studying at the L.A. City College. At 18 she decided to leave her studies to join Billy Rose's Aquacade, where she was spotted by an MGM talent scout. Like starlets Lana Turner, Judy Garland and Kathryn Grayson before her, she was put into a Hardy Family film with Mickey Rooney, *Andy Hardy's Double Life* (1942). After being billed nineteenth in *A Guy Named Joe* (1943), she shot to stardom in her third film, *Bathing Beauty* (1944). *Bathing Beauty* started out as an average Red Skelton vehicle, first called 'Mr Co-Ed' then 'Sing Or Swim', but Esther's superb figure and pretty features were heightened by Technicolor to such an extent that her part was built up and the title changed. She played a swimming instructor at a women's college, and the picture ended with a spectacular water-ballet (staged by John Murray Anderson) set to the 'Blue Danube' with alternate jets of water and flame bursting from a pool. 'Variety' said that Williams was 'pulled to stardom by her swimsuit straps'. The movie was a bigger hit than anyone anticipated, and MGM spent the following decade hiring writers to invent scripts which did little more for Esther than allow her to get

wet. She would later remark, 'All they ever did for me at MGM was to change my leading men and the water in the pool.'

Esther was a bathing suit designer in *Neptune's Daughter* (1949), who naturally demonstrates her creations herself; she played Annette Kellerman, the Australian swimming champion who first introduced the world to the one-piece bathing suit in *Million Dollar Mermaid* (1952), swam the English Channel in *Dangerous When Wet* (1953), co-starring her third husband Fernando Lamas, and doubled as secretary and aqua-star in *Easy To Love* (1953). As *On An Island With You* (1948) and *Pagan Love Song* (1950) were both set on South Sea islands, Esther was given ample opportunity to strip down to her stylish swim suits and take the plunge. Although she commented that 'My pictures are put together out of scraps they find in the producer's wastebasket', they were bubbly entertainments and the aquaballets (some staged by Busby Berkeley) were often breathtaking in their scope.

After the belly-flop *Jupiter's Darling* (1955), the studio for whom, at the box-office, she had grossed over $80 million, let her go without even a goodbye or a thank you. In September 1976, she sued MGM for $1 million, claiming they had no legal right to utilise sequences from her films in *That's Entertainment* (1974) without consulting her about it or offering to share profits. The matter was settled out of court. The former prima ballerina of the water tried her hand at dramatic roles at Universal, including *The Unguarded Moment* (1956) as a schoolteacher sexually attacked by one of her pupils, but left films in 1961 to invest in a business called Esther Williams Swimming Pools. RB

Shelley Winters

Real name Shirley Schrift
Born St Louis, Missouri, 18 August 1922

Shelley Winters grew up in New York and was attracted to the theatre while still a schoolgirl. She did some modelling and amateur acting, then appeared on the 'Borscht Belt' before gradually working her way up to reasonable roles on Broadway, when she was signed to a film contract by

Columbia in 1943. Arriving in Hollywood when it was still operating like a 'dream factory', she got the standard treatment dished out to hundreds of aspiring young and attractive starlets. Her initial studio assessment read: 'The hair's too dark blonde and kinky, but we can straighten and bleach it. Forehead too low; we'll take care of that with electrolysis. Eyes slant the wrong way . . . nose too wide . . . lips too thin . . . teeth crooked . . . Shoulders too broad, bosom too flat, waist not narrow enough, hips too wide, legs knock-kneed, wobbly walk, and speech work needed.' Although there was a lot of attention paid to her appearance during her years at Columbia, she was never given a chance to demonstrate her talent as an actress. Instead she was used to decorate a number of weak escapist vehicles, like her bit role as a harem girl in the Technicolored *A Thousand And One Nights* (1945).

In spite of this treatment, some indication of her determination to succeed as an actress was her postwar choice of career rather than marriage, divorcing her 'war husband' in 1946. Although Shelley looked forward to returning to the theatre after leaving Columbia, she hung on in Hollywood long enough to land the prize role of the young waitress who becomes the mistress of a mentally unbalanced, middle-aged stage star (Ronald Colman) who finally murders her in *A Double Life* (1948). A serious black-and-white picture, effectively directed by George Cukor and making use of New York locations, it was the first of Shelley's many down-to-earth and victimised heroines, and this *film noir* part suggested that there was a very real future for her in pictures. Unfortunately, she was under contract to one of the smaller of the major studios where she was typed as a 'blonde bombshell', Columbia's answer to Lana Turner, perhaps. All her best roles were on loan-out to other studios. She went to Paramount for *The Great Gatsby* (1949) and got her biggest break there, cast as the sad and plain working girl romanced, then rejected and finally murdered by Montgomery Clift in *A Place In The Sun* (1951), directed by George Stevens. This performance earned her an Oscar nomination and proved for the first time that she could really act, given the chance. At MGM she joined an all-star cast in the board-

room drama, *Executive Suite* (1954), followed by two powerful dramatic pictures for United Artists in 1955: *The Night Of The Hunter* was directed by her old friend and acting teacher, Charles Laughton; she played a widow who falls for the charms of Robert Mitchum's murderous preacher and ends up surreally floating at the bottom of the river. And in the film version of Clifford Odets's play about Hollywood, *The Big Knife* (1955), she was a struggling bit player who meets a sad end.

Returning to her first love, the theatre, for a few years, Shelley was only attracted back to Hollywood by the opportunity of working again with her favourite director, George Stevens, on a subject dear to her heart – *The Diary Of Anne Frank* (1959). Her playing of a Dutch housewife and mother trying unsuccessfully to cope with life under the pressures of the Nazi occupation – the first of her more mature, character roles, earned Shelley a supporting actress Oscar. During the following years she appeared mainly in serious, black-and-white pictures, most often cast as earthy, and not always entirely respectable, mothers – in *The Young Savages* (1961), *Lolita* (1962) and, winning her a second supporting Oscar, Elizabeth Hartman's parent in *A Patch Of Blue* (1965).

Ever since becoming a star Miss Winters demonstrated a commendable determination to continue developing as an actress, studying at the Group Theatre in New York and mixing theatre and film work. Her stage roles had ranged from Stella in 'A Streetcar Named Desire' to 'Two for The Seesaw' and 'The Night Of The Iguana' during the 60s, and she even played the mother of the Marx brothers in 'Minnie's Boys'. In films she was not afraid to work with the newer, younger generation of directors like Frankenheimer, Kubrick and Joseph Strick during the 60s, Curtis Harrington and Paul Mazursky in the 70s. Similarly, she was not above working for the smaller 'exploitation' companies like American International if the role and the script were right. Thus, she was extremely effective as the mother of the first

in S.O.B. (Paramount, 1981)

juvenile American President (Christopher Jones) in *Wild In The Streets* (1968), and threw herself wholeheartedly into her lively depiction of the notorious Ma Baker in *Bloody Mama* (1970) for Roger Corman. She continued active in pictures and TV movies throughout the 70s and on into the 80s, winning her last Oscar nomination for a gutsy mother in *The Poseidon Adventure* (1972). Shelley's eventful and often turbulent private life has been set down by her in an entertaining book, 'Shelley', covering her various love affairs (John Ireland, Burt Lancaster) engagements (Farley Granger) and marriages (Vittorio Gassman, Anthony Franciosa), and close friendships with everyone from Marilyn Monroe and Howard Hughes to Charles Laughton and Marlon Brando. JF

with Ronald Colman in A Double Life *(Universal, 1948)*

Teresa Wright

Born **New York City, 27 October 1918**

Teresa Wright had only worked briefly in the theatre and was just experiencing her first success on Broadway in 'Life with Father' when she was signed to a contract by independent producer Sam Goldwyn. She was extremely fortunate in her early film career which included three pictures for director William Wyler and one of the best 40s Hitchcocks. Miss Wright was, in fact, nominated for Oscars for her first three film performances. In order to provide a suitable vehicle to introduce her to film audiences, the role of Bette Davis's daughter in *The Little Foxes* (1941) was expanded from the original play. She was excellent in this, and in her following role as Gary Cooper's young girlfriend and then wife in *The Pride Of The Yankees* (1942), and won the supporting actress Oscar in 1942 for her appealing performance as Greer Garson's daughter in *Mrs*

in 1943

Miniver. (This was one of the rare examples in the Academy's history when the same actress was Oscar-nominated in both the lead and supporting categories in the same year.) Friendly and pretty, she was in danger of being typecast as the girl-next-door. But, in *Shadow Of A Doubt* (1943), Hitchcock put her wholesome image to good use and stretched her abilities when he cast her as Charlie, the small town girl with the same name as, and a dangerous love-hate relationship with, her Uncle Charlie (Joseph Cotten) who turns out to be a murderous schizophrenic. She responded superbly and her sensitive performance contributed to the success of this highly original work. Another nice daughter in *The Best Years Of Our Lives* (1946) was followed by a more interesting and complex role opposite Robert Mitchum in Raoul Walsh's *Pursued* (1947), but her later roles were less interesting. Miss Wright retired in 1958 but was seen again in some TV movies during the 70s and on screen in *Roseland* (1977), and *Somewhere In Time* (1979). JF

Jane Wyman

Real name **Sarah Jane Fulks**
Born **St Joseph, Missouri, 4 January 1914**

Jane Wyman's mother pushed her in the direction of the movies at an early age, but with little success. She did, however, break into show business as a singer on the radio after she left school, and moved on to Hollywood where she appeared regularly as a bit player. In fact, from 1935 through 1944 she played in over forty pictures, most of them long forgotten, with such titles as *The King And The Chorus Girl* (1937), *Torchy Plays With Dynamite* (1939) or *Tugboat Annie Sails Again* (1940), this latter co-starring Ronald Reagan, one of her fellow contract players at Warner Bros. whose first wife she became in 1940.

In 1945 Miss Wyman got her big break when she was cast in the sympathetic part of alcoholic Ray Milland's long-suffering girl-friend in Paramount's Oscar-winning *The Lost Weekend*. Again on loan-

out, this time to MGM, she was nominated for an Oscar for her performance as the severe pioneer wife (of Gregory Peck) and mother (of Claude Jarman Jr) in *The Yearling* (1946). Finally her own studio, Warner Bros., cast her in a role worthy of her in 1948 (the same year that she divorced Reagan) as the intelligent deaf mute girl in *Johnny Belinda* (1948). Although she won an Oscar for her moving performance, the roles which followed were not memorable. Her demure appearance and worried air were assets in dramatic roles, but clearly limited the range of her parts and confined her to mainly women's pictures like *The Blue Veil* (1951) and *Magnificent Obsession* (1954), both of which earned for her further Oscar nominations. But *Magnificent Obsession* was her biggest box-office hit, and there was a rather more interesting follow-up with the same director (Douglas Sirk) and star (Rock Hudson) in *All That Heaven Allows* (1955). She did few films after 1956, working mainly in TV with her own series, 'The Firestone Theatre', and most recently starring in 'Falcon Crest'. JF

with Ray Milland in The Lost Weekend *(Paramount, 1945)*

Robert Young

Born **Chicago, Illinois, 22 February 1907**

One of the most easy-going but hard-working MGM stars of the second rank, Robert Young averaged six pictures per year over an eleven-year stretch from 1931 through 1941. He appeared opposite many of the top female stars in Hollywood in some of their most forgettable pictures like *New Morals For Old* (1932) with Myrna Loy, *The Bride Walks Out* (1936) with Barbara Stanwyck and *The Emperor's Candlesticks* with Luise Rainer.

A quiet-spoken, dark-haired, genial actor, Young grew up in California and had some stage experience at the Pasadena Playhouse before he broke into films. By the late 30s his parts finally began to improve. He appeared in three pictures directed by Frank Borzage and starring Margaret Sullavan, most

in 1945

notably *Three Comrades* (1938) and *The Mortal Storm* (1940), and two with King Vidor: He was the adventurous artist who joins Rogers' Rangers on their wilderness adventures in *Northwest Passage* (1940), and was given the title part in *H.M. Pulman Esq.* (1941), undoubtedly the most important role of his career. He gave an excellent performance as the Boston blue-blood businessman and family man torn between home and Hedy Lamarr. Vidor had fond memories of working with Young whom he referred to as '... a director's dream, thoroughly prepared for every scene he works in, with a maximum of enthusiasm and intelligence.' A few other good roles followed, as Dorothy McGuire's husband in *Claudia* (1943) and the pipe-smoking detective in the *film noir* message picture *Crossfire* (1947). But he virtually retired from films after 1951 and began a new career in TV extending up through the 70s when he appeared in a number of TV movies, most recently reunited with Dorothy McGuire in *Little Women* (1978). JF

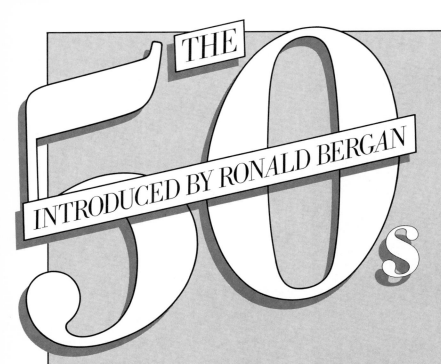

THE 50s

INTRODUCED BY RONALD BERGAN

'I *am* big. It's the pictures that got small,' says Gloria Swanson, as forgotten silent star Norma Desmond, in Billy Wilder's *Sunset Boulevard* which opened in August 1950. The film ambiguously juxtaposed Hollywood's baroque past with the more prosaic present. Swanson, Buster Keaton and Erich von Stroheim appeared as ghostly witnesses of the silent era, while William Holden represented the brash new generation. It was in the 50s, around the industry's jubilee, that the most perceptible changes took place.

The 50s brought entertainment into America's living rooms. As entire families clustered around the small screen, the TV generation was born, and the cinema suffered accordingly.

Although audience figures had already started to decline in 1947, the main cause for drastic reduction in cinema admissions was laid at the door of the one-eyed monster that was proliferating throughout the USA in the early 50s. As Samuel Goldwyn commented, 'Why should people go out and pay money to see bad films when they can stay home and see bad TV for nothing?' While Senator McCarthy was seeing reds under every bed, film moguls saw the box in people's living rooms as the real enemy. Jack Warner stipulated that no TV set was to be seen in a Warner Bros. picture. Television, which was added to the list of taboos, was seldom mentioned except in a satirical context as in the MGM

musical *It's Always Fair Weather* (1955), and in Elia Kazan's *A Face In The Crowd* (1957), a biting attack on the manipulation of the masses by TV. Billy Wilder remarked that 'it used to be that films were the lowest form of art. Now we have something to look down on.'

Bwana Devil (United Artists, 1952) was the first film to be made in 3-D, a short-lived, unsuccessful novelty. Here, photographer Joseph Biroc operates the immense and unwieldy 3-D camera – actually two cameras, one on either side of a central image splitter.

The existence of a financial competitor to Hollywood produced good effects, and bad. One of the worst was the industry's panicky reaction to the threat, by believing that big is beautiful. The pictures might have got small, but the screens certainly got larger. Desperate to entice people away from the twenty-one inch black-and-white screen, a series of complex devices and gimmicks were offered the public. The campaign to win back audiences began in 1952 with United Artists' *Bwana Devil* in 3D ('a lion in your lap'), and *This Is Cinerama*, which gave spectators the sensation of riding a roller-coaster. In 1953, 20th Century-Fox's CinemaScope made its appearance with *The Robe*, followed by Paramount's Vistavision in 1954, and *Around The World In Eighty Days* (1956) launched the 70mm Todd-AO process. The size of the screen, to a large extent, dictated the content of the movies, so that *Knights Of The Round Table* (1954), *Land Of The Pharaohs* (1955) and *Helen Of Troy* (1956) filled the screens if not the theatres.

However, the need to cram every inch of the screen with spectacle was an expensive operation and the films seldom recouped their costs. In contrast, there was a more interesting device for getting people to leave their TV sets for a movie theatre: controversial and adult subjects, deemed unsuitable by TV's commercial sponsors for family viewing at home, could be aired in the cinema. So if one wanted to hear words like 'virgin' and 'seduce', one would have to go out to see Otto Preminger's *The Moon Is Blue* (1954), which was released without the Production Code's Seal of Approval. It helped to create a permissiveness that wrested Hollywood from the puritan values that had gripped it for so long. Independent producers were also breaking the hold of the big studios, and tackled more daring subjects, delving into areas that Hollywood had previously shied away from. But in the first years of the decade, the long shadow of a small man was being cast over the film industry. Joe McCarthy, the senator from Wisconsin, was the prime force behind the House Un-American Activities Committee's second series of hearings which began in March 1951. As a result, 212 people involved in film making were blacklisted. It all took place in the climate of the Cold War, and the hot war in Korea demanded patriotism and all-American activities from the population. Although Hollywood was made jittery, liberal themes continued to be explored and, before and after McCarthy's downfall, the tenets on which American society was based were being questioned. The Red Indian was sympathetically treated in films like *Broken Arrow* (1950) with Jeff Chandler, and *Apache* (1954) with Burt Lancaster. Racial intolerance was examined in *No Way Out* (1950) and *The Defiant Ones* (1958), drug addiction in *The Man With The Golden Arm* (1955) and *A Hatful Of Rain* (1957), and juvenile delinquency in *The Blackboard Jungle* (1955). With the Korean war over and wounds beginning to heal, Stanley Kubrick was able to make *Paths Of Glory* (1957), one of the screen's most powerful anti-militaristic statements.

Nevertheless, whatever the size of the screen, no matter how important the subject, it was stars, above all, that the public always paid to see. Of those of an earlier era, Bette Davis opened the decade by playing a fading actress in *All About Eve* (1950), her last great role; Judy Garland made a sensational comeback in *A Star is Born* (1954), while Ingrid Bergman returned to Hollywood from exile to win an Oscar for *Anastasia* (1956), and Fred Astaire blithely continued to dance after having announced his retirement in 1945. Stars, like pin-up boy Tony Curtis, gradually changed their images.

Wearing a controversial dress and playing up her sex symbol image, the late, great Marilyn Monroe entertained the troops in Korea in 1954.

Frank Sinatra, skinny crooner of the 40s, made a second career for himself when he won the role of Private Maggio in *From Here To Eternity* (1953) and the Best Supporting Actor Oscar. The film also saw Deborah Kerr rescued from lifelong gentility as the adulterous wife, making love to Burt Lancaster on the beach as the waves pounded in. Lancaster himself emerged, with Kirk Douglas, as the most versatile and adventurous of the stars of the 50s. In fact, they were among those who gained greater independence by going freelance, and by becoming producers themselves.

This new independence was one nail in the coffin of the studio system. With overheads becoming impossibly high, with TV encroaching, with changes in the status of actors, producers and directors, the dissolution of the system was becoming inevitable, and would be complete by the mid-60s. Meanwhile, independently financed films and studio product existed, warily, cheek-by-jowl in the 50s.

The most dramatic change in screen acting derived from a group of stage actors and directors who had formed the Actors Studio in New York in 1948. It was there that the acting technique known as 'The Method' was advanced. It was influenced by the teachings of the Russian stage director Konstantin Stanislavsky who stressed a more instinctive approach to acting, the performers arriving at their interpretation of a role through seeking equivalent emotions in their own experiences. The actor who more than any other typified the Method school, was Marlon Brando. Others such as Rod Steiger, Eli Wallach, Montgomery Clift, Joanne Woodward, Anthony Perkins, Karl Malden, Paul Newman and James Dean benefitted from his example. Many thought there was madness in The Method, and it became the most caricatured of all acting styles with its mumbling delivery, shrugging of shoulders, fidgeting and scratching. Humphrey Bogart explained, 'I came out here with one suit and everybody said I looked like a bum. Twenty years later, Marlon Brando comes out with only a sweat shirt and the town drools over him. That shows how much Hollywood has progressed.' Joan Crawford, a remnant of past glamour, claimed 'I don't believe you want to go to the theatre to see somebody you can see next door.'

But, it was precisely because the growing youth audience could imagine the new stars living next door, that made them particularly attractive. With youth culture beginning to infiltrate the movies in the 50s, it was possible for the first time for young people to identify with certain stars. Brando projected an anti-conformist image, and Dean was the personification of adolescent rebellion and despair. As an alternative to the new wave of anarchic performers, the 50s still produced a number of stars in the glamorous Hollywood tradition such as Ava Gardner, Susan Hayward, Elizabeth Taylor, Rock Hudson, Grace Kelly, Audrey Hepburn, Tab Hunter, Charlton Heston and Doris Day. However, the predominant iconography of the fifties still remains Brando in leather sitting astride a motor cycle in *The Wild One* (1954), or the boyish blond features of James Dean, forever a prisoner of the period, or the wide eyes of Marilyn Monroe, who did not live much beyond the decade in which she made her name. The ghosts of the 50s are still there to haunt us.

1954 saw Marlon Brando as a motorcycle hoodlum in The Wild One *(Columbia). The brooding, rebellious anti-hero and his powerful machine brought youth a new and durable icon, the 'bike' culture – a phenomenon whose repercussions extended well into the 60s.*

Anouk Aimée

Real name **Francoise Sorya**
Born **Paris, France, 27 April 1932**

'C'est Moi. C'est Lola', sings Anouk Aimée in Jacques Demy's *Lola* (1960) in a cabaret to sailors on leave. The 30s had the Lola-Lola of Marlene Dietrich in *The Blue Angel* (1930), and the 50s had Martine Carol as *Lola Montes* (1955). Anouk Aimée was the sexual 60s version. As Lola, warmth and romance was breathed into the tall, aloof, enigmatic beauty, solemnity always lurking behind those big brown eyes. Moving easily from French to English, American and Italian films, she offered a promise of love, but revealed that the promise could not be fulfilled. In her private life, her own four marriages also denote love's transience.

Poet and screenwriter Jacques Prevert created the role of a modern day Juliet for her in *The Lovers Of Verona* (1948). In Alexandre Astruc's short, *The Crimson Curtain* (1951), she literally dies of a broken heart in her lover's arms. She is the mysteriously beckoning vision of love lost in George Franju's *The Keepers* (1958), as the girl the hero meets on the dunes outside the asylum, and in *Un Soir ... Un Train* (1969), she is part of Yves Montand's dream. Lola reappears nine years later in Demy's *The Model Shop* (1969). Older she might have been, but certainly not much wiser, posing to satisfy the sexual fantasies of photographers in Los Angeles. *Justine* (1969) was another of her beautiful, unattainable women with a past.

Known simply as 'Anouk' for the first part of her film career, she was the daughter of an actor and actress. She studied acting and dancing in France and England, the latter sojourn helping her to feel at home in English-speaking roles later. Anouk made her screen debut at the age of fourteen in *La Maison Sous La Mer* (1947). She attracted attention in *The Lovers Of Verona*, and soon after starred with Trevor Howard in *The Golden Salamander* (1949), a British film set in Tunisia, in which she played a strange girl who involves Howard in gun running. Another British film was French writer George Simenon's murder story featuring Claude Rains, *The Man Who Watched The Trains Go By* (1952).

Anouk made no films during her first marriage to Left Bank nightclub owner, Nico Papatakis, from 1952 to 1954. (He was later to direct three films.) She resumed work in Astruc's first feature, *Les*

in The Journey (MGM, 1958)

with Trevor Howard in The Golden Salamander (Rank, 1950)

Mauvaises Rencontres (1955), in another doleful role, followed by Julian Duvivier's version of the Zola classic, *Pot-Bouille* (1957). Set in the more recent past, *Montparnasse 19* (1958) enabled her to use her features convincingly as a model for Modigliani (Gérard Philipe). At the same time, she made her first American film (for MGM) as an attractive Hungarian freedom fighter in *The Journey* (1958), in opposition to Yul Brynner's Russian officer during the 1956 Hungarian revolution. It was a small but effective part.

Except for *Lola*, she never became part of the French New Wave, as her contemporary Jeanne Moreau did. Anouk preferred to film in different countries, never happy to stay put for long. This contributed to the break-down of two further marriages. She played the role of a French resistance fighter helping stoical Virginia McKenna in the British-made, *Carve Her Name With Pride* (1958), and one of the lesbians fleeing the wrath of God in the made-in-Italy spectacle *Sodom And Gomorrah* (1961). Also in Italy, for Vittorio de Sica on a bad day, she was one of an international cast playing Neapolitans awaiting the Day of Judgement in *Il Giudizio Universale* (1961). Two of the best films she appeared in were by Federico Fellini, also filmed in Italy. Having her voice dubbed did not detract from

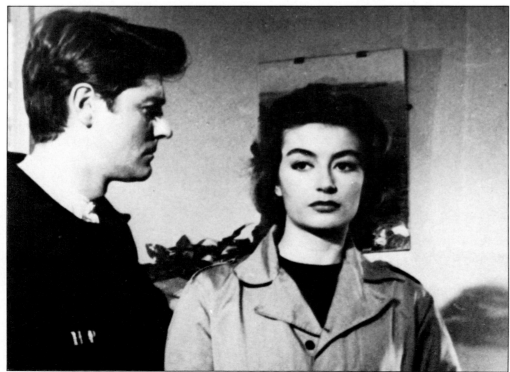

in La Tête Contre Les Murs (1958)

her sensuous performances. As the sex-hungry, significantly named Maddalena in *La Dolce Vita* (1960), she is brought by Marcello Mastroianni to a prostitute's bed to make love. In Fellini's 'cinema confession' *8½* (1963), she played the important role of Mastroianni's bespectacled wife.

However, it was Claude LeLouche's Oscar-winning *A Man And A Woman* (1966) that brought Anouk Aimée's name and face to the consciousness of a wide cinema audience. As the widow of a stuntman, now in love with a racing driver (Jean-Louis Trintignant), she just about makes tolerable this glossy women's magazine love story set at the *trés snob* seaside resort of Deauville.

In 1969, Anouk's feline beauty graced three dreary films – Sidney Lumet's *The Appointment*, in which she ruins lawyer Omar Sharif; Demy's *The Model Shop*, where she moons around a tatty L.A., and George Cukor's film version of Laurence Durrell's Alexandria Quartet, *Justine*. The latter was a very disappointing film, although Anouk was close to the elusive heroine of the novels. She then retired into marriage with actor Albert Finney, living in England most of the time. When that marriage, too, broke up, she returned to France and run-of-the-mill French films such as LeLouche's prison soap opera, *Second Chance* (1976) with Catherine Deneuve, and *First Love* (1978). One still remembers, however, the tenderness, gaiety and sadness of Lola, driving off in a white Cadillac out of Nantes to fulfil an unknown destiny. RB

Pier Angeli

Real name **Anna Maria Pierangeli**
Born **Cagliari, Sardinia, 19 June 1932**
Died **1971**

Marlon Brando once commented that Pier Angeli was his ideal of feminine beauty. The dark-haired, brown-eyed, Botticelli angel-faced Angeli was discovered by Russian emigré director Leonide Moguy, who cast her as the teenage girl painfully learning about sex in his Italian neo-realist film, *Tomorrow Is Too Late* (1949) and the sequel *Tomorrow Is Another Day* (1950). Although her twin sister, Marisa Pavan, wanted to be an actress, their mother forced Angeli into films first.

The young girl's sensitive playing led Fred Zinnemann to give her the role of the young Italian bride brought to New York by her GI husband in *Teresa* (1951). Although she made an impression on her American debut, she was not offered very interesting parts to follow, usually being cast as a naive girl or patient wife. In *The Light Touch* (1951),

in Merry Andrew *(MGM, 1958)*

shot in Italy, she played an innocent Italian girl caught up unwittingly with art thief Stewart Granger. In *The Devil Makes Three* (1952), shot in Germany, she played an innocent German girl caught up unwittingly in the post-war black market. She appeared in two compendium films, *The Story Of Three Loves* (1953) with Kirk Douglas, and *Sombrero* (1953), set in Mexico. She played twice opposite Paul Newman – as the good woman he finally marries in *The Silver Chalice* (1955), and as Mrs Rocky Graziano in Robert Wise's *Somebody Up There Likes Me* (1956).

In 1954, Angeli married crooner Vic Damone, but they were divorced four years later. Distraught, she returned to Europe permanently, where she appeared in a series of inferior co-productions such as *Sodom And Gomorrah* (1962), and provided the feminine interest in *The Battle Of The Bulge* (1965). In 1971, she killed herself by taking an overdose of barbiturates. Pier Angeli had never really liked her profession or adjusted to the pressures of stardom. Like the women she portrayed, she was too sweet and fragile for this world. RB

Carroll Baker

Born **Johnstown, Pennsylvania, 28 May 1931**

On a cot, far too small for her, lies a young blonde woman, staring ahead and sucking her thumb. This was the 'carnally suggestive' image from Elia Kazan's *Baby Doll* (1956) that was condemned by The League of Decency. Carroll Baker as the chaste child-wife, became the screen's first nymphet, gave rise to the fashion of Baby Doll pyjamas, and was nominated for an Oscar. A new sex goddess had arrived. Sadly, that is almost the end of the story.

The daughter of a travelling salesman, Carroll left Junior College in order to join a dance company. After a brief marriage to a furrier, she set off for Hollywood where she had a bit part in the Esther Williams vehicle *Easy To Love* (1953). Back in New York, while appearing in TV commercials, she studied at the renowned Actors' Studio where she met her future husband, stage director, Jack Garfein. Carroll managed to land herself a number of parts in TV dramas and a role in Robert Sherwood's play, 'All Summer Long'.

When she returned to Hollywood for the part of the daughter of a Texas family in *Giant* (1956), she landed the role of *Baby Doll* at the same time. She made little impression in William Wyler's *The Big*

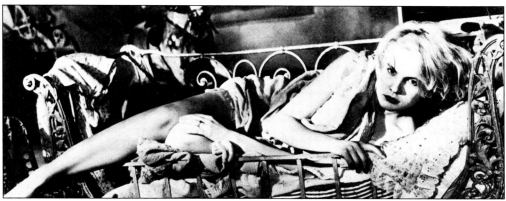

in Baby Doll *(Warner Bros., 1956)*

Country (1958) and *But Not For Me* (1959), and was miscast as the postulant nun in *The Miracle* (1959). Under the direction of her husband, she had a meatier part as a disturbed girl kept prisoner by a would-be rapist in *Something Wild* (1961), but it was a failure. However, Baker had a slight resurgence as a sex object in three soap operas, *The Carpetbaggers* (1964), *Sylvia* (1965), and *Harlow* (1965) in which she was barely credible as the famed platinum blonde star of the thirties.

In 1968, a year before her divorce from Garfein came through, she moved to Italy where she appeared in trashy, soft-porn movies such as *The Sweet Body Of Deborah* (1968), *Orgasmo* (1969) and *Confessions Of A Frustrated Housewife* (1976), the titles of which speak for themselves. Now very much the Adult Doll, she appeared on the London stage in Somerset Maugham's torrid classic, 'Rain', and then a film, *The World Is Full Of Married Men* (1979), made in England. RB

Anne Bancroft

Real name **Anna Maria Louise Italiano**
Born **Bronx, New York, 17 September 1931**

When Anne Bancroft returned to Hollywood for *The Miracle Worker* (1962) after five years on Broadway, it was difficult for filmgoers to believe that she was the same actress who had had such an undistinguished film career previously. Was this powerful, Oscar-winning performer the Bancroft who had played such ineffectual roles as Richard Widmark's wife in *Don't Bother To Knock* (1952), or Indian squaws in *Walk The Proud Land* (1956) and *The Restless Breed* (1957)?

The daughter of Italian immigrants, she was educated at the American Academy of Dramatic Arts and the Actors' Studio. Under the name of Anne Marno, she appeared in TV dramas before taking up a contract with Fox in 1952. After costume dramas such as *Demetrius And The Gladiators* (1954), routine gangster movies such as *The Naked Street* (1955) and westerns, she returned to New York discouraged.

But Bancroft soon made a name for herself on Broadway in two William Gibson plays, 'Two For The Seesaw' and 'The Miracle Worker', for which she received a Tony and the New York Critics' Award. In both the stage and film versions of the

in Seven Women *(MGM, 1966)*

latter, her performance as Anne Sullivan, Helen Keller's teacher, had a vitality and complexity, revealing the character's own psychological needs. Other emotional roles came in *The Pumpkin Eater* (1964) as the much-married, – child bearing-obsessed woman trying to save a crumbling marriage, and

the would-be suicide in *The Slender Thread* (1965). In John Ford's final film, *Seven Women* (1966), she played the atheist doctor in China, representing rationalism over religion.

Although Bancroft had seldom played comedy, she was perfect in the role of Mrs Robinson in *The Graduate* (1968), the alluring older woman who seduces her daughter's boyfriend (Dustin Hoffman). Her output since has been small, but not, alas, necessarily well-chosen: Churchill's American mother in *Young Winston* (1972) and the German countess (with a New York accent!) in *The Hindenburg* (1975). Better roles were as Jack Lemmon's yelling wife in Neil Simon's urban comedy *The Prisoner Of Second Avenue* (1975), and in the soap ballet film, *The Turning Point* (1977), she had a cattish *pas de deux* with Shirley MacLaine.

The star had been under therapy to find out why she had never married, but in the early 'seventies, she became the wife of comedy-writer and director Mel Brooks. As if to reassure Brooks' Yiddishe Momma, the former Miss Italiano played Golda Meier on Broadway. She made an amusing unbilled appearance, dancing the tango with her husband, in his *Silent Movie* (1976), and appeared with him in the remake of Ernst Lubitsch's classic comedy *To Be Or Not To Be* (1983). In 1979, she wrote, directed and acted in *Fatso* starring Dom DeLuise, a comedy about obesity, but it was unsuccessful. RB

Brigitte Bardot

Born **Paris, France, 28 September 1934**

$4,000,000 was the box-office figure earned by Roger Vadim's *And God Created Woman* (1956), and 35-23½-35 was the figure of its star, known to the world simply as BB. A new sex symbol reared its pretty, pouting, kittenish head, one of few to be created outside Hollywood. She was cool, amoral, anti-comformist, childlike and playful, with an insouciant sexuality accentuated by the flopping pony-tail, bare feet and jeans. Bardotlatry was born.

The daughter of an industrialist, Brigitte Bardot

in Shalako (Cinerama Releasing, 1968)

studied ballet from an early age. She began to model when still at school, and at fifteen, she posed for the cover of 'Elle' magazine. Roger Vadim, a young journalist with 'Paris Match' and assistant director to Marc Allegret, introduced himself to Brigitte via her parents. He got her her first film role in *Le Trou Normand* (1952), and they were married the same year. She then had a number of small, coquettish roles, watched over by Vadim who was Allegret's assistant on her best film to date, *Futures Vedettes*

(1954). She brought a bit of oo-la-la to shy medic Dirk Bogarde in *Doctor At Sea* (1955), was charming in modest 19th-century costume in René Clair's first colour film, *Summer Manoeuvres* (1955), and made sexy bit appearances in *Helen Of Troy* (1956), *Nero's Mistress* (1956) and *Mam'zelle Pigalle* (1956). But the first sign of her wanton gamine appeal came as the adulterous wife of a truck driver in *The Light Across The Street* (1955).

. . . And Vadim created Bardot. In his first film, *And God Created Woman*, he teased less fortunate males by displaying his wife in CinemaScope and Eastman Color against the sensuous summer surroundings of St. Tropez. Newly-wed BB's seduction of her husband's brother, getting him to rip off her clothes and take her on the ground, caused a sensation. It was one of the few French films to leave the art houses for the major circuit cinemas. Vadim then continued his baroque, Bardot body worship in further turgid movies such as *The Night Heaven Fell* (1957) – BB driving Stephen Boyd mad with desire – and *Warrior's Rest* (1962) – BB saving a young man from suicide by seducing him.

Vadim and his protégé divorced relatively amicably in 1957, occasionally working together later. The Bardot myth continued to grow as she appeared, wrapped in towels or clad in bikinis, in a series of light sex comedies such as *Une Parisienne* (1957) with old-timer Charles Boyer. She also attempted more serious roles as in *Love Is My Profession* (1958) – judge Jean Gabin is attracted to BB as the accused – and *The Female* (1958), a virtual remake of the Marlene Dietrich-Sternberg *The Devil*

nude. Louis Malle's rather self-pitying *A Very Private Affair* (1962) was based on Bardot's own experiences about being a sex object. She again played a film star very close to herself in Jean-Luc Godard's *Contempt* (1963), a brilliant and sharp comment on international film-making. BB made an appearance as herself at the end of *Dear Brigitte* (1965), about the eight-year-old genius son of James Stewart who has a juvenile crush on her.

Bardot's affairs and antics were seldom out of the headlines of the popular press. Her marriage to German millionaire playboy Gunther Sachs provided a feast for the gossip columnists and photographers. After the divorce, she was seen with a string of different men. 'I live my whole life around my man – work, play, dreams, everything. My lover is the centre of my existence,' she explained. 'When I am alone I am lost. Some actors say they can only really exist when they are playing a role. I can only play a role – only exist – when I am loved.' For her fortieth birthday, a series of seaside nude studies were taken by a young photographer lover and presented to her and the world.

Bardot still found time to make at least one film a year until 1973. Louis Malle's *Viva Maria* (1965) wittily takes off the kind of big production it is – large screen, colour, filmed on location in Mexico – with BB and Jeanne Moreau playing two revolutionaries in Central America, both called Maria. Malle directed her again in one of the three Poe stories in *Spirits Of The Dead* (1967) with Alain Delon. She appeared with Sean Connery in a plodding western, *Shalako* (1968), about European

Bardot (right) in Nero's Mistress *(Manhattan Films, 1956)*

Is A Woman (1935). While making *Babette Goes To War* (1959) in which she played a French agent working for the British, she fell in love with her handsome, 22-year-old co-star Jacques Charrier and they married the same year.

The marriage was a stormy affair from the beginning. The good-looking young couple were immediately exposed to media madness with photographers and journalists pursuing them everywhere. When Brigitte was having her baby, *paparazzi* were climbing onto roofs in order to get photos through the hospital windows. Charrier had a nervous breakdown and attempted suicide, and his wife also suffered from the strain. They were divorced within a year. Brigitte's private life remained in the public domain.

In Clouzot's *The Truth* (1960), she played a lonely and misunderstood girl, a dramatic role about which most people remember her doing a rhumba in the

big game hunters in the West, and in *The Legend Of Frenchy King* (1971), the latter a dismal attempt to repeat the success of *Viva Maria*, by casting Bardot with Claudia Cardinale as female outlaws. Her alluring presence in a film no longer had the power to cause a stir, and she decided to retire from the screen after a last film with her first husband Roger Vadim. It was the arty and salacious *Don Juan 1973* or *If Don Juan Were A Woman* (1973) featuring the former sex kitten, in the title role, actually bedding a number of beauties.

Once the subject of Simone de Beauvoir's serious analysis of her popularity in 'Brigitte Bardot And The Lolita Syndrome', she recently gave a four-hour interview to French TV. She still lives a great deal of the time in St. Tropez, and campaigns internationally for animal rights. Her sex symbol days are over, but the initials BB still evoke the vision of one of France's most seductive exports. RB

Claire Bloom

Born **London, 15 February 1931**

When Claire Bloom, as Lady Anne spits into Laurence Olivier's leering face in *Richard III* (1956) after the crookback has tried to woo her over her husband's coffin, she wishes the spit to be mortal poison. He replies 'Never came poison from so sweet a place.' This describes Bloom's best performances: Jimmy Porter's bitchy mistress in *Look Back In Anger* (1959), the predatory and neurotic suburban housewife in *The Chapman Report* (1962), the black-clad bully in *The Haunting* (1963), the determined independence of Nora in *The Doll's House* (1973) and the cold, calculating, Catholic Lady Marchmain in the TV production of 'Brideshead Revisited' (1981).

During the London Blitz, Claire was evacuated to the USA for three years at the age of nine. When she returned, she was immediately enrolled at the Guildhall School and then at the Central School of Speech and Drama. In her mid-teens, she was already a professional actress, appearing with the Oxford repertory Theatre and then the Shakespeare company at Stratford-on-Avon where she was a notable Ophelia. She made her film debut in a small role in *The Blind Goddess* (1948), and then returned to the stage.

It was the 63-year-old Charles Chaplin who cast her as the ballet dancer in *Limelight* (1952), making the 21-year-old actress into an international name.

in Limelight *(United Artists, 1952)*

Verbose and overly sentimental, the material is transcended by his presence and her poignant interaction with him. In the same year, Claire joined the Old Vic Company and continued to play the classics. This was to be the pattern throughout her career, a division among films, stage and TV.

In between the meaty roles, she was too often asked to be ladylike. She gave good support to James Mason in Carol Reed's *The Man Between* (1953), appeared opposite Richard Burton for the first time in Robert Rossen's over-long, over-serious epic *Alexander The Great* (1956), and was effectively Russian in *The Brothers Karamazov* (1958). Her English sexiness was revealed in *The Chapman Report* of which the director George Cukor commented 'She did all those ignoble things with a beautiful sombre face.' Stolid Martin Ritt directed her in *The Outrage* (1964) as an alleged rape victim and in *The Spy Who Came In From The Cold* (1966) with Burton.

Claire married actor Rod Steiger in 1959, and co-starred with him in two films, *Three Into Two Won't Go* (1969) as his abandoned wife, and in the pretentious science fiction morality *The Illustrated Man* (1969). After their divorce in 1969, Bloom married stage producer Hillard Elkins who produced *The Doll's House*, a well-acted version of the Ibsen play she had performed successfully on the London stage. She has done distinguished work on stage and TV in recent years, such as her Blanche du Bois in 'A Streetcar Named Desire' in the theatre, and a TV production of 'Separate Tables'. RB

Dirk Bogarde

Real name **Derek Van Den Bogaerde**
Born **London, 28 March 1920**

Few movie stars can claim to have written two best-selling autobiographies, two novels and poetry, and sold a drawing to the British Museum. Nor are they in the envious position of living in a 17th-century farmhouse in Provence from where offers of film work are turned down. Dirk Bogarde has reached this position through having had three highly successful film careers. The first was as a J. Arthur Rank contract star and British matinee idol, moving from one production to another without much say in the matter. The second dates from 1961 with *Victim*, leading to more serious and demanding roles in the British cinema, including four films with Joseph Losey. The third was as an international star of Italian, French and German films, working with such directors as Alain Resnais, Luchino Visconti and Rainer Werner Fassbinder.

It all started when this son of a Dutch-born art editor on the London 'Times', studied acting while attending art college. Bogarde did a little acting before being called up to serve in World War II. After five and a half years in the army, he returned to civilian life to start again. He was at first rejected by the Rank Organisation because his 'head was too small', but was later offered a contract after being spotted in a stage play. A few small parts were followed by *The Blue Lamp* (1949). Bogarde recalls in his memoirs, that Basil Dearden, the director, offered him a role in the police drama by saying. 'You could play the snivelling little killer. Neurotic, conceited, gets the rope in the end.' 'That's me!' was the actor's unhesitating reply.

Bogarde had a nice line in 'snivelling little killers' in *Blackmailed* (1951) and *Hunted* (1952), before graduating to the roles of officers and gentlemen in the war heroics of *Appointment In London* (1952), *They Who Dare* (1954) and *The Sea Shall Not Have Them* (1954). His popularity with the general public increased greatly as Simon Sparrow in the *Doctor* series. *Doctor ... In The House* (1954) *... At Sea* (1956) *... At Large* (1957) *... In Love* (1962) *... In Distress* (1963), all about a shy young medic who gets into trouble with girls (not vice versa). He was ridiculously English as *The Spanish Gardener* (1956), but got one of his better roles, as Sidney Carton in *A*

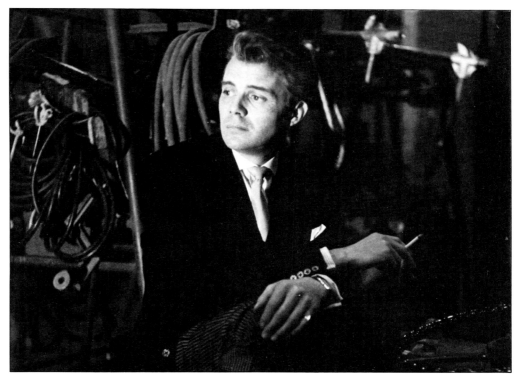

relaxing on the set of Victim *(Rank, 1961)*

Tale Of Two Cities (1958), directed by Ralph Thomas.

But it was a far, far better thing that Bogarde did when he left Rank, than he had ever done. As the respectably married lawyer being blackmailed for his homosexual past in *Victim* (1961), Bogarde felt he had 'achieved what I had longed to do for so long, to be in a film which disturbed, educated, and illuminated as well as merely entertaining ... I had been pointed in the right direction ... I was not to retreat ever again.' The new direction was taken in Losey's *The Servant* (1963) in which he played the unattractive, decadent, power-hungry valet. Also for Losey, he was the adulterous Oxford don in *Accident* (1967), and the elegantly camp, white-haired villain in *Modesty Blaise* (1966).

From his farmhouse in France, Bogarde continued occasional sorties into the film world. Much of his performance in Visconti's rather jackboot-

kissing *The Damned* (1969) ended up on the cutting room floor, so Visconti cast him as Aschenbach in *Death In Venice* (1971). His mannered performance did not have much chance against the sentimentalisation of Thomas Mann's novella with its lashings of Mahler on the soundtrack. In Liliana Cavani's pernicious and titillating *Night Porter* (1974), Bogarde is the ex-Nazi officer carrying out a sado-masochistic relationship with his former concentration camp rape victim, played by Charlotte Rampling. Interesting performances followed in Resnais' *Providence* (1977) as the cynical lawyer son of a dying John Gielgud, and Fassbinder's obfuscating *Despair* (1977) in which Bogarde, affecting a thick German accent, somehow masked the desperation of the proceedings. Certainly, a far cry from some of the cardboard cutout figures he was asked to play at Rank all those years ago. RB

Marlon Brando

Born **Omaha, Nebraska, 3 April 1924**

'Acting is the expression of a neurotic impulse,' Marlon Brando once stated. 'It is a bum's life. Quitting acting is a sign of maturity.' Modern screen acting began with Brando. Unlike the stars of an earlier generation who generally adapted the role to their personality, Brando brought a new realism to the screen. As critic Pauline Kael commented. 'When we watch Brando, the dramatic stage is in him, and the external aggressions against him are the occasions for us to see the conflicts within; the traditional actor's distance and his perfect clarity are gone.' No matter how mannered or misconceived some of his performances have been, he brings an intelligence and intensity to each role. Even when the films – such as *Bedtime Story* (1964), *The Appaloosa* (1966), *Candy* (1968) and *The Formula* (1980) – are unworthy of his talents, there is always something electric happening when he is before the

camera. Only Brando could have asked $3 million for his ten-minute appearance as Superman's father in *Superman* (1978), and got it, or have such a powerful – largely off-screen – presence as Colonel Kurtz in Francis Ford Coppola's *Apocalypse Now* (1979) to justify his top-billed, top-salaried apparition fifteen minutes from the end of the two-and-a-half hour movie.

Brando may often sound, as Rex Reed suggested, 'as if he has a mouth full of wet toilet paper', but an intrinsic part of his characterisation resides in the type of voice he chooses: Mexican for *Viva Zapata* (1952), Japanese for *Teahouse Of The August Moon* (1956), Deep South for *Sayonara* (1957) and *Reflections In A Golden Eye* (1967), German for *The Young Lions* (1958), British for *Mutiny On The Bounty* (1962), Italian-American for *The Godfather* (1972), and an Irish brogue for *The Missouri Breaks* (1976). But he became mainly identified with mumbling, brooding brutes like the character of Stanley Kowalski in *A Streetcar Named Desire* (1951) with his torn and sweaty T-shirt and raw sexuality; or the inarticulate hoodlum biker in *The Wild One* (1954), which made him the leather-jacketed idol of the erotico-anarchic motor-cycle cult; or as the washed-up boxer Terry Molloy in Elia Kazan's classic *On The Waterfront* (1954) speaking the poignant lines, 'I coulda had class. I coulda been somebody. I coulda been a contender instead of a bum, which is what I am.' But Brando does have class, he is somebody, he is more than a contender, he is not a bum.

This symbol of rebellion and unconventionality was born into a middle-class family of French extraction, the name being originally Brandeau. He was a difficult child, so his father sent him to a military academy in Minnesota from which he was

expelled a few weeks before graduating. 'I hated it every day I was there,' he later explained. 'The authorities annoyed me. I had to show respect for those for whom I had no respect.' Young Marlon drifted around for a while before joining his two older sisters, Frances and Jocelyn, in New York. Jocelyn was already an actress and she got him to enrol at the Dramatic Workshop. An actress remembered him as 'the most desirable, sensual young guy I ever saw. He had animal magnetism that grabbed you and a beautiful sensitive face. He could be a charmer: he had star quality and we all knew it.'

After touring in summer stock, he made it to Broadway, at the age of twenty, in 'I Remember Mama', but his meeting with director Elia Kazan and his work with the Actors' Studio was crucial to his development as an actor. It was when John Garfield turned down the role of Kowalski in Tennessee Williams's 'A Streetcar Named Desire' in 1947, that Brando got his big chance in the Elia Kazan production. One critic claimed after the first night, 'It was awful and it was sublime. Only once in a generation do you see such a thing in the theatre.' During the run, he made a habit of changing apartments and women, and gained a reputation for being a rebel. Although he often expressed his contempt for Hollywood, 'that cultural boneyard', he admitted that he was tempted by the money it promised. When it was offered, he took that money and ran, never to tread the boards again.

Brando chose, for his first film, the Stanley Kramer production of *The Men* (1950) in which he played a bitter ex-GI paralysed from the waist down. The conviction he brought to the part was helped by the fact that he had spent some weeks among paraplegics before shooting. He then recreated his stage role in *Streetcar Named Desire* for Kazan, opposite Vivien Leigh, and was nominated for an Oscar. He was also nominated for two other Kazan movies, *Viva Zapata!* and *On The Waterfront*, winning the Oscar for the latter. Another nomination came for his controversial Mark Antony in Joseph Mankiewicz's screen version of Shakespeare's *Julius Caesar* (1953). The initial casting caused a furore, but his eloquent performance won over the critics. 'Brando delivers an actor's *coup* that knocks the film out,' said one, of the famous 'Friends, Romans, Countrymen' funeral oration.

This powerful star further proved his versatility by playing Napoleon in *Desirée* (1954); and pleasantly singing two numbers in a nasal baritone as Sky Masterson in Mankiewicz's *Guys And Dolls* (1955), but returned to Tennessee Williams for the part of the blond guitar-playing drifter in *The Fugitive Kind*

(1960). For his soporific performance in the latter, he became the first actor ever to be offered a one million dollar salary. However, at this period, Brando was suffering a slight decline in his box-office appeal, so he decided to direct his next movie. Allegedly so wasteful was he with Paramount's time and money, that *One-Eyed Jacks* (1960) remains the only film he has directed up to now. It is a long, rambling, self-indulgent western, boasting superb photography and a brooding, Byronic appearance by its star and director.

Brando's personal life has also been in the public eye. In his time, he dated Pier Angeli, Rita Moreno and France Nuyen among others, and was once engaged to French model Josanne Berenger. This ended when he turned up at her apartment for a *tête-à-tête* dinner with another woman. His taste has been mainly for the exotic, and he married Anna Kashfi in 1957, thinking she was Indian, but she was, in fact, of Irish descent. They separated a year later after the birth of a son, and Brando later won custody of the child after a bitter wrangle. In 1960, he married the actress Movita, whom he had known for many years. But while on location filming for *Mutiny On The Bounty*, he met a Tahitian beauty called Tarita, with whom he has two children.

The making of *Mutiny On The Bounty* was fraught with difficulties. It went way over budget, Brando duelled with his fellow actors, and had Carol Reed replaced by Lewis Milestone as director. His choice of roles that followed his foppish Fletcher Christian was not inspired, redeemed only by his fair-minded sheriff of a corrupt town in Arthur Penn's *The Chase* (1966), and his subtle, if not inaudible, stiff-backed closet homosexual major in John Huston's *Reflections In A Golden Eye*. His popularity was restored after a few years in the doldrums by his meticulously delineated character performance as the old Don Corleone in *The Godfather*, for which he was given an Oscar. At the ceremony, an American Indian girl read a prepared statement rejecting the Oscar in order to draw attention to the plight of the Indian, one of Brando's many civil rights' concerns.

He also caused controversy with his role as the anguished middle-aged American in Bernardo Bertolucci's painful *Last Tango In Paris* (1972), who conducts a loveless, joyless, exclusively physical relationship with a young French girl. So explicit and powerful was Brando, that he was threatened with prosecution under Italian law for alleged indecencies committed on screen. Perhaps that was one of the greatest of compliments ever paid to this commanding actor. RB

in The Godfather *(Paramount, 1972)*

in One-Eyed Jacks *(Paramount, 1961)* ▷

in 1969

Rossano Brazzi

Born **Bologna, Italy, 18 September 1916**

'Latins are lousy lovers' wrote Jessica Mitford. Luckily for Rossano Brazzi, Hollywood disagrees. With his Roman profile, soft brown eyes, hair greying slightly at the temples, and soothing Italian accent, Brazzi made a good living as a romantic foreigner on the screen, forever sweeping unsophisticated American women abroad off their feet. He was a girl's wish come true in *Three Coins In The Fountain* (1954), and gave spinster Katharine Hepburn a touch of Venetian romance in *Summertime* (1954); he melted the heart of American nurse Mitzi Gaynor in *South Pacific* (1958) with his dubbed rendering of 'Some Enchanted Evening', and caused Maureen O'Hara to leave her husband in *The Battle Of The Villa Fiorita* (1965). The closest he came to exemplifying Mitford's remark was in *The Barefoot Contessa* (1954), as the aristocrat who marries Ava Gardner only to tell her that a war wound has rendered him impotent.

Rossano left law school in Florence, when his parents were killed by the fascists. He took up acting and made his film debut in 1939. He soon became the romantic lead in a number of mediocre Italian melodramas then, in his first Hollywood film, *Little Women* (1949), gave a touching, if miscast, performance as the hard-up, German professor. He returned to his native Italy in the late 60s and lives there with his wife of many years, the actress Lydia Bartalini and occasionally directs. RB

Richard Burton

Real name **Richard Walter Jenkins**
Born **Pontrhydfen, Wales, 10 November 1925**
Died **1984**

During the much-publicised love-affair with his co-star Elizabeth Taylor during the making of *Cleopatra* (1963), Richard Burton was sent a telegram by Laurence Olivier. It read: 'Make up your mind, dear heart. Do you want to be a great actor or a household word?' Burton replied, 'Both'. He did become a household word, and he had the melodious voice, romantic looks and tragic quality to have become a great actor.

One of thirteen children of a Welsh coal miner, Richard managed to get a scholarship to Oxford with the help of his school teacher, Philip Burton, from whom he took his stage name. He started as an actor at Oxford and at the Liverpool theatre, before joining the RAF from 1944 to 1947. On returning, he gained his first film role in Emlyn Williams's *The Last Days Of Dolwyn* (1948), met his first wife Sybil Williams, and was acclaimed on the stage for his performance in Christopher Fry's 'The Lady's Not For Burning', a role which he repeated on Broadway. This led to a contract with Fox, and *My Cousin Rachel* (1952) opposite Olivia de Havilland.

In between yawning CinemaScope movies, Burton found time to build a reputation as a Shakespearean hero in Hamlet and Othello at the Old Vic. Only a glimmer of these great roles came through in plodding epics such as *The Robe* (1953), and *Alexander The Great* (1956), and soggy soap operas like *The Bramble Bush* (1960) and *Ice Palace* (1960). Only in Nicholas Ray's war drama *Bitter Victory* (1958), did he have a chance to display his poetry and power.

After a run as King Arthur in the Broadway musical 'Camelot', Burton was cast to play Marc Antony in the multi-million dollar production of *Cleopatra*. What went on off-screen was more interesting than the four hours traffic of the film. By the end of shooting, Elizabeth Taylor and Richard Burton had left their respective spouses (hers at the time was Eddie Fisher) for each other. Because of the public interest in their private lives, they soon became the highest paid couple in movies, averaging a million dollars each per picture.

Burton earned his money by walking through *The V.I.P.'s* (1963), *The Sandpiper* (1965), *The Comedians* (1967), *Boom* (1968) and *Hammersmith Is Out* (1972) with a hangdog expression, while his wife looked beautiful. They duelled raucously in *The Taming Of The Shrew* (1967) and in the three-hour TV drama 'Divorce His Divorce Hers', made while their own marriage was breaking up. However, he

gave one of his best screen performances as the self-loathing professor in *Who's Afraid Of Virginia Woolf?* (1966), before the cycle of divorce, reconciliation, remarriage in 1975 and redivorce in 1976.

He then scowled through 1964's *The Night Of The Iguana* (as a defrocked priest) and *The Spy Who Came In From The Cold* (1965), and delivered eight monotonous monologues in *Equus* (1977). Whether playing a gay hairdresser in *Staircase* (1969), Henry VIII in *Anne Of A Thousand Days* (1969), Trotsky in *The Assassination Of Trotsky* (1972), or as a priest again in *Exorcist II – The Heretic* (1977), he continued to give the impression that he would rather have been elsewhere.

Elsewhere could have been Wales, to which he returned regularly to watch rugby and see his family. Or it could have been the stage. He last played Shakespeare in New York in John Gielgud's production of 'Hamlet', which was filmed in 1964. Burton struggled not only against bad parts, but against illness and alcoholism. His relationship with Elizabeth Taylor had recently resumed professionally on Broadway in Noel Coward's 'Private Lives', an ironic title for the famous couple. Burton was nominated for the Best Actor Oscar six times, but never won that elusive award. RB

in Cleopatra *(20th Century-Fox, 1963)*

Yul Brynner

Born **Sakhalin, Russia, 12 July 1915**

'People don't know my real self, and they're not about to find out,' Yul Brynner once commented. For many years, the man with the luminous dome and the hypnotic Mongolian eyes kept his true origins a secret. But the bald facts seem to be that he was born on an island off Siberia of part-Gypsy parentage, coming to Paris in his early teens. He sang and played the balalaika in nightclubs with a gypsy group. Later, he worked as a trapeze artist with the Paris Cirque D'Hiver, until he was injured in a fall. While studying for a philosophy degree at the Sorbonne, he joined a theatre company which toured America in 1940. There he remained for the duration of the war as French broadcaster at the US Office of War Information, and married the actress Virginia Gilmore.

Brynner made his film debut as a heavy in the narcotics drama, *Port Of New York* (1949), but was not to make another movie for seven years. Then, in his second film, as the despotic, polygamous King of Siam in *The King And I* (1956), he won an Oscar for

best actor. It is a graceful, comic and virile portrayal. He had given over a thousand performances of the role on stage before repeating it on film, played the King again in a TV series and in 1977, returned to Broadway and London in a successful revival, hardly having altered in looks or interpretation over the years.

Keeping the Buddhist monk hairstyle as his trademark, Brynner launched into a somewhat less shining film career. He was at home playing Russians, ancient and modern, in *Anastasia* (1956), *The Brothers Karamazov* (1958), *The Journey* (1959), *Taras Bulba* (1962) and *The Serpent* (1973). Epics such as Cecil B. DeMille's *The Ten Commandments* (1956), as the cruel Pharoah, and *Solomon And Sheba* (1959), suited his expansive and exotic personality. After his success as the leader of *The Magnificent Seven* (1960), he made a number of westerns including, inevitably, *Return Of The Seven* (1966), giving performances that hardly differ from his robot gunfighter in the futuristic *Westworld* (1973).

The cosmopolitan, polyglot Brynner – with his third wife – settled a long way from Siam in 1967, becoming a Swiss citizen. RB

Leslie Caron

Born **Boulogne-Billancourt, France,
1 July 1931**

It was Gene Kelly's memory of a 16-year-old ballerina with Roland Petit's Ballets des Champs Elysées in Paris in 1947, that led to her starring opposite him in the six-Oscar-winning MGM musical *An American In Paris* (1951). Leslie Caron's American-born mother had been a dancer and encouraged her daughter to take ballet lessons at a very early age. When the call came from Hollywood for her to take a screen test, it was a dream come true. The tests were sent from Paris to MGM who immediately offered the young French girl a contract. In the same year, she married George Hormel, the meat-packing heir.

'Dancing before the camera instead of an audience was very confusing,' she remembered. 'Then I learned to imagine an audience, and then it was all right.' Caron's freshness, gamine looks, and flowing dancing, brought her instant stardom as Lise Bouvier in *An American In Paris*. The same characteristics were exploited in a few more musicals with the studio, in which her acting became more assured. She was nominated for a Best Actress Oscar for her charming performance as the French waif in

in Gigi (MGM, 1958)

Lili (1953) opposite Mel Ferrer, after which other little orphan roles, of diminishing appeal, were Cinderella in *The Glass Slipper* (1955), and the girl who falls for her patron, Fred Astaire, in *Daddy Long Legs* (1955).

After Leslie's divorce from Hormel in 1954, she spent a year on the stage in Europe, acting in Jean Renoir's play 'Orvet' in Paris, and in Anita Loos's adaptation of Colette's novel 'Gigi' in London, where she met Peter Hall, the then director of the Royal Shakespeare Company. They were married in 1956, and Leslie left Hollywood to live in England. *Gigi* (1958) was her sumptuous farewell to the screen musical, Caron having, in the words of the song, 'grown up in the most delightful way'.

In England, she attempted a career as a dramatic actress, playing the unwed pregnant girl in *The L-Shaped Room* (1962), and in her husband's stage production of Giraudoux's 'Ondine', with an occasional return to Hollywood for glossy trivia such as *Father Goose* (1964) with Cary Grant. In 1966, Hall divorced her, citing Warren Beatty as co-respondent. Three years later, she married producer Michael Laughlin. After five years of inactivity Miss Caron returned to the screen as a mysterious housekeeper in the French film, *Serail* (1976), in Truffaut's *The Man Who Loved Women* (1977), and as a look-alike Nazimova in Ken Russell's crude biopic, *Valentino* (1977). RB

Jeff Chandler

Real name **Ira Grossel**
Born **Brooklyn, New York,
15 December 1918**
Died **1961**

For a decade the archetypal Universal Pictures action star of the 50s, Jeff Chandler made an average of three movies a year. His prematurely grey curly hair and earnest tanned features were seen in westerns, exotic 'easterns' and in war dramas. He looked uncomfortable in anything where he had to wear an ordinary suit as in *Female On The Beach* (1955) with Joan Crawford, and soap operas, *A Stranger In My Arms* (1958) with June Allyson, and *Return To Peyton Place* (1961). He was better boxing to kill in *The Iron Man* (1951), rescuing Maureen O'Hara on a horse in *Flame Of Araby* (1952), winning Rhonda Fleming with a sword in *Yankee Pasha* (1954), wooing Jane Russell in *Foxfire* (1955) and winning the war in *Red Ball Express* (1952), *Away All Boats* (1956) and, in his last film, *Merrill's Marauders* (1962).

Chandler actually served as an officer during World War II, before entering films in 1947. Although effectively, he always played on one note, he was nominated for an Oscar as Best Actor for his role as Apache Chief Cochise in *Broken Arrow* (1950), a part he repeated in *Battle At Apache Pass* (1952). He died at the age of forty-two of blood-poisoning. RB

Cyd Charisse

Real name **Tula Ellice Finklea**
Born **Amarillo, Texas, 8 March 1921**

The camera seems to track for ever along a pair of crossed female legs. It moves up to reveal a *femme fatale* with a Louise Brooks hairdo, teasing Gene Kelly by balancing his straw hat on the end of her foot. It was in 'The Broadway Ballet' from *Singin' In The Rain* (1952) that the beautiful, long-limbed, sexually dynamic dancer Cyd Charisse first made an impact. Later in the ballet, she is seen in a vision as warm and inviting, a mile-long white veil blowing in the wind. In a few minutes, Charisse's film persona is encapsulated – at first cold and aloof, later melted by the love of the right man. In *The Band Wagon* (1953), she is the supercilious ballet dancer to Fred Astaire's hoofer until they dance together sublimely in 'Dancing In The Dark'; in *Silk Stockings* (1957), she is the stern Russian commissar who gives in to Astaire's capitalistic charms, and in *It's Always Fair Weather* (1955), she is haughty with Gene Kelly until he corrects her Shakespeare.

Cyd's mother was a ballet fan who made her daughter take lessons from the age of eight. She joined Colonel de Basil's Ballet Russe de Monte Carlo in her teens, marrying her dance instructor, Nico Charisse during a tour of Europe. On their return, they opened a dance school together in Hollywood. In 1943, she had bit parts in a couple of films under the name of Lily Norwood, but became Cyd Charisse in 1946, when she signed with MGM for whom she made the majority of her movies. Before *Singin' In The Rain*, she was seen smiling prettily and pirouetting through a number of dance cameos in *Ziegfeld Follies* (1946), *Till The Clouds Roll By* (1946) – dancing with Gower Champion – and *Words And Music* (1948), and had a charming number with Judy Garland in *The Harvey Girls* (1946), without a hint of the sexiness which characterised her appearances just a few years later.

With the decline of the musical, Charisse took on a number of straight dramatic parts in *Twilight For The Gods* (1958), an action picture with Rock Hudson, *Two Weeks In Another Town* (1962) as Kirk Douglas's promiscuous ex-wife, and in *Party Girl* (1958), where she at least had a chance to dance in a leopard skin dress. Cyd's body was far more eloquent than her voice or face, and she began to appear rarely on the screen. She teamed up with her second husband (since 1948), crooner Tony Martin, in a series of nightclub revues, and in 1976 they wrote a dual autobiography. RB

in The Search *(MGM, 1948)*

Montgomery Clift

Real name **Edward Montgomery Clift**
Born **Omaha, Nebraska, 17 October 1920**
Died **1966**

As Private Prewitt in *From Here To Eternity* (1953), Montgomery Clift refuses to box for his platoon and is therefore beaten up and humiliated. Boxing would have given him the chance to become part of the system in which there is no room for ethics and by resisting, he is crushed by it. In Alfred Hitchcock's *I Confess* (1953), he is a priest alone with the knowledge of a murderer's confession, refusing to betray the secrets of the confessional although he himself is accused of the crime. As George Eastman in George Stevens's *A Place In The Sun* (1951), he lives with the guilt of having let his pregnant girlfriend, Shelley Winters, drown, and in *Lonelyhearts* (1959), he is racked with guilt as the agony columnist dishing out advice to the lonely and unhappy, until he tries to get involved with the pain of the world. Likewise, he is the neurosurgeon in *Suddenly Last Summer* (1959), trying to get at the truth behind mental patient Elizabeth Taylor's breakdown, and as *Freud* (1962) in John Huston's biography, he finds the key to a patient's trauma by delving into his own infant sexuality. All doomed heroes, loners or, like the title of one of his last films, *The Misfits* (1961).

Off screen, Clift was all these things too. Sensitive, introspective, self-destructive. A personality that expressed itself on film as if afraid of what the camera would reveal. Hesitant, diffident and often tortured, there were at least three faces of Monty Clift. The early public one of the dark, romantic, handsome star of the fan magazines; the face of extraordinary beauty marred after a car accident in 1957, and the private face of drink, drugs and a series of unloving homosexual encounters. Although the accident itself had not really disfigured him too seriously, it seems to have scarred his character much more, and his narcotics intake increased, making him more difficult to work with. The motor crash happened during the filming of *Raintree County* (1957), one of three pictures he had made with his friend and confidante Elizabeth Taylor. A macabre game can be played by audiences while watching this sub-*Gone With The Wind* to try to spot the difference between those scenes shot before the accident and after. Director Edward Dmytryk went out of his way to make sure that the recently recovered Clift was never seen in full face.

Monty started acting at a very early age in amateur productions, and was already in summer stock at 14. A year later, he made his Broadway debut in 'Fly Away Home', and then appeared in Thornton Wilder's 'The Skin Of Our Teeth' and 'Our Town'. Later, he was encouraged by Elia Kazan to extend his range by using the Actors' Studio in New York. His first screen role was as John Wayne's adopted son in Howard Hawks's *Red River* (1948). Clift's edgy angularity was set off against Wayne's macho security, thus creating a tension that gives this western a depth it might not otherwise have had.

The release of *Red River* was delayed, so the public's first glimpse of Clift in films was in Fred Zinnemann's *The Search* (1948). Only the hard-boiled would find their eyes unmoist in this tale of a war orphan in a ravaged Berlin. Bosley Crowther in 'The New York Times' wrote that 'As the American officer who 'adopts' him, the young American actor Montgomery Clift, gets precisely the right combination of intensity and casualness into the role.' Clift was nominated for the Best Actor Oscar, and in the year of the release of his first two movies, he was featured in a 'Life' magazine cover story, 'Look'

magazine presented him with its Achievement Award naming him 'the most promising star on the Hollywood horizon', and 'The Motion Picture Herald' pronounced him 'the star of tomorrow.'

He did not exactly justify these plaudits in the uninteresting roles in his next two films: the dashing fortune-hunter in *The Heiress* (1949), William Wyler's academic adaptation from Henry James, in which he coldly jilts spinster Olivia de Havilland; and as a pilot in the documentary-style *The Big Lift* (1950) about the Berlin airlift. More complex, and more satisfying, was his go-getter in *A Place In The Sun*, with Shelley Winters and Elizabeth Taylor, all three seen in wonderful close-ups. After working again with Zinnemann on *From Here To Eternity* as the sensitive soldier, and with Hitchcock on *I Confess*, Monty travelled to Italy to co-star with Jennifer Jones in Vittorio De Sica's *Indiscretion Of An American Wife* (1953). Almost entirely set in the railway station in Rome, it is a tiresome hour-long farewell between Jones as the wife and Clift as her lover. It was De Sica's first use of big stars, but it did nothing for Clift's career.

Four years away from the screen of drifting and 'finding himself', ended with *Raintree County* and the car crash, but he continued to work immediately after his recovery. As the victimized soldier in Dmytryk's *The Young Lions* (1958), he was outshone by Marlon Brando and Dean Martin. In *Lonelyhearts*, not a successful translation of Nathanael West's bitter novel 'Miss Lonelyhearts', he seemed crushed both by the role and by Robert Ryan's scowling newspaper editor. In Joseph Mankiewicz's overheated *Suddenly Last Summer*, he is little more than a catalyst, merely providing cues for Katharine Hepburn and Elizabeth Taylor. Clift is again strangely passive in Elia Kazan's impressive *Wild River* (1960), and further insecurity is revealed in John Huston's symbol-laden *The Misfits* (scripted by Arthur Miller). Here, Clift was an unwilling roper of wild horses in a film that has the smell of death about it. (It was both Clark Gable's and Marilyn Monroe's last film.)

More pathos and neurosis were expressed in Monty's last films. He was one of the 'star' witnesses in *Judgement At Nuremberg* (1961) as a mentally disturbed concentration camp victim, and behind whiskers in Huston's *Freud*, he formulates the Oedipus complex theory, a world of meaning in his eyes. Curiously enough, during the shooting of *Freud*, he had an operation to remove cataracts from both his eyes. His final film before his death of a heart attack at the age of 45, was a bleak, French espionage movie called *The Defector* (1966) in which he once again played a loner, the role he had played for most of his life. RB

with Olivia de Havilland in The Heiress *(Paramount, 1949)*

Joan Collins

Born **London, England, 23 May 1933**

'If you've got it, flaunt it', could be sultry, dark-haired beauty Joan Collins's motto. She's been flaunting it ever since her screen debut in 1952. She was immediately cast as wayward cockney girls in low key British dramas such as *I Believe In You* (1952) and *Cosh Boy* (1953), and in *Turn The Key Softly* (1953) as an ex-jail-bird. She had a 'naughty' role in *Decameron Nights* (1952), and first showed her curvaceous figure in *Our Girl Friday* (1953), in which she was the only girl among three men wrecked on a desert island. Difficult to believe that Joan had spent two years at the Royal Academy Of Dramatic Art, and had made her London stage debut in Ibsen's 'A Doll's House' 1946.

Separated from her husband, actor Maxwell Reed, the 21-year-old English girl began a career in Hollywood in Howard Hawks's *Land Of The Pharaohs* (1954), purring as Jack Hawkins's Nefertiti-like wife. Needless to say, she did not play the title role in *The Virgin Queen* (1954) but Elizabeth I's rival, offering no competition to Bette Davis, however. Looking gorgeous enough to kill for, Joan landed the plum role of Evelyn Nesbitt Thaw in *The Girl In The Red Velvet Swing* (1954), the show girl involved in the sensational society murder of the 1900s. In further Fox CinemaScope offerings, she was ship-wrecked with Richard Burton in *Sea Wife* (1957), looked unhappy on a horse in *The Bravados* (1958), and was the cause of Paul Newman and Joanne Woodward's marital problems in the witless comedy, *Rally Round The Flag Boys* (1958).

Marriage to Anthony Newley got her to alternate between Europe and the USA. In England, she actually replaced Dorothy Lamour in the last of the 'Road' films, *Road To Hong Kong* (1962), although Lamour had a cameo role to compensate her and the audience. The 'versatile' Newley directed his wife in the Fellini-inspired flop, *Can Hieronymous Merkin Ever Forget Mercy Humppe And Find True Happiness?* (1969), a title and film enough to put a strain on any marriage. It did. They were divorced soon afterwards.

Married for the third time and settled in London, Joan Collins started a lucrative career producing and appearing as the sexy older woman in soft-porn stuff such as *The Stud* (1978) and *The Bitch* (1979). Still as lovely as ever, she launched a book and video on beauty hints, and appeared on stage in 'The Last Of Mrs Cheyney' wearing a variety of stunning frocks as the shady lady. Not all went well, however. Her young daughter suffered a terrible accident and was near death, only surviving due to faith, according to Miss Collins, and her marriage broke down. But she rode out her troubles to become the Queen of American TV soap opera in 'Dynasty', as the woman you love to hate. RB

in Island In The Sun (20th Century-Fox, 1957)

Broderick Crawford

Real name **William Broderick Crawford**
Born **Philadelphia, 9 December 1911**

A stocky figure, loud mouth, bullish features and personality, fitted Broderick Crawford for the roles of a crooked politician and upwardly mobile gangster, two of his finest performances. For his hard-hitting portrayal of the Huey Long-type senator, Willie Stark in Robert Rossen's *All The King's Men* (1949), Crawford won a Best Actor Oscar. As Harry Brock, the *nouveau riche* hoodlum in *Born Yesterday* (1950) who wants to give class to his dumb blonde mistress, he is the butt of Judy Holliday's immortal delivery of the line, 'Drop dead!'

It took Broderick Crawford, the son of vaudevillian Lester Crawford and comedienne Helen Broderick, twenty five films in twelve years before he became a star. Playing mostly dumb oxen and heavies, his films included *Beau Geste* (1939), *Seven Sinners* (1940) – as Marlene Dietrich's companion – and the lead in the comedy-thriller, *The Black Cat*

in Between Heaven And Hell (20th Century-Fox, 1956)

(1941). On Broadway in 1937, he was a critical success as Lenny, the giant with the mind of a child, in John Steinbeck's 'Of Mice And Men'.

After war service, he made a few films, including *Slave Girl* (1947) and *The Time Of Your Life* (1948), before Rossen insisted on a comparatively unknown actor for the lead in *All The King's Men*. However, few interesting roles followed. He was the heavy in a number of westerns like *Lone Star* (1952), fighting Clark Gable for Ava Gardner, and as the husband Gloria Grahame wants knocked off in Fritz Lang's *Human Desire* (1954). Four years as the lead in 'Highway Patrol' on TV, gave him little time for work in films in the late 50s, although he appeared as a bumbling hoodlum in Fellini's *I Bidone* (1955), and as a nasty seaman in *The Decks Ran Red* (1958). Much of the 60s he spent in Italy and Spain making westerns and epics. As well as 'Highway Patrol', Crawford starred in the TV series 'King of Diamonds' and 'The Interns'. After a serious motor accident, he came back in full force as Hoover in *The Private Files Of J. Edgar Hoover* (1977), a character not too distant from Willie Stark. RB

Richard Conte

Real name **Nicolas Peter Conte**
Born **Jersey City, New Jersey, 24 March 1914**
Died **1975**

It was fitting that Richard Conte, near the end of his life, was given a role in *The Godfather* (1972), Francis Ford Coppola's apotheosis of The Mafia and The Family. For decades, Conte had been part of the Italian-American ethos as popularly interpreted by Hollywood film-makers.

The son of an Italian barber, he had a variety of jobs, including messenger boy and truck driver. It was while working as a performing waiter at a Connecticut resort that he was spotted by Elia Kazan, who offered him work at his Neighborhood Playhouse in New York. His raw vitality soon gained him parts on Broadway, mostly as working-class heroes, and in 1943 he signed a contract with Fox.

Conte began in a series of war films, *Guadalcanal Diary* (1943), *A Bell For Adano* (1945), and two Lewis Milestone movies, *The Purple Heart* (1944) and *A Walk In The Sun* (1946), usually as the amiable Italian of the regiment. His 'ordinary man's' looks suited roles in Henry Hathaway's semi-documentary thrillers, *13 Rue Madeleine* (1947) and

in The Raiders (Universal, 1952)

Call Northside 777 (1948). He gradually became harder and more cynical in B gangster films such as *Under The Gun* (1951), *The Big Combo* (1955) and *The Brothers Rico* (1957). Light relief came in *Full Of Life* (1957), as Judy Holliday's husband, but he was back on the wrong side of the law in several films, including the biblical epic, *The Greatest Story Ever Told* (1965), as Barabbas. His last film was, typically, an Italian Mafia movie called *No Way Out* (1972). RB

Tony Curtis

Real name Bernard Schwartz
Born Bronx, New York, 3 June 1925

In *The Last Tycoon* (1976), 51-year old Tony Curtis is seen as Rodriguez, the former swashbuckling star of the screen, now insecure, impotent and whining, afraid to face his public. Curtis, with tongue in the cheek and lump in the throat at the same time, evokes the days when his greasy DA coiff was the height of young men's fashion, and he swept Piper Laurie off on his steed in *The Prince Who Was A Thief* (1951) and *Son Of Ali Baba* (1952).

Tony's background had similarities with those of the delinquent movie dramas of the 50s. The son of an immigrant Jewish tailor, young Bernard Schwartz grew up in a tough neighbourhood where he joined a street gang to survive. His education was minimal, but he did learn a bit of acting at the local settlement house. He continued to act in amateur productions in the navy during the war – he had joined up at seventeen and was wounded at Guam. On his return, he took acting lessons and worked at the Dramatic Workshop in New York, before touring the 'Borscht Circuit' with a stock company. Universal Pictures, who were searching for young talent at that stage, offered him a contract in 1949.

As Anthony Curtis, he was given bit parts in seven movies, three of them westerns, before the studio's publicity machine turned him into a star in preparation for his top billing in the lush Arabian Nights adventure, *The Prince Who Was A Thief*. The new, young heart-throb appeared in all the fan magazines prior to the film's release. He was trained in fencing, riding, speech and deportment at the school in Universal City. The movie was a box-office hit, and Tony began to scent the sweet smell of success. In the same year, he married sweet MGM ingenue Janet Leigh in a much-publicised wedding.

The many films Curtis made between 1951 and 1957, were unpretentious, enjoyable Hollywood staples. Light comedies: *No Room For The Groom* (1952) with Tony as an ex-GI married to Piper Laurie and his in-laws; *So This Is Paris* (1955), as a sailor on leave in the French capital. Sports dramas: Tony as a boxer in *The Flesh And The Fury* (1952) and *The Square Jungle* (1956). In the former, he is quite touching as a deaf-mute, having only to grunt for most of the film. After an operation, he learns to speak like Tony Curtis. In *All American* (1953), the humour is limited to jokes about the length of footballer Tony's hair. With Piper Laurie again in *Johnny Dark* (1954), he is a racing-car designer-driver. War movie: *Beachhead* (1954) had Tony reliving some of his actual experiences against the Japanese. Social drama: *Six Bridges To Cross* (1955) had Tony reliving some of his childhood experiences in the slums as a hoodlum who can't go straight. He also co-starred with his wife in *Houdini* (1953), and in *The Black Shield Of Falmouth* (1954) as a mediaeval English knight.

The latter role caused much hilarity among the critics who quoted the line, 'Yonda lies da castle of my fodda', as an example of Curtis's Bronx accent in whatever part he undertook. But he was soon to prove that he was not just a pretty face with a pretty bad accent. In Alexander MacKendrick's *Sweet Smell Of Success* (1957), Curtis is uncompromisingly loathsome as Sidney Falco, the avaricious, obsequious press agent. His is the whining clarinet to Burt Lancaster's bass bassoon played against the jazzy dazzle of New York by night. All Tony's hard upbringing and experience is there in the role that predates Robert De Niro's in Scorsese's *Mean Streets* by sixteen years.

The following year, Tony received a Best Actor Oscar nomination for Stanley Kramer's *The Defiant Ones* (1958), a chain being the heavily clanking symbol binding racist Curtis to Sidney Poitier as two escaping prisoners. In *Kings Go Forth* (1958), he is blithely unconcerned that Natalie Wood's father was black, unlike his GI buddy Frank Sinatra. Slightly retrogressively, he appeared in loin cloths in two

in Sweet Smell Of Success *(United Artists, 1957)*

sombre, protracted epics, *The Vikings* (1958) and *Spartacus* (1960), upstaged by Kirk Douglas in both. But he wore neither loin cloth, toga, uniform, nor Arab headgear for his greatest role: high-heeled shoes, flapper's frock, a string of pearls, a pretty little hat and a long dark wig was the apparel needed.

Boldly feminine, exuding sisterly warmth, with a high-pitched voice and alluringly made-up eyes, Tony Curtis's performance in Billy Wilder's *Some Like It Hot* (1959) is the best drag portrayal in the cinema, unequalled until Dustin Hoffman's Curtis-inspired *Tootsie* (1982). His stylish comedy offers a triple treat. As his wise-guy self, as a woman, and as a facsimile of Cary Grant to lend class to his seduction of a doubly gullible Marilyn Monroe. By some happy chance, Tony was co-starred with Grant in his next picture, *Operation Petticoat* (1959) in which he does his accomplished, energetic con-

artist act. This was perfected in *The Great Imposter* (1961) in which he played a Navy surgeon, a Trappist monk, a teacher and a prison officer.

In 1962, his 11-year-old marriage to Janet Leigh was dissolved, leaving a great gap in his life. He was soon to leave Universal after thirteen years. The separation and the change led him to seek guidance on a psychiatrist's couch. Meanwhile, darkened slightly, Curtis gave a moving portrayal of Ira Hayes, the Pima Indian, who was one of the marines to raise the flag at Iwo Jima in *The Outsider* (1962). With delicacy, he charted Hayes's tragic descent from war hero to alcoholic.

In 1963, Tony married German actress Christine Kauffmann, twenty years his junior. His career became rather an up and down affair, playing in more than his fair share of inane sex comedies, the most bearable being *Sex And The Single Girl*, (1965) with Tony as a scandal sheet editor wooing psychologist Natalie Wood. Also with Wood, he played The Hero, immaculate in white and displaying a row of glinting teeth in Blake Edwards's spoof of silent screen comedy, *The Great Race* (1965). The reunion with Alexander MacKendrick after ten years, *Don't Make Waves* (1967), a comedy about a swimming pool salesman, produced the sour smell of failure. Also a failure was Tony's marriage, which ended after four years.

As a change in direction from trivia such as *Boeing Boeing* (1965) with Jerry Lewis, and *Not With My Wife You Don't* (1966), Curtis, wearing a false nose, gave a startling performance as the schizophrenic plumber Albert de Salvo, known as *The Boston Strangler* (1968). In 1971, he joined Roger Moore in the short-lived TV series, 'The Persuaders'. Tony's dramatic and comic gifts were generally wasted in the 70s, on such international co-productions as *Casanova And Co.* or *Some Like It Cool* (1977) with Britt Ekland. He also played stooge to a lot of kids in *The Bad News Bears Go To Japan* (1978), and to the mummified 86-year-old Mae West in *Sextette* (1978). In 1977, he published his first novel entitled 'Kid Andrew Cody and Julie Sparrow.' The boy from the Bronx may yet have more surprises in store. RB

in Some Like It Hot *(United Artists, 1959)*

with Natalie Wood in Sex And The Single Girl *(Warner Bros., 1964)* ▷

in Hound Of The Baskervilles (*United Artists, 1959*)

Peter Cushing

Born **Kenley, England, 26 May 1913**

It is difficult for those whose blood freezes at the sound of the name Karloff to feel the same frisson on hearing Peter Cushing, a name more apt for an accountant than the interpreter of Baron Frankenstein and Count Dracula in a multitude of British horror movies since 1957. Cushing managed to overcome this xenophobia and retain his name and his terrifying reputation.

He had been a surveyor's clerk before studying at the Guildhall School of Music and Drama, and made his stage debut in 1935. Four years later, he was playing character parts in Hollywood films such as *The Man In The Iron Mask* (1939), directed by James Whale who made Karloff's *Frankenstein* (1931), and *A Chump At Oxford* with Laurel and Hardy. In 1957, Hammer Film Productions started a lucrative and lurid series of horror pictures with *The Curse Of Frankenstein*, in which Cushing played the Baron. Aside from a few reincarnations of Basil Rathbone vehicles such as Sherlock Holmes and the Sheriff of Nottingham, he remained condemned to walk the night for the rest of his career in films like *The Brides Of Dracula* (1960), *The Evil Of Frankenstein* (1964), *Frankenstein Created Woman* (1967), *Dracula AD 1972* and *Count Dracula And His Vampire Bride* (1978), but he was also one of Darth Vader's evil advisors in *Star Wars* (1977). RB

Doris Day

Real name **Doris von Kappelhoff**
Born **Cincinnati, Ohio, 3 April 1924**

In recent years, Doris Day advertised margarine on American TV, a natural continuation of a film career in which the butter blonde with the honey voice spread creamy, wholesome, goodness. Her sunny smile and freckled face were seen in over a dozen fluffy Warners' musicals between 1948 and 1955, a period in which she was voted by servicemen in Korea as 'the girl we would most like to take a slow boat back to the States with.' From 1959 until her retirement from the big screen in 1968, the girl-next-door became the urban woman, defending her honour and independence in a series of glossy Universal sex-battle comedies.

Unlike Doris Day movies, the Kappelhoff life has not been all sunshine and roses. She was seriously ill as a small girl, and a car accident blighted a promising dance career at fifteen. As a result, she took up singing, taking her name from one of her favourite songs, 'Day By Day.' She sang on the radio and in clubs, before becoming a popular vocalist

with the Bob Crosby and Les Brown bands, and on records. While on the road, at seventeen, she married a 'psychopath musician', as she later called him. Her second marriage five years later, was equally disastrous.

Luck, however, was on her side, when Betty Hutton got pregnant just before the shooting of *Romance On The High Seas* (1948), and director Michael Curtiz suggested Doris Day, who was thus top billed in her first film. The freshness of her singing and personality blew the cobwebs off the stale plots, unimaginative choreography, and heavy direction of *My Dream Is Yours* (1949), *Tea For Two* (1950), *The West Point Story* (1950), *Lullaby Of*

with Kirk Douglas in Young Man With A Horn (*Warner Bros., 1950*)

Broadway (1951) and *April In Paris* (1952). Better were the two small town idylls co-starring Gordon MacRae, *On Moonlight Bay* (1951) and *By The Light Of The Silvery Moon* (1953). Day also handled a few dramatic roles with ease; as trumpeter Kirk Douglas's long-suffering girlfriend in *Young Man With A Horn* (1950), as Ginger Rogers's sister in *Storm Warning* (1951), about a Ku Klux Klan murder, and in *The Winning Team* (1952), a lugubrious baseball biopic, as Ronald Reagan's wife, laying on her charm thickly to compensate for his lack of it.

In 1951, Doris married Marty Melcher, former talent scout and road manager of the Andrews Sisters. They formed a joint company in 1952, which produced most of her films. The following year, she gave one of her gutsiest performances as the tomboyish *Calamity Jane* (1953) opposite Howard Keel, singing the Oscar-winning and chart-topping song, 'Secret Love', touchingly. Looking more glamorous than ever before, Doris sang over a dozen ballads as torch singer Ruth Etting in *Love Me Or Leave Me* (1955), her first film at MGM. Back at Warners, she appeared in one of her liveliest musicals, *The Pajama Game* (1957), as the head of the Sleeptite factory's workers' grievance committee who falls in love with the foreman.

After bringing down a plane singlehandedly in *Julie* (1956), and interrupting the action in Alfred Hitchcock's *The Man Who Knew Too Much* (1956) by singing her biggest hit, 'Que Sera, Sera', she joined Universal to star opposite Rock Hudson in *Pillow Talk* (1959). This highly successful combination and formula was repeated in *Lover Come Back* (1962) and *Send Me No Flowers* (1964), with Cary Grant in *That Touch Of Mink* (1962) and with James Garner in *Move Over Darling* (1963) and *The Thrill Of It All* (1963). In them, according to feminist critics Jane Clarke and Diana Simmonds, Day

'confronts the male and forces him to modify his attitudes and behaviour. Moreover, saying no to manipulative sexual situations is not the same as clinging to one's virginity'. With characteristic wit Groucho Marx put it another way: 'I've been around so long, I can remember Doris Day before she was a virgin,' he said.

Doris was one of the top ten box-office stars, male and female, in the USA throughout the 60s. She was also one of the highest paid. However, in her last films, she began to show her age without adjusting to more suitable roles. It seems a pity that she did not have the courage to accept Mike Nichols's offer to play Mrs Robinson in *The Graduate* (1967) – a plum role that eventually went to Anne Bancroft. When her husband died in 1968, it was revealed that he had squandered and embezzled most of her life's earnings of $20 million, leaving her broke. After recovering from an understandable nervous breakdown, she hosted 'The Doris Day Show' on TV for four years, a series Melcher had contracted for her to do without her knowledge. In 1974, she was awarded $22 million in damages from the lawyer who had helped Melcher in the disastrous mismanagement of her business. 'Que sera, sera. What will be will be.' RB

in 1955

James Dean

Real name James Byron Dean
Born Marion, Indiana, 8 February 1931
Died 1955

In 1978, a film called *September 20, 1955* was released. For those in the know, the title was self-explanatory. It was the date on which James Dean met his death while driving his silver Porsche to Salinas to participate in their autumn racing car event. It happened at 5.58 pm at the intersection of Highway 41 and Route 466. A car in front had refused to let Dean, who was travelling at 115 miles an hour, overtake it. The young actor was found with his neck broken, and his mechanic Ralph Weutherich was left a cripple. Not since the death of Valentino had there been such collective hysteria. As Phillipe Labro, the French director, wrote, 'Everybody claimed him: the homosexuals and the beatniks, the intellectuals and the truckdrivers, old ladies and young girls of 14, children from the country and those of the city, the thinkers in New York and the sunlovers of California, he belonged to everybody; that is to say he belonged to nobody.'

The James Dean myth is still as potent today. There are fan clubs all over the world. A newsletter is put out called 'Jimmy's Memories'. There exists a James Dean Memorial Foundation, and there is a bust of Dean in the University of Princeton's Hall of Fame, as well as one in the place of honour in the hall of Fairmount High where he went to school. In 1957, Robert Altman co-directed *The James Dean Story* which contained stills, home-movies and interviews, and in 1982, Altman directed *Come Back To The Five And Dime, Jimmy Dean, Jimmy Dean*. In *Badlands* (1974), Martin Sheen's actions and posture are directly influenced by Dean. There is even a tale that Dean was so horribly disfigured in the accident, that he has been in hiding under another name for three decades. This fame, more in the realms of myth and legend is, although fanned by Warner Bros. publicists, nevertheless genuine. What is truly remarkable is that it rests on only three movies, all made in 1955, the year of his death at the age of 24.

This extraordinary icon of late 20th-century youth was born in a small town in Indiana, the son of a dental technician. His mother had a passion for poetry and gave him Byron as a second name. When he was eight, his beloved mother died of lung cancer and he was sent to stay with his aunt and uncle on a farm. The myopic boy (his eyes always had a screwed-up look), entered Fairmount High and excelled in sports. At the same time, he became interested in art and literature, learned to play the

in Rebel Without A Cause *(Warner Bros., 1955)*

clarinet and bongos, did Yoga and walked around the conservative town in blue jeans and leather jacket. After graduating from high school, he went to California. In order to buy a new Triumph, he did some TV commercials. He enrolled at UCLA and joined James Whitmore's drama group, attempting

in Giant *(Warner Bros., 1956)*

Malcolm in 'Macbeth' of which the local paper remarked, 'The young man who portrays Malcolm has no stature and would make a very poor king.' Through the acquaintance of a journalist, Bill Bast, and others in the film world, he managed to get himself bit parts in three movies. In Samuel Fuller's *Fixed Bayonets* (1951) he is seen as a frightened soldier; in the Dean Martin-Jerry Lewis comedy, *Sailor Beware* (1951), he is a boxer's second, and in *Has Anybody Seen My Gal?* (1952), he enters a drugstore and asks for an ice-cream.

In 1952, Dean went to New York where he was able to watch some classes at the Actors' Studio, but after an audition he felt like 'a rabbit being vivisected.' He then got parts in some TV dramas and a play called 'See The Jaguar' which ran for six performances. But he was noticed by producer Billy Rose who engaged him for the role of the pederastic Arab boy in Gide's 'The Immoralist'. This led to a screen test at Warner Bros. and a seven-year contract. It was Elia Kazan who asked for him to play Caleb Trask in *East Of Eden* (1955). 'Because he was uneasy, his behaviour was sometimes odd and capricious,' Kazan remembered. 'Working with Jimmy was like working with a very gifted animal. I don't say that in any way to disparage him. It was essential to approach him indirectly and to await the result. One never knew what would happen. My only hope was to strike a chord and it was only afterwards that I saw if I'd succeeded.' Jimmy was perfect as the complex and disturbed adolescent,

with his animated shoulders, tortured postures, extravagance of gesture, studied hesitancy, untamed animal sensitivity. It was the beginning of an era of stars with whom the young could really identify. In his films, a young person's anguish is at the centre, and adults are seen through his eyes.

The desperate father-son relationship, and the need to be loved and understood as an individual, is also at the core of Nicholas Ray's inappropriately named *Rebel Without A Cause* (1955), the film which will forever by synonymous with its star. It is the disenchanted cry of youth, alienated from the adult world. In his last role as Jett Rink in George Stevens's *Giant* (1956), Jimmy is again the rebel and outsider, but in the second half, middle-aged and rich, in grey wig and moustache, he is far too youthful in gesture and voice to be convincing. Perhaps, as someone suggested, he might have become just another actor had he lived. His next film was to have been *Somebody Up There Likes Me* with Pier Angeli, the girl he had wanted to marry. On the day of her marriage to Vic Damone, he waited in his car outside the church for the couple to emerge and then sped along the highway. Dean had wanted to experiment with everything. There had been drugs, and both men and women in his life. It is difficult not to interpret his three films today as prologues to his early death. RB

with Raymond Massey (right) in East Of Eden *(Warner Bros., 1955)*

Sandra Dee

Real name Alexandra Zuck
Born Bayonne, New Jersey, 23 April 1942

In the nostalgic musical *Grease* (1978), about growing up in a fantasized 50s, there is an appropriately evocative song called, 'Look At Me, I'm Sandra Dee.' Pert, petite, blonde Sandra Dee was the sweetheart of the teen set from the late-50s to the mid-60s, and her films now provide instant nostalgia and/or nausea, depending on your taste.

In her early teens, Sandra was a model and TV actress, before making her film debut as the youngest of four sisters living in New Zealand during World War II in MGM's *Until They Sail* (1957). This was followed by the title role in Vincente Minnelli's *The Reluctant Debutante* (1958), in which Miss Dee played Rex Harrison and Kay Kendall's daughter(!). In the next few films, she was to be awash in soap opera; as Teresa Wright's illegitimate daughter in *The Restless Years* (1958), and as Lana Turner's daughter in the remake of *Imitation Of Life* (1959) and *A Portrait In Black* (1960), both

glossy Ross Hunter productions for Universal.

Max Steiner's insistent theme from *A Summer Place* (1959), emanated from Juke-boxes everywhere, and Dee and her blonde male equivalent, Troy Donahue, made love to its strains on the Maine coast, at the start of the 'sexually permissive' era. After her marriage to pop idol Bobby Darin in 1960, the favourite couple of the fan magazines appeared together in *Come September* (1961) representing the younger generation vs Rock Hudson and Gina Lollobrigida as the older; and as newly-weds in *If A Man Answers* (1962), and *That Funny Feeling* (1965), the latter barely amusing.

Sandra made a poor replacement for Debbie Reynolds in *Tammy Tell Me True* (1961) and *Tammy And The Doctor* (1963); played the daughter of the American ambassador in love with the Russian ambassador's son in Peter Ustinov's *Romanoff And Juliet* (1961), and James Stewart's rebellious daughter in *Take Her, She's Mine* (1962). In fact, she played everybody's daughter. Her role as Bobby Darin's wife ended in 1967, and fewer films came her way. There is not much work these days for a 42-year-old teenage star. RB

John Derek

Real name Derek Harris
Born Hollywood, 12 August 1926

Anyone who has been married to both Ursula Andress and Bo Derek, must have something. Now bearded and greying, John Derek is still attractive to women. In the 50s, he was the dashingly handsome young hero of adventure films, rated by his teenage female fans as a 10 on the scale of male beauty. He was Robin Hood in *Rogues Of Sherwood Forest* (1950), disguised as the Count of Monte Cristo in *Mask Of The Avenger* (1951), rescued a sheik's daughter in *The Adventures Of Hajjii Baba* (1954), and assisted the Persian poet *Omar Khayyam* (1967) to overcome his enemies. Derek was also a football idol who put education first in *Saturday's Hero* (1951), and a boxing priest in *The Leather Saint* (1956) who put his opponents to sleep with his Sunday punch quicker than his sermons.

John Derek's father was a writer and his mother an actress. They helped him to get a contract with David O. Selznick when he was seventeen, but he had only two walk-on parts before being called up for war service. On his return, he made an impact as the 'pretty boy' from the slums on trial for murder in Nicholas Ray's *Knock On Any Door* (1949). Few good roles followed, apart from complex cowboys in *The Outcast* (1954), and as James Cagney's riding companion in *Run For Cover* (1955). After cross-

ing the wilderness as Joshua in Cecil B. DeMille's *The Ten Commandments* (1956) and fighting to establish the State of Israel in *Exodus* (1960), he decided with commendable ambition to produce, direct, and photograph his own films.

He co-produced and appeared with his then wife Ursula Andress in a B thriller, *Nightmare In The Sun* (1965), and directed her in *Once Before I Die* (1966),

as the only woman among a group of American soldiers fighting Japs in the Phillipines. In the mid 70s, the marriage collapsed because of his wife's affair with Jean Paul Belmondo. Under Derek's eagle eye, Bo Derek blossomed opposite Dudley Moore in *Ten* (1979), and he himself directed his young second wife in *Tarzan Of The Apes* (1982) in which she dominated as Jane. RB

in Run For Cover (Paramount, 1955)

Angie Dickinson

Real name Angeline Brown
Born Kulm, North Dakota,
30 September 1931

Howard Hawks once expressed in an interview that he liked women who looked young but seemed older. Like 'Feathers' in his *Rio Bravo* (1959) as played by Angie Dickinson. The sexual interplay between her and John Wayne is such that nobody questions the twenty-eight year difference in their ages. Sensual, direct and active and yet discreet, feminine and unaggressive, Angie fits well into Hawks's world of male cameraderie. In fact, she is a woman among men.

She is virtually the only woman in the buddy-buddy heist movie, *Oceans II* (1960), the queen in the Sinatra 'rat pack'. Independent and caring, Dickinson has been cast as a nurse four times; hopelessly in love with doctor Richard Burton in *The Bramble Bush* (1960), struggling as a missionary nurse in the Belgian Congo in *The Sins Of Rachel Cade* (1961), as a sexy midwife being lusted after by the men of an Italian village in *Jessica* (1962), and

helping Gregory Peck as *Captain Newman MD* (1963) in a wartime hospital.

Angie had an all-American upbringing. School in a small town, college at Glendale, winner of a beauty contest and marriage to college football hero Gene Dickinson. She entered movies with a bit in the Doris Day musical *Lucky Me* (1954), and after a few small parts, was given the role in *Rio Bravo*. From time to time, she was offered a chance to show her stuff as in two crime thrillers, Don Siegel's *The Killers* (1964) and John Boorman's *Point Blank* (1967). In contrast to her foul play in these films, she is touching as sheriff Marlon Brando's wife in *The Chase* (1966).

TV benefited from her presence in the 'Police Woman' series in the mid-70s, and so did her second husband, composer Burt Bacharach. She was back on the big screen in 1979 with *Klondike Fever*, and separated from her husband. She is now very close to Brian De Palma, the director of the voyeuristic *Dressed To Kill* (1980), in which Angie is stabbed in an elevator, á là Hitchcock. In this movie, which offended feminists everywhere, she showed that she has matured into a cool, beautiful and accomplished version of her 50s self. RB

Troy Donahue

Real name **Merle Johnson Jr**
Born **New York City, 27 January 1936**

'If Troy Donahue could become a star, then I could become a star,' sings a character in the Broadway musical 'A Chorus Line'. It is a put-down of the well-built, blond, blue-eyed juvenile of the 60s, very popular with young audiences during the period of 'generation gap' movies. Troy could aptly be described as a male Sandra Dee.

He studied journalism at Columbia University, but acting took up most of his time. After appearing in stock, his beach-boy's good looks got him into the TV series 'Surfside 6' and 'Hawaiian Eye'. In the movies, he started out as part of Universal's stable of young talent, making his screen debut in *Man Afraid* (1957) as a teenage burglar who gets killed in the first few minutes of the movie. In *This Happy Feeling* (1958), he took off a 'method' actor, but spent most of his small part staring at a wounded seagull and willing it to fly; and in *Monster On The Campus* (1958), he was one of the students terrified by a giant fish. Not much more edifying were *Voice In The Mirror* (1958), a drama about alcoholism, *Summer Love* (1958), rock 'n roll rubbish, and *Wild Heritage* (1958), a family western.

In Douglas Sirk's melodrama *Imitation Of Life* (1959), Troy had a small but significant role as Susan Kohner's boyfriend who rejects her when he finds out she has black blood. But it was Warner Bros. that shot him into mini-star status in four soap-operas directed by Delmer Daves: *A Summer Place* (1959), as Sandra Dee's teenage lover on a Maine beach; *Parrish* (1961), as a young tobacco grower in Connecticut having trouble with three seductive girls (and with his lines); *Susan Slade* (1961), as a shy horse doctor who marries Connie Stevens who is pregnant by another man; and *Rome*

Adventure (1962), in which Suzanne Pleshette opts for the American Troy over the Latin charms of Rossano Brazzi.

Donahue and Pleshette were married in 1964 – a union which lasted for little over a year. They co-starred in Raoul Walsh's cavalrymen vs Injuns western, *A Distant Trumpet* (1964), with Troy as an expressionless lieutenant defending a fort. His brief time in the limelight was coming to an end with *My Blood Runs Cold* (1965), in which he believes he's in love with a girl from a past life, and *Come Spy With Me* (1967), in which he played a secret agent in the Caribbean. After four years away from the screen, he returned with his clean-cut looks dirtied up as the Charles Manson-like figure in *Sweet Savior* (1971), a nasty exploitation movie. Things have changed greatly in the film business when Troy Donahue knifes people during an orgy. In *The Godfather Part II*, he appeared as a weak WASP intrusion into the Family, a role which eloquently looked back to his obsolete image. RB

in On The Double *(Paramount, 1961)*

Diana Dors

Real name **Diana Fluck**
Born **Swindon, England, 23 October 1931**
Died **1984**

'There was a brand new star being launched in America called Marilyn Monroe. And the press, in their usual fashion, had retaliated with me as the British answer. How many times, I reflected with amusement, had I been tagged as the British answer to someone or other,' wrote Diana Dors in her lively autobiography 'Swingin' Dors'. Not long after Diana had entered films at the age of 15, she was dubbed 'Britain's answer to Betty Grable' and 'The girl who looks like being a baby Lana Turner in British films.' But the big, brassy, buxom blonde managed to stay English, very much her own woman, and to survive passing fashion to remain a popular personality.

Diana was star-struck from a very early age, and changed her name from Fluck to Dors (her grandmother's maiden name) as soon as she started to have serious show business ambitions. Modelling herself on Betty Grable, she entered a beauty contest at 13, lying about her age and winning third prize. After a year at the London Academy Of Music and Dramatic Art, she signed a contract with the Rank

Organisation. The best of her early roles was as Charlotte, the sluttish maid in David Lean's version of *Oliver Twist* (1948).

The Rank Organisation set up a school to train young artists under contract to them. They called it the Rank Charm School. Diana loathed it and entertained her fellow pupils with a song:

'I signed a contract with my friend J. Arthur Rank
My dressing room was lousy and the films all stank.
He handled his films like flour, brother,
With corn in one hand and the sack in the other.'

Among the 'films that stank', were a British western called *Diamond City* (1949), *Dance Hall* (1950), and *Lady Godiva Rides Again* (1951) with Diana Dors in the much publicised title role. More interesting parts came later, giving her a chance to be considered a serious actress. Without make-up, she played a good-time girl in prison in *The Weak And The Wicked* (1954), and a convicted murderess in the death cell in *Yield To The Night* (1956); she also displayed a pleasing comic talent in *An Alligator Named Daisy* (1955) and *A Kid For Two Farthings* (1955).

In 1951, Diana married Dennis Hamilton. It was a difficult marriage due to his drinking, bursts of temper, jealousy of Diana's success, and petty larceny. In fact, he had been convicted for theft and smuggling offences. Nonetheless, the marriage lasted over six tempestuous years. Always with an eye on publicity, Diana caused a sensation with her mink bikini at the Venice Film Festival in 1955, posed everywhere during the Cannes Festival, and made a splash at a Hollywood party when she and some of her guests were pushed into a pool. A Hollywood paper commented, 'Go Home, Diana and take Mr Dors with you.' The films she made in Hollywood, *The Unholy Wife* (1957) with Rod Steiger, and *I Married A Woman* (1958) with comedian George Gobel, were far from successes.

With her second marriage to comedian Dickie Dawson and the raising of children, Diana began to lead a calmer existence. As weight and age crept up, she played more character roles on stage and TV, making only rare film appearances, her best being as the huge, sex-hungry woman in Jerzy Skolimowski's *Deep End* (1970). She was a highly entertaining guest on TV chat shows, including her own. Her third marriage was to actor Alan Lake who once commented 'If they had named the 'Titanic' Diana Dors, it would never have sunk.' Alas, after a courageous and much publicised fight against cancer, the unsinkable and gifted Miss Dors succumbed to the illness, in 1984. RB

with Geoffrey Keen in Yield To The Night *(Associated British, 1956)*

Kirk Douglas

Real name Issur Danielovitch Demsky
Born Amsterdam, New York,
9 December 1916

Lust For Life (1956) could quite easily have been the title of Kirk Douglas's autobiography instead of Vincente Minnelli's biopic of the painter Vincent Van Gogh, in which the actor's physical likeness to the artist was hallucinatory. Kirk Douglas has stuck out his prominent canyon-cleft chin with passionate intensity for some three decades, hardly letting up for a moment and refusing to grow old gracefully. It was while being hit on that famous chin as the ruthless boxer Midge Kelly in Mark Robson's *Champion* (1949), that he first became a dynamic force in American cinema.

As befits the man who played Midge Kelly, Van Gogh and the rebel slave *Spartacus* (1960), the young Issur, son of poor Jewish-Russian immigrants, had to struggle to make a name for himself. Working as a waiter, bell-boy and even professional wrestler, he paid for his education at St Lawrence University and then at the American Academy of Dramatic Arts. After a few small parts on Broadway, he joined the Navy for service during the war. In 1945, he returned to Broadway and radio acting, but was soon signed up by Hal Wallis for pictures.

Kirk made an impressive debut as Barbara Stanwyck's weak and bitter husband in *The Strange Love Of Martha Ivers* (1946), and already revealed his

neurotic strain as the Orestes character in the film version of Eugene O'Neill's *Mourning Becomes Electra* (1947), and as the sadistically smiling gangster standing between Robert Mitchum and freedom in Jacques Tourneur's *film noir Out Of The Past* (1947). As the boxer in *Champion* who alienates his friends and family, deceives women and doublecrosses the manager who helped him get to the top, Douglas nonetheless managed to elicit a certain amount of sympathy for the character.

However, there are few more unscrupulous characters in cinema than the sensation-seeking newspaperman, Chuck Tatum, in Billy Wilder's sardonic *Ace In The Hole* (1951). Douglas, needing a scoop, delays the rescue of a man trapped in a cave by a rock fall in order to build up the story. The man dies. Douglas brilliantly expresses his disdain for everyone in the hick town and for the world in general. In *Detective Story* (1951), he played a detective whose own ethics become twisted because of his constant dealings with criminals. At the beginning of Minnelli's *The Bad And The Beautiful* (1953), originally titled 'Tribute To A Bad Man', a director, actress and writer tell, in flashback, their reasons for hating film producer Jonathan Shields. As Shields, Douglas gives one of his most powerful portraits of an egocentric heel driven by overwhelming ambition. Scenes from the film are shown in the semi-sequel, *Two Weeks In Another Town* (1962), in which the star played a has-been actor determined to make a come-back.

After working on *The Bad And The Beautiful* together, Minnelli and Douglas wanted to make *Lust For Life*. For the part of Van Gogh, Kirk grew a beard, and had his hair reddened, as well as hiring a French artist to teach him to paint crows. His wife Anne, in an article for 'The Saturday Evening Post', wrote, 'Kirk always brings his roles home with him . . . He came home in that red beard of Van Gogh's, wearing those big boots, stomping around the house – it was frightening.' Kirk later explained his attraction for the role. 'Aside from his burning genius, the thing that attracted me to Van Gogh was his loneliness. Anyone who has experienced loneliness can understand his story. Van Gogh's tragedy was that of a man who needed other people so badly that he couldn't admit it even to himself.' A revealing statement that seems to say as much about Douglas as about Van Gogh. His portrayal won him the New York Film Critics' Circle Award, the Foreign Press Award and a Best Actor Oscar nomination.

The western has given this rugged, individualistic performer freedom to express his energy, demonstrated in films such as Howard Hawks's *The Big Sky* (1952), in which he has a finger amputated, and *The Indian Fighter* (1955). In *Man Without A Star* (1955), he rides free, avoiding the fences that are

beginning to enclose the land until he gets caught in barbed wire, and he is 'the last cowboy' in *Lonely Are The Brave* (1962), being hunted portentously over the highways by helicopters and trucks. In 1955, Douglas ensured his independence by setting up Bryna Productions and later Joel Productions, for whom he was able to direct and star in the off-beat western *Posse* (1975).

Kirk cast himself as a bearded, peg-legged pirate in his first film as director *Scalawag* (1973), the sort of rollicking comedy role he obviously enjoys playing, as if to compensate for his earnestness elsewhere. He played extravagant, likeable rogues in *20,000 Leagues Under The Sea* (1954), as the harpooner; the cocky inmate of an Arizona prison in the 1870s in Joseph Mankiewicz's *There Was A Crooked Man . . .* (1970); 'Doc' Holliday in *Gunfight At The OK Corral* (1957), and as Dick Dudgeon, *The Devil's Disciple* (1959). His co-star in the last two was Kirk's old friend Burt Lancaster. They also appeared together in the prison drama *I Walk Alone* (1948), and John Frankenheimer's *Seven Days In May* (1964) about a military takeover of the US Government. Frankenheimer once commented that Kirk 'wanted to be Burt Lancaster all his life.'

Douglas is less interesting in the straightforward war heroics of *In Harm's Way* (1965), *The Heroes*

in The Vikings *(United Artists, 1958)*

Of Telemark (1965), *Cast A Giant Shadow* (1966), as Colonel Mickey Marcus who built Israel's army, and as General Patton in *Is Paris Burning?* (1966), worlds away from his idealistic Colonel Dax in Stanley Kubrick's bitterly ironic and anti-militaristic *Paths Of Glory* (1957). As the defence for three soldiers on an unjust court martial charge, Douglas shows his mastery of delivering lines that express bubbling anger and sarcasm. He could easily go over the top on occasions, such as his self-pitying theatricality in Elia Kazan's *The Arrangement* (1969), but was also able to play intellectual and reserved characters like Jeanne Crain's husband in Mankiewicz's *A Letter To Three Wives* (1949) who only wants to listen to his Brahms record but has a radio soap opera forced on him, and the gentle 'gentleman caller' in *The Glass Menagerie* (1950). He is admirably restrained as the architect who has an affair with his married neighbour, Kim Novak, in *Strangers When We Meet* (1960). Recently, he brought maturity to the juvenile psychokinetic trash of Brian De Palma's *The Fury* (1978) as the father looking for his lost son. Kirk's own son, Michael Douglas is a successful TV and film actor, as well as a producer and director. RB

with Mara Corday in Man Without A Star *(Universal, 1955)*

in Sign Of The Gladiator (American International, 1958)

Anita Ekberg

Born **Malmo, Sweden, 29 September 1931**

'The immaturity of the American Male – this breast fetish,' the director Frank Tashlin once commented in an interview. 'There's nothing more hysterical to me than big-breasted women – like walking leaning towers.' Anita Ekberg was a beautiful, tall, voluptuous leaning tower, referred to punningly in the title of Tashlin's *Hollywood Or Bust* (1956). Fellini, demonstrating the 'immaturity' of the Italian Male, placed Ekberg in a key position in his frieze of decadent modern Rome in *La Dolce Vita* (1960), and in Fellini's 'The Temptation of Dr Antonio' episode from *Boccaccio '70* (1962), she is the sex object on a poster, brought to life to envelop a little puritanical doctor.

As her acting ability was limited, Tashlin and Fellini had found a way of using the former Miss Sweden of 1951 in erotic satire. Anita came to the USA for the Miss Universe contest and stayed to appear in a number of Hollywood films. After her three-year marriage to actor Anthony Steel ended in 1959, she continued her career mostly in Italy. She was a delicious stooge to Jerry Lewis in *Artists And Models* (1955) and *Hollywood Or Bust*, and to Bob Hope in *Paris Holiday* (1958) and *Call Me Bwana* (1963), but had a chance to actually act in King Vidor's *War And Peace* (1956), as Henry Fonda's unfaithful wife. In latter years, she put on a great deal of weight to become the heaviest sex object around. RB

Tom Ewell

Real name **Yewell Tompkins**
Born **Owensboro, Kentucky, 29 April 1909**

On Broadway in 1960, Tom Ewell appeared in 'The Thurber Carnival', a review based on the drawings and stories of the American humourist, James Thurber. With his ski nose and doleful dog's eyes, Ewell is a Thurber cartoon come to life, the ordinary man confronted with big-breasted blondes.

Ewell started acting while attending the University of Wisconsin. He worked as a salesman at Macy's, before getting his first break on Broadway in 1934, but did not make his screen debut until 1949, when he played Judy Holliday's husband in *Adam's Rib*. He is most remembered as the grass-widower in Billy Wilder's *The Seven Year Itch* (1955), saved from adultery by Marilyn Monroe. After Monroe, it was Jayne Mansfield and Sheree North in *The Girl Can't Help It* (1956) and *The Lieutenant Wore Skirts* (1956), respectively, who gained his attention. Also at Fox, he drank whiskey throughout *Tender Is The Night* (1962) and sang to a cow in *State Fair* (1962). Ewell now appears mostly on TV where he is 'Doc' in 'The Best Of The West'. RB

José Ferrer

Real name **José Vincente Ferrer de Otero y Cintron**
Born **Santurce, Puerto Rico, 8 January 1912**

When Betty Comden and Adolph Green wrote the role of Jeffrey Cordova (played in the end by Jack Buchanan), the artsy director and ham actor for *The Band Wagon* (1953), they were thinking of José Ferrer. But Ferrer is intellectual rather than artsy, flamboyant rather than hammy. In fact, in the 40s on stage and the 50s on screen, he revealed an exceptional versatility. On stage, he was a brilliant Iago to Paul Robeson's Othello in 1942, as well as romping around as 'Charly's Aunt'. On screen, he walked on his knees as Toulouse-Lautrec in John Huston's *Moulin Rouge* (1953), as well as dancing and singing as Sigmund Romberg in Stanley Donen's *Deep In My Heart* (1954). In his fourth film appearance, he won a merited Oscar for his dynamic, sonorous, comic and moving *Cyrano De Bergerac* (1950), a role he repeated in Abel Gance's *Cyrano And D'Artagnan* (1964).

The Puerto Rican born actor-director came to the USA as a child. He studied architecture at Princeton, but gave it up to go on the stage. On Broadway since 1935, he established himself as a leading light for over a decade, sometimes performing with his first wife Uta Hagen. The Dauphin in *Joan Of Arc* (1948) was his first film role, and he followed it with Dr Korvo, the crazy hypnotist in Preminger's *Whirlpool* (1950). He directed seven so-so films between 1955 and 1962, starring in five of them, including *The Shrike* (1955), *The Great Man* (1956),

in Whirlpool (20th Century-Fox, 1950)

Cockleshell Heroes (1956) and, as the persecuted French army officer Dreyfus, *I Accuse* (1957).

'Mr and Mrs,' sang Ferrer and his third wife Rosemary Clooney in *Deep In My Heart*. That song ended in the 60s – a period when he was generally playing evil foreigners such as the Mahdi in *Lawrence Of Arabia* (1962), Herod in *The Greatest Story Ever Told* (1965), and the crew-cut anti-semite in *Ship Of Fools* (1965). More recently, he was the sinister doctor in Billy Wilder's *Fedora* (1978) and Athos in *The Fifth Musketeer* (1979), a reminder of his greatest role, Cyrano. RB

Mel Ferrer

Real name **Melchior Gaston Ferrer**
Born **Elberon, New Jersey, 25 August 1917**

There is much about Mel Ferrer that is like Robert Cohn, the elusive Hemingway character he played in *The Sun Also Rises* (1957). Like Cohn, he is a cosmopolitan, linguist and Hispanophile. He seems a melancholy wanderer, moving from country to country, film to film, producing, directing, acting. A difficult man to pin down.

The son of a Cuban-born surgeon, Mel had to support himself after he dropped out of Princeton. He edited a newspaper, wrote a children's book, acted in summer stock, danced in the chorus of Broadway musicals and was a disc jockey. In 1940, he was struck down by polio, but resumed his varied career soon afterwards. Besides acting, he directed a

in 1960

film for Columbia and assisted John Ford on *The Fugitive* (1947). During this time, he had gone through two marriages.

Mel Ferrer made his screen debut in 1949. His acting was often wooden and soporific, but could be soulful, intelligent and even witty. His best moments have been as the swashbuckling villain in *Scaramouche* (1952); the rival for Marlene Dietrich's affections in Fritz Lang's western *Rancho Notorious* (1952); the crippled puppeteer in *Lili* (1953); one of the three beaux from whom Ingrid Bergman has to choose in Jean Renoir's *Elena Et Les Hommes* (1956), and a sensitive Prince Andrei to Audrey Hepburn's beautiful Natasha in King Vidor's *War And Peace* (1956).

His marriage to Audrey Hepburn took place after they had co-starred on Broadway in 'Ondine' in 1954. After their divorce in 1968, Ferrer suffered a heart attack, but returned to appear in a weird mixture of Spanish, French, Italian and German productions. RB

in The Seven Year Itch (20th Century-Fox, 1955)

Ava Gardner

Born Smithfield, North Carolina, 24 January 1922

Some bright studio publicist in the 50s came up with the slogan of 'The World's Most Exciting Animal' to describe Ava Gardner. Absurd, maybe, but who other than this dark-haired, deep-voiced beauty with the distinctive cleft chin and panther-like sexuality could lay claim to as much? In *The Barefoot Contessa* (1954), as the girl from the Madrid slums who has become a film star and countess, she kicks off her shoes and dances with gypsies. There is something of the gypsy and adventuress about her, expressing an enjoyment of life no matter what the role. The sort of woman who will kick off her shoes and begin to dance at any moment and in any situation. This

devil-may-care attitude pervades both her on- and off-screen personality.

One of six children of a poor farmer, Ava has told of an unhappy and deprived childhood. At 18, set to become a secretary, she visited her married sister in New York. Her brother-in-law, a photographer, took some pictures of her and sent them to MGM's casting department. Not long afterwards, she was given a screen test in New York and offered a seven-year contract. On arrival in Hollywood in 1940, Ava found that she was one of many starlets hired by MGM to be groomed for possible stardom. They were given lessons in drama, diction, make-up and fashion, and posed for publicity pictures long before they appeared in a film. One would have to look very hard to find Ava Gardner in her first movies, *We Were Dancing* (1942), *Hitler's Madman* (1943), *Du Barry Was A Lady* (1943) and *Music For Millions* (1944). However, in 1942, her name became known because of her rather unlikely marriage to America's most popular star, the diminutive Mickey Rooney. It was said that a press agent went along on the honeymoon, and the marriage lasted only 17 months. A couple of years later, Ava married bandleader Artie Shaw. He tried to educate her in everything, from what to say to what to read. The marriage lasted seven months.

After appearing as George Raft's moll in *Whistle Stop* (1946), the 24-year-old beauty made the breakthrough from starlet to star in Robert Siodmak's neon-lit thriller, based on Hemingway, *The Killers* (1946), in which she set up sparks with Burt Lancaster (in his screen debut). She caught the eye as the second female lead in *The Hucksters* (1947), with Deborah Kerr and Clark Gable, and, appropriately, as the love goddess in the otherwise poor *One Touch Of Venus* (1948). Her Venus-like allure cast her in *Pandora And The Flying Dutchman* (1951) as a girl who resembles the one for whom the Flying Dutchman (James Mason) is condemned to sail the

seas forever. But she was far happier away from mythological beauties, finding satisfaction in the torrid climes and more down-to-earth roles of Siodmak's *The Great Sinner* (1949) about gambling fever, co-starring Gregory Peck, and a melodrama set in New Orleans with Robert Mitchum called *My Forbidden Past* (1951).

Many vocalists were mooted for the part of the mulatto Julie Laverne in MGM's lavish Technicolor remake of *Showboat* (1951), but producer Arthur Freed insisted on Gardner. She was screen-tested, dubbing to a Lena Horne recording. There was a dispute as to whether or not to allow her to do her own singing. The studio was against it, but the star got her way. However, after the first screening, they removed her voice and substituted that of Annette Warren. 'I really tried in *Show Boat*, but that was MGM crap,' she told Rex Reed. 'I wanted to sing those songs – hell, I've still got a Southern accent – and I really thought Julie should sound a little like a Negro since she's supposed to have Negro blood. Christ, those songs like 'Bill' shouldn't sound like opera. So what did they say? 'Ava, baby, you can't sing, you'll hit the wrong keys, you're up against real pros in this film, so don't make a fool of yourself' Pros!' Despite these undermining disputes, Ava gave an extremely moving performance.

While still battling with MGM, she married Frank Sinatra in 1951, during a low point in his career. He accompanied her to Kenya for the filming of John Ford's *Mogambo* (1953), during which they continually fought and made up. At one stage, Ava threw away a mink coat Sinatra had bought for her as a peace offering. On-screen, as the good-time showgirl, she finally won Clark Gable over an insipid Grace Kelly, and was nominated for a Best Actress Oscar for the role. Other films set her in exotic locales. She appeared the ideal Hemingway heroine in *The Snows Of Kilimanjaro* (1952) with Gregory Peck, and as the playgirl Lady Brett Ashley in *The Sun Also Rises* (1957) with Tyrone Power, filmed in Paris and Spain. Again, in Europe, she was Joseph Mankiewicz's *The Barefoot Contessa*, and went to India for her most demanding role as an Anglo-Indian fighting for her identity in George Cukor's *Bhowani Junction* (1956).

After her stormy marriage with Sinatra ended in 1957, Ava left Hollywood to take up residence in Madrid where she led a 'jet set' existence, making occasional movies. She was one of the last people on earth, with Gregory Peck and an assorted company

with Robert Sterling in Show Boat *(MGM, 1951)*

after a nuclear bomb in *On The Beach* (1959), and relieved the monotony of *55 Days At Peking* (1963) by sporting an array of Orry-Kelly gowns. Before leaving Hollywood, MGM had offered her the role (later taken by Elizabeth Taylor) of Maggie in Tennessee Williams's *Cat On A Hot Tin Roof* (1958). However, a few years later, she did get a chance to enter Tennessee Williams country in John Huston's *The Night Of The Iguana* (1964), as the owner of a run-down Mexican hotel. There, she was at her earthy best, enjoying the satisfaction of young beach boys and a drink or two. It was the sort of role she always revelled in, instead of merely being asked to look beautiful, as with Empress Elizabeth in *Mayerling* (1968), and Lili Langtry in *The Life And Times Of Judge Roy Bean* (1972).

Now of 'a certain age' and putting on weight, Miss Gardner lives in London and makes sporadic appearances in non-masterpieces. She was well cast as Luxury in the disastrous USA-USSR production of *The Blue Bird* (1976), and participated in a few disaster movies such as *Earthquake* (1974), *The Cassandra Crossing* (1977) and *City On Fire* (1979), where the ravages of time are less noticeable than the ravages around her. RB

in The Night Of The Iguana *(MGM, 1964)*

with Charlton Heston in 55 Days At Peking *(Allied Artists, 1963)* ▷

Vittorio Gassman

Born **Genoa, Italy, 1 September 1922**

The great lover Casanova and the great actor Kean, have both been played by Vittorio Gassman. However, his outstanding, dark good-looks have shown him on screen as more Casanova than Kean. Gassman's reputation in Italy as a great actor derives from his work in the theatre for over four decades, including many memorable Shakespearean roles and the productions of his own company – the Teatro Populare Italiano.

Vittorio left his law studies in order to enrol at the Academy of Dramatic Art in Rome. He had been in the theatre for some time before he made his film debut in 1946., Although he appeared in costume melodramas like *Il Cavaliere Misterioso* (1948) as Casanova and *Il Sogno Di Zorro* (1952), it was his roles in two neo-realist films with Sylvana Mangano, *Bitter Rice* (1948) and *Anna* (1951), which led to a Hollywood offer. The two years he spent in Hollywood, were as brief as the period of his stormy marriage to Shelley Winters, with whom he co-starred only once, in Robert Rossen's muddled Italian-made romance, *Mambo* (1954).

In 1953, he played a man on the run in two low key dramas, *The Glass Wall* and *Cry Of The Hunted*. In *Sombrero* (1953), he was dashing, and in *Rhapsody* (1954), he portrayed a romantic violinist who finally chooses his fiddle in preference to spoiled Elizabeth Taylor. He was the perfect handsome seducer of Audrey Hepburn's Natasha in King Vidor's screen version of *War And Peace* (1956), and used gypsy charms on Carroll Baker in *The Miracle* (1959).

Gassman was seen in a number of routine Italian films, but the many light comedies he made with director Dino Risi, revealed him as an accomplished comic actor. For his role as the blind ladies' man still pursuing women in Risi's *Scent Of Women* (1975), he won the best actor award at the Cannes Film Festival. Robert Altman recently cast him as the father of the groom in *A Wedding* (1978), and in the allegorical *Quintet* (1979), in which he had to utter lines like 'Hope is an obsolete word.' RB

in A Virgin For The Prince *(Gala, 1965)*

John Gavin

Real name **Jack Golenor**
Born **Los Angeles, 8 April 1928**

Every time Julie Andrews looks at her handsome boss John Gavin in *Thoroughly Modern Millie* (1967), she sees his teeth glinting as he poses, pipe in hand, and she hears a heavenly choir. He is a solid, All-American and boring character, an amusing self-parody of the image the handsome Gavin projected in nine movies between 1958 and 1961. He was looking at himself from the perspective of six years away from the screen.

In those days, appearing mostly in lush Ross Hunter productions for Universal, Gavin seemed to be getting the sort of roles Rock Hudson had played a few years before, but he suffered from the comparison. He was inadequate as Ernest Graeber, the German soldier in Douglas Sirk's World War II romance, *A Time To Love And A Time To Die* (1958), but provided a well-built shoulder for Lana Turner to lean on in Sirk's *Imitation Of Life* (1959), and Susan Hayward in *Back Street* (1961) to cry on. His conventional masculine good looks were not enough in comedies such as *A Breath of Scandal* (1960) with Sophia Loren, or in the title role, with Sandra Dee, of *Romanoff And Juliet* (1961). Hitchcock recognised that his stolidity was necessary to *Psycho* (1960), and cast him in the role of Janet Leigh's lover to contrast with the abnormality of the rest of the proceedings.

Before entering films, Gavin spent from 1952 to 1955 as an air intelligence officer in the US Navy.

with Vera Miles in Back Street *(Universal, 1961)*

He has been president of the Screen Actors' Guild. He is seen rarely on the big screen these days, but turned up in *Jennifer* (1978), a college horror flick, and in the umpteenth version of *Heidi* (1979). During his six-year absence from the cinema, he appeared in the TV series, 'Destry' and 'Convoys'. It was like old times when he appeared in the TV soap serial, 'Rich Man Poor Man' in 1976. RB

Mitzi Gaynor

Real name **Franceska Mitzi Gerber**
Born **Chicago, 4 September 1930**

For the coveted role of Nellie Forbush in the film version of Rodgers and Hammerstein's *South Pacific* (1958), the director Joshua Logan wanted Elizabeth Taylor, and composer Richard Rodgers wanted Doris Day. They settled for Mitzi Gaynor. What seemed her biggest break, turned out to be her last musical and one of her last movies. The film was ploddingly and garishly directed, and Mitzi, as the little girl from Little Rock, did not have enough star quality to compensate.

A cute, sprightly dancer-singer with a little turned up nose, Mitzi was descended from the Hungarian aristocracy. Her mother, a former ballerina, took her to ballet classes when she was four. At twelve, the little girl was a member of the *corps de ballet* of the Los Angeles Civic Light Opera Company. Eight years later, she made her film debut for Fox in a Betty Grable musical, *My Blue Heaven* (1950), singing 'Live Hard, Work Hard, Love Hard'. This she seemed to do as the star of two minor musical biopics about two forgotten entertainers, Lotte Crabtree in *Golden Girl* (1951) and Eva Tanguay in *The-I-Don't-Care-Girl* (1953). She also worked hard as one of the vaudeville family in *There's No Business Like Show Business* (1954), but Fox decided not to renew her contract. That's show business!

In the same year as leaving Fox, she married talent agent Jack Bean who got her work at Paramount in *Anything Goes* (1956) with Bing Crosby, and *The Joker Is Wild* (1957) opposite Frank Sinatra. But she proved most appealing in her only MGM movie, George Cukor's *Les Girls* (1957), in which Mitzi provided an interesting contrast to Kay Kendall and did a delightful send up of the Marlon Brando movie *The Wild One* (1954), dancing with a leather-clad Gene Kelly.

Following the failure of *South Pacific*, Mitzi, always the 'cockeyed optimist', made a few light comedies, including *Happy Anniversary* (1959) as David Niven's wife of thirteen years, and *Surprise Package* (1960) as a chorine involved with jewel thief Yul Brynner. She has kept working in theatre, nightclubs and on TV. RB

in Bridge On The River Kwai *(Columbia, 1957)*

Alec Guinness

Born **London, 2 April 1914**

In the 30s, playgoers were stunned by his modern dress Hamlet at the Old Vic. In the 40s, they saw his memorable Richard III and Coriolanus at the same theatre, while filmgoers were marvelling at his Fagin in *Oliver Twist* (1948), and his playing of all eight members of the d'Ascoyne family in *Kind Hearts And Coronets* (1949). In the 50s he created the role of Sir Henry Harcourt-Reilly in T.S. Eliot's 'The Cocktail Party' on stage in London and New York, and was delightful in a series of Ealing comedies such as his timid bank clerk turned gold robber in *The Lavender Hill Mob* (1951), and the head of a gang posing as musicians in *The Ladykillers* (1955). In the same decade, his stiff-upper-lip portrayal of Colonel Nicholson, the prisoner of war held by the Japanese in *The Bridge On The River Kwai* (1957), won him the New York Film Critics' Award, the British Academy Award, and the Oscar. In the 60s, he triumphed once again in the theatre as T.E. Lawrence in Terence Rattigan's 'Ross', and on screen he made impressive appearances in epics such as *Lawrence Of Arabia* (1962), *The Fall Of The Roman Empire* (1964) and *Doctor Zhivago* (1965). A new generation discovered him in the 70s when he played Obi-Ben Kenobi in *Star Wars* (1977), uttering, 'May the force be with you,' that became a catch-phrase among young people. In the 80s, he was the crusty grandfather of *Little Lord Fauntleroy*

(1980) and will feature in David Lean's *A Passage To India*. In the 90s, Alec Guinness...

In 1953, the distinguished critic Kenneth Tynan wrote that 'were he (Guinness) to commit murder, I have no doubt that the number of false arrests following the circulation of his description would break all records.' This describes Guinness's ability to become the characters he plays. 'I try to get inside a character and project him,' he explained. 'One of my own private rules of thumb is that I have not got a character until I have mastered exactly how he walks.' Often, he has only to lift an eyebrow to express a world of meaning. His dexterity and subtlety have made him a consummate film actor. TV also suits this master of understatement as witnessed by his George Smiley in the seven part production of John Le Carré's 'Tinker, Tailor, Soldier, Spy' in 1979, and its sequel, 'Smiley's People' in 1982.

Guinness has created a multitude of flesh and blood characters, bringing out pathos in villains such as Fagin or even Hitler in *Hitler – The Last Ten Days* (1973), attempting to avoid any caricature. There is also humanity and depth to the historical figures seen against the conditions that made them, such as Disraeli in *The Mudlark* (1950), Marcus Aurelius in *The Fall Of The Roman Empire*, Prince Feisal in *Lawrence Of Arabia*, and Charles I in *Cromwell* (1970). His Pope Innocent the Third brought some dignity to the flower-child rompings of Zeffirelli's *Brother Sun, Sister Moon* (1973).

In contrast, are the comic performances as little men like George Bird in *Last Holiday* (1950), who mistakenly thinks he has a short time to live, and the scientist in *The Man In The White Suit* (1951) who invents a fabric that will never wear out, or Jim Wormold, the vacuum cleaner salesman who inadvertently becomes *Our Man In Havana* (1960). One of his more recent comic creations was the blind butler in *Murder By Death* (1976), confusingly called Bensonmum. Remarkably, the reserved Guinness is almost as much at home with extrovert figures such as the eccentric painter Gully Jimson in *The Horse's Mouth* (1958), which he scripted himself, and as the fiery, red-haired Scots soldier in *Tunes Of Glory* (1960). There have been a couple of miscalculations, such as his wooden Prince courting Grace Kelly in *The Swan* (1956), and the embarrassing Japanese businessman in *A Majority Of One* (1961).

Guinness's first job on leaving school was as a junior copywriter with an advertising firm. When he was fired, he took acting lessons with Martita Hunt, who soon dismissed him saying he would never achieve anything as an actor. (They later worked together on *Great Expectations* – 1946, and she was forced to eat her words). He gained a scholarship to

in The Horse's Mouth *(United Artists, 1958)*

Fay Compton's Studio of Dramatic Art, and left there a prize pupil. He soon began to get stage work, and joined an illustrious Old Vic company which included John Gielgud and Laurence Olivier in its ranks. In 1938, he began a long and happy marriage to the actress Merula Salaman.

During the war years, Guinness was in the navy, describing the period thus: 'I acted being a naval officer, a very small part, but a long, long, run.' After the war, he made his film debut proper (he had had a walk-on in a musical called *Evensong* – 1934) as Herbert Pocket in David Lean's *Great Expectations*. It was the beginning of a prestigious career that brought him a knighthood in 1959, an Oscar for Best Actor in 1957, and a special Oscar at the 1980 Academy Award ceremonies – as well as two-and-a-half per cent of the profits of *Star Wars*. RB

Julie Harris

Real name **Julia Anne Harris**
Born **Grosse Pointe, Michigan, 2 December 1925**

What an extraordinary figure 17-year-old Julie Harris cut as the scrawny, scruffy, short-haired Frankie in her first screen appearance in *A Member Of The Wedding* (1952). Fred Zinneman's film, unusually using all the actors from the original stage production, was an excellent transposition of Carson McCullers's play about growing pains, and Julie with her pointed, freckled face and sour little voice, was brilliant as the confused, dreamy and aching adolescent. Fifteen years, and only eight films later, she was back in McCullers territory as the neurotic invalid wife of Brian Keith in John Huston's *Reflections In A Golden Eye* (1968), who cuts her nipples with a pair of scissors. It was a pale-faced, fragile performance, but there have been few films that could contain this highly individual and sensitive will-o'-the-wisp performer.

Julie came from a banking family and was sent to finishing school. She then trained at the Yale Drama

School and at the Actors' Studio. In 1950, she became an overnight sensation on Broadway in 'A Member Of The Wedding', and has since won many Tony awards for her stage work. In her second film, Elia Kazan's *East Of Eden* (1955), she is glowingly youthful opposite James Dean, bringing comfort and understanding to his adolescent anxiety. She revealed another side to her talents in *I Am A Camera* (1955), as Sally Bowles, the fun-loving girl in decadent Berlin before the war. However, the theatre, including Juliet at Stratford, Ontario in 1960, kept her a great deal from the screen, and most of the films she did make were ill-chosen.

After the feeble farrago of *The Truth About Women* (1958), she played a simple Irish Girl in *Sally's Irish Rogue* (1958), an unbelievable social worker in *Requiem For A Heavyweight* (1962), did a frightened child/woman bit in *The Haunting* (1963), smoked endless cigarettes as a parent worried about drug addiction in *The People Next Door* (1970), and appeared in *The Hiding Place* (1974), a well-meaning film produced by Billy Graham's Evangelistic Association. Outstandingly gifted, Miss Harris should have been saved from roles such as these. RB

Laurence Harvey

**Real name Lauruska Mischa Skikne
Born Yomishkis, Lithuania, 1 October 1928
Died 1973**

It is unwise, but difficult not, to associate Laurence Harvey with the role of man-on-the-make Joe Lampton in *Room At The Top* (1958). There is something of Lampton's coldness and ambition about Harvey's screen persona in almost everything he did. His handsome but stiff features, and his carefully enunciated speech, made him an unsympathetic figure. In fact, he was perfectly cast as the brainwashed assassin in John Frankenheimer's *The Manchurian Candidate* (1962).

Harvey emigrated with his Jewish parents from Lithuania to South Africa when he was a child. Unhappy at home, he enlisted in the South African navy at the age of fourteen by lying about his age. This was discovered and he was sent home. After acting with the Johannesburg Repertory Theatre, he joined the army when he was fifteen, and served in North Africa during the war. Immediately afterwards, he went to England where he entered the Royal Academy of Dramatic Art. Restless as ever, he stayed three months before joining a theatre company in Manchester. It wasn't long before he reached the London stage and had made his screen debut by 1948. He was to return to the stage from time to time during his career in Sheridan, Shaw and Shakespeare, as well as playing the lead, King Arthur, in the London production of Lerner and Loewe's 'Camelot'.

In the 50s, he was already playing leads in many British films, including a stunt motor-cyclist in *The Scarlet Thread* (1951), a hoodlum in *I Believe In You* (1952), and a member of a gang of robbers in *The Good Die Young* (1954), which co-starred his future wife Margaret Leighton. He appeared in his first Hollywood movie, *King Richard And The Crusaders* (1954), as a brave Scottish knight fighting the heathens as well as a bad script. He did not have the same excuse for his colourless performance in the Italian-made *Romeo And Juliet* (1954). He was amusingly straight-faced amidst the chaos around him in *I Am A Camera* (1955) and *Three Men In A Boat* (1956), but was unintentionally funny as the British officer blinded in the desert in *Storm Over The Nile* (1955), the third and weakest version of *The Four Feathers*. After his success in *Room At The Top*, and as the opportunistic talent scout in *Expresso Bongo* (1959), he returned to Hollywood.

in 1963

He was literally and figuratively on his high horse as Colonel William Travis in John Wayne's *The Alamo* (1960); left Elizabeth Taylor in the lurch in *Butterfield 8* (1960); was a Southern gentleman who stands by as his wife is raped by a bandit in *The Outrage* (1964); and was miscast as the young doctor who arouses spinster Geraldine Page's emotions in *Summer And Smoke* (1961), and as Somerset Maugham's lame hero Philip Carey in *Of Human Bondage* (1964). He was also shamefully at the centre of the action in the trashy *Walk On The Wild Side* (1962) while Jane Fonda, Anne Baxter and Barbara Stanwyck stood on the side lines.

Back in England, Harvey was effectively cynical in John Schlesinger's *Darling* (1965), and repeated his touchstone role of Joe Lampton in *Life At The Top* (1965), this time deprived of Simone Signoret and therefore as bloodless as the film's hero. In his last years, struggling against cancer, he divorced Margaret Leighton and married the widow of Harry Cohn, former boss of Columbia. He appeared again with Elizabeth Taylor in a stinker called *Night Watch* (1973) and starred in and directed *Welcome To Arrow Beach* (released 1974). RB

with Simone Signoret in Room At The Top *(Romulus, 1958)*

Jack Hawkins

**Born London, 1 September 1910
Died 1973**

Solid, unemotional, British dependability in peace, and especially war, was the main commodity offered by the stern, hawk-nosed, avuncular figure of Jack Hawkins. Standing on the bridge coolly issuing orders as the captain in *The Cruel Sea* (1953), reassuring pilots between cups of tea from the operations room in *Angels One Five* (1952), commanding troops on the bomb-stricken island in *Malta Story* (1953), training officers for jungle warfare in *The Bridge On The River Kwai* (1957), or, as Colonel Allenby, reprimanding *Lawrence Of Arabia* (1962). It was difficult to discern whether he was imitating real British officers or they were imitating him. In *The Intruder* (1953), Hawkins was an ex-colonel who turns detective; and in *The League Of Gentlemen* (1960), he used his army officer experience in planning a robbery. Hawkins himself served in India during the war and was made a colonel in charge of the Entertainment Unit.

In peacetime, on screen, Hawkins carried on the war against crime by wearing a raincoat and firmly asking questions about a murder in *The Fallen Idol* (1948), and playing an inspector in *The Long Arm* (1956) and *Gideon Of Scotland Yard* (1958). He was

in Bridge On The River Kwai *(Columbia, 1957)*

also a harassed newspaper editor in *Front Page Story* (1954), and sympathetic as a speech teacher of a young deaf child in *Mandy* (1952). Occasionally, he could be a baddie, like the sadistic captor and torturer of Cardinal Alec Guinness in *The Prisoner* (1955), or the German game hunter in *Rampage* (1963), or the cruel Roman Quintus Arrius in *Ben Hur* (1959), but then they weren't British. He was rather absurd as the despotic Khufu in Howard Hawks's *Land Of The Pharaohs* (1955).

Jack Hawkins began acting at a very early age, making his film debut at twenty in *Birds Of Prey* (1930) and appeared in over a dozen films in smallish parts. He married actress Jessica Tandy in 1932, but they divorced in 1940 before he joined up. He returned from the war with new authority, and began to make a reputation for himself on both sides of the Atlantic. However, in the early 60s, cancer of the throat was diagnosed. Although his voice got huskier and he suffered pain, he courageously continued to work in films, ironically playing Marlow, the narrator of *Lord Jim* (1965). In 1966, he lost his voice entirely after an operation on the larynx. He refused to stop acting and, with his voice dubbed, usually by Charles Gray, he was lost in vast epics such as *Waterloo* (1970), *Nicholas And Alexandra* (1971) and *Young Winston* (1972), and was one of the critics murdered by Vincent Price in *Theatre Of Blood* (1973). RB

in I Want To Live! *(United Artists, 1958)*

Susan Hayward

Real name **Edythe Marrener**
Born **Brooklyn, New York, 30 June 1918**
Died **1975**

They didn't come any gutsier than Susan Hayward. The redhead with the up-tilted nose, deep warm voice and heavy eyelashes, made suffering her fortune. She received five Oscar nominations for her pains, finally winning the Best Actress Award for her role as Barbara Graham, the prostitute who went to the gas chamber in *I Want To Live!* (1958), which focused on Graham's last hours in the death cell. Susan was first nominated for *Smash-Up: The Story Of A Woman* (1947), as a former nightclub singer who gives up her career for her husband and then starts hitting the bottle, one of her earliest showy performances. Her second nomination came for *My Foolish Heart* (1950), a weepy in which she is a lonely girl in love with pilot Dana Andrews who fails to return from a mission. Then in two biopics of singers, *With A Song In My Heart* (1952) about Jane Froman (her voice perfectly matching Susan's own contralto) whose career was interrupted when she was badly injured in a plane crash which left her in a wheel-chair; and *I'll Cry Tomorrow* (1956) about Lillian Roth's battle against booze, which she finally won with the help of Alcoholics Anonymous.

Suffering was something that Susan Hayward knew all about at first hand. In 1954, her ten-year marriage to actor Jess Barker ended, followed by an acrimonious court case over the custody of their twin sons. When Susan lost, she took an overdose of sleeping pills and was hospitalised, just prior to the shooting of *I'll Cry Tomorrow*. One of her visitors was Lillian Roth who encouraged her to get better. Some years later, she contracted cancer, presumably on location in the Nevada Desert while filming *The Conquerer* (1956), due to radiation left over from A-bomb tests. Co-stars John Wayne, Agnes Moorhead and the director Dick Powell, all died of cancer. Hayward, aged only 56, succumbed to a brain tumour.

Susan came from a modest family who put her through commercial high school. She began earning a living as a photographer's model, which led to her being one of the many candidates chosen to test for the role of Scarlett O'Hara in *Gone With The Wind* (1939). After a few bit parts at Warners, she moved on to Paramount and better things, such as the sweet Southern belle in Cecil B. DeMille's lusty adventure film *Reap The Wild Wind* (1942); Fredric March's spoilt fiancée before he meets Veronica Lake in René Clair's *I Married A Witch* (1942), and the rich bitch on deck lusted after by stoker William Bendix in the film version of Eugene O'Neill's *The Hairy Ape* (1944). It was Universal, however, who gave her the chance to first reveal her emotional depths in *Smash-Up: The Story Of A Woman*.

Just after Susan's own smash-up and before *I'll*

with Barbara Parkins (centre) in Valley Of The Dolls *(20th Century-Fox, 1967)*

Cry Tomorrow, Lillian Roth remembered being visited by her at the Beverly Hills Hotel. 'It was early afternoon and she arrived in her black Chinese pajamas with a coat thrown over them. We talked several hours. By the time she left I didn't know whether she was imitating me or I was emulating her. We were both so emotional about things, that when we faced each other it was like looking in the mirror. I was looking at Lillian and she was looking at Susan.' Unlike in *With A Song In My Heart*, Susan sang her own songs in the Roth role. Although she was terrified at first, she made a vocally pleasing and efficient job of it. Her performance revealed, without any gloss, the degradation and ugliness of alcoholism.

When Hayward wasn't suffering, she was smouldering. At Fox, she showed a frank sexuality in Biblical epics as Bathsheba to Gregory Peck's King David in *David And Bathsheba* (1951), and Messalina in *Demetrius And The Gladiators* (1954) dallying with Victor Mature. She turned up in the African jungle, bringing comfort to Gregory Peck in *The Snows Of Kilimanjaro* (1952), bearing medicines to the natives in *White Witch Doctor* (1953), and shooting Zulus beside Tyrone Power in *Untamed* (1955). In *Garden Of Evil* (1954), she is desired by the men she has hired to find her husband in the Mexico of the 1850s. Strong women were also in her line. Hayward was the designer in the garment

in David And Bathsheba *(20th Century-Fox, 1952)*

industry of *I Can Get It For You Wholesale* (1951) who'll step on anybody to get what she wants, and the fiery oil-woman in *Tulsa* (1949), involved in wildcat drilling. She was also *The President's Lady* (1953), that is Rachel Jackson, the married woman Andrew Jackson (Charlton Heston) fell for. One of her most pugnacious roles was as Arthur Kennedy's wife in Nicholas Ray's *The Lusty Men* (1952), trying to dissuade him from the tawdry rodeo life.

The star's roles in the 60s soap operas, became almost self-parodic with her all-stops-out approach. She was in a glossy remake of *Back Street* (1961), in the part previously better played by Irene Dunne and Margaret Sullavan, and also in the remake of the Bette Davis vehicle *Dark Victory* (1939), retitled *Stolen Hours* (1963), in which she goes blind just before dying radiantly, and in a more cloying manner than her famous predecessor. Hayward also played Bette Davis's daughter in *Where Love Has Gone* (1964), and was a monstrous grande dame in *Valley Of The Dolls* (1967). Strangely, Fox wanted her in 1963, to play *Cleopatra*, but she wisely declined. It was a pleasant relief to see her in a sophisticated comedy *The Honey Pot* (1967), one of her last films. RB

Audrey Hepburn

Real name Edda Hepburn van Heemstra
Born Brussels, Belgium, 4 May 1929

'Titism has taken over the country, but Audrey Hepburn singlehanded may make bosoms a thing of the past. The director will not have to invent shots where the girl leans forward for a glass of scotch and soda,' commented Billy Wilder while making *Sabrina* (1954) with the elfin beauty whose delicate features, big brown eyes and boyish figure provided a refreshing antidote to the mammary mania of the 50s. She was a wistful woodland sprite who strayed for a short period into modern civilisation and disappeared again. She had the kind of fragility and feyness that could easily become mannered and wear thin. Perhaps she was aware of this when she retired from the screen in 1967 at the age of 38, only to make a misconceived and desultory comeback nine years later, unlike Ondine of the myth who returned to the water for ever.

It was apt that Audrey should have been born in the country of Mélisande, of an English banker and a Dutch baroness. When her parents divorced, she was sent to boarding school in England. While visiting her mother in Holland during the school holidays, war broke out. She spent World War II in Nazi-occupied Arnhem, where she attended the local school and took ballet classes at the Conservatory. After the war, she took up a ballet scholarship in London, where she also modelled and took drama classes with Felix Aylmer, which led her to the cinema. She had minute parts in the Robertson Hare farce *One Wild Oat* (1951) and the Ealing comedy *The Lavender Hill Mob* (1951). In the same year, she played a cigarette girl in *Laughter In Paradise*, and had leading roles in *Young Wives' Tale*, and the French film *Monte Carlo Baby* (1951) filmed on the Riviera. It was while shooting the latter, that she met French novelist Colette who insisted she play the title role of 'Gigi' on Broadway in the Anita Loos adaptation from her novel. She did, and was a success. (She was later offered the role in the MGM film version of 1958, but turned it down.) The play led to her being cast opposite Gregory Peck in William Wyler's enchanting light comedy, *Roman Holiday* (1953). For her first performance in an American film as the incognito princess who finds romance with a newspaperman in Rome, she received the Oscar for Best Actress, rather in recognition of her novel gamine charms than any

great acting ability. Soon after the excitement of the Oscar ceremonies had died down, Hepburn received the Tony award for her portrayal of Giraudoux's 'Ondine' on Broadway. In 1954, she married Mel Ferrer, her co-star in the play. It was his third marriage and her first.

Billy Wilder directed her with tenderness in *Sabrina*, for which she was Oscar-nominated as the chauffeur's daughter desperately trying to choose between contrasting brothers, stuffy tycoon Humphrey Bogart and playboy William Holden. 'Time' magazine noted that 'Hepburn's appeal, it becomes clearer with every appearance, is largely to the

imagination; the less acting she does, the more people can imagine her doing, and wisely she does very little in *Sabrina*. That little she does skilfully.' Now certainly a star, Hepburn was perfectly cast as the radiant child-like Natasha in King Vidor's mammoth *War And Peace* (1956), and gave a sympathetic performance opposite her husband as Prince Andrei. Ferrer was only 12 years her senior, but in many of her films she was romanced by much older men. As the music student in Wilder's bittersweet comedy *Love In The Afternoon* (1957), she was painfully smitten by wealthy playboy Gary Cooper, 28 years her senior; and in Stanley Donen's *Funny Face* (1957), Fred Astaire, 30 years older, was the

photographer Pygmalion who transforms her shop-girl Galatea into an exquisite, top fashion model. In the latter film, Audrey got to dance with Astaire, sing a solo, 'How Long Has This Been Going On?', and wear a Parisian wardrobe designed by Hubert de Givenchy (who became her favourite designer, making five more films with her).

Mel Ferrer directed his wife as Rima, the Bird Girl, in *Green Mansions* (1959), an adaptation of W.H. Hudson's South American fantasy, but her child-of-nature was not exotic enough, and it was her first film flop. But in the same year, she was again nominated for an Oscar for her performance as the troubled Sister Luke in Fred Zinnemann's *The Nun's Story* (1959), a film that treads far too softly for far too long. However, Hepburn is effective as the Belgian nun brought to question her faith in the Congo, although in most of her following performances she too often substituted coaxing smiles and innocent charm for characterisation.

In 1960, the Ferrers made their home in Switzerland with Audrey making occasional sorties to Hollywood. She gave a superficial performance as an Indian girl brought up by white settlers in John Huston's bombastic western *The Unforgiven* (1960); and received her fourth Oscar nomination for her ingratiating Holly Golightly in Blake Edwards's sugary *Breakfast At Tiffany's* (1961), in which she sang Henry Mancini's hit, 'Moon River'. She seemed a little adrift as the schoolteacher accused of having a lesbian affair in Wyler's *The Children's Hour* (1962); and made a reasonable attempt at cosmopolitan sophistication in Donen's flashy Hitchcockian thriller *Charade* (1963), saying to Cary Grant, 'Won't you come in for a minute? I don't bite, you know, unless I have to.' Of *Paris When It Sizzles* (1964), 'The New York Times' wrote, 'Miss Hepburn, sylph-like as ever, seems slightly bewildered by the trumped-up zaniness in which she is involved.' The credits mentioned 'Miss Hepburn's wardrobe *and perfume* by De Givenchy', and another critic commented that the perfume couldn't be smelt but the picture could.

My Fair Lady (1964) was the most expensive picture in Warner Bros.' history with Hepburn receiving $1 million and top billing, ousting a disappointed (and eminently more suitable) Julie Andrews for the role of Eliza Doolittle. She was hopelessly inadequate as the cockney flower girl, but ravishing as the Cecil Beaton fashion plate 'lady'. Douglas MacVay in 'The Musical Film' regrets that Audrey's 'heavenly' voice was dubbed by Marni Nixon but 'her non-musical impact is unique... Those lashes, quietly drooped: that sudden gaze of clear wide eyes, lips parted, gravely tender: that sweep of dark hair delicate from neck slender: that voice, a bell soft-scooped...' Hepburn did provoke this kind of adulation and critic's hyperbole.

While playing the disillusioned wife bickering with Albert Finney in Stanley Donen's skin-deep anatomy of a marriage, *Two For The Road* (1967), her own marriage was breaking down, partly due to Ferrer's adultery. He had produced the cleverly contrived chiller *Wait Until Dark* (1967) with Audrey gaining her fifth Oscar nomination as a blind girl terrorised by three thugs. A little after, she had made the acquaintance of an Italian psychiatrist, nine years her junior, who had always been a great admirer. Much to the amusement of the world's press, his name was Dr Dotti. On hearing that her marriage was on the rocks, he motored to Switzerland and helped her over a bad time. They were married in 1969, a year after her divorce from Ferrer came through. She went to live in retirement near Rome as Mrs Dotti.

She made her return to the screen after nine years' absence in Richard Lester's monotonously autumnal *Robin And Marian* (1976), as Maid Marian twenty years on, now an Abbess. Hepburn simpers throughout, casting off her wimple at one stage to make love to a grizzled Sean Connery as Robin Hood. After appearing in the abysmal soap opera *Bloodline* (1979), Audrey returned to Italy and her two children. RB

with Gregory Peck (right) and Eddie Albert in Roman Holiday *(Paramount, 1953)*

in My Fair Lady *(Warner Bros., 1964)* ▷

Charlton Heston

Real name Charles Carter
Born Evanston, Illinois, 4 October 1923

'There's a special excitement in playing a man who made a hole in history large enough to be remembered centuries after he died', Charlton Heston once commented. He should know after playing Moses, John the Baptist (*The Greatest Story Ever Told* – 1965), Mark Antony (twice), Cardinal Richelieu, Henry VIII (*The Prince And The Pauper* – 1977), Andrew Jackson (*The President's Lady* – 1953, *The Buccaneer* – 1958), Buffalo Bill (*Pony Express* – 1953) and General Gordon (*Khartoum* – 1966). His deep, solemn voice was even used as the voice of God in *The Ten Commandments* (1956). Their qualities of leadership have clearly rubbed off on him, as he was president of the Screen Actors' Guild for six years and is chairman of the American Film Institute.

Heston had a classical theatre training, studying speech and drama at Northwestern University. After three years in the Air Force, he started a professional career in stock and on Broadway. His Shakespearean performances on CBS TV brought him to the attention of Hollywood, where he made his debut in *Dark City* (1950). For his second film, Heston was cast by Cecil B. DeMille in *The Greatest Show On*

Earth (1952), as the tough circus owner. He continued to play unflinching, unemotional strong men in *The Savage* (1952), *Ruby Gentry* (1952), *Arrowhead* (1953) and *Lucy Gallant* (1955), before DeMille raised him to the Bibilical heights as Moses in *The Ten Commandments*. 'If you can't make a

career out of two DeMille's, you'll never do it', Heston remarked.

The cold, piercing blue eyes, the strong jaw, and tall and muscular carved figure, equipped Heston with the ideal monumental look for roles in epics. He reached the peak of his career in the title role in *Ben-Hur* (1959), winning an Oscar for his brawny performance. Other interminable epics included *55 Days At Peking* (1963), and *The Agony And The Ecstasy* (1965) in which he played Michelangelo. 'Heston hits the ceiling' wrote 'Time Magazine'. However, his heroic impassivity was effective in Anthony Mann's *El Cid* (1961) with Sophia Loren, and was interestingly fallible in modern dress in Orson Welles's *Touch Of Evil* (1958) as a Mexican lawyer with a black moustache.

Heston's popularity was maintained as the representative of *homo sapiens* in *The Planet Of The Apes* (1968) and *Beneath The Planet Of The Apes* (1970), and as an immovable fixture in disaster movies such as *Airport* (1975), *Earthquake* (1974) and *Gray Lady Down* (1978). As a throwback to his pre-Hollywood days, he ambitiously attempted Mark Antony in *Julius Caesar* (1970) and *Antony And Cleopatra* (1972), the latter being stolidly directed by himself. It is a relief to find him as Cardinal Richelieu in Richard Lester's *The Three Musketeers* (1974) and *The Four Musketeers* (1975), with his tongue firmly in his cheek. RB

William Holden

Real name William Franklin Beedle.
Born O'Fallon, Illinois, 17 April 1918
Died 1981

The bullet-riddled body of Joe Gillis (William Holden) lies face downwards in a swimming pool at the start of Billy Wilder's superb *Sunset Boulevard* (1950). The dead man's voice takes up the narration. What sort of story would William Holden have told after being found in his Hollywood apartment some days after he died?

He grew up a handsome, clean-cut, all-American

boy, expected to go into his father's chemical business. However, on a trip to New York in 1937, he became stagestruck. On returning to California, he joined the Pasadena Workshop Theater. A Paramount talent scout spotted him in a play, he was tested, put under contract and groomed for stardom. But it was Columbia who gave him his first screen role as *Golden Boy* (1939), the violinist who is forced to become a boxer. In 1941, he married a

young actress called Brenda Marshall. Columbia bought half his contract, and the golden boy worked hard between the two studios, usually playing boy-next-door types and young servicemen, in films such as *Our Town* (1940), *I Wanted Wings* (1941) and *The Fleet's In* (1942), before he enlisted in the Air Force where he served until 1945.

On the films he made between 1945–1950, Holden commented, 'I got into a rut playing all kinds of nice-guy meaningless roles in meaningless movies in which I found no interest or enjoyment'. An exception was as a psychopath in *The Dark Past* (1949), but his image really changed in *Sunset Boulevard* as the washed-up screenwriter playing gigolo to faded silent star Norma Desmond (Gloria Swanson), for which he received an Oscar nomination. He was quietly effective as Judy Holliday's mentor in *Born Yesterday* (1950), and then won the Best Actor Oscar for his portrayal of the cynical prisoner-of-war in Billy Wilder's *Stalag 17* (1953).

In the 50s, Holden was one of the most popular and highest paid stars, appearing in war dramas –

Submarine Command (1952) and *The Bridges Of Toko-Ri* (1955); comedies – *The Moon Is Blue* (1953) and *Sabrina* (1954); and was effecting as the loner in *Picnic* (1956). For his role in *The Bridge On The River Kwai* (1957), he received 10% of the gross, making him a multi-millionaire. In 1959, he moved with his wife and two sons to the tax-haven of Switzerland. The 60s found him globe-trotting, drinking heavily, spending time at the Mount Kenya Safari Club in Africa which he founded, and making occasional mediocre films. He was also linked romantically with other actresses, particularly his co-star in *The Lion* (1962), Capucine. Brenda left him in 1963, and they were divorced seven years later.

In his final years, Holden began to represent the male menopause in the violent *The Wild Bunch* (1969) and *Network* (1976). Someone once said of Holden, 'When you look at him, the map of the US is right there on his face.' Billy Wilder's *Fedora* (1978), reflects a changing Hollywood, and William Holden's sunken-cheeked, puffy, heavily-lined face records that change. RB

Judy Holliday

Real name Judith Tuvim
Born New York City, 21 June 1922
Died 1965

In the late 30s, Judy Holliday started her career in show business as a switchboard operator backstage at Orson Welles's Mercury Theater. Her last screen role was as a naively meddlesome answering service operator in Vincente Minnelli's musical, *Bells Are Ringing* (1960). In between, she appeared in revues and cabaret with lyricists Betty Comden and Adolph Green; had bit parts in a couple of Carmen Miranda musicals at Fox; upstaged Katharine Hepburn in her scenes as a dim-witted murder suspect in George Cukor's *Adam's Rib* (1949); and won the Best Actress Oscar in her first major role as Billy Dawn, the dumbest of dumb blondes in Cukor's *Born Yesterday* (1950), the role she had played successfully on Broadway.

Her delightful Billy Dawn, with the squeaky voice, innocent wide eyes and baby dimples, hiding her intrinsic common sense, set the pattern for the rest of her career. With only slight variations of the character, Judy appeared in two further Cukor comedies, *The Marrying Kind* (1952) and *It Should Happen To You* (1954), the latter co-starring the skilled and versatile Jack Lemmon. They also made

a good comedy team in *Phffft!* (1954), the title referring to the way their marriage went. After playing the not-so-dumb blonde stockholder in *The Solid Gold Cadillac* (1956), she got the chance to extend herself in the Jules Styne, Comden and Green musical *The Bells Are Ringing*, on Broadway, and opposite Dean Martin on film. She died tragically of cancer at the age of 43, and with her went an exceptional comic talent. RB

Rock Hudson

Real name Roy Scherer
Born **Winnetka, Illinois, 17 November 1925**

When little Roy Scherer's mother remarried, he took his step-father's name and became Roy Fitzgerald. When he entered the movies, he was transformed into Rock Hudson. He had never acted before in his life. At Warners, on his first film, Raoul Walsh's *Fighter Squadron* (1948), 38 takes were needed before he got a line right. In a few years, he was a leading man at Universal, and by the 60s was one of the ten top box-office stars, male or female, in the United States. How to become a film star in eight easy lessons.

First: Be tall, dark, beefy and handsome. Second: Find an agent who will package and sell you. Third: Change your name to something butch and Anglo-Saxon like Rock Hudson. Fourth: Have your teeth capped, take lessons in drama, singing, dancing, fencing and riding. Fifth: Be willing to pose for as many beefcake publicity stills as possible even before you've made a film. Sixth: Gradually learn your craft from film to film. Take any part offered and stay with one studio for as long as possible. Seventh: Try to vary your parts, changing from westerns to dramas, weepies to comedies. Eighth: When age is creeping up on you and your looks aren't what they were, and film roles are not offered as frequently, then go into TV and do some stage work.

After graduating from high school and working as a mailman, Hudson joined the Navy where he spent World War II as an airplane mechanic. On his return to civvies, he drove a truck and worked as a repair man, before an agent saw his film potential. Although his first acting job was at Warners, it was at Universal where he served his apprenticeship, starting with small parts in crime dramas such as *Undertow* (1949), *I Was A Shoplifter* (1950), *One Way Street* (1950) and *Shakedown* (1950). In a further two films in 1950, he played a football player in the unpretentious college comedy *Peggy*, and a Red Indian in Anthony Mann's *Winchester '73*. He started to work his way up the billing as a gangster in *The Fat Man* (1951), a pilot in *Air Cadet* (1951), a pirate in *Double Crossbones* (1951), a heavyweight

in Battle Hymn *(Universal, 1957)*

the director Douglas Sirk. In the latter, James Dean had a walk-on part. Four years later, he was to co-star with Hudson in *Giant* and to represent the antithesis of Hudson's type of traditional star. Meanwhile, Hudson continued his progress by being top-billed for the first time in *The Lawless Breed* (1953) as a gunman in the early west, under the direction of Raoul Walsh for whom he had made his debut as a stumbling amateur. This was followed by *Seminole* (1953), as a West Point graduate with a liberal view of the Indians, which led to his playing the red-skinned title role in Douglas Sirk's *Taza, Son Of Cochise* (1954).

However, Sirk recognised that Hudson's stolid virtues and good masculine looks were perfectly suited to the filmic equivalent of every woman's dream lover in magazine stories, and so cast him in a series of rich, ripe and glossy Ross Hunter-produced tearjerkers that made him into a major star. He had just the right mixture of lightness and solemnity in *The Magnificent Obsession* (1954) as the playboy who

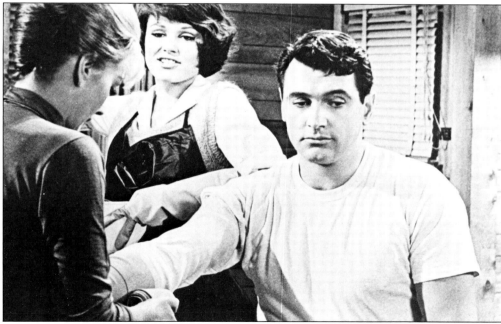

with Paula Prentiss (centre) in Man's Favorite Sport *(Universal, 1964)*

boxing champ in *The Iron Man* (1951), a gambler in Mann's *Bend Of The River* (1952), and a rancher in Budd Boetticher's *Horizons West* (1952).

In *The Scarlet Angel* (1952), he gained leading man status as a sea captain courting saloon girl Yvonne De Carlo, and was the juvenile lead in the pleasant comedy set in the 20s, *Has Anybody Seen My Gal?* (1952), the first of eight films he made with

becomes an eye-surgeon in order to restore the sight of Jane Wyman whose blindness he has caused in an auto accident. In *All That Heaven Allows* (1955), Wyman flies in the face of convention by marrying her gardener, Rock Hudson, a much younger man. Among the alcoholism, impotence, disease and destruction of *Written On The Wind* (1956) about an oil-rich 'Dallas' type family, Hudson is the only

normal character around. Sirk got virtually the same cast together (Hudson, Robert Stack and Dorothy Malone) for *Tarnished Angels* (1958) about stunt flyers, in which Rock showed new depths as a drunken newspaper man.

Rock continued to be a man of 'soap' in *One Desire* (1955), as a gambler fought over by Anne Baxter and Julie Adams; as a surgeon who saves the life of the wife he thought he had lost 10 years before in *Never Say Goodbye* (1956); and in Sirk's *Battle Hymn* (1957), as a World War II flying priest who makes amends for having bombed a German orphanage by air-lifting Korean orphans to safety during the Korean war. His performance as Frederic Henry in the plodding remake of *Farewell To Arms* (1957) earned him the, not entirely unmerited, Harvard Lampoon award for the worst actor of the year. It was time for him to find a new direction.

He found it in the frothy bedroom comedy *Pillow Talk* (1959), in which he played a song-writer who shares a party line with Doris Day. Although no Cary Grant, Rock showed a reasonably light touch where required. This was followed by similar comedies with plush sets and gorgeous costumes such as *Lover Come Back* (1961), *Send Me No Flowers*

with Mary Castle in The Lawless Breed *(Universal, 1953)*

(1964) (with Day again); *Come September* (1961) and *Strange Bedfellows* (1965) with Gina Lollobrigida; and *A Very Special Favour* (1965) with Leslie Caron. Whether he played a scientist, a hypochondriac, a wealthy businessman, a prim oil executive, or an advertising man, he sported the same casual air. In Howard Hawks's *Man's Favorite Sport?* (1964), Hudson was the author of a best selling book on fishing who has never fished in his life. After these extremely puerile and unfunny, shenanigans, it was not surprising to see him going 'straight' again. He is the automaton man restored to youth in *Seconds* (1966), John Frankenheimer's mixture of parody and drama, which was followed by the robot-like war heroics of *Tobruk* (1967), *Hornet's Nest* (1970) and the Cold War yarn, *Ice Station Zebra* (1968).

There were routine westerns like *The Undefeated* (1969) and *Showdown* (1973), and Hudson's only musical, *Darling Lili* (1970), with Julie Andrews. He seemed amused to find himself in soft-porn merchant Roger Vadim's *Pretty Girls All In A Row* (1971) as a college counsellor who murders campus nymphettes, but few others were. In 1978, he toured and 'sang' in the Broadway musical 'On The Twentieth Century', appeared in the disaster movie *Avalanche* (1978), and made TV series such as 'McMillan And Wife'. One way or another, Rock Hudson is seldom out of sight. RB

Tab Hunter

Real name **Arthur Gelien**
Born **New York City, 1 July 1931**

'He had a face that was so handsome that it didn't look real,' George Abbott, the director of *Damn Yankees* (1958) told Michael Druxman in 'From Broadway To Hollywood' about the casting of Tab Hunter in the role of the baseball player who sells his soul to the devil. 'He could have been a composite man created by God ... or the devil.' However, Abbott went on to complain about the inadequacies of his singing and dancing in the musical, and the critics had their usual go at his acting. But the all-American blond pin-up boy still retained his popularity with teenagers throughout the 50s.

At the age of fifteen, the athletic Hunter lied about his age and joined the Coast Guard. Without any drama lessons or acting experience, he made his film debut in Joseph Losey's social drama *The Lawless* (1950). He wore very little as a marine shipwrecked with Linda Darnell in *Island Of Desire* (1952), military uniform in *Battle Cry* (1955) and William Wellman's *Lafayette Escadrille* (1958), cowboy outfits in *Gun Belt* (1953) and *Gunman's Walk* (1958), and was an unlikely German sailor in *The Sea Chase* (1955). He and Natalie Wood made a handsome couple in a western, *The Burning Hills* (1956), and in a strained comedy, *The Girl He Left Behind* (1956). In uniform again, he was the soldier no less a woman than Sophia Loren fell for in the soap opera, *That Kind Of Woman* (1959).

Apart from 'The Tab Hunter Show' on TV, and some stage work, notably Tennessee Williams's 'The Milktrain Doesn't Stop Here Anymore', he made a few movies in the 60s which still exploited his beach boy looks such as *Ride The Wild Surf* (1964) until middle age forced him into character roles. RB

in 1956

Shirley Jones

Born **Smithton, Pennsylvania, 31 March 1934**

Corn was as high as an elephant's eye, literally and figuratively, in the number of musicals featuring dewy-eyed, wholesome blonde singer Shirley Jones, as ordinary as her name. She became a star in her first film, *Oklahoma!* (1955) as, the farm girl in love with cowboy Gordon MacRae. Also with MacRae, she sang and acted sweetly in *Carousel* (1956), made before *Oklahoma!* was released, so sure were Fox of her star quality. In *April Love* (1957), she was the pretty girl on a Kentucky ranch who falls for Pat Boone. In River City, Iowa, in *The Music Man* (1962), Shirley was 'Marian The Librarian' whose love persuades con-man Robert Preston that he can actually teach the town's youth to play musical instruments.

So identified did she become with these sugary, virginal roles, that the Motion Picture Academy were shocked into giving her an Oscar for Best Supporting Actress when she played a blowsy hooker in Richard Brooks's *Elmer Gantry* (1960). She was thereafter a little more sexy in John Ford's *Two Rode Together* (1961) and in the sick comedy, *Bedtime Story* (1964) tricking tricksters Marlon Brando and David Niven, but she reverted to type in Vincente Minnelli's somewhat sugary *The Courtship Of Eddie's Father* (1963).

Shirley Jones had appeared on stage in musical-comedy before making films, and in cabaret with her husband, singer-dancer Jack Cassidy. (He died in a fire in 1976.) In the early 70s, she co-starred with her stepson David Cassidy in the popular TV series, 'The Partridge Family'. Shaun Cassidy, the teenage star of TV's 'The Hardy Boys' is her son. RB

in I Aim At The Stars (Columbia, 1960)

Curt Jurgens

Real name **Curd Jürgens**
Born **Munich, Germany, 13 December 1912**
Died **1982**

Whenever a producer wanted a Teutonic heavy or a Nazi with a heart of gold, they always seemed to call upon Curt Jurgens. It was as a Nazi pilot in the German film, *The Devil's General* (1955), that he became known outside his own country. In *The Enemy Below* (1957), he was the U-boat captain opposing Robert Mitchum as the US enemy above. He was the anti-semitic officer faced with Jewish Danny Kaye in *Me And The Colonel* (1958), the famous Nazi scientist Wernher von Braun in *I Aim At The Stars* (1960), and he played assorted Nazis and German officers in *The Longest Day* (1962), *Miracle Of The White Stallions* (1963), and the tribute to the RAF, *Battle Of Britain* (1969).

Actually, Jurgens spent the war in a concentration camp in Hungary for political undesirables, because of derogatory remarks he made about Dr Goebbels. He had previously been a journalist, but was encouraged to go on the stage by his first wife, actress Louise Basler. Most of his films before the war were operettas and costume melodramas. In 1955, he began his international film career. In France, with Brigitte Bardot in *And God Created Woman* (1955), and in Hollywood, besides Nazis, he was a Chinese general in *The Inn Of The Sixth Happiness* (1958). Unfortunately, he failed to erase the memory of Emil Jannings in the misconceived remake of *The Blue Angel* (1959). One of his last roles was as the arch-villain in the James Bond movie, *The Spy Who Loved Me* (1977). Jurgens was married five times, once to the exotic Hungarian actress Eva Bartok. RB

Howard Keel

Real name **Harry Clifford Leek**
Born **Gillespie, Illinois, 13 April 1917**

Many viewers of TV's 'Dallas' will, while watching the handsome silver-haired gentleman playing Clayton Farlow, remember the tall, self-confident baritone whose rich voice reverberated through many an MGM musical of the 50s. One expects him at any moment to burst out into a rendition of 'Where Is The Life That Late I Led' which he sang with such gusto in *Kiss Me Kate* (1953).

The life Howard Keel led began as the son of a coal miner. While working for an aircraft firm, he used to entertain his fellow workers in song. He made his professional debut in a West Coast production of 'Carousel' in 1945, which led to the role of Curly in the London production of 'Oklahoma!'. While in England, he made his first film, a little thriller inappropriately called *The Small Voice* (1948). When He made his successful Hollywood debut in *Annie Get Your Gun* (1950), a critic dubbed him 'A Gable who sings'.

Keel and Esther Williams made an odd couple in *Pagan Love Song* (1950) and *Texas Carnival* (1951), but his pairing with Kathryn Grayson in *Show Boat* (1951), *Lovely To Look At* (1952) and *Kiss Me Kate* worked beautifully. Irving Cummings, the producer of the latter, wanted Laurence Olivier, but Keel convinced him by making a screen test. The peak of his career was reached as Jane Powell's hillbilly husband in *Seven Brides For Seven Brothers* (1954). With the decline of the musical, to which the idiotic *Jupiter's Darling* (1955) and the tedious *Kismet* (1955) contributed, Keel became just another competent actor in routine westerns like *Red Tomahawk* (1967) and *The War Wagon* (1967), and as St Peter in *The Big Fisherman* (1959). RB

Grace Kelly

Born **Philadelphia, 12 November 1928**
Died **1982**

Once upon a time there lived a beautiful girl brought up in a wealthy Catholic Irish-American family in Philadelphia. She attended good schools in her home town, before going to New York to study at the American Academy of Dramatic Arts. Determined to prove that she could earn her own way, she did modelling on the side, as well as TV commercials. After appearing in a few plays on Broadway, she was invited to Hollywood where she soon became a famous film star, appearing in eleven movies and winning an Oscar as Best Actress for *The Country Girl* (1954). While attending the Cannes Film Festival in 1955, she met Prince Rainier III of Monaco at a reception given at his palace. A year later, she left Hollywood to become Princess Grace of Monaco in a spectacular marriage ceremony held

with James Stewart in Rear Window *(Paramount, 1954)*

in the principality. She resided in the splendid palace overlooking the bay with her Prince Charming and their three lovely children, Caroline, Albert and Stephanie... But the fairy tale does not have the traditional happy ending. While driving along the winding high roads along the Riviera, with her daughter Stephanie, she suffered a stroke. The car plunged off the road and Princess Grace was killed. The world was shocked, and a huge memorial service was held for her in Monaco.

At first, Grace Kelly seemed no more than a rather insipid, though undeniably pretty blonde in a bit part in *Fourteen Hours* (1951), and as Gary Cooper's patient bride in *High Noon* (1952). Her patrician beauty became more evident in John Ford's *Mogambo* (1953), although she paled beside Ava Gardner as the rival for game hunter Clark Gable's affections. However, during the shooting, she became intimate with Gable, and they might have married had Grace not felt that the 27-year age difference was too great. For her role as Donald Sinden's straying wife in the film, she was nominated for a Best Supporting Actress Oscar.

Although she was under contract to MGM (they initially bought *Cat On A Hot Tin Roof* for her), Kelly made most of her films on loan to other studios. It was in three Alfred Hitchcock pictures that her sex appeal was best revealed. She was Hitchcock's ideal 'cool blonde', to be violated in certain situations. She proved an unwilling victim of Ray Milland's murder plot in *Dial M For Murder* (1954); she was James Stewart's society girlfriend who is nearly murdered as a result of his voyeurism in *Rear Window* (1954), and was the delectable prey of a jewel thief in *To Catch A Thief* (1955), filmed only a few miles from her future home.

In vivid contrast to these spoiled sophisticates, Grace's role as the bitter, dowdy wife of an alcoholic singer (Bing Crosby) in *The Country Girl*, was an

attempt to prove she could be more than just glamorous. It is a good, perceptive performance, but many felt she received the Best Actress award for having the courage not to wear much make-up or elegant clothes. Having made her point, she quickly returned to undemanding decorative parts in *Green Fire* (1954) and *The Bridges At Toko-Ri* (1955).

Her last two films were tailor-made for her. *High Society* (1956) co-starred her again with Bing Crosby, whom she dated for a while. The Catholic widower thought that Kelly would make him a perfect wife, but the age gap was again an obstacle. However, they made a pleasant duo singing 'True

Love', her first and last singing assignment. When MGM heard of her impending marriage to the Prince, they quickly dusted off a play by Molnar and cast her as a Princess about to be Married in *The Swan* (1956) as a rehearsal for her real-life royal role.

Despite a great many offers to return to the screen, Grace Kelly always regretfully refused. She carried out the duties required of her, gave prizes at the Monte Carlo Rally, and performed charity readings of poetry around the world. She was a diligent mother, and spent some time in Paris when her daughter Caroline was studying there. On or off screen, she continued to play the role of a star. RB

Kay Kendall

Real name **Justine McCarthy**
Born **Hull, England, 1926**
Died **1959**

In a small, quiet and intimate cemetery in Hampstead, London, lies the grave of the lovely, tall and elegant Kay Kendall whose brilliant comedic talent flared for a short while before she died of leukemia in the prime of her life and beauty, aged 33. The simple gravestone and a handful of minor movies are all we have to remember her by.

Kay was the granddaughter of Marie Kendall, the stage performer, and her own parents were dancers. At 13, she was already in the chorus of shows at the London Palladium, and later toured with her sister in a variety act. In 1944, she began to make brief appearances in British musicals such as *Champagne Charlie* (1944), *Waltz Time* (1945), and *London Town* (1946). After a few years in provincial theatre and early TV, Kay returned to the cinema, but still made little impact. She was genteel beside Diana Dors in *Dance Hall* (1950) and *Lady Godiva Rides Again* (1951), hardly noticeable in the Vera-Ellen musical set in Scotland, *Happy Go Lovely* (1951), and wasted in heavy dramas such as *Street Of Shadows* (1953), and *The Square Ring* (1953) in which she played a boxer's girlfriend waiting on the sidelines. In *Curtain Up* (1952), a modest comedy about a repertory theatre company, she showed some of her comic abilities.

However, in a quaint British comedy about vintage cars, *Genevieve* (1953), she suddenly took up a trumpet at a jazz club and began to play it lustily. A star was born. The roles got bigger and a little better. She was a medical student's girlfriend in *Doctor In The House* (1954) with Dirk Bogarde; formed the 'ideal TV couple' with Peter Finch in *Simon And Laura* (1955); and was one of polygamist Rex Harrison's seven wives in *The Constant Husband* (1955). She was to become the much-married Harrison's real-life third wife in 1957.

Kay was never told that she had only three years to live in 1956, but her friends knew of it. When asked by her doctor what she wanted most in life,

in 1955

she replied 'Rex Harrison'. Both Rex and his then wife, Lilli Palmer, were aware of the situation. After they divorced, he married Kay – a marriage that was painful for him in many ways, because he realised that she would soon die. Meanwhile, Kay launched into a Hollywood career.

In her first American film for MGM, she was perversely cast against type as a maiden in distress rescued by Robert Taylor in the dull spectacle *Quentin Durward* (1955). Kay became virtually the only thing worth seeing in her last movies. In George Cukor's uninspired musical *Les Girls* (1957), she played one of three girls in a cabaret act with Gene Kelly. Her three show-stopping numbers included 'You're Just Too, Too!' with Kelly, and a drunken version of the 'Habanera'. She sparkled as Rex Harrison's wife with a difficult daughter in Vincente Minnelli's trivial *The Reluctant Debutante* (1958), and considerably lightened the plodding proceedings in Stanley Donen's *Once More With Feeling* (1960), in which she played a harp hilariously. Sadly, it was her last film. RB

Burt Lancaster

Real name Burton Stephen Lancaster
Born New York City, 2 November 1913

When Warner Bros. decided to make *Jim Thorpe – All American* (1951), a biopic of the greatest all-round athlete that America has ever produced, they naturally thought of the greatest all-round athlete the cinema has ever produced. Burt Lancaster exults in physical action, even in repose he is like a panther about to spring. He outleaped and outswashbuckled Fairbanks and Flynn in *The Flame And The Arrow* (1950) and *The Crimson Pirate* (1952); he rip-roared across the west in *The Kentuckian* (1955), *The Hallelujah Trail* (1965), *The Professionals* (1966), and *The Scalphunters* (1968); he heroically fought the Nazis in *Run Silent, Run Deep* (1958) in a submarine, as part of the French resistance in *The Train* (1964), and as a major holding off a German attack on a Belgian castle in *Castle Keep* (1969); and he fought the Viet-Cong in *Go Tell It To The Spartans* (1978), and Zulus in *Zulu Dawn* (1979), while often flashing the broadest grin ever committed to film. But there is far more to this smiling action man than meets the eye.

The son of a postal clerk, young Burton grew up

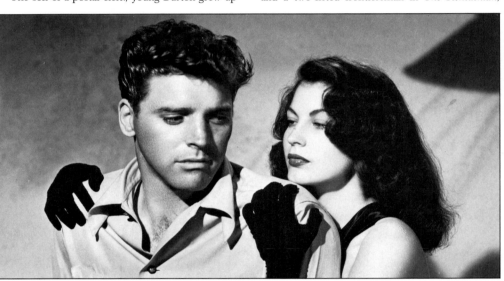
with Ava Gardner in The Killers *(Universal, 1946)*

in a tough section of Manhattan's Upper East Side. An excellent sportsman at school, he won an athletic scholarship to New York University, but left soon after to form an acrobatic act with his friend Nick Cravat. They appeared in circuses, vaudeville and nightclubs as Lang and Cravat, but split up when they didn't get enough bookings to make ends meet. Cravat later joined Lancaster again as his side-kick in the romantic, acrobatic spoofs, *The Flame And The Arrow* and *The Crimson Pirate*, and Burt's circus experience came in handy in *Trapeze* (1956). Lancaster had to take on less exciting jobs such as department store salesman and refrigerator repair man, before World War II gave him the action he needed. After service in North Africa and Italy, he returned to New York and odd jobs.

The story goes that he was 'discovered' in an elevator by a stage producer who asked him if he would read for a Broadway play. He got the part in 'The Sound Of Hunting' which only ran a few weeks, but he was spotted by agent Harold Hecht who got him a Hollywood contract. In 1948, they were to form their own production company, Hecht-Lancaster, later joined by producer James Hill. Mark Hellinger bravely cast the unknown actor in the lead of his production *The Killers* (1946), opposite Ava Gardner in her first big role, and directed by Robert Siodmak, the master of *film noir*. As the ex-boxer waiting in a sordid hotel room to be killed, Lancaster made a striking debut. The sombre, handsome curly-headed 33-year-old, was then cast in a series of low key underworld melodramas. He was behind

bars in Jules Dassin's taut prison drama *Brute Force* (1947); a bitter ex-con in *I Walk Alone* (1948), finding the outside as tough as inside; a murderer on the run in London in the nasty thriller *Kiss The Blood Off My Hands* with Joan Fontaine (1948); Barbara Stanwyck's murderous husband in *Sorry Wrong Number* (1948); and was fatally attracted to Yvonne De Carlo in Siodmak's bleak crime story *Criss Cross* (1949). At the same period, he also played Edward G. Robinson's bespectacled and embittered son in *All My Sons* (1948). Not many flashing smiles or leaping about in these.

The beginning of the 50s found Burt smiling for the first time in a light comedy, *Mister 880* (1950), and proving his athletic prowess in *The Flame And The Arrow*, *Jim Thorpe-All American*, and *The Crimson Pirate*, the latter uncharacteristically directed by Siodmak. He impersonated Thorpe with vigour and a certain pathos, and did a good job of suggesting him in football, baseball and on the track. *Ten Tall Men* (1951) was a tongue-in-cheek foreign legion tale, *South Sea Woman* (1953) a high-spirited farce with Virginia Mayo, and *His Majesty O'Keefe* (1954), another pirate romp set in the South Seas. In the horseplay western *Vera Cruz* (1954), he was an ebullient, grinning foil to Gary Cooper's stoicism; and a two-fisted frontiersman in *The Kentuckian*,

which he directed himself. One of the greatest of stunt men, Gil Perkins, commented that Burt Lancaster 'has great ability, particularly from heights. He's very well co-ordinated and does high wire and trapeze work. But, of course, he does not do all his own stunts. He can ride a horse pretty good now, but at first he was fairly weak at this. Still, it's true that he's done more things himself than most actors have.'

But this most extrovert of actors was not content for his career to proceed only by leaps and bounds. In *Come Back, Little Sheba* (1952), he contained his athlete's body in that of a broken, middle-aged alcoholic, in a performance of suppressed emotion, even more effective beside the more obvious Oscar-winning histrionics of Shirley Booth as his lonely wife. He gave a forceful performance as Sergeant Warden in Fred Zinnemann's *From Here To Eternity* (1953), his erotic grappling with Deborah Kerr on the beach as the waves pound in, being the most vivid and parodied examples of sexual symbolism in the movies. Further roles that widened his range were the pacifist Indian in Robert Aldrich's *Apache* (1954); the simpleton truck driver courting Anna Magnani in *The Rose Tattoo* (1955); Wyatt Earp to Kirk Douglas's Doc Holliday in *Gunfight At The O.K. Corral* (1957); and J.J. Hunsecker, the megalomaniac newspaper columnist in Alexander MacKendrick's biting *The Sweet Smell Of Success* (1957) with steely eyes glinting behind his glasses. It was one of his greatest achievements, and one of his rare villains.

His Oscar-winning performance in Richard Brooks's *Elmer Gantry* (1960), is the sort of silver-tongued con-man he does with ease, a variation on his Starbuck in *The Rainmaker* (1956), who charms Katharine Hepburn and the rain from the sky. There was not much room for his physical grace in *Birdman Of Alcatraz* (1962) as most of it takes place in a prison cell, but Lancaster's mesmeric performance, ageing from his teens to middle-age, sustains all two-and-half hours, and deserved the best actor award at the Venice Film Festival. The following year, Luchino Visconti needed a big star to finance *The Leopard* (1963), so he asked the man from New

York to play the dying 19th-century Sicilian prince. Lancaster at 50, had begun a series of impressive autumnal roles, usually playing the part of a man who sees his old world crumbling around him. As a man who swims each of his wealthy neighbour's pools, fighting the insidious onset of age in *The Swimmer* (1968), he almost makes the parable convincing. In Aldrich's *Ulzana's Raid* (1972), he played an ageing scout hunting the Apaches; for Visconti again, in *Conversation Piece* (1975), he was a professor who has his ivory tower invaded; and in Louis Malle's *Atlantic City* (1980), he won his second Oscar as a man from another age watching the walls collapsing around him.

Lancaster was one of the first stars to become a producer. The Hecht-Hill-Lancaster company made a number of important films besides those starring Burt. His son Bill wrote the screenplay for *The Bad News Bears* (1976), and played the young version of his father in *Moses* (1976). RB

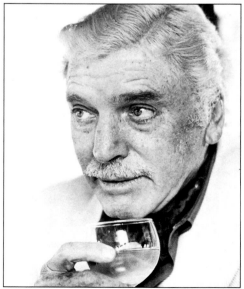
in Atlantic City *(Paramount, 1981)*

in The Rainmaker *(Paramount, 1956)* ▷

Piper Laurie

Real name **Rosetta Jacobs**
Born **Detroit, Michigan, 22 January 1932**

For those who remembered the pert and pretty Piper Laurie at Universal in the 50s, it was hard to believe that the lonely, lame girl in Robert Rossen's *The Hustler* (1961) who commits suicide when rejected by Paul Newman, was one and the same girl. It was a moving and surprising performance. Surprising, because nothing she did before or since touched it. Immediately afterwards, having proved that she could act, she married the film critic Joseph Morgenstern and retired from the screen. She returned fifteen years later, as the loony, fanatically religious mother of Sissy Spacek in Brian De Palma's repulsive-compulsive *Carrie* (1976) for which she was Oscar-nominated, and continued the shock treatment in *Ruby* (1977), as the former gangster's moll haunted by her dead lover, a far cry from the days when she was part of Universal's stable of young talent.

At eighteen, she made her debut in *Louisa* (1950) as a teenager with romantic problems. But strangely, for one so unexotic, she made her name playing Bagdad princesses in lush Arabian Nights adventures with Tony Curtis in *The Prince Who Was A Thief* (1951) and *Son Of Ali Baba* (1952), and with Rock Hudson in *The Golden Blade* (1953). More down-to-earth roles included a flapper in *Has Anybody Seen My Gal?* (1952), a saloon gal in *Dawn At Socorro* (1954), a chorus gal in *Ain't Misbehavin'* (1955), and the only gal in *Smoke Signal* (1955). She recently appeared in the TV soap opera, 'The Thorn Birds' (1983), set in Australia, filmed in California. RB

Jerry Lewis

Real name **Joseph Levitch**
Born **Newark, New Jersey, 16 March 1926**

In *The Nutty Professor* (1963), Jerry Lewis as a bespectacled, absent-minded professor invents a formula that turns him into a cool, good-looking ladies' man, a character bearing a resemblance to Dean Martin. It is a hilarious demonstration that inside every Jerry Lewis is a Dean Martin trying to get out, and of Jerry's Jekyll and Hyde personality. As a performer and director, he can make one wriggle with delight one moment and squirm with embarrassment the next. He sometimes achieves the perfection of his idol Stan Laurel, but although Laurel cried a lot, he was never as sentimental as Lewis. A film he directed, dampeningly titled *The Day The Clown Cried* (1974), set in a concentration camp, is still awaiting release. In Martin Scorsese's *King Of Comedy* (1982), Lewis gave a finely nuanced, restrained and unsmiling performance as a talk show host, and his first four movies as director and star, *The Bellboy* (1960), *The Ladies' Man* (1961), *The Errand Boy* (1961) and *The Nutty Professor*, were quite sufficient to prove that he is a comic talent to be taken seriously.

Jerry Lewis's parents were vaudeville performers and, from the age of five, he would occasionally join their act during the school vacation. When he dropped out of high school, he supported himself with a variety of menial jobs. At 18, he married Patty Palmer, a vocalist with the Jimmy Dorsey band, and became a comic entertaining in the Catskills. In 1946, he met a small-time singer called Dean Martin and they decided to form an act. In a few years, they were the country's top comedy team on stage, cabaret and TV, and it was not long before they signed a contract with Paramount.

They made their debut in *My Friend Irma* (1949), in secondary but scene-stealing parts. *My Friend Irma Goes West* (1950), led to starring roles in a further 14 comedies, generally with Dean, the handsome heel, exploiting his moronic friend Jerry. Among the best of a bad lot were *That's My Boy* (1951), *The Stooge* (1953) and *You're Never Too Young* (1955), and two Frank Tashlin comedies, *Artists And Models* (1955) and *Hollywood Or Bust* (1956), the last films before they split up with bitterness on both sides. Both were beginning to feel restricted by the other's personality.

It was Tashlin who inspired Lewis to direct his own films. In Tashlin's *Who's Minding The Store?* (1963), and *The Disorderly Orderly* (1964), Jerry is like a doll manipulated by a drunken puppeteer, or an animated figure in a cruel cartoon. His own first films are a series of comic sketches linked by a tenuous theme, often using surreal sight gags. Unfortunately, Lewis's later movies deteriorated, with repetition, crassness and sentimentality uppermost. But he remains a big name in the States, mainly because of his annual Labor Day 21-hour TV marathon in aid of children with muscular dystrophy. He himself has six sons. RB

with Richard Haydn (left) in Money From Home *(Paramount, 1953)*

Janet Leigh

Real name **Jeanette Helen Morrison**
Born **Merced, California, 6 July 1927**

When Janet Leigh absconds with $40,000, steals a car, and is viciously stabbed to death while taking a shower in a deserted motel in Alfred Hitchcock's thriller *Psycho* (1960), more was washed away than her blood down the plug hole. She allowed herself to be killed off halfway through the movie, although she was the female star, showed herself undressed in the erotic Peeping-Tom shower sequence, and proved that she could be a tough and sexy blonde, instead of projecting only sweetness and light. Only a few major directors realised this. As a Russian spy in Josef von Sternberg's *Jet Pilot* (1951), she was more than a match for John Wayne; she held her own among the men in Anthony Mann's tense western *The Naked Spur* (1953), and – presaging *Psycho* – was first menaced in a motel in Orson Welles's baroque *Touch Of Evil* (1958).

Janet Leigh had been married twice before she was twenty. While studying music at the College of the Pacific, she was discovered by Norma Shearer

in Safari *(Columbia, 1956)*

who got her an MGM contract, despite her having never acted professionally before. She made her debut as a farmer's daughter in *The Romance Of Rosy Ridge* (1947) opposite Van Johnson, the first in a long line of wholesome ingénue roles. She co-starred with bland Tom Drake in the Lassie film, *Hills Of Home* (1948) and the biopic *Words And Music* (1948, as composer Richard Rodgers's wife), and played Meg in *Little Women* (1949). She was merely pretty in the costume dramas *Scaramouche* (1952), *Prince Valiant* (1954), *The Black Shield Of Falmouth* (1954) and *The Vikings* (1958), the latter two with Tony Curtis whom she married in 1951. They also appeared together in *Houdini* (1953), *The Perfect Furlough* (1959) and *Who Was That Lady?* (1960). The marriage ended in 1962.

Janet danced and sang pleasantly in a few musicals, *Two Tickets To Broadway* (1951), in the title role of *My Sister Eileen* (1955), and in a dark wig as Rosie in *Bye Bye Birdie* (1963). Her appearances on the large screen in the 70s grew more and more rare, but she found time to be frightened by giant rabbits in the ludicrous *Night Of The Lepus* (1972), and by *The Fog* (1979), with her talented and attractive daughter, Jamie Lee Curtis. RB

Gina Lollobrigida

Born **Subiaco, Italy, 4 July 1927**

In the 50s, a French bra ad used the term 'Les Lollos.' People immediately knew they referred to the ex-beauty queen, model and fortune teller's assistant Gina Lollobrigida, known merely by the sensuous sounding name of 'La Lollo'.

She studied as a commercial artist, but soon found herself modelling for others under the name of Diana Loris. Beauty contests led to films, and she first began to be noticed in two French pictures with dashing Gérard Philipe, *Fanfan La Tulipe* (1951) and René Clair's *Les Belles Du Nuit* (1952); in Italy as the fiery village girl after Vittorio De Sica's policeman in *Bread, Love And Dreams* (1953), and *Bread, Love And Jealousy* (1954); and as a girl of easy virtue in *Woman Of Rome* (1954). These roles brought her to the notice of Howard Hughes who offered her a contract, but a dispute over it kept her from working in America for some years.

However, in Europe, Lollobrigida played Humphrey Bogart's wife in John Huston's playful *Beat The Devil* (1954), Esmeralda opposite Anthony Quinn in *The Hunchback Of Notre Dame* (1956), and was the lovely bone of contention between Tony Curtis and Burt Lancaster, on the ground and in the air, in the circus drama *Trapeze* (1956).

At the beginning of her screen career, Gina married her Yugoslav-born manager. For years she had wanted a child, but he felt it would ruin her career. She finally persuaded him but, sadly, they separated soon after her baby was born. Her American films, an uninspiring lot, included *Solomon And Sheba* (1959), *Never So Few* (1959), a clichéd war drama, and two glossy comedies with Rock Hudson, *Come September* (1961) and *Strange Bedfellows* (1965). She returned to Italy, cropping up from time to time in English-speaking films such as *Hotel Paradiso* (1966), and *Buona Sera, Mrs Campbell* (1969). She left the cinema in the early 70s to become a professional photographer and executive with a cosmetics firm. RB

Sophia Loren

Real name **Sofia Scicolone**
Born **Rome, Italy, 20 September 1934**

The story almost reads like an Italian rags-to-riches melodrama, with the titles of some of Sophia Loren's films as chapter headings: *It Started In Naples* (1960), *The Pride And The Passion* (1957), *A Breath Of Scandal* (1960), *Marriage Italian Style* (1964) and *The Millionairess* (1960). Little, skinny Sofia grew up in poverty in the Neapolitan slums, the illegitimate child of a frustrated actress. As she grew, her mother pushed her into beauty contests – she came second in one of them, wearing a dress made from curtains. When she was fifteen, her mother took her to the Cinecittà studios in Rome where they both got jobs as extras on *Quo Vadis* (1951). The now well-developed Sophia exposed her breasts in *Era Lui, Si, Si* (1951), and came to the attention of film producer Carlo Ponti who gave her a contract and groomed her for stardom.

Gradually she was given leading roles such as *Aida* (1953-miming to the voice of Renata Tebaldi), and as the philandering wife in Vittorio De Sica's *Gold Of Naples* (1954). The statuesque, busty Loren soon became known the world over. She was later to

comment, 'Sex appeal is 50% of what you've got and 50% what people think you've got.' She was certainly given a great publicity build-up before her first English-speaking film, *Boy On A Dolphin* (1957) with Alan Ladd. Sophia brought her beauty, vitality and good humour to *Houseboat* (1958) with Cary

Grant, and George Cukor's *Heller In Pink Tights* (1960), but the weighty plaudits came for her unglamorous dramatic role as the mother protecting her daughter in wartime Italy in De Sica's *Two Women* (1961). It won her the Best Actress Oscar.

In 1957, Sophia had married Ponti, 24 years her senior, after he had obtained a divorce in Mexico, but Italian law refused to recognise the divorce and he was charged with bigamy. In 1966, they were forced to renounce their Italian nationality and become French citizens. Loren continued to be an international star, but few of her films were of merit. The declining De Sica directed her in *The Condemned Of Altona* (1962) in which she was unconvincing as a German; *Yesterday, Today And Tomorrow* (1964), *Sunflower* (1969) and *The Voyage* (1974). She was diverting in Stanley Donen's *Arabesque* (1966) with Gregory Peck, and was a blameless participant, co-starring with Marlon Brando, in Chaplin's crudely unfunny *A Countess From Hong Kong* (1967). She was highly acclaimed again for eschewing glamour in *A Special Day* (1977) as the dowdy housewife and supporter of Mussolini.

The Pontis' battle with the Italian law continued. He was sentenced in absentia for currency violations, and Sophia herself recently spent a few weeks in an Italian jail for tax evasion. RB

Shirley Maclaine

Real name **Shirley MacLean Beatty.**
Born **Richmond, Virginia, 24 April 1934**

Webster's dictionary defines the word 'kooky' as 'screwball'. They might have done better merely to note 'see Shirley MacLaine'. 'Screwball' is something infinitely harder, more 30s and 40s, than MacLaine's dumb floozie and heart-of-gold tramp of the 50s, the image indelibly formed in Vincente Minnelli's *Some Came Running* (1959) for which she received an Oscar nomination.

Shirley's drama-coach mother pushed her and her younger brother, Warren Beatty, on to the stage at a very early age. After graduating from high school, she went to New York where she did modelling before getting into the chorus of Broadway shows. Just like the plot of a hackneyed musical, she was understudying Carol Haney in the Broadway production of 'The Pajama Game' in 1954, when Haney broke a leg a few days into the run. Independent producer Hal Wallis saw her and offered her a film contract, and she made her debut in Hitchcock's macabre comedy *The Trouble With Harry* (1955). She then landed the female lead in Mike Todd's star-studded *Around The World In 80 Days* (1956), curiously miscast as an Indian princess. She was engaging in *The Sheepman* (1958), *The Matchmaker* (1958) and *Hot Spell* (1958), before breaking into the big time with *Some Came Running* as the good-time

gal stuck on Frank Sinatra.

After throwing herself around in *Can-Can* (1959), doing an Apache as well as the title dance, and acting no less strenuously, Maclaine was offered her best role in her best film, Billy Wilder's *The Apartment* (1960). As the elevator girl who attempts suicide over her boss, she is the perfect kook,

working beautifully with Jack Lemmon's schnook. Three years later, Wilder cast them together again in the raucously unfunny *Irma La Douce* (1963), in which she played the popular Parisian prostitute, predictably and without delicacy. However, she was nominated for an Oscar for both performances. In *What A Way To Go!* (1964), about a woman who has several husbands, and in Vittorio De Sica's *Woman Times Seven* (1967), playing seven roles, she was vastly overexposed; and as a tart again in *Sweet Charity* (1969), vastly over-emphatic. But she was subtle and moving as the schoolmistress accused of lesbianism with Audrey Hepburn in Lilian Hellman's *The Loudest Whisper* (1962).

Between films, Shirley has been active in many fields. In politics, she worked for Bobby Kennedy in 1968, and campaigned for MacGovern in 1972. She had her own TV show called 'Shirley's World'; produced, wrote and co-directed *The Other Half Of The Sky* (1975), a full-length documentary of a trip she made to China in 1973; and wrote two memoirs, one of which discloses an affair she had with an unnamed British politician, while separated from her husband Steve Parker, a producer of shows in the Far East. After over four years away from screen acting, she returned as the bitchy ex-ballerina who has given up her career for domesticity in *The Turning Point* (1977). She was as excessive as Peter Sellers was restrained in *Being There* (1979), but finally won her longed-for Best Actress Oscar for *Terms Of Endearment* (1984). RB

Gordon MacRae

Born **East Orange, New Jersey,
12 March 1921**

Possessed of an agreeable baritone voice, a manly physique and a blandly good-natured personality, Gordon MacRae might have been a Broadway name at almost any period in its history. That, in the 50s, he achieved Hollywood stardom, was due principally to the fact that he happened to be around when most needed.

His rise to success was almost tediously conventional. As a child, he performed in radio dramas; in his teens, he made a reputation as a big band vocalist; and, following World War II service and some Broadway experience, he was snapped up by a Hollywood talent scout. On the lookout for a personable leading man for Doris Day, Warners cast him opposite her in a modest adaptation of Vincent Youmans's 'No, No, Nanette', *Tea For Two* (1950). This was succeeded by two thick slices of apple-pie Americana, *On Moonlight Bay* and *By The Light Of The Silvery Moon* (1951 and 1953), both visibly influenced by MGM's *Meet Me In St. Louis*. And when the fashion for musicals originally conceived for the screen waned in favour of large-scale adaptations of theatrical hits, his somewhat stagey voice and mannerisms were still in demand: he

played Curly, belting out 'Oh, What A Beautiful Morning' in Rodgers and Hammerstein's *Oklahoma!* (directed by Fred Zinnemann in 1955), and a swaggering carnival barker in the same composers' *Carousel* (1956). MacRae, in short, personified 'the boy next door' – literally in *On Moonlight Bay*, and figuratively throughout his career. DM

Karl Malden

Real name **Mladen Sekulovich**
Born **Gary, Indiana, 22 March 1914**

Since character actors, by their very nature, lack any consistent personal mythology to carry them through good and bad films alike, they are more dependent than stars on an intelligent selection of roles. Thus, were it not already evident from his performances, the intelligence of an actor like Karl Malden could be deduced from the number of major directors with whom he has worked. These include Cukor, Hathaway, Kazan (several times), King, Preminger, Milestone, Vidor, Hitchcock, Brooks, Mulligan, Daves, Brando (in *One-Eyed Jacks*, 1961), Frankenheimer, Ford, Quine and Shaffner. In his best, and most personal, work he has succeeded in exploring depths of moral ambiguity rare in the commercial cinema.

The son of Yugoslav immigrant parents, and instantly recognisable from early youth by his uniquely bulbous nose, Malden started his career with a series of vivid supporting roles in such gritty 20th Century-Fox thrillers as *13 Rue Madeleine*, *Boomerang*, *Kiss Of Death* (all 1947) and *Where The Sidewalk Ends* (1950), before winning an Oscar in 1951 as Blanche DuBois's shy, sweaty suitor in *A Streetcar Named Desire*, directed by Elia Kazan. Again under Kazan's direction, he was sympathetic as a worker's priest in *On The Waterfront* (1954) and wonderfully droll as the middle-aged husband of a Deep South child bride in *Baby Doll* (1956). He

appeared in an almost unbroken sequence of major 60s films (notably *All Fall Down*, *Birdman Of Alcatraz*, the musical *Gypsy*, in which he was a marvellous foil to Rosalind Russell, *The Cincinnati Kid*, *Nevada Smith* and *Patton*); and when Hollywood rejuvenated itself in the following decade, he rapidly became a TV favourite as a detective in 'The Streets Of San Francisco'. Malden's sole directorial credit, the Korean War drama *Time Limit* (1957), proved no less taut and gripping than one of his own performances. DM

Jayne Mansfield

Real name **Vera Jayne Palmer**
Born **Bryn Mawr, Pennsylvania,
13 April 1933**
Died **New Orleans, 1967**

It is not difficult to mock Jayne Mansfield. To start with, the notion of her birthplace being Bryn Mawr, much publicised as Katharine Hepburn's *alma mater*, is irresistibly funny. Her insatiable craving for publicity, her marriage to muscle-man Mickey Hargitay, her heart-shaped swimming-pool, the

'aerial' photographs of her cleavage – all were grist to the tireless mill of columnists and *paparazzi*. The existence of any real talent was certainly open to question, though, in one of the most consistently awful filmographies in cinema history, it was never put to the test.

Mansfield was fired by one ambition – to become a star. And though her principal (and perhaps sole) qualification was a grotesquely voluptuous physique, she worked hard at being professional, with drama classes at the University of Texas and UCLA, innumerable beauty contests and bit parts. In 1955 she created a sensation on Broadway as a dizzy, mutton-headed stunner in 'Will Success Spoil Rock Hunter?' and reprised it in Frank Tashlin's brilliant film version (1957). (The previous year Tashlin had cunningly exploited her as a rock 'n' roll icon in *The Girl Can't Help It*.) It was, however, becoming all too evident that the figure of fun she so cheerfully embodied was not wholly a character role; and her appearances were soon confined to cheap British thrillers, sleazy Italian melodramas and out-and-out porn movies. Her career, culminating with an early and particularly horrific death in an automobile crash, was as tragic in its way as Monroe's. There, unfortunately, the comparison ends. DM

Dorothy Malone

Real name **Dorothy Maloney**
Born **Chicago, 30 January 1925**

Dorothy Malone is one of those performers for whom movie buffs admit to a fondness not quite justified by her place in film history. In a fairly lengthy career, she appeared in few works of distinction, and probably remains most familiar to the general public as Constance MacKenzie in the long-running TV series 'Peyton Place'. Yet she was a talented actress when the role allowed her to be, one capable of projecting a potent blend of cynicism, sexuality and intelligence. She was terrific, for example, as a bespectacled bookstore assistant in *The Big Sleep* (1946), fully deserved her Oscar as a sex-starved oil heiress in Douglas Sirk's luridly

baroque *Written On The Wind* (1956), and was equally moving in the same director's Faulkner adaptation *The Tarnished Angels* (1958).

Malone was spotted by an RKO talent scout while acting in a college play at Southern Methodist University and, as Dorothy Maloney, featured in a number of forgotten potboilers. Later, moving to Warners, she changed her name, the colour of her hair (from brunette to blonde), and from one brand of typecasting to another (nice girl to seasoned floozie, notably in Raoul Walsh's *Battle Cry*, 1955, where her overt sexuality attracted the censor's attention). But not even an Academy Award could salvage a disappointing career; and on those rare occasions when a starring role was offered her (e.g. as Diana Barrymore opposite Errol Flynn in the biopic *Too Much, Too Soon*, 1958), she was invariably ill-served by poor material. DM

Dean Martin

Real name **Dino Paul Crocetti**
Born **Steubenville, Ohio, 7 June 1917**

If Dean Martin's persona were to be resuméd in a single neat formula, it might be 'good company'. This amiable, hard-drinking crooner rarely deigned to give a 'performance' as such: he was content to lend his undemanding presence to a number of films. In the 50s he kept company with Jerry Lewis through a series of record-breaking comedies; in the 60s with Frank Sinatra's 'rat pack' through a series of mildly amusing diversions (*Ocean's 11, Sergeants 3, 4 For Texas, Robin And The 7 Hoods*), apparently made as much for the cast's pleasure as the audience's.

As a young man, Martin had been variously prizefighter, mill labourer, professional gambler and nightclub singer. In 1946, he formed a partnership with the comedian Jerry Lewis; and, already hugely popular on stage and TV, they made sixteen films together, from *My Friend Irma* (1949) to *Hollywood Or Bust!* (1956), the best, because most manic, of which were directed by Frank Tashlin. The team's break-up was an acrimonious one, and Martin looked far more vulnerable than Lewis as a solo performer. Yet, by sheer personality, he retained his following, even offering a handful of impressive performances in *The Young Lions* (1958), *Some Came Running, Rio Bravo* (both 1959) and especially, parodying his own boozy, lecherous swinger's image, in Billy Wilder's *Kiss Me Stupid* (1964).

Martin retired from the cinema in the mid-70s, leaving it much as he had found it. En route, he made a quartet of James Bond spin-offs, (the Matt Helm Movies), as well as some unmemorable westerns, and was the glamorous pilot of the Boeing 747 in *Airport* (1970). DM

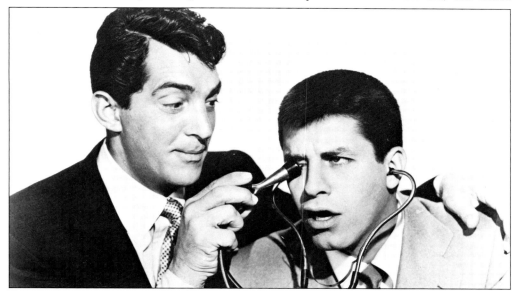

with Jerry Lewis (right) in Living It Up *(Paramount, 1954)*

Marcello Mastroianni

Born **Fontana Liri, Italy, 28 September 1923**

As befits the most celebrated male actor of postwar Italian cinema, Marcello Mastroianni's childhood and youth recall the narrative of some early neo-realist film. Of impoverished peasant origins, he was sent to a German labour camp during World War II, effected a daring escape and went into hiding in an attic in Venice. Drifting into the theatre while at university, he began to acquire a reputation as a member of Luchino Visconti's repertory company; and, with his dark, matinée idol good looks, humanised by a hint of melancholic insecurity, he soon gravitated towards the cinema, then enjoying a recrudescence in his native country. By 1958, when he had completed both Visconti's beautiful adaptation of Dostoevsky's *White Nights* and Monicelli's delightfully wacky farce *Big Deal On Madonna Street*, the parameters of his highly successful career were clearly established.

Mastroianni has acted in scores of films, a high proportion of which were made by major directors: Visconti, Dassin, Fellini, Bolognini, Antonioni, Germi, Malle, Zurlini, de Sica, Petri, Boorman, Polanski, Ferreri and Demy. He was unforgettable as the disillusioned journalist in Fellini's *La Dolce Vita* (1960), becoming the same director's flattering alter ego in *8½* (1963) and again, more recently, in *City Of Women* (1979); poignant and funny as a suicidal gastronome in Ferreri's *La Grande Bouffe* (1973); and, in the cycle of light comedies co-starring Sophia Loren (eg *Yesterday, Today And Tomorrow, Marriage Italian Style, The Priest's Wife*), he could justifiably claim to be the Italian Cary Grant. In short, contemporary European cinema is inconceivable without him. DM

with Anita Ekberg in La Dolce Vita *(Astor, 1960)*

Sal Mineo

Real name **Salvatore Mineo**
Born **The Bronx, New York, 10 January 1939**
Died **Los Angeles, 1976**

Few actors personified that archetypal 50s phenomenon, 'the crazy mixed-up kid', more tenaciously than Sal Mineo, whose career flourished during the decade and died with it. Of Sicilian descent, a troublemaker at school, he was only ten when he made his first appearance on Broadway in Tennessee Williams's 'The Rose Tattoo'. With another theatrical success behind him, as Yul Brynner's son

in 'The King And I', he was signed to play the tormented young Plato in *Rebel Without A Cause* (1955), for which he won an Oscar nomination. Nicholas Ray's melodrama, though dated now, became a movie Bible for a whole generation of teenagers, but Mineo's tragedy was that, while the film made James Dean a star, his own character proved too baby-faced, maudlin and vulnerable to inspire audience identification.

That, alas, was the story of Mineo's career (and, in a sense, his life). In *Crime In The Streets, Somebody Up There Likes Me* (both 1956), *Dino* and *The Young Don't Cry* (both 1957), he continued to play juvenile delinquents, almost invariably hopeless cases. But with age, and despite a second Oscar nomination for his performance as a young Israeli terrorist in *Exodus* (1960), his career began to lose its sense of direction. Mineo worked intermittently on TV and, on Broadway again, directed 'Fortune And Men's Eyes', a prison drama with a powerfully explicit homosexual theme. His last film was *Escape From The Planet Of The Apes* (1971). Then, in 1976, the actor once known as 'The Switch-Blade Kid' was himself stabbed to death in mysterious circumstances. DM

Marilyn Monroe

Real name Norma Jean Baker (or Mortenson)
Born Los Angeles, 1 June 1926
Died 1962

Said Joseph L. Mankiewicz of her, 'Marilyn was the most frightened little girl, who had no confidence in her ability. She was afraid to come on screen. A very strange girl. And yet, scared as she was, she had this strange effect when she was photographed: when she stepped out in front of the camera, the camera liked her. In fact, the camera loved her.' and the former American ambassadress and writer Clare Booth Luce wrote, 'Marilyn's sessions with her studio mirror must have been agonising experiences after she had passed thirty. The hostility and aggressiveness she began to show in her later years (especially to the men who worked with her), the endless changes of clothes and the fits of extreme nervousness just before the cameras began to grind were obvious signs that Marilyn was not destined to grow to a ripe old age. So that, though her death came as a shock, of course, I cannot honestly say that it came as a real surprise.' In effect, if Marilyn Monroe were living today, she would be 58 years old – a strange and perhaps unacceptable image of one of the most beautiful, most legendary women our century has known.

A measure of the uniquely obsessive interest which the whole world has taken in her offscreen personality might be the fact that the name given her at birth, Norma Jean – a name changed in the 40s by 20th Century-Fox's publicity department – is now practically as well-known as that which was to become a household word. So much has been written about Monroe – by hacks and geniuses, by movie directors and hangers-on, by Arthur Miller and Norman Mailer – that the troubled, finally tragic, circumstances of her life and death are probably more familiar to the general public than the plots of her films. For the benefit of any Martian readers, however, it might be worthwhile recounting them yet again.

Her mother, Gladys Pearl Baker (whose maiden name was Monroe), worked as a cutter at various Hollywood studios. Her father's identity has never properly been established, though Monroe discovered at the age of sixteen, when applying for her first marriage licence, that the name which her mother had entered in her birth certificate was that of Edward Mortenson, a baker who had died in a road accident in 1929. She also discovered her illegitimacy. Because of Gladys Pearl's mental instability, Monroe's childhood was a profoundly unhappy, loveless and underprivileged one, spent in a series of foster homes while her mother was confined in psychiatric hospitals. Rape was only the worst of the abuses suffered by the lonely child, who was consistently neglected and humiliated. At the age of nine, she was placed in an orphanage, at eleven she lodged with one of her mother's friends, and at sixteen, a mature and ravishingly beautiful teenager, she married a young worker in a local aircraft factory, Jim Dougherty. Monroe never denied that she accepted his proposal with the sole aim of escaping the endless, literally vicious circle of foster homes; and, only a year later, she attempted suicide, more in a desperate endeavour to call attention to her wretchedness than to end her life.

During the war, with her husband serving overseas in the merchant marines, Monroe took a job as a paint sprayer in an armaments factory, where she was spotted by an Army photographer and invited to pose for morale-boosting pin-ups. The success of these snaps led to a contract with a modelling agency, one which took the first major step in transforming the sullen Norma Jean Baker into the almost supernaturally radiant Marilyn Monroe: it had her brown hair bobbed and bleached blonde. Divorced, she began to make real headway as a cover girl and 20th Century-Fox, after edging out Howard Hughes, signed her to a year's contract in 1946. With her glamorous change of name, plus count-less pin-up portraits, the attention of gossip columnists, singing, dancing and acting lessons, Monroe soon became what today might be termed a 'superstarlet'.

The studio seemed less concerned, however, actually to cast her in any films: her two appearances under this contract were walk-ons in forgotten programmers, *Scudda-Hoo! Scudda-Hay!* and *Dangerous Years* (both 1948). And when the year was up, Fox declined to renew her contract, but she was given a leading role as the daughter of a burlesque queen in Columbia's *Ladies Of The Chorus* (also 1948). She was not very good. So Columbia, too, dropped her; whereupon, unemployed and, as she later put it, 'hungry', she posed for the most famous nude calendar in the world. She received fifty dollars, not an unreasonable fee for a single session, except that the calendar company has since made close to a million in profits.

In 1950 no fewer than six films were released in which she made tiny, but already striking, appearances: the most notable were *Love Happy*, last and weakest of the Marx Brothers vehicles (in which Groucho, informed by Monroe that she is being followed by a strange man, incredulously retorts, 'Only *one*?'); John Huston's atmospheric thriller *The Asphalt Jungle*; and Mankiewicz's *All About Eve*, in which she played a 'graduate from the Copacabana School of Dramatic Art'. By now, as the object of a barrage of publicity, she was a full-fledged star; and

in 1948

when, in 1954, she married the baseball hero Joe DiMaggio, she could justifiably claim to be one of the most famous women in America. With an undulating wiggle of the hips, a breathy delivery that could turn the most innocuous phrase into an unmistakable come-on, and an almost parodically sexy pout, she was the epitome of 50s eroticism, much imitated and yet inimitable.

Her film roles were gradually improving, though, as was demonstrated by *Don't Bother To Knock* (1952), in which she was cast as a mentally disturbed baby-sitter, she was always a trifle stiff and inexpressive in strictly dramatic roles. (Another drama, however – *Niagara* in 1953 – is a key Monroe movie, as she was used by director Henry Hathaway purely as an icon, resplendent in the garish Fox Technicolor of the period.) But her teaming with Jane Russell in Howard Hawks's *Gentlemen Prefer Blondes* (also 1953) was a wonderfully effective casting *coup*. Good or bad, every one of her films constituted a media event. And certain single shots went around the world: for example, that in Billy Wilder's *The Seven Year Itch* (1955), in which she stands astride a New York subway grating with her skirt swirling up over her body. But she herself was dissatisfied. She harboured ambitions as a 'serious actress', one who would be at home in Dostoevsky and O'Neill; and, ignoring the sarcastic

reception which her pretensions met with, she enrolled at the famed Actors' Studio under the personal tutelage of Lee and Paula Strasberg.

Monroe surprised the carpers when, in 1955, she gave an endearing performance as a down-at-heel nightclub singer in *Bus Stop*. Then, in the following year, she amazed both fans and detractors by marrying the dramatist Arthur Miller (later to write a play, 'After The Fall', whose protagonist was a thinly disguised portrait of his ex-wife). And even if Terence Rattigan was not quite in the same league as Dostoevsky, her cultural respectability was further enhanced when she appeared opposite Laurence Olivier in *The Prince And The Showgirl* (1957). Like the original play, the film was a feeble confection, but its failure was completely overshadowed by the smash hit success of Wilder's near-perfect farce *Some Like It Hot* (1959), in which she gave her funniest performance.

Frequently incapable of remembering her lines, demanding take after take of the simplest scenes and almost always late on the set, Monroe had never been the most professional of actresses. But, by the late 50s, things were getting perilously out of control, and more than one major director vowed never to work with her again. During the shooting of her last film, Huston's *The Misfits* (1961, from a script by Arthur Miller), she created problems on almost a daily basis, her regular bouts of depression leading to an overdose of sleeping pills. Relations with Miller, too, were strained, and they divorced only a week before the film's première. Though she recovered to begin work on a new Fox comedy, the ominously titled *Something's Got To Give*, her maddening behaviour finally became such that she was summarily dismissed from the production. A month later, in August 1962, her nude body, an empty bottle of barbiturates beside it, was discovered by her housekeeper.

Marilyn's story, however, did not end there. Her death itself remained an enigma: the question of foul play has often been raised, if never proved; it was revealed that a secret diary had mysteriously vanished from her room, a diary allegedly containing information about her relations with the Kennedy brothers; a private detective even claimed that she had been murdered by the CIA to prevent her from revealing a plot to assassinate Fidel Castro. There have been countless articles and books (one by Norman Mailer), a compilation film, *Marilyn*, a musical version of her life, and an unabated flood of theories, speculations, revelations and memoirs. Perhaps a time will come when the world will tire of pawing over the remains and allow Marilyn – on film – to speak for herself. For though the cameramen may sometimes have cursed her, the camera never ceased to love her – and that, in a sense, is what the cinema is all about. DM

Kenneth More

Born **Gerrard's Cross, Buckinghamshire, England, 20 September 1914**
Died **1982**

Kenneth More was one of the stalwarts of the British cinema, at a period (from the late 40s to the early 60s) when it depended almost entirely on stalwarts. Well aware of his limitations, he seldom strayed beyond them. And, such was the complacency of that cinema (and its audiences), he remained one of its most popular stars during the whole decade.

His private life was as reassuring and uneventful as his film career: two happy marriages, wartime service as a Lieutenant in the Royal Navy (naturally),

Audie Murphy

Born **Kingston, Texas, 20 June 1924**
Died **1971**

Born into a family of desperately poor Texan sharecroppers, Audie Murphy was the most be-medalled American soldier in World War II, his twenty-four decorations including the Congressional Medal of Honor. Through his nationwide fame as a hero, he was turned into a movie actor, in which capacity, however, he remained conspicuously unde-corated. He will probably be best remembered for having played himself in *To Hell And Back* (1955), a film based on his own autobiographical memoir of his war experiences. Certainly, from that point on, Murphy never looked forward.

Though to all appearances a boyish, pudgy-faced innocent, he harboured few illusions as to the value of his filmography. 'The scripts were the same,' he

once laconically remarked of the lengthy series of westerns with which he is associated, 'only the horses were changed.' And, to be sure, such virtually interchangeable titles as *The Kid From Texas, Kansas Raiders, The Cimarron Kid, Duel At Silver Creek*, etc, are hardly calculated to ring down the ages. Yet he was touching as a frightened young Civil War recruit in John Huston's *The Red Badge Of Courage* (1951), oddly effective, even if miscast, as *The Quiet American* (1958), and decidedly unsettling when cast against type as a 'baddie' in Huston's *The Unforgiven* (1960).

In 1968 Murphy was declared bankrupt; two years later, he was arrested on a charge of attempted murder following a violent barroom brawl. Struggling to make a comeback after his acquittal, he both produced and starred in *A Time For Dying* (1971), a strange, elegiac western directed by his friend Budd Boetticher. Though praised by European critics, the film failed to regalvanise either his or Boetticher's career; and it was while they were preparing a second project together that Murphy was killed in a plane crash. DM

and an abortive attempt at fur-trapping in Canada to add the requisite dash of eccentricity. Stardom came with two films: *Genevieve* (1953), an evergreen comedy about the annual London-to-Brighton vintage car race, and *Doctor In The House* (1954), first in a long-running series of medical farces based on Richard Gordon's best-selling novels. More played a similar role in both, that of a cheerful, devil-may-care womanizer, instantly identifiable by his hound-stooth-check jacket, gaudy cravat and cavalry twills. He invested the same kind of character with deeper resonances opposite Vivien Leigh in a stagy film version of Terence Rattigan's drama *The Deep Blue Sea* (1955), and achieved immense popularity as the legless war hero Douglas Bader in *Reach For The Sky* (1956). But he appeared more at ease with 'the deep

in Sink The Bismark *(20th Century-Fox, 1960)*

blue sea' in an absolutely literal sense, in such films as *The Admirable Crichton* (1957, as J.M. Barrie's 'gentleman's gentleman'), *A Night To Remember* (1958, as the captain of the 'Titanic') and *Sink The Bismarck!* (1960). When his film career declined, he moved without resentment into television, scoring a success in the BBC series 'The Forsyte Saga', and eventually retired through ill-health. More had propped up the British cinema as another man might prop up a bar. DM

Patricia Neal

Born **Packard, Kentucky, 20 January 1926**

Perhaps the greatest achievement of Patricia Neal's life is that she is, in the words of the Sondheim song, 'still here'. For though a graceful and affecting actress, and recipient of a merited Academy Award for her performance as a cynical, world-weary housekeeper in *Hud* (1963), she commands our admiration above all for the dignified manner in which she bore and, indeed, overcame, a sequence of tragic blows which might have destroyed a lesser woman. (Her life has been recounted in the TV film *The Patricia Neal Story*, 1981, starring Glenda Jackson and Dirk Bogarde.)

A drama student at Northwestern University and the Actors' Studio, Neal made her Broadway debut in John Van Druten's 'The Voice Of The Turtle' in 1946, then triumphed in Lillian Hellman's 'Another Part Of The Forest'. Her film career began inauspiciously with a modest little programmer, *John Loves Mary* (1949), in which she played Ronald Reagan's war bride; but she attracted attention the same year opposite Gary Cooper in King Vidor's baroque adaptation of the Ayn Rand best-seller, *The Fountainhead*. It was this film, moreover, which first brought her private life to the attention of newspaper columnists: a much-publicised romantic entanglement with her desirable leading man culminated in a nervous breakdown.

With the exception of the British-made *The Hasty Heart* (1951), with Reagan again and Richard Todd, her subsequent roles were unmemorable; and, in 1953, she married the writer Roald Dahl, absenting herself from the screen for four years until Kazan's *A Face In The Crowd*. In 1965, however, she suffered a series of near-fatal strokes which left her partially paralysed, confined to a wheelchair and incapable of articulate speech. Two of her children were also victims of tragedy: an infant son was struck by an automobile and suffered severe brain damage, a daughter died of measles at the age of thirteen. Over the years Neal has made an astonishing recovery, one complete enough to allow her to return to the cinema: she was nominated for an Oscar for her performance as a harassed parent in *The Subject Was Roses* (1968). And it is a testament as much to her talent as to her courage that the nomination was not wholly sentimental in origin. DM

with Gary Cooper in Bright Leaf *(Warner Bros., 1950)*

Paul Newman

Born Cleveland, Ohio, 26 January 1925

In 1982 Gandhimania swept Hollywood's Academy Awards, leaving in its wake two celebrated victims: Steven Spielberg, whose record-breaking fantasy *E.T.* managed to pick up only the merest scraps from the great ascetic's table, and Paul Newman, whose virtuoso performance as the alcoholic, ambulance-chasing lawyer in Sidney Lumet's *The Verdict* was set fair for a best actor Oscar until Ben Kingsley appeared on the scene. What was particularly galling to Newman and his fans was the fact that, though he has been nominated *five* times (the other four films being *Cat On A Hot Tin Roof*, 1958, *The Hustler*, 1961, *Hud*, 1963, and *Cool Hand Luke*, 1967), the capricious little statuette has always eluded him.

Yet he is by common consent not only one of the finest, most versatile actors to have emerged in the postwar American cinema, but one of the few deserving of that much-abused epithet 'super-star'. He is also one of the screen's handsomest, with a pair of blue eyes which he exploits to devastating effect. And, a committed liberal activist who has lent his support to numerous political figures, the industry's most admired man. As David Niven, his co-star in *Lady L* (1963), remarked, 'He is a dedicated professional, totally understanding and generous in his work with others, has a wild sense of humour and somehow manages to consume enormous quantities of beer without putting on a single ounce! He has done more good for Hollywood movies than anyone else I can think of since the great studios virtually collapsed.'

Newman was the son of the owner of a sporting goods store in Cleveland, and was, as a child, already involved in local dramatic groups. His hopes of seeing active service as a pilot in the Naval Air Corps were brought to an end by his colour-blindness: he spent World War II as a radio operator in the Pacific. On discharge, he decided to study economics at Kenyon College, Ohio, but soon switched to his first love, drama – a spell in summer stock (where he met his first wife, Jackie Witte), graduate studies at Yale Drama School and, inevitably, attendance at the Actors' Studio in New York. (Though never exactly a paid-up member of the Method school, and seldom a mumbler on screen, his future film work was clearly influenced by Stanislavskian theories then in vogue.) After his first big break, a Broadway leading role in 'Picnic', a little television experience and, equally significant for the future course of his career, the beginning of his relationship with his second wife, the actress Joanne Woodward, he felt ready for Hollywood.

in 1962

Under contract to Warner Bros., the 30-year-old Newman was given what must have seemed an undreamt-of second break, the leading role in a multimillion-dollar Biblical epic, *The Silver Chalice* (1955). It was, however, a grotesque monument to kitschy religiosity which died at the box-office and might have killed the career of a lesser actor. But, even in such a farrago, Newman positively radiated star quality and, one year later, he was to vindicate the studio's judgement by his portrayal of heavyweight boxer Rocky Graziano in *Somebody Up There*

Likes Me. But 1958 was his *annus mirabilis*: he received rave reviews for his interpretation of Billy the Kid as a retarded psychopath in Arthur Penn's *The Left-Handed Gun*; won a Cannes Festival award for his performance as an itinerant handyman in *The Long, Hot Summer* (based on a trio of Faulkner tales and co-starring Joanne Woodward); and was nominated for an Oscar as the impotent hero of Tennessee Williams's *Cat On A Hot Tin Roof*, directed by Richard Brooks and co-starring Elizabeth Taylor.

Newman was by then one of Hollywood's most popular stars, a position he has maintained to this day. And if, in a career spanning almost three decades, the quality of his films has of necessity varied, that of his own appearances has remained admirably consistent. Of particular note in the 60s were his Israeli terrorist in Otto Preminger's *Exodus* (1960), his laconic pool-player in Robert Rossen's glitteringly squalid *The Hustler*, and the two title roles in *Hud* and *Cool Hand Luke*. (One of the latter film's best scenes saw him win a bet by consuming fifty hardboiled eggs in rapid succession.) And his popularity scaled new, stratospheric heights in 1969 when he partnered Robert Redford as *Butch Cassidy And The Sundance Kid*, a serio-comic western which became one of the most commercially profitable ever made. (The gilt-edged partnership of Newman and Redford re-formed to still greater effect in 1973 for *The Sting*.)

The star's professional life had always been closely linked with that of his wife (they acted together in *Rally Round The Flag, Boys!*, 1958, *From The Terrace*, 1960, *Paris Blues*, 1961, *A New Kind Of Love*, 1963, *Winning*, 1969, and *The Drowning Pool*,

with Elizabeth Taylor in Cat On A Hot Tin Roof *(MGM, 1958)*

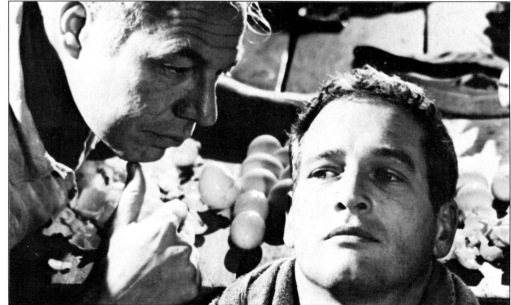

with George Kennedy (left) in Cool Hand Luke *(Warner Bros., 1967)*

1975); and when, in 1968, Joanne Woodward enthused about the novel 'A Jest Of God', he decided to venture into both production and direction. *Rachel, Rachel*, as the film version was called, proved to be a superbly acted, written and directed study of frustrated spinsterdom, suprisingly commercial considering its downbeat subject. Though Newman continued as a producer, he directed only two more features, *Sometimes A Great Notion* (1971) and *The Effect Of Gamma Rays On Man-In-The-Moon Marigolds* (1972), which encased one of Woodward's greatest performances.

His position now seems unassailable. In spite of persistent rumours to the contrary, his marriage is apparently rock-solid. He is one of the most respected figures of the Hollywood community, serving as a US delegate to the United Nations Conference on Disarmament in 1978. He has contrived to maintain an ideal balance between challenging roles and the easier type of popular success. Not least, he has aged well. And, as Pauline Kael wrote, 'I like him so much I always want his pictures to be good, for his sake as well as for my own enjoyment.' In short, the Oscar needs Paul Newman rather more than Paul Newman needs an Oscar. DM

Kim Novak

Real name Marilyn Pauline Novak
Born **Chicago, 13 February 1933**

'Miss Deepfreeze' was the name under which, in the early 50s, Kim Novak toured the United States demonstrating refrigerators, and 'Miss Deepfreeze'

she remained. Though the embodiment of blonde sex appeal, there was a faraway look in her eyes, a sense (underlined by an insecure acting talent) that, whatever her body was doing, her mind was elsewhere. It made her seem, with age, slightly waxy and over-cosmeticised, and her position as one of Hollywood's top female stars lasted a mere half-dozen years.

Of Slavic descent, she was employed as a salesgirl when spotted by a Columbia talent scout and heralded as the successor to an increasingly temperamental Rita Hayworth. For once, the tactic worked. Following routine assignments in a couple of thrillers (*Pushover* and *Five Against The House*, 1954 and 1955), she made a tremendous impression as the heroine of *Picnic* (1956). Her inadequacies – cruelly exposed by two hamfisted biopics, *The Eddy Duchin Story* (1956) and the title role in *Jeanne Eagels* (1957), – were no less brilliantly exploited in Hitchcock's masterpiece *Vertigo* (1958), where her cool, somnambulistic manner accorded perfectly with the film's dreamlike atmosphere. And she displayed her exotic beauty to advantage as a chic urban witch in *Bell, Book And Candle* (1958). A few more interesting opportunities – in *Middle Of The Night* (1959), *Strangers When We Meet* (1960) and *The Legend Of Lylah Clare* (1968) – and her heyday was over. But though her subsequent work is not so much forgotten as ignored, much may be forgiven the woman who, in *Vertigo*, so hauntingly lured James Stewart to his doom. DM

Anthony Perkins

Born **New York, 4 April 1932**

It sometimes happens, paradoxically, that an actor must strive to 'live down', not a poor performance, but a great one. The son of stage and screen actor Osgood Perkins (1892–1937), Anthony Perkins had played gawky, sensitive youths in a number of films before being offered the lead in *Psycho*: Jean Simmons's shy boyfriend in *The Actress* (1953), a Quaker in *Friendly Persuasion* (1956), baseball star Jimmy Piersall in *Fear Strikes Out* (1957) and a long-legged college athlete in *Tall Story* (1960). But it is as the psychopathic motel keeper Norman Bates in Hitchcock's stunning 1960 thriller that he will always be remembered – so much so that, just as Norman literally 'identified' with his dead mother, the actor has become too closely identified with the character he created. That said, his performance remains one of the most amazing in cinema history, as worthy of analysis as the film itself.

in Psycho (Paramount, 1960)

Following his rise to prominence, he settled in Europe, where he worked on a weird joblot of films. He made a plausible Joseph K in *The Trial* (1962), but Orson Welles's adaptation of the Kafka novel was a bloated monstrosity; and his two thrillers for Claude Chabrol, *The Champagne Murders* (1967) and *Ten Days' Wonder* (1972), were also among that director's weakest. Even more dispiritingly, he began to accentuate the tics of his most famous role, eventually reprising it in *Psycho II* (1982), a fairly dire, Hitchcock-less sequel. Perkins, significantly, admitted to having been dominated by his own mother; and it was not until he reached the age of 41 that he married for the first time. DM

Geraldine Page

Born **Kirksville, Missouri, 22 November 1924**

It is perhaps a measure of the uneasy, even grudging respect in which Hollywood holds Geraldine Page that she has been nominated for no fewer than *six* Academy Awards (as best supporting actress in *Hondo*, *You're A Big Boy Now* and *Pete 'N' Tillie*, as best actress in *Summer And Smoke*, *Sweet Bird Of Youth* and *Interiors*), yet does not have a single Oscar on her mantelpiece. Page is fundamentally a stage actress, deeply influenced by the Method school, and only accepts a film role if stimulated by it. Thus her filmography is brief, her mannerisms markedly theatrical in origin, her personality somewhat opaque.

The daughter of an osteopath, she began acting in summer stock, and in 1952 won a New York Drama Critics' Award for her flawless portrayal as a repressed young spinster in Tennessee Williams's 'Summer And Smoke', a role she repeated in Peter Glenville's film version (1961). She was magnificent as the neurotically self-obsessed actress in *Sweet Bird Of Youth* (1962) opposite Paul Newman, and reprised her spinster persona in a weak adaptation of Lillian Hellman's *Toys In The Attic* (1963). When, subsequently, the fad for melodramas of shabby-genteel sexual frustration started to wane, Page worked less regularly, but she gave noted perform-

in 1961

ances as a schoolmistress in *The Beguiled* (1971), as a bitchy matron in *Pete 'N' Tillie* (1972) and, in a return to her ripest Method manner, as the suicidal mother in Woody Allen's overheated homage to Ingmar Bergman, *Interiors* (1978) DM

Jack Palance

Real name Vladimir (or Walter) Palanuik
Born **Lattimer, Pennsylvania, 18 February 1919**

The son of a coal miner, Jack Palance himself worked in the mines before taking up professional boxing. It was not in the ring, however, that he acquired his distinctive appearance – broken nose, taut skin stretched over menacingly angular features. It was the result of plastic surgery after his face had been virtually destroyed when his plane crashed during a World War II bombing mission. First his misfortune, that face was to become his fortune. While understudying Anthony Quinn in Elia Kazan's Broadway production of 'A Streetcar Named Desire', he was invited by the director to play a bubonic plague victim in *Panic In The Streets*

(1950). In 1952 he was nominated for an Oscar as Best Supporting Actor in *Sudden Fear*, then again the following year for the role with which he is still associated in most people's memories – the unforgettably sinister, black-garbed assassin in George Stevens's classic western *Shane*.

Palance, who has not ceased to work in thirty years, played variations on that character in a disheartening number of westerns, most of them mediocre, many of them Italian. That he was capable of more was demonstrated by a cluster of sweatily tormented performances, notably as an anguished Hollywood actor in Robert Aldrich's *The Big Knife* (1955), a hard-nosed army lieutenant in the same director's *Attack!* (1956) and, especially, as the movie producer in Jean-Luc Godard's magnificent *Contempt* (1963) who cynically paraphrases Goebbels: 'When I hear the word 'culture', I reach for my check book.' DM

Sidney Poitier

Born **Miami, Florida, 20 February 1924**

Sidney Poitier forged an essential link between the cheerful, if ultimately demeaning, black stereotypes represented in movies of the 30s and 40s by Stepin Fetchit and Hattie McDaniel and the advent of such sassy, jive-talking super-stars of the 80s as Richard Pryor and Eddie Murphy. Inevitably, with his self-consciously 'soulful' dignity, he came to appear a rather dated, even dubious, model to young black audiences; but this is a fate often reserved for transitional figures, and it would be churlish to belittle his responsibility in the enormous advance made by black performers on the screen.

with Dorothy Dandridge in Porgy And Bess (Columbia, 1959)

Born into a family of poor tomato growers in the Bahamas, he was forced to leave school at thirteen, taking a variety of dead-end jobs before acting in an all-Negro production of 'Lysistrata' in 1946. He appeared to striking effect in a series of 'social problem' films, including *Cry, The Beloved Country* (1952), *The Blackboard Jungle* (1955), *Something Of Value* (1957) and *The Defiant Ones* (1958), for which he was nominated for an Academy Award. After reverting to stereotype as Porgy in Otto Preminger's bloated version of Gershwin's folk opera *Porgy And Bess* (1959), and winning an Oscar as a handyman entangled with some refugee nuns in the mawkish but hugely profitable *Lilies Of The Field* (1963), Poitier scored his greatest success with *In The Heat Of The Night* (1967) as Virgil Tibbs, a black police detective at odds with racist sheriff Rod Steiger in a sleepy Mississippi hamlet. In Stanley Kramer's pussyfooting comedy of mixed marriage, *Guess Who's Coming To Dinner* (1967), he scored a hit, although he was fairly ridiculous as an almost supernaturally eligible black suitor; and, his subsequent roles being increasingly undistinguished, he moved into direction, turning out a number of money-making comedies. Yet, in terms of his influence overall, Poitier is the Richard Wright of Negro performers. DM

Jane Powell

Real name **Suzanne Burce**
Born **Portland, Oregon, 1 April 1929**

Bright, breezy and bubbly, pert, pretty and possessed of a charming coloratura voice, Jane Powell was for a number of years MGM's resident soubrette. The title of one of her most characteristic films, the 1953 *Small Town Girl*, summed up her appeal to perfection: she was the eternal 'girl next door', whose every onscreen romance was her first. Another title, *The Girl Most Likely* (1957), was, however, sadly inappropriate, for the modest small-town musicals in which she thrived were dying: she starred in only two more films before retiring from

in La Strada (1956)

Anthony Quinn

Born **Chihuahua, Mexico, 21 April 1915**

Anthony Quinn is a character actor who, with age, has become more of a character and less of an actor. In a career spanning almost half a century and over a hundred films, he has played innumerable larger-than-life figures, including Chief Crazy Horse in *They Died With Their Boots On* (1941), Eufemio Zapata in *Viva Zapata!* (1952: Oscar for best supporting performance), Attila the Hun in *Attila* (1954), Gauguin in *Lust For Life* (1956: Oscar for best supporting performance), Quasimodo in *The Hunchback Of Notre Dame* (1956), the title role in *Barabbas* (1961), Kublai Khan in *Marco The Magnificent* (1965) and a thinly disguised Onassis opposite Jacqueline Bisset's equally transparent Jackie

the screen at the age of 29.
Already a radio star in her childhood, Powell made her first film appearance, in *Song Of The Open Road* (1944), while still a teenager. Mostly, she was relegated to MGM's second-eleven team; but if such musicals as *Holiday In Mexico* (1946), *A Date With Judy* (1948) and *Nancy Goes To Rio* (1950) loom small in cinema history, they were all agreeable entertainments. In *Royal Wedding* (1951) she acquitted herself well with Fred Astaire, and the peak of her career was unquestionably the effervescent *Seven Brides For Seven Brothers* (1954), in which she partnered Howard Keel. More recently, she replaced Debbie Reynolds in a successful Broadway revival of 'Irene', but a screen comeback seems well-nigh inconceivable. DM

Kennedy in *The Greek Tycoon* (1978). As a consequence, he now seems chronically incapable of incarnating a character who is just life-size. Every role conforms to the same monstrous mould, that of a lusty, rambunctious life force, the epitome of which was *Zorba The Greek* (1964), the film which made Quinn a star but ruined him as an actor.

He was born of mixed Mexican-Irish descent (a potent brew), and married Katherine DeMille, the director's adopted daughter, at the outset of his career in 1937. Notwithstanding such an important connection, he spent almost twenty years playing small roles in small films, most frequently Indian warriors or skulking heavies. Of those subsequent appearances recalled with affection, one might single out his brutish, well-intentioned circus strong man Zampano, befriending Guilietta Masina in Fellini's *La Strada* (1954). That, however, was a long time ago. DM

in 1954

Michael Redgrave

Born **Bristol, England, 20 March 1908**

Father of Vanessa, Lynn and Corin, and himself the child of a theatrical family, Michael Redgrave enjoyed a long, active and not undistinguished innings in the cinema. Yet, perhaps because he simultaneously pursued a stage career of acting, directing and even writing (eg his adaptation of Henry James' 'The Aspern Papers'), he was never to become a box-office name. Though he made his screen debut as the high-spirited, slightly dotty musicologist hero of Hitchcock's *The Lady Vanishes* (1938) and later proved a delightful Jack Worthing in Anthony Asquith's starry adaptation of *The Importance Of Being Earnest* (1952), it was for a series of dry, introspective and often obsessive characterisations that he will be remembered. He was a powerful Orin Mannon in the 1947 film version of Eugene O'Neill's *Mourning Becomes Electra*, winning an Academy Award nomination; disturbingly creepy as an unbalanced ventriloquist usurped by his dummy in *Dead Of Night* (1947); and unforgettably moving as the failed schoolmaster in Asquith's *The Browning Version* (1951, from Terence Rattigan's play).

But Redgrave was increasingly offered smaller parts and even cameos, notably as the reform school headmaster in *The Loneliness Of The Long-Distance Runner* (1962), the poet Yeats in *Young Cassidy* (1965) and the narrator sadly contemplating his younger self in Losey's *The Go-Between* (1971). In the end, a debilitating form of Parkinson's Disease forced him to withdraw from all professional activities: he made a final appearance in Simon Gray's 'Close Of Play' at London's National Theatre, remaining mute throughout the play before speaking its enigmatic curtain line. DM

Steve Reeves
Born **Glasgow, Montana, 21 January 1926**

After having been Mr America, Mr World and Mr Universe, it must have seemed a natural progression for Steve Reeves to take his place among the gods themselves. His showbiz experience limited to flexing his muscles in nightclubs and a bit part in the MGM musical *Athena* (1954), Reeves came to the attention of an Italian showman and occasional film director Pietro Francisci, who was searching for someone to embody (in the literal sense) the title role of his epic, *Hercules* (1959). This was such a success in Italy that it spawned not only an immediate sequel, *Hercules Unchained* (1959), but a whole cycle of cheerfully inconsequential extravaganzas, whose heroes would be pitted against hordes of barbarians or assorted mythological monsters. So Reeves, possessed of no discernible acting ability but a spectacular pectoral development, became a local idol. When producer Joseph E. Levine purchased the films for American release, launching them with almost unparallelled publicity, their leading man achieved international stardom.

He re-surfaced variously as Goliath, Morgan the Pirate, the Thief of Bagdad, Spartacus and Sandokan. The vogue for his type of film, however, proved short-lived; and when it petered out in the 60s (to be replaced by the spaghetti western), Reeves sensibly retired to California to raise horses. DM

in Thief Of Bagdad *(MGM, 1961)*

in 1960

Debbie Reynolds
Real name **Mary Frances Reynolds**
Born **El Paso, Texas, 1 April 1932**

Debbie Reynolds was less of a personality than a well-defined type. Sweet and wholesome, a mildly talented singer and dancer, she differed from such other 'girls next door' as Jane Powell and June Allyson in possessing an exuberant, tomboyish sense of humour, which warded off the threat of saccharine sentimentality. Her passport to movie stardom was a 'Miss Burbank' beauty contest, winning which earned her a contract with Warner Bros. in 1948. It was, however, at the centre court of the 50s musical, MGM, that she flourished, impersonating boop-boop-a-doop singer Helen Kane in *Three Little Words* (1950), then partnering Gene Kelly in that most brilliant of all musicals, *Singin' In The Rain* (also 1950). A series of modest but charming entertainments followed, including *I Love Melvin* and *The Affairs Of Dobie Gillis* (both 1953), *Give A Girl A Break* and *Athena* (both 1954), and *Hit The Deck* (1955) choreographed by Hermes Pan.

Her popularity was boosted by marriage to singer Eddie Fisher (with whom she co-starred in *Bundle Of Joy*, 1956), and the apparently idyllic young couple became the darlings of the fan magazines. And when, in 1959, Fisher divorced her to marry Elizabeth Taylor, Reynolds was widely, and sympathetically, portrayed as a 'wronged woman'. She was starred in *The Unsinkable Molly Brown* (1964), which failed to reach the entertainment heights intended by it, and her subsequent work disappointed. Miss Reynolds's only real success of the 70s came with a lavish Broadway revival of 'Irene'. She is the mother of Carrie Fisher, Princess Leia in the *Star Wars* saga. DM

Jane Russell
Real name **Ernestine Jane Geraldine Russell**
Born **Bemidji, Minnesota, 21 June 1921**

'Mean – moody – magnificent' – such was the alliterative trio of epithets employed by Howard Hughes to describe his discovery, Jane Russell, in *The Outlaw* (1943), and the exposure of her generous bust gave rise to numerous tasteless jokes of the order of 'Jane Russell – *two*good reasons for seeing this picture!' Indeed, through interference from the Legion of Decency, *The Outlaw* was not officially released until 1950.

Russell never quite overcame the kind of prurient attention which her vital statistics received, but she subsequently demonstrated that, if allowed to be humorously self-deprecating rather than moody and magnificent, she was no mean comedienne. It was as

in 1955

Robert Ryan
Born **Chicago, 11 November 1909**
Died **1973**

Robert Ryan was an unusual and interesting man. In spite of the fact that his most haunting performances were as half-demented bigots (eg the anti-Semitic killer in *Crossfire*, 1947; the sadistic Claggart in *Billy Budd*, 1962) or sympathetic characters who were no less psychologically disturbed (eg the coastguard officer in Renoir's strange melodrama *Woman On The Beach*, 1947; the ageing boxer on the run from gangsters in *The Set-Up*, 1949), he himself was a modest, introspective man, a committed liberal activist, and a co-founder of the prestigious UCLA Theater Group.

At Dartmouth, where he was educated, Ryan excelled in various sports, winning the college's heavyweight championship for four successive years.

He drifted aimlessly through a variety of jobs before attending drama classes at the Max Reinhardt Theatrical Workshop in Hollywood. Though he was already playing bit parts in B-movies by the early 40s, it was only after a Broadway appearance as a cynical lover in Clifford Odets's 'Clash By Night' (repeated in Fritz Lang's film version of 1952) that he graduated to starring roles. Ryan was the kind of actor who rarely managed to conceal his own intelligence, irrespective of the film's, thereby lending even routine westerns an unaccustomed toughness and integrity. He was particularly impressive as a crippled ex-soldier out for vengeance in Zinnemann's *Act Of Violence* (1949), as a paranoid tycoon in Max Ophuls's *Caught* (1949), as a racist bank robber in *Odds Against Tomorrow* (1959) and as Larry in John Frankenheimer's adaptation of O'Neill's *The Iceman Cometh* (1973), one of his last performances before his death from cancer. DM

'straight woman' that she proved most effective, making a marvellous foil to Bob Hope in *The Paleface* (1948) and *Son Of Paleface* (1952); to Robert Mitchum in *His Kind Of Woman* (1951) and *Macao* (1952); and, especially, to Marilyn Monroe in Howard Hawks's *Gentlemen Prefer Blondes* (1953). Her plaintive number 'Ain't there anyone here for love?' to a gym full of musclemen more interested in their own splendid torsos than in hers was a cherishable moment. Little more than decorative in Raoul Walsh's 1955 western *The Tall Men* opposite an ageing Clark Gable, she made a surprisingly memorable impression as a cynical dance-hall hostess in the same director's *The Revolt Of Mamie Stover* (1956), whose CinemaScope format provided an apt framework for her spectacular physique. By then, however, her career was almost over; and in the 70s, typically, she found herself advertising bras on television. DM

Randolph Scott

Real name **Randolph Crane**
Born **Orange County, Virginia,**
23 January 1903

Through dozens of films, at first musicals and light comedies, then principally westerns, Randolph Scott seemed the poor man's Gary Cooper or millionaire's Sonny Tufts. These films represented the Old West at its most moral, chivalrous and idealised; they were also, unfortunately, as bland and predictable as Scott himself. Yet, as the years passed, his handsome features growing more rugged and weatherbeaten, he came to be one of the noblest and most dignified exponents of the genre. The cycle of seven Budd Boetticher westerns made for the independent production company Ranown (an amalgam of 'Randolph' and 'Brown', from Harry Joe Brown, his coproducer) are among the best in Hollywood's history: *Seven Men From Now* (1956), *The Tall T*, *Decision At Sundown* (both 1957), *Buchanan Rides Alone* (1958), *Ride Lonesome*, *Westbound* (1959) and *Comanche Station* (1960). And when he retired, after a moving valedictory appearance in Sam Peckinpah's *Ride The High Country* (1962), he was one of the richest men in America, having amassed a fortune in oil and real estate.

Perhaps the greatest compliment paid him was a delicious error in the French subtitled version of *Buchanan Rides Alone*. 'Hi, I'm Buchanan,' Scott remarks on entering a saloon. This was translated as 'Bonjour, je suis Randolph Scott.' DM

Peter Sellers

Born **Southsea, England, 8 September 1925**
Died **1980**

Peter Sellers died of a heart attack at the age of 55. There are actors – not necessarily the greatest – whose deaths inspire in quite ordinary people an impression of personal bereavement. During his lifetime, the odds seemed powerfully stacked against Sellers ever belonging to that enviable category. He had appeared in too many execrable movies. His tantrums on the set, hiring and firing fellow performers and directors at will, had been too well-publicised. Yet when he died, when the tributes poured in and the reminiscences poured out (especially from the best-known of his four wives, Britt Ekland), one could detect behind all the tinselly mourning a genuine sense of loss. It was caused, however, not only by the man's death, but by the widespread belief that, through vanity, opportunism and bad judgement, his truly remarkable gifts of mimicry had too often been squandered on undeserving material.

Sellers was born into a theatrical family and acquired his lifelong loathing of the stage while touring with his parents' music hall act. After leaving the RAF, he worked as a stand-up comic between stripteases at London's notorious Windmill Theatre. Later, on BBC radio, he was one of the founding fathers of 'The Goon Show', an anarchic comedy half-hour still fondly remembered (and revived), and whose influence is perceptible in phenomena as diverse as the Beatles films and the visually and verbally surreal Monty Python Show.

In the cinema, even in minor roles, Sellers made an instant impression. Or rather, innumerable impressions. No other actor in screen history so eerily immersed himself in the characters he played, to the point where Sellers himself was plagued by crises of identity and a feeling, when offscreen, of personal inadequacy. From those early appearances, one still recalls with almost preternatural vividness his gormless Teddy Boy in *The Ladykillers* (1955), his befuddled old projectionist in *The Smallest Show On Earth* (1957) and his Tom-and-Jerry double act with Terry-Thomas in *tom thumb* (1958).

Though initially reluctant to tackle the role, he offered the British cinema one of its greatest character studies as the pompous, hen-pecked shop steward Fred Kite in *I'm All Right, Jack* (1959): so uncanny was his metamorphosis, both physical and vocal, that the film's crew fell uneasily silent when he walked onto the set. And when, the same year, he

brilliantly impersonated a saintly Indian doctor opposite Sophia Loren in *The Millionairess*, he could fairly claim to have become an international superstar. Yet rumours already circulated concerning his monstrously egotistic behaviour. When this could be ascribed to obsessive perfectionism, as with his devastating Clare Quilty in Stanley Kubrick's *Lolita* (1962) or his trio of roles, each bafflingly different, in the same director's *Dr Strangelove* (1964), it was grudgingly accepted as a price to pay for 'genius'. Following a virtually unbroken run of disasters in the 60s and 70s – films sometimes not even released – his colleagues grew less patient, particularly when, after his massive heart attack in 1962, he gave a tactless, anti-Hollywood interview.

Though Sellers became one of the highest-paid actors in the world with his creation of Inspector Clouseau, the accident-prone, tongue-tied sleuth of the *Pink Panther* cycle which began in 1963, both his timing and sense of observation had visibly coarsened; and it was to general surprise that, towards the end of his life, he gave one of his most memorable performances, in Hal Ashby's *Being There* (1979), as Chauncey Gardner, a hypnotically placid bubble floating over Washington and ever about to burst. There was something disturbingly apt about an actor who had confessed to his own lack of identity finally, and hauntingly, breathing life into a psychological nonentity. DM

Simone Signoret

Real name **Simone Kaminker**
Born **Wiesbaden, Germany, 25 March 1921**

The daughter of a Jewish linguist who fled to London during World War II and joined up with De Gaulle's Free French, Simone Signoret supported her family during the Occupation as a typist, and an extra in French films. Her warm, sensuous, 'ghtly overripe beauty and evident talent soon brought her more substantial parts; and by the late 40s, following marriage to the director Yves Allégret, she was a star. Under Allégret's direction, she made two notable postwar melodramas, *Dédée D'Anvers* and *Manèges* (1948 and 1950), then acquired international fame as The Prostitute in one of the most popular of all French films, Max Ophüls's *La Ronde* (also 1950). She consolidated her reputation with a wonderfully moving performance as a golden-hearted whore in Jacques Becker's *Casque D'Or* (1952), as the eponymous heroine of Marcel Carné's *Thérèse Raquin* (1953) and as a scheming mistress in H.-G. Clouzot's uniquely gruesome *Les Diaboliques* (1955).

When the 'thawing' British cinema of the early 60s required an actress of mature sex appeal to play Laurence Harvey's mistress in *Room At The Top* (1960), it turned to Signoret, who won an Oscar for her performance. But her natural if already somewhat blowsy features exposed the empty pretensions of *Term Of Trial* (1962, with Laurence Olivier) and Stanley Kramer's *Ship Of Fools* (1965); and she soon returned to France where, with her politically active second husband, singer and actor Yves Montand, she has become something of an institution among the left-wing intelligentsia. DM

in Games *(Universal, 1967)*

in Revenge Of The Pink Panther *(United Artists, 1978)*

Jean Simmons

Born **London, 31 January 1929**

When she was only fourteen, Jean Simmons was selected to play Margaret Lockwood's sister in a Gainsborough musical, *Give Us The Moon* (1944). The title seemed apt. Within a few years, she had made an enormous impression as the pretty but spoilt Estella in David Lean's *Great Expectations* (1946), as a sulky Nepalese belly dancer in Powell and Pressburger's weird and wonderful *Black Narcissus* (1947), and as Ophelia in Olivier's *Hamlet* (1948), for which she won the best actress award at the Venice Festival and was nominated for an Oscar.

Accompanying her husband, Stewart Granger, to Hollywood in 1950, she became contractually embroiled with Howard Hughes, but disentangled herself to sign up with 20th Century-Fox. Unfortunately, the films which that studio assigned her – such dreary costume epics as *The Robe* (1953), *The Egyptian* and *Desirée* (both 1954) – could not accommodate the playful, almost perverse, intelligence which she had earlier displayed. But her faltering popularity picked up again with such plum freelance roles as Sister Sarah opposite Marlon Brando's Sky Masterson in the 1955 film version of the Broadway musical *Guys And Dolls*; as the mentally disturbed young heroine of *Home Before Dark* (1958); and, especially, in two films for her

second husband, the director Richard Brooks: the powerful *Elmer Gantry* (1960) and the rather more meretricious *The Happy Ending* (1969), for which she was again nominated for an Academy Award. In the mid-70s, after a career that could be described as interesting rather than wholly successful, Simmons retired from the cinema and now resides in California, as lovely as ever, and occasionally appearing on TV in both the US and Britain. DM

Frank Sinatra

Born **Hoboken, New Jersey, 12 December 1915**

An acquaintance of Frank Sinatra once described him thus: 'He's a simple guy who likes to appear complex – or maybe it's the other way around!' Simple or complex, Sinatra eludes any easy analysis. But then, given a career in which he was several times regarded as a has-been, in which he was praised for his philanthropy and damned for the dubious company he kept – not to mention being alternately referred to as one of the most admired and one of the most detested men in show business – this is not too surprising.

He was born in Hoboken, the son of an Italian fireman. Because of the prejudice he encountered as an immigrant's son, he acquired a lifelong hatred of racial and religious intolerance which resulted, in 1945, in his producing an Academy Award-winning short, *The House I Live In*, directed by Mervyn

LeRoy and starring Sinatra himself. He also recorded its title song, which was for many years afterwards included in his repertoire. As a child, Sinatra's idol was Bing Crosby, whose mannerisms he would imitate when requested to sing at dances, weddings and similar social functions. Later, he systematically entered every available talent contest in the area, won first prize on a radio 'Amateur Hour' and was eventually hired as a vocalist with the Harry James and Tommy Dorsey bands. Much of the latter outfit's success was due to the very distinctive phrasing which Dorsey obtained from his horn, and this subtle musicianship was to have a lasting influence on the young crooner. 'I figured if he could do that phrasing with his horn,' Sinatra once remarked, 'I could do it with my voice.' This proved to be no idle boast, for he became, in the 40s, the idol of hundreds of thousands of screaming, swooning bobby-soxers across the United States. Wildly popular on radio and records, he was nicknamed 'The Voice'; and though his first films, such insubstantial but agreeable musical comedies as

Higher And Higher (1943, in which he played himself), *Step Lively* (1944) and *It Happened In Brooklyn* (1947), revealed him to be small, scrawny and emaciated, his physical shortcomings in no way dimmed the ardour of his fans.

Moreover, with appearances in three films co-starring Gene Kelly, *Anchors Aweigh* (1945), *Take Me Out To The Ball Game* and *On The Town* (both 1949), his place in any serious history of the American musical is secure.

In the early 50s, however, Sinatra suffered his first series of setbacks. CBS abruptly cancelled his TV show, and RCA unceremoniously dropped him. He had just divorced his first wife in order to marry Ava Gardner, and the division of property settlement had left him in debt: in addition, his second wife's fame was beginning to overtake his own. Worst of all, he had a haemorrhage of blood vessels in his vocal apparatus which affected the quality of his voice. Sinatra was not ready to retire, however. For the insultingly low fee of $8000 he agreed to play the role of Maggio in Fred Zinnemann's Pearl Harbour drama *From Here To Eternity* (1953), and won an Oscar for that year's best supporting performance. Almost immediately, his career switched gears; and though he was to play Nathan Detroit in *Guys And Dolls* (1955), a snooping reporter (and one of the few bright spots) in *High Society* (1956), Cole Porter's musical version of *The Philadelphia Story*, the title role of Rodgers and Hart's *Pal Joey* (1957), and a French playboy lawyer in another Porter musical, *Can-Can* (1960), he was henceforth to be known principally as a dramatic actor.

Sinatra was nominated for an Oscar for his harrowing performance in Otto Preminger's sensationalist drama of drug addiction, *The Man With The Golden Arm* (1955); was brilliantly sleazy as entertainer Joe E. Lewis in *The Joker Is Wild* (1957); and was surprisingly effective as the GI-turned-writer in Minnelli's lurid melodrama *Some Came Running* (1960). At the same time, his vocal technique had become more sophisticated than ever. With record albums routinely selling millions of copies, record-breaking appearances at nightclubs (and sometimes stadiums) in New York, Las Vegas and London, and TV specials whose viewing figures were stratospheric, Sinatra could claim to be the most famous popular singer in the world. Accordingly, he acquired the new nickname of 'Chairman of the Board of Show Business'.

A group of glittering Hollywood friends had begun to gravitate around him, including Dean Martin, Sammy Davis Jr, Peter Lawford, Joey Bishop and Shirley MacLaine; and the 60s were spent, for Sinatra, indulging the laid-back prankish humour of the so-called 'Rat Pack' in a series of films which, though little more than shindigs with plots, proved consistently successful at the box-office: *Ocean's Eleven* (1960), *Sergeants Three* (1962), *Four For Texas* (1963) and *Robin And The Seven Hoods* (1964). Later in the decade, however, he enjoyed a personal success as a world-weary private eye in *Tony Rome* (1967), *The Detective* and *The Lady In Cement* (both 1968). Though, in 1971, he announced his decision to retire 'from the entertainment world and public life', he blithely continued to make regular show business appearances, giving major concerts. His work for the cinema, on the other hand, has become intermittent and negligible.

Sinatra is almost 70, a veteran of four stormy marriages (his third wife was actress Mia Farrow). His baldness is concealed by a toupee, his scrawniness now but a dim memory. He is one of the wealthiest men in his profession, and since much of that wealth derives from casinos and nightclubs reputed to have powerful Mafia connections, he has frequently been the target of investigative or merely scandal-mongering journalists. And he is by reputation an extremely arrogant man, not averse to physical violence when crossed. Yet the word 'charisma' might have been coined for him, and the show business fraternity will most certainly be diminished on the day its Chairman decides, irreversibly, to resign from the Board. DM

with Gene Kelly (right) in Anchors Aweigh *(MGM, 1945)*

in The Naked Runner *(Warner Bros., 1967)* ▷

Robert Stack

Born **Los Angeles, 13 January 1919**

Robert Stack is one of those actors (another is Phil Silvers) who, after years of sterling service in mostly undemanding film roles, eventually emerged as a TV super-star. Educated at USC in Los Angeles, where he was a noted amateur athlete, Stack possessed rugged good looks, a virile physique and a youthful smile, all of which inevitably led to a career in his home town's most conspicuous industry. At the age of 20, he was chosen to deliver Deanna Durbin's first, and much-publicised, onscreen kiss in a Cinderella-ish romantic comedy, aptly titled *First Love* (1939). His career hummed along for several years, satisfactorily if not spectacularly, though buffs retain a fondness for him

in The Silencers *(Columbia, 1966)*

Stella Stevens

Real name **Estelle Egglestone**
Born **Hot Coffee, Mississippi, 1 October 1936**

'Estelle Egglestone from Hot Coffee, Mississippi' sounds more like one of the characters played by Stella Stevens than her real name and place of birth. She was a delightfully dizzy blonde glamour girl, her easily identifiable sex appeal enriched early on by a precocious knowingness and sensuality probably acquired through her own somewhat eventful private life. She married at 15, mothered a child a year later and divorced her husband only a year after that. She was also one of the most famous *Playboy* cen-trefolds, and one of the few whose careers have been advanced, not jeopardized, by such exposure. Though making her debut with a bit part in Frank Tashlin's mawkish comedy-drama about a showbiz priest, *Say One For Me* (1959), she first attracted attention in the same year as the extravagant vamp Appassionata von Climax in *Li'l Abner*, a charming

film version of the Broadway hit musical based on Al Capp's comic strip. Co-starring with Bobby Darin in John Cassavetes's *Too Late Blues* (1962), she demonstrated that her range was wider than supposed; and she was equally effective in the contrasting comedy styles of Minnelli's gentle satire *The Courtship Of Eddie's Father* and Jerry Lewis's brilliant Jekyll-and-Hyde parody *The Nutty Professor* (both 1963).

Her career gradually lost direction, however, and films like *How To Save A Marriage – And Ruin Your Life* (1968), *The Poseidon Adventure* (1972) and *Cleopatra Jones And The Casino Of Gold* (1975) were hardly calculated to get it back on course. In fact, only one interesting role came her way in the 70s, that of a good-natured prostitute in Sam Peckinpah's elegiac western *The Ballad Of Cable Hogue* in 1970; and in 1979, perhaps feeling, along with her fans, that her talents as a performer were being wasted, Miss Stevens both produced and directed a feature-length documentary, *The American Heroine*. DM

as the young Polish airman who walks out of Jack Benny's soliloquy in Lubitsch's glittering jet-black comedy *To Be Or Not To Be* (1942). In 1954 he played a harassed pilot in *The High And The Mighty*, a hugely successful forerunner of the 70s disaster cycle; and he excelled in two rather more challenging roles for director Douglas Sirk: as an alcoholic in *Written On The Wind* (1957), which earned him an Oscar nomination for best supporting actor, and as a stunt flier in *The Tarnished Angels* (1958).

It was at this period, however, that his celebrity was immeasurably enhanced by regular appearances as G-Man Eliot Ness in one of the most popular and longest-running of TV series, 'The Untouchables'. In recent years, Stack has gleefully parodied his earlier gung-ho image in Steven Spielberg's indigestible slice of custard pie slapstick, *1941* (1979) and, more effectively, in *Airplane* (1981), a spoof of the *Airport* disaster movies and therefore, by extension, of his own *The High And The Mighty*. DM

with Ludmilla Tcherina in Honeymoon *(British Lion, 1959)*

Anthony Steel

Born **London, 21 May 1920**

Not only was Anthony Steel the son of an officer in the Indian Army, a Grenadier Guardsman in World War II and a Cambridge graduate – he really looked the part. His stiff yet somehow also soft-centred good looks were of a type to appeal to schoolboy hero-worshippers rather than to the feminine portion of a film audience, a factor which served him well in a period when the British cinema was almost exclusively concerned with military, naval and colo-

nial heroics. Following a couple of inconclusive roles in *Saraband For Dead Lovers* and *The Blue Lamp* (1948 and 1950), he established himself as a personable leading man in *The Wooden Horse* (also 1950), in which he played one of the POWs plotting to escape from a German prison camp. He appeared as a game warden disgusted with the carnage wrought by ivory hunters in *Where No Vultures Fly* (1951), a film whose box-office success led to an identical sequel, *West Of Zanzibar*, in 1954; and he himself was cast as a big game hunter in *Harry Black* (1958), a humdrum potboiler mysteriously admired in some critical quarters.

A brief spell in Hollywood did nothing for his flagging career; nor did a well-publicised marriage to Anita Ekberg, as Steel remained totally in the shade of his wife's most visible assets. And not one of the numerous Continental films in which he subsequently starred was of the slightest distinction – though one might take a certain perverse pleasure in seeing such a 'Boy's Own Comic' figure turn up in *The Story Of O* (1975), a moonstruck soft-core adaptation of the notorious, pseudonymously published, pornographic novel. When last sighted, Steel was propping up the bar in the long-running British TV soap opera 'Crossroads'. DM

in Waterloo *(Paramount, 1971)*

Rod Steiger

Born **Westhampton, New York, 14 April 1925**

Dropping out of high school at the age of 16 to enlist in the Navy, Rod Steiger served throughout World War II on a destroyer in the Pacific. When discharged in 1945, he continued to be employed by the Navy as a civil servant, while becoming involved with amateur theatricals. His mind made up, he enrolled intially in the Dramatic Workshop of the New School for Social Research, then the New York Theater Wing, and finally the Actors' Studio, at that time the prestigious GHQ of what was familiarly known as the Method school. Steiger was to remain profoundly influenced by Stanislavskian techniques, applying them even in films where they tended to clash incongruously with the more instinctual styles of his co-performers.

Following an unremarked appearance as a psychiatrist in Fred Zinnemann's *Teresa* (1951), Steiger instantly made a name for himself in the title role of 'Marty', Paddy Chayevsky's award-winning TV drama of a pudgy, unprepossessing butcher in the throes of romance (a role taken in the 1955 film version by Ernest Borgnine). It was this success that prompted Elia Kazan to offer him the role of Marlon Brando's brother in *On The Waterfront* in 1954. Their celebrated scene together in the back of an automobile, where Brando makes his much-quoted 'I coulda been a contender' speech, constitutes an extraordinary *tour de force* of fluid direction and nervous, edgy acting; and, in only his second screen appearance, Steiger was justly nominated for an Academy Award.

Presumably as a change of pace, he played the tormented Jud in Zinnemann's *Oklahoma!* (1955), then was outstandingly creepy as a silver-haired and shark-like movie producer in *The Big Knife* (1955 also). It was this film, however, which first intimated in his work a recurrent tendency to overact. Steiger was rarely the kind of 'ham' whose characterisations are all surface – all crust and no bread. In his case, the bias was reversed: as befits a 'Method' devotee, he would contrive rather to suggest that too much was going on *beneath* the surface, even in innocuously written exchanges. He possessed what might be called an obtrusive inwardness, which would surface in an irritatingly limited range of tics and mannerisms. Such was true of Samuel Fuller's curious western *Run Of The Arrow* (1957), where he played an ex-Confederate soldier who becomes an honorary Sioux tribesman; of *Across The Bridge* (also 1957), a limp adaptation of the Grahame Greene novella about a crooked tycoon cornered in a Mexican border town; and of *Al Capone* (1959), with Steiger in the title role. These were, in their way, remarkable performances, yet self-indulgently indifferent to the overall style of the films. And though Sidney Lumet's *The Pawnbroker* (1965) earned him a second Oscar nomination, it is possible to regard his sweaty, neurotic portrayal of a former concentration camp victim sucked into his memories as one of the actor's most oppressively insistent.

Nevertheless, when the rage for 'Method' performers waned, Steiger demonstrated an astonishing adaptability. Burly and heavy-jowled, he was hilarious as an effete embalmer in *The Loved One* (1965); brilliant as the racist sheriff at odds with a black superior in *In The Heat Of The Night* (1967), for which he finally secured an Oscar; and wonderfully droll as a psychotic killer bedecking himself in seven separate disguises (including one in drag) in *No Way To Treat A Lady* (1968).

Unfortunately, his more recent work, often in Europe, has been far less stimulating. He was first-rate in two political thrillers for Francesco Rosi, *Hands Over The City* (1963) and *Lucky Luciano* (1973), but at his tic-ridden worst as Napoleon in the mammoth *Waterloo* (1970) and as Mussolini in *The Last Days Of Mussolini* (1974). And though he made a heroic stab at impersonating Fields in *W.C. Fields And Me* (1976), his casting, like the project itself, was doomed from the start. Indeed, it is not only professionally that the 70s and 80s have proved difficult years for Steiger. Beset by the break-up of his third marriage (he had formerly been married to Claire Bloom by whom he has a daughter, Anna, who is now an aspiring opera singer), by chronic depression, alcoholism and radical heart surgery, he has reportedly retreated even further into a loner's obsessive craving for privacy. It would be Hollywood's tragedy hardly less than Rod Steiger's own if he were allowed thus to stagnate. DM

in No Way To Treat A Lady *(Paramount, 1968)*

Dean Stockwell

Born **North Hollywood, 5 March 1936**

Dean Stockwell was a cute, cheerful, tousle-headed child star who turned into an almost morbidly intense young actor, and it is one of the minor mysteries of Hollywood's arcane thought processes that, still only in his forties, he has all but vanished from the scene. Though born in Hollywood, he was the son of Broadway actors, and made his performing debut, at the age of seven, not on film but in a Theater Guild production of 'The Innocent Voyage'. Signed up by MGM, he was a diminutive charmer in the Kelly/Sinatra musical *Anchors Aweigh* (1945), in *The Green Years* (1946), from the A.J. Cronin story about a young Irish boy and his Scottish grandparents, and in *Song Of The Thin Man* (1947), the last in that series. He then played the title roles in two very dissimilar films: *The Boy With Green Hair* (1948), Joseph Losey's pretentious allegory of mass conformism, and *Kim* (1950), from Rudyard Kipling's novel.

Stockwell first attracted attention in adulthood by partnering Bradford Dillman as the Chicago 'thrill' murderers Leopold and Loeb in the heavy-handed but gripping *Compulsion* (1959), best remembered for its filibuster defence speech by Orson Welles. And if he seemed out of his depth both as Paul Morel in the 1960 version of D.H. Lawrence's *Sons And Lovers* and as Edmund Tyrone in Sidney

in Sons And Lovers *(20th Century-Fox, 1960)*

Lumet's 1962 transcription of O'Neill's *Long Day's Journey Into Night*, in neither film did he shame his far more prestigious co-stars. Since then, for some unexplained reason, his work has ceased to be of interest, ranging as it does from a walk-on in Dennis Hopper's ludicrous *The Last Movie* (1971) to a brief appearance in Henry Jaglom's confused Vietnam drama *Tracks* (1977). DM

Elizabeth Taylor

Born London, 27 February 1932

Since the late 60s the nebulous concept of stardom has been subjected to a systematic inflation of values. In a routine TV series, for example, the status of some obscurely minor supporting performer is usually aggrandised into that of 'guest star'; many of the bizarre menagerie of hangers-on who peopled Andy Warhol's psychodramas dubbed themselves 'super-stars'; and Barry Humphries's outrageous alter ego, Edna Everage, has risen almost imperceptibly from being a 'housewife' to being a 'megastar'. Elizabeth Taylor is neither super-star nor megastar – she is a star. The genuine article. Perhaps the last of a breed that can be traced back to Theda Bara in the teens of this century.

Though she was born in London, her parents were American: her mother a former stage actress, her father an art dealer. In her earliest infancy, she seemed already in training for an eventual career in show business. At an age when other children are learning to stand upright, she was attending ballet classes: such was her precocity (and physical beauty) that, when barely three years old, she performed before the Royal Family. In 1939, a few months prior to the outbreak of war, her parents decided to

return to the US, her father opening a gallery, much patronised by the film colony, in Hollywood's Chateau Elysee. It was in the wake of a visit there by the syndicated columnist Hedda Hopper, and a newspaper article in which she praised not only the beauty of the artworks on display but that of the proprietor's little daughter, that Universal, flushed with the success of their Deanna Durbin musicals, decided to cast 10-year-old Elizabeth in *There's One Born Every Minute* (1942), a low-budget comedy in which she was foil to Carl ('Alfalfa') Switzer, previously one of *Our Gang*.

Not exactly an auspicious debut, perhaps, but she appealed to MGM, who signed her to a 20-year contract. Her first film for that studio, *Lassie, Come Home* (1943), was a huge box-office success: its trivial plot of an impoverished family forced to part with their prize collie dog offered relief from the infinitely greater dramas holding the world stage, and Taylor was as obvious a natural as Lassie herself. She enjoyed another triumph with *National Velvet* in 1944, playing a little girl who trains her horse to win the Grand National; and was equally fresh in *Life With Father* (1947), *A Date With Judy* (1948), and as Meg in a stickily sentimental version of *Little Women* (1949).

Taylor's first truly grown-up role came in *Conspirator* (1949) as a young wife who discovers that her husband (played by her scowling namesake Robert) is a double agent; but it would be more appropriate to date her emergence as an adult

actress from Vincente Minnelli's charming comedy of middle-class domesticity, *Father Of The Bride*, made in the same year. Appropriate because moviegoers who had watched this exquisite creature grow up on screen were now permitted to see her undergo what was, for the period, the only acceptable form of ritual deflowering: a family wedding. The film became one of MGM's biggest money-spinners, especially as the studio had delayed its release to coincide with Taylor's own impending first marriage, to the hotelier Conrad Hilton Jr. For she had blossomed rather more rapidly offscreen than on. While still in her teens, she had dated the 44-year-old Howard Hughes; and when reproached, during the filming of *Conspirator*, for falling behind in her school-work, she tartly replied, 'How can I concentrate on my education when Robert Taylor keeps sticking his tongue down my throat?'

Father Of The Bride (which inspired an uninspired sequel, *Father's Little Dividend*, in 1951) remains as sparky as ever; the Hilton marriage, on the other hand, went stale after only eight months. In 1952, Taylor was married for a second time, and for five years, to the British actor Michael Wilding. During that period, her career flourished, though only one of her films was truly outstanding. George Stevens's *A Place In The Sun* (1951) was an adaptation of Dreiser's 'An American Tragedy' which, by glossing over the implicit anti-capitalism of the original, emphasised the sheer power of mutual sexual passion. As Angela, the young belle of the country club set who tragically gives poor Montgomery Clift ideas above his social station, she was touching, innocent and almost painfully desirable. As the designer Edith Head remarked, 'When

in Cat On A Hot Tin Roof (MGM, 1958)

Elizabeth moved, she looked like sunlight moving over water.' She had also fallen desperately in love with Clift, failing to recognise his homosexuality. A personal entanglement of a like nature occurred during another Stevens film, *Giant* (1956). Taylor had become deeply attached to her co-star James Dean; and when he was killed in an automobile accident before shooting was complete, she was reportedly heartbroken. *Giant* had a success commensurate with its title; and though a large-scale

Civil War drama of the following year, *Raintree County*, was a flop, Taylor's actually rather undistinguished performance (again opposite Clift) earned her an Academy Award nomination.

Divorced from Wilding (who, as an actor, had lived totally in his wife's ever-lengthening shadow), she married the flamboyant showman Mike Todd, begetter of *Around The World In Eighty Days* and backer of the impressive if short-lived optical process Todd-AO. No stranger to flamboyance herself, she made a highly public conversion to Judaism; the engagement was announced at the première of *Around The World*; and her 30-carat diamond ring looked as if it too was in Todd-AO. The marriage, by all accounts a happy one, ended a year later, when Todd's private aircraft, 'The Lucky Liz', crashed with no survivors.

The young singer who had served as best man at their wedding, Eddie Fisher, became Taylor's third husband; this time around, however, she alienated thousands of fans who blamed her for breaking up Fisher's apparently idyllic marriage to Debbie Reynolds. Fortunately, her career was entering its most fruitful phase. She earned two successive Oscar nominations for performances in steamy Tennessee Williams adaptations: as the sexually frustrated Maggie in *Cat On A Hot Tin Roof* (1958); and, offering a suitably overripe display of histrionics, as Katharine Hepburn's mentally disturbed daughter in *Suddenly Last Summer* (1959), a campy yet often compelling study of moral and sexual degradation in which she was partnered, for the last time, by a physically ravaged Montgomery Clift. When she finally did obtain an Oscar, however, it was for a quite unremarkable performance as a call-girl in *Butterfield 8* (1960). Even at the time, it was widely interpreted as a sentimental gesture made less in recognition of her talent than of her recent, near-fatal bout of pneumonia. As another nominee, Shirley MacLaine, put it, 'I lost to a tracheotomy.'

When inflation is taken into account, her next film is arguably still the most catastrophic flop in cinema history: *Cleopatra* (1963). It all but bankrupted its studio, 20th Century-Fox, switched directors in mid-stream (Joseph L. Mankiewicz replacing Rouben Mamoulian), devoured several million dollars as sets remained vacant and actors idle for months on end – and, of course, it united Elizabeth Taylor with Richard Burton, the man whom she was to marry twice and divorce twice, in whose company she would be seen everywhere, and with whom she appeared in no fewer than eleven films. Most of these were unspeakably bad – pointless, pretentious vehicles for a couple whose interest, as far as the general public was concerned, derived almost entirely from the publicity they so assiduously courted. Exception must be made, nevertheless, of *Who's Afraid Of Virginia Woolf?* (1966), Mike Nichols's acid film version of Edward Albee's Pulitzer Prize-winning play, in which Burton gave his last good screen performance and Taylor, raddled and foulmouthed, this time deserved her Academy Award; and of *The Taming Of The Shrew* (1967), in which the Burtons made a spirited Petruchio and Katharina.

Since then, Taylor's choice of roles and films has declined into utter mediocrity, culminating in two musical monstrosities, George Cukor's Soviet-American co-production *The Blue Bird* (1976) and Hal Prince's embarrassingly inept adaptation of Stephen Sondheim's *A Little Night Music* (1977). She chalked up her seventh marriage ceremony and matching divorce, to John Warner, a US Senator who, conceivably on the strength of the attendant publicity, made a preposterous bid for the Presidency. Unlike Cleopatra's, the infinite variety of her beauty has been withered by age and staled by custom. Indeed, she has gradually become so plump and matronly that one English critic, reviewing her in a theatrical revival of Lillian Hellman's 'The Little Foxes', could maliciously compare her to Miss Piggy. Yet there is something endearing about her capacity for survival; and, for better or worse, she is the kind of star of whom one can say, simply, 'They don't make them like that any more.' DM

in The Taming Of The Shrew (Columbia, 1966) ▷

Richard Todd

Real name Richard Andrew Palethorpe-Todd
Born Dublin, 11 June 1919

In British films, Richard Todd was one of the pillars of the 'stiff upper lip' school, but it was not only his lip that was stiff. For most of his quite lengthy career, he was a depressingly wooden actor, as limited in range as in appeal. Though handsome in a baby-faced but humourless, furrowed-brow way, he was a singularly unsexy performer; and it is difficult with hindsight to understand how he ever contrived to achieve, much less maintain, his modest but undeniably authentic stardom.

His career began well. Already a stage actor in his teens, he was one of the founders of the Dundee Repertory Theatre in 1939. As befits someone who would spend much of his time onscreen in khaki, his World War II service in the King's Own Light Brigade and the Parachute Regiment was both distinguished and adventurous. After the war he returned to the stage; then, in 1949, he made three films: a couple of forgotten potboilers and *The Hasty Heart*, in which he played a naive young Scottish soldier coming to terms with the fact of his own imminent death. Co-starring with Ronald Reagan and Patricia Neal, Todd was nominated for an Academy Award; and his performance, which

seemed to inaugurate a future of great promise, remained the high watermark of his whole career.

In the following year, he won the dubious distinction of playing the perpetrator of the notorious 'lying flashback' in Hitchcock's *Stage Fright*, one of the Master's lesser confections. But his popularity

among younger moviegoers was assured when Walt Disney offered him the title role in *The Story Of Robin Hood* (1952), whose success prompted two further historical extravaganzas from the same studio, *The Sword And The Rose* and *Rob Roy* (both 1953). Three films again in 1955: in *A Man Called Peter*, the story of a Scottish minister who became the United States Senate chaplain, he demonstrated that he could deliver an uplifting sermon: as Sir Walter Raleigh in *The Virgin Queen* he laid down his protective cloak as to the manner born; and in *The Dam Busters* – an excellent British war epic with Michael Redgrave heading the cast – he, like the film itself, was buoyed up by Eric Coates's catchily stirring march theme.

Thereafter, his work (and popularity) declined precipitously. There were other war films – *D-Day, The Sixth Of June* (1956), *Yangtse Incident* (1957), *Danger Within* (1959), *The Long And The Short And The Tall* (1961), *The Longest Day* (1962) and *Operation Crossbow* (1965) – but diminishing returns had set in with a vengeance, and the British war film cycle was in any case coming to its exhausted end. Among his last, and worst, films were a campy Italo-German version of *Dorian Gray* (1970), in which he played the painter Basil Hallward to Helmut Berger's ridiculous Dorian, and Michael Winner's British based adaptation of Raymond Chandler's *The Big Sleep* (1978), a film all too aptly named. DM

Peter Ustinov

Born London, 16 April 1921

Packing Peter Ustinov's career into a brief dictionary entry is a peculiarly frustrating task, for the word 'Ustinov' has, as it were, acquired a multiplicity of meanings. Its roots are already entangled: a journalist father of Russian origin (relating Ustinov to Alexandre Benois, the great set designer of the Russian Ballet), an artist mother of French origin. Doubtless a product of such a 'mongrel' background, his versatility is one of the wonders of the world. His

in Billy Budd (Allied Artists, 1962)

initial reputation was made, at the age of 19, as a playwright; and, from the two satires 'The Love Of Four Colonels' and 'Romanoff And Juliet' to his latest, 'Beethoven's Tenth', his best plays are still fairly often performed. He has written several novels, as well as a droll autobiographical memoir, 'Dear Me'. He has directed seven films, scripted many more, and has also been responsible for a number of theatre and opera productions. His career as a film actor stretches over forty years, and he is as much in demand today as ever. Finally, he is perhaps most admired as a wit and conversationalist, displaying his amazing gift for mimicry on chat shows in both Britain and the United States. Though Ustinov can be, and frequently has been, criticised for this Jack-of-all-trades-master-of-none approach

to the arts, it would be churlish to deny the pleasure he has given in his various capacities.

As an actor, he first attracted attention in a Will Hay farce *The Goose Steps Out* (1942), and playing the title role of his own *Private Angelo* (which he scripted, produced and co-directed with Michael Anderson in 1949). Internationally, however, stardom came with his performances as a languid, eccentric Nero in *Quo Vadis?* (1951) and as the ringmaster in Max Ophüls's valedictory film, the much-mangled masterpiece *Lola Montes* (1955). He won an Academy Award for his wily slavemaster in Stanley Kubrick's *Spartacus*: so protracted was its shooting that, as Ustinov recounts, when one of his children was asked what his father did for a living, he replied simply, 'Spartacus.' And a second Oscar was awarded him in 1964 for his clownish, small-time rogue involved in a jewel heist in Jules Dassin's *Topkapi*.

Ustinov's judgement seemed less secure in the 70s; for though he himself was never less than

watchable, he could not salvage such duds as *Hammersmith Is Out* (1972, directed by himself), Disney's infantile *One Of Our Dinosaurs Is Missing* (1975) and the inept science-fiction fantasy *Logan's Run* (1976). But towards the end of the decade, his stock rose spectacularly when he played Hercule Poirot, Agatha Christie's Belgian sleuth, in two recent, enormously successful Christie adaptations, *Death On The Nile* (1978) and *Evil Under The Sun* (1981). (It is doubtful whether Dame Agatha would have approved, for Ustinov bears no physical resemblance to her dapper, diminutive detective.)

His own films as a director constitute a boxful of curate's eggs. A couple are unqualified in their badness (*Lady L*, 1965, *Hammersmith Is Out*); others are diverting if now rather dated (*Private Angelo, Vice Versa*, 1947, *Romanoff And Juliet*, 1961); and only one, his adaptation of Melville's *Billy Budd* (1962), with Robert Ryan as Claggart, Ustinov himself as Vere and Terence Stamp in the title role, can be regarded as a complete success. DM

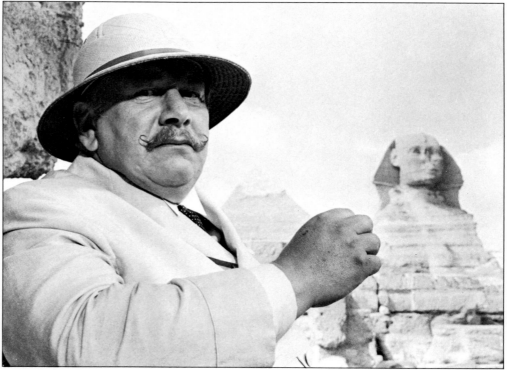

in Death On The Nile (Paramount, 1978)

Vera-Ellen

Real name **Vera-Ellen Westmeyr Rohe**
Born **Cincinnati, 16 February 1926**
Died **1981**

Vera-Ellen was cuteness incarnate; and since cuteness as a commodity is not usually blessed with a long life, her career was correspondingly brief. She was already performing at the age of ten and, with her pert, wide-eyed, effervescent energy, she never seemed – on screen, at least – fully to shake herself out of childhood. But she was an excellent dancer and, after experience as a Radio City Music Hall Rockette, a singer and dancer in Broadway musicals and Billy Rose's Diamond Horseshoe, Hollywood was the logical next step. It was Sam Goldwyn who discovered her, casting her in *Wonder Man* (1945), a jolly musical in which Danny Kaye, Goldwyn's biggest attraction, played a double role. Another Kaye vehicle followed, *The Kid From Brooklyn* (1946), then over to 20th Century-Fox, where she was one of *Three Little Girls In Blue* (also 1946), in company with June Haver and Vivian Blaine.

It is, however, for her appearance in MGM's revolutionary musical *On The Town* (1949) that film buffs remember her most fondly: she played the delectable, elusive 'Miss Turnstiles', forever pursued by and forever evading Gene Kelly. She proved an accomplished partner for Kelly, as she later did for Fred Astaire in *The Belle Of New York* (1952). Two more Hollywood musicals remained: *Call Me Madam* (1953), in which, like everyone else, she was upstaged by the formidable Ethel Merman, and that hardy perennial, *White Christmas* (1954), with Bing Crosby, Danny Kaye and Rosemary Clooney; plus a British-made one, *Let's Be Happy* (1957), set in Scotland. Then her career was at an end. In fact, three of Vera-Ellen's titles contain the word 'happy' (the others were *Love Happy* and *Happy Go Lovely*), and sheer, uncomplicated happiness is exactly what she conveyed. Most unhappily, she died of cancer at the age of 55. DM

with Danny Kaye in White Christmas *(Paramount, 1954)*

Robert Wagner

Born **Detroit, 10 February 1930**

As an actor, Robert Wagner has shown remarkable staying power, especially when one considers that his success in the cinema was effected almost entirely through his dark, boyish good looks. In his youth, certainly, he possessed few other qualifications. He was the son of a wealthy Detroit-based steel executive and his earliest ambition was to enter the same industry himself. But he made his screen debut at the age of 20 and was soon put under contract by 20th Century-Fox where, with his sexy athletic physique and toothpaste-ad smile, he became a teen idol. Though involved with such major directors as Wellman, Milestone, Ford, Hathaway, Fleischer, Ray, Tashlin, de Sica and Blake Edwards, he seldom appeared in a major film and tended to make a striking impression only when clad in swimming trunks, as in *The Frogmen* and

Beneath The 12-Mile Reef (1951 and 1953). In Milestone's guts 'n' glory war film *Halls Of Montezuma* (1951) he played a young Marine, in Ford's *What Price Glory* (1952) a young World War I soldier, and also assumed military rank in *Between Heaven And Hell* (1956), *The Hunters* and *In Love In War* (both 1958), *The Longest Day* and *The War Lover* (both 1962). Wagner appeared to greater effect, however, playing the comic strip title role in the ludicrous but lively *Prince Valiant* (1954), and was quite excellent as the coolly psychopathic killer of *A Kiss Before Dying* (1956), adapted from Ira Levin's almost unfilmable novel.

It would take a very dedicated Wagner-ite to discern much virtue in the actor's 70s film work, though he did become one of television's top attractions in two long-running series, 'It Takes A Thief' and, more recently, 'Hart To Hart' with Stefanie Powers. He was married three times, once to the actress Marion Marshall and twice to Natalie Wood, who tragically drowned in 1982. DM

in Words And Music *(MGM, 1948)*

in A Kiss Before Dying *(United Artists, 1956)*

in 1954

Richard Widmark

Born **Sunrise, Minnesota, 26 December 1914**
Died **1984**

Though Richard Widmark's home town shares the same name as one of the most beautiful of all Hollywood films, and though he has come to seem a fixture of postwar American cinema, his original ambition was to become a lawyer, and he made his screen debut at the relatively mature age of 33. He was raised in Chicago, and enrolled at Lake Forest College as a first-year law student. It was there that, partly because of his wiry, athletic physique, he found himself increasingly involved with its dramatic society, so that, after graduating in 1936, he remained at the college as an instructor in speech and drama. In 1938 he moved to New York, worked steadily on radio and landed a few Broadway roles, in the best of which he was directed by Elia Kazan. It was through Kazan's influence that he was tested by 20th Century-Fox and put under contract.

Few American actors have made quite so vivid an impression with their very first film. *Kiss Of Death* (1947) was, for the period, an untypically vicious little thriller whose nominal stars were Brian Donlevy and Victor Mature. But neither of these somewhat stolid actors stood a chance when confronted by Widmark's manically giggling psychopath of a killer, the highlight of whose existence was gleefully shoving poor, crippled Mildred Dunnock down a flight of stairs. He was nominated for an Oscar – possibly on the strength of that scene alone.

Naturally, having discovered an actor with such a chillingly sadistic line in villainy, the studio was loathe to cast him in any other register; and Widmark was condemned for several years to play variations on the role, notably in the semi-documentary thriller *The Street With No Name, Road House* (both 1948) and *No Way Out* (1950), in which he played a racist hoodlum of whose machinations Sidney Poitier becomes the victim. More challenging for Widmark, perhaps, were two other 1950 roles: that of a small-time wrestling promoter pursued by gangsters through a weird, expressionistically lit London in Jules Dassin's *Night And The City*; and that of a harassed doctor contending with an outbreak of bubonic plague on the New Orleans waterfront in Kazan's *Panic In The Streets*.

Like many contract stars, however, he was forced into a dispiriting number of less stimulating films, which would tend, in Widmark's case, to emphasise an unattractive side of his screen personality, a kind of sneering macho boorishness. It was much to the fore in Lewis Milestone's tub-thumping war film *The Halls Of Montezuma* (1951); in a routine adventure yarn about forest fire fighters, *Red Skies Of Montana* (1952); and in MGM's *Take The High Ground* (1953), where he played a tough Marine master sergeant.

In fact, Widmark was most effective when working with a director of distinction (which is not necessarily the case with every actor). He was excellent in two violent Samuel Fuller thrillers, *Pickup On South Street* (1953: its rabid anti-Communism was altered in several European dubbed versions to an anti-narcotics theme) and *Hell And High Water* (1954); then in two John Ford westerns, *Two Rode Together* (1961) and the elegiacally pro-Indian *Cheyenne Autumn* (1963). On the other hand, he appeared ludicrously ill-at-ease as the idiot Dauphin in Otto Preminger's misconceived adaptation of Shaw's *Saint Joan* in 1957. In Don Siegel's razor-sharp thriller *Madigan* (1968) he scored as a maverick police detective for whom the ends justify even the most dubious of means. So successful was the film that Widmark, who had refused numerous offers to appear on television, was finally persuaded to reprise his role in a long-running TV series of the same name.

An intensely private man, of whose offscreen life little is known (he was married to the scenarist and former actress Jean Hazlewood), his film appearances became increasingly rare latterly, the last memorable one being in Michael Crichton's grisly hospital thriller *Coma* in 1978. But though never quite a star of the first magnitude, his reputation is secure – if, for no other reason, because he shoved Mildred Dunnock downstairs. DM

with Harry Guardino (right) in Madigan *(Universal, 1968)*

Marie Windsor

Real name **Emily Marie Bertelson**
Born **Marysvale, Utah, 11 December 1922**

There is a scene in Stanley Kubrick's thriller *The Killing* (1956) in which a wimpish, would-be hold-up man returns one evening to his drab apartment and his brassily glamorous wife. When he opens the conversation by telling her that he has just witnessed 'something sweet in the subway', she coldly replies, without taking her eyes off her nail file, 'Was it a candy bar, George?' Just as surely as the wimp would be Elisha Cook, Jr, one of the screen's eternal victims, so his wife had to be Marie Windsor, one of its archetypal dames. Tough, scheming and not to be trifled with, as hard as the nails she so obsessively filed and polished, Windsor enlivened many a minor thriller, western or melodrama of the 40s and 50s; and, whatever her ultimate place in cinema history might turn out to be, every buff with a taste for the obscure pleasures of the B-movie has retained a special niche in his affections for her.

in The Killing *(United Artists, 1956)*

Of Mormon parentage, she spent several years as a telephone operator, and was also a former Miss Utah. Somewhat improbably, she trained for the stage under Maria Ouspenskaya, a Mittel-European dowager of countless 30s films. Her first major role came in Abraham Polonsky's powerful *film noir* about the numbers racket, *Force Of Evil* (1948), as a gangster's faithless wife. Most of her work was in a similar vein, so that when, in Richard Fleischer's *The Narrow Margin* (1952), a suspenseful little thriller set almost entirely aboard a train, her gangster's moll turns out in the end to be an undercover policewoman, the revelation could hardly be more shocking. Sadly, apart from *The Killing*, Windsor was never so well used again. But if she was totally preposterous as Napoleon's Josephine in Irwin Allen's no less preposterous *The Story Of Mankind* (1957), it was nice to see her in two casual, light-hearted westerns directed by Burt Kennedy, *The Good Guys And The Bad Guys* (1969) and *Support Your Local Gunfighter* (1971). She had mellowed considerably, but there was still a potent whiff of the 50s about her, and of the *belle dame sans merci* she had so memorably personified. DM

in Splendor In The Grass (Warner Bros., 1961)

Natalie Wood

Real name **Natasha Gurdin**
Born **San Francisco, 20 July 1938**
Died **1982**

Born into a cultivated, cosmopolitan family – her father (of Russian origin) was an architect, her mother a ballerina – Natalie Wood was a precocious child who could, literally, dance before she could walk. The family lived in Santa Rosa, a small Californian township, which served as the location of a film, *Happy Land* (1943), and five-year-old Natalie was given a tiny role. Three years later, when its director Irving Pichel required the services of a little girl for *Tomorrow Is Forever*, a melodrama with Claudette Colbert and Orson Welles, he thought again of Natalie – and so launched her Hollywood career. She was one of the most delightful of screen moppets, cute without ever becoming mawkish, making a strong impression in the whimsical fairy-tale *Miracle On 34th Street* (1947). By 1953, when she appeared in *The Star*, she was 15, a perilous age for child performers; yet the transition from adolescence to young womanhood was a remarkably smooth one, and she never ceased to work during these awkward years.

A petite brunette with dark, melting eyes, she was touching as James Dean's girlfriend in *Rebel Without A Cause* (1955), for which she received an Academy Award nomination; and will be remembered, as long as Hollywood films are, for her role as a pioneer girl kidnapped by Indians and tracked down by John Wayne in what is arguably the greatest of all westerns, Ford's *The Searchers* (1956). Her second Oscar nomination came in 1961 with *Splendor In The Grass*. Kazan's film was 'Romeo And Juliet' transported to a small Kansas town during the Depression, and she and Warren Beatty were inexpressibly moving as its star-crossed lovers. Indeed, the 60s augured well for Wood (by then married to actor Robert Wagner) with two terrific musicals: Leonard Bernstein's *West Side Story* (1961), in which she played the Puerto Rican heroine Maria, and Jule Styne's *Gypsy* (1962), as the stripper Gypsy Rose Lee.

At which point, however, her life, both private and professional, began to seem rather less charmed. She and Wagner were divorced in 1963 (only to remarry in 1972). Following a third Oscar nomination in the same year for *Love With The Proper Stranger*, she made films which were either commercially successful (*Sex And The Single Girl*, 1964, *The Great Race*, 1965) or challenging (*Inside Daisy Clover*, *This Property Is Condemned*, both 1966), but not both. And she caught the attention of the editors of 'Harvard Lampoon', whose distaste for her work prompted them to initiate an annual 'Natalie Wood Award' for the worst actress of the year. Wood took this uncomplimentary homage in good part, but it cannot have helped a faltering career. It was, in any case, outrageously unjust, for if there was a streak of sentimental vulgarity in her screen personality, it was redeemed more often than not by a very genuine emotional intensity.

Apart from Paul Mazursky's timidly subversive comedy of alternative life-styles *Bob And Carol And Ted And Alice* (1969), her later work (for example, *Peeper* (1976), *Meteor* (1978), *The Last Married Couple In America* (1979)) was routine, and it is doubtful whether *Brainstorm*, the last film in which she appeared, would have effected a come-back. The question, however, is academic. Ironically, for someone with a lifelong fear of the sea, she died in a drowning accident before the film was properly completed. DM

in Gypsy (Warner Bros., 1962)

Joanne Woodward

Born **Thomasville, Georgia, 27 February 1930**

The daughter of a publisher, Joanne Woodward always knew that she wanted to be an actress. Her first performing experience was gained in high school, at Louisiana State University, then, professionally, in a small community theatre in South Carolina. While a student at New York's Neighborhood Playhouse, she understudied in the Broadway production of 'Picnic' and began to work steadily in live TV dramas. In 1955 she made her screen debut in a modest western, *Count Three And Pray*; and, in the following year, made a strong impression as the unfortunate college student seduced and murdered by the smooth, preppy Robert Wagner in the film version of Ira Levin's *A Kiss Before Dying*. But she achieved stardom (and won her, to date, sole Academy Award) by playing the extraordinary title role (or roles) in *The Three Faces Of Eve* (1957), the story of a much-publicised victim of split personality. In fact, the film was flat, melodramatic and extremely superficial. Schizophrenia, however, was a modish concept in the 50s and it is probable that, on this occasion, the award went to the virtuosity, not the insight, of her performance.

Woodward is a quintessentially modern actress, expert at capturing the pressures, social, sexual and psychological, besetting women in a man's world, and her characteristic register might be described as 'heightened ordinariness'. She excels at playing

in A Big Hand For The Little Lady (Warner Bros., 1966)

spinsters and slatterns, but always manages to avoid the whiny self-righteousness inherent in such roles by her radiant and never humourless personality. She was memorable as a strong-willed Southerner in *The Long Hot Summer* (1958, based on works by Faulkner), as a young girl struggling to assert her independence in another Faulkner adaptation, *The Sound. And The Fury* (1959) and as *The Stripper* (1963), where she was convincingly blowsy in a role which might have been written for (or about) Marilyn Monroe. Concurrently, she displayed real gifts for screwball comedy in *Rally Round The Flag, Boys!* (1958), *A Big Hand For The Little Lady* (1963) and, especially, as the earthy waitress wife of poet Sean Connery in *A Fine Madness* (1966), directed by Irvin Kershner.

In 1958 she married Paul Newman, who directed her in two brilliant performances, as a lonely, repressed schoolteacher in *Rachel, Rachel* (1968, for which she received an Oscar nomination) and as a sluttish, widowed mother in the awkwardly titled *The Effect Of Gamma Rays On Man-In-The-Moon Marigolds* (1972, for which she received an award at the Cannes Festival). She has since worked with decreasing frequency, but she was very moving as a middle-aged wife hoping to rekindle her marriage in the soapy *Summer Wishes, Winter Dreams* (1973). A vigorous campaigner, with her husband, for numerous liberal causes, Joanne Woodward is now perhaps at a crossroads in her career — a fact which, in view of her superior gifts, makes her future all the more worthy of attention. DM

for most features but simply could not cover *Dolly*'s woefully inflated budget. Putting it succinctly, one might say that the phenomenal success of *The Sound Of Music* brought 20th Century-Fox to the verge of bankruptcy.

Hollywood found its own nouvelle vague *via the 'bike' movie for the youth market. Easy Rider was not the first but it caught the public imagination and steered the film-makers onto a new course. The brainchild of Dennis Hopper (left) and Peter Fonda (centre), it also marked the turning point for Jack Nicholson (right).*

In 1965 20th Century-Fox released *The Sound Of Music*, Robert Wise's adaptation of the Rodgers and Hammerstein musical comedy which boasted Julie Andrews, Christopher Plummer, the Tyrol in Todd-AO, the Nazis, a flock of nuns and the Trapp Family Singers. The movie, which was – and has remained – one of the most commercially successful musicals in Hollywood's history, made millions for Fox and turned out to be one of the worst things ever to have happened to the studio. Convinced that the 'Open Sesame' to astronomical profits lay in big-budget family-entertainment musicals, if possible starring the maudlin yet eupeptic Miss Andrews, it poured millions of dollars into three apparently infallible projects: Robert Wise's *Star!* (1968, a musical biopic of Gertrude Lawrence with the inevitable Julie); Richard Fleischer's *Dr Dolittle* (1967, with Rex Harrison who, having played Higgins opposite *her* Eliza Doolittle in *My Fair Lady*, must have seemed the next best thing to the lady herself); and Gene Kelly's *Hello, Dolly!* (1969, a screen version of Jerry Herman's Broadway hit with Barbra Streisand and Walter Matthau). The first two were disastrous failures at box-offices everywhere (deservedly so, one might add); the third's takings would have been satisfactory enough

Meanwhile, the young actor Peter Fonda and actor-director Dennis Hopper together initiated a project for an inexpensive bike movie. Hopper lacked experience as a director, and it shows in the completed work – but who's counting, for *Easy Rider*, as that inexpensive bike movie was titled, earned somewhere in the region of $35 million. Could this, at last, be Hollywood's New Wave? If you recall (as a number of studio bosses certainly did), the *nouvelle vague* of Truffaut and Godard and Chabrol and Rohmer and Resnais managed to revitalise the French cinema at a period, the late 50s, when it had been in danger of becoming totally ossified. New blood had been pumped into it – and, it is also worth recalling, in art as in war there is nothing cheaper than new blood. Instead of paying worthy, respected and unquestionably experienced directors like Wise and Fleischer small fortunes so that they could go away and lose large ones, it suddenly seemed more reasonable to make movies on such infinitesimal budgets (infinitesimal *only* by Hollywood's own extravagant standards) that profits were all but guaranteed. Roger Corman had been doing just that for several profitable years.

This concurrence of Fox's failure and *Easy Rider*'s success proved to be a major turning-point in Hollywood's history. At first, the industry's reaction was a pedantically literal one: there was a sudden upsurge of interest in focusing, as *Easy Rider* had done, on that nebulous concept 'youth'. Then, following a string of box-office failures, Hollywood began increasingly to question the commercial wisdom of backing specifically youth-orientated features. Though not at the period diagnosed as such, the problem with these movies was that youth, its life-styles, its hopes and fears, its aspirations and occasional bouts of despair, was viewed precisely *as a problem*. Yet, like their elders, the vast majority of young people regarded the cinema as basically an escapist pastime. They tended to shy away from those movies that were directly, and all too self-consciously, aimed at them, preferring the simple-minded but authentic pleasures which had always been Hollywood's stock-in-trade. They wanted to see comedies, fantasies, science-fiction and adventure movies – indeed, all those genres which have been the mainstay of

Phenomenally successful, The Sound Of Music grossed a fortune for 20th Century-Fox and shot Julie Andrews to super-stardom. But the movie ultimately led the studio into a fool's paradise, where its attempts to repeat the formula were dismal failures.

moviemaking since the silent era. At the same time, however, there had to be an injection of new blood. New ideas. And, above all, new – which is to say, young – performers. The movies themselves did not have to be 'about youth', but it was essential that their protagonists be identifiably young.

So the second half of the 60s saw an extraordinary turnover in the faces to be seen in American movies, the kind of turnover, in fact, which had occurred only twice before in Hollywood's history: from the silent to the sound period, in and around 1929; and from the pre- to the post-war period, between 1939 and 1945. No longer was it feasible for directors to cast indiscriminately from the pool of stars who had reigned for almost 40 years and who were, by the mid-60s, near-sexagenarians themselves: in 1965 James Stewart, for example, was 57, John Wayne 58, Henry Fonda 60, Cary Grant 61, etc. And when one of these actors attempted to play the kind of role on which his reputation had been founded – for example, John Wayne as the brutishly tough Vietnam veteran in *The Green Berets* (1968) – it became depressingly evident just how out of touch with contemporary tastes he could be. Notwithstanding its aggressively

which fell victim to the more sanguinary conventions of the Italian brand); and (2) stars so definitively labelled with 60s attitudes as to appear stranded outside of that decade's ideological and socio-political context (the best examples that can be taken from a string of contenders being Elliott Gould, Donald Sutherland and, in Europe, Terence Stamp).

Vanessa Redgrave addressing an anti-Vietnam war rally in London in 1968. The outspoken Miss Redgrave exemplified a new flavour of political involvement among stars which would not have been possible in the studio system of previous decades.

It is not, of course, that they have wholly ceased to be employed: simply that, in the majority of cases, they have found themselves shunted off into television, low-budget European co-production or cameo roles in disaster movies. The more fortunate ones, from a strictly careerist point of view, have continued to work with tolerable regularity; except that, beyond the 60s, their filmographies no longer display any real coherence, one challenging role being followed, perhaps, by a series of hand-me-downs. In a sense, they are less has-beens than might-have-beens.

Hollywood, no one will be surprised to hear, is fundamentally a Darwinian universe, one in which only the fittest, or most adaptable, are equipped to survive. And, in view of the calamitous inroads made by television during this period, and the consequent disaffection of millions of moviegoers from the medium to which they were once so faithful, it is the stars who have had to prove themselves the fittest of all. This is even more urgently the case in the United Kingdom, whose film industry has always been a precarious one, increasingly dependent on American financing and therefore on the product's capacity to 'travel'. As a result, the British stars who have retained their lustre from the 60s are – like Michael Caine, Julie Christie or Sean Connery – those who, without ever forfeiting an essential Britishness, have succeeded in reconciling their national charactristics with international or transatlantic modes of production.

John Wayne (right) found himself out of his depth directing and starring in The Green Berets. *Not simply too old for the role, his supporting stance on American involvement in Vietnam was at odds with that of the 60s generation of moviegoers.*

hawkish political stance, *The Green Berets* might well have enjoyed a degree of favour among younger movie-goers if the sight of an ageing, toupée-topped 'Duke' in battle fatigues had not seemed quite so preposterous.

The young stars who emerged during these transitional years – Hoffman and Eastwood and Nicholson and Streisand and Redford – remain to this day the supreme box-office attractions of the American cinema. And if many were influenced by the great figures who had preceded them – Nicholson (to take only the most obvious case), in whose screen persona can be detected behavioural traces of James Cagney, John Garfield, Clark Gable and even Humphrey Bogart – they themselves were adopted as models and precursors by a succeeding generation of actors and actresses, rising to prominence in the 70s and 80s.

Naturally, there were casualties, those performers who, for whatever reason, were unable to effect a smooth transition from the old to the new Hollywood. Two principal categories may be established: (1) stars whose careers had been launched in the 50s and who depended for their survival on genres which were to atrophy in the following decade (Leslie Caron, Debbie Reynolds, Jane Powell for musicals; Carroll Baker, Kim Novak for a specifically 50s, somewhat steamy, species of melodrama; Tony Curtis, James Garner, Rock Hudson for the type of modest, easygoing Westerns

As far as the movie stars' story is concerned, then, the 60s (in Hollywood, above all) may be viewed as a watershed, a period of deep uncertainty and indecision, no doubt an oblique reflection of the troubled state in which the whole country found itself, plagued as it was by wars (particularly Vietnam), assassinations (most catastrophically of its president), and a growing aversion among younger members of society to the traditional political processes. Hollywood, at least, braving and surviving the upheaval of those years, bequeathed to the 70s and 80s a bright panoply of performers who, by their independence and versatility, have changed the nature not only of what is called the 'star system' but of the movies themselves.

Ursula Andress

Born **Berne, Switzerland, 19 March 1936**

Ursula Andress will always be remembered for one role – that of Pussy Galore in the first of the James Bond thrillers, *Dr No* (1962) – and for one image – stepping out of the waves, a harpoon gun in her hand, like some busty, statuesque Venus in a white bikini. Her name (which easily lent itself to a ribald spoonerism) was made. For, like the film itself, she seemed to herald the racy, sexy and eupeptic 60s which were just around the corner. And, indeed, her presence was deemed necessary, in a fetishistic manner, in two archetypically mod 60s romps, both of them pretty dire: *What's New, Pussycat?* (1965), with Peter Sellers, Peter O'Toole, Woody Allen, Romy Schneider *et al*; and the chaotic Bond send-up *Casino Royale* (1967), with Sellers and Allen again, David Niven, Orson Welles, William Holden *et al*. When the 60s came to an end, so to all intents and purposes did her reign as a star.

Andress left her native Switzerland while still a teenager, becoming part of the fashionable scene in Rome. There, her greatest asset being a startlingly visible physique, she was cast in a number of low-budget potboilers, and might have continued thus

had not Marlon Brando, a friend, introduced her to a Hollywood agent. Paramount was interested, but she declined to study English and the hoped-for contract did not materialise. After the worldwide success of *Dr No*, however, she was suddenly in demand, making a strong impression in the exotic title role of H. Rider Haggard's *She* in 1965. But Andress's powers of histrionic expression were, to put it mildly, limited, and most of her work was decorative rather than dramatic. She was, for example, the foil to France's adored Jean-Paul Belmondo in the effervescent adventure movie *Les Tribulations D'un Chinois En Chine* (also 1965), later earning herself some free publicity by having a love affair with her co-star, an affair which doubtless contributed to ending her marriage to the actor John Derek (the future husband of Bo). She also appeared as a glamorous countess in the World War I aviation movie *The Blue Max* (1966) and as a bank thief in Peter Hall's comedy-thriller *Perfect Friday* (1970), displaying an unexpectedly sharp sense of comic timing.

By the early 70s, however, her career seemed to have come full circle, for her filmography again consisted of little more than cheapo Italian genre movies, the sole exception being a mythological extravaganza, *Clash Of The Titans*, in 1981. There, as always, Andress's performance was, so to speak, only skin deep. DM

in Bus Riley's Back In Town *(Universal, 1965)*

Ann-Margret

Real name **Ann-Margret Olsson**
Born **Valsjobyn, Sweden, 28 April 1941**

Though born in Sweden, Ann-Margret was brought to the United States in her early childhood and grew up in Illinois. In her teens, she became the mini-star of a radio Amateur Hour; then, after a year at Northwestern University, she joined a jazz combo and sang in various nightclubs throughout the United States. With her full-blown, even overblown, physique and sensual blonde beauty, she naturally gravitated to Hollywood, launching her film career with a small but crucial role as Bette Davis's daughter in Capra's *Pocketful Of Miracles* in 1961. Another rather dated remake followed, *State Fair* (1962), in which she was partnered by the antiseptic but extremely popular Pat Boone; and she made a lively impression as a nubile sexpot in *Bye Bye Birdie* (1963), a sprightly musical which spoofed the recent drafting of Elvis Presley into the Army. But though the film's success made her a minor teenage idol, it tended to typecast her in similar roles and delayed by a number of years the possibility of extending her range. For 'range' was not a useful commodity in such films as *Viva Las Vegas* (co-starring Presley), *Kitten With A Whip* (a dreary melodrama of juvenile delinquency). *The Pleasure Seekers* (a remake of *Three Coins In The Fountain*), all of them made in

1964, *Bus Riley's Back In Town, Once A Thief* (both 1965), *Made In Paris* and *The Swinger* (both 1966).

Partly because of this filmography, there seemed by the late 60s something almost sleazy about Ann-Margret, and certainly she had given few indications that a real talent might be lurking under that glamorous, slightly tawdry and determinedly show-bizzy facade. But when she married the actor Roger Smith in 1967, he retired from the (mostly TV) screen to take her career in hand. The result was a major role in *Carnal Knowledge* (1971), a Mike Nichols/Jules Feiffer account of sexual mores among American males covering two decades. Viewed today, the film may have lost some of its power, through Feiffer's cruel and perceptive wit, to oblige spectators to question their own ideas on sexual stereotypes, but it was a huge success at the time, and Ann-Margret's touching performance as a model no longer in the flower of youth won her an Academy Award nomination.

Though it failed to prove quite the turning point she might have expected (her next film, in 1972, was

called *The Train Robbers*), the Oscar near-miss did mean that she ceased to be perceived exclusively as an overgrown sex kitten; and she was nominated again for her performance in Ken Russell's 'rock opera' *Tommy* (1975). Since then, she has not been too fortunate with her screen work. She appeared, with Bruce Dern and Stéphane Audran, in one of the very worst Chabrol thrillers, *Folies Bourgeoises* (1976); in Tony Richardson's doomed endeavour to recapture his *Tom Jones* success with *Joseph Andrews* (1977); and in Marty Feldman's irretrievably ghastly *The Last Remake Of Beau Geste* (also 1977).

Ann-Margret, however, does not depend wholly on the cinema: as a star of TV specials and nightclub spots, she has always been much in demand. And it was while performing at Lake Tahoe in 1972 that she was accidentally thrown from a 22-foot high platform during her show. She took a year to recover (undergoing plastic surgery for facial scars), but recover she did, and it is to be hoped that she will also manage to bounce back from the present slump in her film career. DM

with Elvis Presley in Viva Las Vegas *(MGM, 1964)*

Julie Andrews

Real name **Julia Elizabeth Wells**
Born **Walton-on-Thames, England,
1 October 1935**

In a career spanning two decades, Julie Andrews has made only thirteen film appearances; and, in most of these, her greatest concern would seem to have been to 'live down' the image which has attached to her since the enormous success of *Mary Poppins* (1964) and *The Sound Of Music* (1965). In fact, it could be said that, because of her identification with the role, the phrase 'a Mary Poppins' has entered the language; but the characterisation it suggests, that of everybody's favourite nanny, is one that Andrews has been trying to shake off almost since she completed the film. Brisk and pretty, with a charming soprano voice and a tendency to enunciate her dialogue so clearly that she could be lip-read from a hundred yards away, she has sometimes appeared to find it a strain personifying the more realistic and gritty type of character she so obviously craves to play.

There was not a time in Andrews' life when she was unconnected with some aspect of show business. While still a tot she was already making regular stage appearances with her parents; at the age of 12 she made her debut in London, singing light operatic arias in the 'Starlight Roof' revue; and a year later she took part in the Royal Variety Performance, the youngest soloist ever to perform on such an occasion. When she was 19, she became the toast of New York with her performance in the Sandy Wilson 20s musical pastiche 'The Boy Friend'; then, in 1956, she was invited to create the role of Eliza Doolittle in a musical adaptation of Shaw's 'Pygmalion' written and composed by Alan Jay Lerner and Frederick Loewe. The result, 'My Fair Lady', made theatrical history – and, what is even rarer, deserved to do so. Shaw's play is a minor masterpiece of the British theatre which was turned into a major American musical: the songs were uniformly terrific, the designs (by Oliver Messel) superb, and the leading trio of performers – Andrews, Rex Harrison as a near-definitive Henry Higgins, Stanley Holloway as Doolittle – could not possibly have been bettered. Jack L. Warner, however, did not agree; and when Warner Bros. purchased the film rights to the show, the role of Eliza went not to Andrews (whom Warner considered risky and untested as a movie draw) but to Audrey Hepburn. The film, directed by George Cukor, is almost as delightful as was the stage show; but the credibility of its plot was somewhat diminished by the fact that Hepburn was so precious and chic as to resemble a lady disguised as a flower-seller rather than the other way round.

Andrews was bitterly disappointed at having been passed over; but consolation was offered her by Walt Disney, who cast her as *Mary Poppins* (1964) in the charming musical version of P.L. Travers's books, one in which cartoon sequences were brilliantly interpolated with live actors. The film was a huge hit (a bigger one than *My Fair Lady*), and Andrews won an Oscar for this, her very first film appearance. Already concerned to avoid typecasting, she followed it with *The Americanization Of Emily* in the same year, a curious Paddy Chayefsky-scripted comedy in which she played a British war widow who falls helplessly in love with a smooth American naval officer (James Garner). But she almost immediately returned to the Mary Poppins fold with *The Sound Of Music* (1965), which is still the most commercially successful musical of all time. It did not matter that Rodgers and Hammerstein's schmaltzy show was one of their very worst ('The Sound of Mucus' as some unimpressed wag dubbed it) – from the moment Julie Andrews began to belt out the title number and the Todd-AO cameras panned up over the breathtaking Tyrolean scenery, half the world was conquered, and many spectators, unbelievable as it may seem, were reported to have seen the film over a hundred times.

It was then, just at the height of her triumph, that

in Star! (*20th Century-Fox, 1968*)

Andrews' career began alarmingly to falter, even if, on paper, her various projects must have looked very promising. *Torn Curtain* (1966), for example: an espionage thriller directed by Hitchcock and co-starring Paul Newman. Yet the film was one of the Master's weakest and most contrived confections; and the potentially interesting pairing of Newman and Andrews, including some mildly frank bedroom scenes, came to nothing. *Hawaii*, made the same year, was a rambling historical epic based on James Michener's novel and the kind of film in which the performers are constantly upstaged by the view. *Thoroughly Modern Millie* (1967), however, was an

enchanting 20s musical in which she was perfectly cast, and well-supported by James Fox, Mary Tyler Moore and Carol Channing. Its box-office success suggested to Twentieth Century-Fox and Robert Wise, the studio and director of *The Sound Of Music*, that what they – no less than Andrews – needed now was another large-scale musical built around her personality. What they came up with was *Star!*, a lavish biopic of Getrude Lawrence, using songs by Cole Porter and Noel Coward. The glamorously enticing Lawrence proved, unfortunately, to be light years out of Andrews' range, and the (extremely costly) film turned out to be a monumental flop.

Formerly married to the English scenic designer Tony Walton, Andrews has, since the disaster of *Star!*, worked exclusively with her second husband, the director Blake Edwards. At first, their collaborations were no more appealing than the films which preceded them: *Darling Lili* (1970), an elephantine musical comedy in which she played, of all unlikely things, a German spy; and *The Tamarind Seed* (1974), a tedious romantic melodrama with Andrews and Omar Sharif as a not very alluring pair of lovers. But in the late 70s Edwards hit a relatively lucky streak with a string of personal, often quite brilliant comedies in which his wife would play roles of varying importance. In the hugely successful '*10*' (1979), for example, she was touching as Dudley Moore's girlfriend abandoned for the more spectacular charms of Bo Derek; in the sour, almost jaundiced *S.O.B.* (1981), she created a mild sensation by – gasp! – baring her breasts; and in the wholly enchanting *Victor/Victoria* (1982) she was by turns poignant and hilarious as a woman pretending to be a man pretending to be a woman. Andrews has preserved her great popularity with the general public through some glossy TV spectaculars; and from the evidence of their work together – most recently, *The Man Who Loved Women* (1983) – it would appear that her best hopes for a future in the cinema lie with her husband. DM

with Rock Hudson in Darling Lili (*Paramount, 1970*)

in Catch-22 (Paramount, 1970)

Alan Arkin

Born **New York City, 26 March 1934**

Alan Arkin was born of Russian-German-Jewish parents, and his acting ambitions were formed at an early age. It was, however, as a singer that he originally established a reputation, with a folk-song group named the Tarriers. Subsequently, he joined The Second City, a much-admired company of satirists based in Chicago. (Arkin, in fact, is a highly versatile artist, being, in addition to an actor, the author of several successful books for children, a composer, a photographer whose work has been exhibited and, finally, a film director.) He moved back to New York in the early 60s, made a number of off-Broadway theatrical appearances and, in 1963, created a sensation with his first role *on* Broadway in 'Enter Laughing'. He had another triumph as an obsessively self-analytical New Yorker in Murray Schisgal's comedy 'Luv'; and he received rave reviews as the director of 'Little Murders' (later directing the 1971 film version with Elliott Gould).

Arkin's Hollywood debut came when he played a Soviet submarine commander stranded on America's East Coast in *The Russians Are Coming, The Russians Are Coming* (1966), a role which earned him an Oscar nomination. This was followed by a

couple of less memorable assignments: a cameo in Vittorio de Sica's vulgar compendium film with Shirley MacLaine, *Woman Times Seven* (1967) and the title role of *Inspector Clouseau* (1968), an ill-advised attempt to exploit the celebrated 'Pink Panther' character without either Peter Sellers or Blake Edwards. But in the same year he won the New York Film Critics Award for his unforgettably poignant portrayal of a deaf-mute in *The Heart Is A Lonely Hunter*, an excellent adaptation of Carson McCullers' novel. And he was also terrific as Yossarian (a role that might have been written for him), the desperately sane airman struggling to be certified mad in Mike Nichols's messy film version of the Joseph Heller novel *Catch-22* (1970).

In the 70s he could be described as an actor who was almost invariably better than the material he was given to work with, whether it was as Neil

Simon's middle-class Jewish Romeo in *Last Of The Red Hot Lovers* (1972), as a lunatic cop in *Freebie And The Bean* (1974) or as a gormless driving test inspector in *Rafferty And The Gold Dust Twins* (1975). But he earned his second Award from the New York Film Critics for a charming, nostalgic little comedy of early Hollywood, *Hearts Of The West* (1975), in which he played (hilariously) an excitable hack movie director. His most recent work has been quite undistinguished (though he was by far the best thing in Marshall Brickman's *Simon*, 1980), and it is probably no coincidence that recognition has come to Arkin from New York rather than from Hollywood itself, which has often seemed at a loss to know precisely what to do with him. Curiously, it may even be that his name would be more prestigious today had he remained on Broadway and in the theatre. DM

with Bert Palmer (left) Gwen Nelson and Malcolm Patten in A Kind Of Loving (Anglo Amalgamated, 1962)

Alan Bates

Born **Allestree, Derbyshire, England, 17 February 1934**

Alan Bates has, in the cinema, never given a poor performance – which is not quite the same thing as being a great film star. There is, perhaps, something too shaggily English about his appeal; blandness would be an ungenerous word for an actor who has given so much pleasure, but it happens on occasion that when Bates seeks to convey the intensity of a character's inner life – as with the dotty protagonist of Skolimowski's *The Shout* (1978) – he has recourse to, paradoxically, superficial tics and devices. He is a charmer, and he knows it. He is also, significantly, a notable stage performer, and no fewer than six of his films have been based on theatrical originals: *The Entertainer* (1960), *The Caretaker* (1964), *Three Sisters* (1970, *A Day In The Death Of Joe Egg* (1972), *Butley* (1974) and *In Celebration* (1975).

From a middle-class background, Bates spent his National Service in the RAF, then was caught up in the 50s renaissance of the English theatre. A small part in Tony Richardson's *The Entertainer* led to the leading role in a curious film, Bryan Forbes's *Whistle Down The Wind* (1961), as an escaped convict whom a group of innocent children mistake for Christ. And his promise was confirmed by John Schlesinger's *A*

in Nijinsky (Paramount, 1980)

Kind Of Loving (1962), in which he played (very sensitively and humorously) a young Northerner forced into marriage with his pregnant girlfriend. By the mid-60s, however, the North of England was no longer a fashionable address for film-makers. 'Swinging London' had taken over, and Bates (less inhibited by a working-class accent and mannerisms than

many English actors of the period) adapted with ease to this shift in locale. He was extremely funny as the cynically ambitious anti-hero of *Nothing But The Best* (1964), determined to make good if it killed him (or anyone who might stand in his way).

His first Hollywood assignment, *Zorba The Greek* (1965), proved rather inconclusive, given that he was obliged to perform in the shadow of Anthony Quinn at his most rambunctious. But at the second attempt, in John Frankenheimer's *The Fixer* (1968), he won an Oscar nomination for his portrayal of a Jewish peasant unjustly condemned in Tsarist Russia. His prestige was further enhanced by appearances in two British films of international stature and popularity: Ken Russell's *Women In Love* (1970), in which he gained notoriety by wrestling in the nude with Oliver Reed, and Losey's *The Go-Between* (1971). Unfortunately, when he finally did become a star in America, it was with two of his laziest performances, in *An Unmarried Woman* and *The Rose* (both 1978).

Bates, however, is ageing well, and seems admirably willing to extend his range. Recently, he was quite superb in two TV productions directed by Schlesinger: as Guy Burgess confronting a bemused Coral Browne in *An Englishman Abroad*; and in the double role of a disillusioned politician and a phony Major dining at *Separate Tables* (from Terence Rattigan's play). DM

Warren Beatty

Real name **Warren Beaty**
Born **Richmond, Virginia, 30 March 1937**

Warren Beatty was once described as 'an actor who doesn't like to act'. This curious assessment is based on the fact that, in 23 years, he has appeared in only 17 movies, plus the related fact that he himself produced two of his most successful movies (*Bonnie And Clyde*, 1967, and *Shampoo*, 1975) and more recently took the double mantle of producer-director (*Heaven Can Wait*, 1978, and *Reds*, 1981). Certainly, he is demonstrably 'very much into money', as his sister Shirley MacLaine once suggested, and has proved himself to be such a canny handler of it that he is now one of the richest men of his generation, a millionaire many times over from a series of extremely advantageous percentage deals. Yet his reluctance, as an actor, to rush from film to film, and the fact that he has worked with some of Hollywood's most distinguished directors, would also seem to imply a seriousness about his craft that few others could equal; and that he is willing to take risks from a strictly commercial point of view was spectacularly confirmed by the critical success and box-office failure of his mammoth pet project, *Reds*. Perhaps because of his boyish good looks, dazzling smile and hunky physique, not to mention his offscreen reputation as an insatiable Don Juan, Beatty has consistently been underestimated as a force in current Hollywood cinema.

His mother was a drama coach who directed the first amateur productions in which he, along with his sister, appeared. Later, after a single year at Northwestern University, he studied drama with Stella Adler. But, in this period of a generally charmed life, his progress was a slow and tortuous one; and to eke out a living (especially after a debilitating bout of hepatitis), he worked as a 'rat watcher' in Washington's National Theater, a piano player in a bar and even a bricklayer's assistant. Finally, some good roles started coming his way, on television, in summer stock (notably in 'Compulsion') and on Broadway (in William Inge's 'A Loss Of Roses'). It was there that he was spotted by the director Elia Kazan, who cast him opposite the lovely, vulnerable Natalie Wood in *Splendor In The Grass* (1961), scripted by Inge. *Splendor* might be called a weepie for teenagers, and there was something ineffably poignant about the painful (and ultimately tragic) discovery of first love embodied by two such attractive young performers.

in Reds *(Paramount, 1981)*

In the same year, he appeared as a Via Veneto gigolo opposite Vivien Leigh in an adaptation of Tennessee Williams' sultry novel *The Roman Spring Of Mrs Stone*. The film was stagey and talkative, and the still inexperienced young actor made a somewhat implausible Italian; yet it is worth noting that, when an error of judgment has been made in Beatty's career, it has almost invariably been a case of overreaching, not underreaching. In other words, his worst films are bad because they are pretentious, not mindless. A case in point is John Frankenheimer's *All Fall Down* (1962), again from a William Inge screenplay, in which he played a narcissistic youth whose seduction of an older woman has tragic results: like much of Inge's work, it was glib and meretricious, but it *was* trying to make a statement of sorts about the period in which it was made and the region in which it was set. Robert Rossen's *Lilith* (1964) and Arthur Penn's *Mickey One* (1965) were both curious artefacts to have been produced in Hollywood: the former was a restrained, subtle and often poetic tale of the love between a young therapist (Beatty) and a schizophrenic woman under his care (Jean Seberg); the latter, unfortunately, was one of the most pretentious films ever to have been perpetrated by an American director, a woolly Kafkaesque allegory set in the Chicago underworld. And, perhaps feeling that he was beginning to

alienate large swathes of the moviegoing public, Beatty relaxed in a pair of innocuous entertainments, *Promise Her Anything*, a romantic comedy set in Greenwich Village, and the more modish *Kaleidoscope*, a comedy-thriller set in some of Europe's most elegant casinos (both 1966). Neither was of any consequence, though the former attracted a degree of prurient attention as its leading lady, Leslie Caron, had recently been divorced by her husband, the English stage and film director Peter Hall, who named Beatty as co-respondent.

It was Beatty himself who, in 1967, brought the *Bonnie And Clyde* package – story, stars (himself and Faye Dunaway) and director (Arthur Penn) – to Warner Bros. As the impotent, mythomaniac Clyde Barrow, whose sole ambition is to become Public Enemy No. 1, he gave his best performance to date; and as the producer of this influential, and disturbingly gory, gangster movie, he earned himself a fortune, thereby restoring his slightly tarnished image as Hollywood's wonder boy. He followed this huge success, however, with a film which disappeared from view practically before it was released, George Stevens' *The Only Game In Town* (1970), a dreary melodrama in which he co-starred with an astonishingly frumpy Elizabeth Taylor; then came Robert Altman's quirky, droll and wintry Western *McCabe And Mrs Miller* (1973), a considerable critical success, in which he played a small-time gambler who sets up a brothel in a bleak Northwestern township at the turn of the century.

When it came to his second production in 1975, Beatty again contrived to choose a winner. Hal Ashby's *Shampoo* was perhaps not quite the lacerating satire it so fondly imagined itself to be, but it was a bright, sexy, juicy comedy which gave its star a wonderful role as a Beverly Hills hairdresser who compulsively sleeps with his clients (female), and became one of the top movies of its year. Having hit the jackpot twice as producer, Beatty felt ready to turn to direction; and though the theme of his first choice, *Heaven Can Wait* (1978, and in fact co-directed by Buck Henry), might have seemed a trifle dated and off-beat for the 70s – a middle-aged quarter-back returns to earth in a younger man's body – it earned around sixty million dollars and two Oscar nominations for Beatty (as best actor and best director). With his second directorial effort, *Reds*, he might be said to have paid for his Oscar (as best director) with the film's commercial failure. Yet, however romantic, sentimental and facilely spectacular it may have seemed to some, this double biopic of the American Communist revolutionary John Reed and his feisty companion, the journalist Louise Bryant (Diane Keaton), was a courageous film to make, not only in Hollywood but in Reagan's America. And, from the evidence of his past career, its failure will not deter Warren Beatty from taking future risks. DM

with Faye Dunaway in Bonnie And Clyde *(Warner Bros., 1967)*

in 1970

Jean-Paul Belmondo

Born **Neuilly-sur-Seine, France, 9 April 1933**

Jean-Paul Belmondo, he of the broken nose and thick, sprawling lips, will always be associated with his role as Michel Poiccard, the Bogart-worshipping hoodlum of Jean-Luc Godard's *Breathless* (1960). And because it was Godard's first film (as well as a revolutionary work in cinema history), one tends to imagine that it was also Belmondo's. In fact, the actor had a long, painstaking struggle to make his name, from drama studies at the Paris Conservatory, via theatrical experience in the provinces, to small supporting roles in nine features prior to *Breathless*. Though most of these were the *vin ordinaire* of pre-New Wave French cinema, at least one, the baroque whodunit *Web Of Passion* (1959), was directed by another up-and-coming cinéaste, Claude Chabrol. It was, however, the huge critical and public cult around Godard's film that made Belmondo a star; and though he has remained so, he was only once offered as good a role again, as the tragi-comic anti-hero of Godard's *Pierrot Le Fou* in 1965.

Despite a handful of interesting films in the early 60s – notably, Peter Brook's *Moderato Cantabile*, from a screenplay by Marguerite Duras, de Sica's *Two Women*, in which he co-starred with Sophia Loren (both 1960), Jean-Pierre Melville's *Léon Morin – Prêtre* (1961, in the title role of a priest), and the same director's *Le Doulos* and *L'Aîné Des Ferchaux*, two stylised thrillers of 1963 – he began increasingly to concentrate on 'vehicles': thrillers, adventure movies and acrobatic comedies displaying his own racy personality but hardly advancing the art of the cinema. The best of these were *That Man From Rio* (1964), an amusing, action-filled spy spoof much helped by exotic locations and the presence of Françoise Dorléac, who died soon after in an automobile accident; and *Borsalino* (1970), a lavish tribute to the Hollywood gangster movie in which Belmondo was teamed for the only time with his friend and arch-rival Alain Delon.

But challenging opportunities became rarer and rarer, and his acceptance of the title role in Alain Resnais's *Stavisky* (1974), a characteristically multi-layered study of the notorious 30s swindler, took the French film scene somewhat by surprise. In any case, Belmondo never cared to repeat the experiment. Secure in his pre-eminence, producing many of his films himself, he is all but guaranteed one monstrous hit a year. It hardly matters whether it is called *Le Magnifique*, *L'Incorrigible*, *L'Animal* or *L'As Des As*. For, these days, when you've seen one Belmondo film, you've seen them all – and what is most dispiriting about his career is that the French public seems to prefer it that way. DM

Candice Bergen

Born **Beverly Hills, California, 8 May 1946**

Blonde, well-scrubbed, beautiful and WASPish, Candice Bergen is the daughter of America's best-known ventriloquist, Edgar Bergen, who himself made frequent guest appearances in minor comedy films of the 30s and 40s. She attended an exclusive finishing school in Switzerland, completed her education at the University of Pennsylvania and began work as a model and photojournalist. Bergen is, in fact, a modern equivalent of those genteelly gifted ladies of the eighteenth and nineteenth centuries who were as adept at *petit-point* as at the harpsichord: she is deeply involved in the feminist movement, has written extensively for magazines and television, and is the author of a play, 'The Freezer'. Cinema is by far the strongest bow to her arc, of course, but there is an inescapably dilettantish flavour to her work in it, nevertheless.

Her first role remains one of the best to date. But then, she was ideal casting as the patrician Vassar graduate in Sidney Lumet's witty adaptation of Mary McCarthy's best-selling novel *The Group* (1966). After an unremarkable (and unremarked) appearance in a dreary adventure movie set in China, *The Sand Pebbles* (also 1966), she left for France to play a leading role, mostly riding through Central Park at dawn, in Claude Lelouch's irretrievably meretricious *Live For Life*, and to Greece for the no less ludicrous *The Day The Fish Came Out* by Michael Cacoyannis (both 1967). In 1970, she was effective in two dubious essays in 60s liberalism: as Elliott Gould's girlfriend in the campus comedy *Getting Straight*, and as a liberated young woman who sides with the Indians in the violent revisionist western *Soldier Blue*. But her two best performances were as a ravishing blonde co-ed 'shared' by Jack Nicholson and Art Garfunkel in Mike Nichols's corrosive comedy of male sexual mores, *Carnal Knowledge* (1971); and as the very proper American

in Getting Straight *(Columbia, 1970)*

lady aducted by Berber bandit Sean Connery in John Milius's amusing update of Valentino's *The Sheik*, *The Wind And The Lion* (1975).

Since the latter, her career has hung fire. Not for one moment, in Cukor's *Rich And Famous* (1981), did she and Jacqueline Bisset succeed in making one forget Miriam Hopkins and Bette Davis in *Old Acquaintance*, the film of which it was a remake; and her appearance as the photographer Margaret Bourke-White in *Gandhi* (1982), though a charming tribute to her own efforts in that direction, was little more than a cameo. Bergen, now married to the French director Louis Malle, has made only eighteen films in twenty years, and it seems unlikely that she will become more prolific in the future. DM

in The Group *(United Artists, 1966)*

Charles Bronson

Real name Charles Bunchinsky (later Buchinsky or Buchinski)
Born **Ehrenfield, Penn., 3 November** 1921

Perhaps the sole distinctive feature of Charles Bronson is his massive Easter Island face, tough, craggy and totally inexpressive. Normally, this might be considered a disadvantage to a film star; yet, in Bronson's case, it led to his receiving a Golden Globe Award in 1971 as the world's most popular actor. Though he has starred in few films of distinction, those he does appear in are almost invariably money-makers, since his popularity is not confined to English-speaking peoples. Thus, even if to most buffs Bronson is an unimportant and often antipathetic figure, he certainly cannot be ignored.

His father, who died in his early youth, was a coal-miner of Lithuanian extraction; and, one of a family of fifteen, Bronson himself was obliged to work in the mines on completion of high school. Following World War II service in the Air Force, he became interested in the theatre and, in Philadel-

in Death Wish *(Paramount, 1974)*

in Machine Gun Kelly *(American-International, 1958)*

phia, was briefly engaged as a set designer (!) and walk-on player. In 1949 he enrolled at the Pasadena Playhouse and was soon regularly employed in Hollywood movies, though exclusively in supporting roles. As Charles Buchinski (or Buchinsky) he can be spotted, for example, in two Cukor comedies, *The Marrying Kind* and *Pat And Mike* (both 1952) and two Aldrich Westerns, *Apache* and *Vera Cruz* (both 1954). Changing his surname to 'Bronson' made little difference at first to his onscreen status, but he was cast in the title role of Roger Corman's *Machine Gun Kelly* (1958) and made a strong impression as one of *The Magnificent Seven* (1960). By *The Dirty Dozen* in 1967, his was a familiar enough face, though he had still not, at the age of 46, gained genuine stardom. At which point, he was invited to co-star with Alain Delon in an apparently routine French thriller *Adieu L'Ami* (1968), a huge success in its country of origin; then, in the same year, he was seen as the harmonica-playing, mysteriously unnamed stranger of Sergio Leone's magnificent

Once Upon A Time In The West. And, like any true western hero, Bronson never looked back.

The cheap, often Mafia-inspired thrillers which he made in Europe until his return to the United States in 1972 were, it is safe to say, uniformly dreadful, but they were screened all over the world and made Bronson one of the best-known actors of all time. In America he has retained that popularity, more or less, churning out films whose commercial success would seem to be in direct proportion to the critical drubbing they receive. Thus, the most successful of all, Michael Winner's *Death Wish* (1974), an ultra-violent apologia of urban vigilant-ism, was denounced by numerous commentators as Fascistic, a fact which did not prevent it from being so profitable at the box-office that a sequel was made in 1982, with the same star and director, as *Death Wish II*. In his later films, Bronson has almost always been teamed with the English-born actress Jill Ireland, who also happens, no doubt coinciden-tally, to be his wife. DM

James Caan

Born **Bronx, New York, 26 March 1939**

In the Hollywood community James Caan has been nicknamed 'The Jewish Cowboy', not because of any regular appearances in westerns, but because he continues to participate professionally in rodeos and owns a remarkable stable of horses. At high school and college, he fared better at sports than in his academic studies, supporting himself during summer vacations as a lifeguard, nightclub bouncer and children's camp counsellor. The cinema aside, his greatest enthusiasm is for sports of all kinds; and he is in his private life, by all accounts, a much less nervily urban figure than the character he frequently projects onscreen.

After useful experience in New York's Neighbor-hood Playhouse, Caan made his off-Broadway debut in a production of Schnitzler's 'La Ronde', then turned up in an uncredited role in Billy Wilder's *Irma La Douce* (1963). His rise from bit player to clean-cut, often humorous supporting actor was effected principally through a pair of Howard Hawks

in The Godfather *(Paramount, 1972)*

movies, the forgettable *Red Line 7000* (1965) and the splendid if derivative western *El Dorado* (1967), in which he played, for those already familiar with the same director's *Rio Bravo*, 'the Ricky Nelson role'. Before his breakthrough came with *The Godfather* in 1972, he demonstrated that he was a more versatile actor than had been supposed, by portraying a mentally retarded football player in an earlier Coppola film, *The Rain People* (1969). But it was as Sonny Corleone, a chip off the old Brandoesque block, that he was propelled to stardom; and though, in the intervening years, his career has often been ill-served by his shaky judgment, he remains one of Hollywood's more sought-after actors.

The problem with Caan is not his slightly bland personality and looks, but the fact that he has been associated with rather more box-office flops than is healthy for any actor. Sometimes this has occurred when he took a risk on an intriguing but not cast-iron project (as, for example, with Karel Reisz's turgid, would-be Dostoevskian *The Gambler*, 1974); and sometimes when he took no apparent risk at all (as with Mark Rydell's grisly turn-of-the-century romp *Harry And Walter Go To New York*, 1976, in which he was teamed with Elliott Gould, Michael Caine and Diane Keaton). And though, as the showman Billy Rose, he stood up well to Barbra Streisand in *Funny Lady* (1975), it was on her performance that the film's appeal was predicated.

In recent years Caan has worked in France, making two characteristically idiotic (but immensely popular) films for Claude Lelouch, *Another Man, Another Chance* (1977) and *The Ins And The Outs* (1981); and directed himself in *Hide In Plain Sight* (1980), a sentimental drama centred on a divorced working-man whose children are forcibly separated from him. The film was in Caan's image – modest, affecting, sympathetic and not terribly inspiring. DM

Michael Caine

Real name **Maurice Micklewhite**
Born **London, 14 March 1933**

'When you're born a Cockney,' Michael Caine once told a journalist, 'there's no way to go but up.' Caine was a *bona fide* Cockney all right, born in Bermondsey to a Billingsgate fish-market porter father and a charlady mother. Like many Cockney children born in the 30s, he was evacuated during World War II, returning to find that his parents' tenement flat had been destroyed in the blitz and that home would henceforth be, for the next ten years, a prefabricated shack. He left school at the age of 16, working at various odd jobs: a cement-mixer attendant, a dishwasher in a restaurant, a pastry cook and a construction labourer. National Service followed, one year of which was spent in West Berlin, the other in combat in Korea, where he contracted a form of malaria which would continue to trouble him for a number of years. Demobbed from the army, and in spite of objections from his parents, he made up his mind to become an actor: he would work at Smithfield Meat Market all day to earn his living and attend drama classes in the evening. It was at this period, too, that he decided to change his name – the choice of his new surname was inspired by the play 'The Caine Mutiny'. As he later put it, 'You start getting comfortable with a new name when you first see it in a nice review.'

Good reviews were some way off yet, but Caine had replied to an advertisement in a trade paper for an assistant stage manager in a small repertory theatre, got the job and soon graduated to being a member of the cast – playing, as one might have predicted, mostly Cockney roles. A few TV parts followed, then an unbilled appearance in a British war film, *A Hill In Korea*, in 1956. Until 1964, and his breakthrough performance in *Zulu*, he appeared in a string of fairly dispensable features, the least forgettable of which were Carol Reed's *The Key* (1958), a subdued World War II melodrama starring Sophia Loren, William Holden and Trevor Howard, *The Day The Earth Caught Fire* (1961), a gripping piece of science fiction reflecting the then current fear of nuclear tests in the earth's atmosphere, and *The Wrong Arm Of The Law* (1963), an amusing crime spoof with Peter Sellers. In each case, Caine dutifully did what was asked of him, without any of his performances attracting the slightest attention. 'I look at my early films,' he subsequently admitted, 'and wonder how anyone could have thought I had anything.'

But *Zulu* was different. Caine had originally tested for a Cockney role, but was finally cast as an effete, aristocratic officer: the film was much liked by both critics and the paying public and, given the reviews for his performance, Caine must at last have begun to feel comfortable with that new name of his. His next film, however, constituted an even bigger break. He was chosen to play Harry Palmer, Len Deighton's dry, sarcastic and bespectacled spy in *The Ipcress File* (1965), a film which was so successful that it spawned a couple of sequels, *Funeral In Berlin* (1966) and *Billion Dollar Brain* (1967). Palmer was the anti-James Bond – he seemed fairly minor in the organisation which employed him, he did not invariably sleep with every beautiful woman who crossed his path, he was perhaps happiest pottering about in the kitchen of his flat – and the popularity of these films in a period of Bond mania can fairly be ascribed to Caine's sharp and sardonically funny characterisation. And his reputation reached a new height when he was nominated for an Oscar for the title role of *Alfie* (1966), an unscrupulous womaniser who almost seemed to chat up the camera itself!

After the hat-trick of *Zulu*, *The Ipcress File* and *Alfie*, Caine could afford to be selective; and perhaps he was (or thought he was), but the conjecture is hardly borne out by his incoherent range of projects of a kind endemic to 'international' careers in the 60s. Bryan Forbes' *The Wrong Box* (1966) was a hamfisted travesty of Stevenson's magnificent comic

in Billion Dollar Brain (United Artists, 1967)

novel; *Gambit*, Caine's first Hollywood venture, was a jaunty if derivative heist movie, *Rififi* out of *Charade*; *Hurry Sundown* and *Woman Times Seven* (both 1967) were among the worst films of their respective directors, Otto Preminger and Vittorio De Sica: the first was a bloated, sprawling, cliché-ridden drama, in which Caine was miscast (to put it mildly) as a bigoted Southern racist; the second an episode film built around Shirley MacLaine, with each of seven male actors playing an episode apiece. Nor were *The Magus* (1968), *Play Dirty*, *The Italian Job* (both 1969) and *The Last Valley* (1971) much better, and it seemed for a few years that Caine was no longer terribly interested in upholding any kind of personal image. Having established himself as a star, he appeared to find that status incompatible with being an actor. In this sense (if in no other), his career ran curiously parallel to that of Peter Sellers,

in Zulu (Avco-Embassy, 1964)

another bespectacled 'local boy made good'.

Since the early 70s, however, Caine has succeeded on the whole in maintaining a balance between the kind of immediately accessible work he may feel that his career demands and the more challenging roles through which he can extend his range as an actor. In too many cases, unfortunately, the former have been 'popular' only at the level of intentions: films like *The Black Windmill* (1974), a Don Siegel-directed espionage potboiler, *The Wilby Conspiracy* (1974), a drama set in black Africa, *Harry And Walter Go To New York* (1976), a leaden-footed farce set at the turn of the century, Irwin Allen's *The Swarm* (1978), the disaster movie to end all disaster movies (it more or less did) and *Beyond The Poseidon Adventure* (1979), the same director's attempt to revive the genre after its demise, were far from enjoying the commercial success that would have

been their sole *raison d'être*. And Caine's performances were either predictable (his espionage agent in *The Black Windmill* was little more than an older, wearier Harry Palmer) or bored and expressionless, the steely eyes hardly blinking behind the thick-rimmed spectacles.

Yet, concurrently with these, he could be as excellent as he was in two pastiche thrillers for Mike Hodges, *Get Carter* (1971) and *Pulp* (1972), in which the Chandleresque mythology of private eye novels and films was transferred with surprising success to the 70s. In Joseph L. Mankiewicz's virtuoso adaptation of Anthony Shaffer's Chinese-box thriller *Sleuth* (1972), he and Laurence Olivier made a wonderfully droll and occasionally frightening cat-and-mouse act, his self-consciously *nouveau riche* hair-dresser a superb foil to Olivier's scheming upper-class gamester. And, though the film itself was a somewhat anaemic confection, Caine's performance as a wealthy pulp novelist fantasizing about his wife's (supposed) infidelities in Joseph Losey's *The Romantic Englishwoman* (1975) made it worth seeing. But perhaps the best role in his whole career came in John Huston's adaptation of Kipling's *The Man Who Would Be King* (1975), in which he partnered Sean Connery as two British soldiers who resign from the army in order to set themselves up as deities in remote Kafiristan. The film represented Huston's most successful return to the vein of pure, Stevensonian (and, of course, Kiplingesque) adventure in which he had initially made his reputation as a screenwriter and director, and the earthily witty teaming of Caine and Connery worked so well that one regretted, for once, the impossibility of any sequel to the tale.

In recent years, with the advance of middle-age, Caine has become increasingly indifferent to his star 'image', which means in effect that he will now accept the kind of uningratiating role he would probably have declined only a few years ago. In Sidney Lumet's *Deathtrap*, for example, (1982, and based on a 'Sleuth'-like thriller by Ira Levin), he played a murderous homosexual playwright and shared an on-screen kiss with Christopher Reeve. In *Educating Rita* (1983), a modest British comedy-drama which became one of the 'sleepers' of the year in the United States, he was quite touching as an emotionally deadened scholar whose life is changed through contact with an independently minded working-class student played by Julie Walters: both performers received Oscar nominations for their performances. And he was by far the best thing, co-starring with Richard Gere, in John MacKenzie's clumsy, superficial adaptation of Graham Greene's 'The Honorary Consul', *Beyond The Limit* (1984), as an anti-heroic middle-aged lush. Indeed, given the direction in which his career is currently going, one may hope, and possibly even predict, that at 51 Michael Caine is an actor with a future rather than a past. DM

in A Bridge Too Far (United Artists, 1977) ▷

Claudia Cardinale

Born Tunis, 15 April 1939

Born in Africa of Italian parents, Claudia Cardinale is a quintessentially Mediterranean beauty: smoky dark eyes, lustrous dark hair and a voluptuous figure. She is also one of the tallest of feminine stars, being tall enough to play in Tunisia's national basketball team! In 1957 she won a local beauty contest, her prize being a trip to the Venice Film Festival. It was while studying drama at Rome's Centro Sperimentale film school that she was taken up by the producer Franco Cristaldi, who decided to groom her as a successor to the great Italian beauties of the 50s, Sophia Loren and Gina Lollobrigida (he also married her.) Her first film in Italy, Monicelli's wondrously funny heist spoof *I Soliti Ignoti* (1958), enjoyed exceptional success in the United States as *Big Deal On Madonna Street*; and only two years later Visconti cast her in *Rocco And His Brothers*, another Italian feature to be widely admired. Finally, in 1963, she appeared in two outright masterpieces: in Fellini's *8½* as a symbol of innocent yet earthy

John Cassavetes

Born New York City, 9 December 1929

Somewhat in the manner of Orson Welles, John Cassavetes will be remembered less as an actor than as a director who agreed to act in other people's films in order to finance his own more marginal works. Born into a New York family of Greek immigrant origin, Cassavetes enrolled at the American Academy of Dramatic Arts immediately after graduating from college, and made his professional debut with a stock company in Providence, Rhode Island. His development as an intense, Method-influenced young actor coincided with the golden age of live television drama, in which he became a household face, if not yet a name. Concurrently, he began building up a film career in a pair of gritty, low-budget dramas of social conscience, Don Siegel's *Crime In The Streets* (1956) and Martin Ritt's *Edge Of The City* (GB: *A Man Is Ten Feet Tall*, 1957). It was with his earnings from a popular TV series, 'Johnny Staccato', that he financed his first, independently produced, film, *Shadows* (1961), a sombre inter-racial love story which was made for just $40,000 and won the Critics' Award at the Venice Festival. Two mainstream studio productions, *Too Late Blues* (1962), set in a jazz milieu, and *A Child Is Waiting* (1963), a Stanley Kramer-produced drama about retarded children, were less successful critically and unsuccessful commercially; but Cassavetes had found his true vocation, and acting was henceforth to take a very secondary place to direction.

As a performer, he always has been competent, often more than that, but one sometimes suspected that he was dutifully fulfilling a contractual obligation rather than, as in his earlier TV and film work, investing himself wholly in a character's psychology. Not unpredictably, his best screen performance came in one of his own productions, *Husbands* (1970), about a trio of middle-aged losers on a binge following the death of their best friend. He was also, notably, one of *The Dirty Dozen* in Robert Aldrich's violent war film of 1967; Mia Farrow's husband who 'lends' her to a devil-worshipping sect in *Rosemary's Baby* (1968); and the villain whose life is brought to a literally explosive conclusion in Brian De Palma's absurd yet diverting shock thriller *The Fury* (1978).

Perhaps the greatest service rendered him by this unsatisfactory acting career was that it helped him become an extraordinary director of other people, most memorably of his wife Gena Rowlands. Under her husband's direction in films like the aptly titled *A Woman Under The Influence* (1974), *Opening Night* (1977), *Gloria* (1980) and *Love Streams* (1984), Rowlands has matured into one of the American cinema's greatest assets. DM

in The Pink Panther *(United Artists, 1964)*

purity; and in Visconti's sumptuous adaptation of Lampedusa's *The Leopard* as the *nouveau-riche* heiress Angelica.

Thereafter, with rare exceptions, her career is almost totally devoid of interest. A Hollywood sojourn in the mid-60s produced a mixed bag of films, in none of which was she really tested: *The Pink Panther*, *Circus World* (both 1964), *Blindfold*, *The Lost Command* and *The Professionals* (all 1965). Visconti used her once more, in his melodrama of incest *Sandra* (1965), but she lacked the sheer technique to carry off such a delicate role. It was nice to find her, however, in Sergio Leone's magnificent spaghetti Western *Once Upon A Time In The West* (1968), especially as she seemed as warm, sympathetic and desirable as ever. More recently, apart from a fleeting glimpse of her in Visconti's *Conversation Piece* (1975) and a slightly more extended one as Klaus Kinski's patroness in Herzog's *Fitzcarraldo* (1982), her filmography has consisted of a string of Italian titles totally unfamiliar to the moviegoing world at large. The relative failure of her career to develop, however, is more a comment on the parlous state of contemporary Italian cinema than on any question of personal inadequacy. DM

in The Killers *(Universal, 1964)*

Richard Chamberlain

Born Beverly Hills, California, 31 March 1935

Few contemporary careers illustrate more acutely the dangers of typecasting than Richard Chamberlain's; his also demonstrates the fact that, whereas the cinema has perhaps become too fragmented of late for typecasting to be as rigid as it once was, in television it can act as a stranglehold on an actor's future. Chamberlain became virtually a household name with his playing of handsome young Dr Kildare opposite Raymond Massey's wise old Dr Gillespie in a long-running TV series based on the original MGM movies with Lew Ayres and Lionel Barrymore. It made his name, and he has been struggling to kill the image of an earnest yet sexy young medic ever since.

Born, raised and educated in the heart of the Hollywood movie colony, he served two years in the Army, partly in Korea. With his boyish, cleancut good looks, however, he was a natural for the cinema, and, in the wake of his TV success, was at first offered challenging roles in Richard Lester's *Petulia* (1968), Bryan Forbes's disastrous adaptation of Giraudoux's *The Madwoman Of Chaillot* (1969)

in The Music Lovers *(United Artists, 1971)*

and Ken Russell's delirious *The Music Lovers* (1971), in which he was, under the circumstances, a tolerably plausible Tchaikovsky. At the same time, in an endeavour to extend his range even further, he attempted some Shakespeare (including 'Hamlet') on the British stage. The 70s were somewhat rocky for him, given that he appeared in two of the decade's very worst films, *The Slipper And The Rose* (1976), a hideously twee version of the Cinderella tale, and *The Swarm* (1978), most ludicrous of disaster movies. But he redeemed himself somewhat with an effectively taut performance as an Australian barrister defending a group of aborigines accused of ritual murder in Peter Weir's *The Last Wave* (1979), even if the film's blend of primitive mysticism and contemporary social comment did not quite come off. Most recently, his greatest success has been in the medium which launched his career: he starred in two mammoth TV series, 'Shogun' and 'The Thorn Birds'. Whatever their viewer ratings, neither will add to his reputation as a serious actor. DM

Julie Christie

Born **Chukua, Assam, India, 14 April 1941**

Born on her father's tea plantation in India, Julie Christie was sent to England for her schooling. After studying art in France, she decided to become an actress and attended classes at London's Central School of Speech and Drama. This was followed by her professional debut in the theatre with a repertory company in 1957. Her first big break came when she was offered the title role in a popular TV science fiction series 'A For Andromeda'. At that period, she was in her late teens and a beguiling blonde beauty, an English rose, yet already with the rakish, liberated quality she was to epitomise so memorably in the 60s. Her film debut was fairly inauspicious, however. A farce in the traditional British mould, *Crooks Anonymous* (1962) had a neat idea – an organisation dedicated to reforming criminals through group therapy – but it possessed neither wit nor lightness of touch, and Christie was totally wasted. Ditto with her second, *The Fast Lady* (1963), a *Genevieve* spinoff. And, oddly enough, she had a lesser role in her third, John Schlesinger's *Billy Liar* (also 1963), as the dream girl in Tom Courtenay's life who tries to persuade him to leave his provincial home town for the siren attractions of London. By the end of the film, Courtenay remained unconvinced – but a whole generation of male moviegoers had succumbed to this mini-skirted apparition swinging out

in Darling *(Avco-Embassy, 1965)*

of his life. *Billy Liar* made Christie a star, one who was viewed as the very embodiment of 60s England – she was beautiful in a completely uncosmeticized way, and the Americans were mad about her. She later said of that period, 'You could be someone without having to be glamorous. I know I wasn't. I never could get my hair together or anything like that. I was criticised for that quite a lot in England; perhaps not in America, because they were too gaga over English people then to criticise.'

Her celebrity was consecrated in Schlesinger's *Darling* (1965), a film written by Frederic Raphael specially for her: the script was glib and not quite as witty as it imagined itself to be, but – as an ambitious young model in a cynical, fashion-obsessed milieu – Christie contrived to be both ice-cold and radiant (quite a feat!), fully deserving the Academy Award which she won for her performance. After this, anything short of David Lean's *Dr Zhivago* (also 1965) would have been an anti-climax. Not that the film version of Pasternak's novel was any kind of a masterpiece – but it was a gigantic commercial success, and the role of Zhivago's mistress Lara was, in a way, the 60s' Scarlett O'Hara. Christie, needless to say, rose to the occasion. Now the leading British film actress, and much in demand, she could afford to choose her roles on

other than strictly financial considerations. And if not all of her films have emerged as quite the exciting projects they must have seemed on paper, a glance at her filmography will reveal the intelligence with which she has made her choices. Following her international triumph in *Zhivago*, it was hardly a surprise that Truffaut, in some respects a certified 'woman's director', would wish her to star in his first (and, to date, only) English-language film, an adaptation of Ray Bradbury's science fiction novel *Fahrenheit 451* (1966). The title refers to the temperature at which books burn; and, though visually superb, the film is perhaps more concerned with books than with people. As expected, Christie was excellent – in a thankless role (co-starred with Oskar Werner). Conversely, though the wilful farm girl who destroys the lives of three men in Schlesinger's adaptation of Thomas Hardy's *Far From The Madding Crowd* (1967) seemed tailormade for her talents, she never got the hang of it, striking one as altogether too modern and urban.

From 1968 on, she worked principally in Hollywood, still very much concerned to maintain the high standards she had set herself. Richard Lester's *Petulia* (1968) was an interesting failure (though highly rated in some quarters). But she was excellent as one of the illicit lovers in Joseph Losey's *The Go-Between* and as the businesslike whore in Robert Altman's *McCabe And Mrs Miller* (both 1971 and both among their respective directors' best films). Again, if Nicholas Roeg's would-be baroque thriller *Don't Look Now* (1973) was not to everybody's taste, Christie followed it with a couple of box-office blockbusters: Hal Ashby's *Shampoo* (1975), in which she notoriously fellated Warren Beatty underneath an elegant dinner table, and Beatty's own whimsical fantasy *Heaven Can Wait* (1978), which gave her a rare opportunity to play light, frothy comedy.

Towards the end of the 70s, however, she seemed to drop out of sight, and there were rumours that she had given up the cinema in order to devote herself to the feminist movement and the campaign for nuclear disarmament, of which she is a strong supporter. She purchased a farm in a rather remote

part of England and lived far from the madding crowd of media people by whom she was once mobbed. The rumours proved unfounded; yet in the 80s her choice of roles has become far more personal, quite clearly reflecting her political and ideological views. Thus she has starred in a trio of films based on novels by women: Doris Lessing's *Memoirs Of A Survivor*, Rebecca West's *Return Of The Soldier* (both 1981) and Ruth Prawer Jhabvala's

in Heaven Can Wait *(Paramount, 1978)*

Heat And Dust (1982), directed in India by James Ivory. Most radically, she agreed to accept a nominal fee to appear in a BFI Production Board film *The Gold Diggers* (1984), directed by Sally Potter and made with an all-woman crew. Some, no doubt, will hark back nostalgically to that insouciant dolly bird of the 60s; others will acclaim such independence and strength of purpose from a member of the profession referred to by Hitchcock as 'cattle'. DM

with Omar Sharif in Dr Zhivago *(MGM, 1965)*

Sean Connery

Real name Thomas Connery
Born Edinburgh, 25 August 1930

Sean Connery's early years hardly seemed to prepare him for the role which launched his career and with which he will always be associated. Born in Edinburgh of working-class parents – his father was a lorry driver and his mother a charlady – he left school at the age of 15 and enlisted in the Royal Navy. On his discharge, he worked intermittently as a lifeguard, bricklayer and even coffin polisher, becoming an amateur bodybuilder in his spare time. It was this last occupation which finally helped him escape from the round of dead-end manual jobs. In the late 40s, he was offered the chance to pose for swimming-trunk advertisements, which led to his being cast as a member of the chorus in the London stage production of Rodgers and Hammerstein's 'South Pacific'. Infected with the acting bug, he started working in small repertory companies throughout Britain; possessing a strong accent which, even to this day, he has been unable (or perhaps unwilling) to shake off, he frequently played Scottish roles. Handsome and virile in a tough, proletarian manner, he gradually broke into television and cinema, though for many years playing fairly minor roles. Among his credits from this period were *Hell Drivers* (1957), a violent, Holly-

in The Man Who Would Be King *(Columbia, 1975)*

wood-inspired melodrama about lorry drivers, *Action Of The Tiger* (also 1957), a routine adventure yarn from the veteran director Terence Young, and *Another, Time, Another Place* (1958), a three-handkerchief weepie about a doomed World War II love affair which starred Lana Turner, Barry Sullivan – and, third on the credit titles – Sean Connery. He was selected by Walt Disney to play the male half of the romantic interest (the other half being Janet Munro) in a coy, sentimental piece of Oirishry about leprechauns, *Darby O'Gill And The Little People* (1959), which enjoyed a fair degree of popularity among younger audiences. But his career was not exactly taking off when, from among a number of contenders and to general surprise, he was chosen in 1962 by producers Harry Saltzman and Albert R. Broccoli to incarnate Ian Fleming's secret-agent hero James Bond. Fleming's Bond was an ultra-smooth gentleman spy, equally at ease in gaming casinos and underground torture chambers, knowing precisely which fork or which pistol to use, depending on the circumstances. Connery's Bond was a somewhat rougher diamond, but in some ways a more sympathetic character since blessed with a wry sense of humour. In any event, the first Bond film, *Dr No*, was a sensation; and, despite increasing impatience at being so typecast, Connery starred in six more. *From Russia With Love* (1963), *Goldfinger* (1964), *Thunderball* (1965), *You Only Live Twice*

(1967) and *Diamonds Are Forever* (1971) appeared in regular succession (though a less successful George Lazenby Bond, *On Her Majesty's Secret Service*, interrupted the sequence in 1969, when Connery announced his retirement from the role). And, in 1983, when Roger Moore seemed to have made the part his own, the original star, greying at the temples, returned for one last fling in *Never Say Never Again*, donating his fee (estimated at a million dollars) to a charitable organisation which he himself has founded to aid deprived Scottish children.

Bond made Connery a millionaire and it would have been no more than understandable if he had been willing to allow the role to swallow him up. It is to the actor's credit, however, that almost from the very beginning of his success he had been on the lookout for more challenging assignments. Thus he

in Diamonds Are Forever *(United Artists, 1971)*

worked with Hitchcock on *Marnie* (1964); played a rebellious inmate of a British military prison in Sidney Lumet's *The Hill* (1965); and gave a wonderfully eccentric performance as a bohemian poet in Irvin Kershner's *A Fine Madness* (1966). And when the Bond years were finally over (with the exception of his valedictory reappearance in the 80s), Connery gleefully shed not only his toupee but all the inhibitions to which sex objects and superstars may be prey, and concentrated on character parts. In this vein, he was particularly outstanding as a British soldier with delusions of grandeur in Huston's *The Man Who Would Be King* (1975), as an ageing Robin Hood in Richard Lester's *Robin And Marian* (1976), and as a middle-aged man in love with a younger woman in Fred Zinnemann's underrated *Five Days One Summer* (1982). DM

Tom Courtenay

Born Hull, England, 25 February 1937

A peaky, underfed-looking youth, the son of a ship painter, Tom Courtenay belonged to that generation of actors, many of them from working-class backgrounds, who reversed the accepted codes, practices and conventions of the British theatre in the early 60s. After studying at the Royal Academy of Dramatic Art, he made his debut in an Old Vic production of Chekhov's 'The Seagull', in which he was spotted by the film-maker Tony Richardson. It being a period when both film and stage directors were prepared to take a chance on comparative unknowns, Richardson cast him as the non-conformist Borstal Boy in his adaptation of Alan Sillitoe's *The Loneliness Of The Long-Distance Runner* (1962), a role which made him famous overnight. This initial promise was confirmed when, in the theatre, he replaced Albert Finney as the North Country Walter Mitty locked into his fantasies in 'Billy Liar', later repeating it for John Schlesinger's 1963 film version. And, to complete a striking trio, he was first-rate as a sensitive young World War I deserter in Joseph Losey's *King And Country* (1964).

Yet Courtenay's film career spluttered through the 60s and stalled, almost definitively, in the following decade. This was due partly to a thriving theatrical success (notably as Norman in Alan Ayckbourne's inter-related trio of farces 'The Norman Conquests') and partly to a rather incoherent selection of projects, which included *King Rat*,

in King Rat *(Columbia, 1965)*

Doctor Zhivago (both 1965), a grotesque Greek-British co-production *The Day The Fish Came Out* (1967) and, more convincingly, a straightforward, harrowing adaptation of Solzhenitsyn's *One Day In The Life Of Ivan Denisovich* (1971), in which he played the title role of a Gulag inernee. In 1984, he reprised with great success his stage performance as a cajoling, bullying, homosexual aide to a great, if flyblown, actor-manager in *The Dresser*. DM

Alain Delon

Born **Sceaux, France, 8 November 1935**

The product of a broken home, Alain Delon had a stormy childhood. He was frequently expelled from school, worked as a butcher's boy and, at the age of 17, joined the French marines and served as a parachutist in Indochina during the siege of Dien Bien Phu. Back in Paris, he was briefly a porter at the meat and vegetable market in Les Halles, which was where, in 1956, he was 'discovered' for the cinema. After a trio of forgotten potboilers, he won international stardom as Patricia Highsmith's charmingly amoral anti-hero Ripley in René Clément's *Purple Noon* (1960), a sun-drenched thriller and still one of the best screen adaptations of Highsmith. And since, at 25, Delon was breathtakingly good-looking, dark and Italianate, it was not a surprise that he should, in the same year, be given the leading role in Visconti's *Rocco And His Brothers*, whose success only confirmed the existence of a new European heartthrob.

The early 60s were perhaps his most interesting years, for he made in rapid succession Clément's delightful comedy of turn-of-the-century anarchism,

Quelle Joie De Vivre (1961), Antonioni's strange and beautiful drama of social alienation, *The Eclipse* (1962, with Monica Vitti), and Visconti's stupendous *The Leopard* (1963), in which he played the dashing and cynical young revolutionary Tancredi. There were other, less challenging, roles, of course – mostly in swashbucklers and thrillers – which were accepted as the kind of chore every actor is obliged to perform in order to maintain his position in the public eye.

Yet, with increasingly rare exceptions, such are the genres Delon has chosen to concentrate on ever since; and though they have made him (*ex aequo* with Jean-Paul Belmondo, whose career has run curiously parallel) the most popular male star in French cinema, they have immeasurably compromised his reputation as a serious actor. The exceptions were, notably, Jean-Pierre Melville's austere study of the Parisian underworld, *Le Samourai* (1967), and Joseph Losey's allegory of the Occupation, *Mr Klein* (1976), in which Delon played (brilliantly) the icily sinister title role. Unfortunately, when he himself turned to direction in the 80s, the films which he churned out were indistinguishable from the hack work he had appeared in for over two decades. Moreover, his standing as a screen 'tough guy' was enhanced when, in 1968, he and his former wife, the actress Nathalie Delon, were implicated in one of France's most sensational political scandals. The discovery of his bodyguard's corpse in a garbage dump led to revelations of sex and drug orgies involving a host of personalities from the worlds of politics and show business. Though Delon emerged as a somewhat shady figure, it seemed only to reinforce his filmic credibility. DM

Catherine Deneuve

Real name **Catherine Dorléac**
Born **Paris, 22 October 1943**

Adopting her mother's maiden name for her own career, Catherine Deneuve was the daughter of a veteran French stage and screen actor, Maurice Deneuve, and the sister of actress Françoise Dorléac, who was tragically killed in a road accident in 1967. While still at school, she made her screen debut in a comedy, *Les Collégiennes* (1967), and was taken up by the director Roger Vadim, by whom she had her first child. Vadim cast her in only one feature, a grotesque adaptation of Sade, *Vice And Virtue* (1963), and it was not until the following year that she properly established herself. In 1964 she made three films, including Jacques Demy's incredibly popular, lollipop-hued operetta *The Umbrellas Of Cherbourg*, in which she was a charming, not too saccharine, heroine. It was a measure of Roman Polanski's foresight that, on the strength of that performance, he chose her to play the mentally unbalanced protagonist of *Repulsion*, filmed in London in 1965. For Deneuve's best subsequent work was done with directors who realised the potential for refined sadism in sullying her exquisitely beautiful, coldly porcelain features; and one of the great lost opportunities of film history is that she and Alfred Hitchcock never met, for she was an archetypal Hitchcock heroine.

In *The Young Girls Of Rochefort* (1967), she worked with Demy again (and, for the only time, with her sister Françoise): because screened in Britain and the United States in a crudely dubbed version, the film has been underestimated, but it is an enchanting homage to the MGM musical and a far more vigorous fantasy than that which made both Demy's and Deneuve's names. It was, however, in the same year that she gave her most memorable performance in one of the greatest, most truly erotic, films ever made: Luis Buñuel's *Belle De Jour*. As the bored and frigid *bourgeoise* who finds sexual fulfilment as an 'afternoons only' prostitute, Deneuve (like her character) drew the finest of lines between cool self-assurance on the surface and raging sexual instincts underneath. In a second collaboration with the great Surrealist, *Tristana* (1970), she was hardly less remarkable as a determined young woman mapping out her independence in the repressed society of Spain in the 20s.

By the early 70s, she had become the leading female star in French cinema, a rank which is still indisputably hers. She has worked a few times in Hollywood, most recently in Aldrich's *Hustle* (1975) and the turgid Foreign Legion drama *March Or Die* (1977), but it is for European work with such directors as Bunuel, Demy, Truffaut (*The Last Métro*, 1980) and Ferreri that she will be best remembered. Deneuve is also very much her own woman in private life: though she was briefly married to the photographer David Bailey, the father of her second child is Marcello Mastroianni. DM

Sandy Dennis

Born **Hastings, Nebraska, 27 April 1937**

A little of Sandy Dennis goes a long, long way. Which is a pity, for she is without question an extremely talented actress, one possessed of a quite brilliant technique. Unfortunately, both in drama and comedy, she tends invariably, and monotonously, to give the same performance; and she constitutes, in effect, a curious case of wilful self-type casting. Whiny and insecure, ravaged by tics and mannerisms, forever nursing some warm secret hurt to her breast (which is itself on occasion the source of that hurt), she often succeeds in alienating the spectator no less than her character does the others in whatever film it happens to be.

In her teens she acted in a local stock company, and soon lit out for New York to study under Lee Strasberg at the Actors Studio. Her first appearances were on tiny off-Broadway stages; but, graduating to mainstream theatre, she scored a notable double by winning two Tony Awards in successive years for 'A Thousand Clowns' and 'Any Wednesday'. This was turned into a hat trick with an Oscar as best supporting actress in *Who's Afraid Of Virginia Woolf?* (1966), in which she played George Segal's timorous young bride. Another memorable appearance was her dedicated teacher contending with a tough slumland school in *Up The Down Staircase* (1967). But she was already maddeningly 'sensitive' and quivery in *The Fox*, an adaptation of D.H. Lawrence's novella about a Lesbian relationship, in *Sweet November*, a lamebrained 'liberated' comedy (both 1968) and *That Cold Day In The Park* (1969), an early Robert Altman film in which she played a spinster who, on impulse, picks up a hippie in Central Park.

There is little to be said about her roles in the 70s, which were intermittent and undistinguished. She did make a comeback of a kind, however, in another film by Altman. *Come Back To The Five And Dime, Jimmy Dean, Jimmy Dean* (1982) was a surprisingly poignant transcription of a not very good play about a twenty-years-on reunion of the James Dean Fan Club in a small Texas hamlet; and, with absence perhaps making the heart grow fonder or, at least, more indulgent, Dennis seemed particularly impressive as a dowdy, middle-aged woman whose sole achievement in life – bearing a child of the actor she idolised – turns out to be illusory. Basically, it was the same performance as before, but one realised afresh just how well-observed it could be. DM

Faye Dunaway

Born **Bascom, Florida, 14 January 1941**

There is a passage in Joan Crawford's autobiography which reads: 'Of all the actresses, to me only Faye Dunaway has the talent and the courage to make a real star.' It is not certain whether the formidable Crawford would actually have approved of Dunaway's portrayal of her in the campily excessive film biopic *Mommie Dearest* (1981), but she recognised a soulmate when she saw one. If it were not for Dunaway's existence, one might have said that, after making Joan Crawford, they broke the mould; but, as long as Dunaway is splendidly chewing up the scenery, that mould will remain intact. She herself has drawn parallels between herself and Crawford, as well as with a number of other ruthless, strong-willed women she has been pleased, as an actress, to impersonate. On television for example, she played Evita Peron in a drama of that name, the American evangelist of the 20s, Aimee Semple McPherson, in 'The Disappearance of Aimee', and Wallis Simpson, the Baltimore divorcee who became the Duchess of Windsor in 'Portrait: The Woman I Love'; and one of her most noted roles in the cinema was that of the gun moll Bonnie Parker in *Bonnie And Clyde* (1967). 'These women all had something in common,' she once remarked. 'They had tremendous force of will and they were determined to make their own destinies. And they were also passionate people.' And, so that one is unlikely to miss the implied connection, she went on, 'I knew very little about Evita before playing the part. The Argentine is a long distance away, let alone Los Toldos, where she was born, a mere speck on the map. But I have my own Los Toldos, which is something I can relate to. It is Bascom, the tiny town in northern Florida near the Alabama border where I was born. I, too, wanted power over my own life. I had known the anger and frustration of the poor Southern girl struggling against poverty. Lots of people were amazed I could play Bonnie Parker. But for me it was not amazing; I'm a Southern girl who's been through a depression or two of my own.'

In fact, her father was not, as one might imagine after such an impassioned tirade, some poor share-

in Network *(MGM, 1976)*

cropper, but a career Army officer; and the young Faye very rapidly escaped from Bascom, as she was educated in various American and European cities, wherever her father was stationed. She returned to her home state to attend the University of Florida, continuing her higher education at the School of Fine and Applied Arts in Boston University, where she studied theatre arts. Determined to become an actress, she arrived in New York and successfully auditioned for the Lincoln Center Repertory Company in 1962, under which aegis she appeared in 'A Man For All Seasons' and Elia Kazan's production of Arthur Miller's 'After The Fall', whose protagonist, played by Dunaway, was a thinly disguised portrait of Miller's former wife, Marilyn Monroe. But she had set her sights on the cinema and, after some off-Broadway experience, made her film debut in Elliot Silverstein's bizarre comedy-drama *The Happening* (1967), in which she played a member of a band of beachcombing vagrants who accidentally kidnap a top Mafia gangster (Anthony Quinn). Then, fol-

lowing an appearance in one of Otto Preminger's trashiest sagas, *Hurry Sundown* (also 1967), she landed the role of Bonnie Parker. Though few people besides its producer-star Warren Beatty and director Arthur Penn had much faith in the commercial potential of *Bonnie And Clyde*, the film proved to be a (controversial) smash hit: Dunaway was nominated for an Oscar and was an overnight sensation. Her tall, statuesque, green-eyed beauty was more immediately evident in *The Thomas Crown Affair* (1968), a smooth, silky crime caper in which she was teamed with Steve McQueen and dazzled in a series of glamorous gowns, as if the costume designers were overjoyed to discover a 60s actress capable of doing them justice.

There were a couple of misfires (John Frankenheimer's *The Extraordinary Seaman*, a nautical farce which received few release dates, and *A Place For Lovers*, an imbecilic three-Kleenex weepie from Vittorio de Sica, in which her co-star was Marcello Mastroianni, both 1969), then she worked again with Elia Kazan on the film version of his novel *The Arrangement* (also 1969), a flawed but underrated and often powerful portrayal of a successful middle-aged business tycoon (Kirk Douglas) approaching the crossroads of his life. It flopped at the box-office, however, as did Jerry Schatzberg's outrageously pretentious *Puzzle Of A Downfall Child* (1970), in which, playing a photographic model with psychological problems, she was decked out in a series of hopefully Sternbergian confections (i.e. feathers to the fore), but remained resolutely, obstinately un-Marlene-like. She was good in Arthur Penn's pro-Indian satire *Little Big Man* (1970) but, as the film's title itself seems to indicate, it was very much the property of her leading man, Dustin Hoffman. Dunaway, in short, badly needed, not only a hit, but a hit from which she herself might benefit. And she got one. In Roman Polanski's superb private eye pastiche *Chinatown* (1974), she was cast as a velvety *femme fatale* with the darkest of secrets in her closet; and, no less successfully than her co-star Jack Nicholson, conjured up that smoky old Bogartian magic, she vividly evoked a whole gallery of such Janus-faced ladies in Hollywood's past.

Dunaway relaxed as a splendidly maleficent Milady in Richard Lester's back-to-back burlesques of Alexandre Dumas, *The Three* and *Four Musketeers* (1974 and 1975), in *The Towering Inferno* (1974), and in Sidney Pollack's gripping, suspenseful espionage thriller *Three Days Of The Condor* (1975). And the Oscar which had twice eluded her was finally awarded for a gloriously over-the-top performance in *Network* (1976), as a TV executive whose obsession with the ratings extends even to her romantic interludes with William Holden. Like the film's third star, Peter Finch, who also won a (posthumous) Oscar, she seemed to have understood that the only way to make Paddy Chayefsky's top-heavy script come alive on the screen was to emphasise its comic elements; and, together, they made what might have been a satire of rather strained solemnity into a thoroughly enjoyable piece of Grand Guignol. Her playing, however, foregrounded the campy side of her persona, her headlamp-like eyes and clothes-horse physique; and even if this constitutes, for some of her fans, her whole *raison d'être*, it may well make it more difficult in the future to cast her in serious and genuinely challenging roles. Films like Irvin Kershner's *The Eyes Of Laura Mars* (1978), a heady concoction of modish visuals and gory horror effects in which she played a morbid, Helmut Newton-like fashion photographer who is startled to find her snaps coming to life, and Frank Perry's *Mommie Dearest*, may possess their own peculiar and perverse pleasures, but they surely do not satisfy an actress who, when she chooses to, can powerfully commandeer the screen as if it were her own private space. The 80s will therefore be very much a watershed in her career – and, given that her most recent film was Michael Winner's brutishly vulgar remake of the Margaret Lockwood vehicle *The Wicked Lady* (1983), it cannot be said that the omens are positive. DM

in Bonnie And Clyde *(Warner Bros., 1967)*

in Chinatown *(Paramount, 1974)* ▷

Clint Eastwood

Born San Francisco, 31 May 1930

Clint Eastwood was a true child of the Depression, and an early boyhood spent following his father, who pumped gas for a living, along the West Coast of America conjures up an almost Fordian image of deprivation. His education, fragmented by these peregrinations, was a scanty one, though he finally graduated from high school in Oakland. Thereafter, he drifted around on his own, working as a lumberjack in Oregon and serving as a swimming instructor when in the army. On the GI Bill he attended business administration classes at Los Angeles City College and, in 1954, married a young model whom he had met on a blind date. Though he had not yet properly formulated the ambition, he had long had a hankering to become an actor and persuaded Universal to give him a screen test. A contract duly followed, under which he made brief, be-careful-not-to-blink-or-you'll-miss-him appearances in such routine programmers as *Revenge Of The Creature*, *Francis In The Navy*, *Lady Godiva* and *Tarantula* (all 1955) and *Never Say Goodbye*, *The First Traveling Saleslady* and *Star In The Dust* (all 1956).

The studio declined to renew the contract, however; and Eastwood was toying with the idea of giving up the profession altogether, when quite by chance he was spotted in the outer office of CBS Television and offered the role of Rowdy Yates, the deputy trail boss in a new western series 'Rawhide'. (For the record, his superior – both on the trail and the credit titles – was an actor named Eric Fleming.) 'Rawhide' ran for eight complete seasons, from 1959 to 1965, and made Eastwood a household, if not yet a cinema, name. But he grew increasingly dissatisfied with the weekly grind; since his CBS contract made it difficult for him to make films in the States, he accepted a flat fee offer in 1964 to star in a low-budget spaghetti western by a totally unknown director, Sergio Leone's *A Fistful Of Dollars*. In it he played the monosyllabic, supercool, poncho-clad 'Man With No Name', a fair description of Eastwood's standing among European audiences. Happy to have supplemented his income but not feeling inclined to boast about his European excursion, he returned to further episodes of 'Rawhide'. When suddenly the unthinkable happened – that cheap, *ersatz* western, of which he was probably a little ashamed, turned out to be a phenomenal success all over the world. He and Leone worked on two further westerns, *For A Few Dollars More* (1965) and *The Good, The Bad And The Ugly* (1966), which, on their release, made Eastwood the biggest American star – outside of America.

in 'Rawhide' (TV)

Startled by the competition from Europe, the Hollywood studios soon recalled that Americans too were fond of spaghetti – with plenty of tomato sauce. So, somewhat to the chagrin of purists, they began to concoct westerns on the Italian model, flinty, laconic and very much more violent than the homegrown counterpart: one of the first was *Hang 'Em High* (1968), starring Clint Eastwood, now a Man With A Name. Though he continued to make

in Magnum Force (Warner Bros., 1973)

westerns until the whole genre went into decline (culminating in the *Heaven's Gate* fiasco in 1980), Eastwood gradually acquired a brand new persona, albeit an updated variation of the old one: that of a callous, steely-eyed renegade cop never above taking the law (in the form of a Magnum revolver) into his own hands. *Coogan's Bluff* (1968), his first movie in collaboration with Don Siegel, was a transitional work, for in it he played a Westerner, a deputy sheriff in pursuit of an escaped prisoner, let loose in New York. But before he and Siegel finally had a commercial breakthrough in 1971 with *Dirty Harry*, Eastwood turned up in a number of undemanding entertainments, notably Alistair MacLean's *Where Eagles Dare* and the musical *Paint Your Wagon* (both 1969). He then worked with Siegel again on a strange Gothick melodrama, *The Beguiled* (1971), in which he played a wounded Union soldier who takes refuge during the Civil War in a girls' school presided over by Geraldine Page. Even more disturbing was his own directorial debut (and still arguably his best film as a director), *Play 'Misty' For Me* (also 1971), in which he cast himself as a smooth, sexy disc-jockey haunted by an adoring, and mentally unbalanced, fan. However, if 'Misty' is not a film to watch late at night, it would be hard to think of any time of day for which *Dirty Harry* might be regarded as suitable viewing. One of Eastwood's greatest successes (so much so that he reprised the character in *Magnum Force*, 1973, *The Enforcer*, 1976, and *Sudden Impact*, 1983 – indeed, whenever he badly needed a hit), it is a thoroughly reprehensible work, a racist, sexist and indulgently violent

in The Good, The Bad And The Ugly (United Artists, 1966)

apologia for vigilante justice; and its defence by a number of reputable critics, who choose to describe it as 'ambiguous', beggars belief.

The pattern which Eastwood's career would follow was now clear: though personally remaining as cool and passionless from one type of film to another, he would henceforth divide his energies between movies which attempted, however half-heartedly, to stretch their western or thriller genre conventions, and sheer brute entertainments. Of the latter there is little to be said. The best of them (Michael Cimino's *Thunderbolt And Lightfoot*, 1974, *Every Which Way But Loose*, 1978) constituted junk food, easily digested, easily forgotten; the worst (the 'Dirty Harry' films, *The Eiger Sanction*, 1975, *Firefox*, 1982, both directed by Eastwood) were just junk. Of much greater interest were two westerns in which he directed himself, *High Plains Drifter* (1973), still very much Leone-influenced, and *The Outlaw Josie Wales* (1976), in which he allowed his hero a degree of emotional vulnerability rare in his work. From recent evidence, however, it would appear that the strictly 'commercial' Eastwood is winning out over the actor/director who was once willing to stretch himself in, at least, every other film. Though hardly one of Hollywood's major tragedies, it is nevertheless, given his public popularity, a pity. DM

in A Doll's House *(Paramount, 1973)*

Edith Evans

Born **London, 8 February 1888**
Died **1976**

If wit in an actor or actress may be defined as the capacity to make an audience laugh at a line of dialogue which, on the page, offers little indication of that quality, then Edith Evans was one of the wittiest actresses in the world. Her incomparable delivery of Lady Bracknell's exclamation 'A handbag!' from Oscar Wilde's 'The Importance Of Being Earnest' caused the line to resonate like an epigram; and her reprise of the role in Anthony Asquith's 1952 film version is, in its way, one of the supreme moments of screen comedy.

Though far more celebrated for her stage appearances, notably in Restoration comedy, Dame Edith made two silent films – or three, if one includes her hauntingly mute role as the sinister Countess in Thorold Dickinson's baroque adaptation of Pushkin's *The Queen Of Spades* (1949). It was not until the 60s, however, that she started to work regularly in the cinema; and, whatever the quality of the individual films, she herself was invariably an unalloyed delight. She was absolutely hilarious in Tony Richardson's Oscar-winning *Tom Jones* (1963), both eccentric and dignified as Lady Gregory in the biopic of Sean O'Casey, *Young Cassidy* (1965) and, in a superb courtroom scene, stole *The Madwoman Of Chaillot* (1969) from under the noses of her prestigious co-stars. But it was her portrayal of the lonely, half-demented old woman trapped in a world of illusions in *The Whisperers* (1967) which proved to film audiences that she was not only a great character, but a great character actress. There was truly nothing like this Dame. DM

Mia Farrow

Real name **Maria de Lourdes Villiers Farrow**
Born **Los Angeles, 9 February 1945**

Elfin, urchin, gamine – such are the epithets most frequently employed by critics to describe Mia Farrow. Yet her sprite-like features were actually the consequence of an early polio affliction. As the daughter of director John Farrow and actress Maureen O'Sullivan, she was a typical Hollywood child, practically weaned on 'Variety'. After appearing in an off-Broadway production of 'The Importance Of Being Earnest', she made her screen debut as a replacement for Britt Ekland in *Guns At Batasi* in 1964. Then, fey and wistful, her haunting eyes devouring a skull-beneath-the-skin face, she was ideally cast as the hapless young wife unwittingly pregnant by the Devil in Roman Polanski's *Rosemary's Baby* (1968).

There followed a wispy comedy-drama with Dustin Hoffman, *John And Mary*, and Joseph Losey's weird *Secret Ceremony*, in which she co-starred to intriguing effect with Elizabeth Taylor (both 1969). Critical opinion was sharply divided, however, over her performance in Jack Clayton's *The Great Gatsby* (1974), where she was in any case rather upstaged by Robert Redford's dazzling array of silk shirts. And nothing of much significance has come her way since, save a recent trio of starring roles for Woody Allen (with whom she has been romantically involved): *A Midsummer Night's Sex Comedy* (1982), *Zelig* (1983) and *Broadway Danny Rose* (1984). If she has nevertheless managed to remain consistently in the public eye, it is perhaps due to two much-publicised marriages, to Frank Sinatra and André Previn. DM

in 1979

Albert Finney

Born **Salford, England, 9 May 1936**

For the kind of talent, accent and physique that he possesses, Albert Finney was born at exactly the right moment. The son of a North Country bookmaker, he won a scholarship to the Royal Academy of Dramatic Art (with Alan Bates and Peter O'Toole as fellow students) and subsequently made a reputation for himself as 'the new Olivier' in a sequence of classical, primarily Shakespearean, plays.

But the English theatre and cinema were at a watershed, with the kitchen sink replacing french windows as an essential prop; and, blessed with burly, working-class good looks and a sexily brooding presence, Finney shot to stardom in both media simultaneously: as 'Billy Liar' on the London stage and as the rebellious young anti-hero of Karel Reisz's *Saturday Night And Sunday Morning* (1960). The boisterous, ribald and hugely successful *Tom Jones* (1963) revealed a great gift for comedy, confirmed in a more intimate vein by Stanley Donen's *Two For The Road* (1967), in which he was delightfully paired with Audrey Hepburn.

Yet, despite incidental triumphs as a director (*Charlie Bubbles*, 1967) and producer (the private eye spoof *Gumshoe*, 1971), Finney's film career has become increasingly unfocused. Though, outrageously made-up as Hercule Poirot in *Murder On The Orient Express* (1974) and Daddy Warbucks in the musical *Annie* (1981), he could be inconsequentially entertaining, there remains the sense of an enormous but sadly wasted potential. His sober, moving performance opposite Diane Keaton in Alan Parker's *Shoot The Moon* (1981), however, suggests that Finney may yet surprise us. DM

Peter Finch

Real name **William Mitchell**
Born **London, 28 September 1916**
Died **14 January, 1977**

It was somehow typical of Peter Finch's whole career that he should win a posthumous Oscar – for his flamboyant performance as a mentally unbalanced newscaster in Sidney Lumet's *Network* (1976). Though he proved one of the medium's more subtle and versatile leading men, there was a disjunction between his public 'hell-raiser' image and some enigmatic inner stillness in his personality, which prevented him from ever making it to the highest reaches of stardom.

His childhood was famously eventful. Probably illegitimate, he was farmed out at an early age to a Bohemian grandmother who, he subsequently claimed, sold him off to a Buddhist monk in Madras. After a period of begging and meditation in India, he was dispatched to Australia where he became, in turn, a court reporter, artist's model, vaudeville stooge – then a popular radio and cinema actor. Encouraged by Sir Laurence Olivier, he decided to emigrate to England, where he gradually made a reputation in such films as *The Wooden Horse* (1950), *The Story Of Robin Hood* (as the Sheriff of Nottingham, 1951), *Father Brown* (1954) and *Simon And Laura* (1955).

Finch excelled as rugged, cynical but fundamentally sensitive characters in *A Town Like Alice* (1956) and Fred Zinnemann's *The Nun's Story* (1959), and seemed more at ease than most actors sporting khaki amid tropical surroundings (notably in *Elephant Walk*, *The Shiralee*, *Robbery Under Arms*, *Windom's Way*, *The Sins Of Rachel Cade* and *The Flight Of The Phoenix*). Paradoxically, however, it was in two homosexual roles, as Wilde in *The Trials Of Oscar Wilde* (1960) and the quietly long-suffering doctor in John Schlesinger's *Sunday, Bloody Sunday* (1971), that he gave his most moving performances. DM

225

Jane Fonda

Born New York City, 21 December 1937

Perhaps the measure of Jane Fonda's current prestige is the fact that, though the daughter of one of the greatest actors in the American cinema, she has made the name which they share her own. Or, to put it more succinctly, the word 'Fonda' these days does not automatically refer to Henry (and certainly does not refer to her brother, the actor Peter). This is all the more remarkable in that her success by no means came overnight, or on her father's coat-tails; and that, for a lengthy period of her career, she was unofficially blacklisted by the Hollywood industry, and indeed by a substantial number of moviegoers. Though her choice of films is still very much conditioned by her political views and strong commitment to anti-Establishment causes, she has recently contrived with amazing success to integrate these positions into the accepted codes and practices of American film-making, so that the admiration (or, from another sector of the population, suspicion) in which she was once held is now coupled with widespread, unquestioning popularity. Her second husband, the political activist, Tom Hayden, said of

in Klute (Warner Bros., 1971)

her climb back into general public favour, 'It's important that Jane be restored to legitimacy now, when she's active, and not in the twenty-first century, which usually happens to controversial people. Lillian Hellman is very 'in' now, but she wasn't not too long ago. I'm very impressed by how rapidly Jane's image has started to reverse itself. It's not just her doing: it's a sign that the country has been changing.'

As the daughter of Henry Fonda, Jane was brought up in a totally film-orientated environment on the West Coast. Her mother was Frances Seymour Brokaw, the widow of a multimillionaire, who married Fonda in 1936 and who died, when Jane was 12, by slitting her throat in a sanatorium where she had been confined after a series of nervous breakdowns. (Jane, it is said, only discovered the facts of her mother's suicide when a high school classmate casually handed her a magazine containing the story.) Notwithstanding this early trauma, her childhood was a privileged one; and when Henry took the lead in the smash-hit Broadway comedy 'Mister Roberts', she and Peter moved in with their grandmother who owned a mansion in Greenwich, Connecticut. At this period, acting for Jane was solely confined to high school plays, except for a couple of appearances with her father: in an Omaha Community Theatre production of Clifford Odets' 'The Country Girl' and a summer stock performance of 'The Male Animal'. Her early ambitions lay elsewhere; and, though she dutifully attended (and graduated from) Vassar, she finally upped and left for Paris to study art. On her return to New York, suddenly deciding that she was, after all, her father's daughter and encouraged by Lee

Strasberg, she signed on at the Actors Studio, paying for her courses by modelling work (she was twice featured on the cover of *Vogue*).

1960 was the breakthrough year: she made her Broadway debut in 'There Was A Little Girl', winning the New York Drama Critics Circle Award and the magazine 'Theater World's award as the season's most promising actress; and she starred in her first film, *Tall Story*, a charming tale of athletics and romance in which she was partnered by Anthony Perkins. A number of films followed, none of them too distinguished but permitting her still callow talent to mature: *Walk On The Wild Side*, an adaptation of Nelson Algren's lurid novel of life in a

in Nine To Five (20th Century-Fox, 1980)

New Orleans brothel; *The Chapman Report*, a Cukor-directed farrago based on the findings of the Kinsey Report in which she played a frigid young housewife; Tennessee Williams's *Period Of Adjustment* (all 1962); and *Sunday In New York* (1964), a cute, rather stagey comedy in which she co-starred with Rod Taylor.

Her personal and professional life drastically changed direction in that same year when she went to France to make *La Ronde*, a new version of the Schnitzler play which had been turned into a film classic several years before by Max Ophüls. The director this time around was Roger Vadim, celebrated as the Pygmalion of Brigitte Bardot and purveyor of oh-so-French pieces of filmic froth. Fonda fell under his spell, married him and settled in Paris; the films she subsequently made under his direction – *The Game Is Over* (1966), one episode of the compendium film *Spirits Of The Dead* (1968), in which, before a roaring fire, she was required to flirt with her brother Peter, and the comic-strip extravaganza *Barbarella* (also 1968) – were all as wretchedly bad as Vadim's work has been in general, but they did enable her to change, once and for all, her slightly dowdy, sophomoric image. Father Henry was reportedly mistrustful of his new son-in-law, and there was a deal of sensationalist press publicity; but Fonda remained friendly with her ex-husband after their divorce and, though critical of the way she believes he has treated women exclusively as sex objects, has never made any slighting remark about him personally.

Another turning point in her life came in 1969, when she visited India for the first time. 'I had never seen people die from starvation before or a boy begging with the corpse of his little brother in his arms . . . I met a lot of American kids there, hippies from wealthy or middle-class families in search of their individualistic metaphysical trips. They accepted that poverty. They even tried to explain it away to me'. On her return to California, where the contrast with the spectacle of wretchedness which she had just witnessed could not have been more flagrant, she began to speak out on various burning issues in the United States: the plight of the Native Americans (formerly the Red Indians), the Black Panther movement, her support for which earned her numerous enemies and even alienated her father,

and, of course, the anti-Vietnam movement. Her films began to reflect, if ever so slightly at first, such a concern for social issues. Sidney Pollack's *They Shoot Horses, Don't They?* (1969) was an adaptation of Horace McCoy's celebrated novel exposing the material desperation underlying the 30s cult of marathon dance contests (Fonda earned an Academy Award nomination for her performance); and in Alan Pakula's *Klute* (1971), a multi-layered psychological thriller, her performance as an articulate middle-class call girl was influenced by her burgeoning interest in the feminist movement (and secured her a best actress Academy Award).

Fonda's more radical inclinations were aired in a pair of documentaries, *F.T.A.* (1972), the cinematic record of an anti-war USO show featuring herself and Donald Sutherland, which might be regarded as a subversive updating of the old *Hollywood Canteen* format, and *Introduction To The Enemy* (1974, co-directed by herself, Tom Hayden and the cinematographer Haskell Wexler), an account of her much-criticised trip to North Vietnam; as well as in a curiously muted film she made for Jean-Luc Godard, *Tout Va Bien* (1972), which co-starred her to no very great effect with the Communist-sympathising French singer and actor Yves Mon-

in They Shoot Horses, Don't They? (Cinerama, 1969)

tand, and made as much as possible of their off-screen images. But life must go on; and Fonda also turned up in a number of films whose political charge was more diffuse: *Steelyard Blues* (1973), in which she again worked with Sutherland, was a modish jumble of anti-conformist clichés; *A Doll's House*, Losey's rather academic film version of the Ibsen drama, gave her the opportunity to play Nora, one of the great precursors of contemporary feminism; and Cukor's eye-bogglingly hideous Soviet-American co-production *The Blue Bird* (1976) might have been justified as the movie world's contribution to easing East-West relations (even if, in the event, the film was barely released outside of Russia).

In fact, it was only in the late 70s that Jane Fonda finally succeeded in getting her act together, as it were: with the Vietnam war becoming increasingly little more than a memory, and America falling victim to a kind of collective amnesia, she was able to channel her political energies into a series of more localised issues, ones which lent themselves well to cinematic treatment. Thus such successes as *Julia* (1977), Fred Zinnemann's moving treatment of a Lillian Hellman memoir set in Fascist Europe (Fonda played Hellman herself and was nominated for an Oscar); *Coming Home* (1978), Hal Ashby's chronically soft-centred study of the plight of disabled Vietnam veterans (for which she did win an Oscar); and *The China Syndrome* (1979), a highly commercial thriller seeking to alert audiences to the dangers of nuclear power. Most moving of all, perhaps, and on a much more personal note, was her graceful tribute to her dying father in his last appearance (and their sole film together), *On Golden Pond* (1981). Her reconciliation with the American cinema was complete. DM

with John Phillip Law in Barbarella (Paramount, 1968) ▷

James Fox

Born **London, 19 May 1939**

Like his elder brother Edward, James Fox was – and looked – very much a product of their shared background: Harrow and the Coldstream Guards. It was a background also shared by many of the characters he played, upper crust weaklings, wealthy, well-spoken, well-meaning and a little unbalanced. Unfortunately, the most memorable portrait of this type, and the highlight of Fox's career, came early on, in only his third film, Joseph Losey's *The Servant* (1963). Aided by a brilliant Harold Pinter screenplay, Losey chillingly traced the growing ascendancy of the corrupt manservant Barrett (Dirk Bogarde) over his too acquiescent young master.

in The Servant *(Commonwealth United, 1963)*

Thereafter, Fox's appearances tended to decline into silly ass parody, as in *Those Magnificent Young Men In Their Flying Machines* (1965) and *Thoroughly Modern Millie* (1967). In fact, were it not for *Performance* (1970) it would be possible to write him off as a one-role actor. In Nicolas Roeg's fascinating if not wholly successful film, Fox was cast against type as a gangster on the run swapping roles with a jaded pop star hermit (Mick Jagger), and proved eerily plausible. And it was perhaps the somewhat decadent atmosphere of *Performance* which prompted him to abandon the cinema for almost a decade and dedicate himself to an obscure evangelist sect. Fox has, however, recently resurfaced to work in television, and it would be foolhardy to predict the future course of his career. DM

James Garner

Real name **James Baumgarner**
Born **Norman, Oklahoma, 7 April 1928**

It was Marshall McLuhan who first characterised television as the quintessentially 'cool' medium, most effective when maintaining its audience in a state of passive receptivity. One need look no further for an explanation of James Garner's outstanding success on the small screen, originally in the serio-comic western series 'Maverick', then as the genial, unflappable private eye of 'The Rockford Files'. Cinema, however, is notably 'hotter' as a medium; and Garner, a likeable, funny and good-looking performer, has never really come to terms with its very different parameters.

His early years were a classic example of American picaresque. A high school dropout, he was wounded in the Korean War and awarded a Purple Heart, then aimlessly tackled an odd assortment of jobs, from laying carpets to modelling swimsuits. Drifting into show business, he quickly became a personable, laid-back leading man in such hits as *The Great Escape* (1963), *The Thrill Of It All* and *Move Over, Darling* (both 1963, both co-starring Doris Day), and *The Americanization Of Emily*

Jackie Gleason

Real name **Herbert John Gleason**
Born **Brooklyn, New York, 26 February 1916**

It was as a sergeant in the tragi-comic *Soldier In The Rain* (1963) that Jackie Gleason spoke what might be his epitaph. Contemplating the reflection of his rotundity in a full-length mirror, he wryly muttered: 'It isn't easy to be a fat narcissist.'

Gleason is today a multi-millionaire and, at least in the United States, an authentic superstar, but nothing ever came easily to him. Growing up in Brooklyn poolrooms, he won a talent contest at the age of 15, and for years afterwards toiled indiscriminately in carnivals, vaudeville shows and seedy nightclubs. In the 40s, there were frequent appear-

in The Hustler *(20th Century-Fox, 1961)*

(1964, with Julie Andrews). His career subsequently suffered a decline, the only films being offered him were jokey thrillers and westerns, and he looked thoroughly ill-at-ease as the Chicago hoodlum in love with Julie Andrews and forced to question his sexual prejudices in Blake Edwards' *Victor/Victoria* (1982). Significantly, his own film and TV company is named Maverick Productions. DM

ances on stage and in films, without his visibly enriching either medium. Paradoxically, it was the more modest TV screen which managed to contain this immensely egocentric individual – his popular sitcom 'The Honeymooners' was one of America's longest-running. Simultaneously, Gleason was happily accumulating a fortune from the sales of record albums of his own compositions.

Only twice has the cinema exploited to the full his gargantuan personality: as Minnesota Fats in Robert Rossen's moodily atmospheric *The Hustler* (1961), playing pool, in Paul Newman's company, as to the manner born (which, of course, he was) and earning an Oscar nomination; and as the spluttering, apoplectic sheriff in eternal pursuit of Burt Reynolds in *Smokey And The Bandit* (1977), one of the most successful comedies in film history. DM

Ruth Gordon

Real name **Ruth Jones**
Born **Wollaston, Massachusetts, 30 October 1898**

In her autobiography, *Myself Among Others*, Ruth Gordon wrote: 'Shakespeare died when he was fifty-two. If *I* had, I'd never have been in *The Matchmaker* or met Mia Farrow or been on the Joey Bishop Show or flown sixty-seven times across the country or won an Oscar or eaten papaya...' Or perhaps appeared in this book. For though she had already played bit parts in silent films, lent support to Garbo in *Two-Faced Woman* (1941) and Bogart in *Action In The North Atlantic* (1943), married Garson Kanin and, in collaboration with him, written screenplays for four George Cukor movies, *A Double Life* (1948), *Adam's Rib* (1949), *The Marrying Kind* and *Pat And Mike* (both 1952), besides adapting her own semi-autobiographical play 'Years Ago' as *The Actress* (directed by Cukor in 1953), she is most likely to be remembered for two juicily ripe performances in her seventies.

In Roman Polanski's *Rosemary's Baby* (1968), she played a maleficent Manhattan witch, and her dry corncrake delivery and eerily eccentric presence won her an Academy Award as Best Supporting Actress. And in Hal Ashby's black comedy *Harold and Maude* (1971), she went gloriously over the top as a 79-year-old swinger conducting a lyrical love affair with baby-faced Bud Cort, almost sixty years her junior. If, after initially being either panned or ignored, Ashby's film eventually became a cult favourite, it was in no small measure due to its aged, yet somehow ageless, heroine. DM

in The Big Bus *(Paramount, 1976)*

Gene Hackman

Born San Bernardino, California, 30 January 1931

Though born in California, Gene Hackman was raised in Danville, Illinois, where his father was employed as a journeyman pressman. He quit school at the age of 16 and enlisted in the Marines, serving three years before being discharged. In his late teens he already harboured a desire to act; but, uncertain as to how he might achieve this ambition, he moved to New York and drifted through a series of jobs, including those of truck driver, soda jerk, shoe salesman and restaurant doorman. Thanks to the GI Bill, he was able to study draughtsmanship, journalism and TV production, and worked on and off for a number of years in these various fields. So that he was already past 30 when he finally decided to take a stab at the theatre, enrolling in the Pasadena Playhouse school near Los Angeles. As a result of these classes, on his return to New York he began to find steady employment in summer stock and off-Broadway productions. When at last he landed a leading Broadway role, playing opposite Sandy Dennis in the hit comedy 'Any Wednesday', it was brought to the attention of the Hollywood director

in The French Connection *(20th Century-Fox, 1971)*

with Ned Beatty (left) in Superman *(Warner Bros., 1978)*

Robert Rossen, who chose him for his last film, *Lilith* (1964), a moving love story set in a mental institution. Hackman's role was a small one (just a single scene), but it so impressed the film's star, Warren Beatty, that he cast him in *Bonnie And Clyde* in 1967 as Clyde's brother Buck, a role which brought him an Oscar nomination as best supporting actor. After solid if uninspiring appearances in such films as Frankenheimer's *The Gypsy Moths* (1969), about a group of barnstorming parachutists, and *Downhill Racer* (also 1969), as skier Robert Redford's tough-but-with-a-heart-of-gold trainer, Hackman picked up a second nomination for his disturbing portrayal of a 40-year-old son still living in his father's shadow in *I Never Sang For My Father* (1970), co-starring Melvyn Douglas.

At this period of his career, then, Hackman was what might be called 'an actor's actor'. A wonderfully naturalistic performer, capable of breathing life into dull roles and, especially, of interesting the spectator in the inner conflicts of characters distinguished only by their surface ordinariness, he was much respected by the profession but felt to be too uncharismatic, and perhaps too old, to carry a film by himself. His status changed with an extraordinary performance in William Friedkin's hugely successful *The French Connection* (1971), as the neurotically obsessed narcotics cop Popeye Doyle. (He repeated it to lesser effect in the 1975 sequel, *The French Connection II*). This time Hackman won the Oscar, and at the age of 40 had become a Hollywood star. Not all of his subsequent work has been equally memorable (he made rather heavy weather of his role as a priest in *The Poseidon Adventure*, 1972, and sank along with co-stars Burt Reynolds and Liza Minnelli in that rickety old tub, Stanley Donen's *Lucky Lady*, 1975) but, at his best, he has given some of the most intelligent performances of recent years. He was absolutely superb, for example, in another of his obsessive portrayals, as the guilt-ridden Catholic wiretapping expert in Francis Ford Coppola's brilliant thriller *The Conversation* (1974); hardly less so as a private eye in Arthur Penn's *Night Moves* (1975); and by far the best thing (indeed, the only thing) in Nicolas Roeg's preposterous *Eureka* (1983), in which he played a man for whom the acquisition of fabulous wealth has destroyed all purpose in life. And if all this suggests a monotonously heavy performer, it should be said that he made a most amusing evil genius in the blockbusting *Superman* (1978). DM

Richard Harris

Born Limerick, Ireland, 1 October 1932

In a period when most actors have come to accept that an 'image' of impeccable and unstinting virility is no longer a prerequisite of screen stardom, Richard Harris has continued to purvey a kind of swaggering macho boorishness, only occasionally humanised by the odd sign of inner torment or tenderness. The great influence on his style, from the evidence of many of his films, was Brando; but it is a pity that, with only a few exceptions, it is the mannered, masochistic and hypervirile side of Brando on which his performances are based.

in This Sporting Life *(Rank, 1963)*

He studied at the Royal Academy of Dramatic Art, then joined Joan Littlewood's Theatre Workshop group, attracting particular attention in a production of Arthur Miller's 'A View From The Bridge'. His earliest film roles were by no means unimpressive, but they were characterised by a somewhat exaggerated Irishness in accent and mannerisms: e.g. *Shake Hands With The Devil*, *The Wreck Of The Mary Deare* (both 1959) and *A Terrible Beauty* (1960). Though he had a leading role in Lewis Milestone's 1962 remake of *Mutiny On The Bounty*, it was his performance as a ruthlessly ambitious rugger player in Lindsay Anderson's *This Sporting Life* (1963) which propelled him to international fame, earning him both an Oscar nomination and an acting award at the Cannes Festival. The Brando influence was there, but the role had a certain depth to which Harris rose, so to speak. And, on the strength of it, Antonioni cast him opposite Monica Vitti in his not altogether successful drama of social and psychological alienation, *The Red Desert* (1964).

The promise, however, was never fulfilled. His characterisations had at first a degree of substance – as a dashing sea-captain in *Hawaii* (1966), as King Arthur in the film version of Lerner and Loewe's *Camelot* (1967) and as a Pinkerton detective in *The Molly Maguires* (1970). But, as he gradually began to acquire the reputation of a 'hell-raiser' offscreen, he seemed no longer to pay much attention to the way his career was drifting. From a string of forgotten potboilers, mostly tough adventure yarns, one might single out the curious pro-Indian drama *A Man Called Horse* (1970), with Harris as an English aristocrat captured by the Sioux and ultimately converted to their way of life. It was so successful that it inspired an equally effective sequel, *The Return Of A Man Called Horse*, in 1976. Otherwise, the balance-sheet is very much in the red. DM

David Hemmings

Born Guildford, England, 18 November 1941

David Hemmings was a boy soprano with the English National Opera, notably in works by Britten, until his voice broke. His next activity was painting. Though soon expelled from art college, he managed at the age of 15 to hold a successful one-man (or one-boy) exhibition of his work in a small London gallery. This was followed by nightclub singing, acting on television and in the theatre. His earliest films were produced by the Children's Film Foundation (apart from a tiny role in Preminger's *Saint Joan* in 1957), but he was making no particular headway until Michelangelo Antonioni cast him as a trendy young photographer confronted with the ambiguity of the image in *Blow-Up* (1966). Hemmings' performance was perfectly competent, if little more than that, but the extraordinary critical and commercial success of the film gained him a somewhat unmerited international fame. Simply by dint of having appeared in *Blow-Up*, he found

in The Long Day's Dying (Paramount, 1968)

himself suddenly in demand. His boyish features, both cherubic and decadent, popped up in a bizarre collection of films, from *Camelot* (1967) to Roger Vadim's comic strip-inspired *Barbarella* (1968, with Jane Fonda), from Tony Richardson's surprisingly resonant version of *The Charge Of The Light Brigade* (1968) to the crass spectacular *Alfred The Great* (1969), in which he played the title role.

In the 70s his films got progressively worse (who now recalls *Voices, Mr Quilp, The Squeeze, Deep Red* or *The Disappearance*?); and, endlessly restless and versatile, he switched to direction. His first efforts, *Running Scared* and *The 14* (1972 and 1973) were totally undistinguished but, for *Just A Gigolo* (1978), he brought off a memorable coup by coaxing Marlene Dietrich out of retirement to co-star with David Bowie. The film was worth seeing for its casting alone – there could certainly be no other reason. Hemmings (formerly married to glamorous actress Gayle Hunnicutt) is also the author of several novels, whose place in literature would seem to be comparable to that held by his films in cinema history. DM

Dustin Hoffman

Born Los Angeles, 8 August 1937

In March 1812, the 24-year-old Lord Byron woke up the morning after the publication of 'Childe Harold' to find himself famous. The rather un-Byronic 30-year-old Dustin Hoffman must have had a similar experience on the morning of December 22, 1967 after the opening of *The Graduate*. The 'New York Times' called him 'an amazing new star' and the 'New Republic' wrote, 'he is the best American comedian since Jack Lemmon.' But Hoffman very nearly didn't get the role which was to change his entire life.

By 1966, after eight years of struggling to make a living from his chosen profession, the young actor was at last beginning to make a name for himself as a character actor in the New York theatre. Off-Broadway, he had played a limping homosexual Nazi in 'Harry, Noon and Night' and a spinsterish Russian clerk in 'Journey Of The Fifth Horse' for which he won an Obie. But when Mike Nichols, who had been searching for a male lead for *The Graduate* for six months, offered Dustin a screen test, he initially turned it down. He told Nichols, 'I don't think I'm right for the role. He's a kind of Anglo-Saxon, tall, slender, good-looking chap. I'm short and Jewish.' When Hoffman started acting in the 50s, the ideal male stars were Rock Hudson and Tab Hunter. No wonder Hoffman felt that Nichols was making a mistake. It was only after Dustin Hoffman came along that the names and faces of movie stars reflected more accurately the diversity of ethnic groups in America, opening up the floodgates for Barbra Streisand, Al Pacino, Elliott Gould, Robert De Niro, and Richard Dreyfuss. During the screen test, Dustin forgot his lines, tried to look tall, but acted tired and disinterested. He flew back to New York relieved that he had no chance of being so miscast. A few days later, he got a call to tell him he had been given the role. A year later, he was nominated for a Best Actor Oscar.

More than any other of the 'new breed' of star, Hoffman is a character actor. Even the role of Benjamin Braddock in *The Graduate* was a character role for him. The 30-year-old had to play someone 10 years his junior, a feat far more difficult for an actor than ageing, although Hoffman's perennially 'boyish' personality was a help. He had the maturity to suggest Ben's immaturity, and his Off-Broadway experience and off-beat looks brought a freshness to the role that an 'Anglo-Saxon, tall, good-looking chap' might not have done. Moving into more obvious character acting territory was his petty conman, Ratso, in John Schlesinger's *Midnight Cowboy* (1969). With his greasy hair, pallid complexion, bad teeth and gammy leg, he presented a man who could easily merge into the seedy atmos-

phere of a 42nd Street diner. But the film was sentimentally conceived, with Hoffman in a Margaret Sullavan role, dying just as he reaches Miami, the place of his dreams.

Hoffman, like Peter Sellers, is happiest behind a mask. He is an uneasy romantic figure in *John And Mary* (1969), bringing a sensitive half-smile to the 'ordinary' John characterisation. However, his 'modern' interpretation of a 121-year-old man looking back on his life as an adopted Red Indian in Arthur Penn's *Little Big Man* (1970), concurs with the attempted demystification of the western legend. His intensive research, and ability to think himself into his roles, has sometimes produced a number of mannered impersonations: colluding with Sam Peckinpah's exaltation of eye-for-an-eye slaughter in *Straw Dogs* (1971) as a man of reason forced into violence; emoting behind thick spectacles as a prisoner in *Papillon* (1973); self-consciously playing down his persona as Carl Bernstein in *All The President's Men* (1976); dreadfully earnest and acting

in The Graduate (United Artists, 1967)

young again in Schlesinger's tawdry *Marathon Man* (1976); and plainly uncomfortable opposite the willowy Vanessa Redgrave in *Agatha* (1978), trying to compensate for his lack of height by a preening, actorish manner. But he is impressively unsettling as the bitter, middle-aged ex-con in *Straight Time* (1978). However, comedy is Hoffman's best vein. He gave his most daring, self-stretching performances as the outrageous and tragic nightclub comedian Lenny Bruce in Bob Fosse's *Lenny* (1974); as the divorced father in *Kramer Vs Kramer* (1979) trying to cope with a young son; and in his brilliantly deft comic double in *Tootsie* (1982), self-mocking as a pretentious avant-garde actor and instantly likeable as Dorothy, whom he based on his mother Lillian, 'an earthy, gutsy, courageous woman with a great sexual sense of humour.'

Dustin's father was a prop man at Columbia Studios. His mother was star-struck and named him after Dustin Farnum, the silent screen cowboy. Because of his height (he is 5ft 6ins) and 'the worst case of acne in L.A.', he was very insecure in his teens, an insecurity that continued into middle-age and the need for regular psychoanalyst sessions. 'Only my analyst has ever understood me,' he once said. After dropping out of college in his freshman year, he joined the Pasadena Playhouse where he became friends with Gene Hackman. When Hackman left for New York, Dustin decided to try his luck there. 'I wanted to fail away from home', he commented. In New York, he worked at a variety of jobs including shop-assistant at Macey's and attendant in a mental hospital. There followed the years of stock and off-Broadway before *The Graduate*.

In 1969, Hoffman married Anne Byrne who gave up a dance career to be a wife and mother. Six years later, bored and irritated by Dustin's running around she took up dancing again. The marriage began to break up around 1977, at the same time as Dustin was involved in a multi-million dollar legal battle with First Artist Productions over *Straight Time* and *Agatha*. He accused them of seizing control of the pictures and not allowing him a 'final cut' as specified in his contract. They, in turn, sued him for 'repeatedly refusing and neglecting to prepare the final cut of *Straight Time* and making derogatory statements concerning the picture.' It was while filming *Kramer Vs Kramer* that life imitated art and his own marriage ended. But he finally won an Oscar (he had been nominated three times before). 'I want to thank divorce', he said in his acceptance speech. In the same year, he married Lisa Gottsegen, 17 years his junior, and they now have two children. Hoffman has the reputation for being a difficult man to work with, but the result of his perfectionism has made him an exciting and surprising personality. 'I'm successful beyond my wildest dreams, but the same person is still on the analyst's couch,' he has said with frankness. RB

Glenda Jackson

Born **Birkenhead, England, 9 May 1936**

The daughter of a bricklayer and builder, Glenda Jackson was raised in a strict Presbyterian household, a fact which may have helped shape her rebellious, anti-conformist image and abrasive personality. She made the decision at 16 to leave school, join an amateur dramatics group and study at the Royal Academy of Dramatic Art. During the 50s and early 60s, she gained repertory experience, but was forced to eke out her income by moonlighting as a chemist's shop assistant. In 1964, she was invited by Peter Brook to join his Theatre of Cruelty revue (later filmed as *Tell Me Lies*, 1968), then to play the

in Women In Love *(United Artists, 1969)*

mad Charlotte Corday in Peter Weiss's 'The Persecution And Assassination Of Jean-Paul Marat As Performed By The Inmates Of Charenton Under The Direction Of The Marquis De Sade' (a title generally abbreviated to 'Marat/Sade'). Under Brook's direction, both she and the play created a sensation first in London, then on Broadway and eventually in the 1967 film version. Her performance in Weiss's drama was a totally (and very effectively) theatrical one; and it was not until 1969, when Ken Russell cast her as Gudrun Brangwen in his free adaptation of D.H. Lawrence's *Women In Love*, that Jackson could be called a full-fledged film actress, winning both an Oscar and the New York Film Critics Award.

With high, almost Slavic cheekbones and deep, piercing eyes, Jackson is forbiddingly attractive rather than pretty, and she was well cast in another of Russell's flamboyant flights of fancy, the Tchaikovsky biopic *The Music Lovers* (1971), in which she played the homosexual composer's nymphomaniac wife. Fortunately, John Schlesinger's *Sunday, Bloody Sunday* (made the same year) offered her the chance to avoid being typecast as a neurotic, hysterical virago: as a woman who discovers that she shares her young lover with a middle-aged male doctor (played by Peter Finch), she gave a graceful, affecting performance. And the breadth of her range was further displayed when she picked up a second Oscar (one rather generously offered, it has to be said) for her delightful teaming with George Segal in the romantic comedy *A Touch Of Class* (1973).

Subsequently, Jackson's work has proved a disappointment. Her comic vein was exploited in *House Calls* (1978, with Walter Matthau) and *Lost And Found* (1979, with Segal), but neither quite recaptured the minor key perfection of *A Touch Of Class*. Losey's *The Romantic Englishwoman* (1975) and Altman's *Health* (1979) were among the feeblest efforts of their respective directors. And her preposterous Sarah Bernhardt in *The Incredible Sarah* (1976) was strictly for aficionados of unintentional humour. She did score a personal success as the eccentric poet Stevie Smith in *Stevie* (1978); but this was, significantly, adapted from a stage original, and it may well be that her future career lies principally in the theatre. DM

Jack Lemmon

Real name **John Uhler Lemmon III**
Born **Boston, 8 February 1925**

When questioned on the name of the performer he most admired and envied, the actor-comedian Tony Randall replied, 'Jack Lemmon', adding that he considered him the world's greatest actor. One's immediate reaction is that Randall's judgment must have been clouded by the fact that he himself might be regarded as a poor man's Lemmon. Yet, on reflection, one begins to realise what a remarkable asset Lemmon has been to the American cinema, an actor whose timing and delivery are so flawless as to constitute a source of pleasure distinct from the dialogue he is speaking or the character he is playing. And though seen principally in terms of comedy, the sardonic comedy of urban frustration and inadequacy, he has offered a wide range of dramatic portrayals – most recently, his bewildered father in Costa-Gavras' *Missing* (1982), for which he received an award at the Cannes Festival.

Lemmon came from a wealthy family (his father was president of a doughnut company), and completed his education at Harvard. After World War II service in the navy, and employment as a radio, TV, off- and, briefly, on-Broadway actor, he made his film debut in 1954 in a pair of Judy Holliday comedies, *It Should Happen To You* and the bizarrely titled *Phffft!* Re-viewing them today, one is astonished to note how his comic persona was already fully formed, awaiting only refinement in the films to come. He won his first Oscar as the wheeling-dealing Ensign Pulver in *Mr Roberts* (1955), following it with wacky characterisations in a quintet of Richard Quine comedies: *My Sister Eileen* (1955), *Operation Mad Ball* (1957), *Bell, Book And Candle* (1959, in which he played a chic Manhattan warlock), *It Happened To Jane* (also 1959) and *The Notorious Landlady* (1962). Meanwhile, there had taken place one of the two crucial meetings of his professional life – with the director Billy Wilder, who cast him opposite Tony Curtis and Marilyn Monroe in his evergreen farce *Some Like It Hot* (1959). (It was to Lemmon that Joe E. Brown addressed what is surely the most famous closing line in cinema history: 'Nobody's perfect!') He was

in The Apartment *(United Artists, 1960)*

even better in his next Wilder film, *The Apartment* (1960), as an ambitious junior executive who 'lends' his apartment to his womanising superiors. Lemmon made five more films with Wilder, in three of which he co-starred with the other important figure in his career, Walter Matthau: *The Fortune Cookie* (1966), *The Front Page* (1974) and the best-forgotten *Buddy Buddy* of 1981. Curiously, the teaming worked more effectively in *The Odd Couple* (1968), a straightforward adaptation of Neil Simon's Broadway hit in which they were perfectly mismatched, and *Kotch* (1971), in which Lemmon directed Matthau as a gruff senior citizen struggling to end his days with dignity.

The 70s and 80s have been uneven in opportunities, though he well deserved his Oscar as a disillusioned middle-aged businessman in *Save The Tiger* (1973) and was excellent as the harassed scientist in *The China Syndrome* (1979). But then, Lemmon has never really given a bad performance; and, if nobody *is* perfect, he has perhaps come closer to it than almost any actor of his generation. DM

with Walter Matthau (right) in The Odd Couple *(Paramount, 1968)*

Malcolm McDowell

Born Leeds, England, 15 June 1943

Malcolm McDowell's early life was of the colourful, incident-crowded type one associates rather with American actors. The son of a North Country publican, he was a rebellious public schoolboy and was given his first job assisting his father behind the bar. Later he found employment in a coffee factory, then was appointed a door-to-door representative for the firm in his native Yorkshire. Experience in a repertory theatre on the Isle of Wight led to an engagement with the Royal Shakespeare Company, where for eighteen months he held a spear in various productions. Playing a bit part in Ken Loach's *Poor Cow* (1967), he was spotted by the director Lindsay Anderson, who cast him in the leading role of his award-winning *If...* (1968), a tendentious, over-ambitious but immensely racy exposé of the British public school system. Seldom has an actor's screen persona been so conclusively defined by a single film: rakish, arrogant and anti-establishment, boyishly attractive even at his most vicious, McDowell's Mick Travis was the prototype of almost every

significant role he was subsequently to play. In the violent, futuristic *A Clockwork Orange* (1971), for example, Stanley Kubrick turned the same character into a brilliantly etched, poster paint caricature; and it is a tribute to McDowell that, though its cold, wilfully ugly visuals are of breathtaking virtuosity, one finds it nevertheless difficult to imagine another actor playing the loathsome Alex with just the right degree of satanic charm.

McDowell made two further appearances for Lindsay Anderson, for whom he seems to have become something of a talisman: as Mick Travis, yet again, in *O Lucky Man!* (1973), a picaresque, hopefully 'Brechtian' satire whose narrative derived from many of the actor's own youthful experiences; and, more briefly, in *Britannia Hospital* (1982), a scattershot political farce and the lowest ebb of its director's uneven career. The lowest ebb of McDowell's, however, was without question the egregious title role in Bob Guccione's idiotic masturbation fantasy and animated centrefold, *Caligula* (1979), whose action, such as it was, might have taken place inside Travis's head. McDowell is married to the American actress Mary Steenburgen, with whom he acted in *Time After Time* (1979). DM

in If... (Paramount, 1968)

Steve McQueen

**Real name Terrence Steven McQueen
Born Slater, Missouri, 24 March 1930
Died 1980**

The young Steve McQueen was a juvenile delinquent from a broken home; and though he came as an actor to personify the cool, poker-faced loner who takes care never to let life get the better of him, there remained in his persona, right to the very end, something of the underlying edginess of that delinquency. It made him a considerably more interesting actor than his filmography, or even his immense personal popularity, might suggest; and one can only regret that he was born too late to develop his gifts with individualistic directors such as Ford, Wellman or Hawks and too soon, in a sense, to work with Scorsese, Altman or Coppola.

After his parents' divorce, he was raised at an institution called Boys' Republic in Chino, California – little more, in fact, than a reform school. As a teenager, he was already on the road, drifting from temporary job to temporary job, ending up, in the traditional manner, as a beach bum. A spell in the Marines followed, during which he spent over forty days in the brig on AWOL charges. Discharged, he

in Bullitt (Warner Bros., 1968)

began drifting again, then decided to study acting at New York's Neighborhood Playhouse, making his professional debut, incongruously, at a Yiddish theatre on Second Avenue. Like almost every young actor of his generation, he attended classes at the famed Actors Studio (whose influence can be detected in some of his early film work), then replaced Ben Gazzara in the leading role as a junkie

in 'A Hatful Of Rain' on Broadway. His first film role was a bit in the Rocky Graziano biopic *Somebody Up There Likes Me* (1956); and in 1958 he actually played a lead, though only in a grotesque science fiction B-movie titled *The Blob* (it was re-released many years later on the strength of McQueen's name). In a gritty thriller, *The Great St Louis Bank Robbery* (1959), he was a footballer turned criminal; in a turgid World War II melodrama *Never So Few* (also 1959) he played fourth fiddle to Frank Sinatra, Gina Lollobrigida and Peter Lawford.

But it was two films for the director John Sturges

with Tuesday Weld in The Cincinnati Kid *(MGM, 1965)*

which finally established him as a star. *The Magnificent Seven* (1960), a western remake of Kurosawa's *The Seven Samurai*, depended very much on teamwork playing, but McQueen gave a standout performance as a sardonic gunman. And there was no question as to who was the star of *The Great Escape* (1963), whose highlight was an extremely gripping motorcycle chase with McQueen, a car- and motorcycle-racing enthusiast, performing every stunt himself. (Other manifestations of this enthusiasm were a racing documentary, *On Any Sunday*, and the fictional *Le Mans*, both 1971.) In spite of this newly acquired superstardom, however, his career continued with a trio of modest dramas in which he was surprisingly effective and touching in introverted

roles: Ralph Nelson's *Soldier In The Rain* (1963), about a young G.I.'s devotion to his master-sergeant (played by Jackie Gleason); Robert Mulligan's *Love With The Proper Stranger* (also 1963), a contemporary love story filmed almost entirely on location in New York; and Mulligan's *Baby, The Rain Must Fall* (1965), a curiously muted rural drama. Then it was back to his supercool persona with four big hits: *The Cincinnati Kid* (1965), *Nevada Smith* (1966), *The Thomas Crown Affair* and *Bullitt* (both 1968), the latter best remembered for one of the most spectacular car chases in film history.

In the 70s his appearances became more intermittent, and it was reported that he had turned increasingly temperamental, rejecting more scripts than he was prepared to accept. For Sam Peckinpah he made two vastly different films in 1972: *Junior Bonner* was a subtle, rather melancholy study of an ageing rodeo star, *The Getaway* a real thick-ear thriller (whose co-star, Ali McGraw, McQueen married and subsequently divorced). He dutifully turned up in *The Towering Inferno* (1974) and even had a misguided go at Ibsen (*An Enemy Of The People*, 1979). Two minor films remained (*Tom Horn*, 1979, and *The Hunter*, 1980), then a long bout with cancer, to which he finally succumbed at the age of 50, DM

Lee Marvin

Born **New York City, 19 February 1924**

Appropriately enough, Lee Marvin once claimed that his sole training as an actor occurred when he was serving in the Marines during World War II. 'It was the only way to survive,' he said. 'I was terrified from the moment the fighting started until the moment it ended. That's what I mean by having to act. You couldn't show you were afraid, so you had to pretend to be tough.' With conspicuous success, Marvin has been pretending to be tough on-screen for over thirty years. Even so, it comes as something of a surprise to discover that he was born in New York of a well-to-do family: his mother wrote a monthly column in a fashion magazine, his father was an executive in an advertising agency. Invalided out of service when a Japanese shell splinter landed him in hospital for over a year, he was invited by chance to take a bit part in a local stock production. Growing increasingly interested in acting as a profession, he joined the American Theatre Wing, played a number of roles off-Broadway and finally arrived on the Great White Way in a dramatisation of Herman Melville's 'Billy Budd' in 1951. It was in that year, too, that he made his film debut with a small role in a raucous service comedy called, none too inventively, *You're In The Navy Now*.

However, tough and scowling and ruggedly good-looking, Marvin was seldom to be cast in comedies:

in 1962

westerns and thrillers were his beat, and he would appear in dozens of them before ever seeing his name above the title. Some notable early appearances were in Fritz Lang's *The Big Heat*, a powerful *film noir* of 1953 whose most notorious scene had him throw scalding coffee into Gloria Grahame's face; *The Wild One* (1954), the very first (and frequently banned) 'bike movie' in which he was

Marlon Brando's villainous sidekick; and John Ford's melancholic western *The Man Who Shot Liberty Valance* (1962). Another, very dissimilar Ford film, the old-fashioned *Donovan's Reef* (1963), allowed him to display a real gift for comedy, a gift exploited in the spoof western *Cat Ballou* (1965), in which his dual performance as a grizzled, alcoholic old gunfighter and his murderous twin won him an Academy Award. So, after years of being consigned to the foothills of movie credit titles, Marvin had at last reached the top. And, as a star, he contrived to appear in some of the most memorable 'tough guy' movies of the 60s and 70s, while lending ever greater depth to his brutal, often psychopathic persona: Richard Brooks's *The Professionals* (1966), Aldrich's *The Dirty Dozen* (1967), John Boorman's complex thriller *Point Blank* (also 1967), the same director's *Hell In The Pacific* (1968), in which Marvin and the Japanese actor Toshiro Mifune played two soldiers marooned on a desert island, and Aldrich's *Emperor Of The North Pole* (1973). Light relief was provided by his unexpected appearance in the musical *Paint Your Wagon* (1969), in which he was called upon to 'sing', which he did in a gravelly monotone.

Only one of his recent roles stands comparison with these – the nameless sergeant of a World War II squad in Samuel Fuller's masterly *The Big Red One* (1979) – and Marvin has become rather more famous as the man sued (unsuccessfully) for half his fortune by his live-in girlfriend, a suit which gave the word 'palimony' to the language. DM

in Little Miss Marker *(Universal, 1979)*

Walter Matthau

Real name **Walter Matuschanskavasky**
Born **New York City, 1 October 1920**

In the Jewish-Russian world from which Walter Matthau is descended, a sneeze is a listener's sign of incredulity at a tall story. In Matthau's own case, that sneeze might be his improbable and unpronouncable surname which, he claims, was given him by his father, a Russian Orthodox priest who disappeared from view soon afterwards. Whatever the truth of that assertion, he was raised in New York's Lower East Side, and at the age of 11 was already in show business, selling soft drinks at a Yiddish theatre and, for fifty cents extra, taking the occasional bit part on stage. After distinguished World War II service, he enrolled at the New School's Dramatic Workshop, acted in summer stock and eventually made it to Broadway, where his progress from walk-ons to star billing proved no less slow and cautious. Concurrently, he had begun to appear in film supporting roles: though most frequently cast as a villain, he was impressive as a disillusioned liberal journalist in Kazan's *A Face In The Crowd* (1957). But, at the time, there seemed little reason for his status ever to improve. Matthau was not a conventionally (or even unconventionally)

handsome man. With large, flat feet, a shambling gait and the face of a bloodhound with a hangover, as well as a legendary grouchiness second only to that of W.C. Fields (undoubtedly, the greatest influence on his screen persona), he must have appeared an unlikely candidate for stardom. Yet Neil Simon was prescient enough to spot his comic potential and wrote a play, 'The Odd Couple', to demonstrate it. The rest is, as they say, history.

Matthau created a sensation on Broadway as the slobbish stumblebum Oscar (and was equally irresistible in the 1968 film version). Then Billy Wilder cast him as an outrageous shyster lawyer opposite Jack Lemmon in *The Fortune Cookie* (1966), and not only did Matthau win an Academy Award but a new comedy team was born. (They subsequently played together in *The Odd Couple*, *The Front Page*, 1974, and *Buddy, Buddy*, 1981, the latter two by Wilder; and Lemmon directed Matthau in an Oscar-nominated performance as a crotchety senior citizen in *Kotch*, 1971.) Matthau's personality is so intoxicat-

ingly potent that he works best when confronted with some similarly larger-than-life figure. Thus, he was effectively cast opposite Barbra Streisand in *Hello, Dolly* (1969), Elaine May in *A New Leaf* (1971), Carol Burnett in *Pete 'N' Tillie* (1972), George Burns in another droll Neil Simon adaptation (and another Oscar nomination for Matthau) *The Sunshine Boys* (1975) and Glenda Jackson in *House Calls* (1978). Like Fields before him, moreover, he makes a hilariously funny childhater, notably as the down-at-heel coach of a Little League baseball team in *The Bad News Bears* (1974) and as Damon Runyon's Sorrowful Jones in the 1979 remake of *Little Miss Marker*. Though he is now Hollywood's leading comic actor, Matthau has not deserted the genre in which he was earliest employed: he was excellent, for example, in a pair of thrillers, *Charley Varrick* (1973) and *The Taking Of Pelham One Two Three* (1974), whose final shot consists of a marvellous close-up portrait of his lugubrious, jowly and wholly lovable features. DM

with Elaine May in A New Leaf *(Paramount, 1971)*

234

Jack Nicholson

Born Neptune, New Jersey, 22 April 1937

In 1969, after Bruce Dern turned it down, Jack Nicholson gratefully accepted the role of a soft-spoken, alcoholically befuddled Southern lawyer in Dennis Hopper's *Easy Rider*, a 'bike movie' co-starring the director and Peter Fonda. In a period when many of Hollywood's major studios faced near-bankruptcy because the extravagantly budgeted entertainments on which they had pinned their hopes were dying at the box-office, Hopper's inexpensive little programmer ended up grossing over $35,000,000. It also made Nicholson a star. It was not only because, like the character he played, he had been around and it showed on his sharp, humorous, world-weary features, but also because, unlike his great precursor Brando, and unlike the rising young stars who followed him, Nicholson bestrode two distinct generations of acting styles. He possessed the pugnacity of a Cagney, the virility of a Garfield, the diabolic charm of a Gable. At the same time, he was without question an embodiment of the 60s and 70s and remains so of the 80s. It is well-nigh impossible to imagine the modern American cinema without him.

What makes him so sympathetic, in an age of facile overnight success, is that stardom came slowly to him. Before his revelatory appearance in *Easy Rider*, he had played mostly small roles in no fewer than nineteen films, many of them drive-in fodder. He was no Hollywood wunderkind. His father had deserted the family home when Nicholson was still a child, so that it fell to his mother, who ran a beauty parlour, to raise him and his two sisters. Visiting one of these sisters in California, he landed a job as an office boy in the cartoon department at MGM; and acquiring a taste for live-action cinema, he trained as an actor with a small group called the Players Ring. A number of TV assignments followed, almost entirely in soap operas, and he made his screen debut as a hoodlum in a Roger Corman quickie called *Cry Baby Killer* (1958). More of that ilk followed – including minor roles in *Studs Lonigan* (1960) and *The Little Shop Of Horrors* (1961), in which he played a deliriously masochistic dental patient – until he met Monte Hellman and, with him, made two low-budget, vaguely experimental westerns, *The Shooting* and *Ride The Whirlwind* (both 1966), which are still admired by many critics.

After the success of *Easy Rider*, however, Nicholson found himself suddenly in demand for totally mainstream, big-budget projects. The first, Minnelli's curious and uneven musical about hypnosis *On A Clear Day You Can See Forever* (1970), misguidedly cast him as a wealthy hippie who shares a dispensable exchange with Barbra Streisand on a rooftop patio: though he was also asked to sing, his solo number was cut from the final print. Fortunately, this was immediately followed by Bob Rafelson's *Five Easy Pieces* (also 1970), a film suffused with the troubled self-questioning of the Vietnam period; Nicholson's characterisation as a middle-class drifter who both rejects and is rejected by the American Dream won him his first Academy Award nomination. (Subsequently, he was to work with Rafelson on *The King Of Marvin Gardens*, 1972, another complex dissection of the 'pursuit of happiness', and *The Postman Always Rings Twice*, 1981, an adaptation of James M. Cain's classic thriller, as sexually explicit as the original novel.)

In 1971, as well as giving brilliantly varied performances as an insatiable womaniser in Mike Nichols' *Carnal Knowledge* and as a mercurial fantasist in Henry Jaglom's indigestibly whimsical *A Safe Place*, Nicholson directed his own first feature, *Drive, He Said*, a quirky allegory of the deep divisions of feeling and opinion in post-Vietnam America. (The film proved a failure both critically and commercially, but it gave him a taste for direction which he was to indulge a second time in 1978 by making *Goin' South*, an irreverent little romantic comedy set among the Dakota Badlands in

in The Border *(Universal, 1982)*

the late 19th century.) As an actor, however, it now seemed that he could not put a foot wrong. There was hardly a major director in Hollywood who was not eager to work with him; and with each new film he demonstrated that his range could encompass raucous comedy and psychological drama, thrillers and westerns. He could appear both magnetically attractive and malevolently ugly – on occasion within the space of a single film, as was the case in Stanley Kubrick's *The Shining* (1980). In Hal Ashby's *The Last Detail* (1973) he played a hell-raising yet ultimately sensitive petty officer who discovers his own entrapment in the Navy mirrored in the fate of the young prisoner he has been detailed to accompany to the brig; in Polanski's *Chinatown* (1974) he was brilliant as a smalltime private eye in 30s Los Angeles sucked into a fetid morass of incest and corruption. For both performances he received an Oscar nomination.

After films with the Italian Michelangelo Antonioni (*The Passenger*) and Mike Nichols (*The Fortune*), Nicholson finally secured his Oscar for a brilliant performance in Milos Forman's *One Flew Over The Cuckoo's Nest* (1975) as the rebellious inmate of a mental hospital whose anarchic attitude to the

institution and its staff cause him to be forcibly lobotomised. One might contest Forman's somewhat modish view of mental illness but not the exuberant virtuosity of Nicholson's performance. And so it continued, one major film after another: Arthur Penn's eccentric western *The Missouri Breaks*, followed by Elia Kazan's Pinter-scripted adaptation of Scott Fitzgerald's *The Last Tycoon* (both 1976), with Nicholson reportedly sighing at the end of each working day, 'Another day, another twenty thousand dollars . . .' His most recent notable roles have been his brilliant thumbnail sketch of Eugene O'Neill in Warren Beatty's *Reds* (1981) and his plain-guy astronaut in James L. Brooks' *Terms Of Endearment* (1983).

Throughout his career Jack Nicholson has been a taker of risks, and for the health of the American cinema and the sanity of its public, one can only hope that he will long continue to do so. For, as Richard Corliss wrote in 'Time' magazine, 'he can embody as much of the twentieth century American male – sexy, psychotic, desperate, heroic – as any movie star today'. DM

in Chinatown *(Paramount, 1974)*

in One Flew Over The Cuckoo's Nest *(United Artists, 1975)*

Ryan O'Neal

Real name Patrick Ryan O'Neal
Born Los Angeles, 20 April 1941

In some respects, Ryan O'Neal's early life is more interesting than his career in films. He was born of show business parents: his father, Charles O'Neal, was a screenwriter for both cinema and television and an occasional novelist; his mother, *née* Patricia Callaghan, had formerly been an actress. O'Neal was left very much on his own as a child, however, spending most of his time swimming and surfing on the beaches of Southern California (even working for a spell as a lifeguard). As an adolescent, he mooched across America, then around Europe; on one memorable occasion, he was arrested for assault and battery during a wild party in New York and spent 51 days in jail. Meeting up with his parents in

Munich, he made his first professional appearance before a camera. They were scriptwriters on a TV series entitled 'Tales Of The Vikings'; and, as Ryan was an expert all-round athlete (and had taken part in several amateur boxing bouts), he was hired as a stuntman on the show.

Back in California, he began to work quite regularly in television, though almost always in small supporting roles. But his first taste of success came when he was chosen to be a member of the cast of 'Empire', a western series which enjoyed some popularity. Its run was nothing, however, to that

enjoyed by 'Peyton Place', the TV spinoff from the immensely successful 20th Century-Fox film, itself based on Grace Metalious' best-selling novel. O'Neal played in over five hundred episodes of what was, at the time, the most popular soap opera on American television, so that his boyish, rather soft features were familiar to millions of housewives across the country. Untested by the rigidly superficial dramatics of 'Peyton Place', his acting ability, on the other hand, was something of a mystery.

In 1969 he made his first film, *The Big Bounce*, a low-budget second feature in which he played a misfit veteran drifting helplessly into criminality. Yet his TV popularity was already such that, in his next film, he was given the leading role – above Michael Crawford and Charles Aznavour. This was *The Games* (1970), a Michael Winner-directed study of the gruelling preparations undergone by long-distance runners for the Olympic Games. Apart from the climactic race itself, the sole interest of the film (certainly from O'Neal's point of view) was that it had been scripted by Erich Segal, professor of English literature, enthusiastic marathon runner and, not least, author of one of the truly bestselling novels of recent times, 'Love Story'. Coincidentally, *Love Story* itself was about to be filmed; and O'Neal was one of more than three hundred aspirants who auditioned for the role of Oliver Barrett IV in this weepie to end all weepies. The rest is, if not quite history, then a very familiar story: O'Neal won the role (and an Oscar nomination), Ali McGraw played his lover and wife dying ever so gracefully (leukemia looked good on her), and the film reaped untold

in The Games *(20th Century-Fox, 1970)*

millions for the brave producers who went out on a limb to make the thing. Notwithstanding the shadow of an Oscar, however, O'Neal's acting ability was *still* something of a mystery. (Unwisely, but not unpredictably, Segal, O'Neal *et al* attempted to rework the miraculous formula in 1978 with *Oliver's Story*. This time it was not the heroine but the film itself that died.)

In 1971 he teamed up with William Holden as *The Wild Rovers*. If its title was intended to suggest kinship with Sam Peckinpah's *The Wild Bunch*, it could hardly have been more misleading: Blake Edwards' western was slow and lyrical, less of a violent action movie than a gentle character study. But, for O'Neal, its box-office failure was more than compensated for by the huge success of Peter Bogdanovich's consciously Hawksian screwball farce *What's Up, Doc?* (1972), in which he co-starred with Barbra Streisand. This was not so much a study of character as of personality: its plot (in any case, impossible to recount) mattered less than the behavioural charms of its star coupling. And if O'Neal's bumbler of a hero was a too calculated crib of Cary Grant in a similar role in *Bringing Up Baby*, he, Streisand and the film were often very funny – especially with a last-minute crack at his *Love Story* persona. Bogdanovich's next, *Paper Moon* (1973), lovingly shot in what might be called Fordian black-and-white (ie mostly greys), proved no less successful, a delightfully picaresque tale of a small-town con man (O'Neal) and the foul-mouthed little girl with whom he finds himself saddled. The precocious tyke was of course Tatum, Ryan's daughter (by his first

with Ali McGraw in Love Story *(Paramount, 1970)*

marriage to actress Joanna Moore), and the youngest performer ever to win an Oscar. (Bogdanovich and O'Neal worked together one last time on a disaster of monumental proportions, *Nickelodeon*, 1976, a humourless, charmless and endless evocation of cinema's prehistory).

Stanley Kubrick's *Barry Lyndon* (1975) was a masterpiece, a breathtakingly beautiful fresco of greed, egotism and corruption in 18th-century Europe. But though its narrative was deliberately cold and dispassionate, it is still difficult to understand why Kubrick should have chosen O'Neal to incarnate the title role (instead of, say, Malcolm McDowell): rather than suggest the character's lack of passion, he played him *with* lack of passion – resulting in a bland performance which tended to leave a blur at the centre of the film.

Since then, moreover, there has been little of note in O'Neal's career: he was suitably chilling in the title role of Walter Hill's pretentious thriller *The Driver* (1978); mildly amusing opposite Streisand in *The Main Event* (1979); and queasy, as well he might be, as a cop teamed with John Hurt in *Partners* (1982), a crude anti-homosexual joke. But O'Neal is still only in his early forties, with plenty of time to get his career back into shape – and there is always the example of Tatum to spur him on. DM

Peter O'Toole

Born **Connemara, Ireland, 2 August 1932**

It is the ironic and not wholly unjustified fate of ham actors to end their careers playing .. ham actors. The most celebrated case was John Barrymore; without doubt, the most recent significant example is Peter O'Toole, who was indeed cast as a larger-than-life TV personality in Richard Benjamin's satire *My Favorite Year* (1982). That O'Toole is, and has always been, a ham is surely no longer in question: the fiasco of his recent stage 'Macbeth', a production (and a performance) of such toe-curling awfulness that it turned into a campy cult triumph, represented no more than a redundant confirmation of this long-suspected fact.

Though born in Ireland (and on occasion almost caricaturally 'Irish'), O'Toole was brought up in the English city of Leeds, where his father (oddly, like Albert Finney's) was a bookmaker. He left school at an early age to become a messenger boy for the 'Yorkshire Evening Post', from which modest position he graduated to junior reporter. However, he had also involved himself in local amateur dramatics and, after two years of national service in the Navy, he joined the Old Vic company in 1955. It was a period of renewal for the English theatre, one allied to an obsession with surface realism, usually working-class in origin; but his elongated, slightly fey good looks, patrician voice and ethereal manner were obviously more suited to a leading man in the cinema. After a few supporting parts (most notably as a government official among the Eskimos of Nicholas Ray's *The Savage Innocents*, 1960), he shot to international stardom in the title role of David Lean's *Lawrence Of Arabia* (1962), for which he was nominated for an Academy Award. His next role, as King Henry II in *Becket* (1964), brought him a second nomination (he was to play the same monarch again, *and* be nominated again, in *The Lion In Winter*, 1968, certainly a unique case in the history of the cinema). But his *Lord Jim* in 1965 (by Richard Brooks out of Conrad) seemed to be conceived virtually as a reprise of T.E. Lawrence; and already the suspicion was aroused that O'Toole was a self-indulgent actor gradually being devoured by his own mannerisms.

in Lawrence Of Arabia *(Columbia, 1962)*

Though he displayed a charming gift for light comedy in *What's New, Pussycat?* (1965) and, especially, *How To Steal A Million* (1966), in which he was partnered by his own elfin female equivalent, Audrey Hepburn, it was increasingly hard to cast O'Toole in interesting films, so precious and, in the worst sense, theatrical had his on-screen personality become. In consequence, from the mid-60s on, he tended to be associated with a string of heavy international co-productions, most of them examples of filming-by-numbers: eg *The Bible* (1966);

The Night Of The Generals (1967), a ponderous thriller about a Nazi general committing his own private murders; the James Bond spoof *Casino Royale* (1967); *Great Catherine* (1968), a ridiculous, Shaw-inspired biopic of Catherine of Russia co-starring Jeanne Moreau; and *Goodbye, Mr Chips* (1969), a laughably inept musical of James Hilton's novel which, no less laughably, earned O'Toole his fourth Oscar nomination. In the 70s he fared little better; and though, on both stage and screen, *The Ruling Class* (1972) offered him a role to chew up the scenery with, that of a mad aristocrat who takes

himself for Christ, it was a disaster both at the box-office and as a work of art (needless to say, however, O'Toole was nominated yet again.)

Now in his 50s, and with years of high living behind him, O'Toole has the lean, streaky features of a debauched greyhound; and if he enjoyed a personal success both in *The Stuntman* (1978), as a megalomaniac film director (Oscar nomination No 6), and in *My Favorite Year*, it is becoming more and more difficult to see how he can fruitfully contribute to a medium whose realism mercilessly exposes the inflated and the pretentious. DM

in My Favorite Year *(MGM, 1982)*

George Peppard

Born **Detroit, Michigan, 1 October 1928**

In a career spanning over a quarter of a century, George Peppard has made one first-rate feature, Blake Edwards' *Breakfast At Tiffany's* (1961), and three fairly engrossing ones, *The Strange One* (1957), *Home From The Hill* (1960) and *The Blue Max* (1966) – which leaves a grand total of twenty-two out-and-out duds. Nor can this be wholly ascribed to bad luck. Peppard, although good-looking, is without question the least interesting of current male stars (if, indeed, he can be considered such), the least capable of taking the spectator by surprise. There would seem to be no latent emotional depths in his personality; and it is almost impossible to cast him against type, since the type he represents has never been too clearly defined. In fairness, it must be said that Peppard himself has been conscious of, and frustrated by, this inability to make a stronger impression. In 1978, he mortgaged his home and plunged himself into debt in order to produce, write, direct and star in a melodramatic thriller, *Five Days From Home*. It flopped at the box-office, however, which only meant that he was ever after condemned to the type of role from which he had so dearly hoped to escape.

His father was a building contractor, his mother a singer in light opera; and, after experience in summer stock and studies at the Actors' Studio in New York, he began to make a name for himself in live TV dramas and on Broadway. His debut film was *The Strange One*, a somewhat morbid study of life in a Southern military academy. *Pork Chop Hill* (1959), a war drama, and Minnelli's *Home From The Hill* both advanced his career; the ludicrous Kerouac adaptation, *The Subterraneans*, in 1960 had precisely the opposite effect. In *Breakfast At Tiffany's*, however, a witty and sophisticated film of Truman Capote's celebrated novella, he co-starred with Audrey Hepburn and some of her lustre seemed to be shed over him. Yet it was immediately followed

in 1963

by Carl Foreman's bloated, pretentious war film *The Victors* (1963), which contained a peculiarly grotesque love scene between Peppard and Melina Mercouri; *The Carpetbaggers* (1964), a film as bad (and almost as successful) as Harold Robbins' tawdry bestseller; and *Operation Crossbow* (1965), a dreary World War II epic with Sophia Loren.

From that point on, with the exception of the exciting aviation film *The Blue Max*, it was downhill all the way. Such titles as *What's So Bad About Feeling Good?* (1968), *Pendulum* (1969), *The Executioner* (1970), *One More Train To Rob* (1971), *The Groundstar Conspiracy* (1972) and *Race For The Yankee Zephyr* (1981) were hardly calculated to effect a comeback; and, as one might have predicted, Peppard finally fetched up on television, starring in a crime series, 'The A-Team', a category to which, in the cinema, he has, alas, never belonged. DM

Donald Pleasence

Born Worksop, England, 5 October 1919

Or Donald un-Pleasence? Rarely can an actor's name have seemed more inappropriate. Pleasence, a small bald man with unnervingly beady eyes, has played many villainous characters in a long career on stage, television and the cinema; what makes him a particularly sinister figure on-screen, however, is rather his gallery of ostensibly sympathetic characters, mostly weak-willed, obsessive, ferrety creatures flailing helplessly to ward off the repeated blows of an unkind fate.

in The Night Of The Generals *(Columbia, 1967)*

He began acting on stage in 1939, then joined the RAF: taken prisoner in Germany, he organised P.O.W. camp concerts. After the war, he steadily made a name for himself as a character actor in both provincial theatres and the West End of London, later touring in the United States with a company led by Laurence Olivier. He made his film debut in *The Beachcomber* (1954), a comedy-drama set on a Pacific Island and based on a story by Somerset Maugham. Pleasence appeared in a number of 50s films, including the first version of *1984* (1956), the umpteenth version of *A Tale Of Two Cities* (1958), Tony Richardson's adaptation of the John Osborne play *Look Back In Anger* (1959) and *Sons And Lovers* (1960, from D.H. Lawrence's novel) – as well as a string of minor horror movies in which he was invariably cast as the villain. (He played, for example, the title role in *Dr Crippen*, 1963.) But it was as the pathetically scheming old derelict in the film version of Harold Pinter's *The Caretaker* (also 1963) that he first properly impinged himself on the consciousness of the moviegoing public.

A few roles in Hollywood films followed – in George Stevens' pompously reverential *The Greatest Story Ever Told* (1965) he was cast, not unpredictably, as the Devil – but it was another off-beat British production which offered him one of his best-ever roles. In Roman Polanski's wry, vaguely Surrealist black comedy *Cul-De-Sac* of 1966, Pleasence gave a terrific performance as the humiliated husband of faithless Françoise Dorléac, a performance which contrived to be at the same time funny, sinister and invested with genuine sentiment. Changing pace, his evilly owlish Blofeld in *You Only Live Twice* (1967) was perhaps the most effective of all James Bond's adversaries; he was in the contentious *Soldier Blue* (1970), and was disturbing as a white-garbed zombie in George Lucas's first feature, the arty but not uninteresting *THX 1138* (1971).

Pleasence has made dozens of films; and, though they have been of necessarily varying quality, he himself has always been a pleasure to watch. The most notable have been the nostalgic memoir of early Hollywood *Hearts Of The West* (1975); Elia Kazan's underrated version of the uncompleted Fitzgerald novel *The Last Tycoon* (1976), in which he played a self-satisfied English screenwriter inducted into the rudiments of Hollywoodese by Robert De Niro; and John Carpenter's *Halloween* (1978), as a psychiatrist himself alarmingly in need of psychiatric treatment. DM

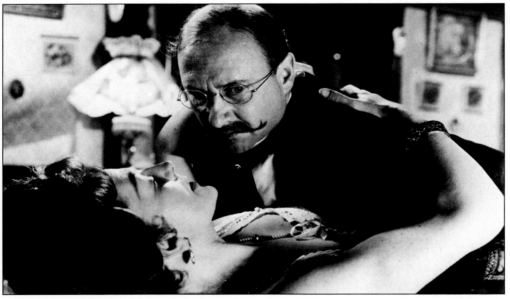

with Coral Browne in Dr Crippen *(Warner Bros., 1963)*

Elvis Presley

Born Tupelo, Mississippi, 8 January 1935
Died 1977

Strictly speaking, Elvis Presley's place in the history of the cinema is an extremely tenuous one. Of the thirty-three films in which he starred, no more than half-a-dozen are of the slightest interest, the others being a horrendous miscellany of insipid, barely distinguishable 'entertainments', few of which will have been seen by any but the most rabid of his fans. Yet his fame as a popular singer was, and still is, so widespread that, purely as a phenomenon, he simply has to be taken into account.

The facts of his life are well-known, especially since the recent publication of Albert Goldman's scabrous biography. Presley was the survivor of identical twins, and moved with his family in his early teens to Memphis, Tennessee. While working as a cinema usher and truck driver, he was already performing locally as 'The Hillbilly Cat'. In 1953, he made an amateur recording as a present for his mother; it was sent to a small recording company for which he made a number of singles; *these* were heard by an RCA Victor executive who put the young hopeful under contract. In 1956 his recording of 'Heartbreak Hotel' went around the world, as did the image of a sensuous, hip-wriggling rock 'n' roller with dark, smoky eyes, long sideburns and a permanent sneer on his lips. Though idolized by a whole generation of teenagers, and though by the time of his death he had sold an estimated 600 million singles and albums, 'Elvis the Pelvis', as he was soon nicknamed, was also feared and mistrusted as a pernicious influence: when he appeared on the family-audience 'Ed Sullivan Show' on television, the cameramen had strict instructions to cut him off at the waist.

Presley's first film, *Love Me Tender* (1956), was a derivative Civil War western which might easily have starred any young contract actor, and it was not until his second, *Loving You* (1957), that Hollywood began to realise how much his films would benefit (commercially) from being tailormade to his precise talents, personality and image. Thus his third, *Jailhouse Rock* (also 1957), was a tough prison drama starring Elvis as a convict redeeming himself with his guitar: it had a score by Lieber and Stoller and remains perhaps the most satisfying of all his films. In 1960 *G.I. Blues* exploited the highly publicised event of his drafting; but just as the army seemed to smooth out much of the disturbing rebelliousness of his persona, so this film, like those which followed, presented a more hygienic Elvis, ingratiatingly conformist and physically chubbier. Without exception, his subsequent work in the cinema would conform to the same pattern, as witness such titles as *Fun In Acapulco* (1963), *Roustabout* (1964), *Tickle Me* (1965), *Spinout* (1966), *Speedway* (1968) and *The Trouble With Girls* (1969). Of far more interest to

genuine devotees of popular music were the two documentaries, *Elvis – That's The Way It Is* (1970) and *Elvis On Tour* (1972), filmed during his concert and nightclub appearances in the early 70s, when he made an astonishing comeback – his impact undiluted – as a public performer.

It was in this period, however, that his health began seriously to deteriorate, partly as a result of the junk food to which he was addicted, partly as a result of his doctors' indulgence in the matter of stimulant and depressant drugs on which he had become equally dependent. He gradually withdrew into his $100,000 mansion Graceland, situated on the renamed Elvis Presley Boulevard in Memphis, where he led an increasingly Howard Hughes-like existence behind heavily guarded walls. And it was there that in 1977, when he was only 42, he was found dead of a heart attack. For a few hysterical fanatics, of course, Elvis 'will never die'; for those less dewy-eyed, but nevertheless respectful of the young man who changed the whole nature of popular music, the real Elvis Presley had died a long, long time before. DM

Vincent Price

Born St. Louis, Missouri, 27 May 1911

It may seem absurd to consider Vincent Price as a star of the 60s, given that he made his screen debut in 1938 and appeared in dozens of films before the decade in question. Yet, though a familiar figure (and voice) to earlier generations of moviegoers, Price played only a few romantic leads at the beginning of his career and was thereafter – until 1960, that is – confined to supporting roles, most frequently as weakwilled, rather effete young lounge lizards or caricaturally etched historical figures (of which he played more than his fair share – Sir Walter Raleigh, the Duke of Clarence, the Mormon founder Joseph Smith, Cardinal Richelieu, Casanova, Omar Khayyam and, though not precisely a historical figure, the Devil).

His languorous manner and unmistakably cultivated voice were the result of his early upbringing and education. Upon graduating from high school, he was given, not a new raccoon coat, but a Grand Tour of Europe's cultural capitals; and he later took a degree in art history and English from Yale. (Price, an art-buying consultant for Sears Roebuck and a notable collector himself, has written several books on the subject, as well as on his other abiding passion, cookery.) After establishing himself on the London stage and Broadway, he launched his film career at Universal, for which studio he played the Invisible Man in one of the later productions of that series, *The Invisible Man Returns* (1940). At 20th Century-Fox, he appeared in a number of major movies, including *Laura* (1944), as Judith Anderson's sarcastic milksop of a gigolo, John M. Stahl's *The Keys Of The Kingdom* (1945), most incongruously as a missionary priest, the same director's delirious Technicolor melodrama *Leave Her To Heaven* (also 1945) and Joseph L. Mankiewicz's *Dragonwyck* (1946), as the haughty, sadistic husband who terrorises poor Gene Tierney in a mansion on the Hudson. In truth, however, Price was not much of an actor: he never discovered the secret of giving a strong portrayal of weakness, and his straight-faced villains were often risible.

His career declined in the 50s, though he prepared himself for his ultimate niche as a star by appearances in a string of low-budget, though on occasion diverting, horror movies: eg *House Of Wax* (1953), *The Mad Magician* (1954), *The Fly* (1958), *The Return Of The Fly* and *The Tingler* (both 1959). Then, in 1960, he was cast by the whizz kid producer-director of exploitation movies, Roger Corman, as Roderick Usher in an adaptation of Edgar Allan Poe's *The Fall Of The House Of Usher*. The film, a lurid, vulgar but vastly entertaining travesty of the distinguished original, was a smash hit, and Price's hammy, demented Roderick set the joyously campy tone of a cycle on which he and Corman were to collaborate six more times. These were *The Pit And The Pendulum* (1961), the openly parodic *Tales Of Terror* and *The Raven* (1962 and 1963), *The Haunted Palace*, a cavalier amalgam of Poe and his epigone Lovecraft, the visually striking *The Masque Of The Red Death* and *The Tomb Of Ligeia* (all 1964). Right up to the 80s, Price was to star in a string of cheap horror flicks, but only his two 'Phibes' vehicles (*The Abominable Dr Phibes*, 1971, and *Dr Phibes Rises Again*, 1972) possessed even a hint of the panache of the Poe series.

Price today seems to have abandoned the cinema for the more civilised pleasures of *haute cuisine* (he has cooked on TV), his art collection and the company of his third wife, actress Coral Browne. He will be remembered fondly; for, as the English critic Gilbert Adair once wrote, 'Every man has his Price – and mine is Vincent.' DM

in The Masque Of The Red Death *(American-International, 1964)*

Charlotte Rampling

Born Sturmer, England, 5 February 1945

To employ an outmoded, even disreputable, term, Charlotte Rampling has *class*. A sensuous, dark-haired stunner with high, prominent cheekbones and a curiously 40s, Lizabeth Scott-like manner, she is a Hitchcockian heroine who never worked with Hitchcock, a Buñuelian victim who never met Buñuel. When one attempts to compare her to other actresses, it is of Lauren Bacall and Gene Tierney that one thinks, rather than someone of her own generation – and it is no doubt for that reason that her eternally promising career has never quite taken off and looks unlikely to do so now. This fact may well be of little consequence to Rampling, however, who is happily married to Jean-Michel Jarre, a millionaire composer, the producer, director and lead performer of two internationally successful record albums, 'Oxygène' and 'Equinoxe'.

She is the daughter of Godfrey Rampling, an Army officer who also represented the United Kingdom at the 1936 Olympic Games in Berlin and won a gold medal in athletics. In 1955, Colonel Rampling was attached to NATO headquarters just outside Paris, and Charlotte received a classical French education: her gift for languages has enabled her to appear in French and Italian as well as English-speaking films. She returned to England in the early 60s, at the height of the 'Swinging London' period; and, being tall, slim and leggy, was soon employed as a model and cover girl. Though glimpsed briefly in the Albert Hall sequence of Richard Lester's wittily modish *The Knack ... And How To Get It* (1965), it was a feeble Boulting Brothers heist movie, rather unwisely titled *Rotten To The Core* (also 1965), and the archetypically 'swinging' *Georgy Girl* (1966), in which she played Lynn Redgrave's chic room-mate, that launched her as a leading young actress of the British cinema.

But London ceased to swing soon after, and Rampling went to Italy to play a minor but important role in Visconti's shrilly operatic melodrama of the rise of Nazism, *The Damned* (1969), and Giuseppe Patrone Griffi's lurid adaptation of *'Tis Pity She's A Whore* (1971). Her English-speaking films were a very mixed bag – they included *The Ski Bum* (1971), *Corky* (1972) and John Boorman's visually extravagant piece of thick-ear science fiction *Zardoz* (1974) – but she became an international star by playing a former concentration camp internee who relives a sado-masochistic love affair with her Nazi tormentor in Liliana Cavani's *The Night Porter* (also 1974), a film as odious as it was idiotic.

In recent years Rampling would seem to have allowed her family life to take precedence over her career: it would be difficult to detect any real coherence in the jumble of films, good and bad, which she has rather distractedly consented to grace. The best of these (though not always for her performance) have been Dick Richards' surprisingly idiomatic remake of Chandler's *Farewell, My Lovely* (1975), in which she made an appropriately slinky Velma; Woody Allen's little-liked *Stardust Memories* (1980), in which she seemed more ravishing than ever; and Sidney Lumet's ultra-conventional but gripping courtroom drama *The Verdict* (1982). DM

in Farewell, My Lovely *(Avco-Embassy, 1975)*

Robert Redford

Real name **Charles Robert Redford Jr**
Born **Santa Monica, California,
18 August 1937**

Blond, athletic and devastatingly goodlooking, Robert Redford has been for almost a decade the American cinema's leading male attraction. And since, in a way, he strikes one as such a creature of the cinema, such a *born* film star, it comes as quite a surprise to discover that (a) it was never his youthful ambition to act, and (b) before his first film appearances, he was an extremely experienced, admired and successful stage actor. In one respect, at least, he totally conforms to a mythic stereotype: he is – as, with his tousled blondness and peachy complexion, he appears – a Californian. The son of a Santa Monica accountant, he attended the University of Colorado on a baseball scholarship, choosing that particular Northern state because it was close to mountains for climbing and skiing. At this stage of his life, sports were Redford's passion, and he excelled also at swimming, tennis and football. Yet, rather like the character he was later to play in *Downhill Racer* (1969), he soon became frustrated with the demands made upon what he called 'test-tube athletes'. 'I never knew what it was like to just enjoy a sport. I was always out there grovelling to win. You begin to fear not winning.' His inattention to baseball practice at college finally led to his losing the scholarship, and in 1957 he dropped out altogether. At high school he had displayed a certain talent as a caricaturist, and he now decided that he would seriously study art. To this end, he did what all hopeful young American artists did in the 50s – he went to Paris. Then, after bumming around the continent of Europe for almost a year, hitching rides and living mostly in youth hostels, he was forced to the realisation that, as a painter, he was derivative and third-rate. And so, uncertain of his future, he returned home to the States.

Yet, curiously, it was his visual sense which finally pointed him in the right direction. Deciding that he might be better suited to theatrical scenic design than high-art painting, he enrolled at the Pratt Institute in Brooklyn; and, because it was suggested to him that, if he really wished to understand the principles of scenic design, he ought to put himself in the actor's place, he concurrently attended drama classes at the American Academy of Dramatic Arts. Though Redford never learned to buckle down to acting as an institutionalized academic subject like any other ('At the Academy I got the space and the opportunity to expand and form myself as an actor, but I didn't learn to act'), it was his attendance there that led to his first professional engagement on Broadway. One of his instructors was also stage manager of the hit comedy 'Tall Story' and required an athletic type to play a basketball player in a crowd scene. From that he went on to a slightly more substantial role in a drama about a nuclear physicist, 'The Highest Tree', which proved, on two counts, to be an unhappy memory for Redford: it ran only twenty-one days and, during its try-out run, his first child (he had married in 1958) died tragically and mysteriously in its crib.

His theatrical roles gradually increased in importance, until in 1963 he was given the lead in Neil Simon's phenomenally successful farce about newly-weds setting up a precarious household in Manhattan, 'Barefoot In The Park'. (Redford subsequently starred in the 1967 film version opposite Jane Fonda.) He remained with the play for one year of its four-year run, but never worked in the theatre again. For he had already made one trip to Hollywood, to appear in a curious little film about a sadistic young American soldier in Korea, *War Hunt* (1962). Redford, in a minor but important role, got some good notices, but was prevented from making another film for two years because of difficulties raised by the terms of his contract with the film's producers. Instead, he worked regularly on television, mostly on the kind of one-off drama shows

in The Candidate *(Warner Bros., 1972)*

which have long since disappeared from American TV schedules, such as 'Playhouse 90' and 'Alfred Hitchcock Presents'.

In 1965, he returned to the big screen in an embarrassingly bad adaptation of Robert Shaw's novel 'The Hiding Place', characteristically re-titled *Situation Hopeless – But Not Serious*. His co-star was Alec Guinness, which would surely have been an interesting experience for the young actor, but the film did no better in public screenings than at its press show, and is without any doubt the worst Redford was ever involved with. Much more intriguing, though no more commercially successful, was Robert Mulligan's *Inside Daisy Clover* (1966), taken from Gavin Lambert's Hollywood-based novel. It was a major role for him, that of a mentally unbalanced screen idol, but there was a snag: the character, as written, was homosexual. Redford accepted the challenge, though he not unperceptively shifted the sexual bias: 'I'm interested in playing, if anything, someone who bats ten different ways,' he said. 'Children, women, dogs, cats, men, anything that salves his ego. Total narcissism.'

Though he had become, by general agreement, The Man Most Likely To Be A Superstar, it was rather his acting abilities that he continued to test, in such films as Sidney Pollack's *This Property Is Condemned*, scripted by Francis Ford Coppola from a one-act play by Tennessee Williams, and Arthur Penn's rather sweaty drama of the Deep South *The Chase*, in which he co-starred with Marlon Brando and Jane Fonda (both 1966). Neither of these made much of an effect at the box-office, so that it was useful for Redford, as a star, to follow them with *Barefoot In The Park* and, especially, George Roy Hill's record-breaking western (perhaps the last real hit in one of the proudest genres of the American cinema), *Butch Cassidy And The Sundance Kid* (1969). Though originally intended for Butch, Redford ended up playing Sundance to Paul Newman's Butch, and their exuberant teaming as a pair of very human outlaws, clownishly foiled by their own myths, made the film among the most popular of its decade. Naturally, given the Hollywood motto of 'If at first you succeed, try again', George Roy Hill in 1973 paired Redford and Newman once more to even greater commercial effect with *The Sting*; though, when Redford went it alone with Hill on *The Great Waldo Pepper* (1975), a bright, engaging and visually delightful homage to the barnstorming pilots of the 20s, the result, for some reason, had much less audience appeal.

Oddly, in view of his phenomenal popularity, plus the fact that he had turned down, or would turn down, such films as *The Godfather*, *The French Connection* and *Who's Afraid Of Virginia Woolf?*, Redford's next four appearances were in minor works, both from a commercial and a purely aesthetic point of view: *Downhill Racer*, in which he did a lot of his own skiing; Abraham Polonsky's heavy-handed 'liberal' Western *Tell Them Willie Boy Is Here* (1970); a facile motorbike movie 'trailing in the fumes of *Easy Rider*', as one critic drily put it, *Little Fauss And Big Halsy* (also 1970); and a mindlessly entertaining caper movie, *The Hot Rock* (1972). *The Candidate*, in which he was first-rate as a Kennedy-like politician suffocating in smoke-filled rooms, and *Jeremiah Johnson*, in which, heavily bearded, he played a 'mountain man' in the Rockies (both 1972), helped to restore his prestige at the top end of the market; while *The Way We Were*, a piece of romantic fluff with political pretensions in which he gracefully played second fiddle to Barbra Streisand, and *The Sting* (both 1973), kept him up there as the country's top-ranking male star.

'I wanted Gatsby badly,' Redford has said. 'He is not fleshed out in the book, and the implied parts of his character are fascinating.' In the event, alas, Jack Clayton's film version of *The Great Gatsby* (1974) did not so much flesh the character out as doll him up. Loved the clothes, hated the movie – that was the consensus of opinion. Another project dear to Redford's heart, however, met with a much more positive response from critics and public alike. This was *All The President's Men* (1976), based on the bestselling book by Bob Woodward and Carl Bernstein recounting the tenacious way in which they uncovered and exposed the Watergate conspiracy. Redford had always been a committed liberal and was instrumental in putting the package together, with Alan Pakula as director and Dustin Hoffman as co-star. Though everyone was wary of its commercial possibilities, it turned out to be such a success that it was dubbed 'the *Jaws* of the Potomac'.

Today, Redford's standing as an actor could hardly be higher; added to which, for his first directorial assignment, *Ordinary People* (1980), he won an Academy Award. Though maintaining a Manhattan apartment, he lives for much of the time on a gigantic 7,000-acre estate in Utah (a dedicated conservationist, he has even written a book on the subject). Happily married and jealous of his private life, he is one of the more admirable figures in contemporary cinema. DM

Vanessa Redgrave
Born **London, 30 January 1937**

Born into a celebrated English theatrical family – father Sir Michael, mother Rachel Kempson, sister Lynn and brother Corin – Vanessa Redgrave was an almost legendary stage performer, giving in *As You Like It* the definitive Rosalind of her generation.

Though punctuated by regular Academy Award nominations, her film career has proved much less distinguished, partly through bad judgment, partly because of her prickly temperament and strongly held political views. It certainly started well. She made a dazzling impression as David Warner's ex-wife in *Morgan – A Suitable Case For Treatment* (1966), receiving her first Oscar nomination; then, in the same year, confirmed her promise with cameo roles in *A Man For All Seasons* (as Anne Boleyn) and Antonioni's *Blow-Up*. And, though Karel Reisz's biopic was coolly received, her flamboyant performance in the title role of *Isadora* (1968) was also considered Oscar-worthy. But it can only have been financial considerations that attracted her to such films as *Murder On The Orient Express* (1974), *The Seven Per Cent Solution* (1976) and *Bear Island* (1979).

Offscreen, however, Miss Redgrave has remained a headliner – whether divorcing the director Tony Richardson on the grounds of adultery with Jeanne Moreau, bearing an illegitimate child to Franco Nero (her co-star in *Camelot*, 1967), aggressively canvassing for the Workers' Revolutionary Party or making a political speech at the 1978 Academy Awards ceremony. That she still has much to offer the cinema was demonstrated by her haunting (and haunted) performance in the title role of Lillian Hellman's *Julia* (1977), finally winning one of the most merited Oscars in recent years. DM

in Isadora (*Universal, 1968*)

Oliver Reed
Born **Wimbledon, London, 13 February 1938**

A nephew of the British director Sir Carol Reed, Oliver Reed ran away from home in his teens and drifted through London, scraping a livelihood as a bouncer in a Soho nightclub, a boxer and cab driver. Though he can just be glimpsed in a few well-known British films of the early 60s (*The Angry Silence, The League Of Gentlemen, No Love For Johnnie, The Rebel*), his career took off when he landed the title role in a cheap but commercially successful Hammer horror production, *The Curse Of The Werewolf* (1961).

Reed, a burly, bull-faced, excessively macho performer and notorious public 'hell-raiser', has seldom worked with a director of distinction or personal style, but he was well employed by Ken Russell in three delirious (and controversial) films: as Gerald in D.H. Lawrence's *Women In Love* (1969: it made headlines with a scene in which Reed and Alan Bates wrestled nude before an open fire); as the libertine priest Grandier in *The Devils* (1971, adapted from Aldous Huxley); and as the Teddy Boy holiday camp host in The Who's rock opera *Tommy* (1975). Otherwise he has most often been associated with Michael Winner, and a jaundiced observer might be tempted to remark that they fully deserved each other. Coincidentally, perhaps, Reed gave his most satisfying performance as a vicious Bill Sikes in his uncle's jolly *Oliver!* (1968, from Lionel Bart's stage musical). DM

in Sitting Target (*MGM, 1972*)

in 1971

Lee Remick
Born **Quincy, Massachusetts, 14 December 1935**

Young actors and actresses on the brink of a professional career can seldom afford to be discriminating about their first films, yet these will occasionally determine the way a personality is perceived for years afterwards. Lee Remick was already an experienced dancer and stage actress when, in 1957, she made a sensational film debut as a nubile, sexy drum majorette in Elia Kazan's *A Face In The Crowd*; and, though she has since portrayed an extensive range of characters, the image of a teasing but eventually obliging flirt has proved a difficult one to shake off.

Admittedly, such roles as Tony Franciosa's co-quettish wife in the Deep South melodrama *The Long Hot Summer* (1958) and the alleged rape victim whose panties form a vital part of the evidence in Otto Preminger's racy courtroom drama *Anatomy Of A Murder* (1959), encouraged such an image. But she was deeply affecting as Jo Van Fleet's widowed daughter in *Wild River* (1960) and magnificently plausible as Jack Lemmon's alcoholic wife in *Days Of Wine And Roses*, for which she was nominated for an Oscar in 1962.

Like many stars launched in the late 50s, just prior to Hollywood's radical 'face-lift' in the following decade, she has found it hard to pursue a consistently stimulating career – films like *The Omen* (1976) and *Telefon* (1977) added little to her reputation. Yet, though miscast as one of *The Europeans* in James Ivory's fey 1979 adaptation of the Henry James novel, she nevertheless gave a witty performance, and she is one of those rare actresses guaranteed to age well. DM

Jason Robards, Jr
Born **Chicago, 22 July 1922**

As befits his date of birth, everything seems to come in twos for Jason Robards, Jr. The son of a celebrated stage and film actor (who made over 100 films, and last appeared in *Wild In The Country* with Elvis Presley, and died in 1963), he was present at the bombing of Pearl Harbor and received the Navy Cross; thirty years later, he almost died in a violent automobile accident.

After the war, Robards settled in Greenwich Village, where, following a time-honoured tradition, he drove a cab while struggling as an actor in radio soap operas and live TV dramas. He was in his mid-30s when, in successive years, critics unanimously lauded his powerful performances in two Eugene O'Neill plays, 'The Iceman Cometh' and 'Long Day's Journey Into Night'. And another two *anni mirabilis* were 1976 and 1977, when he won Oscars for *All The President's Men*, in which he played the 'Washington Post' managing editor, Ben Bradlee, and *Julia*, as the novelist Dashiell Hammett opposite Jane Fonda's Lillian Hellman.

Over the years, in fact, the craggy, intelligent Robards has impersonated an amazing variety of historical figures: the playwright George S. Kaufman in *Act One* (1963); Al Capone in *The St. Valentine's Day Massacre* (1967); Doc Holliday in *Hour Of The Gun* (1967); the sewing machine magnate Singer in *Isadora* (1968); and Governor Lew Wallace, author of *Ben-Hur*, in Sam Peckinpah's *Pat Garrett And Billy The Kid* (1973). Ironically, and to complete the doubles, he relived his Pearl Harbor experience in *Tora! Tora! Tora!* (1970). DM

in The Night They Raided Minsky's (*United Artists, 1968*)

Cliff Robertson

Born **La Jolla, California, 9 September 1925**

A former journalist and merchant seaman, Cliff Robertson began acting in the theatre, making his film debut in *Picnic* (1956), opposite William Holden, Rosalind Russell and Kim Novak. With the exception of a few mildly challenging opportunities – in Raoul Walsh's emasculated but intriguing adaptation of Norman Mailer's classic war novel *The Naked And The Dead* (1958), Samuel Fuller's violent urban thriller *Underworld USA* (1961) and Franklin Shaffner's caustic film version of the Gore Vidal play *The Best Man* (1965) – his career has been mostly routine, no doubt because his clean cut, Ivy League features make him awkward to cast in offbeat roles. Yet he was quite exceptionally disturbing as the mental retardee whom surgery transforms into a genius overnight in *Charly* (1968), for which he won a deserved Academy Award.

Robertson twice made the headlines, on neither occasion to his advantage. In 1962, he was personally selected by President Kennedy to impersonate the young JFK as a World War II Navy hero in *PT-109*, but the film passed virtually unnoticed. And in 1977, he accused David Begelman, then the highly successful production chief of Columbia, of having embezzled $10,000 in his name. Though this proved to be only the tip of an iceberg of corruption, and the actor's claim was completely vindicated, it was Begelman who continued to thrive in Hollywood while Robertson was blacklisted for three years. That's show business. DM

Maximilian Schell

Born **Vienna, 8 December 1930**

There are, it's claimed, 'good' Oscars and 'bad' Oscars: a good one will raise an actor's career to new, unsuspected heights; a bad one risks stunting its growth. Maximilian Schell won an Academy Award as Best Supporting Actor for his disturbing performance as a defence attorney in Stanley Kramer's *Judgment At Nuremberg* (1961), thereafter being offered a series of forgettable roles in which he might have been replaced by any number of German or Austrian immigré performers. Films like *The Reluctant Saint* (1962), Vittorio de Sica's catastrophic version of Sartre's *The Condemned Of Altona* (1963), Jules Dassin's lightweight comedy-thriller *Topkapi* (1964) and *Krakatoa, East of Java* (1969) were all very differently received, but none will be remembered for his contribution.

Schell was born into a literary family, all four children of which became actors (most notably, apart from himself, his sister Maria). Raised in Switzerland after the Anschluss of 1938, he was educated there and in Germany; and, attracting attention in a Broadway drama, 'Interlock', he was signed up to play a Nazi officer (not for the last time

Romy Schneider

Real name **Rosemarie Albach-Retty**
Born **Vienna, 23 September 1938**
Died **Paris, 1982**

Though Romy Schneider's father, Wolf Albach-Retty, was a respected figure on the Viennese stage and screen, it was her mother's name which she

in Forever My Love *(Paramount, 1962)*

George C. Scott

Born **Wise, Virginia, 18 October 1927**

George C. Scott is commonly referred to as a 'character actor' in view of his remarkably extensive range: he played a sly, sardonic prosecuting attorney in Otto Preminger's *Anatomy Of A Murder* (1959), a detective of the old school in John Huston's parodic thriller *The List Of Adrian Messenger* (1963), the pot-bellied, cigar-gnawing General 'Buck' Turgidson in Stanley Kubrick's *Dr. Strangelove* (1964), Abraham in Huston's *The Bible* (1966), the title role in Franklin Shaffner's *Patton* (1970) and a surrogate Hemingway figure in Shaffner's adaptation of *Islands In The Stream* (1977). Oddly for a character actor, however, Scott is almost always the same person on screen, vigorous to the point of pugnacity, acting with his chin the way other actors do with their eyes – yet revealing, in his own eyes, unsuspected depths

in Krakatoa, East Of Java *(Cinerama Releasing, 1969)*

in his Hollywood career) in *The Young Lions* (1958). But his dark, matinee idol good looks were perhaps too dated for the changing cinema of the 60s and 70s; and, though he earned further Oscar nominations for *The Man In The Glass Booth* (1975) and *Julia* (1977), his reputation will ultimately rest on his films as a director – lush, academic adaptations of Turgenev and Von Horváth. DM

adopted when she herself became a professional actress. Magda Schneider is best remembered as the sweet but doomed ingenue of Max Ophüls' *Liebelei* (1933), but she also featured in numerous romantic and musical films during the interwar years, later emerging from semi-retirement in the 50s to play secondary roles in her daughter's first successes. For, in her teens, Romy was already the most popular young star of the German-speaking world – a more *gemütlich* Annette Funicello, perhaps – as 'Sissi', the future Empress Elizabeth, in an extremely sentimental cycle of films about the Austro-Hungarian royal family. These included *Sissi* (1956), *Sissi – Die Junge Kaiserin* (1957) and *Sissi – Schicksalsjahre Einer Kaiserin* (1958).

With a genuine talent, one surprisingly subtle and versatile, revealed in Luchino Visconti's cruelly witty episode 'The Job' in *Boccaccio 70* (1962), in Orson Welles' adaptation of Kafka's *The Trial* (of the same year), and in Otto Preminger's mammoth *The Cardinal* (1963), she seemed set for a major international career. But, as has happened with too many stylish European actresses, she was utterly wasted in Hollywood. And, following a much-publicised romance with Alain Delon, most of her later work was done in France (where she was a particular favourite of the director Claude Sautet in such middlebrow, middle-class dramas as *Les Choses De La Vie*, 1970, *César And Rosalie*, 1972, and *Une Histoire Simple*, 1978). Before tragically dying of a heart attack at the age of 44, Romy Schneider had movingly reprised her most famous role as Elizabeth, Empress of Austria in Visconti's *Ludwig* (1973). DM

of humour and intelligence.

Off screen, too, this star is an explosive personality. He is an aggressive perfectionist, incapable of suffering fools, gladly or otherwise. Following his much-publicised statement that the Academy Awards ritual was a nauseating, self-congratulatory 'meat parade', the Academy called his bluff with an Oscar for *Patton*. Admirably as good as his word, Scott contemptuously declined the bait.

In recent years, worthwhile roles have become scarce, and he himself directed a couple of films, *Rage* (1972) and *The Savage Is Loose* (1974), both of mildly liberal ideology. DM

in Patton *(20th Century-Fox, 1970)*

George Segal

Born **New York City, 13 February 1934**

George Segal is an actor whose films seem to turn up with astonishing regularity when one is travelling by air. Which is not to suggest that there is some aspect of his talent particularly conducive to in-flight viewing – merely that, since his on-screen personality had been shaped, he has displayed a certain reluctance to test or extend it. The upmarket light comedies in which he has come to specialise are perhaps, if one wished to be cruel, the cinematic equivalent of airline meals – pretty enough to look at, not unfilling, but bland, bland, bland. All of which would matter very little, did one not harbour the suspicion that Segal might have enjoyed a

in 1968

considerably richer career; for he possesses the gift – one shared by the actor he most resembles, Jack Lemmon, of making neurotic behaviour not only funny but genially sympathetic.

He was educated at Columbia University, then worked variously as a janitor, theatre usher and jazz musician before being conscripted into the army. Following his demobilization, he appeared on the New York stage and was one of the original members of Theodore J. Flicker's satirical revue 'The Premise'. (In spite of a busy film career he has continued to appear on Broadway, nor is he a stranger to American television). His film debut was in a strictly routine hospital soap opera titled, none too originally, *The Young Doctors* (1961), followed three years later by *The New Interns*. His graduation from such unstimulating material was effected through a single film, Mike Nichols' adaptation of the Pulitzer Prize-winning play by Edward Albee, *Who's Afraid Of Virginia Woolf?* (1966). Burton and Taylor were magnificent as the tired middle-aged professor and his frump of a wife who vent the long-simmering frustrations of their own unhappily childless marriage on two hapless guests, a young lecturer in biology and his understandably nervous wife. Perhaps the greatest compliment one can pay Segal and Sandy Dennis in the latter roles is that they were rarely overshadowed by the virtuoso histrionics of their seniors: Dennis won an Oscar, Segal a nomination.

In the same year he starred in an intriguing espionage thriller about the activities of neo-Nazis in contemporary Germany, *The Quiller Memorandum*. Intriguing partly because it was scripted by none other than Harold Pinter, who lent the dialogue a characteristically gnomic flavor; and partly because Segal's nervy, wholly American acting style clashed fruitfully with the dry, understated sarcasm of his co-star, Alec Guinness. In 1968 he made two memorable if not completely successful films, Roger Corman's *The St. Valentine's Day Massacre*, a lively but over-familiar account of the celebrated gangland

murders, and Sidney Lumet's *Bye Bye Braverman*, a very New Yorkish comedy about a group of Jewish intellectuals who meet at the funeral of an old friend. As the latter film proved, Segal's forte was contained harassment – he cornered the market in a register which one might describe as hangdog urbanity. This was seen to advantage in Irvin Kershner's *Loving* (1970), a touching, often very funny study of a New York illustrator who finds that his family life, professional ambitions and extra-marital involvements are all settling into parallel ruts; in *The Owl And The Pussycat* (same year), a pleasantly raunchy farce in which he teamed up with Barbra Streisand; and in the very amusing black comedy *Where's Poppa?* (same year), which cast him as a bachelor who decides to kill off his aged and importunate Momma (the delicious Ruth Gordon).

But if one single year were to be considered the highlight of his whole career, it would have to be 1973. On paper, *A Touch Of Class* might not have seemed anything too special: a fairly plotless romantic comedy, of a type found commonly in every period of film history, an apparently uninspired teaming – Segal and Glenda Jackson – and a trite, catchall title. Yet the result was a delight, with Segal as the brash executive who falls for the formidable Jackson during an encounter in Spain. It boosted his career, and earned her an Oscar. With director Melvin Frank and writer Jack Rose, the partnership was established again for *Lost And Found* (1979), a comedy in which Segal and Jackson play a pair of academics who meet and squabble on the ski slopes. As is the way with sequels, however, this second film left one wondering if perhaps one had not overrated the first: Segal did his usual, by then ultrafamiliar, number and his co-star seemed sour and abrasive beyond the demands of the comic plotting.

His second film of 1973 was Paul Mazursky's *Blume In Love*, as Californian in spirit as, say, *Bye Bye Braverman* was East Coast. A comedy both romantic and satirical – about a husband who spends the whole film recovering the wife he has alienated at its start – it benefited from a quite daring flashback structure which meant that, though much of it took place in the United States, it was in fact set in Venice throughout. And its final scene, with Segal, Susan Anspach and the camera waltzing round the Piazza San Marco to the strains of the 'Liebestod' and all the peripheral lovers of the film united at last (including, slyly, an updated Gustav

von Aschenbach and his slightly dubious Tadzio), was a cherishable moment.

It was also, unfortunately, the last moment in Segal's career when he succeeded in humanising the hysteria underlying his persona with a lovable, shaggy surface charm. It was perhaps the roles he was offered (or chose to play), perhaps the fact that he had, by the mid-70s, squeezed out every ounce of human juice left in the character – whatever, the remainder of his career (with a single exception) is of interest mainly to the in-flight movie bookers of airline companies. The exception was Robert Altman's *California Split* (1974), a free-wheeling, semi-improvisational study of compulsive gambling (the title is professional jargon for cut-throat poker) enhanced by one of the director's brilliant, multi-textured sound-tracks. Virtually plotless, it followed the meanderings of two punters (Segal and Elliott Gould) through various poker parlours (with many of the supporting roles taken by the real McCoy), finding themselves betting on just about everything, including the whimsical challenge of naming the Seven Dwarfs. Segal and Gould made such a wonderfully laid-back and eccentric pairing that, even after the film had run its course, one felt like spending lots more time in their company.

The same, alas, could never be said of *The Black Bird* (1975), a limp send-up of *The Maltese Falcon* and the whole 40s private-eye genre; of *The Duchess And The Dirtwater Fox* (1976), a charmless jumble of western parodies and slapstick in which Segal was teamed with Goldie Hawn; or of *Fun With Dick And Jane* (1977), a totally unsuccessful parody, and sometime apologia, of the capitalist way of life, in which it was distressing to see Segal and his co-star, Jane Fonda, make such heavy weather of the simplest scenes. *Rollercoaster* (also 1977) was just what its title suggests, a mildly scary fairground ride, with Segal consistently upstaged by the silly Sensurround process; *Who Is Killing The Great Chefs Of Europe?* (1978) was an indigestible gastronomic farce which prompted the immediate rejoinder 'Who cares?'; and *The Last Married Couple In America* (1979) might have prompted a no less swift response of 'Let's hope so!'

Given the direction that Segal's career has been taking over the past few years it is difficult to know where it can now go; but it might be worth recording the fact that one of his latest films, made in 1981, was ominously titled *Carbon Copy*. DM

with Patrick O'Neal (left) in King Rat *(Columbia, 1965)*

in Bye Bye Braverman *(Warner Bros., 1968)* ▷

Omar Sharif

Real name **Michael Shalhoub**
Born **Alexandria, Egypt, 10 April 1932**

Though born in Egypt, Omar Sharif is actually of Lebanese origin, and it was when he began acting in Egyptian films that he converted to Islam and changed his name to the arch-Egyptian one of Omar El-Sharif. With his soft, melting eyes, extravagantly long eyelashes and curly black hair and moustache, he was everybody's notion of a sensuous, smouldering but ultimately gentle Oriental Prince; and, forty or fifty years ago, he might well have become one of Hollywood's most adulated superstars. Yet the type of codified, somewhat kitschy sense of romance he traded in has never quite gone out of style, so that, if his career has been an extremely mediocre one, it is probably the result of his own atrocious judgment. Certainly, one often had the impression that his mind was elsewhere – perhaps on the bridge tournaments at which he is a recognised world master, perhaps on the numerous famous women – Barbra Streisand, Catherine Deneuve, Dyan Cannon – he has courted over the years.

Before breaking into the international market, he had quickly risen to become Egypt's top male star, an ascension aided by his marriage to Faten Hamama, the country's top female star. (They were later divorced.) From this period of his career, the only film at all familiar to Western audiences is *Goha* (1957), directed by Jacques Baratier. But when David Lean cast him in *Lawrence Of Arabia* in 1962, he became virtually overnight an international star and was nominated for an Oscar as best supporting actor. Whatever one's opinion of Lean's contestable epic, however, it towers over every single film in which Sharif subsequently appeared. From *Lawrence* to Lean's *Doctor Zhivago* in 1965, for example, his filmography reads: *The Fall Of The Roman Empire, Behold A Pale Horse, The Yellow Rolls-Royce* (all 1964), *Genghis Khan* and *Marco The Magnificent* (both 1965). *Zhivago* was, in many respects, a

in Lawrence Of Arabia *(Columbia, 1962)*

travesty of Pasternak's novel, as Sharif's performance was a travesty of its protagonist; nevertheless, as a middlebrow romantic spectacle with a larger-than-life heart-throb in the lead, it worked rather well, breaking box-office records throughout the world. Yet, no sooner was it completed than Sharif returned to the likes of *The Poppy Is Also A Flower* (1966), *The Night Of The Generals* and *More Than A Miracle* (both 1967).

His next commercially successful venture was William Wyler's biopic of Fanny Brice, *Funny Girl* (1968), in which, co-starring with Barbra Streisand, he played the Jewish gangster Nick Arnstein. (Though his acceptance of the role made him for

many years *persona non grata* in the Arab world, he reprised it in Herbert Ross's sequel *Funny Lady*, 1975.) Thereafter, he landed himself with comic regularity in some of the most notoriously bad movies ever made: eg *Che!* (1969), in which he was a preposterous Che Guevara to Jack Palance's Castro; Sidney Lumet's *The Appointment* (also 1969), a romantic melodrama booed at Cannes and barely released; *The Last Valley* (1971), an allegorical epic set during the Thirty Years War, which was also how long the film itself seemed to last; and *Inchon* (1980), a biopic of General Douglas MacArthur financed by Sun Yen Moon. As an actor, then, Omar Sharif is a wonderful bridge player. DM

in Battle Of Britain *(United Artists, 1969)*

Robert Shaw

Born **Westhoughton, England, 9 August 1927**
Died **1978**

Robert Shaw's father, a physician and a self-confessed alcoholic, committed suicide in 1939, and the young Robert was raised in Scotland and Cornwall. Already interested in his teens by acting as a career, he enrolled at the Royal Academy of Dramatic Art and first performed professionally in Stratford-on-Avon, at the Shakespeare Memorial Theatre. For seven years, he played mostly minor roles there and at London's Old Vic. His film debut

came in *The Dam Busters* (1954), but he did not really begin to make an impression until 1963, when he played both a cold-blooded assassin in the second James Bond thriller, *From Russia With Love*, and a gentle, lobotomised misfit in the film version of Harold Pinter's *The Caretaker*. He was excellent in the title role of a young Irish immigrant in Montreal in *The Luck Of Ginger Coffey* (1964), then was nominated for an Oscar for his robust performance as Henry VIII in Fred Zinnemann's *A Man For All Seasons* (1966). Shaw continued to portray rather tough, impassive characters in a variety of films, but he was notably eloquent as three historical figures: General Custer in *Custer Of The West* (1968), the

Spanish explorer Pizzaro in *The Royal Hunt Of The Sun* (1970, an adaptation of Peter Shaffer's play), and Lord Randolph Churchill in *Young Winston* (1972).

In 1973 he graduated almost imperceptibly to leading roles: on a modest scale in *The Hireling*, a quietly affecting film version of L.P. Hartley's novel in which he played a classbound chauffeur hopelessly in love with an aristocratic young lady (Sarah Miles); and on a worldwide scale in *The Sting*, as the all-powerful gang boss gleefully conned out of a fortune by Newman and Redford. Because of his undoubted intelligence, however, there was usually something almost sympathetic about his villains, no matter how frightening and sinister. Such was the case with *The Taking Of Pelham One Two Three* (1974), a diverting heist movie about the hijacking of a New York subway train; and, especially, with his melancholy Sheriff of Nottingham in Richard Lester's nostalgic tale of heroes (and villains) grown old and tired, *Robin And Marian* (1976). But though he ended his career as the star of some variable adventure movies, including *Swashbuckler* (1976), *The Deep* (1977) and *Force 10 From Navarone* (1978), he will perhaps be best remembered for his grizzled old sea-dog, the poor man's Captain Ahab, in Steven Spielberg's *Jaws* (1975).

Shaw, it must be added, also made a considerable reputation for himself as a novelist and playwright. His books, including 'The Hiding Place' (adapted, very feebly, for the cinema as *Situation Hopeless – But Not Serious*, 1965, with the improbable pairing of Robert Redford and Alec Guinness) and 'The Man In The Glass Booth' – were admired by literary critics; and the latter work, concerning the trial in Israel of Adolf Eichmann, was turned into a play which ran successfully in London and on Broadway. Very much a family man, with ten children from three marriages (the second to actress Mary Ure), he died suddenly of a heart attack at the age of 51. DM

in Othello (Warner Bros., 1965)

Maggie Smith

Born **Ilford, England, 28 December 1934**

The fact that Maggie Smith has twice been the recipient of Oscars (for *The Prime Of Miss Jean Brodie*, 1969, and *California Suite*, 1978) and twice a nominee (for *Othello*, 1965, and *Travels With My Aunt*, 1972) suggests a rather more distinguished film career than has actually been the case. Though a supremely brilliant stage actress, she has rarely succeeded in adapting her mannered high-comedy style to the more diffuse demands of the cinema; her characterisations, even if they have won the regular

support of the Academy's voters, tend to be too highly-pitched, too self-conscious – in a word, theatrical. Another criticsm which might be levelled against her is a certain reluctance to act *with* other performers: she tends to work all alone in a corner, as it were, oblivious to what is going on around her.

The daughter of a professor in pathology at Oxford, she trained for the theatre at the Oxford Playhouse School, making her West End debut in the kind of modest 'intimate' revue in vogue during the 50s. After her 1959/60 season at the Old Vic, she was invited by Sir Laurence Olivier to join the National Theatre, where she soon triumphed both in drama (eg as Desdemona to Olivier's Othello, a

performance she repeated in the subsequent film version) and comedy (eg her wonderfully witty and idiomatic performances in 'The Beaux' Strategem' and 'The Recruiting Officer'). Her film career started less auspiciously with a couple of forgotten programmers, *Nowhere To Go* (1958) and *Go To Blazes* (1962); but as a mousy, sat-upon secretary in *The V.I.P.s* (1963) she stole several scenes from her prestigious co-stars. She was also effective as Rex Harrison's secretary in Joseph L. Mankiewicz's stylish updating of 'Volpone', *The Honey Pot* (1967) and as Peter Ustinov's roguish accomplice in a diverting heist movie *Hot Millions* (1968). But the role she will always be remembered for in the cinema, one in which her rather dry, brittle, calculated manner was perfectly attuned to the material, was the eponymous Edinburgh school-mistress haranguing her awe-struck charges, her 'crème de la crème', in *The Prime Of Miss Jean Brodie*. Smith (whose co-star was her then husband, the actor Robert Stephens) carried the film on her not-so-frail shoulders, and her piercing voice and 'naice' Lowlands accent rang in one's ears long after the closing credits. An Oscar-winning performance if ever there was one!

In later years, she frequently returned to the stage (notably in Stratford, Ontario); and with two memorable exceptions, she has primarily appeared in film cameo roles: eg in *Oh! What A Lovely War* (1969); *Murder By Death* (1976), a whodunit spoof in which she and David Niven parodied Myrna Loy and William Powell; *California Suite*, in which she won an Oscar for playing an actress who fails to win an Oscar; and a pair of Agatha Christie extravaganzas, *Death On The Nile* and *Evil Under The Sun* (1978 and 1981). The exceptions were *Travels With My Aunt*, George Cukor's charming adaptation of the Graham Greene 'entertainment' in which she played the eccentric title role, and James Ivory's *Quartet* (1981), where she looked very much a creature of the 20s. On the whole, however, Smith has been more of a scene-stealer than a genuinely filmic actress. DM

Terence Stamp

Born **London, 1940**

Like his father, a tug captain on the Thames, Terence Stamp is a Londoner through and through. Wishing to become an actor, he applied for and won a scholarship to the Webber-Douglas drama school. A spell in repertory followed – then in 1962 came the break of a lifetime. Peter Ustinov was casting his film version of Herman Melville's *Billy Budd* and looking for a beautiful young man to play the title role. More on the strength of his appearance than his experience, Stamp was given the part, and managed to convey the essence of Melville's angelic innocent so well that he received an Oscar nomination. After a minor role as a brash student in *Term Of Trial* (also 1962 and starring Sir Laurence Olivier), Stamp landed another plum role – one almost as difficult as Billy Budd. In William Wyler's *The Collector* (1965), an adaptation of the best-selling novel by John Fowles, Stamp played an antisocial young lepidopterist who kidnaps a young woman (Samantha Eggar) in the hope that she will eventually come to love him. In truth, the character was more of a literary conceit than a fleshed-out human being; but Stamp was touchingly shy and graceless and won the best actor award at that year's Cannes Festival.

Accompanied everywhere by his girlfriend, the model Jean Shrimpton, Stamp became one of the leading lights of the 'Swinging London' scene in the 60s, and it was in that modish spirit that he sent up his somewhat rarefied image in Joseph Losey's espionage spoof *Modesty Blaise* (1966), playing Willie Garvin to Monica Vitti's glamorous Modesty. In the following year, he appeared as Sergeant Troy in John Schlesinger's turgid and interminable adaptation of Hardy's *Far From The Madding Crowd*, then adjusted to the miserabilist kitchen-sink natu-

in 1962

ralism of Ken Loach's *Poor Cow*. In 1968 he made two quite extraordinary films in Italy, one of them exploiting the slightly Satanic quality of his beauty, the other allowing him his last fling at Billy Budd-like purity. *Spirits Of The Dead* was a three-part film based on a trio of Poe's 'Tales Of Mystery And Imagination'. The first, by Vadim, was trite and meretricious; the second, by Louis Malle, flat and academic. But the third, Fellini's 'Toby Dammit' or 'Never Bet The Devil Your Head', was a vertiginous fable in which Stamp, an alcoholic actor, is pursued by Satan in the form of a sweet little girl with a large white beach ball. The second of his Italian films was Pasolini's *Theorem*, a weird allegory about an angel

who changes the lives of a bourgeois family by sleeping with each of them in turn.

At which point Stamp, a quintessentially 60s creature, seemed to vanish with the decade. His subsequent films were an obscure bunch – from *The Mind Of Mr. Soames* (1970), in which he was cast as a patient brought out of a lifelong coma at the age of 30, to Peter Brook's unconvincing account of the early years of G.I. Gurdjieff, *Meetings With Remarkable Men* (1979). In *Superman* (1978) and *Superman II* (1980), however, he made an amusing arch-villain by the name of General Zod. From angel to devil, from Budd to Zod – such has been the curious itinerary of Terence Stamp. DM

Barbra Streisand

Real name **Barbara Streisand**
Born **Brooklyn, New York, 24 April 1942**

Perhaps the wittiest and wisest thing ever said about Barbra Streisand was an apparently paradoxical remark made by her ex-roommate, a woman who had known her during her early uphill struggle. 'Barbara,' she said, 'has settled for more.' 'More', in her case, might be the kind of gilt-edged, 100% stardom she has enjoyed for almost two decades, a pre-eminence which not even bad movies and ugly rumours of megalomania have managed to chip away. Streisand has appeared in a dozen features to date, in every one of which she has been the undisputed star, and the thought of her sliding down a credits list to even second or third place is simply mind-boggling. But what was intended by the phrase 'settled for? Probably that she decided early on in her career that the usual processes of learning and maturing, which commonly presuppose a willingness to listen to and take advice from others, were not for her. Apart from a few years at the beginning, she has managed, quite simply, to skip the intermediate rungs of the ladder; and the 26-year-old woman who played Fanny Brice in *Funny Girl* way back in 1968 was, by all accounts, just as sassy, self-assured and tyrannical as the 40-year-old woman who produced, directed, composed, scripted and starred in *Yentl* (1983). In short, there has been no *growth* in her career, merely *expansion*.

She was born, as is evident from her voice and manner, in Brooklyn, of middle-class parents: her father, who died when she was still a baby, taught English and psychology in a local high school; her mother, prior to her marriage, had harboured certain show business ambitions even, in her youth, making a test recording of Sigmund Romberg's ballad 'One Kiss'. Little Barbara was something of an ugly duckling, with a gawky physique and an imperfect face, marred by a famously long and prominent nose. And though she never did grow up into a swan, it may be said that, by sheer force of personality, she succeeded in making conventional swans seem insipid and characterless. There has usually come a moment in a Streisand film – so regularly, indeed, that one has sometimes wondered whether it is written into the contract – when her leading man gazes at her in wonderment and stammers out, 'Why, you're – you're *beautiful!*' And it is a measure of Streisand's capacity to silence

doubts – never mind out-and-out criticism – that this line is never met with incredulous giggles. Her beauty is by no means skin deep – but beautiful she most certainly can be when she chooses.

In any event, despite her awkward features, she was from childhood driven by a desire for fame in the sphere of entertainment. While studying at the Malden Bridge Summer Theater in upstate New York (where she had immediately sought the leading role in their production of 'The Teahouse Of The August Moon' – notwithstanding the fact that the character was male), she eked out a living as a waitress in a Chinese restaurant. Later, poverty-stricken in New York and spending most of her free time attending auditions, she worked as a switch-board operator and theatre usherette. Her first break was winning (as a singer, when she yearned to be a straight actress) a nightclub talent contest in Green-wich Village, which led to regular appearances on the city's late-night circuit and even a handful of television spots. Al Ramrus, a writer on a minor, un-syndicated talk show, in which she featured, wrote this description of her at that period: 'She was like the *essence* of every confused, not-very-attractive girl who wanted extravagantly more out of life than birth or circumstances could possibly give her. Her voice, her life-style, were almost fictional – like a bad 20th Century-Fox musical – that I told her that whether she could sing or not she was going to be a star.'

Finally, in 1962, she landed a small role in a Broadway musical 'I Can Get It For You Wholesale': small as written, the part of a frumpy office clerk with man problems, as played by Streisand, literally stopped the show. Though a few of the critics were unkind about her kookie appearance, none questioned the fact that a great new star had burst on the scene. With her inimitable way of handling a song, she quickly became one of New York's most sought-after performers, gracing elegant supper clubs and guest spots on TV shows; and the consecration was complete when, in 1964, the leading role of 'Funny Girl', Jule Styne's terrific musical biography of another 'ugly duckling', Fanny Brice, made her the toast of the town. At the same time, CBS signed her to a multi-year, multi-million dollar contract for a series of albums, all of which were to enjoy tremendous popularity. During the out-of-town run of 'Wholesale', she had married the show's leading man, Elliott Gould, by whom she has a son; when her fame started to outstrip his, however, the marriage degenerated into an endless round of recriminations and regrets, and they were divorced in 1968.

Streisand's Broadway triumph was repeated in the film version of *Funny Girl*, for which, in an almost unique tie with Katharine Hepburn, she won an Academy Award; during its shooting, she had a much-publicised affair with her co-star (if anyone can be said to *co*-star with such a force of nature), Omar Sharif. And though everyone, herself included, believed her to be much too young, it must have seemed that the only possible follow-up to a success of such magnitude was the title role of matchmaker Dolly Levi in the upcoming film of the longest-running Broadway musical of all time, *Hello, Dolly!* (1969). In the event, the doubters were both right and wrong. Wrong about Streisand herself, whose funny and vibrant performance quashed any doubts as to the character's age – it simply ceased to be a problem. But right about how her need to meddle with practically every aspect of the shooting might unbalance the film. *Hello, Dolly!*, directed by Gene Kelly, turned out to be an elephantine spectacle quite out of tune with the tastes of film audiences, and it was a box-office disaster. Moreover, Streisand's not always productive interference alienated both co-stars and crew. On one occasion, when she stomped off the set in fury, Walter Matthau shouted, 'Just remember, Betty Hutton once thought *she* was indispensable!' and was greeted with a round of applause from the assembled technicians. (Later, he remarked – understandably if, one trusts, hyperbolically – 'I have more talent in one of my farts than she has in her whole body.')

Her next musical, Minnelli's *On A Clear Day You Can See Forever*, co-starring Yves Montand, also flopped (though Streisand had rarely looked more seductive); and she wisely decided to shift gears by making a trio of more modest comedies: *The Owl And The Pussycat* (1970), in which she played a call girl meeting cute with George Segal; Peter Bog-danovich's hugely successful Hawksian comedy-thriller *What's Up Doc?* (1972), whose highlight was her glorious rendition of Cole Porter's 'You're The Top'; and *Up The Sandbox* (also 1972), in which she gave an effective, astonishingly restrained perform-ance as an ordinary New York housewife.

From the mid-70s on, each of Streisand's films (apart, perhaps, from a couple of comedies in the vein of those mentioned above: *For Pete's Sake*, 1974, and *The Main Event*, 1979) has been, if nothing else, an event; and she herself has gradually moved from being a widely resented power-behind-the-throne to being the total mistress of her own show business destiny. Sidney Pollack's *The Way We Were* (1973) was a self-indulgent, soft-centred tale of love and leftism in the 30s and 40s entirely predicated on the charismatic coupling of Streisand and Robert Redford. *Funny Lady* (1975) was Her-bert Ross's less successful sequel to the Fanny Brice story, in which, on a clear day, you might just have spotted the rest of the cast. And, directed by Streisand's former hairdresser, now inseparable companion, Jon Peters, *A Star Is Born* (1976) was a pop-orientated remake of the Wellman and Cukor films of the same title. It was strictly for fans – whose numbers, if the film's commercial success may be taken as a guide, were legion – but it earned her a second Academy Award for the composition of the song 'Evergreen'.

In the early 80s, she purchased the rights to Isaac Bashevis Singer's novella about a young woman at the turn of the century who is obliged to disguise herself as a boy in order to study the Torah. The result, *Yentl*, has proved to be another public triumph for her, even if critics carped and Singer himself publicly expressed his disapproval of the whole project. Yet such criticisms are perhaps short-sighted. For by not only producing and directing, writing and composing this mammoth project, but also singing every one of its seventeen songs and playing both the female and, in a sense, *male* leads, Barbra Streisand has achieved what she probably always set out to do – she has metamorphosed herself into a film. In a dreary age of committees and compromise, long may she reign! DM

with John Richardson in On A Clear Day You Can See Forever *(Paramount, 1970)*

Donald Sutherland

Born **St. John, New Brunswick, Canada, 17 July 1934**

Before becoming a star, Donald Sutherland had appeared to no very striking effect in a joblot of eleven films, from *Dr Terror's House Of Horrors* (1965) to *Oedipus The King* (1968). He had also, earlier, been a disc jockey at a Nova Scotia radio station, a student at the London Academy of Music and Dramatic Art and a stage actor in several English plays. But it was in 1970 as the gangling, spaced-out, irreverent surgeon Hawkeye Pierce in Robert Altman's Korean War satire *M.A.S.H.*, one of the key films of its period, that he made his reputation: he could even have been described, with his co-star Elliott Gould, as something of a cult figure. Sutherland thereafter selected his projects with care, so that, aside from the statutory portion of undemanding roles that is every actor's lot, he was impressive as a moviemaker with 'director's block' in Paul Mazursky's messy but interesting *Alex In Wonderland* (1970); a mad clergyman in Jules Feiffer's *Little Murders* (1971); an enigmatic cop in Alan Pakula's *Klute* (1971); a tormented parent in Nicolas Roeg's thriller set in a cold, wintry Venice, *Don't Look Now* (1973); and as the eponymous sensualist in *Fellini's Casanova* (1976), his heavily made-up features as marbly as if stamped on a coin.

His involvement with political activism has remained strong since the 60s and he featured prominently in the filmic record of Jane Fonda's anti-war troop show *F.T.A.* (1972), which he also co-scripted, co-produced and co-directed. DM

in Klute (Warner Bros., 1971)

in An Almost Perfect Affair (Paramount, 1979)

Monica Vitti

Real name **Maria Louisa Ceciarelli**
Born **Rome, 3 November 1931**

One of the glories of film history is that series of passionate love affairs conducted on-screen between certain directors and actresses. Couples which spring to mind are D.W. Griffith and Lillian Gish, Josef von Sternberg and Marlene Dietrich, George Cukor and Katharine Hepburn, Jean-Luc Godard and Anna Karina – and, of course, Michelangelo Antonioni and Monica Vitti.

Ravishingly beautiful as only Italian blondes can be, Vitti proved to be an ideal interpreter of the Antonioniesque woman – a cool, complex, alienated victim of existential *ennui* – in four major works of postwar European cinema, *L'Avventura* (1960), *The Night* (1961), *The Eclipse* (1962) and *The Red Desert* (1964). No contemporary study of the medium was without its illustration of her posed enigmatically against the lonely expanse of a white wall, or overshadowed by some glass-and-cement tower block looming out of an industrial wasteland.

Yet the virtual monopoly which Antonioni held over Vitti in the early 60s tended to obscure the fact that she was no passive Galatea requiring a Pygmalion to breathe life into her: to general surprise, she has turned out to be an expert light comedienne. Since breaking professional and emotional ties with him, she has starred in a sequence of commercially successful Italian farces, the best-known being *The Pizza Triangle* (GB: *Jealousy Italian Style*, 1970). Few of these admittedly minor efforts have been considered worth exporting, but Vitti seemed the essence of Swinging London verve and chic as the eponymous heroine of Joseph Losey's spoof *Modesty Blaise* (1966). DM

Jon Voight

Born **Yonkers, New York, 29 December 1938**

Jon Voight's (surprisingly brief) filmography reads like a roll call of all that is 'liberal' in contemporary Hollywood: *Midnight Cowboy* (1969), *Catch-22* (1970), *The Revolutionary* (1970), *Deliverance* (1972), *Conrack* (1974), *Coming Home* (1978). And, considering his blond, boyish features and 6ft-2ins athletic frame, this craving to be taken seriously at any cost commands respect, even if his judgment has not always kept pace with his good intentions.

Of Czech descent, the son of a professional golfer, he was an avid participant in amateur dramatics at his Yonkers high school and at Catholic University, from which he graduated in 1960. Moving easily from Broadway (notably in 'The Sound Of Music') to off-Broadway, from summer stock to TV, he inevitably gravitated towards the cinema. After a trio of minor, forgettable roles, he was offered the chance of a lifetime – to play Joe Buck, the pathetic huckster turned hustler in John Schlesinger's *Midnight Cowboy*. His haunted pretty-boy features lent real emotion to an otherwise vulgar, though widely admired, study of Manhattan low life; and, along with his co-star Dustin Hoffman, Voight was nominated for an Academy Award.

If he appeared most impressive in John Boorman's *Deliverance* as a thoughtful city dweller cast adrift in the heart of the Deep South's darkness, it was for his performance as a crippled anti-war Vietnam veteran, involved with Jane Fonda, in Hal Ashby's wet and woolly *Coming Home* that he finally secured the Oscar that earlier had eluded him. DM

in 1980

Liv Ullmann

Born **Tokyo, 16 December 1939**

Though, like many of Ingmar Bergman's repertory company, the radiant and well-scrubbed Liv Ullmann strikes one as archetypically Swedish, she is in fact of Norwegian stock, born in Japan where her father, an engineer, was stationed, and raised in Canada. After his death, she returned to Norway with her mother and it was not long before she gained prominence there on both stage and screen.

In the mid-60s occurred the meeting of her life – with Bergman, then at the height of his prestige as a director. Bergman's public and private involvement with her was so complete – they both divorced their respective spouses – that the films they made together would be inconceivable with a different actress. *Persona* (1966), *Hour Of The Wolf* and

in Lost Horizon (Columbia, 1973)

Shame (1968), *The Passion Of Anna* (1969), *Cries And Whispers* (1972), *Scenes From A Marriage* (1973) and *Face To Face* (1976) are psychodramas of such emotional intensity as to be almost embarrassing to watch.

The other side of that intensity, in both director and actress, tends to be a snivelling Scandinavian dourness, depressingly evident in the two works on which they collaborated again following Ullmann's abortive sojourn in Hollywood: *The Serpent's Egg* (1977) and *Autumn Sonata* (1978). Ullmann became internationally famous by seeming profoundly Swedish. When she herself 'went international', in such disasters as the embarrassingly idiotic *Pope Joan* (1972), the musical remake of *Lost Horizon* (1973) and *The Abdication* (in which she played Queen Christina of Sweden, 1974), she seriously compromised her standing as an actress. And there is still a question-mark hovering over her future career. DM

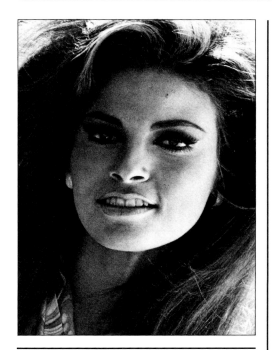

Raquel Welch

Real name **Raquel Tejada**
Born **Chicago, 5 September 1940**

No matter how posterity judges her as an actress, Raquel Welch's position in the history of publicity is secure. By the end of the 60s, she had appeared in seventeen films, not one of any real distinction – a fact, however, which did not prevent her from becoming literally world-famous. Three crucial factors contributed to this fame: her own ruthless determination to make the grade; her involvement with a promoter named Patrick Smith, who no less ruthlessly set about merchandising his client; and the kind of voluptuously Amazonian physique fantasised about by male spectators from the age of 12 onwards. When her Alpine breasts could be displayed to such advantage in the prehistoric designer bikini she sported in *One Million Years B.C.* (1966), it scarcely mattered that the film's dialogue consisted mostly of grunts. Indeed, these aptly achoed the grunts emitted by the male portion of its audience.

Welch's early years constituted a long preparation for her ultimate stardom; a drama course at San Diego State College, repertory theatre experience, modelling, bit parts in potboilers and some minor plastic surgery. The problem is that, as a star, Welch has found it impossible to avoid being typecast as a campy icon, most notoriously in the title role of the execrable *Myra Breckinridge* (1970). And though she was quite poignant as James Coco's put-upon companion in *The Wild Party* (1975), and a revelation as Lauren Bacall's replacement in the Broadway musical 'Woman Of The Year', her future looks none too promising. DM

Michael York

Born **Fulmer, England, 27 March 1942**

Pretty without being effeminate, athletic without being muscle-bound, well-spoken without being aggressively 'cultured', Michael York would seem to possess every quality required for movie stardom. That, in the event, his career has never truly taken off is less the sign of some incipient lack of talent than of the rapidly changing needs of contemporary cinema. The kind of dashing, devil-may-care roles for which his physique suits him do still exist, but they are either Shakespearean (Lucentio in Franco Zeffirelli's *The Taming Of The Shrew*, 1967, and Tybalt in the same director's *Romeo And Juliet*, 1968) or parodic (d'Artagnan in Richard Lester's *The Three* and *Four Musketeers*, 1974/5, and Beau Geste in Marty Feldman's *The Last Remake Of Beau Geste*, 1977). When cast in straight romantic, nostalgic or historical tosh, he can appear quite impossibly stiff and dated – as in *Alfred The Great* (1969), in which he was King Guthrum, *Lost Horizon* (1973), *Murder On The Orient Express* (1974) and the preposterous courtroom whodunit, *Conduct Unbecoming* (1975).

A few directors have succeeded in teasing more

ambiguous performances out of him. Joseph Losey in *Accident* (1967); Hal Prince, who slyly exploited the campy appeal of his boyish good looks in an uneven but amusing black comedy, *Something For Everyone* (1970); and Bob Fosse who, in a piece of inspired casting, selected York to play the languidly homosexual 'Christopher Isherwood' to Liza Minnelli's ripe Sally Bowles in *Cabaret* (1972). DM

Susannah York

Real name **Susannah Yolande Fletcher**
Born **London, 9 January 1941**

It was Susannah York's misfortune not to have been born thirty years sooner: her delicate English rose charm, made more beguiling by lively, intelligent eyes and an aura of unstated sexuality, would have established her as the kind of respectable but flighty heroine often found in British films of the 40s. As it is, her somewhat incoherent career has made less of an impression than her undoubted talents deserved. After graduating from the Royal Academy of Dramatic Art, and a spell in repertory and pantomime (years later, she made a delightful Peter Pan), she first attracted attention as an adolescent girl trembling on the brink of womanhood in *The Greengage Summer* (1961). She soon gained an international reputation with appearances in *Tom Jones* (1963) and *Freud*. The dubious principle underlying John Huston's biopic of Sigmund Freud (played by Montgomery Clift) was to concentrate the great man's discoveries in a single 'composite' patient; and York made a brave stab at this hysteria-laden and impossible role.

She managed to retain her dignity in Robert Aldrich's crass drama of lesbianism, *The Killing Of Sister George* (1968), and well deserved her Oscar nomination for a touching performance as a marathon dancer in *They Shoot Horses, Don't They?* (1971). But perhaps her most challenging experience was Robert Altman's underrated *Images* (1972), in which she played a schizophrenic author of children's books whose fantasies begin to materialise in disturbingly real fashion. Her own, highly successful children's tale, 'In Search Of Unicorns', was quoted at length in the film. DM

in The Seventh Dawn (United Artists, 1964)

Tuesday Weld

Real name **Susan Ker Weld**
Born **New York City, 27 August 1943**

If one limited one's data to her filmography alone, one could be forgiven for dismissing Tuesday Weld as an irretrievably minor starlet, as witness such dispiriting titles as *Rock, Rock, Rock!*, *Because They're Young*, *Sex Kittens Go To College* and *The Private Lives Of Adam And Eve*. Certainly, a far more prestigious list could be compiled of those films which, out of bad judgment, she turned down eg *Lolita*, *Bonnie And Clyde* and *True Grit*.

Yet, despite Weld's blonde sex-kitten image (and her adopted name), the cult which has recently grown up around her is more justified than most. As Steve McQueen's girlfriend in the sad comedy *Soldier In The Rain* (1963), and again in *The*

in 1980

Cincinnati Kid (1965), she was possessed of a touching, almost trembling, vulnerability, rarely shedding a tear yet somehow conveying the impression that tears were never far away. In George Axelrod's curious satire *Lord Love A Duck* (1966), she showed a real aptitude for screwball comedy; while, conversely, as a sexy high-school psychopath in *Pretty Poison* (1971), she managed to be both scary and funny.

That there has always seemed something oddly off-balance about Weld is perhaps due to an unenviable private life. At the age of three, she already supported her family as a child model and TV performer. She suffered her first breakdown at nine, was an alcoholic at ten and attempted suicide at twelve. Later, she was briefly married (to Dudley Moore), divorced, and saw her house burn to the ground. Miraculously, none of these wheels has succeeded in breaking so exquisite a butterfly. DM

THE 70s

INTRODUCED BY MARK Le FANU

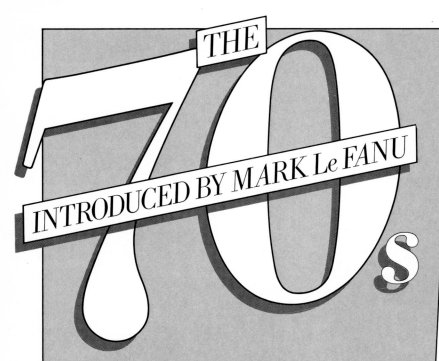

The break-up of the old fashioned structure of the studio system that had first become noticeable in the early 60s continued apace to the end of the decade and into the beginning of the 70s, accelerated by the truly disastrous box-office returns across the board for the years 1969–1971. Later on in the 70s Hollywood was to stage a dramatic comeback, seemingly with all the odds against it. But one of the side-effects that can be put down to the final collapse of the old command structure, *circa* 1970, was the final emancipation of the actor and the actress from a sort of wholesale bondage to contract. In cinema's 'golden age' – the 20s, 30s and 40s – it was customary for a studio to place an actor that it liked under a five, or a six, or a seven year contract (alternatively: engaging him for a specified number of movies). The usually generous financial provision and the guaranteed security were supposed to make up for the inconvenience occasioned by the otherwise almost wholesale curtailment of personal liberty.

The 70s consolidated the era of the independent producer-director, and brought a new strain of creativity to cinema art. Adventurous, versatile and intellectual, as well as commercial (witness The Godfather *and* Apocalypse Now*), Francis Ford Coppola was in the vanguard.*

As we know, however, it didn't. The glamorous public side of the lives of the stars, recounted in numerous magazine articles and fed by the avid publicity machine, ran counter, in too many cases, to the truth of the matter. The memoirs of the stars of the middle period of the century – Lana Turner, Joan Crawford, Margaret Sullavan – provide some of the most melancholy reading matter in the entire history of biography. It would be wrong to claim that modern 'post-contractual' actors and actresses are immune from

stress: from the divorces, suicides, addictions, and falls from grace that plagued their predecessors so sorely. But it must be helpful for the stars of the 70s (and 80s), to be able to live where they want to – on East Coast or West Coast or neither – and bring up their families like ordinary people.

The laconic and macho star of westerns and violent thrillers, Clint Eastwood was one of a number of actors who turned director during the 70s. Here he lines up a take for Breezy *(Universal, 1973) which starred, not Eastwood, but one of the durable 'old guard', William Holden.*

The increasing fragmentation of the studio structure led, then, to a merciful slackening of pressure on the private lives of the stars. There wasn't, any longer – and quite simply – so much at stake. Cinema is, and always will be, an industry full of heavies – there are too many mixed interests tied up in it for it to be anything else – but the tyrant with his fat cigar who, on a whim, could play havoc with your private life had now become a relic of yesterday. Greater relaxation, then; less hypocrisy. It leads to nicer, saner people – actors included. The remaining vestiges of the neurotic paternalism which treated them like pampered children to be bribed, praised or upbraided, had vanished.

Hollywood itself, however, as we have said, recovered remarkably well. Once the dust had settled and the studios had reorganised themselves (usually by amalgamation with some larger industrial conglomerate) there poured out a stream of pictures which for richness, variety and intelligence compare with the very best of the past. Contrary to what is often stated, the 70s were fine years for cinema.

The entrepreneurial confidence responsible for all this is locked up in the American genius. Talented men, fortunately, abound in each generation, expert at raising capital and making it work for them. First there are the money men. But then there are the producers and directors. Increasingly, at the top end of the market, the two functions become difficult to separate. Starting with Francis Ford Coppola, whose success with *The Godfather* (1970) at the beginning of the decade was seminal, and going on in due course to Martin Scorsese, Steven Spielberg, George Lucas, Robert Altman, Michael Cimino, Brian De Palma, John Milius etc., the 70s saw emerge a veritable academy of original directorial talent, men in the grip of a personal vision, and determined, where necessary, to extend the bounds of cinema to accommodate it.

Naturally, a rich time for directors is also a rich time for actors. For the new kind of film, it could be said, came new kinds of actors and actresses. The stars of the 60s – Jack Nicholson, Robert Redford, Clint Eastwood, Warren Beatty etc. – belong culturally to the protestant American tradition. The terrific input forged in the 70s by Roman Catholic Italian-American directors (Coppola again; also Scorsese and Cimino) meant the stars took on a more ethnic, one might almost say, a more European, colouring. Al Pacino and Robert De Niro are in this respect key stars of the decade – though

The Italian-American contingent of actors and directors contributed a new strain of vigorous realism to the decade. In the forefront were Robert De Niro (left) and Martin Scorsese, on set here for Taxi Driver *(Columbia, 1976). The uniquely gifted De Niro portrayed a Vietnam veteran running amok in Manhattan, in a film which violently mirrored the concerns of its time.*

the effect is to be seen right across the board, not only in the major roles, but also (and even especially) in the character parts, making one aware of an incredible fund of talent that might otherwise have lain dormant, or discernible only in theatre. Here again, actually, *The Godfather* with its occasional recourse to subtitling (for example, in the 'Sicilian' scenes in Part II) provides a sort of allegorical picture of the 70s, with the three non-Italian stars (Robert Duvall, James Caan, Diane Keaton) being constantly edged out of the way in favour of actors who were – or who (in the case of Brando) looked as if they were – Italian.

Naturally, to these simple observations there are exceptions; and the 70s, as well as being the decade of De Niro, Pacino, John Travolta, Sylvester Stallone etc., is also the decade of Burt Reynolds and Sissy Spacek: than whom, in their completely different ways, no stars could be more purely 'American'.

But in a way it does give us the clue. It is fascinating to watch the 70s with hindsight, noticing the key moment of emergence of stars who will subsequently become famous. Who, for instance, could have said at the beginning of the decade as between (say) Robert De Niro and Michael Sarrazin, which of the two at its end would be the stronger and better known star? The 70s are an identifiable period in the sense that one is able to be present at the the *blooming* of talent. Men and women like De Niro, Travolta, Spacek, Reynolds, Meryl Streep and Diane Keaton start the decade in obscurity, and then by their own efforts (but also by the luck of being offered the right films) end up established in the pantheon.

A word or two about acting 'style': the invocation of 'authenticity', begun in the 50s among actors like Brando and Dean, steadily gained ground in the 70s. A star, in the past, was the incarnation of a particular stereotype. When the stereotypes were good of their kind there was much fun to be had in meeting them in as many situations as the ingenuity of the screenwriter could muster. One knew that the exercise was artificial; but it was supported by a tactful aesthetic separation between *what* the stars represented on stage, and *who* they represented as private individuals. (As I have remarked, it didn't, as far as personal happiness went, let them off in the end any lighter). What we see in the 70s, however, is the slackening of this comedic insouciance. The old stars scarcely even *acted*. But the new stars act away as if their lives depended on it. There is an earnestness – a theatricality – in 70s cinema that might more properly be devoted to performing Ibsen at the National Theatre. The lessons of Stella Adler and the Actors Studio have been taken to heart and interiorised. The 70s was a decade of studious professionalism.

As the attendance in cinemas during the 70s continued remorselessly to decline (though huge box office successes in individual films make up for the decline financially), so, finally, there might be a tendency to think of the cultural phenomenon of the 'star' as itself being on the wane. Nowadays, a whole generation

Jack Nicholson consolidated his position as a star who could command the box-office in the 70s (and 80s). Here, he discusses a point with director Roman Polanski (left) during filming of the masterly Chinatown *(Paramount, 1974).*

of older people seldom go to the cinema at all. It is possible to meet quite intelligent people who have never heard of Robert De Niro. (Unthinkable in the 30s, the equivalent *homme sage* denying an acquaintance with Gary Cooper). As for the younger generation, *their* heroes are pop stars and tennis players. Alternatively: robots and computers (fed, of course, by movies like *Star Wars*). Television and the advent of the modern successful soap opera (*Dallas*, *Dynasty* etc) have, in addition, transferred our focus of interest to the smaller screen – both literally and metaphorically diminishing the concept of glamour.

Still, one oughtn't be too pessimistic. However close in kind the two media appear, finally they are extraordinarily different. Cinema remains throughout the 70s great and unique; the testing-ground of quality; the goal to which professionals aspire. The vigour and resourcefulness of the medium – as well as its capacity for renewal – may be glimpsed, one hopes, in the following pages.

By the 1970s, the movie star as icon to the nation was largely superseded by the TV star. An almost hysterical public adulation was (and still is) accorded to J.R. and Sue-Ellen of 'Dallas' soap-opera fame. In real life they are Larry Hagman and Linda Gray.

Alan Alda

Born **New York City, 28 January 1936**

If Woody Allen suggests the neurosis of the comedian, Alan Alda temporarily suggests the opposite. The spritely, grey-eyed and preppy-looking actor has about him an enviable aura of competence and sanity. Best known, of course, as 'Hawkeye' in television's longest-running comedy series M*A*S*H (inaugurated 1974), he is equally at home in the theatre and in the cinema, for which latter category he not only acts (*The Mephisto Waltz*, 1971, *Same Time Next Year*, 1978, *California Suite*, 1979), but directs (*The Four Seasons*, 1981) and writes screenplays (*The Seduction of Joe Tynan*, 1979). An astonishingly versatile fellow. When one hears further that he is the successful son of a successful father (the Italian-born Robert Alda, star of many Broadway musicals), that he has been happily married to the same wife for 26 years, that he has three beautiful daughters, and that he campaigns regularly for feminist and liberal causes, one might be tempted to draw the conclusion that he is altogether too much of a good thing – a 'subject for prompt canonisation', in the words of an (ironical) lady journalist. Actually, however, it is impossible not to like him. His boyish good spirits and irrepressible satiric energy add up to a genuine charm. The world of entertainment is the richer for his talents and initiative. ML

Woody Allen

Real name **Allen Stewart Konigsberg**
Born **1 December 1935**

Presumably in the past there have been stars who have looked as odd as Woody Allen, but on the whole they have not taken, as Woody does, the role of romantic lead. Admittedly, he sends himself up: that is the name of his humour. Yet on the other hand, the women playing opposite him – Mia Farrow, Diane Keaton, Mariel Hemingway – are exceptionally pretty, and he usually ends up getting his way with them. If one directs one's own films as well as starring in them there would seem to be an invitation to egotism. Paradoxically, however, this is how the public likes it. The great actor-directors, Chaplin, Keaton – and while one is about it, Clint Eastwood – know instinctively the right level at which to pitch their public persona. Their private characteristics are transformed, as if by magic, into a

in Zelig (Warner Bros., 1983)

lucid public property. There operates, in such a gift, not so much exhibitionism as generosity.

The history of Allen is suggested in two distinct phases, what we might call a pre-*Annie Hall* and a post-*Annie Hall* period. Up until 1978 everything is relatively straightforward. The films of this earlier phase, with their mad and memorable titles – *What's New Pussycat?* (1965) *What's Up Tiger Lily?* (1966), *Take The Money And Run* (1969), *Bananas* (1971), *Play It Again Sam*, also *Everything You Always Wanted To know About Sex But Were Afraid To Ask* (both 1972, an amazing year), *Sleeper* (1973), *Love And Death* (1975) – are full of delightful and surrealistic inventiveness, a sort of spiced up version of the Marx Brothers, permissively brought up to date and injected with a fine colour photography. These films are like genial nightmares. It is as if their protagonist goes to sleep over a book or a movie, only to be swept up helter-skelter into the intrigues of its plot, which (by valiant effort) he then transforms back again into an image of his manic anxieties. These anxieties are usually rather simple (will he get the girl? and does he deserve her? the self-deprecating humour of Groucho). Their fun and delightfulness lie not only in the abundance of excellent one-liners, but also, as it were, plastically: in the variety of vividly-evoked landscapes – from 19th-century Russia (*Love And Death*) to 22nd century futurism (*Sleeper*) – that are conjured up in the course of his dreaming.

With *Annie Hall* the emphasis changes. Fantasy gives way to the exploration of real-life relationships. Sequences which up till now had been staccato, swift and disjointed, in the throwaway manner of revue, became thoughtful and expansive and designed to accommodate subtlety. The comedy is as lissom as ever; but in addition something new is being aimed for. What shall we call it? A freedom of reminiscence, a continuity of destiny, a resonance of memory: all those things, in short, which one associates with proper serious cinema.

Annie Hall, in the event, was an enormous success, winning Oscars for best film, best director and best scriptwriter. Yet it is possible to ask whether this new mode was entirely an improvement. To some it seemed that a milieu that had hitherto been satirised (the neurotic New York intelligentsia) was in danger of being taken at face value. Where previously there had been a healthy gap between Allen himself, and the semi-educated sophisticates whom he made fun of, he seemed

momentarily in danger of joining them. A further criticism might be this: that the continuing reliance on one-liners, in this new phase of seriousness, had become an evasion of artistic responsibility. The jokes which had once been so liberating began all of a sudden to *pre-empt* experience, parcelling it up neatly into the staleness of epigram and truism. Woody Allen was becoming (according to a certain number of critics), something he had never been before – hectoring, moralistic and smug.

That, admittedly, was to see things in their worst possible light. And there were reasons to be more optimistic. For one thing his humour – his gaiety – never really did desert him. The jokes (or the one joke, in its numerous incarnations) poured out as copiously as ever. Then again, when you looked closely you saw that Allen had become serious without losing hold of his decency. One saw for the first time what a great portrayer he is of women. Self-obsessed he might be as an actor, but as a director and screenwriter his energies are always generous, outward-going and appreciative. He wants only to find the conditions in which the actresses he admires can flourish to their natural advantage. *Annie Hall*, then, is a poem addressed to Diane Keaton. *Interiors* (1978), a film given over entirely to an exploration of mothers and daughters, offered wonderful roles to Keaton, Mary Beth Hurt and (an older woman) Geraldine Page; *Manhattan* (1979) celebrates the delicate adolescent beauty of Mariel Hemingway; *Stardust Memories* (1980) offered a pleasant role to the French actress Marie-Christine Barrault (Charlotte Rampling and Jessica Harper are also nicely cameo'd); while *A Midsummer Night's Sex Comedy* (1982) and *Zelig* (1983) re-discovered, after an interval of absence from the screen, the loveliness and gentleness of Mia Farrow.

Allen began his career as a writer of gags for television. Prodigiously talented with the pen, his literary essays appear from time to time in 'The New Yorker'. He is a more than competent jazz-clarinettist. He could have chosen any career that he wanted (one hasn't mentioned his skill as a nightclub performer). Instead he chose to become a film-maker and an actor-comedian. What impresses more than anything in his subsequent career is a sort of manic professionalism, a refusal to rest on his laurels. He brings to the construction of comedy the formal daring, the visual perfectionism, that belongs to the very best film-makers in whose ranks he undoubtedly now features. It is difficult to discuss the rhythms of a film in writing; but the editing of his later movies has a wonderful suppleness and suavity. Easier perhaps to appreciate the painterly qualities of a film like *Manhattan* (with Gordon Willis's beautiful black and white wide-screen photography). Then again, *Stardust Memories* aims at Fellini – but, equally pointedly, gets there! *Zelig*, in this light, for sheer surprise and originality surpasses all previous efforts: the mixing of 'original' and invented footage, to pastiche the period of the 30s, has a virtuosity about it – and a happiness in the execution – that one hasn't seen in American cinema since the time of *Citizen Kane*.

Meanwhile, Woody continues to talk away, never at a loss for an epigram. His voice beneath the New York Jewish vowels is clear-timbred and pleasant. For some reason no one can fathom, his face and his figure are naturally photogenic in the cinema. In real life his balding crown and crumpled appearance – myopia screened behind glasses – causes him to resemble nothing so much as an over-worked college professor. On screen he is transformed by his energy. Has one noticed how often in his films he becomes airborne? In *Love And Death* he is shot through a cannon; in *A Midsummer Night Sex Comedy* he is kitted out with primitive wings; in *Sleeper* he takes to an airscooter; with *Bananas* he quite literally bounces to freedom. His genius seems to be to put into effect plastically the content of everyone's daydreams.

With *Broadway Danny Rose* (1984), his latest, that restless intelligence, and capacity to invent forms, appear happily as undiminished as ever. ML

with Diane Keaton in Play It Again Sam *(Paramount, 1972)* ▷

Jacqueline Bisset

Born Weybridge, Surrey, 13 September 1944

There is something of a mystery about Jacqueline Bisset's reputation. What is the basis of her renown? 'Newsweek' in 1977 voted her 'the most beautiful actress of all time'. But Beauty is in the eye of the beholder. In truth, there are and will be many actresses as beautiful as she is – some of them possessing the additional bonus of acting ability. Without endeavouring to be ungallant, part of it can be put down to luck. Her Scottish-French parentage, allied to a natural reticence, gave her, at the beginning of her career, a 'class' that was appreciated (one is talking about the mid-1960s). Since then she has clung tight and prospered. Evidently there is iron in the soul. Hand in hand with her film career she has pursued a successful secondary line in property dealing. This, coupled to the reputed salary of a million dollars for each film she accepts, has managed to make her 'rich' as well as 'famous' – in

fact (with Joan Collins) one of the richest women in Hollywood.

After small parts in reputable British films – *The Knack* (1965), *Cul-de-Sac* (1966), *Two For The Raod* (1967) – and a cameo in *Casino Royale* (1967), she settled permanently in California. Her career got under way opposite Sinatra in *The Detective* (1968). Roles followed in *Bullitt* (1968), *The Life And Times Of Judge Roy Bean* (1972), *Day For Night* (1972) and *Murder On The Orient Express* (1974). Her smouldering sexiness was given full reign in *The Deep* (1976). The clinging wet T-shirt was the subject of a famous poster. Bissett sued to have the image withdrawn, but lost. In *The Greek Tycoon* (1978) she impersonated another Jacqueline, Onassis, fooling no one who mattered, but benefiting her bank account greatly. Follow-ups have included *Rich and Famous* (1981), *Class* (1983), and, currently, from Malcolm Lowry's novel, *Under The Volcano*. The latter takes her back up the ladder of intellectual aspiration, co-starring with Albert Finney for director John Huston. ML

in 1977

Karen Black

Real name **Karen Ziegler**
Born **Park Ridge, Illinois, 1 July 1942**

Karen Black belongs to the breed of educated (Northwestern University, Illinois), theatre-trained actresses who specialise in playing uneducated roles – hookers, waitresses, women-on-the-loose, in varying degrees of desperation and resourcefulness. An instinctive and generous sensuality singles her out and distinguishes her from the more extreme perils of neuroticism (as exemplified in an actress like Sandy Dennis). She can be criticised for her mannered theatricality; but on the other hand, to her credit, she is something of a humorous survivor, and has starred in a number of good movies.

In *Easy Rider* (1969) she was an acid-tripping whore; the following year in *Five Easy Pieces* – perhaps her best film to date – she was the waitress picked up and deserted without ceremony (in a petrol station) by a disgruntled Jack Nicholson. *Portnoy's Complaint* (1972) failed to make out of the

in Nashville (Paramount, 1975)

film the success that had been enjoyed by the novel (perhaps unsurprisingly, given the scabrous subject matter). And two adaptations from American classics – *The Great Gatsby* (1974) and *Day Of The Locusts* (1975) – remain, to subsequent viewing, obstinately plot-bound and ponderous.

Rather at a low point in her career, Black agreed to play the part of the stewardess in *Airport 75* (piloting down the stricken jumbo, apparently oblivious to the need of a rudder!). Sanity was restored, somewhat, and professional esteem re-established in Robert Altman's fine movie *Nashville* (1975). A year later she found herself playing Fran, a diamond thief, another marginal and outcast, in a witty charade by Hitchcock *Family Plot* (the last film he completed). Two recent first-rate performances – in Altman's *Come Back To The Five And Dime, Jimmy Dean* (1982), and as a neurotic housewife going mad in the African sun in *The Grass Is Singing* (1983) adapted from Doris Lessing's powerful novel – prove her to be as resourceful and energetic as ever. More recently still she has appeared in Henry Jaglom's *Can She Bake A Cherry Pie?* ML

Jeff Bridges

Born **Los Angeles, 4 December 1949**

If Jeff Bridges did not quite succeed by the end of the 1970s in making it to the highest grades of superstardom, it is probably because of his sheer uncomplicated niceness. It is rather an ambiguous quality. With wonderful exceptions (Gary Cooper, Cary Grant spring to mind) we seem to like our male stars to be moody and mean: to possess a touch of truculence, like Brando, or a hint of brooding destiny, like Dean. Bridges is incredibly untragic. His striking good looks ought to single him out as a natural leader of men. But something in his character – a privacy or gentleness – holds him back from asserting himself too flamboyantly. He tends to be the irresponsible second-in-command, rather than the aggressive initiator. The son of Lloyd Bridges, and elder brother of Beau, those boyish good looks of his, even now in the 1980s, seem to delight in their youthfulness, and obstinately refuse to mature.

Bridges, for all this, has starred in some of the more interesting films of the decade. His career got off to an excellent start with an Oscar nomination for the role of Duane, the defeated football hero, in *The Last Picture Show* (1971). The following year he was cast as a feckless country boy in Robert Benton's grim parable about the corruption lurking in paradise, *Bad Company*. The same productive year he put in a memorable performance as a struggling young boxer in John Huston's fine movie *Fat City*. In *Thunderbolt and Lightfoot* (1974), the oddly unfocussed directorial debut of Michael Cimino (*Heaven's Gate*, *The Deer Hunter*), he was a fugitive

on the run through the icy mountain valleys of Montana, in the company of a jokey Clint Eastwood. Next, the trials and tribulations of a Hollywood extra were amusingly chronicled in Howard Zieff's *Hearts Of The West* (1975) – the rumbustious physicality of Bridges accounting for, in large degree, the memorable charm of the enterprise.

Stay Hungry, which he made the following year for director Bob Rafelson, is probably the most personal of his movies. Bridges plays an isolated young man from an upper-class family, brought up in the modern deep South. Gradually he becomes involved in the intrigues of his neighbouring township, centred on a contest of bodybuilders. A fine and pleasant aspect of American culture is demonstrated by the wit and ease with which he abandons his restrictive class background, and mingles with social 'inferiors'. There is something typical and American and optimistic about such behaviour, and Bridges is the actor to exemplify it. *Heaven's Gate* (1980), however, was a major disaster. Resuscitated three years later with much of its original footage restored, the filmmakers, for whatever reason, omitted to restore fully the role of the saloon-keeper. (In the original Bridges had this much larger part, sharing the favours of a delectable Isabelle Huppert, along with Kris Kristofferson and Christopher Walken). *Cutter's Way* (1981), on the other hand, was a superb success: a powerful, anarchic treatment of footloose veterans from the Vietnam War, it was dynamic, popular cinema in the best crafted traditions of Hollywood. Recently there has been the Disney movie *Tron* (1983), memorable for its computerised animation; but also for a nice performance by Bridges in one of the film's few human roles. ML

in The Last American Hero (20th Century-Fox, 1973)

Ellen Burstyn

Real name **Edna Rae Gillooly**
Born **Detroit, Michigan, 7 December 1932**

If proof were needed that Hollywood is occasionally open to talent and not merely fixated on youth, then the career of Ellen Burstyn provides it. She was 38 when she found her first triumph in the cinema, playing the seductive Southern belle, mother of Cybill Shepherd, in Bogdanovich's *The Last Picture Show* (1971). Prior to this time there is a history of hard work and dedication – years of apprentice drudgery on stage, television and dance-floor. Having left home at 18, the longed-for break came in the late 60s when she put herself back to school, taking lessons with Lee Strasberg at the Actors' Studio. Two small film parts came out of this: opposite Rip Torn in Joseph Strick's *Tropic Of Cancer* (1970), and opposite Donald Sutherland in *Alex In Wonderland* (Paul Mazursky, 1970). These led on in turn to *The Last Picture Show*.

Now that she was the centre of attention (the Bogdanovich film having won her an Oscar nomination), offers for other interesting parts materialised. *The King Of Marvin Gardens* (1972), for director Bob Rafelson, turned out to be one of the best small movies of the 70s, a story of failure and defeat, notable for a paradoxical warmth of human feeling and an almost Chekhovian happiness. *The Exorcist* (1973), was a more official project in which Burstyn played the possessed child's mother – well enough to earn her a second nomination.

All this seems preparation for the finest role in her career, that of the young widow from the Mid-West who sets out, son-in-tow, to make a new career for herself, in *Alice Doesn't Live Here Anymore* (1975). The project sprang directly from her desires and experience, and, more than the director's (it was Martin Scorsese), the film should really be called hers. The incidents of struggle and comedy are narrated with a gay, funny, forceful, wistful assurance. It was feminism without the ideology, the portrait of a mother both beautiful and resourceful.

In a sense all these awards – and nominations for awards (five Oscar nominations in all) – tell their own story. Ellen Burstyn is an 'actress's actress'. Broadway recently has reclaimed her. It is unsurprising that she should be attached to the theatre, for the theatre is still the actor's medium. Her most recent film triumph – *Same Time Next Year* (1978) – is a transfer from a Broadway success. And more recently still, she has played Sarah Bernhardt on the boards to French and American audiences. ML

with Kris Kristofferson in Alice Doesn't Live Here Anymore *(Warner Bros., 1975)*

James Coburn

Born **Laurel, Nebraska, 31 August 1928**

It could be argued that James Coburn has never really recovered from the adulation he received in the 1960s for his starring role in the two Flint capers (*Our Man Flint*, 1966, *In Like Flint*, 1967) – satires on Bond, but belonging in essence to the same fantasy world of gadgets and beautiful girls, in which the problems of nations are solved by the twinkling of an epigram. The physical prowess of Coburn – that strong lean frame and weather-tanned visage, that ready smile with its superabundance of ivory teeth – masks a rather light personality. For all his irony and elegance, he seems a character fundamentally adrift from himself. The passion for fast cars, the dabbling in Buddhism and mysticism, the much publicised and disastrous mistakes in his private life (throwing over, in 1977, his wife of many years' standing for the songwriter Lynsey De Paul; then throwing *her* over too) point to an unresolved insecurity.

The work continues to flow: 18 films over the last decade. He continues to be handsomely rewarded. He started in westerns – he was the knife-thrower in *The Magnificent Seven* (1960) – and it is in this genre that he has managed to find some of his best roles, notably as the US Marshal Garrett in Peckinpah's lurid, noble elegy of the dying West, *Pat Garrett And Billy The Kid* (1973); also in such films as *The Last Hard Man* (1975), *Bite The Bullet* (1974) and Sergio Leone's *Duck You Sucker!* (1972). He might still be interesting in comedy, if the comedies would only materialise. ML

Jill Clayburgh

Born **New York City, 30 April 1944**

The advance of the Women's Movement during the course of the 70s signalled the decline of the starlet. A premium is now on actresses who look as if they are able to take part in life's battles. Really, however, it is not perhaps so different from the way it has always been: Jill Clayburgh has her ancestry in tough, pretty, feisty actresses of the past like Margaret Sullavan and Barbara Stanwyck. Without conceding her femininity, she can split a wisecrack with the best of them. Her skill is to suggest that she is coming apart at the seams, while holding onto an unquenchable elegance. Her voice is rich and deep, with subtle modulations of mockery. On screen she gives the impression of enjoying herself; as when, in Michael Ritchie's excellent *Semi-Tough* (1976), she fends off the rival advances of Burt Reynolds and Kris Kristofferson. At ease in comedy, she can be witty and moving. Of course she is rather neurotic. But her neuroses do not make her unsympathetic. Strength and vulnerability in her personality are balanced in delicate equilibrium.

Clayburgh's best-known role to date has been that of the modern pretty woman whose husband walks out on her, in *An Unmarried Woman* (1978). No begging, in this drama, for her husband to come back to her: she divorces him promptly, and finds another man. Her feminism, elsewhere, is pictured as linked to a career. In *Starting Over* (1979), again with Burt Reynolds, she plays a self-sufficient nursery-school teacher who moves in when his marriage is foundering; Claudia Weill's *It's My Turn* (1980) makes her a professor of mathematics; in *La Luna* (Bertolucci, 1979, one of her best roles) she is an international opera singer. Twice she has had legal careers: in *First Monday In October* (1981) she is the first woman judge in the Supreme Court. More recently, in the (not very successful) Costa-Gavras film about terrorism, *Hannah K* (1983), she plays an American Attorney caught up in the troubles in the Middle East.

Despite these ambitious projections, in her private life she is modest and ordinary. Married to playwright David Rabe, she lives simply in New York, enjoying the pleasures, such as they are, of city life: jogging, shopping and the occasional visit to museums and art galleries. ML

Robert De Niro

Born **New York City, 17 August 1943**

Robert De Niro is evidently a screen actor of the first order. But is he exactly a 'star'? The sort of easygoing popularity with audiences that is enjoyed by Clint Eastwood and Burt Reynolds seems to be missing from his character. There is something intense and intimidating – something relentless – about his professionalism, as if the only people he cared to be judged by were his fellow artists. His career is marked out by a quality of singlemindedness, a sort of interior battle with the self, willing him on to ever greater feats of virtuosity. Even when he turns to comedy, as increasingly he seems to be doing (*King Of Comedy*, 1983, and the current *Brazil*, 1984), it is with the underlying aim of mastering a new skill, adding a new technique to his armoury. His most obviously lighthearted films – *New York, New York* (1977) and *King Of Comedy* spring to mind – are comedies only by accident, sustained as much by rage as by laughter.

Lest this make him appear altogether too unlikeable an actor it ought to be added that there is a softer and gentler side to De Niro's nature. In *The Last Tycoon* (1976), not otherwise much of a success, the interest of the film – and its faithfulness to the Scott Fitzgerald original – lay in De Niro's ability to project into Monroe Stahr the true and touching qualities of a gentleman. He is a gentleman, too, though of a harder and narrower sort, in the part of the younger Corleone in Coppola's fine sequel to *The Godfather* (*Godfather II*, 1974). The princely courtesy with which, in that movie, he addresses subordinates and relatives comes to the fore again in *The Deer Hunter* (1978) as a sort of diffused gallantry towards comrades and friends. There is a generous, mature and thoughtful side to his playing here to set against those other occasions – perhaps rather too many – when he finds himself cast as an obsessive.

Obsession is the key to De Niro's career: he excels in the portrayal of haunted and lonely outsiders, men who are possessed of some furious but unproductive curiosity, and whose subsequent behaviour in the pursuit of their quest, becomes to all intents indistinguishable from madness. This is the role – though portrayed in a comic focus – that he took on for Brian De Palma in the first films he ever acted in, 'underground' shorts of the late 60s with names like *Hi Mom!*, *Greetings* and *The Wedding Party*. Such films (he plays an avid pornographer in two of them) now have a mainly period interest, though it is

in Raging Bull (United Artists, 1980)

interesting to catch a foretaste of talents – particularly, talents of improvisation – that were to be cashed in in the great films of the 70s.

A more arresting obsessiveness – and an altogether greater role – came about with *Mean Streets* (1973), in which De Niro plays the irresponsible street hoodlum Johnny Boy, cast against Harvey Keitel. The film was a first rate achievement, breaking new ground for American cinema in showing, for small-scale independent ventures, the way forward into the future. Nothing about it is so memorable as this performance of De Niro's, which, springing up suddenly out of nowhere (it is only a secondary part) imposes itself with the force of a hurricane. *Mean Streets* was directed by Martin Scorsese. For the rest of the decade the two men were to work together frequently. They have made so far four further films in partnership: *Taxi Driver*, *New York, New York*, *Raging Bull* and *King Of Comedy*. It might be said that it was De Niro's good fortune to find himself in the company, at an opportune moment, of a man who was soon to show himself one of the greatest of contemporary directors. But the contention works the other way round. It was equally Scorsese's good fortune, at the beginning of his career, to come across Robert De Niro. They stand together now as one of the permanent creative cinematic partnerships, like John Wayne in his partnership with Ford. The lower-middle-class, street-wise, city culture of Italian immigration, a significant slice of East Coast American society – different from, though in many ways as 'epic' as Ford's Wild West – owes its international illumination to their tireless endeavours.

After *Mean Streets* came *Godfather II*. The part of Corleone gained De Niro an Academy Award (for Best Supporting Actor). Subsequently (1975) he was invited to star in *1900*, Bertolucci's massive, broad epic of recent Italian history. The timorous aristocrat Alfredo brought to De Niro's playing a soft and somewhat feminine suppleness. For the first time he disported himself in the buff (with delectable Dominique Sanda); but his doing so here, however, pointed up its general rarity. De Niro is an ascetic, a traditional and a private actor (if the adjectives are not contradictory). Not for him the casual nudity of Richard Gere or Gerard Depardieu. Sex appeal, as such, isn't a part of his vanity. His body, when displayed, is displayed for the purpose of battery (as

in *Raging Bull*); or for gruelling physical exercise (as in the famous 'training scenes' in *Taxi Driver*).

This relentless interior urging-of-himself-on is the special characteristic of De Niro. Film acting, for him, is not so much the imitating of professions, as their actual acquisition and conquest. After *Taxi Driver* (1976), plying the streets of New York, he might have set himself up as a cabbie. Hours were spent with George Auld, prior to *New York, New York*, in learning to master the saxophone. *Raging Bull* (1980) produced one of the most authentic, detailed, interior portraits of a boxer ever filmed. For *True Confessions* (1982) he cast himself into the company of priests, and mastered the Catholic liturgy. *King Of Comedy* (1983) was preceded, as are all his films, by a period of concentrated study, aiming, on this occasion, to pierce the secrets of that hardest profession of all, the job of the stand-up comedian. De Niro is the sort of actor of whom prodigious tales are told, of feats of endurance and sacrifice, mortifications of the soul and the body. Such feats might all have been ludicrous and literal – the very negation of the actor's art – were it not that each transformation is accompanied by a kind of inner grace, a fineness, a seriousness, unmatched in contemporary cinema. *Raging Bull* won him the coveted Oscar for Best Actor; yet his finest performance is perhaps that of Vronsky in the previous movie *The Deer Hunter*. Rarely has one seen screen acting that combines at the same time such steely self-control and decorum, with such secret inordinate passion. His projection here blazed with authority – as honed and as tempered as the sheet steel from the mills of Clairton, Pennsylvania, in whose furnaces he was pictured as working.

That is the central point to make. Over the course of sixteen films, he goes on from strength to strength. Not one of his films, so far, has been a failure. This fact alone separates him from his contemporaries. Actors with whom he started his career have long since been overtaken. In this most precarious of professions De Niro's choice of role has been achieved with an enviable, gilt-edged assurance. He knows how to stay sufficiently in the public eye: to be on the scene, without becoming a bore. To this end his private life is carefully guarded. Married to the black singer Diahnne Abbott, he is the father of a son, Raphael, born in 1976. Recently, rumour has linked his name with that of another black singer, Helena Springs. He rarely gives interviews. He refuses to endorse books or publicity. His whole life is contained in his acting. Each of his undertakings is a relentless exertion of will power. ML

in The Godfather, Part II (Paramount, 1974)

in The Deer Hunter (Universal, 1978)

in New York, New York (United Artists, 1977) ▷

Bruce Dern

Born **Chicago, Illinois, 4 June 1936**

The first time Bruce Dern appeared on the big screen, he played the thuggish yokel who beat up Monty Clift in Elia Kazan's *Wild River* (1960). He was a real nasty piece of work and continued to be so, although it didn't justify having his hands chopped off in *Hush Hush ... Sweet Charlotte* (1964), or having his head bashed in by a poker in Alfred Hitchcock's *Marnie* (1964). He was a creep and psychotic in a series of westerns – killed by John Wayne in *The War Wagon* (1967), hunted by Clint Eastwood in *Hang 'Em High* (1968), and outwitted by James Garner in *Support Your Local Sheriff!* (1969). Dern had the wild look of someone on speed, drugs and bikes, in Roger Corman's youth-orientated movies, *The Wild Angels* (1966) and *The Trip* (1967), and in *Psych-Out* (1968), was another acid-head whose death is the ultimate trip to him.

Dern's high-powered background could not be further from the overheated world he inhabits on screen. His grandfather had been governor of Utah, and he was the nephew of Roosevelt's Secretary of

in The Great Gatsby *(Paramount, 1974)*

War, and the poet-playwright Archibald MacLeish. Following his own footsteps, Bruce dropped out of college and took up acting. After studying at the Actors' Studio, he began to get roles on stage and on TV. His angular features, and combustible energy soon cast him as scrawny heavies. But by the early 70s, this persona was translated into the counter-culture of the day. When his friend Jack Nicholson made his directorial debut with *Drive He Said* (1970), Dern was effectively cast as the bullying, latent homosexual basketball coach who wants to win at all costs. In *The King Of Marvin Gardens* (1972), he gave a detailed performance as Nicholson's hustler brother.

Dern's range was extended as the botanist in space in *Silent Running* (1972) and, still further, as Tom Buchanan in the over-glossy *The Great Gatsby* (1974). He then showed a gift for sharp comedy in *Smile* (1975) and Hitchcock's *Family Plot* (1976). He was nominated for a Best Supporting Actor Oscar for the role of Jane Fonda's hawkish, demented husband in the sentimental *Coming Home* (1978), and continued to chill as the creepy cop pursuing Ryan O'Neal through a *film noir* landscape in *The Driver* (1978). RB

Richard Dreyfuss

Born **Brooklyn, New York City, 1948**

Chubby, freckled, short and frequently bespectacled, Richard Dreyfuss seems an unlikely star. But the Dreyfuss case is a good example of the aesthetic change that had started in American films in the mid-60s. In Steven Spielberg's quasi-religious fantasy *Close Encounters Of The Third Kind* (1977), Dreyfuss is the representative ordinary mid-western guy chosen by the soppy, little green men to take off with them in their flying saucer. Before taking off for the stellar regions, he had spent his childhood in Brooklyn and Queens, the son of a lawyer. He started acting at nine, after his family moved to L.A. As he was a registered conscientious objector during the Vietnam war, he had to leave college and work for two years in an L.A. hospital as alternative service. By the early 70s, he was getting parts on Broadway and in California, as well as on TV. After making an impression as Baby Face Nelson in *Dillinger* (1973), he was given the role that was to make him a star. *American Graffitti* (1973) was George Lucas's dreamy vision of adolescent life in a small Californian town in 1962, with Dreyfuss as the intellectual among the kids.

He demonstrated a range of bouncy mannerisms as a go-getter in *The Apprenticeship Of Duddy Kravitz* (1974), but was more restrained in the interesting *Inserts* (1976) as Boy Wonder, a film director forced to make porno movies in his own home. Dreyfuss, as an icthyologist, was somewhat outacted by 'Bruce' the shark machine in *Jaws* (1975), and was overwhelmed by the special effects in *Close Encounters*, but his nervy comic technique was given full rein in his Oscar-winning role in Neil Simon's *The Goodbye Girl* (1977), managing to make an irritating character appear endearing. As the paralysed patient in *Whose Life Is It Anyway?* (1982), Dreyfuss proved he has more talent in his head alone than many actors have in their whole bodies. RB

in Whose Life Is It Anyway? *(MGM, 1982)*

Robert Duvall

Born **San Diego, California, 5 January 1931**

'I love the smell of napalm in the morning,' says Robert Duvall as the mad, war-loving Colonel Kilgore in Francis Ford Coppola's two-and-a-half hour nightmarish Disneyland ride through Vietnam, *Apocalypse Now* (1979). Kilgore is certainly a carica-ture of the American military, but Duvall gives him a terrifying reality, presenting a man only as insane as the war around him. Duvall's brief appearance is central to the film, and full of impact.

The son of a rear-admiral, Duvall, with his stern features, fixed gaze and gleaming forehead, seemed born to play psychotic soldiers, gangsters or cops. There has always been a recognition in American films that the line between the military, the mobs-ters and the police is a fine one, and Duvall walks it with perfect equilibrium. He played a disturbed soldier in *Captain Newman M.D.* (1963), was driven crazy by the boorish heroes of *M*A*S*H* (1970), and was a Nazi officer in *The Eagle Has Landed* (1976). Still in uniform, he was a toned down version of Kilgore in *The Great Santini* (1979), portraying a peace time officer unable to think outside the military code even when it comes to his relationship with his family. He played hoodlums in *The Outfit* (1976) and *The Killer Elite* (1975), and cops in Coppola's rambling *The Rain People* (1969) and in *True Confessions* (1981).

Duvall was educated at Principia College, Illinois before doing two years military service. He then joined the Neighborhood Playhouse in New York, and won various acting roles on and off Broadway. At one stage, he shared an apartment with the then struggling Dustin Hoffman and four others. His break came in Arthur Miller's 'A View From The Bridge' on Broadway in 1963 with another new-comer, Jon Voight. Since his screen debut as the simple-minded recluse in *To Kill A Mocking Bird* (1963), Duvall has been the supporting actor *par excellence*. There is no better example than in *The Godfather I* and *II* (1972 and 1974) as Tom Hagen, the go-between, confidant, and retainer to the all-

powerful Corleone family. His strong and discreet performance holds the family, and, indeed, the two *Godfather* films, together.

Gradually, Duvall has emerged as a star in his own right. He recently stated that he wantd to make films about good people. The result was his Oscar-nominated role as the has-been country-and-western singer in *Tender Mercies* (1983), in which he not only sings well, but is able to generate a warmth denied him for most of his previous career. RB

in The Rain People *(Warner Bros., 1969)*

Marty Feldman

Born **London, England, 1933**
Died **1983**

It was inevitable that with his pint-sized figure, nasal London accent and huge bulging eyes, Marty Feldman should have turned to comedy. The eyes were a result of a disease he suffered as a child, but he managed to turn his facial defects to his advantage by using them to comic effect. It must be said that most of his rather crude and limited comedy lay mainly in his animated eyes. Nevertheless, he was a versatile little man who entered show business as a musician in variety where he also began writing comedy material. With Barry Took, he wrote a number of popular British radio and TV shows including 'Beyond Our Ken' and 'Round The

Horne'. In 1967, he wrote scripts for himself in a TV show called 'Marty' which turned out to be equally popular in Germany.

In 1969, he appeared in the film version of Spike Milligan's *The Bed-Sitting Room*. Mel Brooks made him part of his team in *Young Frankenstein* (1974) in which Marty played a hunchbacked leering Igor, and in *Silent Movie* (1976) which suited his visual humour. Along similar Brooksian film spoof lines, he played Gene Wilder's side-kick in *The Adventures Of Sherlock Holmes' Smarter Brother* (1975), directed by Wilder with a certain flair, and his own *The Last Remake Of Beau Geste* (1977), uneven to say the least. He also directed, co-wrote and starred in *In God We Trust* (1980) which had a limited release. His last film appearance was in the painfully unfunny pirate romp *Yellowbeard* (1983), before his premature death of a heart attack. RB

in In God We Trust *(Universal, 1980)*

Edward Fox

Born **London, 13 April 1937**

A product, like his brother James, of Harrow and the Coldstream Guards, Edward Fox trained at the Royal Academy of Dramatic Art and made his screen debut in *The Mind Benders* (1963). He then worked steadily throughout the 60s in a series of not particularly rewarding films: a pair of raucous Michael Winner comedies, *The Jokers* and *I'll Never Forget What's 'Is Name* (both 1967), Richard Attenborough's *Oh! What A Lovely War* (1969) and *The Battle Of Britain* (also 1969). Even as a relatively young man, he was proficient at cruel or pompously blinkered roles, often in the military; and, the less boyishly goodlooking of the two, he found his career somewhat overshadowed by that of his brother. His

chance came in 1971, when Joseph Losey cast him as the gentle Viscount Trimingham who befriends the young protagonist of *The Go-Between*; and he subsequently achieved a measure of international fame (not entirely maintained) as the robotic, ruthlessly dedicated gunman who almost succeeds in assassinating General De Gaulle in Fred Zinnemann's adaptation of the Frederick Forsyth bestseller *The Day Of The Jackal* (1973).

In the 70s Fox surfaced in a dispiriting miscellany of films, from Losey's *Galileo* (1975), as the Grand Inquisitor, to Winner's grotesquely misjudged remake of *The Big Sleep* (1977), but made a much stronger impression as Edward VIII in the lavish television series 'Edward And Mrs Simpson'. His most memorable recent role saw him as a cruel and uncomprehending British officer in Attenborough's multi-Oscared *Gandhi* (1982). DM

Elliott Gould

Real name **Elliott Goldstein**
Born **Brooklyn, New York, 29 August 1938**

The son of a classic 'stage mother', Elliott Gould was an accomplished little dancer, singer and actor by the time he was eight years old. He was also a child model, an occasional TV personality and a frequent performer on the so-called 'borscht belt' in the Catskill resorts. From chorus boy in the Broadway production of 'Irma La Douce' he made it to leading man in another musical 'I Can Get If For You Wholesale': though it flopped, it remains a date in Broadway history for having introduced Barbra Streisand, whom Gould subsequently married. The marriage lasted five years, beyond which point he could no longer endure living in his wife's shadow and being referred to, not always absent-mindedly, as 'Mr Streisand'. The year of their divorce, however, was also that of his screen debut in *The Night They*

Raided Minsky's (1968). One year later, he won an Oscar nomination for his performance in *Bob & Carol & Ted & Alice*; two years later, his irreverent army doctor, Hawkeye, in Robert Altman's *M*A*S*H* made him a cult figure; and three years later, voted America's top male star, he appeared in Ingmar Bergman's *The Touch*. But such a crowded itinerary was to take its toll. A mental breakdown led to two years of unemployment, from which he was rescued by Altman who cast him as Philip Marlowe in his brilliant update of *The Long Goodbye* (1973).

Gould was uptight, but witty enough to realise it; confused, but lucid enough to know that the world was, too. For a few years, with his prodigious mongrel charm and self-deprecating humour, he personified the whole post-60s generation. Deprived of that precise context, however, he became just a shaggily eccentric leading man and made few subsequent films of value. He is, indeed, one of the saddest and most curious cases in contemporary American cinema. DM

in 1978

Goldie Hawn

Born **Washingon, D.C., 21 November 1945**

With bright, impertinent features peeking out from beneath a cascade of soft blonde hair, Goldie Hawn looks (and sometimes sounds) like some pampered lapdog; and the epithets commonly applied to her have been 'dizzy', 'kookie', 'wacky', and the like. It is an enchanting persona as long as it lasts, though perhaps not one to be spun out indefinitely. As the daughter of a musician, she was encouraged from childhood to attend ballet and tap-dancing classes; and, when studying drama at American University, she paid her tuition fees by managing a dance studio. After some repertory work, and a brief appearance in a little-seen Disney film *The One And Only, Genuine, Original, Family Band* (1968), she became a TV superstar on the enormously popular comedy show, Rowan and Martin's 'Laugh-In'. Then, with her first major film role, as Walter Matthau's

mistress in *Cactus Flower* (1969), she won an Oscar as best supporting actress.

Until she took her career in hand by becoming her own executive producer with *Private Benjamin* (1980), however, Hawn starred in disappointingly few successful and/or stimulating movies. Her natural ebullience cruelly exposed the tired mannerisms of Peter Sellers in *There's A Girl In My Soup* (1970); her irrepressible sense of fun served only as relief from the shrill sentimentality of *Butterflies Are Free* (1972); and neither she nor George Segal could make anything of the vulgar slapstick of *The Duchess And The Dirtwater Fox* (1976). Best were Steven Spielberg's *Sugarland Express* (1974), though it flopped at the box-office, and Hal Ashby's *Shampoo* (1975), though she was only one of several butterflies fluttering around hairdresser Warren Beatty. But *Private Benjamin*, a very funny farce about a scatterbrained young woman mistakenly inducted into the army, was a huge success – and Hawn is perhaps her own best producer. DM

Ben Johnson

Born **Pawhuska, Oklahoma, 13 June 1920**

Perhaps the very last authentic cowboy to make a career in the movies – a tradition stretching back to the teens of the century – Ben Johnson came of mixed Irish-Cherokee descent. His early years were spent as a rodeo steer roper, at which he became world champion in 1953. Having been hired by Howard Hughes as a horse wrangler for *The Outlaw* (1948), he soon found regular employment in Hollywood as a double and stunt man. It was John Ford who made him an actor by casting him as a cavalry sergeant in *She Wore A Yellow Ribbon* (1949) and *Rio Grande* (1950). Though he was, unusually, offered the title role in Ford's strange, elegiac epic

in The Last Picture Show *(Columbia, 1971)*

Wagonmaster (1950), Johnson's quiet good looks and blandly sympathetic personality seemed to typify him as one of nature's supporting actors. His was a familiar, even reassuring, presence in such classic westerns as *Shane* (1953), Marlon Brando's *One-Eyed Jacks* (1961) and *The Wild Bunch* (1969).

By casting him against the grain as a corrupt tycoon in his characteristically violent thriller *The Getaway* (1972), Peckinpah revealed that Johnson was a more expressive and versatile performer than his reputation allowed. But it was as Sam the Lion, the ageing movie theatre owner in Peter Bogdanovich's *The Last Picture Show* (1971), that Johnson was finally able to demonstrate that he possessed real star quality, even if the Oscar he received for his performance was that of Best Supporting Actor. DM

Tommy Lee Jones

Born **San Saba, Texas, 1948**

A series of powerful, low-keyed performances in gritty and interesting movies established Tommy Lee Jones, by the late 70s, as an actor to be looked out for. Son of a Texan oil-rigger, trained at Harvard and on Broadway, he moved to California in 1976, taking a lead role (as an uneducated criminal) opposite Yvette Mimieux in the Roger Corman picture *Jackson County Jail*. Subsequently Jones has specialised in playing cussed, tough and uningratiating men, pitched at an angle against the system, but preserving, nonetheless, in their chosen paths, a certain inner life and integrity. In *Rolling Thunder* (1977), a semi-exploitation thriller, he plays a Vietnam veteran on the rampage. In *The Executioner's Song* (1982) he is the murderer Gary Gilmore.

Martin Ritt's *Back Roads* (1981) has him as an Alabama ex-boxer down on his luck accompanying Sally Field in search of better times in California. In *The Eyes Of Laura Mars* (1978) he plays a psychopathic police detective. One of his most memorable roles to date has been that of the famous millionaire recluse in *The Amazing Howard Hughes* (1978, made for CBS television). He will be remembered, too, for his role as Sissy Spacek's husband, Doolittle – all at once tender, rough, jealous and solicitous – in Michael Apted's Oscar winning country-and-western drama, *Coalminer's Daughter* (1979).

Married for the second time, wealthy, and socially reclusive, he lives now in his native Texas, where he keeps a string of polo horses for a hobby. His hands are as large as a German baker's; his face is jowled, and uninviting of confidences. He is like a rather formidable Nick Nolte, of whom one would hope to see more in the course of the 1980s. ML

Diane Keaton

Real name **Diane Hall**
Born **Los Angeles, 5 January 1946**

The key question about Diane Keaton is whether she is merely a 'kook'. Is there real acting talent behind that dimpled, ever so slightly mannered charm? Or is she only a lightweight? The fact that, along with thousands of other people, one may once have been rather in love with her, only makes the question more piquant.

Right from the start Keaton's fate has been linked with Woody Allen's: the stage version of 'Play It Again Sam' in 1970 had been – after a short interval as leading lady in 'Hair' – her first major role in the theatre. In the film version (1972) she is delightful. Glamorous enough not to give in to a character as wretched, self-dramatising and unprepossessing as the one played by Allen, her surrender when it comes has a touching and tender generosity.

Two subsequent films for Allen gave her two distinctly contrasting careers. In *Sleeper* (1973), projected forward into the 22nd century, she plays a literary intellectual hostess of the sort one meets, if not in life, then in one's occasional nightmares. She excellently sends herself up. And how witty Allen is in both knowing and showing her foolishnes. But she was allowed to incarnate a quite other sort of woman in *Love And Death* (1975), where she played a countess in Napoleonic Russia who knows how to use her seductiveness. The film has something of the amateur and home-made about it, but Keaton dazzles with a performance of malicious tender naughtiness.

This brings one to *Annie Hall* (1977), presumably where the trouble commences. It doesn't help that the film was so popular. Retrospectively speaking, nothing makes people so obstinate as the memory of a fashion that, for a brief season, held vigorous and undisputed dominion. Diane Keaton's outfit – scarf and felt hat, canvas jacket and floppy trousers – not to mention casually slung shoulder bag – was wonderfully original at the time. But a reversion to elegance in the later 70s has left it stranded.

Ingenuousness was the problem with the role. 'Huh? Gee. Well. That's great! Isn't it? Wow.' It is possible to be just too accommodating. Her vulnerability kept getting the better of her. One might be forgiven for preferring the straight-haired, calm and ironic persona of *Play It Again Sam*, to this frizzy-haired, liberated and inarticulate damsel who now encountered us strumming her guitar. Was it the real Diane Keaton? Or was she still playing a role? One examined the matter carefully; and reluctantly, if not necessarily correctly, concluded the former.

And then again: Diane Keaton's reserves as an actress, we can see now, had *not* been used up in the role. For almost simultaneously she appeared in a totally different incarnation, that of a tormented and sexually adventurous Catholic primary school teacher, in Richard Brooks's melodrama *Looking For Mr Goodbar* (1977). The violence of this film was disliked by some, but the film keeps its distinction. Keaton's performance, without becoming exhibitionist, is serious and brave beyond the call of duty,

and she doesn't baulk at showing her nakedness on the screen. The grim determinism of the movie is illuminated by her frenetic and touching sexuality.

In *Interiors* (1978), she holds onto this fine vein of seriousness, while reverting to a more inhibited character. Renata, one of a trio of sisters in an artistically-inclined family of women, thinks of herself as an accomplished poet. To the audience it becomes clear that the film concerns itself with the falseness of this pat self-description. Her soul has been frozen by gentility; she breathes the thin rarefied air of narcissism. Where previously – in *Sleeper* – Keaton had mocked this condition, she now illuminated it with sober precision.

A few films are missing to tie up this sketch of her career. In *Reds* (1982) she plays Louise Bryant, the combative, bohemian lady journalist, companion (though never the wife) of Warren Beatty's John Reed. Offscreen the stars developed a liaison; the acting that came out of it gives a sense of depth and excitement to a story that otherwise, runs the risk of looking somewhat academic.

Shoot The Moon, directed by Alan Parker and released the same year, keeps up the heat of the psychodrama. What a fiery actress she is, one has to concede at last! Here she plays the abandoned wife of Albert Finney. It is a role that goes right back to her first appearance in cinema as the wife of Al

in Looking For Mr Goodbar *(Paramount, 1977)*

Pacino – waspish, delicate, neurotic and finally cast aside – in *The Godfather* (1970).

Keaton has never married in private life and one feels that now, at the age of 38, she would like to. Fame and a successful career have their reward; but they also have their price. What they cost seems to be becoming clear in an increasing sombreness of her acting. A 'kook' she is not. And neither is she intellectually frigid. Judging from her career so far, one can look forward to more surprises. ML

Harvey Keitel

Born **Brooklyn, New York, 1947**

As much as Robert de Niro's, the career of Harvey Keitel demonstrates a difference between actor and star. If he is a star it is not through any prompting of his own. He dislikes the concept and proscribes the expression, in conversation, with flinty concision. ('The term has no substance whatever.') Still he has found himself, and not presumably by accident, in some of the most interesting films of the decade – not, invariably, in the leading role but sufficiently frequently for him to have acquired fame and notice. If 'taking the leading role' in a film is the same thing as 'starring', it is a description he will have to bear.

Another reason for reluctance may perhaps be put down to physique. He has the stocky, bullish gait of a character actor. Like Cagney and Robinson before him, what is lacking in good looks, is made up for by energy and presence. Yet the toughness of Cagney and Robinson had, for its reverse side, a certain fastidious dandyism. So it is with Keitel. One remembers in *Taxi Driver* (1976) the pimp's long painted fingernail, as he sways in the lurid semi-darkness clutching Jody Foster to his bosom.

This dandyism is an intriguing characteristic. Keitel's hair, in *Taxi Driver*, came down to his shoulders. In *The Duellists* (1977), where he plays an officer of the Hussars, it is braided into side-hanging bangles. The young-man-on-the-make in *Mean Streets* (1973) has his suits laid out by his mother (and his shirts have monogrammed initials). A

cynical elegance is brought to the part of the goatee-bearded professional international terrorist in James Toback's *Exposed* (1982). More recently still, in *Order of Death* (1983), as a corrupt police officer, there is a deft, precise way of holding a newspaper (folded on either side of the centre, making it a vertical prayer scroll), and the same thing goes for his manner of choosing cigars and pouring measures of whisky. The persona is Keitel – wise to the street – but also aesthetically oriented. He seems to like roles in which social expectations are subtly subverted, as happens in *Bad Timing*, (1980), where the Austrian police inspector sports a Harvard degree and a secret obsession with opera. In *Fingers* (James Toback, 1978) this tendency is taken to its furthest extreme when Keitel plays a Mafia hit man who is at the same time a cultured concert pianist.

One is not sure what to make of all this: his best role to date, after all, is still the working-class immigrant Bartowski in Paul Schrader's brilliant factory drama *Blue Collar* (1978). Other fine films of the 70s, to whose success his acting has contributed, include *Alice Doesn't Live Here Anymore* (1975), *Buffalo Bill And The Indians* (1976), *Welcome to L.A.* (1977) and (with Jack Nicholson) *The Border* (1982).

The ex-Marine, Method-trained actor remains a mysterious private individual as well as a ferociously hard worker, and it is difficult to predict his eventual place in the pantheon. He is a penetrating and powerful actor, but there is something about him that is a trifle dour and humourless. Perhaps it is simply the price he charges for holding onto a jealously-guarded privacy. ML

in Mean Streets (Warner Bros., 1973)

Margot Kidder

Born **Yellow Knife, Canada, 17 October 1948**

Margot Kidder appeared in eight films, some of them not at all bad, before she shot to fame in the part of Lois Lane, Superman's girlfriend, in the screen's first adaptation of the comic-book (1978). Whether she will be able to capitalise on this fortune remains a matter of conjecture. *Superman II* (1980) was, from her point of view a step forward, giving her the opportunity to display a nice line of knowing sexy irony. She almost captured the film from her co-star Christopher Reeve. (Indeed it could be said she did capture it, by managing to lure him to bed.) Quarrels, however, with the films' producers resulted in the part being severely curtailed (11 lines in all) in the sequel, *Superman III* (1983). Concurrent projects – *Willie and Phil* (1981), *Heartache* (1981, made in Canada), *Some Kind Of Hero* (1982, made with short-term boyfriend Richard Pryor), and *Trenchcoat* (1983) – failed to find critical enthusiasm.

Contrary to the image of sensible Lois Lane, her private life has tended towards the bohemian. An instinctive, raunchy, non-intellectual woman, she seems vulnerable to false starts and dubious career decisions. (In the mid-70s she posed naked for 'Playboy'.) Previous films include Brian De Palma's excellent *Blood Sisters* (1973) and, starring against

in Some Kind Of Hero (Paramount, 1982)

Robert Redford, *The Great Waldo Pepper* (1975). Divorced twice – her marriage to actor John Heard lasting a mere six weeks – she has recently married again, this time to veteran French film director Philippe De Broca. ML

Klaus Kinski

Real name **Claus Gunther Nakszynski**
Born **Sopot, Danzig (now Poland), 1926**

The Polish-born, German speaking actor (father of Nastassia) Klaus Kinski existed, in the recent past, as a phenomenon of film-acting energy. In a career that has taken him from Germany in the 1950s, through Italy and France, finally hence to America, he has appeared in an astonishing estimate of 200 movies. The object of the exercise appears to have been simply the amassing of a fortune, in which goal he has certainly succeeded, even though it meant turning down offers of parts from directors as distinguished as Visconti, Pasolini and Fellini that

in Love And Money (Paramount, 1982)

were not deemed sufficiently lucrative. One European director of a younger generation did manage to capture him. This was the German Werner Herzog; and it is on the basis of four films for Herzog made over the last decade that Kinski's name will go down in the history books.

The first of these (1971) was *Aguirre, The Wrath of God*, the story of a Peruvian river expedition in search of the lost El Dorado. The fierce, noble demeanour of Kinski as the expedition's deluded leader, cradling in his arms the body of his daughter (transfixed by an Indian arrow) remains ineffaceably memorable – a permanent addition to cinema's evanescent iconography.

A decade later Herzog returned to the same source – another story but the identical myth – in *Fitzcarraldo* (1982), an international success. This time round Kinski played a 19th-century enthusiast determined to establish an opera house in the middle of the South American jungle. His efforts are doomed and heroic (they include the famous shifting of a paddle-steamer over a mountain). But the pleasure of this film, when measured against the earlier one, lay precisely in its untragic ebullience. Herzog discovered the impossible combination of an epic that was happy, and a defeat that left the audience exalted.

Meantime, back in Europe, two films – *Nosferatu* (1978) and *Woyzeck* (1979) – harnessed Kinski's talents further to an exploration of German romanticism. They were by and large successful. Kinski's acting has always been broad and gothic, and these two films offered ample scope for the exaggerated, operatic gesture he delights in. Divorced from Herzog's visionary projects, Kinski's acting will seem mannered and irritating. Inside them, however, his style is an apparition of genius. ML

Liza Minnelli

Born Los Angeles, 12 March 1946

One night, Judy Garland woke her husband, film director Vincente Minnelli, and said, 'I have a name for the baby if it's a girl. How about Liza? Liza Minnelli. It will look so good on a marquee.' Given the child's antecedents, it was most likely that Judy's prognostication would be fulfilled. It was not easy for Liza to find her own place in the spotlight away from her mother's long shadow. As a performer, she is too close to Judy to avoid comparisons, and audiences old enough to have been fans of her mother since childhood, were slow to accept her. The two have a similar intensity, warm vibrato, the blend of pathos and humour, and an over-eagerness to communicate with their audiences. Even their looks are often eerily alike, although Judy became a giant pixie while Liza has remained a tall and gawky waif. Both walked the perilous tightrope between personal neurosis and public persona. But Liza has kept her balance and not fallen fatally as her mother did. Liza is really in her element on stage, where her enlarged emotions and audience contact are given the space that films have not provided. Apart from *Cabaret* (1972) and *New York, New York* (1977), her film career has been unfortunate. It is noticeable that she is at her best in the latter when she emulates Judy by relaxing in, rather than reacting against, her mother's legacy.

Named after the Gershwin song 'Liza', she used to bounce around to music long before she could walk. At a very early age, she was taken to dancing lessons at the studios of Nico Charisse, Cyd's ex-husband. Liza made her screen debut at two-and-a-half years old as the daughter of Van Johnson and Judy Garland in the final shot of *In The Good Old Summertime* (1949). A film set became a familiar place from early childhood, a place where she would always hang around watching her parents work, and she grew up exposed to all the glamorous people that would visit their home, often curling up under the piano to listen to their conversation. But after her parents divorced when she was five, Liza never remained in one place very long. Mother and father each had six months custody of her every year, and the precocious girl was shuttled back and forth between them, attending over sixteen schools, including one in Annecy, France and the Paris Sorbonne.

The child's education in show business, however, wanted for nothing. At seven, Judy permitted her to dance on stage at the Palace Theater, New York, while she herself sang 'Swanee'. Four years later, Liza was watching from the wings while her mother performed at a Las Vegas nightclub. The audience seemed to be too busy eating, drinking and talking to pay much attention to Judy. She stopped singing, walked over to Liza, led her onto the stage and introduced her. Left alone, Liza sang some of her mother's songs, including 'The Man That Got Away'. In a movie version, the child would have stilled the audience, but they continued to pay little attention. Nevertheless, Liza had her first taste of cabaret. 'You were terrific', Judy commented. As Liza told Gerold Frank, Judy's biographer, 'I couldn't sing worth a damn then – it was nice of Mama to say that to me.' More formative stage experience followed. Liza played the title role in a school production of 'The Diary Of Anne Frank' that toured Israel. Judy, in the audience, cried all the way through a performance into a powder puff as she didn't have a handkerchief. But when Liza was playing the third lead in an off-Broadway revival of 'Best Foot Forward' in 1963, Judy pretended to have forgotten the date of the first night in order to prevent her presence from detracting from her daughter's.

Among the many schools Liza attended, was the School of Performing Arts in New York. But her best teacher was her famous mother. Judy taught her that singing was acting. 'You never lose the thought behind the word. You are not just singing a note,' she explained. Liza continued to learn nightly, when

she appeared with her mother at the London Palladium in 1964. There was never any rivalry or jealousy between mother and daughter, but Judy dominated the show, cruelly exposing Liza's inexperience and encouraging a sentimental complicity between her and the audience and between her and Liza. However, Liza came into her own the following year in the title role of the Broadway musical 'Flora, The Red Menace' for which she received a Tony award. She was introduced by her mother to Peter Allen, one of the singing Allen Brothers, and they were married in 1967.

In the same year, she made her adult screen debut opposite Albert Finney in Finney's first film as director, *Charlie Bubbles* (1968), in which she lightened the gloom somewhat as the kind of kook that Shirley MacLaine had been playing for a decade. She then took her self-conscious mannerisms to an irritating extreme as Pookie Adams, a neurotic college girl who calls everyone who disagrees with her, a 'weirdo', in *The Sterile Cuckoo* (1969). The role got her nominated for an Oscar in a poor year. In Otto Preminger's *Tell Me That You Love Me, Junie Moon* (1970), she played a physically scarred girl whose sexual hangups are illustrated by

a lurid flashback. The film was as shrill as her performance. A further demonstration of the way a kookie crumbles was given in Stanley Donen's hapless *Lucky Lady* (1975), with Liza as an idiotic floozy in a blonde wig. Not much better than this crude comedy, was her long-awaited collaboration with her father, in the disastrously twee *A Matter Of Time* (1976). The hope that Vincente Minnelli would be able to recapture the great days of his musicals with Judy (*Meet Me In St. Louis*, 1944, and *The Pirate*, 1948) through his daughter, was soon shattered. The world had changed and Liza had gathered a young and modern audience. She was not suited to the role of a French chambermaid learning about love and life from Contessa Ingrid Bergman, a part which called upon her to burst inappropriately into song once or twice. She was also wasted in an underwritten supporting role to Dudley Moore's drunken playboy in *Arthur* (1982).

It is plain that she needs stern direction in the cinema, and she received it in her two best roles. The brashness that covers the insecurities of her character was perfectly suited to the brashness that covered the insecurities of Berlin in the 30s in Bob Fosse's *Cabaret* (1972). As Sally Bowles, an American nightclub singer, she was too good a singer to be found in such a sleazy dive as the Kit Kat Club, but who cared? Her songs were put over with such bite and passion, and her acting carried a moving conviction. The Oscar that she won is as much a tribute to Fosse as to Liza. As the singer in Martin Scorsese's entertaining pastiche of a 40s movie, *New York, New York*, Liza was able to play the sort of role worthy of her mother, and did so with comparable power and vulnerability. The French, indeed, have dubbed her *La petite Piaf Américaine*. By now she had divorced Peter Allen and married Jack Haley Jr, the son of the actor who had played The Tin Man opposite Judy in *The Wizard Of Oz* (1949). Now she fell under Martin Scorsese's spell. Her second marriage ended. Scorsese started directing her in the Broadway musical 'The Act', but Gower Champion came in to bring his musical know-how to it. Liza triumphed and won a Tony. In 1984, she made another hit on stage in 'The Rink' as Chita Rivera's daughter. The time has long passed when she had to justify her existence as an individual, with an identity separate from her mother's, by spelling out her name, 'L-I-Z-A – Liza with a zee. That's me'. RB

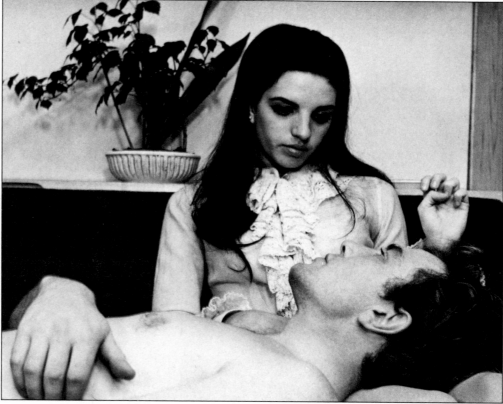

with Albert Finney in Charlie Bubbles *(Universal, 1968)*

in Arthur (Warner Bros., 1981) ▷

Roger Moore

Born **London, 14 October 1928**

Sean Connery bowed out of the Bond role after his sixth effort (*Diamonds Are Forever*, 1971), handing over the reins to Roger Moore who carried on the series through the 70s. Like the Kabuki theatre of 19th-century Japan, the formula is always the same, but amenable to infinite adjustment. The successive waves of fashion whose rise and fall elsewhere affect the arts profoundly, fail to make an impression on its watertight, rocksure foundation. The personality of

in 1980

Moore, habitually dismissed as a lightweight, is thus adequate enough for the purpose. He has forged for himself, if he never before possessed it, the lightness of touch, the insouciance, the humour, of a genuine star. Polled by the 'Daily Express', seven out of ten women still prefer Connery. One can't however imagine this news rendering Moore the slightest bit ruffled. His ironical eyes are Olympian. He has a true artist's freedom from vanity. He is a gentleman.

The changeover went smoothly enough with *Live And Let Die* (1973), the 'Voodoo' Bond, with action set in the Caribbean. *The Man With The Golden Gun* (1974), set in the Far East, is probably the poorest in the series; *The Spy Who Loved Me* (1977) and *Moonraker* (1979) are full-blown exercises in gadgetry, with incredible sets by Ken Adam, the one beneath the depths of the ocean, the other circulating in outer space. *For Your Eyes Only* (1981) attempts, intelligently, to come back to earth again, with settings in exotic Southern Europe. *Octopussy* (1983) transports us to India.

Meanwhile, spurred on by the return of Connery in *Never Say Never Again* (1983), another Bond with Moore, *From A View To A Kill*, is in current preparation (for which the star's salary is reputed to be an awesome £2 million).

Moore has come a long way from humble beginnings. (His father was a policeman in South London). After training at RADA, he found small parts in British films, before following his second wife, the singer Dorothy Squires, to America. The film roles in Hollywood, after an initial promising start, didn't materialise. The marriage was unhappy, ending later in acrimonious divorce. (Now an exemplary *paterfamilias* – one of the pleasantest things about him – he has been married to his present wife Luisa for 23 years, and is the father of four children.) Then, at last, two television series in Britain, 'The Saint' (1962–67) and later, with Tony Curtis, 'The Persuaders', made him famous, thanks to the entrepreneurial efforts of Lord Grade. Nor, to his credit, has the star rested on his laurels. Besides the Bonds, Moore has made a number of successful comedy and adventure films in recent years: *The Wild Geese* (1977), *Escape To Athena* (1978), *North Sea Hijack* (1980), *The Sea Wolves* (1980) and *The Cannonball Run* (1981). ML

Franco Nero

Real name **Franco Sparanero**
Born **Southern Italy, 1942**

Franco Nero likes to joke that his most famous role, Lancelot to Vanessa Redgrave's Guinevere in the film version of the musical *Camelot* (Joshua Logan, 1967), almost put paid to his career. Raised to a pinnacle of fame in his native Italy – almost as great as that of Clint Eastwood in America – and by much the same means, as hero of a series of Spaghetti Westerns (the so-called 'Django Cycle', directed by Sergio Corbucci), he as near as anything blew it all by being seen to *sing* (for heaven's sake!) mounted on a warhorse, and from within the confines of a clanking suit of armour.

But one recovers. Nero has never taken his acting more seriously than it deserves, resting content on the whole to let his sultry Latin looks see him through the worst. He works hard at his chosen profession (he has appeared in over 60 films), but only, one suspects, so as to enjoy more keenly the moments of pleasure in between. He has a pleasant villa outside Rome; he grows his own vines; he is apparently a generous host.

in Tristana *(Maron, 1970)*

Rather more famous for his looks than for his talent, his name – in default of other matters – has frequently been linked with the names of beautiful women. The major liaison of his life has been with Vanessa Redgrave, whom he met on the set of *Camelot* and with whom, for six years, he battled in a tempestuous relationship. (A son was born to the couple in 1970). Recently the couple have been together again on film, Tony Palmer's ill-fated *Wagner* (1983) in which Nero played a chief of police. But the shooting of their different scenes in Vienna took place on separate days, thus sparing an encounter in the flesh.

With 60 films behind him it would be unusual not to have had a few critical successes. Nero has worked with good directors – with John Huston in *The Bible* (1966: Abel to Richard Harris's Cain); with Buñuel in *Tristana* (1970: as the artist); with Chabrol in *The Musicians* (1975). *The Virgin And The Gypsy* (Christopher Miles, 1970) was well received by critics and public. The fairly disastrous *Pope Joan* (1970), with Liv Ullmann and *The Monk* (Aydou Kyrou, 1972) still enjoy a certain cult popularity. *Force 10 From Navarone* (Guy Hamilton, 1978), with Edward Fox, Robert Shaw and Harrison Ford, is an exciting adventure film, and recently he has appeared with Ursula Andress in an epic – *Red Bells* (1981) – directed by no less than Sergei Bondarchuk. ML

Nick Nolte

Born **Omaha, Nebraska, 1941**

The great stars who came to fame in the 60s – Redford, Newman, Eastwood, Caan – continued to diffuse their glamour as powerfully as ever into the 70s. Meanwhile, unsurprisingly, hot on their trail comes a generation of promising younger actors who, as the 70s have moved into the 80s, begin to show – more than mere sex appeal (which attribute can be taken for granted) – a toughness, an authority, an integrity of character that mark them out from their contemporaries. A representative list of such actors (neither quite in the 70s, nor 80s) would have to include Richard Gere, Christopher Walken, Robert De Niro, – and, certainly, Nick Nolte.

Nolte is a Nietzschean actor, by which it is implied that his restless physical energy, exactly like Robert De Niro's, is essentially serious, and harnessed to the service of his art. Both men are, in the strictest sense, intellectual rather than popular actors, with discriminating standards about the kind of film they will allow themselves to act in. Nolte appeared in *The Deep* (1976) – but hated it (he refers to the pain of 'competing against Jacqueline Bissett's T-shirt'). Two very lucrative assignments have been turned down by him – the first being to take part in the sequel to the immensely successful television series 'Rich Man Poor Man', in which (as Tom Jordache), he had originally acquired stardom and fame. The second – if true, even more notorious – was to play Superman in the original movie.

If in the event he passed over *Superman*, it was for the role of Neal Cassady in *Heart Beat* (1978), John Byrum's pictorial, poetic version of the Jack Kerouac story. Somehow the symbolism is appropriate. Cassady was a bohemian and a hell-raiser, a charming, witty rebel whose intellect was kept sharp by an opposition to all forms of establishment. That is rather like Nolte. Mainly, he finds himself playing roles involving men whose lucid despair is disguised behind passionate energy. *48 Hours* (1983), with Nolte as a policeman yoked to a black criminal, is

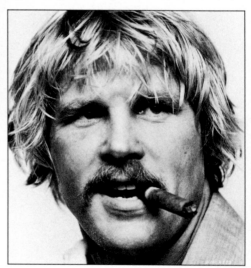

in 1977

simply the best film to date of director Walter Hill. In *Dog Soldiers* (1977: American title *Who'll Stop The Rain?*) he plays an educated dope smuggler drawn into the game, in the wake of Vietnam, by a sort of gambler's need for excitement and adventure. In *Under Fire* (1984), he is a liberal reporter during the war in Nicaragua, whose uncovering of the truth leads paradoxically to the confounding of friends, and the victory of establishment interests. In *North Dallas Forty* (1979), a grim, gritty saga of football life, his is the consciousness that perceives what the younger footballers are incapable of realising, the sadness and the exploitation which are inherent in the national pastime. All these films are, in the best sense of the word, dissident: small-scale, textured, finely crafted and imagined: in a word, an addition to the canon. ML

Al Pacino

Real name **Alberto Pacino**
Born **New York City, 25 April 1940**

Of Sicilian descent, Al Pacino was raised in New York's South Bronx by his mother and grandparents, his father having left the family. From his earliest childhood he was an actor, that is, a show-off: he would spend every free moment (and frequently played truant) at the movies, which he then acted out at home for his grandmother. This enthusiasm led to acceptance by Manhattan's High School of Performing Arts (of *Fame* fame), though even there his congenital resistance to discipline and academic studies emerged and he dropped out when he was only 17. He then drifted through a series of temporary jobs until he had saved enough to pay his tuition at Herbert Berghof's acting school; concurrently, he auditioned for and received a number of small parts off-Broadway. After two years of study at the Actors Studio, he won an off-Broadway award (the Obie) for his performance as a psychotic in 'The Indian Wants The Bronx', capping that with Broadway's own award (the Tony) for playing a junkie in 'Does A Tiger Wear A Necktie?'.

His screen debut came in a totally forgotten film *Me, Natalie* (1969); but, two years later, it was another performance as a drug addict, in Jerry Schatzberg's *Panic In Needle Park*, which brought him to the attention of Francis Ford Coppola who was searching for a young, not too famous actor to play Michael Corleone, heir to Don Vito, in The

in The Godfather, Part II (Paramount, 1974)

Godfather (1972). Though his co-stars Brando and De Niro were both infinitely better-known than Pacino, it was he who had the pivotal role of the whole saga, the only role which truly developed (and moved to centre-stage in Coppola's sequel *The Godfather Part II*, 1974). He was nominated for an Oscar, and his darkly intense, goodlooking features and small, muscular build were now invested with star quality. Between the two *Godfathers* he made a somewhat old-fashioned on-the-road movie for Schatzberg, *Scarecrow* (1973), in which he and Gene Hackman played a pair of poeticized hoboes; and was nominated for a second Oscar for his richly

in Serpico (Paramount, 1973)

faceted performance as the obsessive, hippiesque cop *Serpico* in Sidney Lumet's film. (His third nomination was for *The Godfather Part II*.)

Always the bridesmaid, Pacino was a nominee yet again for what is perhaps his most brilliant performance to date – as the homosexual bank robber hoping to use the proceeds to pay for his lover's sex-change operation in Lumet's *Dog Day Afternoon* (1975). Though he was omitted from the nomination lists for 1977 (his sole appearance had been in Sidney Pollack's grotesquely sentimental melodrama *Bobby Deerfield*), there he was again in 1979

for *... And Justice For All* (1979), a slick, specious indictment of the American legal system directed by Norman Jewison.

Pacino chooses his parts with deliberation, and has, in consequence, made only a dozen films in a career spanning fifteen years. If, in any particular year, none of the scripts which he is offered stimulates him, he will simply return to the theatre: most recently, for example, in the Broadway production of 'The Basic Training Of Pavlo Hummel', for which he received his second Tony. He has taken risks which were hardly justified by the results: William Friedkin's repulsive *Cruising* (1980), in which he played an undercover cop sucked into the S and M scene in New York's gay bars. And let his hair down in 'commercial' films which never managed to find their audience: his foray into hip, wise-cracking comedy, *Author! Author!* (1982). But his is one of the most compelling presences in the current American cinema; and, whatever the wisdom of remaking Howard Hawks' classic *Scarface* in 1983, as Brian De Palma has done, the existence of Al Pacino (in the title role) as the agent of its violence might already be considered sufficient reason. DM

Valerie Perrine

Born **Galveston, Texas, 3 September 1944**

Tall, talented, tender and tantalizing, Valerie Perrine is an actress starved of meaty parts. Over a decade ago, she was nominated for the Best Actress Oscar for her role as Lenny Bruce's long-suffering wife, the stripper Honey Harlowe in Bob Fosse's *Lenny* (1974). Her touching and funny performance was not outshone even by Dustin Hoffman's virtuosity in the title role. She has since made a living playing various sexy, dumb broads, without being asked to over-extend herself.

Valerie's father was an army officer and her mother a former showgirl. Because of her father's profession, she spent much of her childhood in Japan and other overseas army posts. After studying for a short period at the universities of Arizona and Nevada, she got a job as a topless showgirl in a Las Vegas nightclub. Like many other young people in the 60s, the future screen actress went hippie. She embarked upon drugs, communes, the novels of Herman Hesse and all the other assorted rites of the

in 1974

cult, before finding herself in Los Angeles on welfare.

One of the literary heroes of hippie culture was Kurt Vonnegut. Valerie made her film debut in George Roy Hill's *Slaughterhouse Five* (1972), based on his 'time-tripping' novel, and made an impression as a beautiful, outer-space Hollywood starlet named Montana Wildhack. In *The Last American Hero* (1973), she played an amoral stock-car racing groupie who has the hots for any driver that wins. After her success in *Lenny*, she was cast in another biopic as the 'Me' in the title of *W.C. Fields And Me* (1976), bringing some flesh to the cardboard character of Carlotta Monti, Fields' mistress for the last fourteen years of his life. She did what she could as Lex Luthor's stereotyped dumb-blonde girlfriend in *Superman* (1978), also cropping up in *Superman II* (1980). Appearing as a top New York model who promotes The Village People in the crass disco movie *Can't Stop The Music* (1980) did nothing to further her career, but a role as the sexy, affectionate wife who has aspirations beyond her husband Jack Nicholson's income in *The Border* (1981), showed what she is capable of, and perhaps her real opportunities will now come along. RB

Burt Reynolds

Born **Waycross, Georgia, 11 February 1936**

If the box-office was the only yardstick of success, then Burt Reynolds could rest easily on his laurels. The Number One attraction for four successive years from 1979 to 1981, his films have grossed well over $400 million, and *Smokey And The Bandit* (1977), the ultimate drive-in smash, was second only to George Lucas's *Star Wars*. But Reynolds has long yearned for critical acceptance, an earnest ambition constantly undermined by his image as genial macho man, laid-back master of the one-line put-down on Johnny Carson's 'Tonight' show, and coy 'Cosmopolitan' centrefold. He wants to be Cary Grant, and has attempted the role in the 80s in *Rough Cut* (a distant cousin of *To Catch A Thief*) and *Paternity* (which feebly stirred the embers of *Bringing Up Baby*). But the star's wolfish grin echoes Gable's swagger rather than Grant's contained, astringent style. Grant had a disturbingly dark side, glimpsed in *Suspicion* (1941) and *Notorious* (1946), but Burt's alter ego is often troubled, a bit confused, and almost desperately eager to please. His vulnerability has been artfully exploited by Robert Aldrich in his two most interesting films, *The Longest Yard* (1974) and *Hustle* (1975), but his vast audience prefers him in the role of the sly good ol' boy of *White Lightning* (1973) and *Gator* (1976), always a bit sharper than anyone expects, outwitting fat, ugly rednecks and trading raunchy banter amid the mayhem of hurtling automobiles.

He was brought up in Palm Beach, Florida, where his father, a former cowboy, was chief of police. On his father's side, his grandmother was a full-blooded Cherokee Indian. At Florida State University he was a football star, but an automobile accident wrecked his chances of a professional career with the Baltimore Colts. He drifted into acting at Palm Beach Junior College, and then tried his hand in New York, where he supported himself with stunt work, as well as a stint as a bouncer at Roseland. He had a part in Charlton Heston's Broadway revival of 'Mr Roberts' and, in January 1959, arrived in Hollywood, having signed a seven-year contract with MCA-Universal. He was cast as the second lead in a TV series, 'Riverboat', where he struck up a friendship with stuntman Hal Needham, an important figure in his later career and the director of *Smokey And The Bandit* (1977), *Hooper* (1978) and *The Cannonball Run* (1981).

After a year in 'Riverboat', he was released from his contract, appeared in a Broadway production of 'Look, We've Come Through' and then returned to California to play Quint Asper, the blacksmith in the long-running 'Gunsmoke' series. In 1966, he starred in 'Hawk', in which he played a half-Indian detective. It foundered after four episodes – two of which

in Deliverance *(Warner Bros., 1972)*

he directed – at about the same time as the collapse of his marriage to the English actress Judy Carne (the 'Sock It To Me' girl of Rowan and Martin's 'Laugh In'). His last television series was the shortlived 'Dan August' (1970).

Reynolds had made his big-screen debut nine years earlier, in *Angel Baby* (1961). In the 60s he strolled through a string of routine films: *Operation CIA* (1965), *Impasse* (1968), *Skullduggery* (1970) and Sam Fuller's *Shark* (1970), although he gave a relaxed performance, encouraged by Angie Dickinson's warm sexiness, in *Sam Whiskey* (1969), and in *100 Rifles* (1969) nimbly stole the show from Raquel Welch and the humourless Jim Brown. The big break came with John Boorman's *Deliverance* (1972), in which Burt played Lewis Medlock, the bow-wielding believer in the need for man to come to terms with Nature. His high-definition performance transformed him into a major personality star, a position cemented in the same year by his appearance, tastefully naked, in 'Cosmopolitan' magazine. The film and the centrefold reflected the two poles of his appeal – as a fantasy drinking buddy for Middle American men and as the dream lover for their wives. Reynolds's amused acknowledgement of this iconic status quickly took him from the pages of 'Cosmopolitan' to the culture chic of Andy Warhol's 'Interview' magazine. Nor was he slow to guy his own image, appearing as 'the Switchboard' in the 'What Happens During Ejaculation' segment of *Everything You Always Wanted To Know About Sex But Were Always Afraid To Ask* (1972). He followed *Deliverance* with *Fuzz* (1972), a broadly comic

reworking of Ed McBain's '87th Precinct' novel, in which he dressed up as a nun to stake out a criminal. After *Shamus* (1973), an offbeat private-eye tale in which Burt easily outdid Philip Marlowe in the number of times he managed to get beaten up, he slipped easily into the country boy role of Gator McCluskey, in *White Lightning* (1973). In Reynolds's own words, Gator is 'an ordinary guy who does extraordinary things but still has his Egg McMuffin in the morning'.

After *The Man Who Loved Cat Dancing* (1973), a sluggish Western whose filming was interrupted by the suicide on location of his co-star Sarah Miles's manager, he moved into a higher gear in Robert Aldrich's *The Longest Yard* (1974). Reynolds was Paul Crewe, a washed-up football star who has 'sold out' his team and is now serving time in the state pen. Pressganged into training and playing in a prisoners' team to give the ferocious guards' squad a work out, he is presented with a simple ultimatum – if he doesn't 'throw' the game, his stay will become indefinite. Aldrich went on to tap the star's underlying hesitant streak in *Hustle* (1975), a film noir companion piece to his *Kiss Me Deadly* (1955), in which Reynolds was cast as a divorced cop living with call girl Catherine Deneuve. She stays on the game, making erotic phone calls to her clients while he listens. The mid-70s saw a disappointing run of films: *WW And The Dixie Dancekings* (1975); Stanley Donen's feeble comedy-thriller *Lucky Lady* (1975), which contrived to waste the talents of Reynolds, Liza Minnelli and Gene Hackman in equal measure; and Peter Bogdanovich's lumbering homage to the 30s musical, *At Long Last Love* (1975). Burt almost succeeded in extricating himself from this disaster with some engagingly amateurish hoofing, breathlessly murmuring, 'I don't get enough exercise' at the height of a strenuous routine. There was another flop with Bogdanovich, *Nickelodeon* (1976), set in the early days of cinema. Then the actor followed the trail blazed by Clint Eastwood, directing himself in *Gator*, sometimes appearing to be doing it by numbers, but nonetheless dispensing buckets of shaggy dog charm.

Smokey And The Bandit (1977) cast him as the Bandit, an ace trucker running a 900-mile gauntlet pursued by Jackie Gleason's Sheriff Burford T. Justice. In Michael Ritchie's *Semi-Tough* (1977) he sparred with footballing buddy Kris Kristofferson over classy Jill Clayburgh. He returned to directing again in *The End* (1978), playing against type as a man on the edge of middle age who is told that he has only a short time to live. An ambitious comedy, aiming to milk its laughs from the Great American Taboo, death, it lost its nerve half way through and sputtered out in a rush of Mel Brooks-type slapstick. In *Hooper* (1978) he returned to the style of his early television days, playing an ageing stunt king with creaking joints, persuaded by ambitious tyro Jan Michael Vincent to go for the biggest stunt of them all. Alan J. Pakula's *Starting Over* (1979) stranded him, dithering, between ex-wife Candice Bergen and mistress Jill Clayburgh; *Rough Cut* (1980) had Burt as a retired jewel thief tempted out of retirement by Lesley-Anne Down, but the mood fell flat; in *Paternity* (1981) he revealed a deft comic touch, paying Beverly D'Angelo to bear his child; then there was a flight to familiar territory in *The Cannonball Run* (1981), a coast-to-coast auto race adventure. *Sharky's Machine* (1981), in which he again directed himself, cleverly combined his flair for laconic fallibility with the commercial demands of mainstream macho. At the film's 'climax', the chief villain is literally bodily ejaculated from the top of a skyscraper - a jokey aside on the director/star's status as a phallic symbol.

Norman Jewison's *Best Friends* (1981), co-starring Goldie Hawn, was an old-fashioned romantic comedy with both stars playing it to the hilt and walking off at the end into a glowing Californian sunrise. After this, there was an air of inevitability about his lazy collapse into the abundant embrace of Dolly Parton in his role of the sheriff in *The Best Little Whorehouse In Texas* (1982). RC

with Goldie Hawn in Best Friends *(Warner Bros., 1981)*

in The Best Little Whorehouse In Texas *(Universal, 1982)* ▷

Gena Rowlands

Born **Cambria, Wisconsin, 19 June 1934**

Gena Rowlands has been married to the film director and actor John Cassavetes for thirty years and has successfully combined her acting career with bringing up a family of three children. The solidity of the marriage bond, and the enduring happiness that has come from it, are a palpable part of her film personality, never so much in evidence, paradoxically, as in roles dealing with breakdown and suicide. Thus, such distress as she displays on screen is always a stress that results from getting further *into* a relationship, never from avoiding it or reneging on it. One feels this is something very personal. The embracing humanism, seriousness and maturity of her acting is relatively rare in contemporary American cinema. And it is as far from Hollywood's superficial glamour as it is from the celluloid conception of the opposite pole of neuroticism.

She has made six films under Cassavetes's direction, four of them in the last decade. In *Minnie and Moskowitz* (1971), a superficially incredible comedy, she plays a middle-class woman who falls for the car-parking attendant at her place of work (the Los Angeles County Museum). A film that starts in darkness and moves slowly into light, its serious sub-theme is the necessity for love and commitment. Altogether it is better than its kooky, eccentric premise might suggest. *A Woman Under The Influence* (1974) is her most serious film, a devastating portrait of breakdown, and yet not, for all that, without flashes of residual humour. One feels that each incident is given a chance, not 'weighted' towards optimism or pessimism. The acting, at all events (Peter Falk is the co-star), is stunning.

With *Opening Night* (1977) she again portrays breakdown, this time of an actress forced by an accidental death to confront aspects of her personality she would rather not know about. But, typically for Cassavetes and his star, it is the therapy – provided by agent, producer and fellow actors – that is concentrated on, not the disaster. Finally, *Gloria* (1979) is an excellent witty tale of a woman on the run from the Mafia, shielding a 10-year-old boy. The story is exciting enough; but it is the oddity of detail, and the natural warmth of affection between woman and child – the gutsiness of their response to adversity – that are liable to stay in the memory.

Earlier films with Cassavetes include *Faces* (1968) and the somewhat sentimental *A Child Is Waiting* (1963). She has starred against Frank Sinatra (*Tony Rome*, 1967), Kirk Douglas (*Lonely Are The Brave*, 1962) and Charlton Heston (*Two Minute Warning*, 1976). A handsome comfortable woman to look at, she has green eyes, a blonde complexion and an %nvariably pleasant speaking voice that may have something to do with the Welsh-descended community (Cambria, Wisconsin) in which she was raised, and to which she returns every year. ML

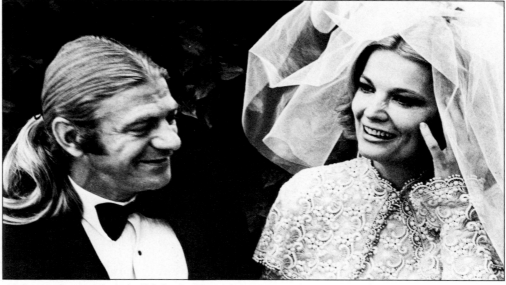

with Seymour Cassel in Minnie And Moskowitz *(Universal, 1971)*

Susan Sarandon

Real name **Susan Tomaling**
Born **New York, 4 October 1946**

The quirks of fame are odd. How much belongs to luck and how much to talent is forever imponderable. The career of Susan Sarandon, which started in 1970, had taken in, until recently – along with some interesting work – too many indifferent films to hold out hope for the ultimate accolade. Is she more interesting than, say, Shelley Duvall? or Jessica Harper? or Barbara Hershey? Probably not. Then came *Atlantic City USA* (1980) and an Academy award nomination for her role as Sally, the waitress who washes her breasts in the juice of fresh lemons, and who, picked up by Burt Lancaster, dreams of departing for Morocco. It was a film about the heroism of delusion and the bravery of the imagination. Suddenly, in this nice small part, one saw that she did have talent. And elegance. The relationship with Louis Malle, the film's director, subsequently over, has obviously been important for her confidence. (He had directed her once previously, in *Pretty Baby* (1978), where she had the role of the child prostitute Brooke Shields's mother.) Co-incidentally it turns out she is excellent on the stage, though her film career has held up without formal acting training of any kind.

A tall, squirrel-eyed, angular beauty, she was first seen to effect in Billy Wilder's comedy *The Front Page* (1974); then briefly, before falling off the wing of a bi-plane, in *The Great Waldo Pepper* (1975). She was the dewy-eyed innocent Janet in *The Rocky Horror Picture Show* (1975). The end of her marriage

in Pretty Baby *(Paramount, 1978)*

(to the actor Chris Sarandon) led to a nervous breakdown in 1976. Evidently she recovered with resilience, though a number of wasteful roles followed. Recently, post-*Atlantic City*, she has played Ariel in Paul Mazursky's version of *The Tempest* (1982). She was vampirised sexily by Catherine Deneuve in *The Hunger* (1983). Now she plays opposite Richard Dreyfuss in a 'serious comedy' called *The Buddy System* (1984). The occasional wildness of the past seems slowly to be adapting to the more sober demands of ambition. Thus one looks forward to her future work with some interest, though with not a little trepidation. ML

in In Search Of Gregory *(Universal, 1969)*

Michael Sarrazin

Born **Quebec City, 22 May 1940**

This tall, intense-eyed actor had a brief ride of fame at the end of the 60s and beginning of the 70s. As a successful actor in his own right, and long-term boyfriend of one of Hollywood's most glamorous stars, Jacqueline Bissett, his prosperity and future success would seem to have been sufficiently sewn up. It would only be a matter of time and of consolidation. But after a splash in 1972, the parts never seem to have materialised in sufficient quantity or quality. If Michael Sarrazin had started off a step ahead of actors like Harvey Keitel and Robert De Niro, the truth is that now he is a long way behind them.

Why should this be? Impossible, probably, to speculate: character and good luck are far too mysteriously entwined to be disentangled. His handsomeness, perhaps – those staring eyes – had always about it something gaunt and frightening, so that he came over like a slightly demented version of Anthony Perkins. His skinny frame and smallish head, surmounted by a copious coiffeur, kept him boyish-looking, when other actors (for example Keitel, De Niro) were experimenting with older and more strongly-written parts. The sense of rebelliousness combined with ultimate failure, that he projected so well as Jane Fonda's marathon dance partner in Sidney Pollack's powerful Depression movie, *They Shoot Horses Don't They?* (1969), ironically seems to have clung to his own career. But he is excellent and sensitive in *The Pursuit of Happiness* (Robert Mulligan, 1971), one of the better youth movies that Hollywood was currently dabbling in. He is funny in *For Pete's Sake* (1974), sufficiently spooky in *The Reincarnation of Peter Proud* (1975); and sexy in *Scaramouche* (1976). Recently, after a break in Canada, he has appeared in *The Seduction* (1981), with Morgan Fairchild. Perhaps middle-age will bring renascence. ML

Telly Savalas

Real name **Aristotle Savalas**
Born **Garden City, New York,
21 January 1925**

A heavy is always a heavy. Telly Savalas makes Kojak a charmer, but judging by his looks alone it won't come as a surprise to learn that, in the earlier part of his career, the roles played by this Greek-descended actor (a first generation American) were of the mean, tough and brutish variety. In *The Dirty Dozen* (Robert Aldrich, 1967) he was 'Maggot', a religious-maniac rapist in World War II – nastiest of a nasty bunch of

in Buona Sera, Mrs Campbell *(United Artists, 1968)*

criminals sent out on special operations behind enemy lines. He played a bullying Foreign Legion sergeant in *Beau Geste* (1966); and a similarly loutish cavalry sergeant, named Tibbs, in *McKenna's Gold* (1969). In *The Scalphunters* (Sidney Pollack, 1968) he was a psychopathic bounty hunter. *On Her Majesty's Secret Service* (1969, the Lazenby Bond) saw him as Blofeld,

the head of SPECTRE. The same kind of remarks cover the same sort of roles in the surge of films – sometimes as many as five a year – that Savalas made, mainly in Europe, at the end of the 60s and the beginning of the 70s, prior to his commitment to 'Kojak'.

Naturally there were exceptions, where a sort of innate decency and humour were able to come to the fore. Comedy was assayed, quite successfully, with Gina Lollobrigida, in *Buona Sera, Mrs Campbell* (1968). And the two roles for which he has received Academy Award nomination – as a tank sergeant in *The Battle Of The Bulge* (1965), and as a prisoner in *Birdman Of Alcatraz* (1962) – were notably generous and gentle.

His coming to acting was an accident. Until 1959 he was a public servant and television producer. Asked by a colleague to look out for an actor able to play a part demanding mastery of European accents, he went to the audition himself, and was accepted. (The baldness, incidentally, came later: George Stevens requested it for the role of Pontius Pilate in *The Greatest Story Ever Told*, 1965).

Fame as Kojak was likewise an accident, and almost never happened. Based as he was in London in the early 70s, Savalas was happy making films in Europe that were lucrative, if not very distinguished (mainly spaghetti Westerns and horror). CBS television asked him to return to America to play the cop in a three-hour 'special project' they were preparing, to be called *The Marcus-Nelson Murders* (1971). Savalas accepted – only on the assurance that a series, for which the show was filmed as a pilot vehicle, was unlikely in the event to materialise.

Matters, of course, turned out differently. The show took off, and ran for eight years, until 1980. Subsequent offers – eg to play a lawyer named Hellinger in a new series *Hellinger's Law* – haven't, at the moment of writing been taken up. Savalas has always paced his work well, and in any case has other interests to fall back on. He writes and directs and travels. The gravelly voice, which reputedly sends shivers through the heart of millions of women, can currently be heard in British cinemas before the main feature, extolling, in witty advertisements, the virtues of a famous Caribbean rum. ML

Roy Scheider

Born **Orange, New Jersey,
10 November 1935**

Without much, in his younger days, enjoying a star's adulation Roy Scheider now, towards the middle of the 80's finds himself, almost unobtrusively, as a bankable Hollywood leading man. Like many successful actors in current cinema he started off on the New York stage where, since the beginning of the 60s (as Mercutio in 'Romeo and Juliet'), he has had parts in some 80 productions. His lean, ascetic good looks, as distinctive in their way as Paul Newman's, might have been expected to make him a star sooner if it had not been that the theatre is less 'glamorous' than the cinema. In addition, it should be said that (like George C. Scott, another actor whom he resembles) there has anyway been a 'character' edge to his personality. The two factors combined have meant that for much of his cinema career he has found himself playing second string – to Gene Hackman in *The French Connection* (1971); to Robert Shaw and Richard Dreyfuss in *Jaws* (1975); to both Dustin Hoffman and Sir Laurence Olivier in *Marathon Man* (1976).

The breakthrough into leading roles was achieved quite late, then, with *All That Jazz* (1977), a musical written and directed by Bob Fosse which, besides winning the Golden Palm at Cannes, earned Scheider an Oscar nomination. It is scarcely a traditional musical, treating as it does of a serious, even melancholy subject (the trauma of open heart surgery). It struck many as purely an exercise in bad taste. But the tortuous and introspective writhings of its plot brought to Scheider's playing (also, of course, to his dancing and his singing) a maturity – a depth of feeling – beyond the

in Jaws *(Universal, 1975)*

range of almost any actor one can think of.

The presence of Scheider in any movie is a guarantee of its enjoyment. There is a sort of quiet, discreet professionalism to his movement that mocks the pretentions of flashier, more theatrical film stars. Confident and earnest in action, his face in repose has a beautiful gentle quality, mingling equally sadness and humour. One senses (as one also does with Eastwood or Newman) that he is capable of accomplishment, and can be relied on in moments of danger. Such indeed, more or less, have been his roles in the two 'Jaws' films (*Jaws* and *Jaws II*, respectively 1975, 1978); also his part in William Friedkin's excellent, underrated *Wages Of Fear* (1981); and latterly again in the helicopter drama *Blue Thunder* (1983). ML

Martin Sheen

Real name **Ramon Estevez**
Born **Dayton, Ohio, 3 August 1940**

The features of Martin Sheen are smooth and neatly shaped, rather than striking or handsome. He has contrived to become a star without seeming to have to project a personality. A bit like the actor Robert Vaughn, the neutrality of his person makes him an ideal presence in those fictional-factional 'specials' that have recently become a feature of television. In *Blind Ambition* (CBS, 1981) he impersonated John Dean in the Watergate scandal; in *Kennedy* (NBC/Central, 1983) he played the President himself – exceptionally well and convincingly. Elsewhere, his cameo appearances in worthwhile projects have remained merely at the level of the bland – as for instance in *Gandhi* (1982), where he plays the reporter who, sent out by his paper to get at the truth, finds himself converted to the cause.

It is a little like his own recent trajectory. The experience of performing in Attenborough's film drew him back to the Catholic Church, as well as convincing him that acting, in future, wasn't everything. A liberal in a profession consisting largely of liberals, he is now apparently unwilling to undertake roles that contribute in any way to the world's overburdened weight of violence: scruples which – things being what they are – are virtually guaranteed to restrict his future choice of role. (These scruples were ready to operate with *Kennedy*, until his wife Janet persuaded him that, on the contrary, acting the role would encourage understanding, thereby having a good rather than a bad effect in the long run.) At any event, he seems very serious about this at present, to the extent of talking about going to prison if necessary for his beliefs in disarmament.

He was born 44 years ago, of Spanish and Irish parents, into a poor but decent and hardworking household. Tough, wiry and ambitious, he had already enjoyed a decade of success on the New York stage before the film *Badlands* (Terrence Malick, 1973) catapulted him to wider public notice. Since the film involves what is usually taken to be the killing spree of a youthful teenager, it is odd to reflect that Sheen was 32 when he made it. The tendency to play subtly disturbed characters – a tendency against which he is now rebelling – was continued in his best-known film to date, Coppola's *Apocalypse Now* (1979), where he took on the role of the American soldier Willard, entrusted to hunt down Marlon Brando in the jungle.

Fantastic difficulties were experienced making this epic. Sheen in fact suffered a heart attack. It is plausible to speculate that this experience, more than anything else, set in motion the new way of thinking about his craft that later came to a head in the filming of *Gandhi*. If so, his appetite for work remains surprisingly undiminished. For, in addition to the TV spectaculars, there have been five movies in the past four years, and one waits with curiosity the future products of Sheen's choices. ML

in Badlands *(Warner Bros., 1973)*

Sissy Spacek

Real name Mary Elizabeth Spacek
Born Quitman, Texas, 25 December 1949

Four gifts are needed to succeed as a movie-actress: luck, talent, will-power and looks. In Sissy Spacek's case the last of these attributes is the hardest to anatomise. In certain lights she is the very epitome of the teenage American girl. With her long golden hair, her fair freckled skin, her wide-set, blueish-green eyes (enormous irises!) one can imagine her a popular cheerleader in some little, unsophisticated Texan township, her teeth fresh out of braces.

Already, however, there is something a bit odd; at the age of 24, in *Badlands* (1973), she was playing a girl of 15, almost more convincingly than a teenager herself could play the role. Ordinary in one sense – no actress more so – there is an uncanny, ethereal, almost retarded aspect to her beauty. Her skin is ever so slightly too pale, her eyes ever so slightly too piercing. She seems at times like a creature from another planet altogether.

This is the aspect that was seized on by Brian De Palma for his adaptation of the Stephen King novel *Carrie*, when casting around for an actress to play the psychically disturbed high school pupil who develops (against the taunts of her schoolmates) telekinetic powers of revenge. If there is a single image from Sissy's films that stands in the memory, it is surely, from early on in the movie (1976), the

in Missing *(Universal, 1982)*

stricken misery of her face in the girls' locker room, responding to a barrage of sanitary sticks that have been let fly at her by her fellow students on discovering her ignorance of menstruation. Much more than the grand guignol climax (outstretched arms, body and head plastered in gore) the pathos of this shot, with her large white breasts and streaky tear-stained visage, stands as an emblem of the actress, and an icon of her disturbing film presence.

She grew up, in Texas, with no more ambition than to be a moderately good guitarist and country-and-western singer. At the age of 18, however, a brother to whom she had been close fell ill with leukemia, and so – to get her out of the way at a difficult time – her parents sent her off to New York to stay with her cousin Rip Torn. Under the encouragement of Torn and his actress wife Geraldine Page she enrolled in the acting classes of Lee Strasberg. This didn't last more than a few months. Soon she found herself her first small part in a movie, playing a teenage waif from the Chicagoan mid-West whom Lee Marvin rescues, drugged and naked, from a cattle pen, in Michael Ritchie's lurid thriller *Prime Cut* (1972).

Even films as bad as this aren't two a penny. The role was a small one, and she still needed the 'break' which every actress has to have once in her career. It

was provided in the following year by *Badlands* (Terrence Malick, 1973), where she played the companion of a young small-town tearaway (Martin Sheen) in a mad (but oddly innocent) journey of mayhem and murder across the plains of central North America.

Two factors made the film touching and memorable: the first was the extraordinary elegance – the formal rigour – of its construction, which seemed to by-pass the strictures of traditional morality, elevating an icy beauty in to the midst of the young couple's fecklessness and crime. Central to this effect were the voice-over extracts from the girl's diary – suggestions for the phrasing of which had been given by Sissy herself – which in prim, almost ladylike tones (copying the style of romance magazines) recounted the grim adventure as if it were no more than a picnic excursion, and lent the film an extraordinary poignancy.

After the deserved success of *Badlands* a couple more roles exploited the same vein of slightly spooky innocence. Aside from *Carrie*, there was Robert Altman's *Three Women* (1977). About this latter work one could probably say that there isn't a stranger film in all the 70s. Spacek was cast as Pinky, a vulnerable child-woman (again from the heartland of Mid-West America) rescued at the start of her first job in California by an equally forlorn, but marginally more sophisticated, colleague (Shelley Duvall), who takes her off to share a condominium on the edge of the Mojave Desert. In this dotty environment – colourful, laid-back, Mexican, drug-haunted – her personality slowly begins to take on the personality of her rescuer. Until, that is, a catastrophe involving the baby of a third woman (Janice Rule) precipitates her back into infancy. It is wonderful to watch Pinky's meekness convert by stages into confidence, aggression, finally almost into humanity. Did it matter that Altman himself, the director, was unsure whether his film was tragedy or comedy? The utterly original particularity of its slow, dreamy rhythms – its cruel and fantastic iconography, its desert-blown sadness – place it among the memorable movies. Aside from *Coal Miner's Daughter* (1980) it is Sissy's great role and the proof – if proof were needed – of her extraordinary versatility as an actress.

A subtle change now came over her roles. The bare-chested agency maid vacuuming the floors of rich people's apartments in Alan Rudolph's *Welcome*

to L.A. (1977) is eccentric and scatty, but John Byrum's *Heart Beat* (1979), where she plays Neal Cassady's (Nick Nolte) wife, the woman companion of the beat poet Jack Kerouac, was her chance for the first time to take on a genuinely adult character – a chance taken lightly and deftly, in this small, agreeable movie, that succeeds in converting Kerouac's odyssey into a series of tableaux unmistakably inspired by Hopper.

Next came the great film, *Coal Miner's Daughter* (1980), with Tommy Lee Jones, the major staging post of her career so far: a dramatised account of the legendary (and still-living) country and western singer Loretta Lynn, raised out of nowhere, married at 13, mother of four children by 18, but possessed, through all this time, of some indomitable talent, spirit and will-to-survive that take her to the highest reaches of her profession. It is a terrific role for Spacek, both in its public and its private aspects – above all, perhaps, in the subtle and truthful interaction between the two. So many films about singers are finally stories of defeat – stories about *not* being able to stand up to the pressure. Here was a film that showed determination and courage paying off, without, however, in any way glossing over the genuine knocks on the journey.

For this tender and heartfelt portrayal, much of the music of which was provided by her own guitar, Spacek received, in 1980, the Academy Award for Best Actress. The two films that have followed – *Raggedy Man* (Jack Fisk, 1981) and *Missing* (Costa-Gavras, 1982) – are both very good of their kind (the latter, a political thriller set in a fascist South American republic and co-starring Jack Lemmon, won the Golden Palm in the Festival at Cannes.) Fisk, who directed *Raggedy Man*, is her husband, a former art-director responsible for the fine visuals of *Badlands* and *Heart Beat*. A child was born to the couple in July 1982. Recently, a joint portrait of her and her husband appeared in the London 'Sunday Times' colour magazine showing Spacek, very much the country girl, dressed in tartan shirt and jeans, and leaning against the flanks of her husband's stallion. The upper part of Fisk, on the horse, is invisible; but his presence is palpable and reassuring. The portrait evidently emerges out of happiness. Nothing now could be further from the moon-faced anxiousness of her earliest appearances on celluloid. Her striking good looks, finding their home at last, are wonderfully normal and ordinary. ML

in Coal Miner's Daughter *(Universal, 1980)*

Sylvester Stallone

Born **New York City, 1946**

'In comes this big lug who weighed 220 lbs, didn't talk well and acted slightly punch-drunk,' recalled film producer Irwin Winkler. 'He said he had an idea for a boxing script and he wanted to star in it.' The story of how Sylvester Stallone, an unknown supporting player, came from nowhere to become champion of the Motion Picture industry overnight,

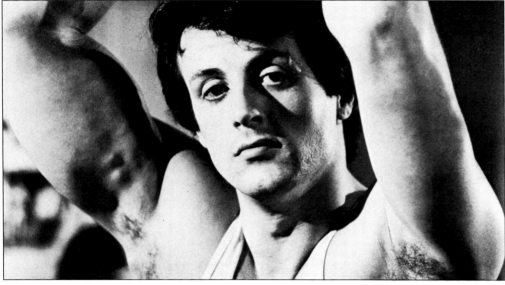

in Rocky *(United Artists, 1976)*

parallels the plot of *Rocky* (1976), the American dream come true. Winkler and Robert Chartoff offered Stallone $300,000 plus but, although he was down to his last dollar and his wife Sacha was pregnant, he asked for only $75,000, a percentage of the profits, and the lead. It was a shrewd move. *Rocky* turned out to be one of the biggest box-office hits for twenty years, grossing millions and winning three Oscars. Stallone was nominated for best Actor and Best Screenplay. (He claimed to have written the latter in three-and-a-half days). Like the character of Rocky Balboa, Stallone was the poor boy who made it good in 'the golden land of opportunity.'

But the rocky road to fame was a bumpy one for the son of Sicilian immigrants who grew up in the tough Hell's Kitchen section of New York. The product of a broken home, he spent many years farmed out to foster parents. A big lad, Sylvester was expelled from fourteen schools as a trouble-maker, before graduating from Philadelphia's Devereux-Manor Hall for boys with 'behavioral problems.' Luckily, he gained an athletic scholarship to the American College of Switzerland, a school for the rich. In order to supplement his pocket money, he sold hamburgers and, as proctor of the men's dorm, he would charge the students' girlfriends a five-franc-an-hour bedroom entrance fee. He then studied drama at the University of Miami where he alienated the professors by insisting on reciting his own monologues. He left before graduating.

In New York, he made the rounds of auditions for plays, keeping himself alive by doing a variety of jobs from cleaning out animal cages to ushering in a theatre. When turned down by Sal Mineo for a part in an off-Broadway production because Mineo said he wasn't intimidating enough, Stallone grabbed Mineo by the lapels. 'Am I intimidating you now?' he asked. Mineo gave him a frightened yes, but not the part. However, he did appear nude in an off-Broadway drama called 'Score', played a hoodlum in Woody Allen's *Bananas* (1971), and the mugger who chases Jack Lemmon in *The Prisoner Of Second Avenue* (1975). He also played surly gangsters in *Farewell My Lovely* (1975) and *Capone* (1975) while, at the same time, writing depressing scripts that nobody wanted. But he did write some of the dialogue for the teen nostalgia movie *Lords Of*

Flatbush (1974) in which he shared the lead with Henry Winkler. Other parts included 'Machine Gun' Joe Viterbo in his Peacemaker car in Roger Corman's campy and violent sci-fi comedy, *Death Race 2000* (1975), and its follow-up, *Cannonball* (1976).

Although Stallone was born in 1946, *Rocky* seems to have been influenced by 'every single goddam Warner Bros. epic' of the 30s. However, the streetwise dialogue and Stallone's self-mocking good-hearted pug make the rags-to-riches clichés and simple, sentimental situations palatable. Stallone played a heavyweight boxer nicknamed 'The Italian Stallion' (Stallone in Italian – an 'in' joke) who gets a chance to become champion of the world. The fight ends in a draw, allowing Stallone to make a sequel, and a sequel. And a sequel. Part of the success of these films has been Stallone's total identification with the character. 'I've met three presidents and they called me Rocky', he said. 'I suppose it's flattering really.' He never uses a stunt man, and – admirably – has elected to train rigorously like a boxer for six months before each movie.

The triumph of *Rocky*, naturally enough, changed his whole way of life, and fame went to his head for a while. He began to live it up, separated from his wife, had an affair with Susan Anton, reunited with his wife, separated and reunited again. Stallone has also attempted to prove that he is not a one-role man. A sort of cross between Robert Mitchum and Lee J. Cobb, he co-wrote and starred in *F*I*S*T* (1978) about a corrupt Union boss. Norman Jewison's direction is shallow, and Stallone's performance is all bombast, jowels and droopy eyes. He wrote, directed and starred in *Paradise Alley* (1978), as well as singing the title song. The movie is set in Hell's Kitchen in the year of his birth, and as a hustler who exploits his younger brother in the wrestling ring, Stallone delivers his lines fortissimo in case the audience can't believe their ears. As with the *Rocky* pictures, the deprived are viewed through the lens of corn and sentimentality.

The star is rather more restrained in the puerile POW tale *Escape To Victory* (1981), directed by the once-distinguished John Huston. In a soccer match between a team of Nazis and prisoners, Stallone, as an energetic goalie, saves a goal to save the match but not the film. Inevitably, given his mumbling macho image, he played a New York cop in *Nighthawks* (1981), a mindless action movie that pretends to say something about terrorism and politics. He is a Vietnam veteran who gets his bloody revenge on a sheriff who has run him out of a small town in *First Blood* (1982), a routine blood-and-guts drama tailored to his personality. He used his familiar, simple, gut technique as the director and co-writer of *Staying Alive* (1983) which starred John Travolta. The director helped build up Travolta's body for his role as a dancer in a disco-ballet called 'Satan's Alley' (Stallone's in-reference to *Paradise Alley*), an effort well-reflected in the star's torso.

After *Rocky II* (1979) and *Rocky III* (1982), Stallone signed a $30 million deal for *Rocky IV*. He is in tune with his audience. 'I identify with the charm and comedic survival of the people in the streets,' he has stated. But he believes that even the wealthy are able to identify with Rocky. 'We all basically want acceptance. Even the rich want to be accepted for what they are, not for their money.' Nevertheless, Rocky seems to hang out a hope to the underprivileged that they can make it to the top without brains; the films are really opiates, lulling people away from responsibility and change, the latter something their creator may have to adapt to if his survival is to be a long one. RB

directing Rocky III *(United Artists, 1982)*

Meryl Streep

Born **Basking Ridge, New Jersey, 1951**

No one has any doubts about Meryl Streep's class as an actress, but people are divided about her beauty. The features, it is said, are too elongated. There is a problem with that nose of hers which, in full face, is thought by some (falsely, in the event: it is straight as a prow) to be crooked. No one, however, disputes the beauty of her skin, transparent mother of pearl with the faintest flushings of rose, and the dignity of her clear blue eyes. Born and brought up in America, she brings to her roles a sort of European elegance, allowing her somehow, beyond her birthright, to share in the glamour of a Garbo or a

in The French Lieutenant's Woman *(United Artists, 1981)*

Bergman. She is one of those actresses – the very definition of a beauty – who bring out the painter in directors, urging them on to rival feats of portraiture. So the fierce red hair of *The French Lieutenant's Woman* (Karel Reisz, 1981) is Pre-Raphaelite; while paler and creamier colours in *Sophie's Choice* (Alan J. Pakula, 1982) hint at the Renaissance and Botticelli. Surely the mobility of her features in that latter film is extraordinary: thin-lipped and pinch-faced one moment, with her hair plastered swarthily to her crown; then the next moment, as the flashback gives way to the present, radiantly glowing and beautiful.

One of the strengths of Meryl Streep as an actress is an ambiguity as to whether she is confident or shy. At times she is as shy as an animal: she seems like one of those timid, aristocratic gazelles at their waterhole who take flight at the first scent of danger. At other times one thinks that no contemporary actress has a stronger, more commanding presence. And this may be because she really *is* an actress, trained on the classical boards. Streep was raised in a middle-class family. The origin of their name is Dutch (ironically, in view of Meryl's propensity for portraying spiritually tormented gentiles, Jewish Dutch). Her father was a pharmaceutical executive, her mother a commercial artist, and she herself was educated at Vassar and Dartmouth. The decisive moment of her career came immediately after, however, at Yale, where she enrolled at the University's famous drama school. The plays she performed in her three years at New Haven – numbering an impressive 40 in all – gave her a sense of the classical, and a basis in the European tradition, that have animated all her subsequent film work.

The body of this work is not yet very large. (That is the point: she is still a rising star). Starting with *Julia* in 1977, she has appeared in nine films over the last seven years – ten if we count the television drama *Holocaust* (1978). In keeping with her mysteriously 'foreign' allure, she tends to be cast in roles that emphasise an independent sexuality – ex-wife or mistress, disrupter rather than upholder of marriages. In *Manhattan* (1979), a comedy, she

leaves her husband (Woody Allen) for another woman. In *Still Of The Night* (1982) she is the rich sophisticated mistress of a murdered auctioneer. The title of *The French Lieutenant's Woman* (1981) may be said to speak for itself. Wonderfully elegant and independent in *The Seduction of Joe Tynan* (1979) as a Southern belle career woman, she 'seduces' Senator Alan Alda away from his wife Barbara Harris. In *Kramer Vs Kramer* (1979) – her most celebrated role to date – she is the object of bitter divorce proceedings against a put-upon husband (Dustin Hoffman). Finally, the love affair in *Sophie's Choice* (1983) is doomed and fathomless, a journey beyond the bounds of normal morality.

But it would be wrong, for all that, to suggest that she is incapable of portraying normal emotion or faithfulness. On the contrary, the memory of her children, in *Sophie's Choice*, partakes precisely of this deep human passion. And a mistress, too, may be faithful – as is the French Lieutenant's woman to her vanished, invisible ideal. One of the most touching of Streep's roles to date is that of an abandoned girlfriend – left behind in the supermarket by Christopher Walken, in *The Deer Hunter* (1978), as he goes off to fight in Vietnam. Her performance in

in Kramer Vs Kramer *(Columbia, 1979)*

these films is generally thought to be impeccable. A different question concerns the quality of the films themselves. Three of them may be considered as flawed in conception. There is, in retrospect, something unsatisfactory and automatic about Robert Benton's *Kramer Vs Kramer*. The feminist case having been stated in films like *An Unmarried Woman* (Paul Mazursky, 1978, with Jill Clayburgh), it is almost as if there were a statutory necessity to come up with the reverse side of the coin; to say that men can be pleasant and women can be selfish is to

put it a little too glibly, but the film fails, perhaps, to find a proper sense of irony or satire. Meryl Streep's performance, however, in the witness box, arguing the custody of her child, remains in the memory with a vivid and electric intensity. (It won her an Oscar for the Best Supporting Actress.)

The French Lieutenant's Woman has a flaw equally fundamental. It is split into two different stories; but a shortage of space prevents either of the two parts from coming to a head in a destiny. The stories are supposed to interact, but in fact they remain resolutely separate – sketches towards a life rather than the picture of a complete life itself. In the longer, Victorian, episode we are troubled by our inability to see into the heart of the heroine, this ravishing red-headed governess. Is she in love with the hero (Jeremy Irons, a geologist)? or is she in the grip of a mania (the memory of her vanished French officer)? To know whether she is *serious* or *mad* would alter our view of her character. But the filmmaker himself is unsure; so that, in the end, the magnificent performance of Streep becomes merely a species of melodrama.

Melodrama, too, in the broadest conception of the word, is *Sophie's Choice*. Streep gives her classiest performance (for which she was duly awarded an Oscar), but once the firework virtuosity of it has died down in the mind – the stunning Polish accent, the chameleon changes of happiness – one is left with a few pressing questions. Is it not vulgar, for instance, to call into action the weight of the whole Jewish tragedy in order to furnish the education of a somewhat ingenuous young writer? Everything, in film and book, is seen through the refraction of 'story'. The fatal hesitation is to doubt in the end whether the famous choice – the surrender or not of her infant – exists outside the novelist's fantasy. Weighed up in retrospect, the dilemma of her sacrifice resembles an elaborate confection. (Oddly enough, however, it has to be said, such objections don't hold against the earlier television film *Holocaust*. That film is all of a piece, and Streep's attempts, in consequence, as the young Aryan German woman, to save her Jewish husband, possess a genuine and memorable poignancy.)

After initial hesitation, Streep had fought like a tigress to land herself the part of Sophie, besieging Alan Pakula in his office. Originally, it was intended for an unknown Czech actress. ('Where is she now?' 'In Czechoslovakia.') Despite misgivings, the role up till now remains the most formidable of her career. Yet other smaller roles should be mentioned. *The Deer Hunter* is as fine a piece of cinema as the 70s produced. In a film about men at arms, Streep's is the residual womanly presence. Her doom and her destiny is to keep a place in her heart for a lover who will never come home to her. Her consciousness is finer than the consciousness of the men she is involved with. Brave, abandoned and weeping, jabbing at the supermarket goods with her price-marker, she manages throughout to maintain the pitiable dignity of a princess.

A far cry from such helplessness is the portrait of the Senator's P.A., Karen Traynor, in *The Seduction of Joe Tynan*. Along with Michael Ritchie's *The Candidate* (starring Robert Redford, 1972) the film is one of the best pictures of politics-in-action to emerge out of the 1970s. Sleek in attire, seductively sexy in her command of Southern vowels, smoothly calculating as to the ultimate advantage or disadvantage of pursuing an affair with her colleague, Streep's is as flawless a portrait of ambition as one has come across in contemporary cinema. Both film and performance are exceptional. The verdict on *Silkwood* (1984) is awaited at the moment of writing.

After a long affair with John Cazale that ended tragically with his death from cancer in 1978, Streep is now married to the sculptor Don Gummer and is the mother of two small children. She lives as privately as possible, dividing her time between an apartment in the Chinese district of Manhattan and a 'nice large' property (92 acres) in upstate New York. Her future would seem to be, on all fronts and deservedly so, assured. ML

in The Deer Hunter *(Universal, 1978)* ▷

John Travolta

**Born Englewood, New Jersey,
18 February 1954**

There are films which so hauntingly embody the values and aspirations of a particular class at a particular period that they all but transcend their own specifically cinematic virtues and shortcomings and, like dance crazes, render criticism irrelevant. Such a film was *Saturday Night Fever* (1977), directed by John Badham.

Taking its inspiration from an article by the rock journalist Nik Cohn, 'Tribal Rites Of The New Saturday Night', it told the story of an inarticulate young Brooklynite, Tony Manero, who shakes off the stultifying routine of his job by transforming himself into a sexually swaggering disco dancer at weekends. The film was a phenomenal hit world-wide, its tie-in record album (with music by The Bee

in Urban Cowboy (Paramount, 1980)

in Grease (Paramount, 1978)

Gees) sold around 10 million copies and a shot of its star, John Travolta, strutting on the disco floor in a dazzling white dude suit became one of the most reproduced (and trend-setting) icons of the 70s. (The total conviction which he brought to the part was all the more remarkable in that, just after shooting started, his lover and companion, Diana Hyland, died tragically of cancer.)

Of Irish-Italian origin, Travolta was a high school dropout who gradually drifted into acting in summer stock, TV commercials and off-Broadway theatre. After a few minor appearances in television dramas and a spell in the touring company of the Broadway

musical 'Grease', he was offered the role of Vinnie Barbarino, a likeable street-smart hoodlum in the TV situation comedy 'Welcome Back, Kotter'. With his toothy smile, his soft, liquid eyes and his spellbinding sexuality, he became an instant phenomenon, his popularity with teenagers soon rivalling that of the Fonz in 'Happy Days', Henry Winkler (an actor whose career initially paralleled Travolta's). *Saturday Night Fever* followed, for which he received both an Academy Award nomination and a rave review from Pauline Kael. And when Randal Kleiser's film adaptation of *Grease* (1978), in which he starred opposite the British export to Hollywood, Olivia Newton-John, made more money than any other musical in cinema history, it appeared that Travolta could do no wrong.

Not so. *Moment By Moment* (1978), co-produced by Travolta and directed by his friend Jane Wagner, was a disastrously inept melodrama with the dramatic impact of a second feature home movie; his role

in *Urban Cowboy* (1980) was merely that of Tony Manero in a Stetson hat; and if Brian De Palma's paranoid thriller *Blow Out* (1981) was in a different class altogether, it was scarcely more successful at the box-office. The tag 'meteoric', which had almost immediately been attached to Travolta's rise to fame, now seemed as if it might prove no less applicable to his fall.

For the moment, however, that fall has been halted by the commercial triumph of *Staying Alive* (1983), a sequel to *Saturday Night Fever* directed by a past master of sequels, Sylvester Stallone. So that his star might acquire the glittering torso on display in this film, Stallone put him through a *Rocky*-like programme of dieting, jogging and weightlifting: afterwards, Travolta could claim with some justification, 'I now feel I've got a physique any professional dancer would die for.' It may well be that, in the end, he will turn out to be just as much of a survivor as Tony Manero. DM

Gene Wilder

**Real name Gerald Silberman
Born Milwaukee, Wisconsin, 11 June 1935**

Like many of the characters he has played, Gene Wilder was the son of a Russian Jewish immigrant: his father prospered in the United States by manufacturing miniature whisky bottles. At the University of Iowa, Wilder began attending drama classes and appeared in summer stock during vacations. On his graduation, now determined to make acting his profession, he left for England, enrolling at the Bristol Old Vic Theatre School. Dissatisfied with traditional English teaching methods (though he did become an expert fencer, which enabled him subsequently to teach the sport for a living in America), he returned to New York, joined the Actors Studio and soon landed his first Broadway role. It was there that he met his future mentor and collaborator Mel Brooks, who was endeavouring to set up a film then titled 'Springtime For Hitler'. In fact, Wilder's screen debut was in *Bonnie And Clyde* (1967), in which he played a nervous young undertaker whisked off on a

in Blazing Saddles (Warner Bros., 1974)

joyride by the eponymous couple. When Brooks finally managed to find backing for his project, its title had changed to *The Producers* (1968), and Wilder's performance as a neurotic accountant enmeshed in Zero Mostel's topsy-turvy schemes won him an Oscar nomination.

Wilder's strength, so to speak, was vulnerability. His most characteristic screen persona is of an ostensibly well-balanced intellectual transformed into a half-demented bundle of neuroses by some major (or even minor) crisis; and he offered variations on it in such comedies as Woody Allen's *Everything You Always Wanted To Know About Sex, But Were Afraid To Ask* (1972), as a doctor in love with his patient's sheep; Mel Brooks' *Blazing Saddles* and *Young Frankenstein* (both 1974); and *Silver Streak* (1976) and *Stir Crazy* (1980), in both of which he was effectively teamed with Richard Pryor. His own films as an actor/director, *The Adventure Of Sherlock Holmes' Smarter Brother* (1975) and *The World's Greatest Lover* (1977) were not notably successful at the box-office; and Wilder, perhaps in consequence, has been absent from the screen for the last few years. DM

John Travolta with Cynthia Rhodes in Staying Alive *(Paramount, 1983)* ▷

THE 80s

INTRODUCED BY DAVID MALCOLM

Hollywood, *circa* 1984, is a living paradox. Indeed, it reminds one of nothing so much as the paradox of the broom whose handle has been replaced as often as its brush. Is it the same broom? Is it the same Hollywood? To be sure, signs of continuity can be detected in the actual, topographical community bearing that name. Actors and actresses, for example, continue to celebrate their rise to stardom by embedding a set of their handprints in the cement forecourt of Grauman's Chinese Theater on Hollywood Boulevard – except that it is no longer called Grauman's, but Mann's. Buoyed up by hopes of fame and fortune, young people continue to pour into the lotus limbo of greater Los Angeles – except that, these days, they are just as likely to be aspiring directors and writers as beauty queens clutching mail order diplomas in mime and dramatic art. The

major studios (such as MGM, Universal and Paramount), whose names and logos haunted our moviegoing adolescence, continue to operate – except that most of them have long since been swallowed up by vast industrial conglomerates, making it near-impossible for a buff to distinguish between, say, the MGM and the Paramount product. Alas, the whole notion of a studio 'look', an identity, a house style, seems to have vanished along with contract players and B movies.

And the movies themselves? There, too, paradox reigns. Few of the rules which guided Hollwood's lucrative progress through the first four or five decades of this century continue to hold good. Consider:

1. *Sequels can never, repeat never, be expected to rival the commercial success of the original.* Yet each successive episode of Sylvester Stallone's *Rocky* saga (we're up to *Rocky III* at the time of writing, but, for Stallone, the sky is obviously the limit) has managed to take in more money than its predecessor(s). As for the *Star Wars* sequels (or prequels or whatever they are), *The Empire Strikes Back* and *Return Of The Jedi* already figure among the most profitable movies in cinema history.

left to right: Mark Hamill, Alec Guiness and Harrison Ford at the controls of their space-ship in Star Wars *(20th Century-Fox, 1977). George Lucas's blockbusting science fiction success set the trend for a new kind of film – and a new kind of star: one whose success rests on his association with his machines, rather than on his own talent or personality.*

2. *To be a success, a movie should contrive to appeal to spectators of all ages.* Here, to be sure, it is possible to argue that the aforementioned blockbusters *do* possess an appeal which bypasses questions of generation. Yet it must be remembered that, of those millions of once regular moviegoers whose principal source of entertainment is currently the TV set or Betamax and who will actually visit a cinema no more than two or three times a year, most tend to select movies of a very different stamp: *Kramer Vs. Kramer, On Golden Pond, Ordinary People, An Officer And A Gentleman. Tootsie* and *Terms Of Endearment.* The commercial success of *Star Wars* and that ilk depends almost wholly on the teen and pre-teen crowd – and on, for Hollywood, the novel phenomenon of massive repeat viewing. As we know, the true fan of Luke Skywalker and Co. is he (or she) who has sat through each of the adventures at least half-a-dozen times. And it may be that what has attracted many adults to these movies is not so much their subject-matter – subject-matter which they would contemptuously reject in book form – as their very success. The kind of intelligent adult to whom it would not normally occur to queue up for a movie about a shark nevertheless finds it hard to contain his curiosity as to just

Deanna Durbin, the 'Watteau Shepherdess of Universal' having her footprints immortalised in cement at Grauman's Chinese Theatre in 1938. Present-day Hollywood nods in the direction of the past by retaining the custom, though the theatre has changed its name to Mann's.

why *Jaws* might have broken every known box-office record in its first weekend on release. Nothing, so it has (too) often been remarked, succeeds like success – and, as Hollywood has discovered, great success can almost automatically be hyped into success of a degree that such tired critics' superlatives as *phenomenal, unheard of* and *unprecedented* for once get it right.

By the 1980s, George Lucas (left) and Steven Spielberg had achieved pre-eminence in the contemporary Hollywood hierarchy, earning admiration for their creative vision and their box-office power. Their latest (joint) venture, Indiana Jones And The Temple Of Doom *(Paramount, 1984) has outgrossed its phenomenal predecessor,* Raiders Of The Lost Ark *(Paramount, 1981).*

3. *If it is to become an authentic box-office triumph, what a movie needs is stars.* Well, it should be patent to even a casual observer of the Hollywood scene that this rule is no longer valid. Most of us, if fielded such titles as *Jaws, Star Wars, Close Encounters Of The Third Kind, Raiders Of The Lost Ark* and *E.T. – The Extra-Terrestrial*, would probably be able to cite the names of a handful of the performers who appeared in them. But are Richard Dreyfuss and Mark Hamill and Harrison Ford and Carrie Fisher what anyone would honestly term 'stars'? Does anyone, on spotting a poster of *Return Of The Jedi*, murmur, 'Mmmm, the new Mark Hamill film...' the way people used to refer to 'the new John Wayne film' or even 'the new Doris Day film'? Were it not for the know-how of producer-director George Lucas, Hamill, a skilful

enough performer and one perhaps capable of a greater depth of characterisation than has been offered him by the role of Luke Skywalker, might easily have ended up playing second fiddle to a Volkswagen in some cute Disney farce. As for Harrison Ford, thirty years ago he would most likely have been a stalwart of the very cheapest, instead of the most expensive, movies around. If the cinema had not transformed itself so radically, he might have been the 80s' Rod Cameron or Rory Calhoun.

Is there, then, no room for stars in the new Hollywood, a Hollywood whose products would seem to be aligning themselves with comic books and video games rather than with novels and plays? The answer, paradoxically, is that not only will Hollywood continue to regalvanize itself on a regular influx of new stars, but that it is in the survival of the star-system, in whatever form, that its very salvation lies. To understand why, one should cast one's mind back to those films – from *Kramer Vs. Kramer* to *Terms Of Endearment* – which have managed to tease out of their homes spectators who had settled, apparently once and for all, for the more domestic, more comfortable, yet also more cramped, pleasures of the small screen. From the cast credits of the half-dozen titles already mentioned, one will note the presence of Dustin Hoffman (twice), Meryl Streep, Henry Fonda, Katharine Hepburn, Jane Fonda, Donald Sutherland, Richard Gere, Jessica Lange, Shirley MacLaine and Jack Nicholson – all of them *stars.* So, quite appart from teenagers frequenting cinemas as though they were video arcades, there is an audience out there willing, if the conditions are right, to be tapped. And what, from past evidence, will most effectively tap that audience is a good, solidly constructed story (either a comedy or a melodrama) and a starry cast. Kids may be more interested in planets than stars (and, it would seem, in any other planet, real or apocryphal, than the one they are living on). But the century-old craving for the glamorous, the charismatic, the larger-than-life has not yet died, nor is it soon likely to do so; and it is safe to predict that, long after Altair 14 and Krypton and the Moon of Endor have waned, there will be stars burning in Hollywood's spotlight-raked sky.

Director Richard Attenborough, his wife, and two of several Oscars for Gandhi *(Columbia, 1982). The film attempted to bring a heroic message of peace to a troubled world, thus continuing the British success in Hollywood begun by* Chariots Of Fire *(20th Century-Fox, 1981)*

The fantasy of Hollywood finally realised – or the ultimate example of life imitating art. President Ronald Reagan, former star of Bedtime For Bonzo, *has achieved 'international' fame at last. There is bound to be a sequel to* The White House Story . . . . .

Nancy Allen

Born **New York City, 1955**

The youngest of three children, Nancy Allen was raised in Yonkers and began attending dance classes at the age of five. Later she enrolled in New York's High School of Performing Arts as a dance major, and also studied at the Lee Strasberg Theater Institute. Her first professional acting experience came in TV commercials, of which she calculates that she has made over one hundred. In 1972, she auditioned for the director Hal Ashby, who cast her in a tiny role in *The Last Detail*. It was enough to interest a Hollywood agent, who insisted that she move to Los Angeles. Though she left New York immediately, she found herself idle for several months in Hollywood; and it was quite by chance that she was invited to read for the director Brian De Palma, then about to shoot his stylishly eerie supernatural thriller *Carrie* (1971). She got the part – consisting mostly of a few giggly scenes as a high school student – and later married the director.

Her subsequent roles were of no great help to her

in Dressed To Kill *(Filmways, 1980)*

career, as, however enticing they might have seemed at the planning stage, the films themselves turned out to be box-office disasters, one of them, De Palma's *Home Movies*, being denied any theatrical release at all. *I Wanna Hold Your Hand* (1978), on which Steven Spielberg was executive producer, concerned the rise of Beatlemania in New York, and was totally out of synch with the volatile tastes of the young audience which it hoped to capture; and Spielberg's own *1941* (1979), a monumental farce about fears of a Japanese invasion in the wake of Pearl Harbor, was a commercial flop. Allen's greatest success to date has been her husband's *Dressed To Kill* (1980), a crypto-Hitchcockian thriller about a psychotic killer on the loose in New York: as one of his intended victims, a prostitute who assists in tracking him down, she brought a highly individual freshness and charm into the otherwise ugly proceedings. Another De Palma thriller, *Blow Out* (1981), in which she co-starred with John Travolta, was less successful, and it is hard to say whether Allen's career will benefit or not from such close association with her husband's work. It will be a pity if her career fails to pick up, since she is both attractive and undeniably talented. DM

David Bowie

Real name **David Jones**
Born **Brixton, London, 8 January 1947**

Few rock singers have had the staying power of David Bowie, a star of the 60s and perhaps an even bigger star of the 80s. His success surely derives from the fact that he maintains a total creative control, not only over his record albums but over the futuristic, multimedia quality of his stage shows. Bowie is above all an image, whose trademark (at least, for anyone not unconditionally a fan of his music) is his own precious, ashen-complexioned (and highly made-up) androgynous appearance. In purely filmic terms, he resembles nothing so much as a star of the silent 20s period, and it is not difficult to imagine him playing opposite a Pola Negri or a Garbo (indeed, in profile, he bears a striking resemblance to the composer, actor and matinee idol *par excellence*, Ivor Novello). Such excessive roles come rather more scarce these days, however, and Bowie's filmography fatally lacks continuity – each of his major films has tended to be *sui generis*, offbeat and virtually unrepeatable. Whether he can integrate his striking, flamboyant personality into a career which will allow of real development remains a question-mark hovering over his future acting.

Though, in 1969, he briefly appeared in a short, *The Image*, and took a bit part in a film adaptation of Leslie Thomas' vulgar bestseller *The Virgin Soldiers*, the first screen role to exploit his ethereal off-screen aura was Nicolas Roeg's *The Man Who Fell To Earth*

in The Man Who Fell To Earth *(British Lion, 1976)*

(1976), which craftily cast him as an extra-terrestrial come to earth in a desperate search for water. Glamorous, charismatic and yet somehow touchingly vulnerable, Bowie carried the film on his frail shoulders and made an instant reputation outside of the rock music milieu. Yet his subsequent work has entirely failed to live up to the promise of that role. It must have seemed a brilliant idea to partner him with the even more exotic Marlene Dietrich in *Just A Gigolo* (1978), but David Hemmings' Anglo-German co-production was a disaster; and *The Hunger* (1982), in which he played Catherine Deneuve's vampire boyfriend, was roundly booed at Cannes, so ridiculous were its visual posturings. Only Nagisa Oshima's *Merry Christmas, Mr Lawrence* (1983), a pretentiously written study of mutual fascination between the commandant of a Japanese POW camp and a British prisoner, suggests that there might be an actor in Bowie, if he is capable of shaking off his orchidaceous pin-up image. DM

Bo Derek

Real name **Mary Cathleen Collins**
Born **Long Beach, California, 20 November 1955**

Not long after the release of Blake Edwards' hit comedy *'10'* (1979), a joke went around the movie community: 'What is 10, 9, 8, 7, 6... etc?' The somewhat bitchy answer was: 'Bo Derek ageing.' Cruel as that may appear, it is a joke that ought to give Derek herself cause for reflection. A beautiful, statuesque, blonde Californian, she has achieved undoubted celebrity after only a handful of films, in most of which she was invited to do little more than look her ravishing self in various stages of *déshabillé*. She will soon be 30, however – an age when the cinema, and its audiences, require even its most exquisite icons to do more than merely prop up the screen like caryatids. And it has to be said that nothing in Bo Derek's work heretofore has intimated that she will be capable of transforming herself from what used to be called a starlet into a genuine star.

in 10 *(Warner Bros., 1979)*

A typical (physical) product of Southern California, she met the former actor John Derek while in her late teens and married him. He became not only her husband but her manager – and, at least in his own mind, her Pygmalion. Thus, apart from a tiny role in *Orca ... Killer Whale* (1977), he refused script after script as unworthy of her talents. The ploy worked: her appearance as Dudley Moore's ideal woman in *'10'* (practically obliterating the presence of Julie Andrews from the audiences' consciousness) made her name internationally known and, for a few months, the image of her voluptuous body in a one-piece bathing costume rivalled those of the screen's greatest stars. Interest in her faded rapidly, however, when she reprised her 'dream girl' image in a snide and much less funny comedy, *A Change Of Seasons* (1980), and, especially, when she appeared as a simpering, scantily clad Jane in her husband's ludicrous *Tarzan, The Ape Man* (1981), of which she was co-producer. Derek's latest film, *Bolero* (1984), was also directed by her husband; and if she proves to be no better an actress than he is a filmmaker, the future will be none too rosy. DM

Richard Gere

Born **Syracuse, New York, 31 August 1948**

Richard Gere was born into a middle-class family in upstate New York, and his first love was not acting but music: at school he quickly mastered several instruments and composed mini-scores for end-of-term theatrical productions. Subsequently, he both composed and performed the score for a production of 'A Midsummer Night's Dream' given by the Provincetown Playhouse, a repertory theatre in which he briefly worked. Following an unsuccessful attempt to launch his own rock group, he began to act off-Broadway, notably in Sam Shepard's play 'Killer's Head'. This experience got him the leading role (played by John Travolta in the film version) of Danny Zuko in the London production of the hit musical 'Grease'. On completion of the run, he was, rather surprisingly, hired by Frank Dunlop to work at the Young Vic, where he was to be seen as Christopher Sly in 'The Taming Of The Shrew'. Gere has never totally cut himself off from the theatre, but consents to appear in only those plays which stimulate him. Thus, at the beginning of his rise in the cinema, he courageously took the part of a homosexual internee in a concentration camp in the harrowing and moving 'Bent'.

Despite Gere's current image as sex object and superstar, he did not make his name overnight and astonishingly few of his films have ever made money for their producers. Thus his first, *Report To The Commissioner* (1975), was a low-budget adaptation of James Mills' best-selling novel about a young cop who accidentally kills one of his (female) colleagues: Gere played a pimp and received a mention in the odd review. He was more impressive as a shell-shocked GI in *Baby Blue Marine* (1976), another film which passed more or less unremarked by critics and customers alike. His third was a very different matter: *Looking For Mr Goodbar* (1977) was a slick, meretricious adaptation by Richard Brooks of a slick, meretricious novel by Judith Rossner. Yet, on the credit side, it could boast an interesting, virtually untapped subject: the phenomenon of the singles bar; a terrific central performance from Diane Keaton; and, a distant third but worthy of inclusion nevertheless, a chilling little cameo from Gere as a violent punk who terrorises Keaton during one of her nocturnal sorties. His promise (a word already used by a handful of critics) was confirmed by Terrence Malick's *Days Of Heaven* (1978), an over-photographed (as novels may be over-written) slice of turn-of-the-century Americana in which he was perhaps the only performer not to be eclipsed by the insistently gorgeous visuals. And in Robert Mulligan's *Bloodbrothers* (also 1978) he was offered

the first role in which he was allowed to be more than a cipher, that of a teenager in the Bronx desperate to free himself from the emotional pressures of his Italian-born parents.

No matter how varied these roles were, however, the slim, goodlooking Gere (goodlooking in a manner that contrives to be both boyish and intense) could still not be regarded as a star. In was in 1979 tha his status definitively changed – even if, curiously, neither of the two films which he made that year came close to being a box-office blockbuster. The first was John Schlesinger's *Yanks*, a sentimental wartime wallow about American GIs stationed in England and a film whose acting honours were stolen from both Gere and Vanessa Redgrave by a young newcomer named Lisa Eichhorn. Gere, nevertheless, possessed considerable behavioural charm, and there could be no denying his sheer sexiness. It was this latter aspect of his persona which was exploited in Paul Schrader's *American Gigolo*, a foredoomed attempt on the director's part to turn his kept-boy hero into an existential figure of suffering and redemption, but also a dazzlingly well-designed view of conspicuous Californian consumerism in which Gere well personified the ultimate status symbol.

So he had established his credentials, as it were,

and all he needed now was a mega-hit. His next film, *An Officer And A Gentleman* (1982), was that mega-hit – to almost everyone's surprise. Said Gere himself, 'I don't think anybody thought it would be

in Beyond The Limit *(Paramount, 1983)*

in An Officer And A Gentleman *(Paramount, 1982)*

the blockbuster success it was. I certainly never did. I did it because I liked the script.' In its release year, this old-fashioned melodrama came second in popularity only to *E.T.* – it was the type of film which somebody who had not been to the cinema in years might choose to see. Gere looked splendidly alluring in his crisp white ducks; and *American Gigolo* was abruptly re-released with the slogan that, in it, he was *neither* officer *nor* gentleman.

Gere is a more interesting though perhaps less instinctual actor than John Travolta, with whom he has occasionally been compared. But the threat to the growth of his career, as with Travolta's, is that his pretty-boy image might eventually obscure the shadowy, vaguely manic-depressive side of his personality. This was certainly the case in Jim McBride's foolish *Breathless* (1983), which was little more than a narcissistic exhibition of its leading man, baring body and soul to various effect; so that it was all the harder to take him seriously in *Beyond The Limit* (GB: *The Honorary Consul*) (also 1983), a well-intentioned but not too effective adaptation of the Graham Greene novel. If he is to avoid a career of fits and starts, such as Travolta's, he will have to decide soon whether he can afford to rely quite so slavishly on his own undeniable sex appeal. DM

in Days Of Heaven *(Paramount, 1978)*

John Gielgud

Born **London, 14 April 1904**

Since his debut at London's Old Vic theatre in 1921, John Gielgud has been widely regarded as (with Olivier) England's (and the language's) greatest actor, blessed as he is with a voice that is one of the glories of the English stage and a capacity to externalise an interior passion or pain without ever resorting to ranting, barnstorming histrionics. What is so remarkable about Gielgud is, no doubt, the ineffable calm, even sweetness, of his theatrical disposition, with the result that his dramatic roles are made all the more powerful for the rigid control which his classical training – allied, again, to that superbly mellifluous voice – maintains over them. His film career, unfortunately, has seldom allowed him to exploit that tension: at least until the late 70s and early 80s, his status remained that of a 'classy' supporting performer, a more prestigious Cedric Hardwicke, perhaps.

His first important screen appearance was as the high-spirited schoolmaster-cum-composer in the 1933 adaptation of J.B. Priestley's comedy of concert-party life, *The Good Companions*. As a result of this, Hitchcock cast him in the *jeune premier* role of the spy Ashenden in his adaptation of a Somerset Maugham novella, *Secret Agent* (1936); but his performance was stiff and unrelaxed, and he proved far more effective as Disraeli in *The Prime Minister* (1941). Gielgud was absent from the cinema between 1941 and 1953, when he made a brilliant Cassius in Joseph L. Mankiewicz's film version of *Julius Caesar*, following it with Chorus in the Italian *Romeo And Juliet* (1954) and Clarence in Olivier's *Richard III* (1955). Until the 70s, he tended to be cast in historical roles, notably as Mr Barrett in *The Barrets Of Wimpole Street* (1956), as Warwick in Otto Preminger's disastrous *Saint Joan* (1957), as Louis VII of France in *Becket* (1964), for which he won an Academy Award nomination, as Henry IV in Welles's *Falstaff/Chimes At Midnight* (1966), for which he ought to have been nominated, and as the Pope in *The Shoes Of The Fisherman* (1968). In 1969,

he was effective in Richard Attenborough's *Oh! What A Lovely War*.

From a very mixed bag of appearances in the 70s, one would certainly wish to single out his unforgettable portrayal of a witty, bilious old novelist struggling to fuse images of memory and imagination into a coherent fiction in Alain Resnais's *Providence* (1977). At its diametric opposite was a ludicrous performance in a ludicrous film, as Seneca in the grotesque 'Penthouse'-backed *Caligula* (also

1977). But it was not until the 80s that Gielgud could fairly be said to have achieved true cinematic stardom. He made several major, and often extremely successful, films, including *The Elephant Man* (1980), *Chariots Of Fire* (1981) and *Gandhi* (1982); but it was with *Arthur* (also 1981) that his name at last filtered down into popular consciousness. As Dudley Moore's urbanely foul-mouthed 'gentleman's gentleman', Gielgud gleefully sent up his own somewhat precious image and, at the age of 77, won his first Oscar. DM

with Dudley Moore (right) in Arthur *(Warner Bros., 1981)*

Nastassia Kinski

Real name **Nastassja Nakszynski**
Born **Berlin, 1961**

Unlike most of the prepubescent film actresses of the late 70s – Jodie Foster, Tatum O'Neal, Brooke Shields – Nastassia Kinski entered films quite by chance. She was dancing in a Munich nightclub when spotted by the wife of director Wim Wenders, who was at that time about to start filming *Wrong Movement* (1975), an adaptation of Goethe's 'Wilhelm Meister'. She was cast in a tiny but haunting role, but it was only after he had decided to

in Tess *(Columbia, 1980)*

use her that Wenders discovered that her father was Klaus Kinski, an actor best known for playing a number of tortured, half-demented protagonists in the films of Werner Herzog, eg *Aguirre, Wrath Of God, Nosferatu, Woyzeck* and *Fitzcarraldo*. (Throughout her short career, Nastassia has rarely allowed interviews to touch on the subject of her father, from whom she has long since been estranged; and it is certain that at no time did he encourage her in a film career). After working with Wenders, she accepted offers indiscriminately, including one film, *The Passion Flower Hotel* (1978), which was virtually softcore porn. Then, perhaps in search of a substitute father, she met and fell in love with Roman Polanski, who had been assigned to photograph models for a Christmas issue of *Vogue*. Their affair lasted a year, at the end of which Polanski suggested that she attend classes at the Actors Studio in New York. Finally, in 1979, he cast her in the title role of *Tess*, an adaptation of Hardy's 'Tess Of The D'Urbervilles'. The film was a worldwide success; and though Kinski was perhaps too immature for the role, as well as being noticeably un-English, she gave a touching performance and revealed a disturbing resemblance to the young Ingrid Bergman.

Since the breakthrough of *Tess*, Kinski has made an astonishing total of ten films, all of them – on paper, at least – major productions by major directors. Her choice of projects is an intelligent one, yet it somehow never seems to translate into either critical or commercial success. In 1980, for example, meeting Francis Ford Coppola at the Cannes Film Festival, she was invited to join the small repertory company at his Zoetrope studio. Their only film together, however, *One From The Heart* (1981), a heavily stylised musical set in a sound-stage Las Vegas, was a catastrophic flop; Kinski was charming

as a tightrope walker but, like the film, her performance was little seen. Nor did Paul Schrader's *Cat People* (1982) enjoy much more acclaim: based on a classic horror film of the 40s by Jacques Tourneur, it cast her and Malcolm McDowell as brother and sister, half-humans and half-panthers. In *Exposed* (also 1981), another ambitious film just too off-centre to make any headway at the box-office, she enjoyed the unique privilege of being 'played', as on a cello, by Rudolf Nureyev: the image was not only startling but genuinely erotic. After *Spring Symphony* (1982), a German biopic of Robert and Clara Schumann, she signed up with Jean-Jacques Beineix, the whizzkid director of *Diva*, to star with Gerard Depardieu in *The Moon In The Gutter* (1983), an adaptation of a David Goodis novel which was filmed on the largest sound stage in Europe, Rome's Cinecitta. The result was unveiled at the Cannes Festival to unanimous disfavour (including that of its male star who refused to attend the press conference and contemptuously dubbed the film 'The Moon In The Sewer'): a monstrously bloated melodrama bombarding the spectator with luridly hollow imagery, it possessed only the degree of life that one can impute to a decapitated chicken.

Is Kinski, then, a jinx? Her own physical beauty is so great – the auburn hair, the grey-green eyes, the pouting lips – that directors are still eager to secure her services. And her various projects – especially *Paris, Texas*, a mammoth 'road movie' directed by the man who discovered her, Wim Wenders – look very exciting indeed. Yet her career so far remains a vivid illustration of the impossibility for an actor or actress to make an intelligent choice of roles based on the 'form' of their collaborators. While that makes it an interesting and informative one from the critic's or historian's point of view, it is in all other respects an unhealthy situation. DM

Jessica Lange

Born **Cloquet, Minnesota, 1950**

in Frances *(Universal, 1982)*

Jessica Lange was born in rural Minnesota, and her whole childhood was spent on the move. Her father was a travelling salesman whose work obliged his family to pull up its roots no fewer than eighteen times before Jessica, quite alone, hopped onto a freight train and moved out for good. Her ambition was to become an actress, and at high school she had already starred in a senior-class production of 'Rebel Without A Cause' – a production which, curiously, was cancelled when one of the students was murdered. After attending the University of Minnesota for a couple of years, she left for Paris to study mime under Etienne Decroux, the former instructor of Marcel Marceau. So began two years of living in tiny hotel rooms, eating in tiny working-class restaurants, performing in the open air and finally landing a job for several months as a dancer at the Opéra Comique. Deciding that there was no future in mime, or for an American actress in France, she once more pulled up the roots which she had begun to establish, abandoned her furnished apartment and the few possession she had gathered around her, and took a plane for New York. There she studied drama under Herbert Berghof and eked out a living by serving in restaurants and doing minor modelling work.

Her chance came in 1976 when she made a screen test for Dino De Laurentiis, who was about to film his remake of the classic Beauty-and-the-Beast adventure movie *King Kong*, and required a fresh young Beauty to be swept off her feet by his gigantic mechanical Beast. Lange – certainly a beauty – won the part: she was whisked off to Hollywood, where both cameras and publicity machine began inexorably to roll. Though *King Kong* was not the disaster a number of outraged critics judged it to be, it all but destroyed Lange's career: her romantic scenes with the Beast aroused only ribald comment, which had been fuelled by an outstandingly idiotic publicity campaign. Lange, for example, was quoted as having

said of Kong's death scene: 'Tears came to my eyes, because I *do* believe in the story.' Despite a seven-year contract with De Laurentiis, she did not work again until 1979, when she played the Angel of Death in Bob Fosse's morbid musical *All That Jazz*, again hardly a role to advance a budding career. Nor did it help that she was pursued by doubtful publicity when it was widely reported that her blind husband, living alone and in poverty in a Bowery slum, was suing her for maintenance not long after she bore a child to the dancer Mikhail Baryshnikov.

Another career misjudgment followed – an inane comedy, *How To Beat The High Cost Of Living* (1980) – then she was cast as Cora, a role once played by Lana Turner, in Bob Rafelson's remake of James M. Cain's *The Postman Always Rings Twice* (1981), and forced the critics to take her seriously for

the first time. Though the film was a box-office failure, Lange revealed a tawdry, dank sexuality that nothing in her career had prepared one for, and her frenzied lovemaking on a kitchen table with Jack Nicholson was disturbingly authentic. Determined to capitalise on her success, Lange fought for her next part – that of the tragic actress Frances Farmer (with whom she may have identified) in the biopic *Frances* (1982) – and totally vindicated herself with a magnificently affecting performance. Though nominated for an Oscar for that role, it was for another in the same year that she actually won it – as the bewildered young TV actress in *Tootsie* who finds herself enmeshed in Dustin Hoffman's cross-dressing deception. With two such performances, and a future full of promise, *King Kong* has become just a bad memory. DM

Dolly Parton

Born **Locust Ridge Hollow, Tennessee, 1946**

'I'm exaggerated in every way, big wigs, big boobs and big rear end. I choose to look that way because it reflects my personality. I want to feel good living inside what I've created.' In effect, as was the case with Mae West or W.C. Fields, Dolly Parton is her own creation, her own David Levine caricature. It is possible to dislike or disapprove of her, but it would seem very difficult to be *disappointed* in her, since her public persona is so much of a piece. And perhaps what is most curious and endearing is the complete denial of erotic charge in her presence, whether on stage or in either of the two movies which she has made to date. It is almost as if the fact of possessing such an outrageously voluptuous figure (one commentator described her as 'a Juliet with her own built-in balcony') has rendered pointless any supplementary come-hither posturing; and there is finally something rather maternal (in a Felliniesque manner) about her whole act.

Locust Ridge Hollow, where she was born, lies deep in Tennessee's Smokey Mountains, home of moonshine whisky distilleries and one of the most underprivileged areas in the whole of the United States. Parton was one of twelve children, and the family's ramshackle two-room house was so isolated that there was no electricity, no television or radio and practically no schooling. She has spoken of a childhood in which she and her brothers and sisters were obliged to sleep head to toe in a single bed, and the only form of entertainment was choir singing at the local church. Her grandparents were all preachers and singers, so that as a child she began to write her own songs: at the age of 12 she made her first public appearance at the Grand Ole Opry, the

in The Best Little Whorehouse In Texas *(Universal, 1982)*

Nashville radio station through whose gates all country-and-western singers must pass on their way to national fame. Unlike the maudlin, self-sacrificing heroines of the songs she heard and sang herself, however, Parton was determined that she would have the good things of this life, without waiting patiently for her reward in Heaven. And the first step towards making these acquisitions was organising her family into a singing group, which subsequently travelled around the Deep South states. As their success grew, so did her personality: she began to emphasise her authentic if improbable bust measurements, her two-inch fingernails, her gaudy pink apparel and a series of cascading blonde wigs, blatantly proclaiming their falseness. Her husband, Carl Dean, whom she married only months after quitting high school, attended to the family homestead in Tennessee; and despite long separations while she cruises the country with her roadshow, their marriage has continued to be one of the happiest in American show business.

Parton's first film was *Nine To Five* (1980), a comedy in which she was rather incongruously teamed up with Jane Fonda and Lily Tomlin as three office secretaries who concoct a scheme to revenge themselves on their inept, sexist boss. It was a jolly enough entertainment and the very dissimilar personalities of its trio of leading ladies bounced off each other in wonderfully droll style. *The Best Little Whorehouse In Texas* (1982) which followed it, was a big, vulgar, well-upholstered film version of the hit Broadway musical, in which Parton, co-starring with Burt Reynolds, simply lent her outsize personality to the proceedings. Whatever their purely artistic merits, both proved to be huge commercial hits, and there can be little doubt that Parton, like some curvaceous ocean liner, has been successfully launched as a movie star of the 80s. DM

Richard Pryor

Born **Peoria, Illinois, 1 December 1940**

At the age of seven, Richard Pryor was sitting in with the band at a Peoria nightclub, where he would meet such visiting greats of the jazz world as Duke Ellington, Count Basie and Louis Armstrong; and at twelve he gave his first performance on a stage, in a community production of 'Rumpelstiltskin'. As a teenager, however, he led a somewhat aimless existence, unhappy at school and making himself extra pocket money by packaging beef at a meat plant, racking balls at his grandfather's pool hall and driving trucks for the small construction firm owned by his father. After two years in the army, mostly spent in West Germany, he returned to his home town and made his debut as a comedian/emcee. As such, he moved around the United States and Canada, endlessly observing his fellow beings and integrating his observations into his act, which he reportedly would polish and refine in an obsessive manner. In the early 60s he had arrived in New York's Greenwich Village, the headquarters of 'alternative humour', and his reputation was soon such that he was dubbed the 'black Lenny Bruce'. By the time he was 30, his success was no longer confined to live performances: he was increasingly in demand for top TV talk shows and musical 'specials'.

His early work in the cinema is wholly devoid of interest – eg *The Busy Body* (1968), *The Phynx* (1970), *You've Got To Walk It Like You Talk It Or You'll Lose That Beat* (1971, and an authentically Pryoresque title, even if he played only a minor part) – and it was not until he was cast as Piano Man in the Billie Holiday biopic *Lady Sings The Blues* (1972) that he began to make an effect with audiences (and won an Oscar nomination). But Pryor was indisputably one of the funniest men in America, black or white, and there was only the briefest lapse before he starred in a series of unambitious but enormously successful comedies, notably *Silver Streak* (1976), *Which Way Is Up?* (1977), *Stir Crazy* (1980) and *The Toy* (1983). Paul Schrader's *Blue Collar* (1978), about three factory workers caught between union and management, gave him a rare serious role; and in Sidney Lumet's adaptation of the black Broadway musical *The Wiz* (also 1978) he was teamed again with his *Lady Sings The Blues* co-star, Diana Ross.

With his ascension to black superstardom, however, Pryor has tended to gloss over what was so remarkable in his stage performances – his hallucinatorily vivid mimicry of pimps and junkies, the scatological energy of his language – and, from that point of view if hardly from a strictly cinematographic one, the highlight of his career remains *Richard Pryor Live In Concert* (1979), a straightforward transcription of his stage show, shoddily spliced together but one of the funniest films ever made and a fitting tribute to Pryor's gifts. DM

in Bustin' Loose (Universal, 1981)

Christopher Reeve

Born **New York City, 25 September 1952**

Despite differences of temperament, physique and nationality, the obvious comparison with Christopher Reeve is Sean Connery. Both shot to stardom (literally, in Reeve's case) in a single heroic role; neither merely assumed that role as given, but shaped it to the contours of his own personality; and if Connery, now in his early fifties, has the advantage over Reeve in having fully established himself as a serious and versatile performer, it very much looks, from the evidence at hand, as if Reeve will be capable of doing likewise.

He is the son of journalist Barbara Johnson and Franklin Reeve, the editor of *Poetry Magazine* and a lecturer at Yale and Wesleyan universities. As a young boy, he seemed already set for a career as a performer: at school he studied piano and voice, sang with a madrigal group, was assistant conductor of the orchestra, and made his stage debut with a small Princeton theatre company at the age of nine.

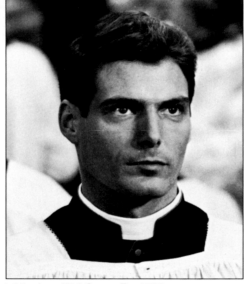

in Monsignor (20th Century-Fox, 1983)

Brooke Shields

Born **New York City, 31 May 1965**

Of the trio of Hollywood nymphets to emerge in recent years (Tatum O'Neal, Jodie Foster and Brooke Shields), the one most likely to effect the delicate transition to mature stardom is Shields, her principal assets being a fashionably leggy physique and a warm, sensuous beauty recalling that of the young Elizabeth Taylor. Already in demand as a model at the age of eleven months, she made her film debut as the victim of a religious fanatic in *Alice, Sweet Alice* (GB: *Communion*, 1977), then became the most notorious child in America for her role as the pre-pubescent prostitute who is auctioned off in Louis Malle's *Pretty Baby* (1978), a sensational yet oddly affectionate evocation of a New Orleans brothel at the turn of the century. Her commercial, if not critical, prestige was enhanced by two soft-focus, soft-core and soft-centred melodramas, Randal Kleiser's *The Blue Lagoon* (1980) and Franco Zeffirelli's *Endless Love* (1981).

In 1983 Shields unsuccessfully sued a photographer for marketing nude pin up shots of her taken when she was only ten years old. The suit was unsuccessful, even though the presiding judge called her 'a hapless child victim of a contract to which two grasping adults bound her'. One of the 'grasping adults' was her mother, the former actress Teri Shields, widely portrayed as a ruthless stage manager of her daughter's career: Brooke herself was reported to be incensed at her persistent interference during the shooting of *Sahara* (1984). DM

Graduating in English from Cornell, he enrolled at Juilliard's drama division and studied under John Houseman. After stints at London's Old Vic and the Comédie Française as part of his master's degree course, he returned to New York and accepted a (villainous) role in a long-running TV soap opera 'Love Of Life'. This led to a Broadway play 'A Matter Of Gravity', which ran for seven months in all and starred Katharine Hepburn, an actress who greatly influenced him. 'What I learned from her was simplicity,' he has said. 'She's a living example that stardom doesn't have to be synonymous with affectation or ego.' Two years later, in 1978, he made his film debut in *Gray Lady Down*, a claustrophobic thriller about a marooned submarine. And in the same year he was selected by the Salkind brothers to incarnate both the title role of *Superman* and his 'mild-mannered' alter ego, Clark Kent. Though the film was in any case a far more satisfying transposition of the celebrated comic strip than anyone had dared to hope, there is no doubt that much of its enormous popular success was due to Reeve's charm, humour and a sense of irony *vis-à-vis* the role which never descended into coyly knowing camp. He actually managed to wear the famous costume as if to the manner born; and if he cannot be said to have created a complex human being, at least he never allowed one to forget that underneath the snakily heraldic 'S' on his chest a real person could be found.

Two sequels were made (in 1980 and 1983): a third is unlikely, however, in view of the meagre returns on *Superman III* and the fact that Reeve has publicly announced his retirement from the role. Of his non-Superman work, one can discount *Somewhere In Time* (1980), a woolly romantic melodrama about a love affair conducted through time travel, and the horribly misguided *Monsignor* (1983), in which he was quite miscast as a priest. But he accepted the challenge of *Deathtrap* (1982), Sidney Lumet's film version of the Chinese-box puzzle play by Ira Levin, in which he played a young homosexual playwright plotting with his lover Michael Caine to murder the latter's wife; and recently became involved in a pair of Henry James adaptations: James Ivory's *The Bostonians* (1984), in which he co-starred with Vanessa Redgrave; and, teamed with Redgrave again, 'The Aspern Papers' on the London stage. DM

in Endless Love (Universal, 1981)

Christopher Reeve in Superman II *(Warner Bros., 1980)* ▷

A star's principal entry will be found on the page denoted in bold type. If a star is mentioned more than once in different contexts on the same page (other than in his or her principal entry), the number of times mentioned is indicated in brackets after the page number.